AFTER ANTIQUITY

A Volume in the Series

MYTH AND POETICS

Edited by GREGORY NAGY

A full list of titles in the series appears at the end of the book.

AFTER ANTIQUITY

Greek Language, Myth, and Metaphor

MARGARET ALEXIOU

CORNELL UNIVERSITY PRESS

ITHACA AND LONDON

The publisher gratefully acknowledges the support of the ILEX Foundation
in bringing this book to publication.

The publisher also gratefully acknowledges a subvention in support of publication
from the Loeb Classical Fund, Classics Department, Harvard University.

First published 2002 by Cornell University Press

Printed in the United States of America

Library of Congress Cataloging-in-Publication Data
Alexiou, Margaret.
      After antiquity : Greek language, myth, and metaphor / Margaret Alexiou.
         p. cm.
      Includes bibliographical references and index.
      ISBN 0-8014-3301-0 (cloth)
         1. Byzantine literature—History and criticism 2. Greek literature,
      Modern—1453–1800—History and criticism 3. Greek literature, Modern—19th
      century—History and criticism 4. Mythology in literature. 5. Metaphor.
   PA5130.M96 A54 2001
   880.9'002—dc21   2001028172

Cloth printing   10   9   8   7   6   5   4   3   2   1

For my mother

Katharine Thomson

in loving memory of Lis
14 December 1936–27 July 2000

Sei   standhaft,   duldsam   und   verschwiegen!

Mozart

Let   no-thing, let no-thing,   no-thing stay to give   of-fence

Purcell

*A living tribute to departed dear ones whose lives and
values give meaning to our work:*

George Thomson † 3 February 1987
Frida Knight † 2 October 1996
Thanasis Kapsalis † 23 August 1999
Aspasia Alexiou † 9 November 1999
Elisabeth Thomson † 27 July 2000

Contents

Foreword

by Gregory Nagy

After Antiquity: Greek Language, Myth, and Metaphor, by Margaret Alexiou, is a work so far-reaching that it tests the limits of the Myth and Poetics series. The title of the volume tells the tale, and so too does the subtitle.

In the case of the subtitle, the tripartite arrangement of language, myth,
and metaphor is asymmetrical. In other volumes published in the series,
language has been correlated with myth or with metaphor. Such symmetries are challenged, however, by the three-way conceptualization of language, myth, and metaphor. One obvious sign of asymmetry in the subtitle
is the fact that myth is missing its twin, ritual. Another sign is less obvious:
metaphor, viewed in terms of Prague School linguistics as the "vertical axis
of selection," is not being paired overtly with its own respective twin,
metonym, viewed symmetrically as the "horizontal axis of combination."

The asymmetry of Alexiou's subtitle—and approach—stems in part
from the author's systematic questioning of attempts to formulate and
apply universal definitions of myth in the ongoing study of poetics and
rhetoric. Other books in the Myth and Poetics series have challenged the
universalization of myth, but Alexiou is the first to extend the challenge to
metaphor. For her, universal definitions of metaphor tend to blur the local
color, as it were, of its uses within the visual world of a given culture.

For other reasons as well, Alexiou downplays symmetries such as myth
and ritual, metaphor and metonym. She resists mutually exclusive dichotomies. In her analysis of Greek traditions, both pairs, myth and ritual,
metaphor and metonym, interweave. As a metaphor in its own right, the
idea of interweaving is particularly apt, since the mechanical process of
weaving combines the cognitive operations of metonymic and metaphorical

thinking. Here is where language, as the first in the triad of language, myth, and metaphor, becomes particularly engaging. Following Wittgenstein, Alexiou develops a ritual interpretation of language. To put it another way, she systematically works ritual into language, into metaphor. Her essential idea here is interdependence.

The same idea is already active in the first part of the title: "after antiquity." At stake here is the privileged status that some classicists ascribe to the time-frame they study, drawing a dividing line between themselves and those whose research takes them beyond classical Greek, into the "post-classical." Alexiou's wording highlights the relativity of such a dividing line—and its arbitrariness. At what point exactly does antiquity stop and post-antiquity begin for a culture mediated by a language with a recorded history starting from as early as the second millennium BCE and extending all the way to the present? This book demonstrates by example the interdependence of studying the postclassical (and the preclassical) along with the classical phases of Greek culture.

Alexiou's expertise is hardly confined to the postclassical. An accomplished classicist in her own right, she inherits the intellectual legacy of her father, the late George Thomson, a pioneer in revitalizing the proud old discipline of classical philology. She inherits equally the intellectual legacy of her maternal grandmother, Jessie Stewart, who was one of Jane Harrison's earliest pupils and her "first First" in classics (archaeology). Alexiou's own distinctive approach to classical scholarship is perhaps best exemplified by her—and Thomson's—deep sympathy for the philological methodology of Walter Headlam's magisterial edition and commentary on the *Mimes* of Herodas. For Headlam, as for Thomson and Alexiou, a true understanding of a given work by a given Greek author requires the internalizing of every relevant piece of evidence from Greek literature, without placing restrictions on the historical time-frame to be covered. Jane Harrison's writings on ritual and religion have also left an enduring mark on Alexiou's work. Alexiou credits Headlam and Harrison—in fact, her Cambridge heritage—with teaching her to think comparatively and to transgress conventional boundaries, although in different spheres. Continuing in this tradition, Alexiou is committed to combining rigorous synchronic analysis with perceptive diachronic reconstruction.

The idea of interdependence extends beyond rethinking the distinction between the classical and the nonclassical. Applying her expertise in social anthropology, Alexiou re-examines various other distinctions well known to classicists and other humanists, such as "standard" and "substandard," "high" and "low," "premodern" and "modern," "written" and "oral," "European" and "non-European," "Western" and "non-Western." Greek culture becomes an ideal testing ground, offering a vast time-span of available evidence. Her perspective on all these distinctions is historical, not absolutist.

Alexiou's historical perspective helps her appreciate the discontinuities as well as the continuities of Greek civilization. Just as important, she consistently tracks the changes that go together with the continuities. A small but telling example is the way she prints the Modern Greek word for "superstitions," *deisidaimoníes*: while the ending gets its "modern" spelling, *-es*, the roots of the compound are written in accordance with their "classical" forms, *deisi-* and *daimon-*, recapitulating the Greek concepts of "fear" and "demon" (the latter word needs to be seen in a pre-Christian sense: it designates some unknown force, larger than everyday life, which cannot be named).

Alexiou's insights into questions of genre illustrate the power and effectiveness of her historical method. She shows, for example, how a lament can modulate into a love song, and the other way around. Such modulations, as she also shows, can best be understood by viewing the uses of genres in their performative contexts, not in the abstract.

The author's sense of history is reflected indirectly in the way she resists theory for theory's sake. She consistently eschews universalism, archetypalism, reductionism. She chooses not to venerate various sacred cows currently pasturing in the field of Greek studies. Included among the venerable notions marked out for sacrificial slaughter are the various cultural constructs of Hellenic "purity"—viewed from outside of Hellenic culture or from within. Native models of Hellenic "purity" run the gamut from the classical purisms of *katharevousa* on one extreme all the way to the anticlassical detoxifications of demotic Greek on the other. Among the non-native models is the facile equation of "proto-Greeks" with "Indo-Europeans," as if the Greek language—and therefore the Greeks—could be viewed as some kind of direct emanation from the reconstructed "proto-language" called Indo-European. Yet another object of Alexiou's criticism is a nationalizing style of ethnography or *laographia* that privileges an overly textualized view of Greek folk traditions. Alexiou shows how both literary texts and folk songs can transgress the generic boundaries that scholars have sometimes imposed. She demonstrates that the four Ptochoprodromic Poems can be fully interpreted and appreciated through a historical and contextualized approach, including comparative use of Greek folk traditions.

Alexiou not only avoids excessive reliance on theory. She actively shuns any form of ideology. Such an overall stance, however, never goes so far as to prevent her from applying methods and modes of thinking that differ, sometimes radically, from those of her own. Though she distances herself from Marxists, deconstructionists, radical feminists, afro-centrists, and so on, she is careful not to avoid active engagement with any of them. One quality is everywhere apparent: an extraordinarily deep empathy for the multiform religious pieties of Greek-speaking peoples throughout the ages.

Alexiou brings together, from fresh perspectives of myth and ritual as defined in the book, not only love songs, lullabies, laments, and mythical songs ("ballads") but also the hymns of Romanos the Melodist (fifth to sixth centuries), the Ptochoprodromic Poems (twelfth century), and their interaction with the storehouse of songs, tales, and traditions now subsumed under the category "folklore." If love songs have been comparatively neglected by serious scholars (in contrast to the laments, with which they share so many ritual and metaphorical codes), then *paramythia* (tales) have been almost universally ignored, even by Greek folklorists, despite the richness and versatility of their narrative modes and imaginative horizons. The author's *Ritual Lament* (1974) opened new horizons on the study of lament, both in literature and ritual; her new book explores a wider range of genres, folk and literary, mythical and ritual, always through the prism of the Greek language in all its diversity of shapes and forms. Alexiou's work on the *paramythia* is intended to provide a new point of departure for discussion and study of the Greek novel, both modern and premodern.

An empathy for all aspects of Greek civilization pervades Alexiou's *After Antiquity*. Just as pervasive is the author's intense intellectual engagement with everything she touches in this book. Testing the limits of what it is to be Greek, she offers the reader a vastly expanded and enhanced understanding of Greek civilization in all its wondrous complexities.

Acknowledgments

This book was conceived more than twenty years ago, when I was Senior Lecturer in Byzantine and Modern Greek at the University of Birmingham, England. Since 1986 I have had the honor of holding the George Seferis Chair of Modern Greek Studies at Harvard University. I would like to record my gratitude to graduate students of both institutions, since I have learned as much from them as they may have learned from me.

I acknowledge debts to many readers of this manuscript. In particular, I thank Gregory Nagy for overall advice and support. I thank the following readers for critical comments and suggestions: Timothy Boyd, Vangelis Calotychos, Michael Hendy, Michael Herzfeld, Yiorgos Kalogeras, Panagiotis Roilos, Anna Stavrakopoulou, Charles Stewart, and Katharine Thomson. Ole Smith's premature death (February 1995) robbed me of my most rigorous reader, but I am grateful for his suggestions on four chapters. Peter Bien's meticulous comments in later stages helped me make crucial revisions. I offer profound gratitude to my Greek family, including my former husband, Christos Alexiou. My thanks for technical assistance on bibliographical references and on the computer to George Syrimis and Thomas Jenkins. But my greatest debt is to the major midwives: Laurie Kain Hart, Alexander Hollmann, Gregory Nagy, and Teresa Jesionowski, each of whom labored with love to deliver this book. Our crowning glory is the jacket illustration, with heartfelt thanks to Ioli Kalavrezou.

Since 1995, when the manuscript was completed, many titles have appeared that I would have liked to include. Two must be mentioned: Roy A. Rappaport, *Ritual and Religion in the Making of Humanity* (Cambridge:

Cambridge University Press, 1999), and Geoffrey Horrocks, *Greek: A History of the Language and Its Speakers* (London: Longman, 1997).

This book could not have been published without a substantial subvention from the Loeb Classical Foundation.

To Gregory Nagy and to Zeph Stewart, I owe many thanks.

M.A.

A Note on Transliteration
and Translations

I have tried to devise my own forms of transliteration, even though they may differ across divergent forms of Greek. If I have not adhered to the system recommended by the Modern Greek Studies Association, it is because I have had to cover a wide chronological range of texts. I suspect that Greekless readers will find such renderings as "poiēsis" less alienating than "píisis." I have used accents in transliteration only where failure to do so might cause confusion, and I have marked long ē and ō as deemed appropriate. I have maintained polytonic accentuation in Greek throughout, with the exception of the papyrus letters, which are rendered without accents.

My translations aim to convey the structure and register of the Greek. Where possible I have retained the original tense and sequence of tenses. I have preferred the Greek convention of punctuation, which introduces direct speech by a dash (—) but does not mark its conclusion in the manner of quotation marks in English, thereby blurring distinctions between direct and indirect speech, dialogue and narration, and creating opportunities for free indirect discourse.

AFTER ANTIQUITY

Introduction: Forward to the Past

This book is a series of investigations of interrelated aspects of Greek language, myth, and metaphor. My aims are to examine the functions of language in defining the contours of myth and metaphor; to analyze the repetitions, ruptures, and transformations in diverse selected texts drawn from the postclassical periods; and to explore the interactions between orality and literacy as a significant factor in determining the resilience of mythical and metaphorical elements in new combinations and contexts, both literary and ritual.

I have chosen texts with the intention of introducing readers to the richness and diversity of the Greek linguistic and cultural heritage. Rather than treat the subject chronologically or delineate a canon, I combine both synchronic and diachronic perspectives, with particular attention to historical contexts, so as to explore new approaches for understanding the processes of continuity and change.

1. Aims and Scope

Part I, "Language," examines the significance of the unusually long documentation for Greek as an isolated member of the Indo-European group of languages. In order to counteract the bias toward structure (*langue*) over usage (*parole*) evident in post-Saussurian structuralist linguistics, attention is paid to the diversity and heterogeneity of the Greek language at key points of its written heritage from the end of antiquity to the emergence of modern Greek. Part II, "Myth," attempts to reach a working definition of myth to include texts transmitted by both oral and literary means. To that end, narrative songs, legends, and wondertales drawn from the rich corpus of folklore collected since the early nineteenth century are examined alongside literary prose texts selected from roughly the same period. Part III, "Metaphor," explores the ritual underpinnings of metaphor, from ritualized activities of everyday life to the folk songs of the life cycle. Finally, I suggest how recurrent metaphors in modern folklore form an integrated and regenerative system, which can in turn be related to the literary and religious texts presented in Part I. In sum, I argue for a diachronic and interdisciplinary approach to language, myth, and metaphor and indicate how the Greek case can illuminate our understanding of other cultures.

There are links among these apparently disjunctive parts. The chronological range of texts discussed under the term "Greek," together with their generic diversity, is deliberate, even if it transgresses boundaries. I wish to challenge the appropriation of "Greek" as defining only the ancient part of the tradition, to the exclusion of its medieval and modern inheritors; to question the validity of universalist, archetypalist, or reductionist theories; and to replace one-way Hellenist perspectives on continuity with a dynamic understanding of interaction, both across various stages of Greek and with contiguous cultures. In other words, we must look forward, backward, and sideways.

2. Some Preliminary Definitions

To give a preliminary review of the contents of this volume, a few comments on my uses of the terms "language," "myth," and "metaphor" are called for. Of the three, "language" would appear to be the least problematic. Appearances, however, may be deceptive. First, the case of Greek, from Mycenean times to the present day, offers an opportunity to study the processes of linguistic change at close quarters and from a diachronic perspective. As Colin Renfrew has suggested, Greek, with its well-documented history and its heritage of diverse forms of language—written and spoken, high and low, standard and dialect—and its long record of lexical borrowings, offers interesting clues as to what determines linguistic makeup or breakup.[1] Martin Bernal's controversial challenge to an idealized concept of the ancient Greeks permits us to take his argument in a different direction and to view the denigration of the Byzantines and modern Greeks on grounds of racial and linguistic "impurity" as a particular form of ideological bias designed to seal off the ancient Greeks from subsequent and lateral contaminations.[2]

Second, quite apart from considerations of how the history and development of the Greek language after antiquity may affect our views of ancient Greek and its role in the diffusion of Indo-European, there are other compelling reasons for taking language as a starting point for this study. The extent to which language, myth, and metaphor are interdependent has received more than a little attention over the past decade from scholars in the humanities, the social sciences, and the sciences.[3] In different ways, the Russian scholars Nicholas Bachtin, his brother, Mikhail Bakhtin, and V. N. Vološinov have challenged Saussurian linguistics by emphasizing that the privileging of system (*langue*) over usage (*parole*) stems from a false dichotomy. For Bachtin, the case of Greek, especially since classical times, has a special contribution to make to the present debate, just because its history has been so complex and diverse. Bakhtin and Vološinov argue that language should be studied not as a homogeneous, isolated abstraction but as a means of interaction and communication and therefore as a social phenomenon in all its actual heterogeneity. Bakhtin points to multiple registers for subtlety of communication and literary expression; to bilingualism, multilingualism, diglossia, and polyglossia as factors in linguistic and literary history; and above all to interaction and dialogue as major signifiers on the textual, synchronic, and diachronic scales. His model provides a useful comparative analogy for Bachtin's diachronic studies of the Greek language. In particular, Bakhtin's concept of the "dialogic imagination" will prove crucial thoughout my study, although I hope to show that it is by no means restricted to the novel.[4]

Third, the transition from orality to literacy, from oral memory to written record, has long been the subject of intense debate.[5] The question is central to all forms of cultural transmission, including myth and metaphor, but let me start with language. It is too often assumed that the transition from orality to literacy has been a unilinear, one-way process: we may admit the interpenetration of oral and literary forms of language, especially in the late-medieval West, but take it for granted that today, literacy, or the "technologising of the word," as Walter Ong has put it, has more or less won out. But, viewed diachronically from antiquity to the present day, the case of the Greek language offers some remarkable paradoxes, past and present. Although "common modern Greek" is now universal currency, people when talking among themselves revert to local idioms and dialects, while making liberal use of "puristic" forms and phrases. They exhibit pride in acknowledging the proximity of ancient to modern Greek, a passive understanding of ecclesiastical Greek, but in everyday discourse they employ dialectal forms not readily comprehended by the outsider. Which of these languages is oral, and which is literary? How have they interpenetrated? The frontiers between local idiom, national language, and cultural heritage are hard to define in terms of a simple transition from orality to literacy.

Chapter 1 provides a historical overview of the Greek language. Chapters 2 to 4 illustrate and analyze diverse texts, both to chart major linguistic changes from the New Testament to the twelfth century—when modern Greek first emerges in literary form—and to set the textual parameters for my analysis of myth and metaphor.

As for myth, oral myth tells stories, but because it forms part of a complex system of thought and expression, its language is associative, involving "thinking in complexes," although the contours of evocation and the resulting stories may vary or be differently determined at each repetition.[6] Greek myths are distinctive because they have been recorded and repeated in the same language ever since the inception of literacy early in the first millennium B.C. It was out of mythology that the earliest philosophy, history, and drama emerged from the sixth to the fourth centuries. As we have them, ancient myths are neither oral nor literary but have been transmitted in diverse and sophisticated literary forms—epic, historiography, lyric, hymn, drama. Yet the number of divergent forms is sufficient to suggest a rich and continuing oral tradition. The rapid and uneven pace of socioeconomic and historical change across the city-states facilitated local diversity and contextual revitalization through ritual and oral performance.[7] Aeschylus' treatment in the *Oresteia* of the myth of the House of Atreus provides just one example of how the fifth-century dramatist could, like the oral poet, draw on a fund of narratives, themes, characters, and associative allusions familiar to his audience through myth and ritual. A new kind of *literary* myth was thereby created. Even at the end of antiquity, Alexandrian poets such as Theokritos and Moschos or the novelists were writing for an educated elite, yet they drew freely not only on a varied literary mythology but also on forms familiar from later oral tradition. Throughout antiquity there was a continuing and creative interaction between myth, poetry, and ritual, between orality and literacy.[8]

Which elements of ancient mythology have been revitalized in the postclassical period, in what forms, and at what levels? What happened to Greek myths, which from an early stage had become the basis of conscious art, after the end of antiquity? Many were transmitted throughout the Byzantine period and beyond as the literary heritage of elites, although this does not mean that they were derivative, imitative, and divorced either from contemporary reality or from parallel forms of popular literature; *mimēsis* (imitation), used in the sense of variation upon classical forms, was the very stuff from which humor and irony, parody and satire were revitalized, especially in the late eleventh and twelfth centuries.[9] As for the Ottoman and modern periods, ancient and medieval myths have been appropriated and reinterpreted by writers and scholars in a constant struggle over the site of "Hellenism" from diverse linguistic, national, and political perspectives. This process of reinterpretation has not been restricted to elites; ancient mythology and religion were absorbed and "translated"—not always at a conscious level—into popular Christianity and have left deep marks on rural culture, as evidenced in Greek folklore as recorded over the past 180 years. Songs and tales have proved a dynamic element, interacting with the literary culture of more differentiated urban societies. The Greek case is special only insofar as past and present interactions between orality and literacy can be documented.[10]

Why Greek myths, which have received no mean share of scholarly attention? Considerable confusion still surrounds the question, crucial for this volume, of how "myths" are related to "folktales." Geoffrey Kirk rejects traditional distinctions based on the presence or absence of supernatural and religious elements but insists on treating folktales as a subspecies of myth, defining them as "traditional tales, of no firmly established form, in which supernatural elements are subsidiary; they are not primarily concerned with "serious" subjects or the reflection of deep problems and preoccupations; and their first appeal lies in their narrative interest."[11] He falls into the common trap of regarding folktales as lacking the religious and social complexity of signification, supposedly to be found only in myth.

Walter Burkert views myth as a special form of folktale, or a traditional tale with secondary, partial reference to something of collective importance (such as sacrificial ritual practice), or a "metaphorical tale."[12] While agreeing that differences between myth and folktale cannot be determined at the level of form or structure (which may differ radically because of modes of transmission), I hope to show in Part II that sacrificial and religious themes are central to many narrative songs and tales drawn from modern Greek folklore, reflecting a cosmology and morality as profound and complex as those of ancient myths. The differences lie in the eye of the beholder, depending on whether the genre is perceived as "high" or "low." One set of distinctions to be explored is that ancient myths tend both to reflect and to oppose dominant religious forms, while modern songs and tales may exploit mythical and fantastic elements without reference to—or even at variance with—officially sanctioned religion. This aspect will be considered in relation to the linked concepts of atonement and reciprocity in the tales, Christian in essence but not always in particular manifestations. Narrative songs and tales provide an invaluable—and largely unresearched—source for the study of popular, or "other," forms of religious belief, coexisting and overlapping with established ones and escaping censorship except when practiced in the domain of ritual. Exorcism and enchantment may have been condemned as "superstitions" (*deisidaimoníes*) by the Orthodox Church, but they bear testimony to belief systems not necessarily grounded in established doctrines and have found tenacious expression in mythical genres.[13]

Several aspects which make Greek myths unusual have been ignored. If elements of ancient myths can be shown to have passed in different forms into diverse later texts, then a framework exists for the study of the diachronic transmission of myth within one culture, thereby affording a valuable corrective to the fashionable comparative analyses of myths in divergent cultures. Further, if modern Greek folklore can be viewed from less Hellenocentric and more historically and geographically appropriate perspectives—the Balkans and Anatolia—some insight into more general patterns of cultural transformation might emerge. As with language, what is needed is diachronic *and* synchronic analysis from broader cultural and historical perspectives.

A diachronic approach to myth can help to show how myth is related to language and metaphor; while synchronic analysis of specific examples can highlight social and historical perspectives, with implications beyond the study of Greece. Two series of questions arise. First, which features of myth tend to be specific to one culture, and which are universal? Do ways of putting together the constituent parts of a story form an analogy with what Roman Jakobson and Morris Halle call the "metonymic" or syntagmatic axis of language (based on contiguity, subsitution, and order), therefore tending to vary according to specific geographical and historical contexts?[14] Conversely, are the recurrent themes and images which define their tone and color (as opposed to "story") more closely linked to the "metaphorical" or paradigmatic axis of language (based on similarity, difference, and selection) and hence more enduring across time? Do myths and metaphors, studied diachronically, resemble a kaleidoscope, in which similar components are re-arranged to provide endlessly shifting pictures? Second, how can social and historical forces be related to the changing forms and functions of myths? What part do fantasy, dreams, and the unconscious play in their creation and perpetuation? Chapters 5 to 8 address these questions, drawing from oral and literary texts in an attempt to suggest how myth and history may be transformed into fiction (*mythistoréma*). Similarities and differences between Greek and other mythical songs and tales suggest that the path toward "modernity" has been uneven in the Greek case.

Some answers may lie in metaphor. Despite the voluminous studies on metaphor in recent years from many perspectives, there is no consensus on what it is and how it functions, beyond a majority view that it is inherent in language and thought. I argue further that there are important ritual dimensions to be explored in the Greek case. Jakobson and Halle's distinction between the metonymic and the metaphorical poles of language, supported as it is by linguistic, literary, and neurological evidence, will be used to suggest that myth and ritual have a share in both axes. Ritualized actions, from everyday life to those performed at each stage in the life cycle, will serve to introduce my discussion of metaphor. Metaphor and metonym form complementary rather than oppositional aspects of figurative language, and for that reason I shall treat metonym as one subset of the wider category of metaphor.

There exists a frequent overlap between literalist and nonliteral language. Modern wondertales, for example, may be told and received as true and not-true in a conscious game with time and place: "there was and there was not" is a common *incipit*, just as "I wasn't there, you weren't there, so who can believe a word of what I say?" is a common ending. Other tellers—especially of ghost stories—achieve their effect by insisting that they witnessed the events themselves: "and I was at the wedding, and see, here is food and drink from the feast to prove it." Tellers make skillful use of literalist devices in the weaving of the tale: "There was an old fisherman who wished he had a child, even if it were only half a child. And in due course his wife conceived and bore half a child."[15]

In discussing the importance of ritual and the interplay of literalist/figurative modes, I draw on the neurological disorder of autism, both from my experience as mother of autistic identical twin sons and from clinical studies. Autism is as relevant to an understanding of language as the clinical studies of aphasia on which Jakobson and Halle based their theory, since aphasia is a dysfunction only of *verbal language*, whereas autism reflects a deeper dysfunction of *communication* or signaling systems. The major problems are not between metaphor and metonym, literalist and nonliteral utterances and interpretations, but rather ones of *contextual understanding* or *inference* and *performative action*. Autistics make up the gap in their signaling systems with self-imposed rituals affecting motor-sensory reactions both to protect themselves from contact with the "outside world" and to derive pleasurable sensations, including those of touch and smell.[16]

There is some evidence to suggest that autistics' thought processes and abilities for performative action may take place through an unusually well-developed form of synesthesia, with heightened visual memory, but that these talents may diminish or disappear with the acquisition of even the most elementary use of language.[17] If metaphor—a kind of "thinking in pictures"—is an essential part of language, that does not mean it cannot function on some level outside language; for this reason it is misleading to suppose, with L. J. Cohen, that "until the linguistic problem [how metaphors are invented and comprehended] has a definitive solution, the psychological one cannot be adequately articulated." Rather, as Dan Sperber and Deirdre Wilson have argued, the art of communication is primarily psychologically—even physiologically—based and only secondarily linguistic. It is an inferential system, which may be encoded and decoded through language, but not by language alone. Ritualized actions, both private and public, remain a fundamental means of communication *outside language* through synesthesia. The behavior of autistics can therefore illuminate the processes of transposing experience and sensation into thought and action at the nonverbal as well as the verbal levels.[18]

Consideration is given in Chapters 9 and 10 to ritual and metaphor in oral speech and folk culture, or to the ways in which the whole manner of thinking and speaking may be figurative. In Greek it is possible to trace the processes by which certain key images are transmitted and transformed. For example, in the songs and stories relating to the life cycle, a complex and infinitely variable parallel is sustained between the human, vegetal, and animal worlds: a young child is a shoot or a seed of grain, a bride is a thick-leaved cotton plant or an orange tree, a young man is a cypress tree, while death is lamented as felling or uprooting. Such image systems are so deeply embedded in the language and in popular consciousness that they can give rise to striking new metaphors in everyday speech if the occasion demands, such as during the Civil War of 1945–49, when a woman who saw her husband brought in dead cried out, Πεῦκο μου "My pine-tree!"[19] Moreover, metaphors (as defined by Jakobson and Halle) are culturally as well as linguistically determined and for this reason are less easily translatable than are metonyms: "White House" can be rendered literally into Greek, but how to convey in English the Greek expression for "the sun has set" (βασίλεψε ὁ ἥλιος), which makes the sun a king whose reign is over? Our difficulty in interpreting metaphors can enrich our own use of language. Andrew Ortony has commented that "metaphors stretch language beyond its elastic limit." In similar terms, the poet and translator Olga Broumas explains how she treats language "like musical elastic," using Greek (from which she translates) to push English (in which she writes) "beyond its normal limits."[20] Metaphor connects disparate things, and, by means of surprising connections, teases us into believing that they are more similar than we would at first imagine.

3. The "Continuity Question" Revisited: Old Debates and New Approaches

A case has been made for reexamining language, myth, and metaphor in the context of Greek tradition as a whole. Let me now review briefly some studies relevant to Greece, then consider the contribution of recent debates between the traditional empiricists, on the one hand, and the various schools of Marxists, structuralists, and poststructuralists, on the other.

"Continuity" is currently an unfashionable term among a wide range of Greek scholars of different persuasions. I shall weigh up the arguments on both sides in general terms. The case against continuity has been argued most forcefully by historians, who have pointed out that comparisons between ancient and modern Greece omit or distort evidence for fundamental changes during the Byzantine and Ottoman periods.[21] Anthropologists too, reacting against E. B. Tylor's "survivalism" in a justifiable validation of modern Greece for its own sake rather than because of its links to the past, have tended to reject diachronic comparison in favor of intensive synchronic field analysis, although the past decades have seen a trend toward diachronic reintegration of history and anthropology.[22] Synchronic perspectives have also characterized structuralist and generative studies in linguistics.[23] While this emphasis may have enhanced the status of both Byzantine and modern Greek studies within each of these three disciplines, it has—unwittingly, perhaps—played into the hands of those classicists whose vision extends beyond antiquity only when Greek is *not* concerned. It has also facilitated the compartmentalization of Greek studies into three discrete categories—ancient, Byzantine, and modern—with concomitant sneers against trespassers, thereby affording others the excuse to marginalize or trivialize postclassical Greek. Surely there is room to pursue both synchronic and diachronic approaches side by side, so long as they take account of the processes of change?

The case for continuity has been dormant, associated with "romantic Hellenism," a product of nineteenth-century nationalism and survivalist theories of culture. Proponents have included, on the one hand, Greek folklorists and linguists intent on proving their claim to the ancient heritage and on disproving the pernicious racism of nineteenth-century attacks on the purity of the medieval and modern Hellenes and, on the other, European and American classical scholars of allegedly romantic or philhellenic leanings.[24] While their various ideological baggages need no longer be taken on board, there is no reason to reject all their results, particularly in the areas of language, religion, and mythology.

What is needed is a reassessment of the *politics* of continuity from a different perspective and according to new models. The old "archaeological model" of Greek folklore, by tracing straight parallels between ancient and modern material or deriving modern ballads from ancient myths, put emphasis on folkloric materials as *pure oral survivals* from antiquity and as *monuments and mosaics* from the past, neglecting changes in context and function. Similarly, according to the "textual model" of the historical-diffusionist school, oral tradition is traced back to the Byzantine period by a process of stemmatics: like classical manuscripts, variants were analyzed in meticulous detail in the hope of unraveling the historical and ethnic origins—or the evolution and diffusion—of particular story and song types. In both cases, tradition is *textualized*.[25]

The painstaking work of these scholars does not have to be brushed aside for us now to develop more sophisticated models for cultural transmission, taking account of the complex interaction between oral and written forms which has operated ever since literacy has existed.[26] Nor are the methodological practices and principles of earlier scholars to be rejected. In textual criticism, Walter Headlam established the principle that in order to edit any classical text, the critic must first become familiar with the changing forms of language known to the Byzantine scribes and scholars who transmitted them. Any form of Greek from any period may be relevant to our understanding of a given text. Nicholas Bachtin—less acclaimed than his brother Mikhail Bakhtin—had a rigorous yet dynamic approach to the principles and processes of linguistic change in Greek.[27] "Philology" is an easy target for certain schools of poststructuralist thought; but no theory of literature or criticism can afford to dispense with close attention to texts and textual traditions.

The major question to be addressed concerns the *kind* of "continuity" we are talking about, and this is where politics come into play. Adherents of survivalism and discontinuity alike rely on a static or idealized model of "Greece." If such notions are rejected as a largely modern fabrication, then "non-Greek" influences can be assessed at each stage of cultural transmission without undermining the integrity of the language and culture as a whole, becoming the focus of inclusion and interaction rather than exclusion. It is here that debates between various schools of criticism can sharpen our focus.

Marxists, in common with structuralists, have sought to explore and interpret underlying structures rather than merely record visible and observable data. Both contest the empiricist view that scholarship can be divorced from the ideologies of its time. In the field of myth, Marx, Mao, and Lévi-Strauss have illustrated the associative and metaphorical nature of mythical thinking and its relation to preliterate thought and language. Whereas Marxists have been concerned primarily with the dialectics of thought in relation to socioeconomic historical change, emphasizing the significance of the supposed transition from "primitive" to "rational" thought and the qualitative distinction between them, structuralists have tended to detach myth and ritual from their historical and socioeconomic contexts in order to reveal the universal patterns of human thought, seen to operate in quasi-metaphysical terms of a complex series of culturally variable binary oppositions. For Lévi-Strauss, history is no more "real" than myth.[28]

Over the past few decades, scholars in different fields have contributed to the debate. In anthropology, Maurice Godelier (1977) and Maurice Bloch (1983, 95–123) have scrutinized the ideas of Marx, Engels, and Lévi-Strauss in the light of recent research, seeking to extract the positive elements of each to develop a new approach, informed by structuralist methodology but grounded in historical and socioeconomic analysis. For Godelier, myth and history in ancient Greece raise vital questions about differences between "traditional" and "modern" societies. Bloch identifies elements in Marx, and above all in Engels, which can be associated with nationalism, evolutionism, and social Darwinism. In particular, he suggests that the objections of contemporary anthropologists to Marxism lie in its adherence to theories of primitive classless society and matriarchy, tentative and incipient in Marx but more fully developed in Engels' *Origin of the Family, Private Property, and the State* and rendered into orthodox dogma by Lenin and the early Russian Marxists.

If we make allowances for the "illusions of the age," from which neither Marx nor Engels were exempt, the gap between anthropology and Marxism is by no means so wide as some would believe. One may ask, is Marxism any longer relevant, now that its political edifices have collapsed? My response is much the same as it is to structuralist and poststructuralist critiques of philology: do we need to embrace Marxist ideological premises to appreciate their contributions to an understanding of socioeconomic factors in the formation and transmission of culture, any more than we need dismiss philology?

In ancient Greek mythology, French classicists have demonstrated the importance of viewing ancient mythical tradition as a whole and in relation to its changing historical times. Jean-Paul Vernant, Marcel Detienne, and Nicole Loraux, among others, have succeeded in defining an underlying mythical-metaphorical system which can be related to social and historical change. Their models form a synthesis of historical and structuralist approaches and provide a starting point for a study of later Greek texts, although this issue is one they fail to address. By contrast, among British Marxist classicists, George Thomson and Richard Seaford have shown less dalliance with structuralism and a greater insistence on dialectics and materialism.[29]

In religion and anthropology, Mircea Eliade has challenged the legacy of positivism, which opposed "myth" to scientific or religious "truth." Yet his insistence on the underlying function of all myths as an attempt to escape from the bonds of historical time and seek eternal return to "illo tempore" tends toward the mystical. Myths are not precluded from being culturally, socially, and historically determined just because they are ahistorical in form. Clifford Geertz sees cultural patterns as symbolic models in two senses, both as a model *of* reality and as a model *for* reality, which simultaneously express and shape perception. He exposes the treachery of such concepts as "logic" when dealing with unfamiliar behavior. However, his overall theory removes culture into the field of perceptions and away from its socioeconomic context.[30]

Questions of interpretation and meaning are central to poststructuralist debates on language, culture, and society. In *Rethinking Symbolism*, French scholar Dan Sperber proposed a new model for the study of myth, replacing the questions "what myths mean" and "what is their underlying truth" with the question "how myth means." In opposition to structuralism and historicism, he develops a theory of symbolic and comparative interpretation to explain how myths function in relation to the society and culture which created them, how myths in one culture derive from the transformation of other myths, and how different kinds of data are transformed into myth by means of mnemonic/symbolic selection. His conclusion is open: myth has no universal meaning, although there may be general areas of focalization, while its evocational fields (both cultural and individual) vary according to the nature of society and experience. Sperber's approach invites new ways of examining the interactions between myth and society. His more recent work, written with Deirdre Wilson, encompasses the study of communication and cognition.[31]

No study of continuity can afford to ignore the force of deconstruction, whether in the form of Jacques Derrida's critique of the nature/culture opposition which underlies the work of so many linguists and anthropologists, or of Michel Foucault's problematization of the concept of "tradition," with its concomitant preoccupations with tracing links, continuities, and similarities. Derrida demonstrates the shifting qualities inherent in all language and modes of interpretation, as well as the false Cartesian dualism of many conventionally opposed categories, such as Voice and Writing. Foucault, in place of traditional methods of analysis, proposes a new model of "archaeological analysis" as a means of determining how the governing rules of transformation in a given discourse may be linked with other discursive practices—in other words, how things change. For Foucault, deconstruction is political: texts and interpretive strategies compete violently for power and domination, while no single method can be validated on its own merits. His studies have proved useful in terms of broader strategies, but unlike Derrida, he has informed few close readings of texts.[32] Positive aspects of French deconstructionists include insistence upon the interrelat-

edness of all forms of discourse and upon the changing power struggle in
determining the dominant texts, interpretations, strategies, and ideologies—an approach not incompatible with the Marxist theories of dialectics
and the class struggle. Negative aspects include verbose opacity, lack of
documentation at crucial points, and, above all, the appropriation by
acolytes of abstruse terminology to form a professionalized critical discourse which obscures the radical potential of the deconstructionist case.
Exaggerated reactions against naïve realism and biographism have led to a
tendency to view interpretive strategies only in terms of "discourse theory," in isolation from the experience of writers and readers.[33]

The past few decades have seen a growing awareness of the importance
of gender studies in the human and social sciences. While considerable advances have been made in developing new theoretical and critical approaches to language, literature, and psychology, particularly in the West,
there has been insufficient reappraisal of the cultural and religious experience of women outside the "first world."[34] A major question I address is,
What role have women played in the creation and transmission of Greek
culture? Important work is being done in the fields of anthropology, soci-
ology, and literature, but links with the past have been relatively neglected.[35]
Western feminists assume a tone of condescension toward their third world
or "developing" sisters, inveighing against veils, clitoridectomy, wife beating, and other easy targets, without deeper analysis of the inhibiting effects
of more individualized but diminished socioeconomic and religious roles
played by women in modern capitalist societies and of the contingent differences in defining concepts of self, body, and property. Certain schools of
feminist criticism are at best irrelevant and at worst detrimental to an understanding of women's actual and potential cultural roles as mediators in
developing countries and across a rapidly changing face of Europe.

Questions of designation and definition arise at this point. What do we
mean by "modern" and "traditional" societies, and how can "Greece" be
described today? Its economy and sociopolitical structures are still transitional between the "third" and the "first" worlds (Greeks call themselves
"second-and-a-half"). Historically, Greek-speaking peoples have experienced transitions which range from the independent city-states of the
ancient world to incorporation with other peoples and languages under
Roman, Byzantine, and Ottoman rules and to unification into a small
nation-state, with subsequent population exchanges negotiated in the aftermath of World War I. Such diversity is not unique, but historical memory
of the past is strong among Greeks everywhere and has tended to shape
their perception of themselves as being different from peoples in modern
industrial and developing societies alike.

Is Greece "West" or "East"? Granted the Orientalist bias inherent in such distinctions, eloquently exposed by Edward Said, my own position which will clarified with reference to specific cases in the course of this book—is that Greeks, to this day and throughout their history, have a share in both. Since the eighteenth century and earlier, and well before the formation of the nation-state, Greek elites have aligned themselves, through education and association, with "Europe," and Greece is today a full member of the European Community.[36] Alliance with the world's more advanced economies has been strengthened by generations of emigration to Europe, North America, and Australia, creating strong ethnic communities and local societies which have invested financial and other resources back into their Greek villages.[37] In terms of popular culture, Greek songs, tales, and dances—and moral values—bear a stronger resemblance to those of the southern Mediterranean and the Near East than they do to our own, and it is this identity that expatriate communities have tended to preserve, through religious and cultural activities. For the purposes of brevity, the terms "Western" and "Greek" will be employed as shorthand for these complex antinomies and dichotomies.

The Western literary canon has been determined on the basis of written texts, until recently the products of male authors. Literary women in the West have had to fight for the right to inclusion on the same terms as men. In Greece, as in other traditional/transitional societies with a long past, orality has played a stronger cultural role: women have promoted moral and religious values, and have preserved the "mother tongue" at times of foreign domination, by telling stories and singing songs in the family context. If woman's voice of lamentation and protest in Greece and other comparable cultures has been appropriated over the ages by male writers, it remains paradoxically true that women can be shown to have contributed more significantly to the common culture than in the West, where the male written canon has been firmly entrenched at least since the Renaissance.[38] As for the present, Karen Van Dyck (1998) has shown that women writers of the so-called generation of the seventies have developed what she calls a "poetics of censorship," first employed as a means of subversion under the military dictatorship (1967–74), into a "poetics of self-censorship," which challenges the orientation of the (male) nationist-demoticist canon that began to be shaped in the 1880s. Thus, in accordance with postmodernist trends, previously discrete categories are merged or scrambled.

Salutary as such developments may be, most of these women writers reflect urban, middle-class, intellectual (and therefore Western-oriented) values and hence are unable to address Greek women (rural, provincial, and urban) who are literate enough to follow the media but whose experience of life places them outside the enclosed time-space of salon, bedroom, and kitchen in which much of the new women's poetry seems to be situated. Greek women writers find themselves at a critical point, whether to jump on a Western literary bandwagon or whether to question the male appropriation of the rich oral heritage of their rural mothers and sisters. Paradoxically, modern Greek literature does not afford supporting analogies to the "war between the sexes," argued by Sandra Gilbert and Susan Gubar to be the starting point of Western modernism at the turn of the nineteenth and twentieth centuries. On the contrary, Greek women writers insist on their right to be acknowledged as poets and novelists, not as "women writers." Their confidence as women stems from their life experience: they do not make a political statement out of gender.[39]

I cannot close this brief survey of theoretical approaches without acknowledging a lasting debt to the fine ethnographies of Greece, most published since my *Ritual Lament in Greek Tradition* (1974). Time and again, when interpreting songs, tales, poems, and stories, I have had recourse to studies of Greek culture in all its multifarious ritual manifestations: dance and song, lament and rejoicing, enchantment and exorcism.

By way of conclusion, I shall comment briefly on what I call linear and cyclical concepts of time and how they may be related to our understanding of Greek language, myth, and metaphor. According to the linear model, life is deemed to start at a particular point (individual birth) and to terminate at a final point (individual death), hence time measures the individual's progression from past to present, from present to future, in a diachronically ordered sequence: time is disjunctive, rather than connective— it does not repeat, nor can it go backward, and is analogous to the grammatical category of *tense* or to the syntagmatic axis suggested by Jakobson and Halle. According to the cyclical model, time is measured not just in terms of the individual's passage through life but also in terms of the generational passage from great-grandparents and grandparents down to grandchildren and great-grandchildren in an unending spiral, which is closer to the verbal category of *aspect* (Eliade's *illo tempore*), or to Jakobson and Halle's paradigmatic axis.[40] All literate cultures combine both linear and cyclical concepts in differing degrees. But whereas the "modernized West" has, at least since the Renaissance, tended to organize thought and religion along the linear model, for traditional and transitional societies, such as Greece today (and ancient and medieval societies with a developed but limited degree of literacy), human life is associated in myth, ritual, and metaphor with the reproductive, as well as destructive, forces of the cycle of nature. It would be simplistic to associate linear time with man's progression from myth to reason (public performance), cyclical time with woman's adherence to ritual and metaphor (household and family), but there *is* a gendered differentiation in Greek which operates on the levels of language, myth, and metaphor. Men have dominated literary discourse, and their language reflects the conflicting social power structures in successive historical periods, from diverse forms of archaizing Greek to the institutionalized demotic of the past decade or so. Women's voice across the ages has been more muted but more subversive, making freer use of dialect tongues and puristic phrases as appropriate to their woven words. Myth in song and tale is linear in its internal structure, cyclical in its frame of reference: it tells a story in coherent syntagmatic units, but it can be stored up and used on other occasions linking past to present and future paradigmatically, through memory. What ritual songs of the life cycle lack in syntagmatic coherence as narratives is compensated by constant metaphorical and metonymic reference to the business of everyday life.

In the corpus of Greek songs and stories collected over the past 180 years or so, the cyclical perception of time is predominant in women's songs and stories of the life cycle, whereas men celebrate individual combative exploits: death may be heroic, but is terminal, and needs women's songs to commemorate and immortalize men's existence. Linear concepts of time have determined how "continuity" has been understood. But if men's writing has defined the Greek literary canon and its interpretation, it has also been indebted to women's perceptions of the life cycle—human, natural, and divine. Cyclical, spiral—even double helical—concepts of time and space may form the basis for new models.[41]

There can be no single theoretical or ideological perspective on language, myth, and metaphor, only a diversity and a plurality of texts and interpretations.

PART I

LANGUAGE

It is convenient . . . to set aside the idioms of the Ancient Greek civilisation. But it is neither convenient nor accurate to speak of a Modern Greek "language". There is no such thing. There is only the present state of Greek.

—N. BACHTIN, *Introduction to the Study of Modern Greek*

Greek Polyglossia:
Historical Perspectives

Greeks have long shared a sense of linguistic continuity and cultural unity, however scattered geographically and divergent their dialects. They have been accustomed to using a wide range of linguistic registers, where parallel forms and words have learned to coexist. As one Athenian woman put it, "the Greek vocabulary records only births, never deaths."[1] It is doubtful whether at any stage in the history of the Greek language there was ever a single, unified form for either speech or writing. Even the so-called Common Modern Greek of the past two decades or so is more a perceived consensus between previously opposing factions than any clearly delineated standard spoken and written practice. The present language situation can best be understood in the wider perspective of the past, not simply as a legacy of two centuries of linguistic controversy.[2]

My concern is to focus attention on the diversity of registers in Greek and the interactions between them, with reference to earlier studies of its recorded history. Combining diachronic and synchronic approaches, Robert Browning charts and analyzes the major changes in linguistic forms from the "common Greek" (the koine) of the fourth century B.C. to the present day. Peter Mackridge is synchronic: in contrast to the normative grammars and studies of the past two centuries, he analyzes "the present state of the Greek language," drawing examples from everyday conversations, the media, and literature, arguing that some kind of "standard Greek" is now a reality, at least in the urban centers.[3] I review some other dimensions of both past and present usages.

1. Distinctive Features of the Greek Language

We may start with a series of paradoxes. Ancient Greek, in common with Latin and Sanskrit, is one of the three major languages on which theories of the origins, diffusion, and history of the Indo-European family of languages have been based. Yet about 40 percent of its vocabulary cannot be identified as Indo-European (I-E), although vocabulary may prove treacherous, especially if the extant texts are of a technical nature.[4] Ancient Greek is closer to the Greek of today than it is to Latin or Sanskrit, which have given rise to the interrelated but independent groups of Romance and Indic languages. While Latin and Sanskrit are "dead" languages, Greek is not. This does not mean that Greek has not undergone profound changes during the two and a half millennia of its recorded history. Rather, as Bachtin and others have shown, the patterns of linguistic change can be systematically recorded, and many of their generative principles are evident from the beginning.

We speak of the history and development of Greek as a single, uninterrupted process; and so it is, in that the major changes can be documented throughout most of its history. Yet undue emphasis on the unity of Greek can mask diversity in forms co-existent at every stage of its development and the extent to which vocabulary and morphology, syntax and phonology, have been modified through contact with neighboring languages and through multilingual communities scattered across the Greek-speaking world from the Black Sea coast to southern Italy. For these reasons, this chapter will draw attention to the general features of Greek polyglossia, while analysis of specific texts, both literary and nonliterary, forms the focus of Chapters 2–4.[5]

A further paradox has more to do with modern preconceptions than with the Greek language. On the one hand, as Bachtin has suggested, whereas classical scholars tend to be ignorant of medieval and modern Greek, few scholars of medieval English literature approach it without a fluent command of the living English language. As he points out, New Testament Greek differs from Homeric Greek more than it does from the modern tongue, being roughly equivalent in difficulty to Shakespeare for the average English speaker today. The relationship between Latin and Italian has been invoked as a parallel, although the differences between them are greater.[6] Latinists speak and read Italian more readily than ancient Hellenists will admit knowing medieval and modern Greek. The reasons lie, I suspect, in Orientalist perceptions of Greece under Ottoman rule and also in what Vološinov has termed philology's desire to restrict its domain to the study of "defunct, alien languages preserved in written monuments."[7] I try to put some life back into those voices from the Greek past. On the other hand, the modern Greek state discontinued the teaching of ancient Greek in schools (1981), while some neohellenists have recently raised doubts on the relevance of ancient Greek.

Some brief examples will demonstrate how a knowledge of ancient Greek (AG) can enrich appreciation of the modern language (MG). On the phonological level, the "narrowing-raising-fronting" of the vowel system, which resulted in the shift from *a* to *ē* in some ancient dialects (Attic *mētēr* versus Doric *matēr*), was operative in determining the further sound shifts *ai* to *e*, *ē* to *i*, *ei* to *i*, *oi* to *ü*, *ü* to *i*. These changes (except the last) can be documented from the beginning of our era, although even today certain dialects have preserved many features of the older vowel system: Maniot and Aeginetan, forms of "Old Athenian," have πάϊδα (*páidha*) instead of standard παιδιά (*pedhiá*), τσουλία (*choulía*) for κοιλιά (*kiliá*).[8] In morphology, stem changes in verbal conjugation can be traced back to late antiquity, so that the vagaries of many of the most common modern verbs may be understood, and better learned, with reference to ancient paradigms. The following chart shows how modern Greek verbs have re-formed imperfective endings consistently on the basis of the ancient perfective stem, which has remained remarkably stable:[9]

Table 1.	Modern Greek		Ancient Greek	
Present	Aorist indicative	Aorist subjunctive	Present indicative	Aorist indicative
πηγαίνω 'I go'	πήγα	πάω	υπάγω	υπῆγον
στέλνω 'I send'	έστειλα	στείλω	στέλλω	έστειλα
μαθαίνω 'I learn'	έμαθα	μάθω	μανθάνω	έμαθον
λαβαίνω 'I hold'	έλαβα	λάβω	λαμβάνω	έλαβον
πίνω 'I drink'	ήπια	πιῶ	πίνω	έπιον
παίρνω 'I take'	πῆρα	πάρω	υπαίρω	υπῆρον

Syntactic changes, such as the loss of the infinitive, declinable participle, and relative pronoun, as well as changes in mood and aspect, can be explained both by internal principles and by the influences of neighboring languages.[10] In vocabulary, while a large number of ancient words has lived on, with semantic shifts, Greek has been as greedy in assimilating foreign loanwords as it has been cavalier about dropping them when no longer functionally relevant, while storing up such words for future literary exploitation.[11] Almost all modern writers have been familiar with the ancient heritage, mostly from the original texts. The reaction against ancient Greek, whether in the educational system or among academics, is the demoticist converse of purism.

2. Diversity and Change: From Ancient Greek to the Koine

From about 1400 B.C. to the present day, the Greek language can be documented in written records (with the largest gap from c. 1200 to 700 B.C.), so that changes can be charted according to major historical and demographic shifts: Prehistoric, Ancient, Hellenistic, Byzantine, and Modern. Each has left traces in the literary and spoken language of the present, while the most crucial changes in the direction of modern Greek are to be found in the Hellenistic *koine* from the mid–fourth century B.C. Linguistic change does not always coincide with the processes of historical change, but it is contingent upon them. From its earliest recorded history, the literary language has shown versatility and flexibility, and these two features have continued to affect written and spoken usage. Homeric Greek is a traditional poetic language, or *Kunstsprache*, comprising features from several dialects but never the spoken language of any one people, and was possibly first committed to writing in the mid–seventh century.[12] The dialects of AG were literary as well as spoken forms, each cultivated for particular genres, regardless of the writer's mother tongue; Attic-Ionic was usual for prose and dialogue; Aeolic and Doric, for hymns and choral odes.[13] Literary dialects differed from actual dialects as preserved in inscriptions, but they were readily understood and served to enrich the linguistic heritage.

The phonetic system of AG includes one important factor which enables us to reconstruct its "tone of voice" rather more than is the case with other "dead" languages: because pronunciation was based on pitch accent rather than on stress, intonation was relatively fixed, hence nuance of meaning was conveyed by variable word order and by a rich fund of particles.[14] The shift from pitch to stress after the classical period was a crucial factor in determining far-reaching changes thereafter.

With the demise of the independent city-states and the unification of the Greek-speaking world under the Hellenistic kingdoms from the mid–fourth century B.C., there arose a new "common dialect" (κοινὴ διάλεκτος). Koine Greek (KG) was a late form of Attic Greek with some standardization, diffused throughout Greece and eastward by the Macedonian armies, forming an interesting parallel to the spread of Low Latin by the Roman legions. It was at this time that the ancient dialects fell into gradual spoken disuse, with the exception of a late form of Doric which survived in parts of the Peloponnese.[15] Meanwhile, writers continued to exploit the ancient literary dialects for verse and strictly classical Attic for prose. The picture of Greek during the Hellenistic period was by no means as simple as the term "common Greek" might suggest. On the one hand, its spoken and written uses were diverse; on the other, literary forms of Greek from

Homer to the classical poets, historians, and orators remained prestigious models. New elites were situated on the eastern peripheries of the Greek-speaking world.

Controversy on questions of language and style dates back to the years following the Roman conquests of the second century B.C. Writers aspired to revive classical Attic and other ancient dialects as a literary medium in place of the contemporary koine, while arguments on "correct" prose style remained long and bitter.[16] "Pure Attic" became a mark of social superiority.[17] In the meantime, there was a growing discrepancy between the language of literary texts, which formed the basis of the educational system, and the spoken languages. With Latin as the language of central administration from the first century B.C. to the sixth century A.D., changes in spoken Greek were rapid, giving rise to new dialect differentiation within the koine still evident in modern dialects.[18] Atticizing grammarians of the period display many features which can be paralleled in the kind of disputes that have continued until recently: they compiled lists of words and forms proscribed as barbarous or vulgar, with "correct" Attic equivalents; they used Attic for writing and for formal and public occasions, but made concessions to the spoken language in private notes and informal writing. They also invented their own hypercorrect Attic forms, as well as resurrecting old ones.[19] The Greek language has never been transparent.

3. Conflicts of Language and Style in the Byzantine Period

Such was the linguistic situation inherited by the Byzantine Empire. The koine remained the basis for spoken Greek, for early Christian writers, and for certain texts either intended for performative delivery or designed for wider dissemination, such as hymns, homilies, saints' lives, and popular chronicles. Attic was still the language of prestige, thus once Christianity was officially established, Attic began—gradually and unevenly—to interpenetrate the Hellenistic koine in religious writings. From the sixth century until at least the twelfth, Attic remained entrenched in the educational and social system. Further major changes in spoken forms of Greek can be postulated for the early and middle Byzantine periods. Like all empires, Byzantium included a large number of peoples whose first language was not Greek, and many who spoke no Greek at all. In a linguistic map of the Empire under Justinian (c. 560 A.D.), Cyril Mango attempts to rectify the overwhelmingly Greek bias of our extant sources by drawing attention to the number and significance of other languages—including Latin, Aramaic, Coptic, and Caucasian tongues. He also cites evidence for multilingualism and bilingualism, especially in the southeast (Syria, Egypt), although he does not stress the significance of the phenomenon for the creation of new literary genres, such as the *kontakion* "hymn," to be discussed in Chapter 2.[20] During the middle Byzantine period (c. 600–1050), major incursions and population shifts saw the penetration of what is now Greece by Slavic and Albanian peoples and, soon after, movements of Turkic peoples across the hinterland of Asia Minor. While the degree of interaction between Greek and other languages cannot be calculated with any precision, the multilingualism of the Empire can be attested by loanwords from Latin, Slavic, Albanian, Arabic, Persian, Celtic, Germanic, Turkic, and other languages in texts from the sixth to twelfth centuries. Many such loanwords, derived mainly from nominal roots, survive in standard and dialect speech to this day. Of these, the number of Latin words for ceremonial, military, and household terms which have remained part of the basic word stock of modern Greek suggests a deep-seated Latin influence on the vocabulary of the spoken language, probably deriving from the use of Latin in the army during the late Roman periods and from its continued use in court ceremonial.[21]

From the late eleventh and twelfth centuries onward, there is a steady rise in the literary use of the vernacular, or forms of Greek evolved from the Hellenistic koine. Contact with the West after the Fourth Crusade of 1204 meant that the lingua franca of trade was Italian, as evidenced by bilingual Greek-Italian nonliterary and vernacular conversation manuals of the twelfth century and after.[22] In areas under Western rule, a good classical education ceased to be a sine qua non of social status, although the learned language continued to enjoy prestige. The earliest compositions of any length in vernacular Greek were in verse. From late-eleventh- and twelfth-century Constantinopolitan court circles there survive satirical and edificatory poems of a literary quality that suggests conscious experimentation with the vernacular on the part of an educated elite, such as the four "Ptochoprodromic Poems," attributed to Theodore Prodromos. These are analyzed in Chapter 4, alongside satire and fiction in learned Greek. From the thirteenth to fifteenth centuries, there survive verse laments, fables, romances, and chronicles, many known to emanate from outside Constantinople. Most are composed in *politikos stichos*, the stressed fifteen-syllable meter of modern oral tradition, and in a form of Greek that has been termed by modern scholars "Byzantine koine," in the absence of identifiable dialect elements and in view of the range of morphological, syntactic, and lexical forms employed.

What kind of language was this—spoken or written, popular or learned? Or are these very dichotomies a simplistic projection onto the past of latter-day concepts? Its nature and origins have been much debated since the 1880s. The problem is central to the literary emergence of modern Greek (for, in all important respects, these texts are in "modern Greek") and concerns its relationship, on the one hand, to spoken forms and oral tradition (not necessarily the same thing) and, on the other, to learned literature. I attempt to outline the major arguments and make my own suggestions.

As for linguistic consistency, if we heed Browning's reminder that "register" is a more accurate concept than "language," the difficulties of mixing learned and vernacular forms disappear, especially since writers experimented with established literary genres.[23] Michael Jeffreys is categorical in his assumption that the Byzantines shared our own preconceptions of linguistic homogeneity, and finds it "difficult to accept the picture of generations of Byzantine intellectuals who experiment in popular language, yet fail to carry their experiments through to the *logical conclusion of a completely vernacular poem*. The education of such men was directed entirely to the *elimination of mistakes from their writing*, towards the preservation of a *uniform linguistic level*. If they decided to experiment with the vernacular, surely at least one man could have been found in several centuries to impose *a similar uniformity on his demotic writing*?" (emphases mine).[24] To explain the lack of uniformity in the (written) vernacular poems (which, it is assumed, cannot have been characteristic of everyday speech), Jeffreys advances the hypothesis of a Byzantine literary Kunstsprache, dependent on a supposedly *oral* tradition in politikos stichos, which admitted variant forms for metrical and oral-formulaic reasons of composition and performance.

While acknowledging the interaction between many forms of Greek in the later Byzantine period, I propose a different explanation—namely, that the "inconsistencies" encountered are precisely those to be expected during the process of adapting the "vulgar tongue" to the written word.[25] First, there was no such thing as modern "demotic" during the twelfth to fifteenth centuries. Second, learned literature of the eleventh and twelfth centuries displays a commensurate variety of forms and registers in its experimentation with mimesis and parody.[26] Third, while paying lip service to "correctness," authors of functional texts had always made concessions to what they call "vulgar Greek" in the interests of intelligibility. As for the forms of Greek actually spoken in the capital, Browning concludes, with judicious caution, that there probably existed "a common tongue in which a great many alternative forms, belonging historically to different dialects, were acceptable. Men from all over the Greek world mingled in Constantinople as they did nowhere else."[27] The currency of non-Greek tongues in everyday use on the streets of the capital has been noted by John Tzetzes, who lists Latin, Hebrew, Alanic, Arabic, Slavic, and

Turkic.[28] This was not new; what is significant is that it was deemed worthy of comment, precisely at a time when Clement of Alexandria's view of language as fixed and "God-given" was debated.[29]

None of our early vernacular verse texts can be dated with any certainty on linguistic grounds.[30] Notions of linguistic unity and consistency have been an obsession among scholars, Greek and non-Greek, from before the birth of the Greek nation-state to the present day (particularly at the turn of the nineteenth and twentieth centuries). It seems safer to attribute the profusion of linguistic forms to the difficulties of recording in writing a spoken form of the language which cannot have been *standardized*, simply because it had never been *written*, than to postulate either an oral-formulaic poetic Kunstsprache or haphazard scribal interference. The earliest vernacular poems are courtly, not "folk," in genre, tone, and context.[31] Much of the vernacular literature of the thirteenth to fifteenth centuries was transmitted anonymously, with an increasing diversification of genres, alongside translation and adaptation of Western models and experimentation with popular songs and fables. Where more than one manuscript of a text is preserved (as with *Digenes Akrites* and many of the romances), the differences are considerable, with frequent interpolations, omissions, and digressions. These factors have misled some scholars into vague notions of "popular tradition" or "low style"—and therefore supposedly "artless"—composition. Closer examination of the manuscripts reveals an awareness of individual style that is often masked by the prevalent editorial practice of conflating different manuscripts of a text into a single, unified version. In particular, the romances of the Palaiologan period (1204–1453) show a degree of sophistication in language, imagery, and composition that is only just beginning to be treated with deserved seriousness.[32] It seems fruitless to speculate on the precise relationship of the new poetic vernacular either to spoken usage or to folk tradition and preferable to regard it as a varied and continuing interpenetration of spoken and written forms, where literary language is conscious artifice.

It remains to review the emergence of the literary vernacular in relation to meter, the fifteen-syllable accentual politikos stichos.[33] The theories advanced to account for its origins are controversial and need not concern us here. Suffice it to say that its connections with the ancient catalectic tetrameter have been questioned, despite Byzantine attestations; Jeffreys's theory of its derivation from a late Roman ceremonial meter (*versus quadratus*) cannot be proved. Its earliest known uses come not from "folk poetry" but from court ceremonial of the ninth century.[34] The few snatches of popular songs and acclamations cited sporadically by chroniclers and historiographers from the seventh to twelfth centuries suggest, as we shall see in Chapter 3, an irregular combination of stressed seven or eight-syllable lines, thus supporting the view of the Swiss musicologist Samuel Baud-Bovy that the origins of politikos stichos ("city verse" or "political verse") are composite, a theory consistent with his observations that the oldest units are probably octosyllabic and heptasyllabic (trochaic and iambic), as in the fragments of Byzantine popular songs and as still current in Maniot and other folk songs. His tentative conclusion that politikos stichos was a spoken rather than a sung meter and that it was a relatively late development in Byzantine tradition accords with the linguistic and literary evidence for the emergence of the vernacular in the Komnene period. It was an urban court phenomenon, which spread rapidly across the Greek-speaking world for narrative verse and written literature during the late Byzantine period, but with no proven origin in song or dance.[35] The earliest modern Greek literature, then, is neither oral nor popular in any meaningful sense but an artful blend of spoken and written forms, drawing on learned, Western, and Eastern models as much as on folk traditions and designed to meet the requirements of audiences across an increasingly diversified and fragmented Greek-speaking world.

4. The Emergence of Dialect Literature: Cyprus and Crete

The five major dialect groups still spoken today are descended from the Hellenistic koine: Peloponnesian, Northern, Cretan, Southeastern, and Cypriot. It is not possible to trace their origins in detail, but Cretan, Cypriot, and, to a lesser extent, Southeastern are well represented in the records and literature of the post-Byzantine period.[36] One of the prerequisites for the development of literature in vernacular dialects is the spread of literacy across a wide range of functions, which gives rise to a new class of relatively unskilled scribes, whose task was not to compose but to take down from dictation all kinds of legal, administrative, and other documents. Dialect is recorded in areas outside Byzantine control, first in legal and administrative documents and later in poetry. The earliest evidence for literary dialects comes from areas under Western rule, notably from Cyprus, Crete, and other islands of the Aegean. From Cyprus under the House of Lusignan in the fourteenth to sixteenth centuries we have legal Assizes, two prose chronicles, and a group of anonymous love poems, all of which display features of the modern Cypriot dialect.[37] The love poems are translations and adaptations of Italian sonnets, retaining original verse forms and drawing sporadically on folk tradition. Dialect archives also survive from fifteenth-century Naxos, while the delightful series of love poems, the *Ero-*

topaignia, or *The Alphabet of Love*, often referred to as "Rhodian," probably belong to the Aegean more widely.[38]

It is above all from the island of Crete, during the period of Venetian rule from 1204 until its capture by the Ottomans in 1669, that dialect can be illustrated most fully. Documents showing dialectal features exist from the end of the twelfth century, rapidly increasing in number from the later thirteenth century onward. From the start, where Greek rather than Italian or Latin is used, it is a form of Cretan dialect, often written in the Latin alphabet and according to the phonological rules of Italian.[39] A break with the Greek alphabet facilitated the recording of a form of vernacular closer to the spoken language. This mode, preferred by many of the Cretan poets and dramatists from circa 1400 to 1669, is not to be attributed to ignorance of the Greek alphabet but to a conscious preference for a different graphical system to record what was perceived as a different form of the language.

It remains to consider the impact of bilingualism and multilingualism in areas under Latin (and especially Venetian) rule. Again, the fullest evidence comes from Crete, although the Cypriot *Assizes* (fourteenth century) and the chronicler Leontios Makhairas (fifteenth century) testify to a comparable diversity on Cyprus. During the sixteenth and seventeenth centuries, Crete could scarcely have been more diverse economically, socially, and ethnically despite a population of no more than 200,000. This number included some 3,000 foreigners—Italians, Jews, Armenians, Albanians, and Germans—registered in Kastro as mercenaries or as engaged in trade and commerce. Judging from the evidence of contemporary documents, the sharpest economic divide fell between the aristocratic and prosperous urban inhabitants of the island and the indigenous urban and rural population. Even here, the interdependence of peasant and feudal lord and of urban laborer and contractor fostered some kind of social and cultural interaction. By the mid–seventeenth century, peasant bands were ready to arm themselves against the Veneto-Cretan aristocracy in the service of the Ottomans.[40]

Crete owed its urban prosperity to Venetian mercantile contacts maintained across Europe from Portugal to England and Holland and southeastward to Ottoman-held territories in Egypt, Syria, Cyprus, and Armenia. From the later sixteenth century, the wars between Venice and the Ottoman empires gave Crete a crucial military and commercial position. Its prosperity owed much to the wars between Venice and the Ottoman Empire from the late sixteenth century.[41] The emergence of new literary genres cannot be explained only by socioeconomic factors, but the cultural diversity, economic prosperity and fertile contacts with the outside world created the conditions under which staged drama in Greek could flourish during the 1570s, for the first time since classical Athens.

Language was a crucial factor in the emergence of drama; here, women had a mediating role. Although the Venetian dialect of Italian was usual for administration and notaries had to be fluent in Italian and literate in Latin, there was no official imposition of Italian. The language of everyday communication was Cretan Greek, which, in the absence of the constraints of archaizing Greek, was cultivated in writing. Venetians permanently settled in Crete were bilingual, but their descendants tended to become hellenized. Thus, Foscarini complains that during the later sixteenth and seventeenth centuries, "la colonia in magior parte e fatta greca . . . hanno del tutto perso la cognitione et intelligenzà della lingua italiana" ("the colony is in greater part Hellenised. . . they have entirely lost the knowledge and understanding of the Italian language").[42] Mocenigo attributes this loss of Italian to the pernicious influence of Greek wives, who brought up their children to be Greek speaking and Orthodox.[43] While the male landowning aristocracy— both Veneto-Cretan and Cretan—were bilingual, their wives and daughters, by virtue of their seclusion and lack of education, spoke only Cretan, tending to remain true to the Orthodox faith (by the mid–seventeenth century, the daughter of dramatist and landowner Marcos-Antonios Foscolos knew no Italian). Italian was the major language of the all-male literary academies, the Vivi of Rethymno and the Stravaganti of Chania. For drama, which provided entertainment for highborn wives as well as foreigners, Cretan Greek became the language of common currency.[44] Tragedy provided dramatists with the opportunity to elevate the Cretan Greek to a degree of sophistication and complexity equal to that of classical Greek and Italian drama; religious drama makes use of ecclesiastical forms; pastoral poetry and drama exploit the more rural dialect of Western Crete. Above all, the urban comedies juxtapose the language of pimps, procuresses, and other "women of the street" with the trilingual, macaronic Greek-Italian-Latin of pretentious pederastic schoolmasters to form an obscenely subversive yet subtle source of verbal humor and dramatic irony through misunderstanding.

5. Forms of Greek in the Ottoman Period

After the fall of Crete to the Ottomans in 1669, many Cretans fled to areas still under Western control, such as the Ionian Isles, taking with them their books and manuscripts, their dialects and oral traditions. It was through the Ionian Isles—never part of the Ottoman Empire—that contact between centers of learning in Italy and the Greek-speaking world was maintained. The learned tradition which dominated Byzantine culture no longer formed part of a centralized system. Although Hellenism was acephalous, the myth of the past—that is, the idealization of its classical and Christian heritages—lived on. It operated on several levels: on the radical reformers influenced by Western humanism who cultivated various forms of Greek derived from the spoken language; on the Orthodox Church; and on the more conservative adherents of archaism. At this stage language disputes took on another aspect that was to become dominant from the late eighteenth and nineteenth centuries: language became identified with the search for national and cultural identity. In the mid–sixteenth century, Nikolaos Sofianos, an enlightened reformer from the Ionian Isles who spent most of his life in Italy, wrote one of the first grammars of the vernacular so that, as he put it, the language could be systematized for use in commerce and as the basis of a reformed educational program.[45] His dreams of educational reform were never realized, and it was not until the later eighteenth century that ideas similar to his own for language reform were seriously developed. Archaizing Greek still enjoyed prestige, and for good reasons: Greek remained the language of the Orthodox patriarchate and of the many Greek administrators of the Ottoman Empire in Constantinople; it was also used for trade and commerce throughout the Ottoman world. Archaism was motivated not just by traditionalist intellectuals (a good many intellectuals were radicals in outlook), but by the realization that it had greater universality than did the vernacular dialects. Its use in schools and churches outside the Greek-speaking areas, especially in the Balkans, afforded a sense of cultural superiority. To promote the vernacular would have meant implicitly denying the exclusiveness of the Greek of the Bible and the classics.

The struggle under the Ottoman Empire between vernacular and learned forms was only one aspect of a further series of contradictions. In one respect the reformers were right: archaism was a linguistic anachronism which had a stultifying effect on creative writing. In other respects, had it not been for the prestige of the ancient language, which acted as a unifying force throughout the period of Ottoman rule, Greek might well have split up into divergent languages, as happened elsewhere in the Balkans. Writers and intellectuals were often educated or domiciled abroad, and their scholarly output was printed at the Greek presses of Jassy, Bucharest, Constantinople, and Saint Petersburg: Greek letters formed a bridge between East and West as between the multilingual elites of the Ottoman world.[46] At the same time, the increasing influence of the European Enlightenment met with disapproval in more conservative quarters of the Orthodox Church, although it would be a mistake to view the Church's role as negative or negligible, especially as regards popular education. Whereas most educated Greeks from the early or mid–eighteenth century despised popular culture for what they saw as a manifestation of Ottoman enslavement, the Church—almost as suspicious of Western ideas as it was inimical to the Infidel—was less remote from the people, and it did disseminate basic literacy.

Alongside secular and religious tracts, there is a third strand in prerevolutionary literary productivity: simple prose tales of local saints and heroes, whose legendary deeds had saved their communities from infidel and barbarian attacks and from natural disasters or who had led their people to new village sites—a veritable blend of popular religion, history, and oral traditions. It was from such humble works as the *Chronicle of Galaxeidi* (1703) or the sermons of Kosmas the Aetolian that the more farsighted precursors of the War of Independence (1821–28), such as Rhigas Velestinlis and the anonymous author of *Greek Nomarchy* (1806), drew inspiration for their own writings in an attempt to bridge the gap between ideals for national liberation and rural reality, where fierce local rivalries often proved stronger than abstract notions of Hellenism.

Meantime, old favorites such as the romances of Alexander the Great, Apollonios of Tyre, Cretan poetry and drama (including Bergadis' *Apokopos*), the pastoral *The Shepherdess* (Βοσκοπούλα), Vitzentsos Kornaros' *Erotokritos*, the anonymous *Sacrifice of Abraham*, and Chortatsis' tragedy *Erofili* were continuously modified in their linguistic forms and reprinted as chapbooks, to be circulated—not without profit—from the Glykys and other presses in Venice to the towns and villages of Epiros.[47] Alexis Politis cites evidence that such texts were recited at weekly gatherings, at the house of the local priest or doctor, so that Greeks under the Ottomans, if no more literate than their Balkan counterparts, were in closer touch with past literary heritage, perhaps because best-loved texts were an inalienable part of their "Greekness" under conditions of Turkish rule.[48]

It was the geographical fragmentation of the Greek mainland and Aegean islands, the uneven patterns of foreign occupation, and the diversity of cultural influences that rendered possible the variegated mosaic of local traditions in music, song, dance, weaving, and copperware techniques, once such a striking feature of Balkan and Anatolian cultures. All sides cherished the illusory hope that Greece could be saved by appeals to her past when the necessary economic and political conditions for an independent nation-state were lacking; yet it was precisely these diverse facets of patriotism in a small people, widely scattered geographically, but with a strong sense of cultural unity and diversity, which kept the concept of Greekness going during its most vulnerable period.

The contradictions and tensions of the prerevolutionary period are best reflected in the works of Adamantios Korais (1748–1833), "father" of *katharevousa*, or "purifying Greek." The term was introduced in the decade 1790–1800, although not used extensively until later, but the concept of "purification," or "beautification," is implicit in Korais' proposed reforms.[49] Korais was caught between two extremes, trying to reconcile the irreconcilables. His new koine was opposed on two fronts: by the archaizers, who represented the interests of the civil administration and church hierarchy of Ottoman Constantinople; and by the more radical intellectuals, who regarded the spoken language as the only viable medium. But because his attempt to steer a middle way reflected the ethos of the most decisive class in the struggle for independence—the mercantile bourgeoisie and the intelligentsia—katharevousa, as it became known during Korais' lifetime, was eventually established as the language of the new Greek nation.

Was this inevitable? The seeds of a national language for Greece as then constituted existed in the dialect of the Peloponnese, which gradually became standardized as it spread to Attica after the provisional administration of 1828 moved from Nafplio to form the first independent government in Athens (1833). But the reform movement was still in its infancy, and conditions did not favor the supremacy of a standardized form of the spoken tongue for another 150 years. Linguistic science was undeveloped, and advocates of vernacular and puristic forms alike could not separate questions of language from emotive issues of patriotism and Hellenism. Early proponents of the spoken language, such as Athanasios Christopoulos in his *Grammar of Aeolo-Doric, That Is of the Present Spoken Language of the Greeks* (1805) and Iannis Vilaras in Η Ρομεηκη Γλοσα [*sic*] "The Romeic Tongue" (1814), justified their position by claiming that spoken Greek was derived not from the Hellenistic koine of the Septuagint and the New Testament but from the ancient Aeolo-Doric dialect and was therefore more Hellenic than any descendant of Attic.[50]

6. After National Independence: Struggles for Hegemony

The fifty years following the establishment of Greece as a nation-state saw an increased polarization in the language controversy and the emergence of the "language question" (Γλωσσικὸ Ζήτημα) in its mature stages. Katharevousa (K) was established as the language of the state, while the term "demotic" ("the people's language" [D]) gained currency from 1818 onward, taking over from earlier designations such as koine, vulgar, or Romeic.[51] There were more conservative dissenters, such as the Soutsos brothers. Extreme proposals followed, vitiated by the fact that their concept of Attic was an artifice. Like their antecedents of the second century A.D., they produced prescriptions and proscriptions.

Since the beginning of the War of Independence (1821–28), several factors had strengthened the advance of D. By the time Athens became the nation's capital, the Peloponnesian dialect was in the process of acquiring national currency as a form of spoken Greek more comprehensible to outsiders attracted to the metropolis than was the local "Old Athenian" dialect. Furthermore, in reaction to Jakob von Fallmerayer's attacks on the integrity of the Greek race, there was a growing awareness of the significance of folklore, with its rich and poetic language, as occurred elsewhere in nineteenth-century Europe.[52] Demotic was cultivated in literature, especially in the Ionian Isles, which had enjoyed political independence during the Ottoman period and were ceded by Britain to Greece in 1864. By the 1880s, the demoticist movement had gained considerable support. What was needed was its establishment on a scientific basis and national prestige.[53]

The debate between purists and demoticists appears to be a straightforward question of language: is K or D the genuine descendant of ancient Greek and *therefore* (according to preconceptions on both sides) the more apt medium for literary expression? From the vantage point of the present, both sides had a case, sharing the assumption that the modern language must be coherent in its relation to the ancient. In fact, by the latter part of the nineteenth century, what was at stake was the literary canon. Jean Psicharis (1854–1929) and Kostis Palamas (1859–1943) played crucial roles in wresting hegemony from the purists and revising the rules of the modern Greek canon. "I cannot be merely the poet of myself," wrote Palamas in the preface to *The Twelve Lays of the Gypsy*. "I am a poet of my age and of my nation" (Thomson 1969, 2). His poems gives expression to the continuity of Hellenism from a new standpoint—that of the outsider, the quintessentially romantic Gypsy with a heterogeneous past. The same sense that imbues his work of poet as "bard of the nation" has inspired male poets ever since, from ideological perspectives as different as those of Angelos Sikelianos (1884–1951), Kostas Varnalis (1884–1974), Yiannis Ritsos (1909–1989), George Seferis (1900–1971), and Odysseas Elytis (1911–1996). It gives priority to *phōnē* "voice" over *graphē* "text," rendering to modern Greek poetry a songlike quality, whether declamatory, prophetic, tragic, or nostalgic. Although different from that of Western modernist or postmodernist poetry, this voice has significant parallels in other non-Western cultures, where the poet still performs in public, retaining something of his mantic character, as in other premodern cultures.

Throughout, Greece has enjoyed the advantages of a heterogeneous tradition. As the poet C. P. Cavafy (1863–1933) once wryly remarked from his outsider's vantage point in Alexandria, the demoticists wanted to throw half of the Greek language into the river, while the purists wished to push the other half into the sea.[54] Cavafy, a near contemporary of Palamas, born in Alexandria and educated during his early life in England, exploits the full range of linguistic registers, eschewing the rhetorical and lyrical modes for the dramatic and ironic, while drawing on the Hellenic past to explore its gaps, interstices, and discontinuities, giving greater emphasis to textual than to oral texts. Often regarded as idiosyncratically "Alexandrian," Cavafy stands in an alternative bibliophile tradition which can be traced back through Emmanuel Roidis and Adamantios Korais to the scholars of Byzantium and of his native Alexandria. Although he founded no school of poetry, his challenge to the demotic poetic canon has continued into the present decade, as poets—men and women—differ not merely in their avoidance of declamation and their greater flexibility of register but also in their perceptions of time, space, and tradition: the sites of "Hellenism" are satirized, parodied, or subverted.[55]

The language of Greek prose fiction has attracted less attention than that of poetry and has followed a different path. Prose was slower to adopt demotic, no doubt partly because there were fewer vernacular models of the kind cultivated in poetry since the twelfth century but, more significantly because poetry/song was deemed a more appropriate vehicle than prose/tales for nationist-demoticist sentiments. While the dominant poetic mode has been declamatory, or what Bakhtin terms "monologic," prose has been more "dialogic," affording a wider variety of registers and styles. General Makryiannis, veteran of the War of Independence, who learned to write in later life expressly to record his experiences, composed his Ἀπομνημονεύματα (Memoirs) and Ὁράματα καὶ Θάματα (Visions and Miracles) during the 1850s in his native Roumeliot dialect. For prose fiction, the preferred registers during the nineteenth century range from "high" puristic Greek to the "mixed" language of the short stories of Georgios Vizyenos (1849–96) and Alexandros Papadiamandis (1851–1911), both of whom draw on registers from dialect to high puristic to convey distance, irony, and, above all, different narrative tones and voices. During the twentieth century, demotic has prevailed as the standard medium, but there is considerable variety in literary use of local dialect, from the Mytilenian colorings of Stratis Myrivilis to the Cretan tones of Nikos Kazantzakis, and a greater experimentation with register than was deemed appropriate in poetry.

The distinctive—if conflicting—qualities of modern Greek literary language may be summarized as follows: First, Greek folk traditions have fed both from and into literary composition in a variety of ways at least since the twelfth century; the poet can still speak—or sing—in a public voice, in accordance with the ancient meanings of ōidē and mélos. Second, alongside the language of folk culture, there has existed the tempering influence of a prestigious and coherent learned tradition, whose terms of reference—again unlike most Western European literatures—can be traced back to late antiquity. Third, there is the religious language, familiar to everyone from its use in the Orthodox liturgy, and frequently exploited in poetry and prose.

These three strands, and discordant elements within them, have often conflicted and attempted to efface each other, especially since writers from the inception of the nation-state have striven to establish a distinctively modern Greek identity. Despite the dogmatic tone of many proclamations, prescriptions, and proscriptions from the second century to the present, in practice interpenetration of linguistic registers has been continuous in Greek, both spoken and written. Just as in the past, before the formation of the nation-state, varied registers—not necessarily conforming to spoken tongues and never standardized—were cultivated in the Ptochoprodromic Poems, the Palaiologan romances, the Cypriot love sonnets, and the poetry and drama of Renaissance Crete, so today diverse forms and styles can be included under the term "modern Greek" and exploited in a variety of ways appropriate to genre and occasion. There is no reason for Greeks to follow Eurocentric notions in privileging Writing over Speech, especially since their medieval and Renaissance past has remained a living part of language and culture in ways radically different from the fate of medieval and Renaissance Latin in Western Europe.

As for "foreign influences," we do not doubt the debt of Cretan literature to Italy, of Greek folklore to neighboring Balkan and Anatolian countries, or of modern poetry and prose to Western Europe. Politically, Greek elites may have been pawns in games played by the greater powers of East and West. Culturally, the classical heritage has remained a source of inspiration for mimetic, tragic, and parodic modes, rather than just a reminder of the "glory that was Greece." A poem by Cavafy (1917) epitomizes the diversity of Greek letters, expressing poignantly the urgency that the past and the "other" be included in the present. The speaker is an Alexandrian of the early seventh century A.D.—just before the Arab conquest—who asks another Alexandrian, Raphael (an Egyptian) to compose an epitaph in perfect Greek for their mutual friend, Ammonis (another Egyptian, whose name suggests the god Amon, "the hidden one"), a poet of Greek who has died at the young age of twenty-nine. It must do justice to his physical beauty as well as his exquisite Greek. What Cavafy is saying, here and elsewhere, is that Greece has always and already been plural in linguistic, literary, and religious terms—and ethnic ones as well.

Γιὰ τὸν ᾽Αμμόνη, ποὺ πέθανε 29 ἐτῶν, στὰ 610

Ραφαήλ, ὀλίγους στίχους σὲ ζητοῦν
γιὰ ἐπιτύμβιον τοῦ ποιητοῦ ᾽Αμμόνη νὰ συνθέσεις.
Κάτι πολὺ καλαίσθητον καὶ λεῖον. Σὺ θὰ μπορέσεις,
εἶσαι ὁ κατάλληλος, νὰ γράψεις ὡς ἁρμόζει
γιὰ τὸν ποιητὴν τὸν ᾽Αμμόνη, τὸν δικό μας.

Βέβαια θὰ πεῖς γιὰ τὰ ποιήματά του—
ἀλλὰ νὰ πεῖς καὶ γιὰ τὴν ἐμορφιά του,
γιὰ τὴν λεπτὴ ἐμορφιά του ποὺ ἀγαπήσαμε.

Πάντοτε ὡραῖα καὶ μουσικὰ τὰ ἑλληνικά σου εἶναι.
Ὅμως τὴν μαστοριά σου ὅληνα τὴ θέμε τώρα.
Σὲ ξένη γλῶσσα ἡ λύπη μας κ' ἡ ἀγάπη μας περνοῦν.
Τὸ αἰγυπτιακό σου αἴσθημα χύσε στὴν ξένη γλῶσσα.

Ραφαήλ, οἱ στίχοι σου ἔτσι νὰ γραφοῦν
ποὺ νἄχουν, ξέρεις, ἀπὸ τὴν ζωή μας μέσα των,
ποὺ κι ὁ ρυθμὸς κ' ἡ κάθε φράσις νὰ δηλοῦν
ποὺ γι' Ἀλεξανδρινὸ γράφει Ἀλεξανδρινός.

For Ammonis, who died at 29 years in 610.

Raphael, they ask you to compose
a few verses as epitaph for the poet Ammonis.
Something very finely felt and polished. You will do it,
you are the one qualified to write as befits
the poet Ammonis, our own.

Of course you will speak of his poems—
but speak also of his beauty,
of his subtle beauty we loved.

Your Greek is always fine and musical.
But we want all your craft now.
Our sorrow and love penetrate a foreign language.
Into the foreign language pour your Egyptian feeling.

Raphael, let your verses be so written
as to contain—you know—our life within them,
so rhythm and every phrase might show that
an Alexandrian writes for an Alexandrian.

(Cavafy 1963b; my translation)

7. From "Diglossia" to "Standard Modern Greek"?

What is "diglossia," and how does Greek compare with other cases? Is there today, or will there be tomorrow, a "Standard Modern Greek" (SMG)? The following seven diagnostic features are summarized from C. A. Ferguson's classic definition of "diglossia" (1959), based on several case studies (including Greek). Diglossia is (1) a relatively stable language situation in which, in addition to the primary dialects of the language (2) which may include a standard or regional standards (3) there is a divergent, codified (grammatically more complex) superposed variety, the vehicle of (4) a large and respected body of literature, either of an earlier period or in another speech community, (5) which is learned largely by formal education and is used (6) for most written and formal spoken purposes, but is not (7) used by any sector of the community for ordinary conversation. Two features emerge: the dichotomy between written and spoken forms and the relative diachronic and synchronic stability of each. Linguists have now modified Ferguson's definition to focus attention on the force of linguistic change, which can produce divergent and fluctuating language situations, and to emphasize the sociolinguistic overlap between bilingualism and diglossia.

For Greek, Ferguson's definition is schematic in three respects. The first difference is linguistic and affects the internal structure of D and K. In common with other "low" languages, D presents divergent morphological and lexical forms, frequently reflecting local dialects, in both speech and writing. Since the sixteenth century, attempts have been made to classify D rules and establish a standardized form, culminating in Triandafyllidis' *Modern Greek Grammar* (1941), reissued in modified form in 1976, as part of the language reforms, for use in primary and secondary schools. Yet these "rules" are rarely followed consistently in either speech or writing: even the most ardent demoticist who advocates the indeclinable form πού for the relative pronoun will use ὁ ὁποῖος for the sake of clarity or insist on νύχτα "night" while using ὀκτώ "eight." Conversely, K has no uniformly standardized forms because there have always been so many degrees of archaism and purism.[56] Katharevousa was a compromise between archaism and colloquialism, formulated in the early nineteenth century and imposed as the official language of the Greek state. In literature, although we may speak of various gradations of learned uses, there is no consistent or homogeneous form. Nikos Kazantzakis commented at the beginning of this century, "Greece has acquired not one but hundreds of *katharevousas.*" [57] One is tempted to respond, "Yes, but then Kazantzakis did his best to create the hundred-and-first demotic!"

The second difference is cultural. Since the 1880s, D has been a major form for creative literature, and during this century it has become the acceptable medium for scholarly writing and administration. Demotic has not in practice been a mark of inferior education or lower social status, despite the attempts of its opponents since the eighteenth century to cast it as the "language of the vulgar mob"; on the contrary, champions of D have come from the radical intelligentsia, while cases of "mixing" occur most fre-

quently in the media and among the less well educated.[58] The cultural prestige of D reflects a more advanced—and qualitatively different–state of the
"low" language than in any other diglossic situation known to me. The reasons are complex and to be explained only partly in terms of literary history: while it is true that the D has been the vehicle of a rich folk culture
and an accepted medium for poetry and prose since the twelfth century, its
high prestige in comparison with Swiss German and the Arabic vernaculars
has to do with conflicting national perceptions.

The third difference is political, affecting the official status of D. From
about 1830 until 1976, K was the official language, used in parliament, the
law courts, the army, and civil administration, although its position in the
educational system was more complicated: D was tolerated in primary
schools, whereas K remained the language of instruction at secondary
schools and at most universities, apart from two brief periods of liberal
rule (1917–20 and 1964–67), which encouraged demotic.[59] The 1976 legislation, introduced by the government of Constantine Karamanlis two
years after the fall of the Junta, stipulated the use of D for educational purposes, removing the clause in the constitution stating that K was the official language of the state. The practical implementation of this clause
proved acrimonious precisely because of the political aspects of the language question. The Left supported D; the Right, especially during the repressive regimes of the 1930s and from 1967 to 1974, hounded D as the
"language of anarchists and communists." It is doubtful whether the language question could have been solved painlessly "if only politics had
been kept out of the dispute," simply because politics remained a reality
so long as K was the language of the state and the instrument of higher
education.

These differences render it doubtful whether the Greek case has ever
been one of "diglossia" as defined by Ferguson and unlikely that either K
or D will prevail with absolute consistency. The two forms cannot be divided into watertight compartments, each with a separate set of syntactic,
morphological, and lexical structures. There are too many shades of each
and a great deal of interpenetration in the spoken and written forms. Some
sixty years ago, the French scholar André Mirambel distinguished five categories of modern Greek, or "états de langues": katharevousa; μικτή "mixed
Greek"; καθομιλουμένη "mixed, everyday spoken Greek"; standard demotic;
and μαλλιαρή "hairy", or ultra-demotic, affected by long-haired intellectuals.[60] To these should be added the influence of Ancient Greek, taught in
secondary schools for up to eight hours a week until 1981; New Testament
Greek, used in church; and the major dialects still spoken. There are no fixed
categories. Today, such "hairy demoticisms" as φτυχιό (πτυχεῖο) "diploma"
have disappeared, while "mixed" and "everyday" Greek reflect shades and

fluctuations between K and D. Intermediate forms provide the basis of the SMG used by urban Greeks with moderate levels of education.[61]

The present situation marks the culmination of a process in which forms of D have encroached on functions of K. Mirambel traces the gradual evolution in the use of written Greek from the nineteenth-century opposition of poetry (D) and prose (K) to the early twentieth-century opposition of literature (D) and that of scholarship and official documents, (K), to the trend in the mid-sixties toward an opposition between technical, scientific, and official writing (K) and critical writing and literature (D).[62] These developments have entailed an increasing range of intermediate forms, especially in the media.

As for developments since 1976, Mackridge's study of the usage of urban Greeks—the first of its kind—shows that the concept of consistency is giving way to flexibility and interpenetration. Yet, does not his insistence on the term "Standard Modern Greek" (SMG) to render κοινή νεοελληνική ("Common Modern Greek") imply an unduly pessimistic prediction for the future of the dialects? Granted, Tsakonian, Pontic, and Old Athenian are dying out, but dialects persist in everyday speech on Cyprus, Crete, and the larger islands, as well as in the towns and villages of northern Greece. Synchronic studies of rural and provincial code switching, together with analyses of literary uses, need to be undertaken before dialectal differences can be characterized as "rather small details."[63]

Since the practice of mixing has proved crucial to recent developments and attitudes have undergone radical revision over the past decade, it will be opportune to summarize the traditional diagnostic distinctions between katharevousa and demotic and to analyze the practical implications of code switching, both negative and positive. First, katharevousa.[64] It has retained the morphology and orthography of ancient Greek but has adopted the principal sound changes of the spoken language, which took place roughly between the third century B.C. and the fifth century A.D. These include the replacement of pitch accent by stress; the "fronting-raising-closing" of vowels; the change from voiced plosives b, g, and d to voiced fricatives v, gh, and dh. The tendency of Greeks to pronounce AG according to modern phonology may be a source of irritation to Western classicists; but, although the pronunciation is unfounded, is it more reprehensible than current ways of reading Chaucer, Shakespeare, and koine Greek? Vizyenos has the educated Greek narrator of "Consequences of the Old Story" get his own back on his German professor's Erasmian pronunciation of Homeric tags by rendering them phonetically into modern Greek, highlighting its alienating effects on the native Greek ear.[65]

In my earlier study (1982), I presented the case of a fictitious Greek student from a northern provincial town, born circa 1952, who graduated in

Philology from Athens University in 1974. Let me update it, this time with a Cypriot example and an African American parallel. Our Cypriot student speaks dialect at home, but the only language of her education at all levels is SMG. If her subject is literature, she receives no encouragement to use the vernacular; nor are any courses offered, even at the highest level, on the history and development of the Cypriot dialect, despite its rich literary and oral heritage and its preservation of archaic lexical and morphological features. She may not be subjected to the same degree of code switching between K and D at her most formative age, as was the case in my earlier example, yet her literary sensibilities must be challenged by constant censure of her mother tongue. With rare exceptions, the Cypriot dialect has been accorded little space in modern literature.[66] Let me now contrast her case with that of an African American student today, whose vernacular is gaining recognition as a medium for creative literature but is regarded as beyond the pale for all forms of academic discourse. Yet even if she becomes a professor, she will use it vibrantly in conversation with other African Americans at all levels of education.[67] There are, of course, differences between the Cypriot and African American experiences, but the complex linguistic heritage of each can prove enriching for literature.

As for the psychological attitudes inherent in K and D, the concept of "purity" and "consistency" is integral to both. Katharevousa entails a "purifying" mentality, its general principle being to conserve language within specified norms and to protect it from fluctuation and change, equated with vulgarism and anarchy. This mentality has been justified by dogmatic appeal to tradition or the prestige of the so-called Helleno-Christian heritage.[68] Yet despite a pescriptive and prospective role in official functions, K has been exploited in creative writing to enhance the dialogic potential.[69] Demoticism, too, has been a national and cultural as well as a linguistic movement. Like the purists, demoticists have invoked past tradition and national pride in support of their case, often using identical slogans. Psicharis proclaimed in 1888, "Language and fatherland are one: to fight for your language and to fight for your country are the same." His dictum has been aptly compared with Korais' earlier statement, "Just as it is true concerning each individual person that a man's character is shown by his speech, so, in the same way, the character of an entire nation is known by its language."[70] Few today would support the extremisms of the demoticist movement of the 1880s, but the concept of "pure demotic" has left marks still evident in both educational and literary theory and practice. As with K, there is a tendency to prescribe and proscribe, privileging consistency of style over clarity of expression.

Here the ambivalent status of the Greek dialects is relevant. Exotic but obsolescent dialects, such as Tsakonian, south Italian, and Pontic, have been analyzed since the late nineteenth century; a dwindling number of speakers are sought out and their speech assiduously recorded. Because these dialects are believed to preserve a greater number of archaic features, they are accorded cultural prestige, while the commoner dialects, such as Northern Greek and Peloponnesian, have been relatively neglected. Similarly, Cretan enjoys "high" status, whereas Cypriot is regarded as "low," although both dialects are more closely related to each other than either is to Peloponnesian (on which SMG is based). Why the difference? Cretan literature of the Venetian period was institutionalized as a link between Byzantine vernacular poetry and the emergence of national poetry in the nineteenth and twentieth centuries. Although Cypriot literary pedigree is as old as Cretan, the island stood outside the nation-state and therefore outside the demoticist movement: to stress Cypriotness is to underline its differences from Hellenism. Cypriot writers have had to contend with the suppression of dialect in writing, the lack of any center for Cypriot dialect studies, and, last but not least, prejudice against the Cypriot accent! Small wonder that some, such as Hektor Patrikios, have turned to archaizing Greek as their literary medium. Yet Cypriot songs and tales are among the richest in Greek folklore, with generations of *poiētárides* ("singers of tales").

In conclusion, if anything can be learned from the past, it is that the concept of linguistic purity has been an obsession since late antiquity which has failed to take account of the constant interpenetration of written and spoken forms and has led to the false assumption that language should be homogeneous. Now that "common Greek" has been established as a basis for education, cannot the richness and complexity of past and present usage be exploited to afford a wider choice of vocabulary and linguistic registers than is available in most modern languages? Literature can retain its dialogic dimensions, while translations of foreign works can avoid the monologic character noted by Bachtin over fifty years ago in George Seferis' demotic rendering of T. S. Eliot's *The Waste Land*.[71]

Bachtin defines the linguistic peculiarity of Eliot's poem as "a continuous shifting from one level of the language to another," describing four major "scales" within this range: (1) the colloquial scale (different varieties or levels of modern colloquial idiom or jargon used to specify the "voice," above all in social terms); (2) the normal scale of poetic diction (different varieties of poetic diction but perceived synchronically, as belonging to the same temporal strata); (3) the diachronic scale (quotation or allusion to different temporal strata and past verbal contexts, used to create dissonance and disruption); and (4) the diaglossal scale (quotation or allusion to various strata of foreign poetic idioms). He then goes on to analyze some differences between English and Greek: on the colloquial scale, English has developed diversified, yet socially stratified, forms of speech at the expense of individual speech variation, whereas Greek permits a greater range of idio-syncratic and regional forms without betraying social status. Conversely, on the diachronic scale, English poets can avail themselves of a range of allu-sion stretching back to Shakespeare and beyond, whereas for contemporary Greek poets (that is, the demoticists of the 1930s), Bachtin argues that the linguistic resources of the past have been excluded. As a result, Seferis, in his translation of *The Waste Land*, substitutes the threefold scale of the orig-inal (colloquial, poetic, and diachronic) with a twofold one (colloquial and synchronic), eschewing K even where appropriate to the context ([1938–39] 1985, 340) and thereby rendering Eliot's discordant voices in less varied tones.

Bachtin's analysis is remarkable for two reasons: it shows an approach to tone and register similar to that of his brother, Mikhail (of whose work he knew nothing at the time); and despite his crusading support for the de-moticist cause (he had been a pupil of Psicharis in Paris), he was clearly fas-cinated by the case of modern Greek. "Why have most of the resources of the past been kept outside the pale of contemporary poetic usage?" he asks in conclusion. "And how, in spite of this, could they have lost every associ-ation with their respective periods? The answer to these two questions is, as we shall see, one and the same" (355–56). Bachtin's third part was either lost or never written. I shall try to uncover these lost voices in the next three chapters.

CHAPTER 2

The New Testament and Its Legacy

In the previous chapter, I attempted to situate Greek polyglossia in the context of its linguistic and literary history. This and the next two chapters will explore its resources with reference to specific texts, literary and non-literary, chosen from the first to twelfth centuries A.D. My selection is intended to highlight some late-antique and Byzantine texts which speak in differing ways across past and present. Bachtin's two questions, "Why have the linguistic resources of the past been closed off from contemporary poetic usage?" and "How could they have lost association with their respective periods?" can be reformulated: "What are the resources of the past, and how have they interacted with subsequent generations?" I hope that readers will bear with three chapters fairly dense with texts; I have tried to ease the burden for the Greekless by putting linguistic commentary in the form of lists, which may be skipped, and longer texts in an appendix. Among the challenges that Byzantinists and neo-Hellenists must face is that readers cannot be assumed to have a prior familiarity with the texts we may wish to analyze and discuss: there is no established canon, let alone an internationally known one. This lack can be turned to advantage, and used to question our preconceptions about what constitutes "tradition."

1. Voices from the Past

Nicholas Bachtin posed but never answered the question of the Greek literary language and its peculiar relationship to time. In a series of late essays, Mikhail Bakhtin raised a number of not dissimilar questions relating to language and literature, time and space. Bakhtin experiments with the terms "speech genre" and "utterance" rather than "language" and "sentence" to emphasize the importance of context and intonation in all human communication.[1] Since his thinking is open-ended rather than clear-cut and since it relates not just to actual speech but to literary—and indeed all artistic—discourse, I shall rephrase some of his major arguments in terms relevant to my own purposes.

Language cannot be fully studied in the abstract terms of a system or code, as has been attempted by various schools of structuralist linguistics and semiotics. The neat diagrams used to illustrate the transmission of the "message" from addresser to addressee leave out the interference which necessarily intrudes on all human communication, such as tone of voice, unfinished sentences, exclamations, unspoken thoughts, and allusions to past conversations. Equally, they reduce the role of addressee to a passive one and therefore underestimate the extent to which the addresser's words and tone are shaped, consciously or unconsciously, by the other's expected response. It is not enough to analyze speech in sentence units or merely for thematic content and style.[2] Only close study of the context, manner, and tone (compositional structure) of the utterance as a whole can determine its "speech genre"—that is, the relatively stable types of utterances developed by each sphere in which language is used. The heterogeneity of speech genres therefore includes oral and written, primary and secondary, from short rejoinders of everyday dialogue to military and other technical treatises, business and personal correspondence, and all literary genres.

On the level of everyday discourse, Bakhtin's view of speech genres as whole utterances finds strong support in the speech patterns and comprehension abilities of autistics with developed language skills. Although their command of vocabulary and grammar may be unimpaired or even above average, it is precisely the dimension of language at the level of speech genre that is missing. Autistics may be superb mimics of other people's mannerisms, intonations, and accents, yet their own speech is curiously one-dimensional and monotonal, as if repeated by rote from "other" utterances (theirs and others', past and present), and hence stereotypical—sounding rather like a voice on an answering machine. They have problems with shifters, such as statement and question markers or first- and second-person pronouns. Their decoding of language is also defective, not so much in their failure to understand individual words and sentences but to infer meaning from context, tone of voice, facial expression, and so on; they simply "miss the point."[3]

Given the complexities of dialogic interaction at the basic levels of everyday speech, it is hardly surprising that secondary speech genres, especially literary ones, are heterogeneous, complex, and difficult to decode.

How can texts, above all texts from the past, be interpreted as whole utterances when so much of their immediate context is missing? Bakhtin insisted that the attempt should be made, keeping in mind, first, the relevance of "speech genres" to literary history (how different kinds of texts make use of varying registers, which change over time); second, the problem of texts as utterance (how texts may be monotonal, using a single register, or multitonal, exploiting multiple registers from different "speech genres"); and third, the study of dialogue and dialogic relations—that is, not statement and counterstatement within a particular text, but dialogue between author and characters, between author and readers (present and future), and across genres and styles, historical epochs, languages, and cultures.

In the case of postclassical Greek we have a remarkable range of "speech genres" to draw on: the Septuagint and the New Testament (NT); hymns, homilies, and saints' lives; orations and treatises on a variety of topics (including military, legal, and administrative matters); law codes and *typika* (monastic foundation documents); scholarly commentaries and lexica; historiographies and chronicles; secular poetry and prose; bilingual conversation manuals; letters, magic incantations, and testaments preserved on papyrus; curse tablets and funerary and other inscriptions; snatches of popular songs and acclamations; even sixth-century tax lists in Homeric Greek—the list is almost endless.[4] Of course, not all genres are represented equally, and there are periods (such as the seventh and eighth centuries) from which little "literature" has survived. Yet despite the superabundance of evidence and the heterogeneity of linguistic styles and forms, it is not possible to reconstruct the actual spoken language of any given period. This is no doubt part of the problem Bachtin had in mind when he noted that in Greek the resources of the past had "lost every association with their respective periods." However, by fusing Bachtin's "scales" with Bakhtin's "speech genres" and "utterances," it becomes possible to recover something of the heterogeneity of past voices and the dialogic interactions between them. To that end, texts will be presented not in strict chronological sequence but according to categories of genre, register, and function: religious literature (New Testament, homilies, and hymns); functional texts (personal letters, an imperial treatise); fragments of popular songs; and twelfth-century secular literature (dialogue, novel, vernacular verse).

2. The New Testament

Although composed in koine Greek of the first century A.D., the New Testament (NT), which helped to shape the language of the liturgy, remains a vital part of oral culture. How much do people really understand? It might be argued that response to the language is emotional, even mystical (although this in itself is an essential feature of the Orthodox faith). Not all priests and cantors are educated: although he never wrote much, my father-in-law, Dimitris Alexiou, served throughout his life as cantor in his parish church of Sklithron, Ayias, *because he knew everything by heart* , but of course he liked to have "the Book" in front of him. The finer points of grammar may have escaped him, but he had internalized the language more completely than many a New Testament scholar and would introduce quotations into everyday conversation. Kostas Takhtsis, in his remarkable novel *The Third Wedding*, conveys the flavor of women's everyday conversation largely because he includes such religious "tags" in the dialogue of his characters.

Let me begin by juxtaposing two short extracts from the Gospel story of the Resurrection as told by Mark and Luke in order to demonstrate the morphological, syntactic, and lexical proximity of KG to MG and to set up a framework for other Christian texts of the early Byzantine period (up to the sixth century A.D.). The New Testament was recorded in the first century A.D. and is now generally agreed to approximate the language of everyday speech.[5] Of the four Gospels, Luke's is the most archaizing, and Mark's is closest to popular idiom.[6] Mark is familiar to all Greeks who attend the Orthodox liturgy on Easter Saturday, when it is read out during the service.

Mark 16:1–8

1. Καὶ διαγενομένου τοῦ σαββάτου, Μαρία ἡ Μαγδαληνὴ καὶ Μαρία Ἰακώβου καὶ Σαλώμη ἠγόρασαν ἀρώματα ἵνα ἀλείψωσιν αὐτόν. 2. Καὶ λίαν πρωῒ τῆς μιᾶς σαββάτων ἔρχονται ἐπὶ τὸ μνημεῖον, ἀνατείλαντος τοῦ ἡλίου. 3. Καὶ ἔλεγον πρὸς ἑαυτάς—Τίς ἀποκυλίσει ἡμῖν τὸν λίθον ἐκ τῆς θύρας τοῦ μνημείου; 4. Καὶ ἀναβλέψασαι θεωροῦσιν ὅτι ἀποκεκύλισται ὁ λίθος ἦν γὰρ μέγας σφόδρα. 5. Καὶ εἰσελθοῦσαι εἰς τὸ μνημεῖον εἶδον νεανίσκον καθήμενον ἐν τοῖς δεξιοῖς περιβεβλημένον στολὴν λευκήν, καὶ ἐξεθαμβήθησαν. 6. Ὁ δὲ λέγει αὐταῖς,—Μὴ ἐκθαμβεῖσθε. Ἰησοῦν ζητεῖτε τὸν Ναζαρηνὸν τὸν ἐσταυρωμένον. Ἠγέρθη! Οὐκ ἔστιν ὧδε! Ἴδε, ὁ τόπος ὅπου ἔθηκαν αὐτόν. 7. Ἀλλ' ὑπάγετε εἴπατε τοῖς μαθηταῖς αὐτοῦ καὶ τῷ Πέτρῳ ὅτι Προάγει ὑμῖν. 8. Καὶ ἐξελθοῦσαι ἔφυγον ἀπὸ τοῦ μνημείου, εἶχε δὲ αὐτὰς τρόμος καὶ ἔκστασις· καὶ οὐδενὶ οὐδὲν εἶπον, ἐφοβοῦντο γάρ.

1. And when the Sabbath was over, Mary Magdalene and Mary [mother] of James, and Salome bought perfumes so that they could come and

anoint him. 2. And very early in the morning of the first [day] of the week, they come to the tomb after the sun has risen. 3. And they were saying to each other,—Who will roll away for us the stone from the door of the tomb? 4. And on looking closely, they see the stone has been rolled away—it was a very big one. 5. And coming into the sepulchre they saw a young man seated on the right, dressed in a white robe, and they were amazed. 6. But he says to them,—Do not stand amazed: you are seeking Jesus of Nazareth, the crucified one; he has risen, he is not here. Behold, the place where they laid him. 7. But go, tell his disciples and Peter that— he goes before you to Galilee: there you will see him, just as he told you. 8. And, coming out, they [the women] fled from the sepulchre, for terror and ecstasy possessed them. They said nothing to anybody, for they were afraid.

Luke 24:1–11

1. Καὶ τὸ μὲν σάββατον ἡσύχασαν κατὰ τὴν ἐντολήν. Τῇ δὲ μιᾷ τῶν σαββάτων, ὄρθρου βαθέως, ἦλθον ἐπὶ τὸ μνῆμα φέρουσαι ἃ ἡτοίμασαν ἀρώματα, καί τινες σὺν αὐταῖς. 2. Εὗρον δὲ τὸν λίθον ἀποκεκυλισμένον ἀπὸ τοῦ μνημείου. 3. Καὶ εἰσελθοῦσαι οὐχ εὗρον τὸ σῶμα τοῦ Κυρίου Ἰησοῦ. 4. Καὶ ἐγένετο ἐν τῷ διαπορεῖσθαι αὐτὰς περὶ τούτου, καὶ ἰδού, ἄνδρες δύο ἐπέστησαν αὐταῖς ἐν ἐσθήσεσιν ἀστραπτούσαις. 5. Ἐμφόβων δὲ γενομένων αὐτῶν καὶ κλινουσῶν τὸ πρόσωπον εἰς τὴν γῆν, εἶπον πρὸς αὐτάς. —Τί ζητεῖτε τὸν ζῶντα μετὰ τῶν νεκρῶν; 6. Οὐκ ἔστιν ὧδε, ἀλλ᾽ ἠγέρη! Μνήσθητε ὡς ἐλάλησεν ὑμῖν ἔτι ὢν ἐν τῇ Γαλιλαίᾳ, 7. λέγων ὅτι δεῖ τὸν Υἱὸν τοῦ Ἀνθρώπου παραδοθῆναι εἰς χεῖρας ἀνθρώπων ἁμαρτωλῶν, καὶ σταυρωθῆναι, καὶ τῇ τρίτῃ ἡμέρᾳ ἀναστῆναι. 8. Καὶ ἐμνήσθησαν τῶν ῥημάτων αὐτοῦ. 9. Καὶ ὑποστρέψ- ασαι ἀπὸ τοῦ μνημείου, ἀπήγγειλαν ταῦτα πάντα τοῖς ἔνδεκα καὶ πᾶσι τοῖς λοιποῖς. 10. Ἦσαν δὲ ἡ Μαγδαληνὴ Μαρία καὶ Ἰωάννα καὶ Μαρία Ἰακώβου, καὶ αἱ λοιπαὶ σὺν αὐταῖς, αἳ ἔλεγον πρὸς τοὺς ἀποστόλους ταῦτα. 11. Καὶ ἐφάνησαν ἐνώπιον αὐτῶν ὡσεὶ λῆρος τὰ ῥήματα αὐτῶν, καὶ ἠπίστουν αὐταῖς.

1. And whereas on the Sabbath they rested according to the command- ment, on the first day of the week at deep dawn, they [the women] came to the tomb, bearing such spices as they had prepared. 2. But they found the stone rolled away from the sepulchre, 3. and on going inside they did not find the body of the lord Jesus. 4. And it happened upon their per- plexity on this—behold, two men stood behind them in shining raiment. 5. Upon their [the women] becoming fearful and turning their faces to the

earth, they [the men] said unto them,—Why do you seek the living amongst the dead? 6. He is not here, but he has risen. Remember how he spoke to you whilst he was yet in Galilee, 7. saying of the Son of Man that he must give himself up into the hands of sinful mankind and be crucified, yet on the third day rise again. 8. And they remembered his words, 9. and turning back from the sepulchre they [the women] announced all these things to the eleven, and to all the others. 10. They were Mary Magdalene and Ioanna [mother] of James; and the rest of the women with them told these things to the apostles. 11. And these words of theirs seemed to them [the apostles] as idle gossip, and they did not believe them.[7]

Morphological changes from AG show the process of unification in Greek verb inflection. A single set of aorist endings (-α, -ες, -ε, -αμε, -ατε, -αν) is used where AG had separate forms for verbs designated as "thematic" and "athematic" (Luke 5: εἶπον, "they said").[8] Mark's ὑπάγετε (imperative of ὑπάγω) in the sense "go" shows the process of eliminating old anomalies in the verbal system (ὑπάγω replaces εἶμι "go," ἀποκυλιῶ replaces ἀποκυλίνδω "roll aside"). Aorist singular endings (-κα, -κες, -κε, extended from the perfect), are applied to the plural (Mark 6: ἔθηκαν "they put"), part of the process of fusion of aorist and perfect tenses, incipient in AG, which led to the disappearance of the AG perfect and to the new formation of a compound perfect in BG and MG.[9] The augment marking the past indicative may be dropped in verbs beginning with a vowel (Luke 6: εὖρον [AG ηὖρον] "they found," cf. MG ἄκουσα, AG ἤκουσον "I heard").[10]

Syntactically, Mark is simple, showing a preference for coordination (parataxis) over subordination; the conjunction "and" (καί) frequently opens sentences and clauses, as well as joining nouns. The main types of subordinate clause are final (ἵνα + subjunctive) and relative (ὅς); there is also abundant use of genitive absolute and participial clauses (although the latter tend to agree with the subject, as in MG).[11] Phrases are short, and there may be a change of subject and tense (from past to historic present) within the same sentence, resulting in a preponderance of personal pronouns. Particles are reduced in number and function (Mark uses only δέ and γάρ). The pitch accent of AG dictated fixed tones of voice but relied on flexible word order and on particles for emphasis and nuance. As pitch gave way to stress in KG, the full range of ancient particles as markers became redundant. Recasting Mark's Greek into AG entails major changes in sentence structure and word order, whereas it can be rendered into MG with only minor adjustments to morphology and vocabulary.[12] The prepositional system also shows signs of reformation: AG prepositions are more restricted in the number, function, and variety of cases they may take.[13] As for adverbs, the juxtaposition of two adverbs is postclassical, signaling the tendency for adverbs to diversify in function (λίαν πρωΐ). Luke's syntax appears more pretentious: he makes greater use of particles, even when not strictly necessary (μέν and δέ)), although the range remains limited in comparison with AG. He uses the relative pronoun ἅ, avoided by Mark, but as in Mark, the same form of personal pronoun αὐτός is employed in all cases, causing some confusion, as is evident in my literal translation.[14] His repertoire of prepositions is larger than Mark's, but they are often redundant according to classical usage. His constructions may be convoluted (ἐν τῷ ἀπορεῖσθαι, preposition + article and infinitive); the genitive absolute in the fourth sentence is gratuitous (strictly speaking, the participial clause should be in agreement with the object of the sentence, αὐτάς).

Turning to vocabulary, with the single exception of Luke's ἔσθης "raiment" (contrast Mark, στολή; cf. MG "uniform"), in both passages words conform to later Attic prose, or to KG usage. Semantic change and lexical innovation can be charted as steps in the direction of MG. For example, ὧδε in the sense of 'here' is found only in KG (AG "then," "so"): in MG this has undergone further transformation to ἐδῶ, by phonetic analogy with its paired opposite, ἐκεῖ "there".[15] Examples of roots which have remained metaphorically alive throughout the history of the Greek language include θεωρῶ (AG "behold, see, perceive, contemplate with religious awe, inspect, review", derived from the noun θεωρός (envoy sent to consult oracle, spectator at festival). While the MG verb θεωρῶ is more restricted in meaning, "consider, regard (as)", the nominal forms θεωρία (K) and θωρά, θωριά (D) have a range of meanings from abstract theory and "contemplation" (K) to concrete "visage, hue, colour" (D).[16] Similarly, ἐκθαμβέω "I am amazed" is found only in KG; yet AG θαμβέω, θαμβαίνω "be astounded, alarmed", related to the nominal root θάμβος ("object of dazzlement, wonder"), has undergone a metaphorical shift in MG to θάμπος "dazzlement, astonishment, darkening," θαμπός "gloomy, opaque," θαμπώνω "dazzle, blur, darken, grow dim" and θάμπωμα "darkening," with consonantal change μβ to μπ).

Despite the differences between Mark and Luke, both texts are distant from AG, especially in syntax and vocabulary. Changes in phonology are masked by conventional orthography, but papyrus letters (to be examined in the next chapter) afford proof of major vowel shifts. While morphology in Mark and Luke has none of the "mistakes" commonly found in the papyrus letters, both show signs of the restructuring of verbal, nominal, pronominal, and prepositional systems; Luke's pretensions to a more literary style are cosmetic. The effect of his "corrections" to Mark's Greek is to move the level of discourse from direct to indirect; whereas Mark uses only direct speech (even after the indirect conjunction ὅτι), Luke makes greater use of indirect clauses, paraphrase, and circumlocution.

For reasons touched on in the last chapter and examined in detail by Browning, Christians who wished to convert cultivated pagans to Christianity tended from the fourth century onward to employ varying forms of Atticizing Greek in their writings and preachings. In addition to evidence cited and discussed by Browning,[17] the following letter from Isidorus to Theognotos (fifth century A.D.) illustrates the tortuous reasoning and pedantic language deemed necessary to justify the "vulgar" language of the Scriptures: According to Thomson 48, n23, himself from Thigne 78.1500

Διὸ καὶ τὴν Θείαν αἰτιῶνται Γραφήν, μὴ τῷ περριττῷ καὶ κεκαλλωπισμένῳ χρωμένην λόγῳ, ἀλλὰ τῷ ταπεινῷ καὶ πεζῷ· ἀλλ' ἡμεῖς μὲν αὐτοῖς ἀντεγκαλῶμεν τῆς φιλαυτίας, ὅτι δόξης ὀρεχθέντες, τῶν ἄλλων ἥκιστα ἐφρόντισαν· τὴν δὲ Θείαν ὄντως Γραφὴν ἀπαλλάττωμεν τῶν ἐγκλημάτων, λέγοντες ὅτι οὐ τῆς οἰκείας δόξης, τῆς δὲ τῶν ἀκουσόντων σωτηρίας ἐφρόντισεν. Εἰ δὲ ὑψηλῆς φράσεως ἐρῶεν, μανθανέτωσαν ὅτι ἄμεινον παρ' ἰδιώτου τἀληθὲς ἢ παρὰ σοφιστοῦ τὸ ψεῦδος μαθεῖν. Ὁ μὲν γὰρ ἁπλῶς καὶ συντόμως φράζει, ὁ δὲ πολλάκις ἀσαφείᾳ καὶ τὸ τῆς ἀληθείας ἐπικρύπτει κάλλος, καὶ τὸ ψεῦδος τῇ καλλιεπείᾳ κοσμήσας ἐν χρυσίδε ἰὸ δγλητήριον ἐκέρασεν. Εἰ δὲ ἡ ἀλήλειδ τῇ καλλιεπείᾳ συναφθείη, δύναται μὲν τοὺς πεπαιδευμένους ὠφελῆσαι, τοῖς δ' ἄλλοις ἅπασιν ἄχρηστος ἔσται καὶ ἀνωφελής· διὸ καὶ ἡ Γραφὴ τὴν ἀλγαειαν πεζῷ λόγῳ ἡρμήνευσεν, ἵνα καὶ ἰδιῶται καὶ σοφοὶ καὶ παῖδες καὶ γυναῖκες τὴν μάθοιεν· ἐκ μὲν γὰρ τούτου οἱ μὲν σοφοὶ οὐδὲν παραβλάπτονται, ἐκ δὲ ἐκείνου τὸ πλέον τῆς οἰκουμένης προσεβλάβη. Ἄν τινῶν οὖν ἐχρῆν φροντίσαι, μάλιστα μὲν τῶν πλειόνων, ἐπειδὰν δὲ καὶ πάντων ἐφρόντισεν, δείκνυται λαμπρῶς θεία οὖσα καὶ ἐπουράνιος.   (Migne 78, 1500)

That is why [the pagans] . . . accuse the Holy Writ of employing, not the elaborate and ornate style, but the humble and prosaic one; yet we, on the other hand, can issue a countercharge against them of self-regard, in that, having once tasted glory, they have taken minimal heed of others; let us then exonerate the truly Holy Writ from reproaches, saying that it has taken heed, not of personal glory, but of the salvation of those who will listen. If it had espoused the lofty speech, let them know that it were better to learn the truth from an ordinary citizen than falsehood from a sophist. For the one speaks simply and to the point, while the other often masks the beauty of truth with falsehood; whence, having decked falsehood with eloquence, he had served poison in a vessel of gold. But if, indeed, truth were to be wedded with eloquence, it has the power to benefit educated men, but for all the rest it will be

useless and not beneficial; hence the Scripture used prosaic language, in order
that ordinary and wise men, women and children alike should learn.

Isidorus' Greek, replete with obsolete optatives, particles (for example,
contrastive μέν and δέ used five times in a short passage, not always
correctly), and a real "zombie," the third-person plural imperative
μανθανέτωσαν, is not easily conveyed in comprehensible English (the
reverse of Bachtin's problem with Seferis' translation of *The Waste Land*,
since English lacks the inflexional complexity of Greek). Yet the questions
faced by early Christendom are all too apparent: how can the everyday language of the Scriptures be explained to the elite? What should be the language of sermons, liturgy, and worship?

As Browning has noted, while homilists were occasionally exhorted to
preach in a language comprehensible to all, John Chrysostom (fourth
century) was interrupted in one of his sermons by a woman complaining that she couldn't understand half of what he was saying.[18] Did
Chrysostom "lower" his style for oral delivery, committing his sermons
to writing in the higher style? We do not know, but archaizing forms are
tempered by frequent rhetorical use of short, and syntactically simple
rhythmic phrases (κῶλα). Inveighing against excessive lamentation and
funerary practices (regarded as subversive pagan practices), Chrysostom
thunders at his congregation as he winds up his homily, driving his point
home with rhetorical use of second-person address, imperatives, and
homely examples:

Ὅταν γὰρ τὸν οὐδὸν ὑπερβῶμεν τῶν τῆς πόλεως πυλῶν, καὶ τοῖς
σκώληξι παραδόντες τὸ σῶμα ὑποστρέφωμεν, πάλιν σε ἐρήσομαι.
Ποῦ πορεύεται ὁ πολὺς ὄχλος ἐκεῖνος; τί γέγονεν ἡ κραυγὴ καὶ ὁ
θόρυβος; ποῦ δὲ αἱ λαμπάδες; ποῦ δὲ οἱ χοροὶ τῶν γυναικῶν; ἆρα
μὴ ὄναρ ταῦτά ἐστι; Τί δὲ καὶ ἐγένοντο αἱ βοαί; ποῦ τὰ στόματα
τὰ πολλὰ ἐκεῖνα; τὰ κραυγάζοντα καὶ παρακελευόμενα θαρρεῖν, ὅτι
οὐδεὶς ἀθάνατος; Οὐ νῦν ταῦτα ἔδει λέγεσθαι τῷ μὴ ἀκούοντι,
ἀλλ' ὅτε ἥρπαζεν, ὅτε ἐπλεονέκτει, τότε μικρὸν παραλλάξαντας
ἔδει λέγειν· Οὐ δεῖ θαρρεῖν· οὐδεὶς ἀθάνατος. Εἰ μέν τίς σοι
κατεσκεύασεν οἰκίας ἔνθα μὴ ἔμελλες μένειν, ζημίαν τὸ πρᾶγμα
ἐνόμισας ἄν· νῦν δὲ ἐνταῦθα βούλει πλουτεῖν, ὅθεν καὶ πρὸ τῆς
ἑσπέρας πολλάκις μέλλεις ἀποδημεῖν. Ἐπίσχες τῆς μανίας, σβέσον
τὴν ἐπιθυμίαν, ...   (Migne 63:811–12)

For when we go beyond the threshhold of the city gates and return, having rendered the body unto the worms, again I will say unto you,—

Whither goeth forth that great crowd? What has become of the shrieks and the din? Where are the torches, where the women's dances? Can it be that these things were but a dream? Then what has become of the shouting? Where are those many mouths—mouths that cried out and bade [people] to take courage, for no one is immortal? Such words should not be said now, when he cannot hear, but then, when he was grasping; when he was seeking profit, with slight variation, they should have said:—It is not proper to take courage, for no one is immortal. If, indeed, someone had built you houses, wherein you were not intending to dwell, you would have considered the affair a loss; but, as things stand, you expect to get rich here and now, whenceforth perchance to depart ere evening. Restrain your madness, quench your desire!

3. The Emergence of a Byzantine Genre: The Kontakion and Romanos

The language of Christian worship, as in the liturgy and the hymns of Romanos the Melodist, remained close to the Greek of the Septuagint and the New Testament. In assessing the achievement of Romanos and his enduring contribution to Greek tradition, we need to address two issues: definitions and transmissions; precedents and precursors.

The word *kontakion* (diminutive of κόνταξ "wooden cylinder around which the papyrus was rolled") gained currency for "rolls of liturgical texts" (including hymns) from the ninth century; its later widespread but specific reference to collections of hymns has been aptly compared with the use of *livret* ("libretto") to refer to the text of an opera by the French scholar, José Grosdidier de Matons.[19] As a hymn form, it originated in the fifth century and flourished until the seventh, when it was superseded by the *kanon*. In content, it is a poetic sermon, sung after the chanting (*ekphōnēsis*) of the Gospel during the liturgy. It comprises verses (*troparia*), each built on a model sequence (*heirmós*), so that all verses share the same metrical and melodic structure; within the verse, there is variation, but each line of each verse has the same number of syllables (*isosyllabismós*) and the same position of tonic accents (*homotonía*). The last line of the first verse is repeated at the end of each succeeding verse, forming a refrain. The verses are linked by acrostich, so that the first letter of each spells out either the alphabet, from alpha to omega, as in the famous *Akathistos Hymn*, or the name of the melodist :ΤΟΥ ΤΑΠΕΙΝΟΥ ΡΩΜΑΝΟΥ [ΤΟΥ ΜΕΛΩΔΟΥ] OF THE HUMBLE ROMANOS [THE MELODIST]. The hymn is introduced by a proem (not included in the acrostich) in a distinct and often more elaborate melody (*koukoúlion*). From the hymn *To Ten Virgins II* we learn that Romanos himself sang the hymn as soon as the reader (*anagnōstēs*) had completed his Gospel readings, with the choir or congregation responding with the refrain. These technical details indicate the complexity of the melodic and metrical forms and origins of the kontakion.

Romanos' kontakia survive in manuscript collections of the tenth to thirteenth centuries, known as *kontakária* "collections of kontakia." The earlier manuscripts contain no musical notation, but from the thirteenth century onward some have a system of dots and signs now transcribed according to Western convention. This indicates not that the hymns were originally recited rather than sung but that their musical performance became more elaborate in the later Byzantine period.[20] The kontakaria are arranged according to the feasts of the Orthodox calendrical year, such as (1) hymns for fixed feast days, starting from September 1; (2) hymns for moveable feasts from Lent to Passion (Triodion); (3) hymns from Easter to Pentecost (Pentekostarion). The kontakia are not always transmitted complete; some are reduced, others truncated to proem and first and last troparia, thus reminding us that the collections were useful records of live performance, handed down and to be handed on. Because they were "live texts," there are signs of rehandling as details were added or subtracted for metrical, stylistic, or theological reasons. Especially prone to alteration was the proem; and that is why many of Romanos' kontakia have two or three. Such "live" rehandling of material may date back to the lifetime of Romanos himself, so we cannot speak of an "authorial archetype" for any one hymn.[21]

What can we reconstruct from the scant, mostly late, Byzantine sources of Romanos' life and work? Born in the later fifth century in the city of Emesa, Syria, possibly of Hellenized Jewish extraction, he served at the Church of the Resurrection in Beirut during his early years.[22] He came to Constantinople during the reign of Anastasios I (491–518), where he was attached to the Church of the Theotokos in the Kyros quarter of the City. According to legend, it was in this church that the Virgin Mary appeared to him in a dream, giving him a scroll (kontakion) to swallow; having done so, he woke up to chant his first Hymn on the Nativity, the first part of which is still sung on Christmas Eve.[23] His main creative period coincides with the reign of Justinian (527–65), whose ethos and dogma he reflects. Of the thousand kontakia he is said to have composed, only eighty-five are extant, and of them some sixty-five are thought to be "genuine"; the acrostic BY THE HUMBLE ROMANOS became a way of paying tribute to the great master's voice. Verses composed after his death allege his Jewish origins but stress his Christian piety.[24]

These details, summarized from later legends, accord with Paul Maas' analysis of datable elements in the hymns, confirming their time of composition as within the Justinian period.[25] Romanos' dogmatic approach, especially his Christology, agrees with Justinian principles. Against heretics and heathens, he calls the Jews τῶν ἀνόμων λαός "people of the lawless ones," and in his hymn *On Pentecost* he invokes antiquity only to play pejorative word games on the names of Homer, Plato, Demosthenes, Pythagoras, and Aratos. This verse does not necessarily prove his ignorance of classical tradition, as has been supposed, although in my view it does indicate his opposition to its intellectual legacy.[26] It is perhaps significant that the first Byzantine poet to shape so distinctively Byzantine a genre should have dissociated himself from the archaizing tradition.

Over the past few decades, critical assessment of Romanos' literary qualities has advanced considerably so that few today would share the view of Maas early this century: "I am afraid that if we were more fully acquainted with the homily of the fourth and fifth centuries, Romanos would inevitably emerge as a second-rate writer."[27] Outstanding features of his finest kontakia include: dramatic and dialogic qualities are not just formal (dialogue between different characters) but conceptual, creating a tragic conflict between human and divine planes; human perspectives are explored in dramatic tension and predominate over dogmatic theology; passionate involvement in every line, never detached or cold, if too "rhetorical" for modern tastes. His imagery has an Aeschylean quality, especially when "leitmotifs" are developed to add allusive significance and multiple dimensions to religious themes. Finally, there is his "architectonic" mode of composition: chronotopes, characters, and themes are built up on chiastic structures, so that time (past, present, future) is merged with space (Hades, Earth, Paradise), while human and divine levels are juxtaposed in constant tension; these "layers" are held in place by dialogue, which alternately balances and varies the pattern and sequence of speakers. Many features of composition are also found in Byzantine art.[28]

Romanos' Greek is close to the colloquial idiom of the Justinian period, as can be confirmed by comparison with contemporary nonliterary papyrus texts and with chronicles, such as that of John Malalas, whose unaffected prose is a valuable source of evidence for linguistic change in the early Byzantine period.[29] But although Romanos' Greek betrays few signs of Atticism, it would be misleading to equate it with the colloquial idiom of his day. Recent studies indicate that he draws freely on the Hellenistic koine of the scriptures, on the liturgy, and even on the vocabulary of AG.[30] His so-called semitisms may have been exaggerated in view of his alleged Jewish origins but should not be dismissed. It is unlikely that Greek was his only language. Although Grosdidier de Matons states that "there is no evidence" that he knew Hebrew or Syriac,[31] interactions between Greek and Semitic are attested from the third century B.C., and there is no reason to suppose that they ended with Roman domination. Given Romanos' passage from Emesa to Beirut, biblical Hebrew and spoken Aramaic (Syriac) surely played some part in shaping his linguistic horizons. It seems safest to conclude that his Greek, an elevated form of koine, was enriched by words and rhythms from both Semitic traditions.

Romanos' kontakia show the influence, whether directly or as mediated by early Syro-Palestinian Christian homilists and prose writers, of Greek rhetorical prose as it emerged in the so-called second sophistic, with a predilection for homoioteleuton, or words with endings of similar sound, to round off phrases. His hymns contain prosodic patterns and rhythms familiar from Hebrew and Syriac psalms and hymns. Scholarly controversy over the origins of the kontakion—Greek or Semitic?—has been posed as either one or the other. Why not both? It is precisely out of such conjunctures that new genres are born.

4. Precursors and Precedents

Few aspects of the kontakion have been as hotly contested as its origins, ever since J. B. Pitra (1876) claimed they were Semitic, not Greek.[32] At about the same time, Eduard Norden pointed out that "antithetical style" is characteristic of both Greek and Semitic religious literature, tracing its roots to common origins in the ancient Mediterranean and Near East.[33] Since then, scholars have emphasized, from differing perspectives, the "Greekness" of Romanos. As Martin Nilsson pointed out, several features of pagan beliefs and cult practices were taken over by Christianity in late antiquity with little change, including the practice of daily hymn singing at the first and third hours of the service, comparable to the "horae canonicae" of Christian liturgy. Nilsson argues that the Christian daily service originated in Greek pagan practice of late antiquity and that it still predominates in the Orthodox liturgy over the Catholic and Protestant tradition of the weekly Sunday service derived from the Jewish Sabbath.[34]

Among the first to compose Christian hymns in Greek was Clement of Alexandria (b. A.D. 150), said to have converted in later life from the pagan mysteries. Although he repudiated the theological content of the mysteries, he absorbed into the language of the new religion key concepts and words from the old, many of them still fundamental to Orthodox Greek liturgy. These include μυστήριον "mystery," or divine secret above human intelligence; τέλειος "one made perfect" or an initiate; ἀγών "contest" as the athletic and spiritual contest of life; λύσις πόνων "deliverance from evil" as the essence of salvation; and φῶς "light" as the mystical expression of godhead.[35] Methodios (d. A.D. 312), writing about one hundred years after Clement, concludes his *Symposium on Chastity*, or *Parthenion* (Συμπόσιον περὶ ἀγνείας), with the *Hymn of Thekla* which survives complete. Composed of twenty-four verses in uncertain meter (possibly Anacreontic) and arranged in alphabetic acrostic, the hymn (ψαλμός) is introduced by two lines of choral response, repeated after each strophe: ἀγνεύω σοί καὶ λαμπάδας φαεσφόρους κρατοῦσα, νυμφίε, ὑπαντάνω σοί ("I keep myself pure for you and holding light-bearing torches, bridegroom, I come to meet you"). These two structural features, acrostic and refrain, with precedents in the Psalms and Lamentations, remained integral to the kontakion. This complex hymn is also remarkable for its sustained use of imagery, as in strophe 6:[36]

> Ζωῆς χοραγός, Χριστέ, χαῖρε φῶς ἀνέσπερον,
> ταύτην δέδεξο τὴν βοήν· χορός σε παρθένων
> προσεννέπει, τέλειον ἄνθος, ἀγάπη, χαρά,
>   φρόνησις, σοφία, Λόγε.

> Guide of life, Christ, hail, light unfading,
> you have received this cry: the chorus of maidens
> addresses you, perfect bloom, love, joy,
>   prudence, wisdom, Word.

The greeting χαῖρε "hail!", in association with the light revealed to the initiate, is a formula central to Greek Orthodox worship, as in the refrains to the *Akathistos Hymn* (χαῖρε νύμφη ἀνύμφευτος "hail bride unwed") and to Romanos' *On the Annunciation* (χαῖρε φῶς ἀνέσπερον "hail light unfading").[37]

In the fourth to fifth centuries, Gregory of Nazianzos (c. A.D. 330–390) and Synesios of Cyrene (A.D. 370–413/414) experimented with language and prosody in their hymns. Gregory's *Hymn to Christ* can be read as stressed octosyllables without violating the rules for the iambic trimeter; in others he employs the hexameter. Synesios combines stress and quantity consistently in octosyllabic and heptasyllabic lines; he also uses Doric forms borrowed from Pindar and incorporates eschatological terms and ideas derived from the mysteries. We know little about the mode of performance for such hymns.[38] If a new hymn form was to be established as an expression of Orthodox dogma and as an integral part of the liturgy intended for public recitation and song, it would have had to accommodate changed speech rhythms and break away from the outward forms of classical prosody. No compromise, however ingenious, could create the basis of an enduring and living hymn form; nor could it easily avoid suspicion of "heresy." At the same time, the diverse contributions of these early hymnographers to later Christian tradition may have been underestimated; new metrical, structural, and linguistic forms had to be evolved, yet the language of religious imagery and thought retained many of its ancient features.[39]

What of Greek prose? The distinctive features of the kontakion mentioned above are isosyllabismos, homotonia, and homoioteleuton. While they may have been new in Greek poetry, in prose they have a considerably longer history. Norden's study of ancient prose style shows that the use of parallel *kōla* (limbs), antithesis, wordplay, homoioteleuton, and conscious manipulation of rhythm can be traced back to fifth-century Attic prose and that some of these features are evident in earlier philosophical verse. He suggests that what he terms the "antithetical style" is hieratic in origin and common to the ancient Greek and Near Eastern worlds. Literary prose writers of the fifth and fourth centuries exploited it for rhetorical effect, but it lived on in simpler form in later philosophical and medical writings and in popular inscriptions from the Hellenistic provinces. By the late classical period, Greek rhetoricians were aware of the artistic possibilities of a developed prose style, using ornamental figures analogous to those of poetry, and rhythm but not meter.[40] By the second century A.D., the cities of the eastern Mediterranean produced a wide range of prose genres in Greek, from Lucian's elegant dialogues to sophisticated fiction and Christian homilies in both Greek and Syriac. "Asiatics" cultivated the use of ἔνρυθμος λέξις (rhythmed diction); "Atticists" despised their style as vulgar and bombastic.[41]

Such linguistic and stylistic conflicts had a complex history in Greek, as we saw in Chapter 1. We have only to turn to Paul's Epistles in the New Testament or to the pagan and Christian prose hymns and homilies of late antiquity to find "isokola" of the type so characteristic of the kontakion. Here is Paul on the resurrection of the soul, rendered into the splendid English of the King James version:

σπείρεται ἐν φθορᾷ, ἐγείρεται ἐν ἀφθαρσίᾳ·
σπείρεται ἐν ἀτιμίᾳ, ἐγείρεται ἐν δόξῃ·
σπείρεται ἐν ἀσθενείᾳ, ἐγείρεται ἐν δυνάμει·
σπείρεται σῶμα ψυχικόν, ἐγείρεται σῶμα πνευματικόν.

(I Cor. 15, 42–45)

It is sown in corruption; it is raised in incorruption: it is sown in dishonour; it is raised in glory: it is sown in weakness; it is raised in power: it is sown a natural body; it is raised a spiritual body.

And an extract from a homily *On the Passion*, attributed to Saint Athanasios (fourth century A.D.), in language which echoes Herakleitos, and is still to be heard in the liturgy:[42]

ἡ γὰρ τοῦ βίου παρουσία τοῦ θανάτου τὴν βίαν ἐνίκησεν . . . Ἐπειδὴ δὲ Χριστὸς ἐξ οὐρανῶν ἀνεφάνη . . . φωνῇ δεσποτικῇ τὰ Ἅδου διηνοίγετο κλεῖθρα, καὶ δεσμώντας νεκροὺς ἀπεδίδουν οἱ τάφοι· καὶ κλῆσις ἐγένετο, καὶ τάφος ἠνοίγετο.

(Migne 28, 1073)

The presence of life has vanquished the violence of death. . . . Since Christ has appeared from the heavens . . . the gates of Hades have opened up at his lordly bidding; and the tombs gave up the dead in their bondage: there was a summons, the tomb opened.

New prosodic and melodic systems could not be created ex nihilo. The Hebrew Psalms were chanted antiphonally, showing three major forms of parallelism: synonymous (same thought reproduced in different words); antithetic (thought reinforced by means of contrast); and synthetic (thought continued from line to line to build up cumulative, or "incremental," effect), as in the following lines:

(1) The Lord, who shall sojourn in thy tabernacle? / who shall dwell in thy holy mountain? (Ps. 15, 1).
(2) For the Lord regardeth the way of the righteous / but the way of the wicked shall perish (1, 6).
(3) Happy is the man that / hath not walked in the counsel of the wicked / nor stood in the way of sinners / nor sat in the seat of the scornful (1, 1).

There is no regular meter, but the lines consist of two balancing parts, sometimes subdivided into three or more sections and often grouped into strophes of equal length.[43]

Three major forms of Syriac religious poetry predate the Byzantine kontakion by one and a half to two centuries: the *memra* (metrical sermon in narrative style); the *madrasha* (lyrical hymn in variable syllabic patterns within each strophe); and the *sôgîthâ* (dialogue poem, usually strophic, with antiphonal responses). The kontakion shares elements with all three forms but is formally closest to the madrasha.[44] A major exponent and practitioner was Ephrem (b. Nisibis, c. A.D. 306), known as "Harp of the Spirit." Ephrem is the most widely known, but he was working from a highly developed tradition, dating back to Bardesanes, which continued to be creatively reworked in Syriac until the eighth century, as suggested by texts recently edited by S. P. Brock. Ephrem's influence as one of the greatest early hymnographers of Christendom may be judged by the number of translations circulating soon after his death in Greek, Latin, Arabic, Coptic, and Georgian, although not all translations may be genuine "Ephrem," or even Syriac, in origin.[45]

5. Romanos' Kontakia *On the Nativity* and *On the Resurrection*

In Byzantine hymnography as in art, time and space are perceived as a series of overlapping and interrelated juxtapositions. As frescoes of the Nativity and the Dormition face each other in the Monastery of Hosios Loukas, where the Virgin holding the infant Christ in swaddling bands is balanced by Christ holding the Virgin's soul, also in swaddling bands, so in Romanos' perception of Christ, the Nativity, Crucifixion, and Resurrection are connected and merged with the Fall and Redemption of man. There is no attempt to depict a moment in time, rather a sense of eternity by first fusing, then reversing, the roles of mother and child, playing on the tensions between grief and triumph.[46]

Romanos' second *Hymn on the Nativity* (also known as *Adam and Eve and the Nativity*; see the Appendix for text and translation) breaks down rational boundaries of time and space, introducing Adam and Eve into the Nativity scene with Mary as *mediatrix* between her human forebears and her human/divine son/father as it moves in dramatic dialogue across past, present, and future, Earth and Hades.[47] Less well known than his first *Hymn on the Nativity* (allegedly inspired by the Virgin in a dream), which deals with the more familiar Nativity story of the shepherds and the Magi, it shows complex use of imagery, drawn from the life cycle of nature.[48]

In the proem the Melodist, addressing the Virgin Mary, introduces the refrain ἡ κεχαριτωμένη "full of grace" (Mary's appellation at the Annunciation) and asserts the ineffable mystery of Christ's birth by allusion to the Psalms (πρὸ ἑωσφόρου, Ps. 109, 3) by means of antithetical pairs (ἀμήτωρ / ἀπάτωρ, ἄσπορον τόκον). Throughout this and other hymns, the Septuagint is evoked to link past prophecy, present fulfillment, and future promise on spatiotemporal levels. The first two stanzas out of a total of eighteen introduce Mary at the scene of the Nativity as the vine tree (ἡ ἄμπελος) who bears Christ, the uncultivated grape cluster (τὸν ἀγεώργητον βότρυν), in her arms as on branches (ὡς ἐπὶ κλάδων ἀγκάλαις). As in Greek folk songs, address is direct, with little use of simile and a blurring of distinctions between metaphor and metonym. She calls him her fruit and her life, praising him for preserving her virginity intact. She acknowledges him as master (δέσποτα) but exults in the fact that the whole of creation (ἡ πᾶσα κτίσις) 'dances together' (συγχορεύει) to celebrate her appellation—for, she claims, "I rule the world" (τοῦ γὰρ κόσμου βασιλεύω). The "high" Mariology of her initial exultation is reversed at the end by her grief at the infant Christ's prediction of his own Crucifixion.

Her cry of joy performs a vital dramatic function: it crosses the boundaries between life and death. Like Demeter's cry for her daughter in the third Homeric Hymn, it reaches the Underworld, where it is heard by Eve, who gave birth in pain (ἡ ἐν ὀδύναις τεκοῦσα τέκνα) but understands its import as one of hope and redemption: Mary has brought forth a branch on which she, Eve, may feed and not die (ταύτην ἣν προέγραψεν υἱὸς Ἄμως, / ἡ ῥάβδος τοῦ Ἰεσσαὶ ἡ βλαστήσασά μοι κλάδον / οὗ φαγοῦσα οὐ θνήξομαι). Tree imagery, introduced in the first strophe, is extended in time and space to link Old and New Testaments, Isaiah's prophecy and Christ's birth, with Eve's faith in future salvation (3). Turning to Adam, she bids him cast off his deathlike sleep (τὸν ἰσοθάνατον ὕπνον), listen to the "swallow's voice" as terminating, once and for all, the wiles of the serpent (ἐμὲ γὰρ ποτὲ εἷλεν ὁ ὄφις καὶ σκιρτᾶ, / ἀλλ' ἄρτι ὁρῶν τοὺς ἐξ ἡμῶν φεύγει συρτῶς) (4). Gradually, the slothful Adam awakens to his wife's "woven words" (ἀκούσας τοὺς λόγους οὓς ὕφανεν ἡ σύζυγος): he opens his ear, blocked by disobedience (οὓς ἀνοίξας ὁ ἔφραξε παρακοῇ) but remains skeptical—the sound is sweet and seductive, but this time it brings no delight, because he is now aware of the dangers of female seduction (γλυκεροῦ ἀκούω κελαδήματος, τερπνοῦ μινυρίσματος, / ἀλλὰ τοῦ μελίζοντος νῦν ὁ φθόγγος οὐ τέρπει με· / γυνὴ γὰρ ἔστιν, ἧς καὶ φοβοῦμαι τὴν φωνήν / ἐν πείρᾳ εἰμί, ὅθεν τὸ θῆλυ δειλιῶ) (5). Eve reassures him, once more through images drawn from nature but now explicitly sensual, that the past has gone by—"sniff the moisture of Mary's offspring, Christ, and burst out in bloom at once, like an ear of wheat in erectness, for spring has reached you!" (Τούτου τῆς νότιδος ὀσφράνθητι καὶ εὐθέως ἐξάνθησον, / ὡς στάχυς ὀρθώτητι· τὸ γὰρ ἔαρ σε ἔφθασεν)—Christ's breath is a cool breeze, enabling Adam to flee the furnace and follow Eve to the scene of Mary's childbirth (6).

In another dramatic transition from Hades to the Nativity scene Adam, now fully aroused, within the same speech (7–8) first declares his renewed hope to Eve and then addresses Mary, kneeling with Eve at the crib. To Eve he acknowledges the advent of spring as, quickened by the smell of Christ's breath (ταύτης νυνὶ τῇ εὐοσμίᾳ ρωσθείς), he sees a new and other Paradise in the "tree of life" (αὐτὸ τὸ ξύλον τῆς ζωῆς) borne by Mary—the first hint of the impending Crucifixion, since the same term is used here and elsewhere for the Cross. To Mary, he pleads as penitent father to daughter (Ἀδὰμ τὸν πρωτόπλαστον / οἰκτείρησον, θυγάτερ, τὸν πατέρα σου στένοντα), asking her to exchange the poverty of the rags he is wearing (woven by the snake, he underlines—ἃ ὄφις ὕφανέ μοι), for she too gave birth in poverty. Eve joins his plea (9), explaining to Mary the harassment she has suffered from Adam since the Fall for having blossomed from his rib. In the next three stanzas (10–12), Mary responds to them with tears, reassuring her parents of her son's mercy and pointing to her intact virginity as proof by allusion to Christ as the burning bush (πῦρ ὑπάρχων ᾤκησέ μου / τὴν γαστέρα καὶ οὗ κατέφλεξεν ἐμὲ τὴν ταπεινήν, cf. Ezek. 3.2). At this stage she is still confident that, as *mediatrix*, she can win her son's immediate compassion. Turning to the infant Christ, she repeats to him Adam's naïve assertion that the snake was to blame for their nakedness (ὁ δὲ τούτων αἴτιος ὄφις ἐστὶ τιμῆς γυμνώσας αὐτούς).

Addressed to God lying in the manger (θεῷ κειμένῳ ἐν φάτνῃ), her words evoke a reminder from Christ that it is only through his will that he now suckles at her breast; the salvation of her forebears, who chose willingly to break the divine command, can only be at the cost of his own sacrifice, willingly suffered (13–14). Mary demands elucidation in terms similar to her lamentations in the hymn *Mary at the Cross*, and Christ affirms the details of his Crucifixion (15–16). She protests, "O my grapevine, they shall not crush you, the lawless ones" (ὦ βότρυς μου, μὴ ἐκθλίψωσί σε ἄνομοι· / ἐβλάστησά σε· μὴ ὄψομαι τέκνου σφαγήν) (17), only to be reassured that his death will be but a sleep of three days from which he will arise to bring renewal to all nature and its creatures (ἐπ' ἀνακαινίσει τῆς γῆς καὶ τῶν ἐκ γῆς). This final message is conveyed by Mary to Adam and Eve in the concluding stanza (18).

There is no sustained precedent for Romanos' bold treatment of the Nativity, which at the moment of Christ's birth dares to look both backward to the Fall and forward to the Crucifixion and Resurrection, juxtaposing God's perfection and infancy καὶ ὥσπερ βρέφος αὐξάνω ὁ ἐκ τελείου τέλειος, 14.2) with the human predicament of hope deferred.[49] In terms of thematic structure, the contradictions may be resolved:

Table 2

MARY	Paradise regained (holy death)	CHRIST
divine motherhood	suppliant to Christ	born of woman
painless birth		in holiness (willing)
	suppliants to Mary	
sinful motherhood		fathers man
painful birth		in sin (willing)
EVE	Paradise lost (sinful union)	ADAM

Such a diagram, while tabulating architectonic and chiastic structure, fails to take account of the mediating yet tragic role of Mary expressed through imagery of nature.

In comparably bold manner, the second *Hymn On the Resurrection* (see Appendix) engages in dialogue with conflicting versions of the story found in the Gospels, examples from which I introduced this chapter. Whereas Mark and Luke conclude with women's fear (ἐφοβοῦντο γάρ) and men's disbelief (καὶ ἠπίστουν αὐταῖς), Romanos, while alluding to all four Gospel versions, credits women as the first to have faith in Christ's resurrection and uses their voices to spread the message of the "coming of spring" to all humankind.

Of the six hymns on the Resurrection, five are concerned with Christ's struggle with death and only one deals throughout with the story as told in the Gospels (Maas-Trypanis 29, Grosdidier de Matons 40). Undoubtedly among Romanos' finest works, it is structured like a fugue in which different voices, themes, and images overlap in counterpoint throughout the twenty-four stanzas, culminating in the Melodist's direct address to God in the final stanza (24). His faith in the miracle of the Resurrection is powerful because still tempered with fear and doubt—*has* lamentation turned to joy, death into life? Faith is expressed not by monologic proclamations but by exploring, through dialogue and imagery, the tensions inherent in the human condition and the contradictions underlying all attempts to record and interpret the divine. And despite the alleged misogyny of the Christian church from the fourth century onward, from which Romanos is not always immune, the hymn celebrates—in contrast to the Gospels, homilies, and commentaries—woman's power to mediate between the human and the divine.[50]

Dialogue predominates. Exchange of interlocutors is present in every strophe, even in the two proems and the concluding stanza, whether as a direct address to Christ/God (Proem I, 24), or in overlapping speakers within the same stanza (6, 9, 10, 19, 23), or in speech within speech, past and present (Proems I and II, 1, 6, 7, 8, 10, 12, 14, 15, 20, 22, 23). Most stanzas combine narration with dramatic representation, although some give only a part of a whole speech (8, 12, 14, 16) or narrate a past event with citation in direct speech (4–5). Apart from dramatic representation, Romanos not only engages in direct dialogue with his Creator (Proems I and II, 24) and audience (refrain) but also with the Gospels, Old and New Testaments, homilies, and commentaries. According to Grosdidier de Matons, his motivation was to dispel disbelief in the Resurrection engendered by the three variant stories as told by Matthew, Mark, and Luke on the one hand, (different only in detail), and with John's somewhat divergent one on the other, by creating a compelling synthesis, credible to all. In so doing he irons out some inconsistencies but introduces new ones.[51] He also makes minor but significant changes of his own so as to place women—above all, Mary Magdalene—at the center of the hymn. Miracles from the life of Christ are carefully selected from the New Testament to contrast the human and the divine and are frequently juxtaposed with Old Testament figures (Jonah, Moses), who are used as *protypa* to indicate fulfillment of past prophecies, as when Mary Magdalene compares her sense of glory on returning from the sepulchre with that of Moses descending from the mountain (14). As for homilists and commentators, Romanos is aware of their attempts to explain the discrepancies but transforms their pedantic correction of inconsistencies into psychological insight; his Mary Magdalene does not doubt Christ's resurrection after he has appeared to her, as occurs rather improbably in Severus, but immediately before when, alone at the sepulchre, she has dismissed the apostles with reassuring words she does not inwardly believe. There is also a constant dialogue with the liturgy, in which rites of baptism, wedding, and funeral are alluded to by means of imagery but transferred to the context of the Resurrection.[52] On the emotional level, the hymn shifts constantly between fear and joy, lament and rejoicing.

Imagery plays a major role. Cosmic, natural, and human forces are subtly exploited in metaphor and metonym to form a chain of images. As in the Easter liturgy, Christ is the sun, who has set beneath the earth only to rise again in renewed splendor (Proems I and II, 1). He controls the breath/spirit of living creatures (τὴν τῶν κινουμένων πνοήν, 2), and emits angelic fire (18). Fire and light also express human love and longing for Christ, who raises Mary's sensual desire to touch him to a divine plane, once more by allusion to the torch-lit procession of the Easter liturgy (12). Fire is in turn juxtaposed with the quenching power of liquids, associated on the human plane with women, on the divine with God. The hymn begins with Christ's message to the myrrh-bearing women (γυναιξὶ μυροφόροις, Proem I) as they weep over his body (δακρύσουσαι, Proem

II), and closes with their message of hope. Perfumes and tears serve the same function, to mediate between the divine and human; in the first stanza, the women compare their gifts of myrrh with those of the Magi at Christ's birth. Whereas the apostles fail to find Christ inside the Tomb, whose space they violate (5, 6), Mary Magdalene's tears and wails (ἐβόα οὐχὶ ῥήμασιν, ἀλλὰ δάκρυσιν, 7) have the power to invoke his presence as she begs to wash his whole body with her tears, recalling John's baptism of Christ (8). Later, dazzled by the lightning and fire of the angel's appearance, the women pray to God as divine rain (ὄμβρος, 18) to quench their thirst, again in terms which evoke the ritual of baptism. Liquids are linked with the tongue and language (γλῶσσα), hence the words of the Word are like raindrops to guide their souls (νῦν ὡς σταγόνες οἱ λόγοι τοῦ στόματος, Λόγε, 19 19), while Mary's inarticulate wails (7) are transformed by Christ's presence into a resonant musical instrument (σάλπιγγι, 12) or into an olive branch to be placed on her tongue (ὡς καρφὸς ἐλαίας, 14) to spread the good news of the Resurrection (16, 23). Coherent speech is related to physical movement and space as well as to meter, harmony and dance; Mary is reassured by the other women that "your utterance [ἐφθέγξω, 16] is upright, neither limping nor lame" (χωλεύει, σκάζον: the terms are also metrical), whereupon she later urges them to dance (στήσατε χορείας 22, 24) and in turn inspires the Melode to song (τῶν ἀσμάτων τούτων, 24).[53] Here again, Romanos draws an implicit, but deliberate, contrast between male and female perceptions. Gregory of Antioch, in his homily on the Myrrh-bearing Women (εἰς τὰς μυροφόρους) has them vying with one another to be the first to bring the good news to the apostles.[54] Romanos transfers this detail to Peter and John, who race to the spot the women had already reached (4); their freedom and daring (παρρησίαν, ἐτολμήσαμεν, 5) is contrasted with the women's blameless courage (θάρσος ἄμεμπτον, 21), which gave them faith without trespass.

Romanos has changed the Gospel story as told in Mark, Luke, and Matthew, where the women did actually enter the tomb. In her plea to Christ to arise, Mary reminds him of his miraculous raising of Lazarus, rescued from the bonds of death (John 11:43–44) and transformed into a runner (δρομαῖον, 8), since the concept of life as a race or contest (ἀγών), rooted in mystical and Christian thought, can be understood either literally (as by Peter and John) or figuratively (by Mary and the women). The tomb is recognized by the apostles as a throne (θρόνος, 5), but the women see it as a fertile bosom (κόλπος, 17) which makes room for God (χωρήσας ὃν οὐ χωροῦσιν οὐρανοί) and (by assonance and wordplay) space for the dance bands (χορείας) of humankind, affording to Christ the chance to trample on death (ἐπάτησας τὸν θάνατον, 23). Christ is the object of longing and desire (πόθος, 3, 6, 9, 11), interlinked with human emotions of love and grief: *póthos* means both physical and spiritual longing. Christ's medical metaphors (10) connect healing on human and divine planes, yet he does not rebuke Mary's sensuality (10), whereas the apostles' audacity in encroaching on his space is met with silence and absence (5–6). Twice the women are graced with the appellation θεοφόροι (god-bearing); twice they bear the message of spring and resurrection (22, 23). If at the Nativity Mary as *theotókos* turned her cry of jubilation into one of lament, at the Resurrection, Mary Magdalene and the myrrh-bearing women, as *theophóroi*, transform lamentation (κλαύσωμεν) into exultation (κράξωμεν) against a backdrop of spring and the renewal of life (22, 23).[55] Tensions between human sensuality and divine love are explored in myth and metaphor.

I have dwelt on Romanos' use of the Scriptures and imagery to suggest that neither myth nor metaphor can be separated from language. Syntactically and morphologically close to the colloquial idiom of the Justinian period and comparable in many respects to the unaffected prose of his time, Romanos elevates the language of the Scriptures, enriched by the vocabulary and rhythms he chose to sing in. Romanos' hymns have a modern textual history of only 120 years or so. Even if no manuscript had survived he would still have left indelible marks on the music of the Greek language and its specific imagery, evident not just in hymnography and liturgy but also, as we shall see, in the erotic novel, vernacular verse, modern prose and poetry, and the love songs of the folk tradition.

CHAPTER 3

Nonliterary Genres: Some
Private and Public Voices

If the language of the Gospels and hymns lived on not just through textual transmission but also through daily performance of the liturgy, the fragmented texts discussed in this chapter could not have survived without evolved levels of literacy. Taken together, they provide evidence of significant linguistic change (including dialect differentiation within the koine) in four nonliterary genres: the personal letter, the technical treatise, public acclamations, and popular songs. They speak to the present in ways different from the religious texts analyzed in the previous chapter and the literary texts to be considered in the next, conveying a sense of urgency to communicate information or emotion.

1. Writing Home

The value of the many hundreds of personal letters preserved on papyrus* lies in the insights they afford into the everyday language and life of a broad cross section of Greek speakers in Egypt from the late fourth century B.C. to the eighth century A.D. The language of the letters is far from homogeneous, reflecting diverse educational levels of writer or scribe; but the orthographical and grammatical "errors" provide incontrovertible proof of major linguistic changes. Whereas the language of papyri from the Hellenistic period has been carefully studied alongside NT Greek, the Roman and Byzantine papyri have often been wrongly interpreted by editors; so that in the absence of a systematic grammar it is premature to draw con-

---

*As explained on p. xvii above, the papyrus letters are rendered without accents.

clusions about whether divergences from the koine reflect the influence of Egyptian (Coptic) speech, foreshadow practices in MG, or perhaps both.[1] I have selected four letters to outline linguistic shifts and three more to illustrate how, beneath the epistolary clichés, we may glimpse the same kind of desperate situations and heartrending emotions in everyday life—shipwrecks and exposure of infants, abductions and prostitution, death and bereavement—as those we shall encounter in the next chapter in the context of the novel.[2]

My first example is an importunate letter from the second century A.D. sent by young Antonis Longos to his mother, who lives in Karanis, a village in the Fayum. We may surmise that there has been a family quarrel arising from some kind of indiscretion on his part and that he is in debt:

Αντωνις Λονγος Νειλουτι τη μητρι πλιστα χαιρειν. Και δια παντων ευχομαι σαι υγειαινειν. Το προσκυνημα σου ποιω κατα αικαστην ημαιραν παρα τω κυριω Σαραπειδει. Γεινωσκειν σαι θελω οτι ουχ ηλπιζον οτι ανεβενις εις την μητροπολιν. Χαρειν τουτο ουδ εγο εισηλθα εις την πολιν. Αιδυσοπουμην δε ελθειν εις Καρανιδαν οτι σαπρως παιριπατω. Αιγραψα σοι οτι γυμνος ειμαι. Παρακαλωσαι, μητηρ, διαλαγητι μοι. Λοιπον οιδα τιποτ αιμαυτω παρεσχημαι. Πεπαιδευμαι καθ ον δι τροπον. Οιδα οτι ημαρτηκα. Ηκουσα παρα του Ποστουμου τον ευροντα σαι εν τω Αρσαινοειτη και ακαιρως παντα σοι διηγται. Ουκ οιδες οτι θελω πηρος γενεσται ει γνουναι οπως ανθροπω ετι οφειλω οβολον; Νειλουτι μητρει απ Αντωνιω Λονγου υειου.   (B.G.U. 846)[3]

Antonis Longos to his mother, very many greetings. And I pray always you are in good health. I make offerings for you every day to Lord Sarapis. I want you to know I didn't expect you would go up to the metropolis. That's why I didn't come to town myself. I was ashamed to come to Karanis, because I go around in rags. I wrote you, I'm broke. Please, mother, make it up with me! Yes, I know I've brought it on myself to some extent. I've been punished, and in the appropriate manner. I know I've been wrong. I heard from Postoumos who came across you in Arsinoitis, and he told you everything at the worst moment. Don't you know I'd rather be lame than realize I still owe anyone an obol? So do come yourself, I beg you. To my mother Nilous from her son, Antonios Longos.

Phonology. Spelling mistakes confirm major shifts from AG to MG.
Vowels show "fronting-raising-closing": η/ι, ει/η, ει/ι (so-called "etacism") αι/ε; ο/ω; ω/ου.

Instability of iota subscript, and of breathings ("psilosis," κατ᾽ ἑκάστην, οὐχ ἤλπιζον), is manifest.

Consonants show degemination (λ/λλ) and dissimilation (σθ / στ).

Morphology. Inflexional systems of verb and noun are restructured: εἰσῆλθα (AG ⁻ον): "weak" endings (⁻α, ⁻ες, ⁻ε) are substituted for AG "strong" ones (⁻ον, ⁻ας, ⁻ε) in singular.

The contracted form of the proper name Ἀντώνης (compare the MG) coexists with formal Ἀντώνιος. Καρανίδαν: feminine nouns of third declension are assimilated to first.

Syntax. Simpler constructions replace more complex ones: the infinitive in greetings (after εὔχομαι and θέλω), ὅτι + indicative (after οἶδα). χάριν τοῦτο (AG χάριν τούτου) may be a phonetic error or may suggest attenuation of the genitive. παρέσχημαι, πεπαίδευμαι, ἡμάρτηκα (cf. διήγηται): perfect and aorist are no longer distinct. τὸν εὑρόντα (AG τοῦ εὑρόντος in agreement with object) marks the reduction of participial forms; compare Romanos' use of masculine participial forms for feminine nouns and the formation of the MG indeclinable active participle from accusative singular. It also suggests the breakdown of the AG case system, evident in indiscriminate use of accusative, genitive, and dative after prepositions.[4]

Vocabulary. Words are used in senses attested only from Attic prose of the fourth century B.C. or from NT Greek: παιδεύω "chastise, punish," παρακαλῶ "beseech, entreat."

The second letter, of about the same date, is from Apion, another young man from the Fayum. A volunteer recruit in the Roman fleet, he writes home on arrival in Italy with news of his voyage, the receipt of passage money, and the new name he has been given. Recruits like Apion came from prestigious orders, drawn from the Greco-Egyptian ruling class; and as one who has passed his *probatio*, with hopes for further advancement, he has been well educated. The spelling is better than that of Antonis, perhaps because it was written by a scribe; yet the Greek shows unmistakable signs of linguistic change:

Απιων Επιμαχω τωι πατρι και κυριω πλειστα χαιρειν. Προ μεν παντων ευχομαι σε υγιαινειν και δια παντος ερωμενον ευτυχειν μετα της αδελφης μου και της θυγατρος αυτης και του αδελφου μου. Ευχαριστω τω κυριω Σερπαπιδι, οτι μου κινδυνευσαντος εις θαλασσαν εσωσε ευθεως. Οτε εισηλθον εις Μησηνους ελαβα βιατικον παρα Καισαρος χρυσους τρεις και καλως μοι εστιν. Ερωτω σε ουν, κυριε μου πατηρ γραψον μοι επιστολιον πρωτον μεν περι της σωτηριας σου δευτερον περι της των αδελφων μου

τριτον ινα σου προσκυνησω την χεραν οτι με επαιδευσας καλως
και εκ τουτου ελπιζω ταχυ προκοσαι των θεων θελοντων. Ασπασαι
Καπιτωνα πολλα και τους αδελφους μου και Σερηνιλλαν και τους
φιλους μου. Επεμψα σοι εικονιν μου δια Ευκτημονος. Εστι δε μοι
ονομα Αντωνις Μαξιμος. Ερρωσθαι σε ευχομαι. Κεντυρια Αθηνονικη.
Εις Φιλαδελφιαν Επιμαχω απο Απιωνος υιου. Αποδος εις χωρτην
πριμαν Απαμηνων Ιουλιανου λιβλαριω απο Απιωνος ωστε Επιμαχω
πατρι.   (B.G.U. 423)[5]

Apion to his father and lord, very many greetings. Above all I pray that you
are well and always in good health and fortune together with my sister and
her daughter and my brother. I thank the lord Serapis that despite my danger at sea he saved me at once. When I arrived at Meseni, I received my
passage money from the Caesar of three gold coins, and things are fine
with me. I ask you then, my lord and father, write me a letter, first about
your well-being, second about my brother and sister, third that I may kiss
your hand, because you educated me well, and for this reason I hope soon
to get promotion, gods willing. Many greetings to Kapiton and my brothers and Serenilla and my friends. I have sent you a picture of myself
through Euktemon. My name is Antonis Maximos. I wish you good
health. Centurio Athenonike. To Philadelphia, for Epimachos, from Apion
his son. Deliver to the first cohort of Apameni for the scribe Julian from
Apion to Epimachos his father.

Apion writes fluently and as correctly as he—or his scribe—knows how.
Orthography is good, with one minor mistake (ἐρωμένον for ἐρρωμένον;
but note ἐρρῶσθαι at the end). He employs a wider range of particles
(μὲν, οὖν, δὲ) and prepositions (πρὸ, διὰ, μετὰ, παρὰ, ἐκ, περὶ, ἀπὸ,
all used with the genitive case) than does Antonis. He knows his "strong"
aorist ending, εἰσῆλθον, but he lets slip the odd morphological and phonological change: χέραν for χεῖρα (MG χέρι "hand"); προκόσαι for
προκόψαι; εἰκόνιν for εἰκόνιον (εἰκών); βιάτικον as transliteration of "vi-
aticum." As is natural in a military context, there are Latin loanwords, showing assimilation by liquid metathesis: χώρτην for cohortem, λιβλαρίω for li-
brario. His vocabulary is consistently KG: εὐχαριστῶ (AG χάριν εἰδέναι),
σωτηρία (ὑγιεία) ἐρωτῶ (παραιτῶ), εὐθέως "at once" (straight). Despite
fluency, his grammar is not all it should be according to strict Attic standards: μὲν is used twice without an answering δὲ; and the genitive absolute
μοῦ κινδυνεύσαντος εἰς θάλασσαν should be an accusative participial
phrase, in agreement with the implied object of the main verb (ἔσωσε "he
saved"). Apion's letter shows how even the best-educated young men could

not but reflect the processes of linguistic change, at least at the level of personal communication.

A different piece is a petulant little outburst from Theonatos, again from the Fayum (second to third centuries A.D.), who complains to his father about not being taken for a trip to the "big city" and about receiving no money. He sounds angry, as if writing in haste:

Θεων Θεωνι τω πατρι χαιρειν. Καλως εποιησες ουκ απενηχες με μετ εσου εις πολιν. Η ου θελεις απενεκκειν μετ εσου εις Αλεξανδριαν ου μη γραψω σε επιστολην ουτε λαλω σε ουτε υιγενω σε ειτα. Αν δε ελθης εις Αλεξανδριαν ου μη λαβω χειραν παρα σου ουτε παλι χαιρω σε λυπον. Αμ μη θελης απενεκαι με ταυτα γεινετε. Και η μητηρ μου ειπε Αρχελαω οτι αναστατοι με αρρον αυτον. Καλως δε εποιησες δωρα μοι επεμψες μεγαλα αρακια. Πεπλανηκαν ημας εκει τη ημερα ιβ οτι επλευσες. Λυπον πεμψον εις με παρακαλω σε. Αμ μη πεμψης ου μη φαγω ου μη πεινω. Ταυτα. Ερωσθε σε ευχομαι. Τυβι ιη. Αποδος Θεωνι απο Θεωνατος υιω.

(Thomson 1966, 47 (no. 20)

Theon to his father Theon greetings. A fine thing you've done: you didn't take me with you to the city! If you won't take me with you to Alexandria, I'll never write you a letter or speak to you or wish you well ever again. But if you do go to Alexandria, I won't take your hand or greet you ever again. Unless you take me with you, that's it! My mother said to Archelaos—he upsets me, get rid of him! Yes, you've done well—sent me a load of chickpeas! They deceived us there on the twelfth day, for you sailed off. So, send for me, please. If you don't, I'll neither eat nor drink. That's it. I wish you health. Seventeenth of Tybis. Deliver to Theon from Theonatos his son.[6]

In addition to the phonological changes noted in Antonis' letter, Theon's misspellings show οι and υ as the same high front round vowel *ü*; γ before front vowels as voiced palatal fricative (*y*) rather than voiced velar fricative (*g*): υἱγένω; and assimilation of consonants (ἄμ μή for ἄν μή). Morphologically, in addition to the consistent preference for "weak" over "strong" verb endings in the aorist indicative (ἐποίησες, ἔπεμψες, ἔπλευσες) and the reformation of third declension feminine nouns as first declension (χεῖραν), we observe the conflation of aorist and perfect: ἀπένηχες < perfect ἀπενήνοχας and aorist ἀπήνεγκες, compare infinitive ἀπενέκαι; πεπλάνηκαν perfect πεπλανήκασι and aorist ἐπλάνησαν, compare MG aorist passive. ⁻ηκαν. The re-formation of the nominative suffix Theon-*atos* from genitive Theon-*as* (nominative Theon) is illustrated in the paradigmatic patterns of many MG nominal endings. Personal pronouns are also in the process of re-formation as in MG: ἐσοῦ is modeled by analogy on ἐμοῦ (cf. MG ἐσύ / ἐσένα, ἐμένα). As for syntax, this brief missive provides ample evidence for the reduction in the number and function of cases (μετ᾽ ἐσοῦ, γράψω σε, λαλῶ σε, υἱγένω σε); the remodeling of tenses and moods (χαίρω, γίνεται, φάγω, πίνω); breakdown of AG negative conditionals, replacing εἰ in protasis with a string of options: ἂν + subjunctive or future indicative; εἰ οὐ for εἰ μή, ἂμ μή + subjunctive; ἂμ μὴ πέμψης "unless you send"; οὐ μὴ φάγω "I really won't eat." This last example suggests the distinction between actions perceived as potential and those perceived as actual, as in MG. As in Mark and many other papyrus letters, his mother's direct speech follows the indirect conjunction "that" (ὅτι ἀναστατοῖ με, "that he upsets me"). The heat of the moment has preserved the tones of voice intact.[7]

Another letter from the Fayum from the same period is close to Antonis' in its clichés, but unusual because written by a girl, Serenilla. Unlike Antonis and Theonatos, she has made it to Alexandria (we do not know why), but she is lonely and desperate for news from her family. Her poignant tone contrasts nicely with the young men's petulance:

Σερηνιλλα Σωκρατη τω πατρι πλιστα χαιρειν. Προ μεν παντων ευχομαι σαι υγιαινιν και το προσκυνημα σου ποιω κατ εκαστην ημεραν παρα τω κυριω Σαραπιδι και τοις συννεοις θεοις. Γεινωσκειν σε θελω οτι μονη ιμι εγω. Εν νοω εχης οτι η θυγατηρ μου ις Αλεξανδρειαν εσσι ινα καιγω ειδω οτι πατερα εχω εινα μη ιδωσειν με ως μη εχουσαν γονεις. Και ο ενιγων σοι την επιστολην δος αυτω αλλην περι της υιας σου. Και ασπαζομαι την μητερα μου και τους αδελφους μου και Σεμπρωνιν και τους παρ αυτου.   (B.G.U. 385)[8]

Serenilla to Sokrates her father, very many greetings. Above all I pray you are well and I make offerings for you every day to lord Sarapis and the rest of the gods. I want you to know that I am alone by myself. Keep in mind that "my daughter you are in Alexandria," so I can see as well that I have a father, so people will not see me as having no parents. And the bearer of this letter, please give to him another about your health. And I greet my mother and my brothers and Sempronis, and those with him.

In addition to the spelling mistakes shared with Antonis and Theonatos, she writes υίας for υγιείας, confirming our suspicion that -γ between front vowels had its present "glide" or "yod" value. She uses KG for the second-person singular "you are" (ἔσσι, AG εἶ) and εἰς + accusative for ἐν + dative.

The form ἐνιγών is obscure (an attempt at the aorist active participle of φέρω, ἐνέγκων?). Like Theonatos, she transfers to direct speech after the conjunction "that" to convey vividly her father's hoped-for response.

It has been stated that few of the personal letters "rise above the epistolary clichés, or transmit the vigour or warmth of a personality."[9] This is true if present-day Western standards of self-expression are applied, but the style accords well enough with attempts by those not used to writing to convey dire straits to close relatives, as I can vouch from my own experience of receiving letters from relatives in Greece who were looking after my autistic son.[10] What are we to make of Ilarion's letter to Alis, his sister (first century B.C.)?

Ιλαριων{α} Αλιτι τηι αδελφηι πλειστα χαιρειν και Βερουτι τη κυρια μου και Απολλω-
ναριν γινωσκε ως ετι και νυν εν Αλεξαν-
δρε[ι]α ⟨ν⟩σμεν· μη αγωνιας εαν ολως εισ-
πορευονται εγω εν Αλεξανδρε⟨ι⟩α μενω
ερωτω σε και παρακαλω σε επιμελη-
θ⟨ητ⟩ι τω παιδιω και εαν ευθυς οψωνι-
ον λαβωμεν αποστελω σε ανω εαν
πολλαπολλων τεκης εαν ην αρσε-
νον αφες εαν ην θηλεα εκβαλε
ειρηκας δε Αφροδισιατι οτι μη με
επιλαθης πως δυναμαι σε επι-
λαθειν ερωτω σε ουν ινα μη αγω-
νιασης
ετους κθ Καισαρος Παυνι κγ.

(P. Oxy. 744)

Ilarion to Alis his sister many greetings, and to Berous my mistress and Apollonaris. Know that we are still in Alexandria. Don't get upset if they make their way together, I shall stay on in Alexandria. I ask you and beg you, take care of the child, and if we get a treat soon, I'll send it up to you. If in the end you give birth, if it is male, let it live, if female, expose it. You told Aphrodisias, don't forget me. How could I forget you? I ask you then, do stop worrying.

We cannot reconstruct the family crisis involved, but Alis is pregnant again and anxious, whereas Ilarion seems to take the exposure of female infants as a matter of course.[11]

Another domestic tragedy is indicated by a letter from Serenos to Isidora (second century A.D.). It is poorly spelled, but the strength of his emotion at their enforced separation and its consequences breaks through epistolary clichés of good wishes for mutual health that are still current in present-day Greek letters (see n. 10 above):

Σερηνος Εισιδωρα τη αδελ-
φη και κυρια πλαιστα χαιρειν.
προ μεν παντος ευχομαι σε υγιαι⁻
νειν και καθ εκαστης ημερας και
οψιας το προσκυνημα σου πυω
παρα τη σε φιλουση Θοηρι. γινοσκειν
σε θελω αφ ως εκξηλες απ εμου
πενθος ηγουμην νυκτος κλεων
ημερας δε πενθων. ιβ Φαωφι αφ οτε
ελουσαμην μετ εσου ουκ ελουσαμην
ουκ ηλιμμε μεχρει ιβ Αθυρ. και επεμ⁻
σας μυ επιστολας δυναμενου λιθον
σαλευσε, ουτως υ λογυ σου καικινη⁻
καν με. αυτην τη ορα αντεγρα⁻
ψα συ και εδωκα τη ιβ μετα των
σων επιστολων εσσφραγιζμενα.
χωρεις δε των σων λογων κε γρα⁻
μματων ο Κολοβος δε πορνην με πεπυ⁻
ηκεν ελεγε δε οτι επεμσε μυ φασειν
η γυνη σου οτι αυτος πεπρακεν το αλυ⁻
σιδιον και αυτος κατεστακε με εις το
πλυν τουτους τους λογους λεγεις ηνα
μηκετι [φ]πιστευθω μου την ενβολην.
εδου ποσα{ρ}κεις επεμσα επι σε. ερχη ειτε
ουκ ερχη δηλοσον μυ.

(P. Oxy. 528)[12]

Serenos to Isidora, his sister and mistress, many greetings. Before all else I pray for your health and every day and evening I make offerings to Thoeris who loves you. I want you to know that since you left me I have led the mourning, weeping by night and lamenting by day. Since we bathed together on Phaophi 12, I never bathed nor anointed myself till Athyr 12. You sent me letters which would have shaken a stone, so much did your words move me. At once I wrote back to you and gave it on the 12th, sealed up with your letters. Apart from your messages and letters [saying], Kolobos has made me a prostitute, he [Kolobos] said that, your wife sent me word that, he [?Serenos] sold the chain himself and put me on the

boat. You say these things to stop me being believed as to the shipment.
See how many times I have sent to you. Whether you are coming or not,
let me know.

My final example is a torn fragment from a letter of condolence, possibly from a former slave to his master on tragic deaths in the family. It was
written in the sixth century:

5
ο εκων σου [
εχαριν γνωσας εξ αυτον τα πε....[
τα τριαντα πεντε φορτια εις πληρες [
και παλιν ανεγνοσα το σκότος το εκ [
πεδια και πολ{λ}υ εληπιθιν και οσε [
10
ηλπιδα σου εσενεφερην λοιπα γα[[ρ
να των αυτων δια τιναν κλαυσο δι[
τι επαθες ομοιος αμμα Ευα ομοιος Μαρια και ζη θεος
δεσποτα μου ουτε
δικιε ουτε εμαρτολε ουτεποτε επαθαν το επαθες ομος δεν ε
αμαρτιε υμον
                              εισιν αλλα
δωξαζωμεν τον θεον ότι αυτός εδωσεν και αυτος ελαβεν
αλλα ευξαι ενα ο
                                                κυριος
15
εναπαυσι αυτοις και και καταξιωσι υμας εδιν εν αυτοις εις τον
παραδεισον οτι κρινον[
τε ε ψυχε των τον ανθρωπων αυτοις γαρ απερθαν εις
κωρφον του
                              Αβ{ρ}ααμ και
του Ισαακ και του Ιακω{β}. αλλα παρακαλω σε κυριε μου με
βαλης
                                        [λυπη]ν εις το ψυ-
χι σου και απολήσις τα πραγματα σου αλλα ευξε ενα ο
κυριος αποστιλη
                                                επι [σ]αι
την ευλογιαν αυτου. Πολλα γαρ καλα εχι ο κυριος και
αθυμουν[τας
                              ευθυμ[ο]υς
20
εισστιν τοις θελοντες απ αυτου ευλογια⟨ν⟩, και ελπιζωμεν εις
τον θεων
                                        οταν δια
τις λο[ι]πις ταυ[τ]ης χαραν πεμ{μ}πι υμα⟨ς⟩ ο κυριως και τον

κυ[ριον] τον
αδελφων υμον.

(P.Oxy.1874)

5   I your willing [
was happy to know from them the . . . . [
thirty-five loads in full [
and again I learned of the darkness that [
children and I was much grieved and as many [

10   hope I brought you, for in the future [
why should I weep for them be [
cause you have suffered like unto Eve, like to Mary, and may God
    live, my lord, neither
just men nor sinners have ever suffered what you have suffered: but
let us glorify God, for he has given, and he has taken away; then pray
    that the Lord

15   give rest unto them and deem you worthy to see through them into
    Paradise whence are judg-
ed the souls of men; for they (?) are departed to the bosom of
    Ab[r]aham and
of Isaac and of Jaco[b]. But I beg you, my lord, do not set
    [grie]f in your so-
ul and disperse your goods, rather pray that the Lord send unto you
his blessing. For the Lord disposeth many good things even the
    sound in heart

for the down in heart

20   to those wishing blessing from him, and may we have hope in God
    whenever throughout
the rest of these (?times) the Lord sends you joy,
my lord and your brothers. [13]

This mutilated piece can scarcely be analyzed, either as an utterance or in linguistic terms. Judging from the phonological and graphical errors (ε for ι, ε for α, ιε for αιοι, ε for οι), the writer's first language may not have been Greek, although liquid metathesis, or "delateralization" (κῶρφον for κόλπον, ἀπέρθαν for ἀπῆλθον) is still current in Greek dialects.[14] As for morphology, the definite article is used for the relative pronoun, as in medieval Greek (τὸ ἔπαθες), while the form δέν would seem to be one of the first attested usages of the contracted form of the negative adverb οὐδέν "in no way," now current in MG as the negative particle "not."

    None of the papyrus letters cited can be read or interpreted without familiarity with MG phonology, morphology, syntax, and vocabulary. As for the relevance of these texts to modern Greek, their linguistic value has long been recognized. What of literature? In his novel *The Third Wedding*, Kostas Takhtsis forenamed Nina's second husband "Antonios" and surnamed Ekavi's husband "Longos," attaching considerable importance to both names at key points and playing on their associations with epitaphs and with Cavafy's poem "The God Abandons Antony." Given the varied registers of Takhtsis' Greek, it is tempting to suppose that he had Antonis Longos' well-known letter in mind in choosing the names.[15] Perhaps Cavafy has come closest to capturing the gaps of such utterances, as in his poem Ἐν τῷ μηνὶ Ἀθύρ, "In the Month of Athyr" (1917), inspired by an attempt to read a consolatory but mutilated funerary epitaph on stone from the Hellenistic period:

Μὲ δυσκολίαν διαβάζω   στὴν πέτρα τὴν ἀρχαία.
"Κύ[ρι]ε Ἰησοῦ χριστέ."   Ἕνα "Ψυχὴν" διακρίνω.
"Ἐν τῷ μη[ν]ὶ Ἀθὺρ"   "Ὁ Λεύκιο[ς] ἐ[κοιμ]ήθη·"
Στὴ μνεία τῆς ἡλικίας   "Ἐβί[ωσ]εν ἐτῶν."
τὸ Κάππα Ζῆτα δείχνει   ποὺ νέος ἐκοιμήθη.
Μὲς στὰ φθαρμένα βλέπω   "Αὐτὸ[ν] ... Ἀλεξανδρέα."
Μετὰ ἔχει τρεῖς γραμμὲς   πολὺ ἀκρωτηριασμένες·
μὰ κάτι λέξεις βγάζω-   σὰν "δ[ά]κρυα ἡμῶν." "ὀδύνην."
κατόπιν πάλι "δάκρυα"   καὶ "[ἡμ]ῖν τοῖς [φ]ίλοις πένθος"
Μὲ φαίνεται ποὺ ὁ Λεύκιος   μεγάλως θ'ἀγαπήθη.
Ἐν τῷ μηνὶ Ἀθὺρ   ὁ Λεύκιος ἐκοιμήθη.

(Cavafy 1963b)

With difficulty I read   on the ancient stone
"Lo[r]d Jesus Christ"   A "so[ul]" I discern.
"In the mon[th] of Athyr"   "Lefkio[s] was l[aid to] rest"
At the mention of age   "he li[ved] the years"
the xxviii shows   he was laid to rest young.
Amidst the effaced I see   "Hi[m] . . . Alexandrian."
Then three lines   much mutilated:
but I can make out some words—like "our t[ea]rs," "pain,"
then again "tears," and   "for u[s] his [f]riends grieving."
It seems to me that Lefkios   was greatly loved.
In the month of Athyr   Lefkios was laid to rest.

(Cavafy 1963b: my translation)

Cavafy transforms the "difficulty of reading" ancient stones into a poem of gaps and interstices, punctuated by flashes of excited fluency when he thinks he has deciphered correctly.[16]

2. Of Purple Pants and Chamber Pots: The Imperial Baggage Train

Turning now to imperial ceremonial, we note in general terms that Byzantine technical treatises from the seventh century onward may use Attic in the preface and the more narrative parts of the text, but less formal levels for detailed inventories and regulations governing military, monastic, and courtly life. Military treatises from Maurice in the seventh century to Kekaumenos in the eleventh testify to simplified morphology and syntax and to extensive lexical borrowing.[17] Monastic *typika* (rules of governance) and *acta* (records for ownership of lands and properties) contain varied levels of style, from legalistic formulations in defining rules and agreements to more colloquial styles in describing land and boundaries.[18] To illustrate in the most striking terms the diversity and complexity of lexical borrowing, I have selected from the appendix, "On the Imperial Wardrobe," to Constantine Porphyrogenitus' treatise *De caeremoniis*, an itemization of what should be included in an emperor's baggage train when on military campaign.[19]

Constantine VII (908–959) came to the throne as a child and learned to leave imperial duties to others. He never went on campaign, preferring to record the duties of imperial rule and ceremony from the seclusion of the imperial palace. His two treatises *De administrando imperii* and *De caeremoniis* nevertheless contain invaluable evidence for linguistic change. Philology alone cannot interpret even words of Greek origin without reference to Byzantine court ceremonial and usage. The high proportion of Latin and other loanwords used for technical items of dress and equipment suggests interactions between late Roman, Byzantine, and Oriental imperial ceremonial on the one hand, and with the kingdoms of the West on the other. While many words in this text are now defunct, some (including non-Greek roots) survive to this day, especially in the dialects.

Latin loan words are assimilated to Greek sound patterns: μινσουράτωρ < mensurator "officer in charge of tent"; βησσάλιον < bessalium "pebble," MG βότσαλο; κόρτης < cohors "tent." Substantival suffixes ending in ‑ιτζιν, ‑ιον, ‑αριον, ‑ωτος, ‑ατος; and prefixes beginning with δι‑, τρι‑, ὁλο‑ (and others of the same type) testify to the morphological adaptation of Greek, Latin, and Slavic elements in the formation of new compounds. Lists make few demands on syntax, but we may note formulaic use of preposition + article and infinitive to express purpose (διὰ τὸ εἰς τὰ σαγμάρια βαστάζεσθαι "for the conveyance on pack-saddles"); the ubiquitous gerund ἰστέον "be it known that," to summarize information; the neuter plural participle ἔχοντα "having" to define a substantival phrase; and the adverbial preposition λόγῳ τῶν "by reason of" to amplify causal clauses.

Vocabulary is baffling; words are familiar, meanings elusive. First, some Greek words which show semantic shifts:

ἀληθινός, adj.: not "true," but "genuine purple"
νερόν, n.: "water" < νεαρὸν ὕδωρ (MG νερό)
ψυχριστάριον, n.: "cooler" (AG ψυχριστός, MG ψυγεῖο "fridge")
ἐπεύχιον, n.: "prayer-rug"
πτενός, adj.: ?fine, transparent < πτερόν "feather"
θάλασσα, f.: not "sea," but "short tunic"
ὑποκαμισοβράκιον, n.: "vest-underpant set"
ὀξέος, adj.
βδέλλιον, n.: not "leech" (AG), but an ornamental motif, embroidered or sewn in gold onto imperial garments ("sequin"): suggestions include "vine palm-leaf motif"; "hornet"; "bee"[20]
ἀετός, m.: not "eagle," but an ornamental motif (double-headed eagle).
περσίκιον, n.: lit. "something Persian", here either "baton" (Hendy) or "pouch" (Haldon)
κολόβιον, n.: "short-sleeved tunic" (AG κολοβόω, "cut")
θεματικός, adj.: "pertaining to the themes"
ἐθνικός, m.: "foreigner"
πιλωτός, adj.: "piled"
τρίμητος, adj.: "of triple weave"
δίσχιστος, adj.: "slit" (Haldon); "separated from" (Hendy)

Latin loanwords and compounds are less enigmatic, perhaps because their use is more specific and their history in court ceremonial easier to trace. Some common examples:

ἄσπρον, n.: "silver coin" < asper (MG ἄσπρα)
ἄσπρος, adj.: "silvery white" (MG "white")
βησσάλιον, n.: "tile" < bessalium (MG βότσαλο "pebble")
ἐξέμπλιον, n.: "pattern" < exemplum (MG ξόμπλι)
μανδίλιον, n.: "napkin" < mantilium (MG μαντίλι)
μανιακάτον, n.: "collar; neck-piece" < manica (MG μανίκι)
σιτλολέκανον , n.: "basin" < situla + λεκάνη (MG)
χαμοκούμβιον, n.: "stool" < χάμω + accumbo
σαγματοπασμαγάδιον, n.: "saddle and shoe set" < sagma + Turkic baçmak (MG pasmaki)

Other loans include:

Arabic φάτλιον, n, "candle" < fatil, (MG φυτίλι "wick"); μασουρᾶτος, adj. "thin-woven" < masura; ἀβδί "cloak" < abdayeh MG ἀβδᾶς)
Sanskrit: σάχαρ, n.: "sugar" < sarkara (MG ζάχαρι)

Slavic: βεδούριον, n.: "vessel" < *vedro* (MG βεδοῦρι)
Celtic: βουλγίδιον, n.: "chest" < *bulga*
Turkic: σκαραμάγγιον, n.: "caftan"; cf. MG toponym Σκαραμαγγᾶς

No word list, however, can convey one's sense of frustration in interpreting the list of requisites as well as the following extracts from two recent translations, one by John Haldon, the other by Michael Hendy. Are chamber pots or saddles required? Divergent interpretations are underlined in both versions.

Σιτλολέκανα ἀργυρᾶ καὶ ἐπιχυτάρια μετὰ ἐνδυμάτων λόγω τοῦ βασιλέως. καὶ ἕτερα ἀσπρόχαλκα καὶ γανωτὰ λόγω ἀρχόντων καὶ εὐγενῶν προσφύγων. πιλωτὰ διβλάττια παχέα καὶ πτενὰ λόγω τοῦ βασιλέως διὰ τὰ χαμόκουμβα· σελλία δύο τῆς προελεύσεως, σελλία τοῦ κουκουμιλίου ὁλόκανα διάχρυσα κοπτά, ἐπιστρώματα ἔχοντα, καὶ ἕτερα ἐπιστρώματα ἄνωθεν συγκαλύπτοντα τὴν κοπὴν τῆς χρείας· καὶ λόγω τῶν εὐγενῶν προσφύγων ἕτερα τοιαῦτα ἀργυροκατάκλειστα δύο. (Reiske 1829, 568 b–c)

(1) <u>Small silver pails</u> and sprinklers with covers for the emperor, and others of <u>polished bronze</u> for officers and distinguished refugees; thick and thin double-bordered <u>cushions</u> for the emperor to recline upon; two chairs for the cortège, <u>chairs for the chamber-pot</u>, of metal gilded with beaten gold, with covers, and with other covers above <u>concealing the space for the latrine</u>; and for the distinguished refugees two other, similar, seats, bound in silver. (Haldon, 1990)

<u>Cast silver bowls</u> and jugs with covers on account of the emperor, and other <u>tinned ones</u> on account of the nobles and high-born refugees. Double-bordered mats, thick and downy on account of the emperor for reclining purposes. Two saddles for procession, <u>saddles of the chamber-pot type</u> (i.e. with tall cruppers), gilded and chased all over in hatch-work pattern, with fitments, and with other fitments on them <u>to cover the chafing of wear</u>. And on account of the well-born refugees, two other such enclosed silver saddles. (Hendy, 1985, 307–8)

I hesitate to take sides, but I cannot see how the Greek συγκαλύπτοντα τὴν κοπὴν τῆς χρείας could possibly mean 'concealing the space for the latrine'.[21] Turning to purple silk underwear, we may compare the same translators' versions:

Τουβία ἐκ τούτων πάντων, τὰ μὲν προκριτώτερα ἀπὸ διβλαττίων ἀετῶν καὶ βασιλικίων ἀμφιεσμένα, τὰ δὲ δεύτερα τούτων ἀπὸ βδελλίων· σφιγτούρια, θάλασσαι καὶ ἀβδία πλατύλωρα καὶ ἀβδία μασουρωτά, τὰ μὲν ἀμφιεσμένα ἀπὸ διβλαττίων, τὰ δὲ καὶ λιτά· ὑποκομισοβράκια διαφόρων ποιοτήτων. ἐπιρρηπτάρια πρῶτα καὶ δεύτερα καὶ τρίτα, ζωστρία ὀξέα διάφορα καὶ ψευδοξέα ἀνὰ νομίσματος ἑνὸς καὶ μιλαρησίων δ′. καὶ ἕτερα ψευδοξέα ἀνὰ νομίσματος α′, καὶ ἕτερα ἀνὰ μιλαρησίων η′. ὑποδήματα ἀδήμινα ζυγαὶ διάφοροι. (Reiske 1829, 470 c–d)

Leggings for all these (garments), those of the best quality with double borders of silk decorated with eagles and imperial symbols, those of second quality decorated with hornets. Shirts, <u>tunics of the sea-pattern type</u>, and mantles, some with broad stripes, others with narrow stripes, some decorated with double, some with single borders. Undershirts with breeches of various qualities; purple-dyed <u>hoods</u> of first, second and third (quality), various purple and false-purple belts valued at 1 nomisma 4 milaresia each; and others at 8 milaresia. Various pairs of <u>red-leather boots</u>. (Haldon 1990)

Hose for all these, the most select being made up with double borders of eagles and imperial symbols, the second quality ones with bee-motifs; bands; <u>short military tunics</u>; cloaks both thick-woven and thin-woven, the one being made up with double borders, the other plain. Sets of vest-underpants of various qualities; <u>gowns</u> of purple of the first, second and third qualities; various belts, purple and pseudo-purple costing 1 nomisma 4 milaresia, and 8 milaresia apiece; pairs of <u>travelling</u> boots. (Hendy 1985, 308)[22]

One is reminded of present-day advertisements, in which the only words of Greek origin are the conjunction "and" and the preposition "with":

μακό πενιέ γκαζέ μερσεριζέ μπλούζα ριγέ σέ μπλέ καὶ άσπρο μέ τιραντες.

gauze-like mercerised sleeveless combed-cotton blouse striped in blue and white with shoulder-straps.[23]

The parallel may not be so far-fetched; as we see in the next chapter, the twelfth-century Ptochoprodromic Poems confirm the vernacular currency of Porphyrogenitus' unusual words (including loanwords) for items of clothing. The point to be emphasized is that in texts of this nature, Greek vocabulary is so slippery that interpretation depends on contextual knowledge of the artifacts, not on philology alone.

3. Fragments of a Byzantine Tradition of Oral Song?

In Chapter 1, I indicated grounds for doubting the oral-epic origins of the poetic language of vernacular literature from the twelfth to the fifteenth centuries (pp. 23-26). If the hypothesis of a lost tradition of oral epic is rejected, there is evidence, albeit scanty and fragmented, of a tradition of oral songs (ἄσματα), which influenced vernacular literature only intermittently because their terse style was unsuited to the demands of longer narrative. Fragments of popular songs and acclamations relating to events from the early seventh century onward are recorded by chronographers and historiographers. Too short to be subjected to the kind of statistical formulaic analysis attempted for vernacular literature, frequently obscene and even banal, they are the closest approximation we possess to Byzantine popular song. Analysis of structure, style, language, and meter will be made as relevant.[24]

One of the earliest targets of popular satire was the emperor Maurice just before November 602. The story goes that the people, dissatisfied with his rule, chose to ridicule the number of children he had, so they found someone who resembled him, sat him on a donkey with a crown of garlic, and, singing a ribald ditty, paraded him around the streets of Constantinople. The following text is preserved independently (with minor metrical and linguistic variations) by three historians, John of Antioch, Theophanes, and Kedrenos, from the seventh, ninth, and twelfth centuries, respectively. I have followed John:

Εὗρεν τὴν δάμαλιν	ἀπαλὴν καὶ τρυφερὰν
καὶ ὡς τὸ καινὸν ἀλεκτόριν	οὕτω αὐτὴν ἐπήδηκε
καὶ ἐποίησε παιδία	ὡς τὰ ξυλοκούκουδα,
καὶ οὐδεὶς τολμᾶ λαλῆσαι,	ἀλλ' ὅλους ἐφίμωσεν.
Ἅγιέ μου, ἁγιέ,	φοβερέ καὶ δυνατέ,
δός αὐτῷ κατὰ κρανίου	ἵνα μὴ ὑπεραίρηται,
κἀγὼ σοι τὸν βοῦν τὸν μέγαν	προσαγάγω εἰς εὐχήν.

1 εὕρηκε TC, δαμαλίδα TC, καὶ τρυφερὰν om. TC. 2 ἀλεκτόριον C, οὕτω C, ταύτῃ T, πεπήδηκε αὐτήν C. 3 ξυλοκώδωνα C. 5 φοβερὲ καὶ δυνατέ, om. C. 7 μέγαν βοῦν C.

He found the heifer	soft and tender,
and like the young cock	he mounted her,
spawning kids	like wooden wart-heads;
no one dares speak,	he's gagged all.
Saint, my saint,	terrible and mighty,

strike his head   to stop him swelling,
then I'll bring in vow   your great big bullock.

The meter is unidentifiable. Maas and Politis (who conflate the three manuscripts), read it as rather awkward fifteen-syllable verse; more convincingly,
Baud-Bovy reads it as an irregular sequence of six, seven, and eight syllables
without fixed stress, but by no means the politikos stichos of later vernacular
literature.[25] As to morphology, while dative and infinitive are still in evidence
(αὐτῷ, λαλῆσαι), we find such postclassical features as the fusion of aorist
and perfect (εὕρηκε, πεπήδηκε); new lexical compounds (ξυλοκούκουδα:
adjectival prefix ξυλο- = "wooden," "dumb" + κουκούδι = "head of a wart"
or "pimple"; cf. MG pejorative ξυλόσοφος for φιλόσοφος); and metaphorical uses of πεπήδηκεν (= mounted) and ἐφίμωσεν (= muzzled, gagged).
The style is terse and allusive; as in the modern folk songs, each line (except
the final punch line) falls into two balancing halves. The final three lines
promising the saint a bull for services rendered (knocking Maurice on the
head), reflect a popular attitude to saints still evident in folk tradition. The address ἁγιέ μου, ἁγιέ can be paralleled in other Byzantine religious texts and
modern "quête songs."[26] The humor depends on obscene metaphorical associations of the animals mentioned (δάμαλιν, ἀλεκτόριν, μέγαν βοῦν).[27]

Seven years later, a derisive couplet in trochaic octosyllables, preserved by
the same sources, was allegedly shouted by the "Greens" of the hippodrome
at the emperor Phokas whenever he turned up late. Again, I follow the text
of the earliest (John frag. 218c):

Πάλιν εἰς τὸν καῦκον ἔπιες,   You've drunk too much again ("out
                                  of the big vessel")
πάλιν τὸν νοῦν ἀπώλεσας.   you've knocked out your mind again!
1 στὸν C, οἶνον C. 2 ἀπέλεκες T, ἀπώλεκες.

                                                        (Politis)[28]

This couplet can be closely matched by two other verses, in the same meter,
recorded in the ninth and tenth centuries, respectively, by Theophanes and
by the Italian ambassador to Constantinople, Liutprand of Cremona, the
first sung by envoy to Michael II during the siege of Saniana, the second
sung against Count Adelbert (*Antapodosis* 2.34):

Ἄκουσον, κὺρ Οἰκνόμε,
τὸν Γυβέριν τί σοῦ λέγει·
ἂν μοῦ δώσῃς τὴν Σανιάναν
μητροπολίτην σε ποιήσω
Νεοκαισαρείαν σοι δώσω.

'Αδελβέρτος κόμης κούρτης
μακροσπάθης, γουνδοπίστης.

Listen, lord Oikonomos,
to what Gyveris tells you:
if you give me Saniana
I'll make you bishop
I'll give you Neokaisaria too.

Adelbertos count of tent
long in sword and short on faith!

2 κοντοπίστις. (Lambros)[29]

Μακρυσπάθης an obscene epithet modeled on the title πρωτοσπα-
θάριος, makes pithy alliterative play on words and titles (κόμης κούρτης).
A similar song in alternating oxytone and paroxytone octosyllables is
recorded by Anna Komnēnē as having been sung about her father, Alexios I,
after he had successfully quashed the conspiracy of 1 February 1081:

Τὸ Σάββατον τῆς Τυρινῆς
χαρῆς, 'Αλέξιε, ἐννόησές το,
καὶ τὴν Δευτέραν τὸ πρωί
ὕπα καλῶς, γεράκιν μου.

(*Alexiad* 1.98)

On Saturday of Cheese Week
—good for you, Alexios, you got it right!
And on Monday in the morning
—off you fly, my falcon!

Anna, in her commentary, renders such vulgar language into elegant paraphrase for the benefit of her readers—but there is no doubt that they were
familiar with the popular idiom.

Most intriguing is a song preserved in three manuscripts, including a
Venetian codex from the sixteenth century (M).[30] Much is obscure because
of the elliptic style, but names and details point to a nasty episode relating to
the Empress Theophano. This beautiful but unscrupulous woman—a publi-
can's daughter—held her first husband, Romanos II, in thrall. On his early
death in 963, his successful general Nikephoros Phokas was acclaimed by the
troops as emperor, so she offered herself in marriage to him to secure her
own position. But Nikephoros II was an aging and unprepossessing asce-

tic—Liutprand of Cremona described him as "a hairy old Cappadocian"— who took holy vows shortly afterward, leaving her free to lavish her attentions on the handsome young Armenian general John Tzimiskes. Together they plotted Nikephoros' murder in his bedchamber on the night of 10–11 December 969, and John was declared emperor; but their plan to marry was thwarted when in 970 the Patriarch insisted—ostensibly in view of her complicity in the murder but in fact to obtain some leverage over John to make him revoke the antimonastic fiscal policies of his predecessor—that John could legitimize his usurpation by marriage to Theodora (also known as "Kalē"), sister of the last legitimate ruler, Romanos II, and Theophano's former sister-in-law.[31] These episodes, covering a period of some ten years, are allusively compressed into seven lines of biting satire:

[Πολλοὶ φόνοι εἰς τὴν ἄκραν τοῦ κάμπου]
Ὁ χαλκεὺς βαρεῖ τ' ἀμόνι καί βαρεῖ τοὺς γείτονας,
ὁ Σινάπης κι ὁ Τριψίδης εἰς τὴν θύραν στήκουσιν,
Θεοφανοῦ ἐπολέμα πίταν καὶ ἡ Καλή τὴν ἔφαγεν.
Ὁποὺ ἐφόρει τὸ διβίκιν τῶρα δέρμαν ἔβαλεν,
κι ἄν τὸν φθάση ἐδῶ ὁ χειμῶνας, φέρε καὶ τὴν γούναν του.
Κουκουροβουκινάτορες, φουκτοκωλοτρυπᾶτοι
εἶσε σέλαν μίας μούλας καυχόκτονο πομπεύουσιν.

3 συνάπτη, πριψίδης Morgan. 4 Θεοφουνοῦ, ἐπόθειν M. 5 φόρειν M. 6 ἐφθάση . . . χειμῶν M.

[Many murders on the edge of the plain]
The smith strikes the anvil and strikes the neighbors too.
Sir Mustard Seed and Grinder stand at the door.
Theophanou fought hard [to bake] the cake, but Kalē ate it.
The one who wore the royal cloak has now donned the leather,
and if winter finds him here, let him bring his fur as well.
Braying-cuckolding trumpeteers, fist fucked,
parade him who vaunted murder on the saddle of a mule.

The song provides a perfect example of the relevance of Bakhtin's insistence on text as utterance, with the fullest possible reference to historical and linguistic context and textual transmission.[32] On the historical level, the proverbially ugly smith suggests Nikephoros Phokas, who "struck the anvil" with his spectacularly successful military campaigns but also "struck the neighbors" with burdensome taxation and unpopular legislation directed against the peasantry and the Church and in favor of the magnates. The names Sinapes ("Mustardseed") and Tripsides ("Grinder") are pejorative and obscene fabrications for imperial hangers-on, "waiting for entry" (to Theophano and thereby to the throne), possibly more specifically to Nikephoros' *parakoimō-menos* (lord of the bedchamber), the eunuch Basil ("the spiced/perfumed one"), and to Tzimiskes. Theophano's thwarted designs on John are indicated by the sexual innuendoes of ἐπολέμα πίταν "she fought [hard to bake the] cake"; the royal purple exchanged for leather could point either to Theophano, who went into monastic exile after the failure of her plot (where she remained until her elder son by Romanos II succeeded to the throne as Basil II in 976), or, more probably, to Nikephoros, who wore monastic garb while still emperor, only to be murdered in the depths of winter. The bawdy bilingual and punning epithets of the penultimate line suggest the troops who helped in the coup, first by murdering Nikephoros, then by acclaiming Tzimiskes emperor: pomp and ceremony at his coronation were marred by the substitution of mule for horse in the imperial parade, required by custom since the "true emperors" (born in the purple to Romanos and Theophano, later to rule as Basil II and Constantine VIII) were still minors.[33]

Linguistically and metrically, the text is MG; this could be due in part to later transmission, but not entirely, given the archaizing propensities of two out of the three transcribers. It can be read only according to MG grammatical and phonetic rules, and the meter is indubitably politikos stichos. There follows a line-by-line commentary:

1. χαλκεύς: "coppersmith" (AG, MG).
βαρεῖ: "strike"; cf. AG βαρόω, semantically influenced by βαρία, "large hammer" < AG βαρεῖα.
ἀμόνι: "anvil", also med. ἀμόνι(ν) < ἀγμόνιον, diminutive ἀκμόνιν (Aesop) < ἄκμων (Hesiod).
2. Σινάπης: suffix -ης replaces learned -ιος for proper names (cf. papyrus letters). Σινάπι < med. σινάπι(ο)ν, dim. AG σινάπυ (= mustard seed).
Τριψίδης: "Grinder" (*in sensu obsceno*), τριψ- < τρίβω + -ίδης (AG patronymic).
στήκουσιν: third-person plural present (with final -ν), med. ἐστήκω, < AG perfect ἔστηκα (ἵσταμαι).
3. ἐπολέμα: third-person singular imperfect (πολεμόω) with semantic shift from "make hostile" to "struggle to".
πίταν: < It. *pitta* (< Lat. *picta*?), or AG πηκτή < AG πίττα (πίσσα), Koukoules.
ἔφαγεν: third-person singular aovist τρώγω (note final -ν).
4. ὁπού: early instance of indeclinable relative pronoun.
ἐφόρει: third-person singular imperfect φορέω "wear" (note semantic restriction from AG).

διβίκιν: < Lat. divitisium "imperial cloak" (cf. Ptochoprodromos).

τώρα: < AG τῇ ὥρᾳ; cf. MG "now."

δέρμαν: (AG δέρμα ⟨ δέρω "to flay" < slang "to beat") "leather (garment)" (note final -ν).

5. κι ἄν: ἄν replaces εἰ/ἐάν in conditional clauses, as in MG.

γοῦναν: < med. Lat. *gunna* (Celtic origin?).

6. κουκουροβονκινάτορες: < Lat. *cucurio* "to bray" or *cucurus* "quiver" + βουκινάτωρ, technical term for "trumpeteer," cf. βούκινον < Lat. *bucina*.

φουκτοκωλοτρυπᾶτοι: compound formed by adjectival prefix of φοῦκτα (MG φοῦχτα = "fist"; cf. χοῦφτα, by antimetathesis, "handful") φουκτίζω < AG πυκτή, πυκτεύω "box'" + infix -κωλο- "arse" < AG κῶλον, esp. hind legs of animal + adjectival suffix -τρυπᾶτοι "with holes."

7. εἰσὲ: cf. MG σε, used alongside AG εἰς, line 2.

σέλαν: < Lat. *sella*.

μούλας: < Lat. *mula*; cf. MG μουλάρι.

καυχόκτονο : compound from prefix καυχ- "boast" and -κτόνος "killing."

Why should the song have been recorded by three independent sources and remembered until the seventeenth century, long after the targets satirized had passed out of living memory? A possible answer is that the scandalous nature of events—brought about by a beautiful but lowborn woman, wife in turn to a legitimate emperor and his usurper, then mistress to another usurper, and mother of two long-reigning sons—served as a premonition of upheaval, for the song was remembered and sung on the eve of the earthquake in Crete (1365) and of the fall of Cyprus to the Ottomans (1570). Perhaps it survived just because its allusive terms of reference, not pinned down to a single imperial ruler, can be appropriated for any corrupt and oppressive regime.

Fragmentary as it is, the evidence suggests that even the explicitly topical and satirical Byzantine songs considered so far share significant metrical, linguistic, and figurative means of expression with modern folk songs: as in the carols (*kálanda*) and quête songs, the most common meter is heptasyllabic and octosyllabic, with variable stress accent (oxytone, paroxytone, and proparoxytone); as in all songs, there is a strong sense of antithesis, alliteration, and wordplay and an abundance of pithy allusion to sexual prowess, both animal and human. Yet the most varied and enduring similarities in Greek song tradition from antiquity to the present day are to be found in seasonal songs, in which religious, ceremonial, and secular events are linked, both ritually and metaphorically, with the months and seasons of the year and with the cycle of activities associated with each.

It is a fitting irony that the longest and most complex vernacular song text to have survived in Byzantine Greek is a "swallow song" (*chelidónisma*), recorded in Latin script from Greek schoolboys in Rome by Canon Benedict for inclusion in the twelfth-century *Liber Politicus* along with *laudes* associated with the Cornomannia festival. Extant in two manuscripts of the twelfth and fifteenth centuries (Cambrai 512 and Vallicellian F-73), the text forms a link between the swallow songs of antiquity and the present day, researched by Michael Herzfeld.[34] Yet modern scholars can only deplore its garbled nature, and the impossibility of its transcription, let alone translation and interpretation. Were the scribes familiar with Greek, or did they take down what they heard as a sort of aide-mémoire? Whatever the linguistic confusion, does the text make sense if measured against the ancient and modern "swallow songs"?

The scribes were sufficiently conversant with ecclesiastical Greek to render liturgical phrases, interspersed throughout the *Laudes,* according to reasonably consistent and comprehensible patterns of word division and transcription.[35] By contrast, in the vernacular song, word division and phonology alike are so bizarre as to suggest an attempt to fit sounds they had only *heard* (as opposed to ones which could also be *read*) into latinized word patterns. If we bear in mind the probability that the dialect of Greek schoolboys in Rome was assimilated to Italian phonology, as are the Greek dialects of southern Italy and Sicily to this day, and that the sound patterns may have been further distorted for the listener because they were set to unfamiliar song units in which natural spoken stress is often at odds with melodic lengthening, the text is not so incomprehensible after all. Aside from word division, phonetic peculiarities abundant in both manuscripts include vocalic confusion between front, middle, and back vowels (i/e, e/a, a/o, o/u), and consonantal confusion between prevocalic gutturals (k´, kh´, gh´), aspirated and unaspirated dentals, voiced and unvoiced (d, t, th), liquids (l/r) and sibilants (s/z), not to mention instability of final -s and -n. Of these, many are attested in MG dialects, while consonants not represented in Italian (kh´, gh´, th´) give rise to fluctuating transcription. It may not be possible to restore the "original" text, which is probably much earlier than the twelfth century if we take account of imperial acclamations dating back to the tenth. Rather than try to correct it according to modern principles of linguistic consistency, as previous editors have done, I have transcribed the song with minimal phonetic alteration, in the belief that scribes at least tried to record what they thought they heard and that the result may be less far from the truth than modern attempts at standardization, especially if we accept the principles of early dialect differentiation within the koine as argued by Andriotis, Browning, and others. English translation is at best conjectural, but I shall try to show that this text is not quite as nonsensical as has been claimed.

Ycodes potachere chere metopanton deoysoro oro
sisto mello o kerasisilthe carpoforunta keagalliunta
tysa galliusi o tyrathanate loinatis paraschu singinunta
10   tegna probatha tinabula damaritinagria timisuntes
colites oscheinus manthanone fige fige febroarie o
martis scediochi yberba yperba februarie kera meta
pantono martis.

. . . .

21   Arxomen protopin kerete pantisode chelido chelido
basilia ysida palino de parinu georgite georgos catha-
panta et tini diaydor kepilu pirgo micodomisa abina
abina via via et kelegasi mimediris istas keras kesto-
25   trima pente pente allapente dicapente exilthes astro-
fores ton angelon simbule simbule kesiskene Aname-
niseo kosmos ylaros keoreon agallias tepedes kallite
seraconta istos colion trecontes gramatha mantan
nontes. O magister ymon o didascalo symon apotes
30   anatholis graphi keana ginosche kelam banini tobagin
tobagin kestostobro otheos eleyson ymas tervices exo
februaris exo o martis tervices anetilento ear II biya-
zusi tubanda II diadadascale o theos sephilacis II
filoponuntus machitasu II tintilogus uti narpasin II tin-
35   tilogu uepatheluntes Romania nica.
Alpha archios ton apanto Bitabisileu y curios Respondent Romaniamen gamma gennate o christos
1   Delta dialogou theicu Ro. Eichete epitisgis zithasion
ferito cosmu Ro. Eichete ita ilos keselin tethateon
proscinumen in gicheni carmoni tempedaon ethasen
o magister garautus apestilen cheroste christe o theos
5   ymon filaxontus prugintas I. Benedicte patriarchen
polistis etesi tondidascalon imon curie filaxon ymon
osipedes isti christi ebreon craicanzontes osanna toy-
conti christo toy o david apotis anatolisto eraranetile
kefocia ianaistas kosmon pantaosothyr.
    (Fabre, *Liber Politicus de Benoit*, 173–74; original line numberings)

1   Οἰκοδέσποτα χαῖρε χαῖρε μετ{ω} πάντων
ὧδε εἰσορῶ ὁρῶ σ' εἰς τὸ μέλλο⟨ν⟩

ὦ χαῖρ᾽, ἔαρ, εἰσῆλθε
καρποφοροῦντα καὶ ἀγαλλιοῦντα
5 τοῖς ἀγαλλιοῦσι ὦ ⟨σ⟩ωτὴρ ἀθάγατε
λο⟨γ⟩ὴν α⟨ὐ⟩τοῖς παράσχου
συγκοινοῦν τὰ τέ{γ}να
πρόβαθα τινάβουλα δάμα{ρ}ι τὴν ἄγρια
τιμῆς ὄντες σκολίτες ὡς κείνους μανθάνονε
10 φύγε φύγε Φεβροάριε ὁ Μάρτης σὲ διώκει
ὑπέρβα ὑπέρβα Φεβροάριε χαίρ{α} μετὰ πάντων ὁ
Μάρτης.—   [Fabre, lines 1–13]
Ἄρξωμεν πρωτωπεῖν {κ}αίρετε πάντις ὧδε
χελιδώ χελιδώ
βασιλιὰ εἰσεῖδα πάλιν ὧδε πάρ⟨ειμαι⟩
15 γεωργεῖται γεωργός καθ᾽ ἄπαντα ε⟨ὐ⟩{τ}υμεῖ
διὰ ὕδωρ καὶ πηλο[ὐ] πύργο μ᾽ οἰκοδόμησα
ἀβήνα ἀβήνα βία βιά⟨ζ⟩ετε κελάδησι
μὴ μὲ δείρης εἰς τὰς χεῖρας καὶ στὸ τρῆμα
πέντε πέντε ἄλλα πέντε δικαπέντε
20 ἐξῆλθες ἀστροφορὴς
τῶν ἀγγέλων σύμβουλε καὶ σύσκηνε.
Ἀναμένει σε ὁ κόσμος ἱλαρὸς καὶ ὡραίο⟨ν⟩
ἀγαλλιᾶστε παῖδες καλοὶ τεσσαράκοντα
εἰς τὸ σχολεῖον τρέκοντες γράμαθα μαντάνοντες.
25 Ὁ μαγίστερ ὑμῶν ὁ διδάσκαλος ὑμῶν
ἀπὸ τὲς ἀναθολῆς γράφει καὶ ἀναγινώσκε⟨ι⟩
καὶ λαμβάνει τὸ βαγίν τὸ βαγὶν καὶ τὸ στ{ο}υρό
ὁ θεὸς ἐλέησόν ἡμᾶς (ter vices)
ἔξω Φεβρουάρης ἔξω ὁ Μάρτης (ter vices)
30 ἀνέτειλεν τὸ ἔαρ (II)
δια ⟨σ⟩οῦ ⟨ζ⟩εῖ τ⟨ὰ⟩ πάντα (II)
δι[α]δάσκαλε ὁ θεός σε φυλάξοι
φιλοπονοῦν τοὺς μαθητάς σου II
τὴν τοῦ λόγου σου τὴν ἄρπασιν II
35 τὴν τοῦ λόγου ἐπα⟨φ⟩έ⟨ρ⟩ουντες· Ῥωμανία νίκα.
Ἄλφα ἀρχη⟨γ⟩ὸς τῶν ἀπάντω Βῆτα βασιλεύει κύριος.
Respondent Romani, amen.   [Fabre, lines 21–37]
Γάμμα γεννᾶται ὁ Χριστὸς Δέλτα διὰ λόγου θεϊκοῦ (*resp.R*)
Εἶ ⟨ἔρ⟩χεται ἐπὶ τῆς γῆς Ζῆ⟨τ⟩α ζωὴν φέρει τοῦ κόσμου
40 Εἶ ⟨ρ⟩χεται ἦτα ἥλ⟨ι⟩ος καὶ σελήν ⟨Θῆτ⟩α ⟨θ⟩εὸν
προσκυνοῦμεν
Ι ἤγγικεν ἡ χαρμονή, τὴμ πηδάει ὅσον ἔ⟨φ⟩θασεν

ὁ Μαγίστερ γὰρ αὐτοὺς ἀπέστειλεν
χαίρ{ο}σται Χριστὲ ὁ θεὸς ἡμῶν φύλαξον τοὺς
προύχ{ι}ντας
I. *Benedicte* πατριάρχην πολλοῖς τοῖς ἔτεσι
45   τὸν διδάσκαλον ἡμῶν κύριε φύλαξον
ὡς οἱ παῖδες οἱ χρηστοὶ Ἑβραίων κρα{ικ}άζοντας
ὡσάννα τῷ ἥκοντι χριστῷ τῷ υἱῷ Δαβίδ
ἀπὸ τῆς ἀνατολῆς τὸ ἔαρ ἀνέτειλε
καὶ φωτιὰ ἡ ἀναστᾶσ' κόσμον πάντα ὁ σωθήρ.

1   Hail, master of the house, hail with all,
       I behold, I'll see you in the future,
       o hail, spring, come hither, bringing fruits
       and rejoicing for those that rejoice;
5   o savior undying, bestow on them worth;
       they share one feeling, children,
       sheep, little bells, the wild heifer;
       for schoolboys in honor
       like them are learning:
10   Flee, flee away, February, March is hard on your heels,
       pass on, pass on, February, hail with all, o you March.—
       Let us begin to recite, hail to all, thus:
       swallow, o swallow,
       I've seen the king, once more I am here,
15   the farmer is tilling, all things with joy filling,
       with water and silt my tower I have built.
       Whip, whip, might fights, they sang:
       Don't whip me on the hands or arsehole,
       five, five and five more makes fifteen,
20   you came out wearing stars
       who counsels and consorts with the angels.
       The world is awaiting you, joyful and fair.
       Rejoice, good forty boys,
       running to school, learning your letters.
25   Your master, your teacher
       from the east he writes and he reads,
       as he takes up the palm, the palm and the cross.
       God have mercy upon all of us.
       Out, February, out, March,
30   spring has arisen,
       through you lives all.

Teacher, may God protect you,
cherish labor in your pupils.
What they seized from yourself

35   they give back to yourself:
                   Romania, conquer!
Alpha, All creatures' leader; Beta, Best reigning ruler,
Gamma, Gift of Christ's birth; Delta, Divine is his word.
E, he came upon Earth; Zei, Zest and life to this world.

40   Eta Is the Sun and the Moon; Theta, The godhead we kneel to.
                   Romania, conquer!
I, It was touched by delight, over whom leapt till there reached
the Master who sent them for us to rejoice.
Christ, our God, protect our nobles.
Blessings on the patriarch, many be his years.

45   Our teacher, Lord, protect him.
Like the good sons of Jews crying out,
Hosanna to Christ, he comes to us the son of David.
In the east the spring has risen,
as fire he has lit up the whole world, our savior.

Commentary

1. meto CV.*

2. oros or V: 4 ceras C: cheras V: ὧδε οὒς ὁρῶ· ὅρισον τὸ μέλλο⟨ν⟩ Krumbacher: εἰσορῶ ὁρῶ [σ']εἰς τὸ μέλλο⟨ν⟩ Tommasini. Both readings are problematic, but perhaps Krumbacher's ὧδε can be combined with Tommasini's to provide the least unsatisfactory sense. If σ' (second-person singular pronoun) is read, to whom should it refer? To the master, or to the swallow? Or perhaps to both, since in lines 13–14 it is the swallow who claims to have seen the emperor. Herzfeld cites parallels from two modern songs, τὸν βασιλιὰ δὲν εἴδαμεν (text 25) and τὸν βασιλιέα εἴδαμε (text 50). I toyed with the conjecture θεὸ⟨ν⟩ εἰσορῶ but rejected it as an unparalleled formulation.

3. o kerasisilthe CV: καιρός Fabre, Maas: ὦ χαῖρ', ἔαρ, εἰσέλθε Tommasini: ὁ κέρας εἰσῆλθε Krumbacher. Tommasini's reading is most convincing, both for its parallels in other Byzantine acclamations (Maas 1912) and for congruence of the imperative with line 6. Fabre's reading is possible (cf. Πάσχα τῶν καιρῶν ἁγίων, p. 172.3, 5–6) but less specific; Krumbacher's "horn of plenty" is tempting in view of the context of the Cornomannia festival, but the need to substitute t- is less easy to justify than the a/o confusion (meto 1, stobro 27).

---

*In the commentary, the line numbers refer to the Greek text.

5. o tyrathanate C: thityr V: corr. Tommasini: πατήρ Maas: loin atis CV: ζωήν corr. Maas (cf. Const. Porph. 358). I have retained λο⟨γ⟩ήν, in medieval sense of moral and spiritual worth (Kriaras, s.v.: Sophianos *Paidag.* 264).

7. singinunta: either συγκινοῦν τα, "[such things] stir feeling in," or, preferably, συγκοινοῦν τα "are in communion with" (Demetrakos).

8. tinabula CV: Krumbacher πτηνόπουλα *BZ* 11.587: πτηνά πολλά Tommasini: πρόβατα, τιν' ἄβουλα Politis: δάμαλιν (for *tintinabula "bells")* Alexiou*: δάμαλιν corr. Tommasini. I have retained the original spelling, in view of the text's frequent fluctuation between l/r.

9. timisuntes colites oscheinus manthanone: σὺν ταῖς λιταῖς Fabre: τιμήσοντες, πολίται μανθάνομεν Tomm.: ἡμεῖς ὄντες σχολητές, ὡς καὶ ἡμεῖς μανθάνομε Baud-Bovy: τιμῆς ὄντες σχολίτες or κι ἡμεῖς ὄντες σχολίτες Herzfeld. It is tempting but not necessary to correct to first-person plural if we read τιμῆς ὄντες (Herzfeld texts 26, 39). Assimilation of person is common in folk song, where "voice" changes swiftly; and in any case, there is a suppressed verb, "honored pupils like them have learned [and we say]."

11. kera meta pantono: least violence is done to the text if we read some form of χαῖρε μετὰ πάντων (cf. line 1) with March either as predicate, "Here is March!" or as subject of implied verb "has come" (cf. line 29).

12. pantisode: πάντες ὧδε.

14. palino de parinu: πάλιν ὧδε πάρ⟨ειμι⟩ is not necessary. Why not παρῆν...οὗ...., "I am here (imperfect KG), whence ...."?

16. diaydor kepilu pirgo micodomisa: I read πηλού as accusative (*u* for *o*), μ' as possessive genitive, "I've built my tower with water and mud." Baud-Bovy identifies tower with nest; cf. ηὗρεν πύρκο κι ἔκατσε (Herzfeld 65 and text 26).

17. abina via via et kelegasi: ἀβήνα whip (Demetrakos). Either βία βιά⟨ζ⟩εται καὶ λέγασι or βία, βιάζετ', ἐκελάδησι: Herzfeld, cf. καὶ χαμ-οκελάηδησε (text 27).

18. kestotrima: τρῆμα (AG τετραίνω "penetrate"): "hole," *in sensu obsceno* (Demetrakos).

19. Herzfeld suggests (66), an arithmetic lesson; cf. ν' ἀγοράζουμεν ἐφτά, νὰ πουλοῦμε δεκαεφτά. Beatings would follow an incorrect answers. The connection with lessons is implied from the first stanza (line 9)

---

*My reading is based on evidence for the apotropaic properties of sheep and cattle bells (*tintinabula*); see Russell 1995, 42. It could, of course, be argued that the scribe substituted "[tin]tinabula" for the *lectio difficilior* and that "bells" are not consistent with the animal species here named. They provide a link between sheep and cattle, however, and are not inappropriate for ceremonial use.

and followed through with the alphabet in the third: pupils progress from "animal sense" to control of numbers and letters.

24. istos colion trecontes: Herzfeld (67) cites Koukoules (73): Φεγγαράκι μου λαμπρό / φέγγε μου νὰ περπατῶ / νὰ πηγαίνω στὸ σκολειό / νὰ μαθαίνω γράμματα / τοῦ θεοῦ τὰ πράματα. gramatha mantanontes: cf. πόσον δρόμον ἔκαμες / κι ἔμαθες τὰ γράμματα (Herzfeld 67, Koukoules 9); also γράμματα βασιλικὰ / ποὺ μαθαίνουν τὰ παιδιά (Herzfeld, text 2).

25. It is hard to say whether the possessive pronoun is first- or second-person plural: perhaps the first is ὑμῶν (= the emperor), and the second is ἡμῶν (= the schoolmaster) (Herzfeld 68).

27. βαγίν·⟨βάϊον, "palm" (Kriaras: Rhodol. B' 276, 476): stobro = στ{α}υρό.

30. ἀνέτειλεν τὸ ἔαρ: cf. ἦρθεν ἡ ἄνοιξις πάλι καλή (Herzfeld, text 13) (Maas 1912).

41. tempedason (V:) tempedaon (C:) ethasen (CV:) ἔφτασεν Maas. *Locus desperandus:* I have retained the original orthography for the verb and suggest τὴμ πηδᾶ,⟨ὄ⟩σον on the grounds that leaping and jumping form a prominent part in Byzantine seasonal games; see Koukoules 1948–55, 1, 94–96, 3, 264–68.

47. ebreon craicanzontes: as Herzfeld points out (84), "shouting against the Jews" is a not uncommon instance of Greek religious anti-Semitism.

This song is made up of three parts, with an epilogue. In the first part, the boys address the "master of the house," announcing the departure of February and heralding the arrival of March in terms which command both the welcome of a deity and the communion between divine, human, and animal worlds. In the second part, the swallow, as harbinger of spring, responds to the boys' greetings with an affirmation that she has indeed built her nest among them, having communed with the sky and the stars. In the third part, the boys respond to the threat of their masters' beatings by reciting an acrostich from alpha to iota. In the epilogue, master, teacher, pope, God, and Christ are fused into one as a symbol of the Resurrection.

The text is problematic but not nonsensical if compared with its ancient and modern Greek counterparts and with the Latin "hymns to spring" interspersed with the Greek in our manuscripts. With the ancient text, cited by Athenaios in the second century A.D. as an old song from Rhodes, it shares an address to the swallow as harbinger of spring and abundance, and a hint that the young boy singers may in the end prove worthy of their elders.[36] With the modern songs it shares many formulaic and structural units, combining seasonal with divine and human greetings in the form of alphabetical and numerical rhymes which have to be whipped out of the boys just as their reward will have to be ripped out of them, as in the ancient text. With contemporary Byzantine texts, such as Ptochoprodromos, the song shares a predilection for the enigmatic game (or the name of the game?), where beatings, beratings, and learning the lessons of the past are similarly juxtaposed with secular and sacred symbolism, according to a nonverbal logic not unconnected to the cycle of the seasons. If this essentially pagan custom of welcoming spring with a chelidonisma was condemned by John Chrysostom in the fourth century and by the Council in Trullo (602), the Byzantine church had done quite a good job in assimilating it to the Orthodox liturgy by the twelfth. As we shall see throughout this book, seasonal rituals of one kind or another provide the latent force for artistic representation.

Next in our survey comes a couplet and an odd line cited as simple verses (στίχοι ἁπλοικοί) in simple diction (λέξει ἁπλοικῇ) by the Cypriot recluse Neophytos Enkleistos of Paphos, of the later twelfth century:

"Ὅτι ὁ ξένος πάντα θλίβεται, ὁ ξένος πάντα κλαίει,
ὁ ξένος πάντοτε θρηνεῖ, παραμυθιὰν οὐκ ἔχων...

Because the foreigner is always grieving, the stranger always weeps,
the stranger all the time laments, having no consolation . . .

Πότε νὰ ὑπάγω εἰς τὰ ἐμά, πότε νὰ ἐπαναλύσω;

When shall I go back home, when shall I return?

These tantalizing snatches of "laments for exile" (τῆς ξενιτειᾶς) can be closely compared not only with the literary examples of the genre in the verse romance *Belthandros and Chrysanza* but also with the structure and formulaic patterns of many modern examples.[37]

Nor is this the only modern genre to have antecedents in Byzantine popular song. There is a tender little love lament about a girl whose lover has left for foreign parts, leaving her to curse the months (of her pregnancy?) in tersely alliterative traditional form. The fragment is preserved in a Venetian manuscript.[38]

"Ἄσπρη ξανθή πανέμνοστη, ὁ κύρκα⟨ς⟩ της μισσεύει,
καὶ ὑπάγει ὁ κύρκα⟨ς⟩ της μακρέα, καὶ τὸ ταξίδ᾿ εἶν μέγα.
Καὶ ἡ κόρη ἀπὸ τῆς λύπης της τοὺς μῆνας καταρᾶται·
Νὰ κῆς, Φλεβάρη, φλέγεις με, καὶ Μάρτη, ἐμάρανές με,
᾿Απρίλη ἀπριλοφόρητε καὶ Μᾶ κατακαμένε,

τὸν κόσμον κι ἂν ἐγέμισες τ' ἀθίτζια καὶ τὰ ρόδα,
τὴν ἰδικήν μου τὴν καρδιὰν τοὺς πόνους καὶ τὰ δάκρυα.

A fair and golden-haired young girl whose lord leaves,
whose lord goes far afield, and his journey is long.
And the girl from her grieving begins cursing the months:
Fire to you, February, you enflame me, and March, you have parched me,
April decked in April, and May, you bescorched,
you may have filled the world with blossoms and roses,
but my own heart is left with labor pains and tears.

Certain features of this song can be paralleled in the longer narrative tradition of the late Byzantine period (the catalogue of months, the complaint of a deserted girl); but its lyrical and allusive qualities can best be matched in the modern song tradition (see Chapter 10).

Fragmentary as it may be, the evidence suggests that there *was* a tradition of Byzantine oral song. It was submerged, it is imperfectly recorded, and—one may ask—so what? For neo-Hellenists, it is significant that many distinctive characteristics are shared with modern folk songs, despite the impossiblility of "counting formulas" from such a tiny sample. For Byzantinists, the pithy and obscene style of the urban satirical songs and the plaintive and lyrical mode of others, rich in imagery and metaphorical allusion, come as a welcome change from the long and sometimes tedious narrative poems. More generally, the songs, in their use of concrete images drawn from nature to comment—favorably and unfavorably—on the human condition, form a specific link, through popular tradition, between the social and political satire of ancient comedy, the Ptochoprodromic Poems, and later comic theater, on the one hand, and between the religious symbolism of Romanos' kontakia and the concept of love in modern folk songs, on the other. The evidence does not suggest a "come-down heritage" or "downward seepage."[39] All culture, high, middle and low, is a matter of interaction, most productively across different languages.

In conclusion to this chapter, let it be noted that none of our texts—letters, treatises or songs—has been transmitted by "high" literary sources. For these and for literary experiments with the vernacular we must now turn to the twelfth century.

CHAPTER 4

New Departures in the Twelfth Century

1. Texts and Contexts

The traditional view of the twelfth century as one of economic decline and cultural decadence has now been seriously challenged. Historically, Michael Hendy's studies have shown that during the period of
Komnene rule (1081–1204), both society and economy display signs of
rapid growth, triggered by territorial losses to the Turks in the Anatolian
plateau and by Alexios I's consolidation of Balkan Thrace. This growth
brought economic expansion and social diversification to the urban centers
and a general increase in urban and rural populations. The negative impact
of Turkic encroachment and of the increased power and privileges of Italian city traders (Genoese and Venetian) has been exaggerated.[1]

Culturally, Alexander Kazhdan's studies on the eleventh and twelfth centuries develop earlier leads by Sofia Polyakova and Herbert Hunger to draw
attention to dynamic changes in literature and culture.[2] Drawing on a
wealth of sources, Paul Magdalino has argued, in his comprehensive analysis of the Empire of Manuel I Komnenos (1143–1180), that the concept of
"literature" in the modern sense is inappropriate for Byzantine texts, which
were composed not to be read but for public performance as part of the
"rhetorical theater," encompassing oral discourses on philosophy and medicine, religion and philosophy, law and politics, "belles lettres" and scholarship.[3] "Theatre," he writes, "is the key to understanding both the aesthetic
and the social functions of high-style literacy in twelfth-century Byzantium." As he points out, the texts as we have them are but the "dry bones"
of a once vibrant and multitoned dramatic experience, not disanalogous to

court ceremonial and liturgy. Performances were fostered by the increasingly complex system of patronage and held not only on ceremonial court occasions but in churches and at gatherings in the private houses of the Komnene aristocracy and the rising bourgeoisie. The implications are considerable. If literature is performatively inseparable from other discourses, it follows that its range of reference will include what for us are "extraliterary" concerns. Ong's polarized perception of "orality" and "literacy" must be redefined to accommodate twelfth-century Constantinopolitan realities, where distinctions between "learned" and "popular", "written" and "spoken" were not as sharply defined as in the medieval West. John Tzetzes wrote his commentaries on Aristophanes for "publication" through oral performance at a small gathering of intellectuals.[4]

Truisms about the imitative and tedious qualities of Byzantine literature have, it is hoped, finally been laid to rest.[5] In addition to reevaluations of particular texts, we now have more comprehensive literary surveys.[6] In this final chapter of Part I, rather than attempt an overview,[7] I illustrate, with reference to three seemingly disparate texts, how the diverse linguistic registers reviewed in the last three chapters were combined in new ways so as to allow considerable experimentation and, more particularly the simultaneous expression of wit and wisdom, humor and seriousness of purpose.

Byzantinists frequently complain that Byzantine literary humor "tries to be clever without being funny," contains "too much slapstick," or is "frequently obsessed with what everyone has to eat."[8] It is perhaps easier to appreciate another culture's history—even tragedy—than it is their sense of humor, simply because we take it for granted that what fails to amuse us cannot, by its very nature, be funny. Yet, as Bakhtin has indicated in his essays on Rabelais, medieval parody differs from its modern literary counterparts. It is not wholly negative but has regenerative—if ambivalent—powers, derived from the use of "images of the human body with its food, drink, defecation, and sexual life." Two types of imagery converge, especially at the crossroads of medieval parody and early Renaissance realism, the one drawn from the culture of folk humor, the other from the bourgeois conception of the individual.[9] Rabelais and his world may seem a far cry indeed from twelfth-century Constantinople. By juxtaposing three texts, composed in different styles and belonging to what for us are diverse literary genres (prose dialogue, erotic novel, vernacular verse), I hope to show that they share the same features of dialogic interaction and regenerative humor as do those discussed by Bakhtin.

The more general questions I shall address are the following: Given the diversity of linguistic registers encountered, what changes can be discerned in perceptions and practices? Was the revival of ancient genres and the re-vitalization of classical myths merely a matter of "slavish imitation"? Or do these processes reflect a distinctively twelfth-century consciousness which can be related to social and historical contexts?[10] Have such texts proved relevant to subsequent literature in the Greek language? Although no direct lines can be drawn between the revival of the ancient romance and the emergence of modern Greek prose fiction, are there perhaps connections to be traced not directly but through language, myth, and metaphor, with comparable modes of perception and representation? These questions will be followed up in Parts II ("Myth") and III ("Metaphor"), above all in a detailed analysis of the short stories by Georgios Vizyenos (1849–96).

So far as literature, scholarship, and art are concerned, there can be no question of decline; but "timelessness" is frequently implied, with connotations of nostalgia and decadence.[11] Socioeconomic and cultural developments cannot be directly correlated, but evidence suggests that the consolidation, at least under the reigns of John II (1118–43) and Manuel I (1143–80), of the socioeconomic expansion which began under Alexios I (1081–1118), gave rise to a new literary consciousness in Constantinopolitan intellectual circles, comparable with, yet significantly different from, developments in the West, sometimes anticipating the Renaissance.

First, attitudes to the past. Antiquity had always provided Byzantine writers with revered models, but during the Komnene period, ancient texts were rediscovered from new perspectives.[12] Eustathios' commentaries on Homer not only provide an unprecedented wealth of scholarly detail but draw constant comparisons between past and present, holding one as mirror to the other;[13] Tzetzes' Aristophanic scholia may deprecate the comic obscenities but explain them fully, never expunging or suppressing them.[14] Aristotle's more obscure treatises, especially the medical and physiological ones, attract philological attention and scholarly debate at the "rhetorical theaters" of Constantinople, while some of his detailed observations on dreams are exploited in the erotic romances of Eustathios Makrembolites and Theodore Prodromos as a means of exploring what has been termed the psychology and physiology of Eros.[15] As for Plato, he may have been frowned upon by church and state, but his works enjoyed unprecedented popularity among the literati and rising bourgeoisie alike.[16] Past and present enter into a new, dynamic relationship: literary imitation of classical models (mimesis) becomes a means of exploiting privileged texts not merely to dignify the present but for purposes of irony, satire, and parody as well.

Second, literary sense and sensibility are qualitatively different, even in works of uncertain authorship. There is a new exploitation of narrative and fictional strategies and an engagement in dialogue with other texts and discourses. Rhetorical genre exercises (*progymnásmata*), practiced since antiquity, are intensified to explore mood, character and scene in biblical and mythical contexts, as in Nikephoros Basilakes' "character sketches" (*ēthopoiēíai*): What words might Hades utter when Lazaros was raised from the dead? Or Mary, on seeing Christ dead on the Cross? Danae, when raped by Zeus in pure gold? Pasiphae, when raped by Zeus in the form of a bull?[17] In his *Katomyomachia* ("Battle of Cats and Mice"), Theodore Prodromos examines how Kreillos might think and act as he rallies his fellow mice to emerge from their dark holes and engage in battle with the Cat.[18] Alongside, and out of, these rhetorical exercises, new genres emerged, such as prison poems and animal fables. Old genres, such as the ancient novel or the tale of a trip to the Underworld, were revived and creatively adapted to contemporary contexts.

Third, language is perceived and played with as inherently rhetorical. Magdalino cites John Tzetzes' comment on one of his letters to Nikephoros Servlias as an example of how easily praise (*épainos*) can be twisted into blame (*psógos*):

> Servilius was a consul and caesar of the Romans. With forceful method and in a rhetorical manner, I say that Servlias is descended from the Servilii. But if someone else wanted, he could have called him Serb Elias. This is the way of the two-tongued rhetor (*rhētoros amphoteroglōssou*), to use facts and names and everything else for "praise" and "blame" as his interest demands.
>
> (*Historiae*, ed. Leone, *Chil.* VII, lines 295–301, p. 267)[19]

Theodore Prodromos, in a letter to the *nomophylax* ("guardian of the laws"), disputes from a Platonic perspective the traditional view of Clement of Alexandria that language is natural:

> I do not praise [Clement] in the *Stromata* where he claims never to strive for eloquence and nobility of diction but to be satisfied with merely the comprehension of sense. *For thus there would be no difference between the cloth seller and the wise man.* I too would have counted language as of meager or no import if we transcended this clay that binds us and could pass through life with naked souls. But since this hulk of the body—I refer to this living statue—has shaped itself around our souls, and, since it is not possible for mental processes to be intimated to us directly, I consider it imperative to rate language as of no secondary importance.
>
> (Migne 133, 1265a–b, emphasis added)[20]

Prodromos locates language and style in the gap separating spiritual and corporeal realms and therefore to be judged relatively rather than absolutely. In this context should be seen the emergence of vernacular verse *from within court circles*, as part of a new confidence in language as a means of exploring multiple levels of expression and signification rather than as an end in itself. As we shall see, the Ptochoprodromic Poems are concerned precisely with the difference between the "language of the cloth seller" and "the language of the wise man."

I shall try here to bring together the salient points of three texts: the anonymously transmitted *Timarion*; Eustathios Makrembolites' *Hysmine and Hysminias*; and the Ptochoprodromic Poems. On the face of it, these texts could scarcely be more different. *Timarion* is a satirical dialogue on the afterlife, composed in the high style. *Hysmine* is an erotic novel—or is it?— again in the high style, but with much simpler syntactic structures. As for the Ptochoprodromic Poems, they are sketches of "low-style life" in vernacular speech, frequently exploiting the "language of the gutter" to explore the "rhetoric of hunger" through metonyms of deprivation and exclusion. All three texts make complex use of classical allusion. By examining in turn their rhetorical and linguistic strategies, I hope to show that the similarities between these three texts are greater than their differences, revealing the authors' awareness of the duplicity of language and the complicity of author/speaker and reader/listener in the narrating process. All three texts, in different ways, are thoroughly dialogic in their use of voice and interlocution, in their manipulation of other contemporary texts and discourses, and, above all, in their reach back and forth between past and present.

2. The *Timarion*

Among the ancient genres to enjoy a resurgence of popularity from the late eleventh and twelfth centuries was the satirical prose dialogue, usually associated with Lucian of Samosatta (A.D. second century). The *Timarion*, although by no means the only such dialogue to have survived, is generally agreed to be the most polished, amusing, and informative.[21] Yet despite the attention it has received from scholars, there is no agreement as to its date or authorship. Estimates have varied from the eleventh to the fourteenth centuries, although general consensus now situates it in the first half of the twelfth century, and recent—if by no means conclusive— attempts have been made by Tsolakis and Beaton to pin it down more finely to around 1110 to 1112.[22] Even less progress has been made on authorship: of the names suggested—Timarion (otherwise unknown), Theodore Prodromos, Nikolaos Kallikles, Michael Italikos—only that of Kallikles would seem compatible with Tsolakis' revised dating, if we dis-

count Timarion in the absence of prosopographical evidence.[23] It is perhaps wisest to retain an open mind and to turn first to the text.

The *Timarion* describes a descent to the Underworld, a favorite theme
in literature and song from Homer to the present day. If the author appears to have appropriated Lucian's form (dialogue) and theme (conversations on the Underworld), not to mention ubiquitous Lucianic "tags," he
has made both form and theme serve different functions: Lucian's dialogues are dramatic re-creations of Underworld scenes, unmediated by a
narrating presence, whereas the dialogue in the *Timarion* between the
narrator, Timarion, and his interlocutor, Kydion, draws constant attention
to the text's narrating instant and to its fictional strategies. Apart from Lucian, the text shares with Aristophanes' *Frogs* the device of an underworld
setting to satirize the recently dead while commenting on current affairs,
and with Plato's dialogues a love of repartee between interlocutors and—
despite the humorous façade—a serious concern with the relationship
between philosophy and rhetoric. It is a pivotal text, engaging in dialogue
with religion (paganism and Christianity) and other major discourses
(medicine, law, rhetoric) and doing so across time (from antiquity to the
twelfth century) and space (from Constantinople to Thessaloniki and
back again, via the Underworld). The text's "chronotopes," to use Bakhtin's
term, are as wide-ranging as those of Romanos, but its perspectives on
life after death, so uncompromisingly secular, could scarcely be more
different.

Because the *Timarion* was intended, and interpreted, as a satire on contemporary society, with humor and irony directed at other discourses, not
to mention corruption and gluttony in high places, the author may have
had good reason to conceal his identity. Less than two centuries later, the
statesman Constantine Akropolites complained in a letter to a friend that
the work should be burned, because, under the guise of erudition, it seeks
to undermine the Christian faith.[24] Such an attack was likely to be taken
more seriously under the Palaiologan regime of the fourteenth century
than in the Komnenian twelfth; yet, if the Doukas-Palaiologos family is a
hidden target, as I have suggested elsewhere, the text was indeed transgressive. A summary with analysis based on my earlier and more partial study,
will provide the context necessary for an appreciation of the text's significance, although the principles of narratology outlined by Gérard Genette
are perhaps less applicable to the oral-performative context of Komnenian
literature than I once thought.[25]

First, the "story." The dialogue is divided into 47 chapters. It opens as the
narrator, Timarion, is welcomed home to Constantinople after a long absence by his friend and interlocutor, Kydion (1). In reply to Kydion's questions, Timarion embarks on his tale of adventures in the Underworld, but

Kydion keeps interrupting with negative comments on his poor narrative style. Timarion describes the comforts and diversions of his outward journey from Constantinople to Thessaloniki, where he attended the famous Festival of Saint Demetrios on 26 October (4–10), and then relates his nightmarish ride back through Thrace, where at some point along the River Hebros (Maritsa) he was stricken by sudden fever, dysentery, and liver disease and robbed of his bile, one of the four alleged "elements" of living beings (11–12). His soul was ripped untimely from his body by two evil demons, who whizzed him down to Hades, first zooming through the atmosphere, then by slow and arduous descent from the earth's crust into the interior—rather as in the surrealist sensations of a dream (13–14). His numerous encounters in the Underworld are vividly described (15–23), as is his trial (24–45), at which Asklepios and Hippokrates, the supreme Underworld medical authorities, declare in an official postmortem that his soul is still incompletely separated from the body and is therefore to be discharged forthwith from Hades, with free passage home in return for a promise of fatted fowl, pork, and sow's belly to be sent down as payment for the presiding Sophist, Theodore of Smyrna, Timarion's former tutor (46).

The dialogue ends with an amusing account of how his soul was wafted back to where his body still lay unburied in a house by the Hebros, then slipped down the chimney and reentered the body via the nostrils. After a shivering night, he returns the next evening (a tough ride for one in such a state!)—And now I'm home, go out and find some newly dead people (νεοθανεῖς), so they can take down the food ordered by the Sophist—only take care not to choose pious and clean-eating men, as they would loathe the enterprise; better to find some of those filthy-eating Paphlagonians, who wouldn't mind making a profit out of trading pig meat, even in Hades. Now it's late, time for home and bed (47).

Second, narrative structure. The dialogue is carefully framed; we begin and end in the narrator's present, ostensibly a pleasant evening's chat with a friend in twelfth-century Constantinople. It may well have been performed at one of the City's informal rhetorical theaters. The close draws us back to the comfort of home, thereby reminding us of our own. The narrated story of past adventures takes us first westward across the Empire through Macedonia to Thessaloniki, then backward in time via the superimposed "mythic perspective" of the descent to the Underworld, introduced by a quasi dream device (12), and finally eastward through Thrace to the point of outset. If the narrating instant is in the present, the story has a "reach" back in time through the centuries of imperial glory to antiquity, occupying the major "extent" (duration) of the narrative.

Locations of narrating instance and story are clearly specified. Constantinople, where the dialogue takes place, is not described; but a double-edged aside from Kydion accuses Timarion of improperly hastening his narrative in order to get back to the City, "like one pursued by Scythian hounds, as if the City were the only hope of salvation" (3).[26] At an early point in the dialogue (5), Timarion claims to be a Cappadocian from "beyond the frontiers" (ἐκ τῆς ὑπερορίου). While Cappadocia had become respectable by the eleventh to twelfth centuries, as the region from which magnates had originated since the tenth, our author, by invoking the past, cannot but suggest proverbial clichés about Cappadocians as "dirty barbarians" in his choice of narrator, specified as an outsider. But if the prevailing narrative voice is an outsider's, the region of the Empire most prominently foregrounded is Thessaloniki, which is both the purpose of his journey and the source of his subsequent travails. Its approach and environs are depicted in topographical detail sufficient for it to be assumed that the author was indeed familiar with this terrain.

Kydion's frequent interruptions to Timarion's story have been ridiculed as disturbing the narrative flow.[27] However, they serve two important functions. They remind the reader of the narrating instant, while casting an ironic side-glance at prevailing narrative conventions: Kydion wants a straight story, told in detail and in proper order from beginning to end, whereas Timarion insists on his own, more complex sequence, accusing Kydion of greed (ἀπληστία) and pardoning himself in advance for omitting reference to every crow, stone, and wayside bramble that may have impeded his ride (3, 64–69; 7, 206–9, 230–31). The interruptions problematize narrative as communication: how many ways are there of "telling a story"? And what does the reader gain by the constant reminders that Timarion is telling his own to a sympathetic, if sometimes bantering, friend? We shall find similar interactions between close friends in Eustathios Makrembolites and, in modern Greek fiction, between educated narrator and uneducated brother in Vizyenos' story "Who Was My Brother's Killer" (1884).

Perspectives of time are as significant as those of place and space. From fictive present (mimetic dialogue) we move through narrated past (Timarion's story) by means of fantasy back across Byzantium to the good old days of antiquity, returning to the point of outset to converge at the end with the present narrating instance. Ideologically, focal conflicts are brought out by mythic perspectives between justice and injustice, wealth and poverty. We are afforded an outsider's review of the Byzantine world, past and present, West and East, with observations on aspects of social, political, and economic life. Interplay between chronotopes is facilitated by dual focalization of dialogue and narrative, which keep Timarion's excursions under scrutiny and control. Far from proving detrimental, the narrative's "discursive and episodic plan" is fully consistent with its medieval nature.[28]

Third, fictional strategy and targets of satire. Byzantinists often complain that Byzantine literature is so addicted to classical citation that it is infuriatingly vague and timeless, with such little unequivocal reference to historical figures and events that, in the absence of external evidence, texts transmitted anonymously are almost impossible to date, let alone attribute to a known author.[29] The *Timarion* does not do so badly on this score: it names explicitly as dead men the Emperor Romanos IV Diogenes (d. 1072), the Armenian general Philaretos (fl. 1072–86), John Italos (trial for heresy 1082, date of death unknown), and Theodore of Smyrna (still active 1112); it also strongly implies Michael Psellos (d. after 1078). Other specific but unnamed figures whose identity cannot be confirmed include: the *dux* of Thessaloniki, the description of whose physical beauty occupies central and maximal space in the entire dialogue; his implied distant relative, the unnamed glutton with grease and cabbage spilling into his beard whom Timarion encounters in Hades; and the "homunculus" (*hemíandron*) trailing after Italos.[30]

To return to the question of date: Tsolakis' revised dating to around 1112 is based, first, on alleged new prosopographical evidence for one Andronikos Doukas, who may be the unnamed dux; and second, on the argument that the text cannot be too distanced in time from the figures presented or else much detail would be lost on the audience.[31] Plausible as it sounds, the hypothesis raises problems: "Doukas" was not an uncommon name, with no fewer than thirty persons called "Andronikos Doukas" in the first half of the twelfth century.[32] More seriously, Theodore of Smyrna was still active in 1112, and it is surely perverse to suggest that Timarion's main guide to the Underworld may have been alive at the time of the dialogue's composition! Rather, the author seems to have followed a deliberate policy of revealing some names and concealing others—including his own— much as novelists today conceal their personal targets.

Timarion's portrait of Theodore is funny but not hostile (Theodore's casuistry secured his acquittal). It functions not merely to poke fun at his former teacher but also to comment obliquely on the question, controversial in the mid–twelfth century, of the relative merits of Aristotle and Plato. According to Magdalino, as "Consul of Philosophers" and successor to Italos and Kyprianos, Theodore was instrumental in the revival of interest in Aristotle, fostered by church and state as an alternative to the more subversive yet popular Platonic tradition. After Theodore's death, the post of Consul lapsed until the 1160s, when Michael "Anchialos" was appointed to counter the alleged Neoplatonism of the anti-imperial Orthodoxy. Despite Anna Komnēnē's imperial promotion of discussions on Aristotle, the works of Plato continued to attract such intellectuals as Michael Italikos and

Theodore Prodromos, whose Lucianic dialogue "Plato-Fan, or Leather-Worker" accords Plato high praise for his "perfect combination of rhetoric and philosophy."[33] Significantly, Timarion encounters neither Plato nor Aristotle during his trip to Hades; yet the ambivalent references to Psellos, Italos, and Theodore suggest the author's awareness of a sensitive issue which originated in the 1070s and whose repercussions reached far beyond 1112. Tsolakis' argument for situating the text at a time when it was still topical can be turned on its head: only "those long dead" could be safely identified. A date around the mid-1140s would be consistent with several details in the text, where the identities of near contemporaries are shrouded in mystery;[34] it also coincides with mounting controversy over the relative merits of Aristotle and Plato, philosophy and rhetoric.

One of the means by which our author succeeds in targeting key motifs and figures is by sophisticated and extensive use of *ekphrasis*, or formal description of place and character, which evokes, synesthetically, sight, sound and movement. Thessaloniki forms the center of the dialogue. Despite its fictional context, the account of the Festival of Saint Demetrios is one of the most detailed descriptions of a medieval fair recorded anywhere: from the Iberian peninsular to the Balkans and Asia Minor, Spanish, Portuguese, French, Italian, Slavic, Bulgaric, and Celtic peoples, as well as those from all parts of the empire, throng to the Festival. Things traded include precious textiles and all manner of goods and animals brought over on the hoof from as far afield as the Black Sea via Constantinople. Even from his hilltop, Timarion can hear horses whinnying, cattle lowing, sheep bleating, pigs grunting, and dogs barking.[35]

Apart from its commercial importance, the Festival also served as a major religious and political event: the dux of the theme (leader of the region) is portrayed as a ceremonial attraction, outshining even the archbishop; yet it is indicative of our author's fictional strategy that the identity of the dux is obscured. Ekphrasis serves several purposes here: it enriches the depiction of topos with specificity of detail, as in the description of the tents, peoples, and goods, and then moves the level of narration from real to symbolic by means of allusion, as in the eulogy of the dux, which, as Hunger observes, "steht im Mittelpunkt der Ereignisse" [stands in the middle point of the narrative]."[36] Here is an extract from the eulogy, describing the approach of his entourage:

Ἵπποι δὲ τούτους Ἀραβικοὶ γαυριῶντες ὑπέστρωντο, μετάρσιοι τὼ πόδε καὶ τοῖς ἅλμασι δεικνύντες ὡς ἀέρος ἐφίενται καὶ τὴν γῆν ἀποστρέφονται· ἐδόκουν συνιέναι καὶ τῆς περικειμένης λαμπρότητος, ὅση ἐν χρυσῷ καὶ ἀργύρῳ τοὺς χαλινοὺς περιέλαμ-

πεν ὥσπερ ὑποτερπόμενοι τῇ τῆς περιβολῆς φανητίᾳ καὶ πυκνὰ
τοὺς τραχήλους περιελλίττοντες τοῖς στιλβώμασιν. οὗτοι μὲν οὖν
οὕτω προσίασιν ἐν εὐτάκτῳ κινήσει καὶ ἅλματι στρατιωτικῷ τὴν
πορείαν ποιούμενοι· καὶ διάλειμμα μικρὸν ἐπὶ τούτοις καὶ ὁ δοὺξ
ἐπῄει γαληνῷ τῷ κινήματι· Ἔρωτες δὲ αὐτοῦ καὶ Μοῦσαι καὶ
Χάριτες προέτρεχον καὶ ὑπέτρεχον. ὦ πῶς ἄν σοι διηγησαίμην,
Κυδίων φίλτατε, τὴν ἐνσκηνώσασαν χαρμονὴν τῇ ψυχῇ μου τότε
καὶ τὸ τῆς ἀγαλλιάσεως πλήσμιον;

Arabian horses were laid beneath them, prancing, with two legs aloft, appearing by their leaps as if desirous of the air and disdainful of the earth.
They seemed to be blended with the radiance surrounding them, such as
shone forth from their reins in gold and silver, as if delighting in the glit-
ter of their harness, and frequently twirling their necks around their
adornments. Such, then, were they, and thus did the approach, advancing
their course in orderly movement and in military step. Afterwards, a short
interval, then the *dux* rode by, with serenity of movement. Afore and beneath him scurried Cupids, Muses, and Graces. O how could I describe to
you, dearest Kydion, the bliss that took root in my soul at that moment,
and the fullness of my cup of rejoicing?

The emphasis on spectator and spectacle in the lead-up to this extract is
made explicit through verbal redundancy.[37] The prancing horses recall the
vocabulary and imagery of the soul's desire to escape its mortality, as expressed in the famous allegory of the charioteer and his horses in Plato's
Phaidros (246a–250c, 253d–257b), a text implied in Michael Choniates'
response to his critics, who try to drag him down to the earthbound display (*epideixis*), preventing him from soaring on the wings of true learning
(I, 7–23; Magdalino 1993, 336–7). I argued earlier (1982/83, 40–42) that the
top-to-toe eulogy of the dux which follows is a veritable montage of embedded classical and biblical allusions; and so it is, although I now think that
the ekphrasis functions not just as parody but also as a dramatic contrast to
the fate that awaited Timarion in Hades.

The eulogy's central position in an overtly satirical dialogue and the textual prominence of the dux (to whom more space is devoted than to any
other individual in the entire text) should alert us to multiple levels of
meaning. On the one hand, we may infer that the dux is "a dandified sissy
of reported aristocratic descent, of ambivalent proclivities, capable of exer-
cising a devastatingly toxic effect on his subjects."[38] On the other hand, the
eroticism of the dux's presence should perhaps be seen as ambivalent rather

than pejorative: as Magdalino argues, "One striking manifestation of change in Byzantine culture in the eleventh and twelfth centuries was the rehabilitation of Eros . . . from puerile thug into something like a legitimate sovereign." The "imperial iconography" of Eros that emerged in the early years of Manuel I's reign is sufficient to explain the foregrounding of eroticism in Timarion's description of a military ruler, especially since the occasion was a ceremonial one.[39] This is not to deny the possibility of satirical intent but to point out the cultural background for such a portrait and Byzantine fondness for ambivalence.

Let us now turn from *ekphrasis*, which signals a change of mood and mode, to *diegesis*. After the eulogy, Timarion describes the sudden onset of his sickness and his nightmarish attempt to ride back to the City in a state of debilitation from lack of food: τούτοις πᾶσιν ἐμπεδωθέντα με, φίλε Κυδίων, ἱππάριόν τι φορτηγὸν ὥς τι τῶν ἐπισαχθέντα ἦγε πρὸς τὸ Βυζάντιον ["So, my dear Kydion, transfixed as I was by all these woes, one of the pack horses carried me towards Constantinople strapped across its back like a parcel"] (12; Baldwin's translation). This passage may well have inspired Vizyenos' description of Georgis' nightmare ride from Constantinople back to Vizye in "The Only Journey of His Life."[40] Medical particularities are described in detail (13). The scene, with the two "shadowy dusty-looking creatures" appearing at his bedside to whisk him off to Hades, conforms with visions and dreams of holy men; yet both context and atmosphere are rationalized and secularized to make a convincing adventure story with incidental realistic touches. As in a dream, Timarion is paralyzed with fear, unable to utter a sound, listening helplessly while his condition is debated (14). Details of the journey are vividly described, evoking classical Hades rather than the Christian Hell (15). The portrayal of the doorkeepers as "just like mountain-bandits" is more effective than the bestial demons of the apocalyptic visions: as in Aristophanes' *Frogs*, Hades is familiarized to resemble a grotesque version of contemporary bureaucracy.

At this point (16), Kydion interrupts to ask Timarion how he managed to see what was going on in Hades if everything was pitch dark? Only the common herd lives in darkness, he replies, whereas people of quality enjoy the privilege of artificial light acording to their status. Despite the author's debt to the Lucianic dialogues, there is an important difference: Timarion's Hades is no salutary and leveling democracy, as is Lucian's, but a replica of social divisions within Byzantine society. Kydion's intervention and Timarion's reply are strategically placed to remind the reader of the gap between past and present—in archaizing but conversational style:

16. ΚΥΔΙΩΝ. Ταῦτα μὲν οὖν, φίλτατε Τιμαρίων, φοβερὰ καὶ αὐτὸς ἥγημαι καὶ φρίττω κἀκ μόνης τῆς ἀκοῆς. ἀλλὰ πῶς ἐν τοσούτῳ ζόφῳ καὶ σκότει τὰς ὄψεις διεσκέψω τῶν πυλωρῶν καὶ τἆλλα, ὡς εἰκός, κατεμάνθανες;

ΤΙΜΑΡΙΩΝ. Φίλε Κυδίων, ἁπλῶς μὲν τὰ ἐν ῞Αιδου πάντα ζοφερὰ καὶ ἀνήλια· ἔχουσι δὲ χειροποίητα φῶτα, ὁ μὲν ἐκ ξύλων καὶ ἀνθρακιᾶς. ὁ δὲ ἐκ κλάδων. ὁ κοινὸς καὶ ἀγοραῖος ὄχλος· ὅσοι δὲ παρὰ τὸν βίον ἐλλόγιμοί ποτε καὶ λαμπρότεροι καὶ λαμπάδας ἀνάπτουσι καὶ ὑπὸ φρυκτωρίᾳ διαιτῶνται λαμπρᾷ· τοιούτους ἐγὼ πολλοὺς ἔγνων παροδεύων τὰς σκηνώσεις τῶν νεκρῶν καὶ τὰς ἑστιάσεις αὐτῶν.

16. KYDION. I think all this is terrible, dearest Timarion, and I shudder just to hear it. But how, in such gloom and darkness, did you manage to distinguish the doorkeepers' faces and to learn everything else you seem to have done?

TIMARION. Dear Kydion, quite simply everything in Hades *is* gloomy and sunless. But they do have artificial lights, this man's made of wood and charcoal, the next one's from branches, that is to say, the common folk. As for men of sometime quality and brilliance, they light up torches and spend their time under brilliant beacon light: I recognized many of them as I passed by the abodes of the dead and their hearths.

Timarion's encounters in the Underworld, unlike those of Odysseus or Aeneas but anticipating those in the work of Cretan poet Bergadis (c. 1400), are with neither heroes nor patriots. He passes a disgusting (but not terrifying) old man eating his Underworld meal of cabbage and bacon, who is not identifiable with any historical figure but is by implication a powerful magnate from Phrygia distantly related to the dux (17–18). The detail of the two mice—fat, sleek, and as big as pigs—that wait to lick the spillings from the old man's beard after he has fallen asleep is yet another variation on a traditional feature of apocalyptic visions, in which mice and other pests in Hell are the souls of the sinful dead.[41] Here, their presence is introduced with realism and humor (much as in Prodromos' *Battle of Cats and Mice*) and given an entirely rational explanation: as earthborn creatures, mice live and multiply in Hades, only occasionally visiting the living by springing up from small cracks in the earth's surface caused by drought (18–19). As for the mythical torments traditional to Hades since Homer (Tantalos, Sisyphos, Tityos), the author singles out as his victim the unfortunate Byzantine emperor Romanos IV (1068–71), whose eyes had been gouged out with particular ferocity after a feast in a tent (20–22). As a new-comer, Timarion is accosted with questions about everyday life on earth, particularly about the price of food. Suddenly, he comes across the barely recognizable slim figure of his former tutor, Theodore of Smyrna, who has clearly benefited from his healthy Underworld diet of asphodels.

The ensuing exchange between Theodore and Timarion is of crucial importance, as yet another example of how the author targets his satire (29). Timarion is horrified to hear that he has to stand trial before the pagan judges of antiquity, Minos and Aiakos, who will be bound, he as-sumes, to be hostile to one of the Christian faith (a "Galilaean"). Not at all, replies Theodore, the pagans are a lot more tolerant of other religions than the Christians, and there is no attempt at proselytization in Hades! It is surely such passages as this, flatly contradicting apocalyptic visions of tor-ments for those of other faiths (especially the Jews), that caused Akropolites to regard the work as subversive of Christianity. There follows an ekphras-tic topos, replete with classical allusion, on the Elysian fields.

The court scene, with Theodore pleading Timarion's case against his captors, Oxybas and Nyktion ("Quickfoot" and "Nightwatch"), is pure parody of legal procedures, in a tradition which can be traced back to Lu-cian and Aristophanes, but with resonances satirizing specifically Byzantine legal and medical malpractices. The case is referred to Hades' top medical experts, Asklepios and Hippokrates, but they are still preoccupied with the case of Julius Caesar's murder, so Theodore and Timarion are free to feed unharmed on nourishing Elysian vegetables (31).[42] On the third dawn fol-lowing (note the deliberate inconsistency of there being a "sunrise" in Hades), the court resumes session. The medical experts are humorously but sympathetically portrayed; Theodore, Timarion's spokesman, wins his case by arguing, first, that Timarion wasn't technically dead and, second, that Oxybas and Nyktion flouted international rules by failing to wait for the statutory rites (on the third, ninth, and fortieth days for Christians), to which peoples of all religions are entitled before removal from earth. Nyk-tion objects that Timarion was a stranger in foreign parts when he "died," thus no one would have bothered to bury him anyway. Then, as now, death in foreign parts was not an enviable experience. The issue is decided only when two more officials, Oxyderkion and Nyktoleustes ("Sharpeye" and "Nightspy"),[43] give Timarion a medical examination and report that parti-cles of blood, flesh, and breath still cling to his soul—a neat inversion of the judgment still pronounced today on disinterred bones during the exhuma-tion ritual: if the bones are clean, they can be placed in an ossuary, other-wise further measures are needed. Here the bones are not clean, and the soul is resurrected in the body.[44] The verdict of the jury is to acquit Timarion. It is read out by a "Byzantine professor," witty but vain, who has been identified as Michael Psellos (1018–78), occupant of the Chair of Rhetoric at the University of Constantinople after its refoundation in 1045.

Timarion spends yet another "night" in Hades and uses the opportunity to meet some philosophers, starting with the pre-Sockratics (43–46). Once more, Byzantine philosophers are his target: John Italos, Platonist philosopher and pupil of Psellos, is named as one who tries in vain to join their august company. Found guilty by special tribunal of lay and church figures in 1082 for holding dangerous and heretical beliefs, Italos had been anathematized and banned from teaching, but not condemned to death. In view of the notoriety of philosophical and religious debates of the later eleventh century, it is significant that he is alluded to at all, albeit in no favorable light.[45] In contrast to the brush-off Italos receives, the Byzantine professor (Psellos again?) is accorded a quiet welcome by the philosophers and a standing ovation from the orators, in terms of exaggerated praise as "Sun King," not dissimilar to Psellos' own exaggerated praise of members of the imperial family. The humor is ironic but nonetheless subversive of Byzantine *mores*. Ancient philosophers do not hold their Byzantine successors in high regard. The Sophists recognize Psellos as one of their own kind for his eloquence and polished diction. The episode confirms my view that the relation between rhetoric and philosophy is a central theme.

What, then, are the major features of this entertaining text? First, in common with other Byzantine writers of the twelfth century, the author employs different levels of Greek, from elaborate syntax and abstruse diction in ekphrastic passages to conversational style, as in Makrembolites' novel. He also displays and exploits to the full his knowledge of classical Greek from Homer to Lucian, in a manner which to us seems excessive but which was much loved at the time. It is through these means—linguistic and stylistic—that he is afforded a certain license: by embedding almost everything potentially controversial or subversive in citations from the ancient Greeks, he can seem to be saying one thing while implying another, in words not his own and for which he is not answerable. It is a kind of irony hard for us to appreciate fully, although not entirely without parallels in postmodern literature.

Second, what does the text tell us about beliefs in life after death? At every point it seems to invert Orthodox Christian dogma: no punishments for the wicked; no Heaven and Hell; no Last Judgment; no moral is implied but rather an intellectual reassessment of the relative merits of antiquity and Byzantium. On each count, antiquity wins out: religious tolerance, reasoned debate, and healthy deathstyle versus religious discrimination and intellectual repression, not to mention the gouty, gluttonous lifestyle of most

Byzantine philosophers and sophists, which not even long spells of Hadean diet have quite managed to cure. We are worlds away from Dante's *Divine Comedy* (early fourteenth century), the first Western medieval text to attempt an integration of classical and Christian conceptions of the afterlife. Yet it is not so far removed from a near contemporary of Dante's, the Cretan poet Bergadis, whose *Apokopos*, "Exhausted," tells a tale of a trip to Hades which pokes fun at religion and popular beliefs and practices of that time.[46]

Third, how representative is this text? We cannot name the author, even if we may be sure that he was no uncouth Cappadocian from "beyond the frontiers" but a highly educated member of Constantinopolitan society. Quite apart from their erudition, one of the functions of twelfth-century writers was to explore—playfully but also seriously—contemporary issues from multiple perspectives. That constitutes the appeal of the *Timarion*, despite its seemingly esoteric nature.

Fortunately, Constantine Akropolites did not burn his copy but sent it on to a friend. The text has survived in a single manuscript, Codex Vaticanus graecus 87, datable to the early fourteenth (or, at the latest, early fifteenth) century. Despite the terrifying near-death experience described so vividly by Timarion, in the end there is something reassuring about his tale of adventures: he *did* get back safely to body, home, and bed; what he found in the Underworld was not the Homeric Hades of glorified women and discontented heroes visited by Odysseus or the threatened torments of Christian Hell or even Lucian's classless utopia but a somewhat improved version of Byzantine society, where class privileges could still be enjoyed, together with the additional promise of a superior judicial system, a healthier death-style, and an absence of religious or racial discrimination. It is a story with a happy ending, like the modern wondertales. By contrast, Bergadis' *Apokopos* disturbs us more deeply with the poet's ambivalent answer to a different question: do the living remember their dead?

3. Eros and the "Constraints of Desire" in *Hysmine and Hysminias*

If I have modified my earlier interpretation of *Timarion*, my assessment of *Hysmine and Hysminias* has undergone radical revision, partly in the light of recent scholarship on the Komnene period in general and on the novel in particular but, more profoundly, as a result of my own close rereading of the text alongside Plato's *Symposion* and *Phaidros*. It is not a "mere love story," as H.-G. Beck claims, with titillating—even pornographic—passages; nor can it be compared without distortion either with its late antique prototypes on the one hand, or with postmodern novels (and sex manuals) on the other.[47] Rather, it is a complex and peculiarly Byzantine reflection on the ambivalent tensions between sensuality and spirituality, exploring sexual behavior—male and female, aggressive and submissive—as well as the boundaries of gender and status (freedom and slavery). It concerns the power of Eros, and the interconnectedness between human, animal, and vegetal life cycles, on the one hand, and the cycles of seasons, planets, and gods, on the other. Such an approach was pioneered by Sofia Polyakova in her interpretation of the novel as an "allegory of love," although she distinguishes the "inner" qualities of Byzantine allegory from the "outer" forms of its Western counterpart.[48] Karl Plepelits has taken this approach to reductive extremes, reading the novel as a straight allegory of Christian love.[49] My own reinterpretation, shaped before I read Polyakova and Plepelits, is based on the premise that the author was attempting to integrate Platonic and Christian concepts of Eros into a new, Komnene synthesis of "Hellenism," while dealing more explicitly than is the case in any other Byzantine romance with the physicality of sex and the maturation of the individual man and woman, whose love, as Beaton has suggested, is immortalized through art.[50]

I cannot do full justice to this complex text here. But before I attempt to summarize some of my results, let us briefly review the reception of the Byzantine novel by the reading public and by literary historians and critics, with specific focus on *Hysmine*, which was, without doubt, the Byzantine novel most widely read, copied, printed, and translated from the thirteenth to nineteenth centuries and among the earliest and most formative texts in the history of modern fiction.[51] For almost three centuries, the Komnene revival of the novel was universally condemned by historians of literature as "slavish imitation."[52] The past two decades have witnessed an almost complete reversal in the critical evaluation of the prose "drama" *Hysmine and Hysminias*, by Eustathios Makrembolites, and three verse novels: Theodore Prodromos' *Rhodanthe and Dosikles*; Niketas Eugenianos' *Drosilla and Charikles* (in twelve-syllable iambic trimeter); and Konstantinos Manasses' fragmentary *Aristandros and Kallithea* (in fifteen-syllable "political verse"). M. Gigante and H. Hunger drew attention to the uses of literary allusion and psychological coloring in Makrembolites' text;[53] these and further studies showed that the other three novels also reflect a genuine attempt to re-create, in a twelfth-century context, a genre which had ceased to exist, containing several allusions to contemporary historical events.[54] Since my own reappraisal of *Hysmine* (1977)—the first to attempt a "rehabilitation" of a single Byzantine novel—several studies have recognized the qualities of innovation and creativity, restoring the Byzantine novel to its rightful place in the history of fiction.[55] It is no longer necessary to offer an apology for the literary quality of these texts, which interact not only with one another but also with other literary and scholarly discourses of the twelfth century, as well as with the later Palaiologan romances of the thirteenth to fifteenth centuries.[56]

Although the four Komnene novels share with their late-antique paradigms the twin overarching structures of love and adventure, replaying themes, episodes, and specific features from twelfth-century perspectives, more remarkable are the innovations, particularly as manifested in *Hysmine*. Consistent use of first-person viewpoint, for the first time in the history of fiction, allows Makrembolites to dispense with everything extraneous to the fictional times and places of Hysminias' actions and emotions: there is no conventional authorial "oral-epic" presentation of the hero, as in Achilles Tatius' *Leukippe and Kleitophon*; nor are there subplots, with their concomitant intrigues, digressions, and recapitulations. Instead, ekphraseis and dreams are used to explore Hysminias' inner world, while diegesis (narration) is artfully constructed (as in the *Timarion*) with regard to time and space: the total fictional time of just over one year is distributed over few more than fourteen days and nights; and the spatial movement is cyclical and explicitly fictional, with only parenthetical reference to geographic location.[57] Yet if the narrative point of view is exclusively Hysminias', the guiding hand is Hysmine's, while the underlying theme is arguably the sanctity and power of Eros the god and the constraints of human desire.[58]

How are these new ventures in fiction to be explained? Before postulating "Western influences spread by the Crusades," we should review Byzantine precedents and Eastern parallels with which they interacted. To begin with, hagiography: Before the revival of the ancient romance in the twelfth century, the most popular narrative genre was the saint's life, composed in varying but more or less popular forms of Greek, prior to the tenth-century reworkings in high style by Symeon Metaphrastes.[59] Christian saints seem improbable models for secular heroes bent on pursuit of Eros, but several key themes and concepts are common to both, even when they move in contrary directions. First, from an early age, both are chosen for a higher quest, by God or by Eros, who reveals the future mission by *semeia* signs in dreams and visions, ekphraseis and art. Second, both saints and lovers must renounce home and family to embark on the higher quest: *anachōrēsis* "withdrawal" into the desert / wilderness / forest / monastery (saints), exploration through travel and adventure in foreign / barbarian lands (lovers). In the course of their trials, saints and lovers are engaged in constant battle with hostile forces, whether in the form of temptation dreams and visions, human impersonations of evil, or divine/demonic opposition and natural forces.[60] In response to fervent prayer, divine providence is manifested to saints and lovers alike to save them from natural disasters, such as earthquakes, storms, and fires, as well as from man-made catastrophes of war, piracy and slavery. Aspiring saints undergo symbolic death in order to be reborn; lovers endure physical death to be miraculously restored. Women cross-dress as men, freeborn men or women may be enslaved. The saint's union with God and immortalization through sanctity have their counterpart in the lovers' reunion with each other and with their families and their immortalization through art. There are important differences in the two genres, most obviously the role of women and the treatment of food and sex. If the saint is on his own (save for divine help) in his fight to abjure all pleasures of the flesh, including the breast on fast days during infancy, lovers act together to remain chaste in the midst of sexual promise and gastronomic delights at pagan festivals. *Timarion* secularizes Byzantine religious discourse on the afterlife, while *Hysmine* sanctifies Eros, tempered by the four cardinal virtues.

The second text relevant to the Komnene novel is the epic romance, *Digenes Akrites*. The Grottaferrata version shares themes of war and adventure with the popular Alexander Romance; other versions, with the saints' lives; and yet others, with the ancient novels, especially those of Achilles Tatius and Heliodoros.[61] As Catia Galatariotou has shown, there is an inherent opposition between Digenes' success as a warrior, associated with life in the *ténda* "tent", and his failure in love, after he takes up settled life in the *oikos* "house", so that "the story of Digenes is one whose major apparent dynamic behind the action is the pursuit of the code of male honour as opposed to . . . shame; but whose real dynamic appears in the end to be the opposition and tension of the sexes, and one man's fruitless pursuit of one woman's unconditional love."[62] In the Komnene and Palaiologan novels, the opposition between warfare and love is differently presented: as soldier of Eros, the warrior god, the hero attempts to conquer the female body as if a fortress; counseled by Sophrosyne, she resists. Successful outcome depends on balancing the tensions between these two.[63]

Third, three Byzantine tales with connections to Eastern narrative traditions dating back to late antiquity are worth mentioning. The earliest attested example is *Barlaam and Ioasaph*, a Christianized reworking into elevated koine Greek of the widespread Eastern *Tales of Buddha*, which gained popularity between the eighth and eleventh centuries. There follow *Stephanites and Ichnelates*, probably translated into Greek during the eleventh century from Syriac and Arabic versions of the sixth-century Sanskrit *Pancatantra*, and the *Book of Syndipas the Philosopher*, an eleventh-century rendering from Syriac of the Persian *Pehlevi*.[64] These texts form a temporal and spatial bridge between antiquity and the twelfth century and between

Byzantium and the East, continuing the legendary traditions about the lives of Alexander the Great, Apollonios of Tyre, Aesop, and Apollonios of Tyana, attested since the third century A.D.[65] Each of these tales in its own way combines a religious or philosophical quest with Eastern travel and adventure, thereby sharing some elements with the ancient romance and others with hagiography. Popular from the sixth to twelfth centuries, the best known have proved formative for oral and literary tale-tellings ever since, from the *Alf-Laylah wa-Laylah* ("One Thousand and One Nights") in the late tenth century to Boccaccio's *Decamerone* in the early thirteenth century, down to oral storytelling traditions today.[66] Common to oral and literary tales is the "frame" device, or "Chinese box" construction, whereby each tale is enclosed within another tale, and within each tale are encoded riddles, proverbs, and enigmas.

Questions of authorship and dating are no less vexed in the case of *Hysmine* than with *Timarion*. Estimates on date range from the 1070s to the 1230s, and I can offer here no more than a summary, with brief notes on my own adherence to somewhere in the mid-twelfth-century. At the one extreme, Plepelits constructs an ingenious but fanciful hypothesis that the name "Eustathios Makrembolites" (not consistently rendered in the manuscript tradition) is a pseudonym and that the author is to be sought behind "Charidoux" ("Charidemos" in some manuscripts), addressed by Hysminias in the first paragraph of the novel, which, he proposes, is a cryptonym for "John Doukas," to be identified with the brother of Constantine X, active between 1057 and 1083, and praised by Michael Psellos for his love of learning, books, and hunting. The idea of a cryptonym is not unattractive, although the deduction from Charidoux to John Doukas is arbitrary; and as we saw in the case of the *Timarion*, trying to find your Doukas in the late eleventh to twelfth centuries is rather like looking for a needle in a Byzantine haystack. Plepelits fails to give any historical or cultural context for dating *Hysmine* so early and at such distance from the other three Komnene novels, with which it shares many features.[67]

At the other extreme, Carolina Cupane, followed by Beaton, inclines toward a late-twelfth-century—even thirteenth-century—date, on the grounds that the figure of "Eros the King," a new departure (as they say) in Greek, was modeled on the French *Dieu d'Amour*, established in Old French and Provençal literature from the twelfth century. She argues that parallels between *Hysmine* and the *Roman de la Rose,* attributed to Guillaume de Lorris, can be explained only by the precedence of the French text, citing a case where Makrembolites may have drawn part of his description of the months from the French *Fablel du Dieu d'Amour,* now dated to the first quarter of the thirteenth century.[68]

Turning from the two extremes (1070s to 1220s), what is the evidence for the mid–twelfth century? Polyakova's citation of Greek and French parallels shows that in each case the Greek is more complete and detailed than the French and is consistent with imagery of gardening, plants, and shrubs which was developed in Greek literature long before the twelfth century and cultivated in the *Progymnasmata* of Nikephoros Basilakes, who also drew on Makrembolites.[69] As for the twelve months, allusion in the French fable is brief and incidental, whereas in *Hysmine*, details are fully developed, corresponding almost word for word not only with an anonymous twelfth-century painter's manual but also with an elaborate Byzantine calendrical iconography and rhetoric, dating from the fourth century.[70] What of Eros the King? Magdalino has now shown that the motif can be traced back to late-eleventh-century rhetoric and art, culminating in the mid–twelfth century with reference to the young and beardless Manuel I, known for his imperiousness and erotic escapades.[71] Finally, Suzanne MacAlister brings to light new data on the use of philosophical treatises in all four Komnene novels, suggesting that "not only do our writers seem to have been closely acquainted with each other's work, it even looks as though they could have discussed their works and delegated among themselves different areas for exploitation."[72] She situates them in the mid–twelfth century and posits that *Hysmine* was probably the first. The general conclusion the reader may draw from these protracted debates is that arguments based on details (names, figures, isolated passages) must remain speculative or flights of literary fantasy; arguments based on cultural and historical contexts carry more conviction.

In my previous analysis of the novel, I paid attention to narrative structure, with consistent use of first-person viewpoint, skillful manipulation of spatial and temporal levels; complex use of classical citation and allusion; and, last but not least, the eroticism and psychological detail in the depiction of Hysminias' awakening love, especially through dreams. These observations remain valid, but they are based on what I now believe to be a partial analysis, with undue weight given to the first part (the awakening of Hysminias' love) and insufficient attention to the second, the lovers' trials. Ostensibly, the first part presents the hero-narrator's "inner," and largely nighttime, world, and the second, his "outer," largely day-time experiences. But that is to read the novel at a linear, one-dimensional level. To redress the balance, I shall try to show how the eroticism is imbued with allegory, intimated in the first part through ekphraseis of Sosthenes' garden and acted out in the second, where it is Hysmine who takes the initiatives necessary for their salvation.

The following summary is abridged from my earlier one, the first since that of J. Dunlop. I have kept the first-person viewpoint and filled out the second half.[73]

Book 1. I, Hysminias, leave my fair native city, Eurykomis, where people are celebrating the feast of Diasia, sacred to Zeus. Elected by lot as herald, my dearest
Charidoux, I am sent off with my cousin Kratisthenes to Aulikomis, where we are
entertained by the wealthy Sosthenes. I walk round his garden and admire the
sculptures surrounding the well. At a banquet held in my honor, Sosthenes' daughter, Hysmine, makes advances to me as she serves wine, but I protest, and her
mother, Panthia, is shocked. At night, Kratisthenes interrogates me on my conquest,
but what do I know of Eros? We go to sleep.

Book 2. I visit the garden with Kratisthenes, and we examine a frieze depicting
in the central scene the four Virtues, Phronesis, Ischys, Sophrosyne, and Themis; then
a beautiful winged and naked youth, armed and seated on a chariot; followed by
throngs of people and animals. At the evening meal, again Hysmine makes immod-
est advances, and again Kratisthenes teases me; I deny Eros as firmly as before, and
we fall asleep.

Book 3. In a dream I see Eros, the figure of the frieze, come to enroll me as slave,
forcibly joining my hand to Hysmine's. Panic-stricken, I tell Kratisthenes I am now
a slave of Aphrodite and must renounce my duties as a herald; but he rebukes me
sharply and goes back to sleep, leaving me to indulge in half-waking erotic fantasies.
Toward dawn I fall asleep; dreaming of caressing Hysmine, I wake up, wet and re-
lieved. At the banquet that evening I respond passionately to Hysmine's advances.

Book 4. Afterwards, I join Hysmine in the garden, pressing attentions upon her,
but she resists. I retire but later return with Kratisthenes to the garden, where we
continue our contemplation of the frieze: the next scene depicts twelve figures, repre-
senting the seasons from March to February. Back to bed, but I slip out in the hope
of finding Hysmine. Noticing my absence, my friend drags me back to bed: after long
arguments, he sleeps, but I go out again on hearing a noise, to find Hysmine alone
by the well. We kiss, bite, and embrace, but she counsels restraint and is called away.
Back to bed, to be admonished by Kratisthenes, I determine to give up Eros and remain loyal to Zeus. I cry myself to sleep.

Book 5. In feverish dreams, I try to make love to Hysmine, dressed as bride, but
Panthia, her mother, catches us in flagrante: a host of avenging women descends,
threatening to tear me to pieces. I cry out out to find Kratisthenes trying to wake me,
for the noise is real: Sosthenes is at the door telling us to get up and greet the crowd
outside, clamoring to crown me as herald. During the festivities, my parents arrive,
to invite Sosthenes and his family to Eurykomis for a return visit. We all sail to Eurykomis, and a lavish banquet is held. At night, while our parents depart to sacrifice
to Zeus Xenios, I go to Hysmine's bed. We swear eternal love, but she refuses to sacrifice her virginity.

Book 6. Woken by mother for yet another banquet, I hear Sosthenes announce
the betrothal of Hysmine to a well-born man from Aulikomis and invite us all to
the nuptials. When our parents go off for propitiating sacrifices for the wedding, I go
to Hysmine's room to lament our lot. Later, I attend the sacrifices, where an eagle

snatches the victim from the altar. Next evening, the omen is debated, and Panthia almost curses Zeus. While our parents are off sacrificing again, Kratisthenes tells me a boat is waiting to take the three of us to Syria, and he goes off to make arrangements. I dream of the sea, waves, dancing young people, and Hysmine's embraces, and we are conjoined by Eros.

Book 7. Parents are away again for sacrifices, and Kratisthenes, on business. I go to Hysmine's bed and tell her of our planned elopement. She agrees but still won't give up her virginity. Embraces are interrupted by Kratisthenes: the boat is about to depart, no time to waste. After prayers to Poseidon the ship sails off in calm seas, but the next day brings a storm. The captain declares the need for a human sacrifice, and the lot falls on Hysmine. As we lament, she cries out to her mother, in league with Poseidon to destroy us, and is cast overboard. My lamentations are so unbearable that I am dumped at the next landing place, where I cry myself to sleep, dreaming of Eros leading Hysmine to me from the waves.

Book 8. I wake to be captured by Ethiopian pirates, who attack the nearby city of Artykomis, sacred to Artemis and known for its virgin springs. They cram their trireme with booty and Greek-speaking captives. Three days later, as the pirates disembark to gorge themselves with food, drink, and sex, we captives are rescued by an army of Greeks, who sell us off as slaves in the city of Daphnipolis at Apollo's shrine. I follow my Greek master and mistress as slave, but my mistress urges me to tell my story over a banquet, which I do. She falls in love with me, leaving me no peace. A year passes, and the time of Diasia comes round again. But here it is Apollo, not Zeus, who is to be celebrated, and it is my master's turn to act as herald in the city of Artykomis, sacred to Artemis. We all depart.

Book 9. Now a servant, I weep to remember past happiness. My right eye twitches—a good omen, according to Theokritos! At the banquet that evening, a maidservant attending my host Sostratos' daughter, Rhodope, looks suspiciously like Hysmine. Next evening, as I lament my servitude, I am handed a letter from Hysmine, telling of her miraculous escape from the storm on the back of a dolphin: I dream of her. Next day, Rhodope, seeing me overcome with emotion, urges me to tell my story. She takes me, fainting, to her bedroom, and summons her servants to attend. One, none other than Hysmine, declares me her long-lost brother. She later warns me that Rhodope is in love with me, and under the guise of our fraternal relationship, she can act vicariously to advance the affair. I dismiss the idea, but Hysmine, citing Euripides, insists that female duplicity is our only path to freedom.

Book 10. Letters and caresses with Rhodope the next day, mediated by Hysmine. My master, the herald, and mistress (also in hot pursuit of me) take our households back to Daphnipolis for celebrations to Apollo. The next night, the masters, accompanied by companions and slaves, sacrifice at the shrine of Apollo, where we find—who else?—my own and Hysmine's parents, lamenting us, their lost children, Panthia is still blaming me for abducting their daughter. After a recognition

*scene, the priest of Apollo declares us free, but the crown is torn from our heads by
my master and Sostratos, who insist we are still their slaves. Appealing to the crowd
for support, the priest pronounces that from now on Greeks shall never be slaves to
Greeks. A lavish banquet follows for all present, and there is general feasting, dancing and singing through the night.*

*Book 11. Next day, back to Apollo's shrine, where the priest offers another feast
and gets me to repeat my story. The priest urges Hysmine to relate hers, but she is
prevailed on to do so only after incurring her father Sosthenes' ire: the detail she
adds to what I knew is that, as she was about to succumb, naked, to the waves, she
was saved by a naked youth, with winged feet and riding a dolphin, to safe harbor,
where she was sold as virgin slave to Rhodope. It is decided that we all go back to
Artykomis, where her virginity can be tested in Artemis' springs. She passes! We
proceed to Aulikomis, where our nuptials are celebrated. This day has no end, but
our story will be immortalized in our book, "Drama of Hysmine and Hysminias."*

It would be perverse to suggest that this is not a love story, enjoyed, as intended, by readers throughout subsequent centuries in numerous manuscripts, printed editions, and translations. Is it anything more? I shall analyze
narrative structure (time and place), interaction between gods and humankind, and symbolic time and space as suggested by the cyclical movements of spheres and seasons, to indicate its allegorical meanings. First,
structure. According to Beaton, it "fall[s] naturally into three distinct parts":
books 1–5, 6–8, and 9–11. Plepelits divides it into four: 1–4, 5–6, 7–9, and
10–11.[74] Such divisions, based on plot and action, are arbitrary. In my view,
the novel's careful time scale has two parallel movements, each covering in
contrasting tempo just over seven consecutive days and nights of narrated
time at the same points of the calendar year, from February to March
(when the Feast of the Diasia was celebrated), with Pisces in the ascendant
and Aries forthcoming. Fictional time is just over one year, with two breaks
in book 8, one minor ("on the third day," 8.8.2), the other major (one year,
8.16.1).

The first cycle opens slowly: by the end of book 4 we are still in the
middle of the third day, but the pace increases in books 5–7 to cover five
nights and four days. After the two breaks, in the second cycle time is more
condensed, and movement is enhanced by the technique of "overlapping"
days with nights, in the manner of an arabesque, each covering two or three
days and nights. Spatial movement balances tempo, so that density of action
matches density of time. In cycle 1, movement is limited—from Eurykomis
to Aulikomis and then Eurykomis (1–7)—then intensified on board the
ship bound for Syria, when Hysmine is apparently drowned at sea and Hysminias is held captive and taken via Artykomis to Daphnipolis, where he is

sold as a slave (7–8). In cycle 2, movement is doubled: from Daphnipolis to Artykomis, Daphnipolis, Artykomis, and, finally, Aulikomis (8–11).[75] Temporal and spatial movements are apparently controlled by four pagan deities: Zeus – Poseidon, Apollo – Artemis; but the lead role is played by Eros, named as Zeus' son and brother to Apollo and Artemis. Eros is no child, as in the ancient romances, but King of all creatures of the universe. Thus, in cycle 1, Hysminias sets out as herald to Zeus (1), becomes enslaved by Eros (2), is torn by conflict between the two, only to be joined with Hysmine by Eros (6). Eros seems to have won the battle with his father, Zeus, so far as Hysminias' allegiance is concerned; but only at the future cost of his favorite, Hysmine, who falls victim to Poseidon's wrath.

In cycle 2, the focal point of action is the shrine to Apollo in Daphnipolis, as the site where Hysminias was first enslaved, where the god's cult is annually celebrated (mirroring the Diasia of cycle 1), and where the lovers are reunited with their parents and eventually set free by Apollo's priest. What is Apollo's role, and how does it signify? At the outset of the annual seven-day festival, Hysminias, under hot pursuit by his mistress for sexual favors, ponders the myth of Daphne, central to the city's cult: the flight of the maiden Daphne, Apollo's pursuit, and her prayer to the earth and metamorphosis into a laurel, from which Apollo creates his immortal crown. The god's attempted rape of Daphne mirrors in myth Hysminias' pursuit of Hysmine in cycle one and that of Hysminias' mistress of himself in cycle 2.[76] A vicious circle? It is the turn of Daphne, Artemis—and Hysmine—to intervene. The festivities are transferred the next day to Artykomis, sacred to Artemis. As Hysminias sits lamenting his lot under the shade of a laurel tree (ὑπεκστὰς δάφνῃ), a young girl (παιδίσκη) hands him a letter, saying, "This letter to you from Hysmine the maiden, your beloved, and now my companion in slavery [ὁμοδούλου]." A slave girl's act of her own free will initiates the reunion of the lovers and breaks the cycle of pursuit and slavery. Further, it is Hysmine who takes the initiative in announcing to Rhodope that she is Hysminias' long-lost sister, and she again who insists, despite Hysminias' objections, on mediating in Rhodope's suit for marriage to Hysminias. Toward the end, after the pair have been set free by the priest of Apollo (a human agent), the final trial is Hysmine's in the springs of Artemis. Only then can Eros make his triumphant entry at the end (11.4).

Throughout, human and divine agents interact. For Hysmine, the storm sent by Poseidon to destroy her in book 7 was brewing from the beginning of the novel, through the figure of her mother, Panthia, who casts a more sinister shadow throughout than does her counterpart over Leukippe in Achilles Tatius' novel. Hysminias renounces his "father," Zeus, and follows

Eros; Hysmine renounces her mother, as she repeatedly notes.[77] The first time Hysmine serves drinks at the initial banquet (book 1), she whispers "greetings" (χαίροις) to Hysminias; the second time, she presses his foot with hers under the table as she tells him, in a low voice, "you hold the cup from a maiden with the same name"; the third time, she will not release her fingers from the cup as she offers it, forcing their hands to a battle of wills (ἔρις οὖν ἐν χερσί, καὶ χεὶρ παρθένου κόρης νικᾷ χεῖρα κήρυκος ἀνδρὸς παρθένου). Angry, Hysminias exclaims out loud in a herald's voice, "You won't give it to me? What is it you want, then?" causing the girl to blush with shame and look to the ground. Panthia gives her a withering look—the "evil eye," in effect: "Panthia turns her eyes on the girl, eyes all anger, all indignant, full of blood. She casts her eyes upon the girl's head, upon her hands, upon her feet, upon her neck; she takes possession [ἔχει] of the girl with her eyes, she consumes her in fury, all of her in rage. Her cheeks turn red . . . then again pallid, as if all the flush had flowed into Hysmine's face" (1.10.1–2). Panthia's next outburst comes in Hysminias' dream, when she catches him trying to deflower Hysmine (5.3.4): fueling her anger with reference to Paris and the Danaids, she has him stripped of his heraldic tokens, then summons an armed band of avenging women to march against him, with Zeus at their lead. The next two incidents concern the sacrifice to Zeus on the occasion of preliminary sacrifices for her daughter's arranged marriage (6.10): as in Achilles Tatius, an eagle swoops down to seize the sacrificial victim from the altar, an omen Panthia laments at length as signaling her daughter's ravishment and death but interpreted the next day by the others as indicating Zeus' disapproval of the match. Furious, Panthia comes near to blasphemy as she protests against offering further sacrifices, until overruled by Sosthenes (6.14.5–6). As for the storm at sea, it is a stock device whereby gods separate lovers in the ancient and Byzantine novel; but, with bold psychological insight, Makrembolites has transferred responsibility from divine to human agency. Presciently, moments before she is cast overboard, Hysmine cries out that Poseidon's wrath is merely divine response to her mother's imprecations: "A mother's curse is raising the storm against me; a mother's arms, raised in prayer to heaven, are driving us to the abyss, drowning us all. Oh tongue of a mother submerging us, oh hands of hers stirring up all these seas, oh seething of her soul overwhelming entirely all our own. . . . But, oh mother, restrain your tongue, as may also Poseidon the storm. Put down your hands, that we may escape the deluge. Spare our souls" (7.11.1–3).[78] It is no surprise to find Panthia at the end still stridently lamenting her daughter's abduction and rape, even as the lovers stand before her at the shrine of Apollo (10.11).

Is it Panthia's opposition to her daughter's free choice of partner, rather than the intervention of gods, pirates, and slave owners, that is the driving force of hostility against the lovers? Her fury might not have been provoked, had Hysminias not spoken "out loud in a herald's voice" to expose Hysmine, when he should have observed silence (as Kratisthenes kept reminding him, in terms recalling the ancient mysteries), and had he been more in control of his own sexual urges, once awakened. These are tempered in cycle 1 by his sense of duty as herald to Zeus, by Kratisthenes (his "alter ego," or father's voice?),[79] and above all by Hysmine herself. It is not self-assertion he has to learn but self-control. His first lesson in cycle 2 is taught him by the Ethiopian pirates, who disgust him by gorging themselves on food, drink, and sex at their earliest port of call after his capture. His second is taught him by his master's wife, more enslaved to Eros than he is to his master. His third confrontation is with Rhodope, Hysmine's mistress, also in love with him as a result of his "story." He despairs at this new complication, yet it is Hysmine's idea to act, as "sister," as *mediatrix* between her lover and her mistress, carrying their letters and vicariously enjoying his embraces. It is a nice insight into the difference between male and female psychology that he regards this behavior as dissemblance, whereas she, ever practical, insists it is their only path to freedom (9.22–23).

Much has been said on the inconsistencies of Hysmine's sexuality and her treatment of Hysminias: she makes unmaidenly advances, whispering in his ear, playing "footsie" under the table, engaging in a "battle of fingers" over the cup, even tickling and kissing his feet as she washes them at his bedside; then, once his passions are aroused, she rebuffs his five attempts at her chastity (two in the garden, three in bed), managing to remain a virgin till the end, as convention required. Even Hysminias' dreams involve no more than "heavy petting" and never jeopardize the final virginity trial. Having once argued that her change of mind "reflects female behavior as viewed by men" and is therefore consistent with the novel's first-person perspective, I am no longer so sure. True, sexually aggressive females are usually married, courtesans, or of lower social status, according to novel convention. But Hysmine's playful advances have an interesting precedent in those of the maiden Chloe, who, although two years younger than Daphnis, is portrayed at fourteen as sexually more mature.[80] Could Makrembolites have had other sources in mind?

The story of Parthenope and Metiochos is mentioned by Lucian and other sources of the second century. a.d. in association with mimes, songs, and dances. Its popularity in the Roman imperial period is further attested by floor mosaics in summer residences situated in the region of Antioch, particularly at Daphne (modern Harbiye).[81] One shows Parthenope and Metiochos seated back to back but gazing intently at each another with evident agitation. A papyrus fragment of the novel's opening chapter (P.Berol.7927) perhaps affords a clue as to the cause of their agitation: at a banquet hosted by Parthenope's father, Polykrates, Metiochos is asked what he thinks of Eros. Metiochos replies that he values philosophy and mythology more highly, thereby incurring the wrath of Polykrates and Parthenope, who casts him a glance full of ire: κἀκείνη δι' ὀργῆς ἔχουσα τὸν Μητίοχον διὰ τὸ μὴ ὡμολογῆσαι τὸν Ἔρωτα μήπω οὐδεμιᾶς ἐρασθῆναι (2.64). The scene offers close and contextual parallels with the first banquet in *Hysmine*. A second mosaic, presumably illustrating a later stage in the story, shows Metiochos looking wistful, with downcast eyes. Parthenope stands behind, looking straight at—and beyond—him, with her left hand outstretched, as if showing him the way. Again, we have a parallel with Hysmine's behavior in cycle 2. We shall never know whether Makrembolites had access to some written version of the romance, no longer extant. But the story, known as ὀρχηστικὴ ἱστορία "dance story" in second-century sources, is attested in performative contexts (song, dance, mime); it is represented in art; and it is associated with a particular locality, Daphne (cf. "Daphnipolis"). This at least raises the possibility, worth further investigation, that Makrembolites could have been familiar with love stories, once celebrated in local cult, where the heroine first initiates the hero into sexuality, then counsels restraint, and finally leads him to the highest level of Eros. In any event, it is clear that such stories were not transmitted by literary texts alone: Hysmine's advances should be viewed not from our own, post-Freudian perspectives of precocious female sexuality but as a ritual dimension of alternating phases of exposure and seclusion, in accordance with the principles of the life cycle.

Eros tells Hysminias in his first dream that Hysmine was "already loving of Eros, and beloved by Eros" (παρθένον...οὕτω φιλοῦσαν Ἔρωτα καὶ φιλουμένην ἐξ Ἔρωτος, 3.8.2) and that he commanded her to disclose "as in a mystery" the similarity of their names; he blesses the pair only after she intercedes on her lover's behalf. Why does she resist his attempts to violate her? After a bout of mutual biting and kissing in bed, Hysminias tries "something more serious" on Hysmine (μήκετι παίζειν ἀλλὰ σπουδάζειν ἐρωτικῶς). She pleads: "Spare my virginity, Hysminias. Do not strip the ears of corn before summer. Do not trample the rose before it puts out its flower pod, nor the grape as yet unripe, lest you press vinegar instead of nectar from the virgin grape . . . I am your sleepless guardian, an inviolable fortress" (5.17.1)[82] Imagery is drawn from cultivation, as in descriptions of the garden (*parádeisos*).

Let us now look more closely at the three extensive ekphraseis, each strategically placed at key turning points and each followed by dialogue:

1.4–5; 2.1–9; 4.5–18. The first describes Sosthenes' garden in terms of an earthly Paradise (μεστὸς χαρίτων καὶ ἡδονῆς, πλήρης φυτῶν, ὅλος ἀνθέων, 1.4.1): beneath the rows of cypress, the thick-shading myrtle, the laurel, and the grape-laden vines grow fragrant violets, roses (some in bud, others in full bloom, and yet others scattering petals), and perfumed lilies— sights and scents so delicious you thought you were in Alkinoos' garden or the Elysian plain—while overhead the trees almost dance together as their boughs intertwine and sway to let in sparkles of sunlight. - A veritable "golden chain," Hysminias tells Sosthenes, evoking not only the Homeric σειρὰν χρυσείην ἐξ οὐρανόθεν πεδιόνδε (Il. 8.19) but also the whole *aurea catena Homeri* of medieval Neoplatonism or the "love chain" joining humans to the powers of the universe.[83] In the midst of the garden stands a well, four cubits wide, its water funneled through a column, fashioned from Thessalian marble and studded with multicolored gems, to form a fountain whose waters gush forth from the beak of a golden eagle into an ornamental bath, around which are engraved a goat with first-born twins, milked by a goatherd, and a hare. Above is an arc of birds—swallow, dove, and cock—each with water noisily gurgling from its beak. Beneath, the base of the well is of white marble flecked with darker shades, so the water seemed to shimmer as if in constant motion. Its sides are constructed of three kinds of marble, from Chios, Lakonia and Thessaly, each separated by an inset of precious, multicolored stones.[84]

A wonder indeed for all the senses! There follows the first banquet, where Hysmine's advances may be seen as Hysminias' initiation and inter- preted as "unseemly" only by her mother and the two young men, Hys- minias and Kratisthenes, whose somewhat lewd schoolboy exchanges close the chapter. As A. R. Littlewood suggests, the garden is a plausible symbol of the heroine's virginity, with sacred connotations. Religious dimensions have been explored by Plepelits, who goes so far as to equate Sosthenes' garden with Paradise/Jerusalem and Hysmine with Christ, interpreting every detail of the garden's artifice with Christian imagery.[85] Byzantine al- legory is more complex than Plepelits allows. The connections between garden, Hysmine, and sanctity of love are elaborated with subtlety as Hys- minias attempts to rape her throughout cycle 1, and returned to at the end of cycle 2 as the sacred site of nuptials (καὶ θύομεν τοὺς γάμους ἐν μέσῳ τοῦ Σωσθένους κήπῳ, 11.18.2).

In the second ekphrasis, Hysminias continues his exploration of the gar- den with Kratisthenes (2.1–8). Together, they wonder at the frescoes on the wall (θριγγίον): the first panel shows four Virtues, painted as maidens: Phronesis (Wisdom), Ischys (Strength), Sophrosyne (Chastity), and Themis (Justice), with Platonic echoes of *dikaiosyne, sophrosyne, andreia, sophia,* from

Agathon's speech in praise of Eros in Plato's *Symposion* (196D). Then a naked and priapic young male, Eros enthroned on a chariot (Hysminias is ashamed to look upon him, but can't keep his eyes off!), with gods, kings and men, beasts and birds, insects and reptiles, in thrall. The young men retire as they engage in lighthearted repartee. Hysminias dreams of enslavement to Eros and toward morning has his first wet dream: war inside him between Zeus and Eros has begun!

The third ekphrasis (4.5) shows us the next panel of the garden frieze, visited by Hysminias and Kratisthenes on the third evening. Twelve men are portrayed, each engaged on different labors: soldier, goatherd, gardener, thresher, reaper, bather, vintner, bird catcher, sower, harbinger, hunter, and an old man around a fire who is reaching from earth up to the heavens. Thanks to the verse inscription, they infer that the men represent human labors in the year's cycle, governed by three seasons—summer, cold, and spring—then retire to debate the scene in philosophical terms recalling the various tributes to Eros in Plato's *Symposion*.[86] Hysminias, whose mind has been more on Hysmine than on Kratisthenes' initiatory explanation (*mustagōgēma*), asks why, if everything in Nature is ruled by the seasons, Eros was not portrayed alongside them? -Ah, replies his friend, you forget that Eros figured on the first panel we saw, for he will submit to no law and is ruled by no seasons. So, infers our hero, if seasons and months are enthralled to Eros, then every particle of time and space—even day and night with all they engender and encompass—must bow to his superior force! (4.20). Eros gives free license to act as we please. Shortly after, seeing Hysmine in the garden beside the well (the centerpiece of the garden and of female virginity), Hysminias flies to her side, his feet "winged by Eros" (4.21.1), to put his new theory into practice. Surprised at his audacity, she gives back as many bites and kisses she receives, sweeter than honey (as in the *Song of Songs*),[87] but resists when he assails her virginity, summoning Sophrosyne and Aidos (Chastity and Shame) to her aid. A war between the fire (*pyr*) of Eros and the water (*hydor*) of modesty ensues, which Hysminias thinks Eros would have won had not a voice from the house summoned Hysmine inside.[88] He retires, to be chastised by Kratisthenes, then relapses into adolescent petulance—never again will he try to embrace Hysmine!

This third sequence of ekphrasis/diegesis, interspersed with dialogue, is a supreme example of the multiple levels of signification in Komnene literature. On the human level, Hysmine's resistance may seem "inconsistent"; yet there are cosmic dimensions too. The Orthodox calendrical year begins, then as now, in March and ends in February, the twelfth, oldest, and most important (if reviled) of the months, in accordance with interpretations of the twelve signs of the zodiac (between Pisces and Aries). August, six months later, marks the turning point between summer and winter and is depicted on the frieze as a bather (*lelouménos*) whose total immersion suggests baptism.[89] For humankind, the calendrical year sets up cosmic strife between Fire and Water: February's fire may promise eternal renewal, but it must be tempered by the waters of August if it is not to consume itself.

Hysmine intuitively knows what the two young men have forgotten from the first panel of the frieze—that Eros the King is preceded by the four female virtues (2.2–11). The rest of the novel could be interpreted as no less than her initiation of Hysminias, through his sufferings and pairs (*páthē, pónoi*) from slavery and female lust, to the highest level of Eros, incorporating Phronesis (wisdom in mediating between her lover and her mistress), Ischys (toughness of soul as well as body), Sophrosyne (modesty and shame, tested by Artemis' springs), and Themis (justice accorded by Apollo's priest, who frees them from slavery to fellow Greeks). Hysmine, too, must overcome female shame (*aidōs*) and tell her story before the nuptials can be celebrated. Why is she so reluctant to do so? (11.11–13).

Images of fire and light predominate in cycle 1, and water—salt and fresh—in cycle 2. Hysmine is sacrificed to the sea; Hysminias gives himself up to tears and penitence, to be saved by Hysmine, whose virginity is tested in Artemis' springs. Having told Hysminias in a letter (8 9.1–2) that "a dolphin from the sea" rescued her from the storm, while Artemis protected her virginity, what she reveals in her recapitulation (11.13–15) has to do with nudity and Eros, beauty and beast: she experienced fear (*phóbos*) of the beast on whose naked back she rode naked, tossed by waves (γυμνῷ τῷ θηρὶ καὶ τοῖς κύμασιν ἐκυκώμην, 11.13.2). Terrified by the beast (*thēra*), who turned out to be her savior (*sotēra*), she was about to jump into the sea when a naked youth with winged feet gave her his hand and led her to safety (μειράκιον...γυμνὸν ἐπὶ δελφῖνος ἑστὼς καὶ αὐτὸ, 11.14.1).[90] The scene suggests Hysmine's sexual union with Eros, but it has the spiritual qualities of an initiation: she has gazed on Eros without the shame first experienced by Hysminias (2.7.2). If Eros initiated Hysminias through fire, he saved his beloved Hysmine from water. Male and female elements have been reconciled in a new concept of Eros.

There is also a play on the numbers three, four, seven, and twelve: three are the seasons; twelve are the months; and seven and a half the number of days over which each cycle of the action is set. The most turbulent interruption occurs from halfway through the seventh book; immortality is promised at the close of the eleventh. In his third recapitulation, Hysminias alters one crucial detail: Eros, earlier said to be on a chariot (δίφρῳ, 2.7,9), is now seated on a throne (θρόνῳ), with day and night attending him. His winged feet, inspired by iconography of the Exapterygos ("six-winged seraphim")),[91] have perhaps incorporated the four Virtues (at 2.7, "winged feet" is rendered by the dual form τὼ πόδε). One recalls Aristophanes' doctrine of Eros from Plato's *Symposion*, that initially there was only one human species, the *andrógynon*, with three genders (male, female, female-male), two faces on one rotating neck, four arms, and four legs, which Zeus split down the middle as a punishment for its daring to reach up to heaven.[92] Since our lovers share the same name, as Hysmine, prompted by Eros, first told Hysminias, the merging of their souls marks the rebirth of both Eros and humankind in a new form, to be celebrated not in the flesh (night is deferred) but in literature. In the course of the novel, Makrembolites has led us from the lowest to the highest level of Eros, as discussed in Plato's *Symposion*, from the physical, physiological, and mythical perspectives to the divine, with the difference that heterosexual love is reinstated, to be enjoyed both in the body and in the spirit: through art, "the divine good" (*to thēion kalón*) can be reached in its purity and indivisibility.

Yet the novel does not ignore the joys of the flesh. No less than fourteen banquets have been served since the opening, almost one for each day in narrated time. In the first cycle these were sacred to Zeus but indulged in only by the immediate families of the two lovers. In the second, we progress from the gross indulgence of pirates to the four feasts sacred to Apollo but hosted by slave owners, to the last three feasts sacred to Apollo and Artemis, at Daphnipolis, Artykomis, and Aulikomis, where people sing and dance together in a manner resembling the participants in a saint's feast (*panēgyris*). Gods, masters, and parents have learned to understand their children, and adolescents have grown up to respect one another, observing the seasons. Eros is king, but conjoined with the Christian virtues.

What is new in the Komnene novel? As in antiquity, it is a "mixed genre," both erotic and religious, light and serious. Aside from the Christian perspective, interest in the psychology of the individual, evident in *Daphnis and Chloe*, is raised to new levels and informed by medical discourse. Allegory is developed in association with the ritual calendar of the months and seasons. We know little about the audience for the ancient novel, but we can say that *Hysmine* was much loved throughout late medieval and Renaissance Europe. Narrative techniques (juxtaposition of ekphrasis and diegesis, with dialogue) have remained hallmarks of the best Greek fiction ever since, as we shall see in Chapter 8.

4. Prodromos and the Politics of Hunger

If *Hysmine* celebrates the pleasures of the flesh, the four Ptochoprodromic Poems, attributed to the learned and prolific writer Theodore Prodromos, lament the lack thereof, although it has to be pointed out that one learns far more about twelfth-century eating habits from the hunger of "Ptochoprodromos" (Poor Prodromos) than from all the banquets in *Hysmine*. In each of the four poems, the addresser adopts a different narrating persona in his begging pleas to imperial patrons. The value of these poems has long been recognized by historians for their unique vignettes of everyday life and their inventories of foodstuffs and items of clothing, and by linguists for their profusion of lexical and morphological forms; but there has been far less unanimity as to their stylistic and literary merits.[93] Three major stumbling blocks seem to have prevented the poems from being taken seriously as "literature": the mixed levels of language, ranging from semilearned Greek to vulgar street slang; the coarseness of the humor; and the discursive, episodic structure. These questions will be fully addressed in an edition I am currently preparing with Michael Hendy; here, I shall review three features: variety of linguistic registers and "speech genres"; narrative structure; and bodily functions as a source of humor. Because the text is more "speakerly" than "readerly" or "writerly," I shall make ample use of direct citation.

Problems of authorship and date differ from those of *Timarion* and *Hysmine*. Can the Poems been written by one man, let alone by Theodore Prodromos, to whom they are attributed almost unanimously in the manuscripts? Can the author of learned discourses, an erotic novel, and rhetorical treatises have composed poems in vulgar—worse, inconsistent—forms of Greek? What is more, the author pays "obsessional attention to what everyone has to eat"; he even indulges in banal scatological humor in a manner deemed unworthy of a writer of Prodromos' education and standing.[94] I have addressed the question of authorship elsewhere (1986b, 32–35), so I restate my position that they are the work of a single author and that there are no objective or external grounds for rejecting the majority of manuscript attributions to Theodore Prodromos. As for vulgar language, it is now accepted that several authors varied their idiom in accordance with genre and content, so that "we may surmise that the Comnenian court did not eschew the fashion for vernacular literature."[95] Despite modifications and interpolations in later manuscripts, the historical kernel of all four poems belongs ineradicably to the twelfth century, as can be determined by datable artifacts (coins and other items of everyday life) and social values specific to the twelfth century, which could not have originated in the economic climate after 1204.[96]

In each of the four poems the poet moves with consummate ease between different levels of language and style, combining a wide range of literary references and "speech genres." Whereas the *Timarion* is conducted throughout on an even level of polite dialogue between two educated young men of equal status, not unlike the intimate conversations between Hysminias and Kratisthenes, in the Ptochoprodromic Poems the poet uses diverse linguistic registers to play on levels of social *difference* and especially on categories of inclusion and exclusion. Nor is it simply a question of using a more formal style in addressing his imperial patron and a vulgar one to convey the speech of artisans (*bánausoi*). Close analysis reveals crafted language and style throughout, as appropriate to the different personae adopted by the narrator in each poem: henpecked husband (I); impecunious paterfamilias with thirteen mouths to feed (II); abused monk (III); starving scholar (IV). Thus, in the proems and epilogues addressed to each patron, the tone is semilearned, importunate yet intimate, persistently playing on the shifting qualities of certain key oppositions: writing and speaking, prose and verse, praise and blame, truth and fiction, humor and wisdom, wealth and poverty, health and sickness.

The poems enclosed by these frames make use of colloquialisms to explore on diverse levels what Beaton has termed the "rhetoric of poverty," or Herzfeld the "politics of hunger."[97] There is a good deal of slapstick humor, with frequent reference to bodily functions and emissions caused by near starvation. It should not be assumed that the Byzantine court of the twelfth century shared our own genteel reservations about using gastronomy as a source of comedy and satire. As the text indicates, base language affords a certain license for base humor, which our author exploits to the full.[98] Second, the narrator suggestively links his hunger with sexual deprivation, in contrast to the gluttony of his interlocutors, be they his wife and family (I), his monastic superiors (III), or his social inferiors (IV). As Herzfeld has pointed out, in the very different context of twentieth-century Cretan sheep stealers, food and sex serve both as a metonym for the repression and oppression of the periphery by the center and as a rhetorical device to appropriate, parody, and invert the authoritarian discourse of church and state.[99] The figurative codes in which this rhetoric is couched are rooted in the Greek language and have remained remarkably constant to this day.

Eight formal addresses frame the four poems, with frequent interventions in the course of the narrated contents. Poem I (MS G) is entitled from "Prodromos, kyros Theodoros, to the Emperor Mavroiannes"—that is, John II (1118-43), known earlier in his reign as "John the Black" on account of his swarthy looks but later as "John the Good" (Kaloiannes) because of his behavior as emperor.[100] The narrator also refers in the Proem to his own past, as he now adopts the persona of a henpecked husband (and father of four), whose wife is constantly complaining that his courtly con-

nections involve him in riotous activities but bring in no hard cash or
goods to the household:

Proem: Τί σοὶ προσοίσω, δέσποτα, δέσποτα στεφηφόρε,
ἀνταμοιβὴν ὁποίανδε ἢ χάριν προσενέγκω
ἐξισωμένην πρὸς τὰς σὰς λαμπρὰς εὐεργεσίας,
τὰς γινομένας εἰς ἐμὲ τοῦ κράτους σου παντοίας;
5   Πρό τινος ἤδη πρὸ καιροῦ καὶ πρὸ βραχέος χρόνου,
οὐκ εἶχον οὖν ὁ δύστηος, τὸ τί προσαγαγεῖν σου,
κατάλληλον τῷ κράτει σου καὶ τῇ χρηστότητί σου,
καὶ τῇ περιφανείᾳ σου καὶ χαριτότητί σου,
εἰ μή τινας πολιτικοὺς ἀμέτρους πάλιν στίχους,
10   συνεσταλμένους, παίζοντας, ἀλλ᾽ οὐκ ἀναισχυντῶντες,
παίζουσι γὰρ καὶ γέροντες, ἀλλὰ σωφρονεστέρως10.3
Μὴ οὖν ἀποχωρίσῃς τους, μηδ᾽ ἀποπέμψῃς μᾶλλον,
ὡς κοδιμέντα δέξου τους, ποσῶς ἄν οὐ μυρίζουν,
καὶ φιλευσπλάγχνως ἄκουσον ἄπερ ὁ τάλας γράφω.
15   Κἂν φαίνωμαι γάρ, δέσποτα, γελῶν ὁμοῦ καὶ παίζων,
ἀλλ᾽ ἔχω πόνον ἄπειρον καὶ θλίψιν βαρυτάτην,
καὶ χαλεπὸν ἀρρώστημα, καὶ πάθος, ἀλλὰ πάθος.
Πάθος ἀκούσας τοιγαροῦν μὴ κήλην ὑπολάβῃς,
μηδ᾽ ἄλλο τι χειρότερον ἐκ τῶν μυστικωτέρων,
20   μὴ κερατᾶν τὸ φανερόν, μὴ ταντανοτραγάτην,
μὴ νόσημα καρδιακόν, μὴ περιφλεγμονίαν,
μὴ σκορδαψόν, μηδ᾽ ὕδερον, μὴ παραπνευμονίαν,
ἀλλὰ μαχίμου γυναικὸς πολλὴν εὐτραπελίαν,
προβλήματα προβάλλουσα καὶ πιθανολογίας
25   καὶ τὸ δοκεῖν εὐλόγως μοι προφέρεται πλουτάρχως.

What shall I dedicate to you, lord, crowned lord,
what kind of recompense or favor can I bring
of equal value to your own bright benefactions,
bestowed in every shape upon me from your might?
5   It happened once before—not so very long ago—
that I, poor wretch, had not a thing to offer you,
appropriate to your might and to your godliness,
as also to your pomp and to your graciousness,
except some verses, political unmeasured ones,
10   restrained in playfulness, but not at all indecent,
—for old men too can play, albeit more wisely so.

> Do not then refuse them, or worse, decide to send them back,
> take them as condiments, although they have no smell,
> and hear with pity what I write in my misfortune.
15   Although I seem, lord, to laugh and play at once,
> I am oppressed by endless grief and burdensome affliction,
> by grave indisposition, and suffering—what suffering!
> Hearing of suffering, don't suppose I have a rupture,
> or any of your graver and less obvious troubles:
20   it's no eyesores, plain to see, nor shivering fever either,
> it isn't heartburn, nor inflammation of the lung,
> no shit-face, no dropsy, no bronchial troubles . . . .
> No, I have a nagging wife whose tongue wags on and on,
> pugnaciously parading parapets and predictions,
25   redundantly recounting me the rightness of her cause.

The narrator sets the scene cunningly. The tone sounds cringing, but nothing is quite what it seems. He wants to give "equal recompense" to the "bright benefactions" (λαμπρὰς εὐεργεσίας - shiny new coins?) he has received from his patron in the past (2–3) but undercuts the implied compliment by offering in return his own ambivalent verses (9–10). He begs his patron to *listen to* what he *writes* (ἄκουσον ἅπερ γράφω, 14; cf. τῶν . . . . ἄρτι γραφωμένων, 32), because he can be playful and serious at the same time (γελῶν ὁμοῦ καὶ παίζων, 15), "clowning wisely" with verses that may lack perfume but not spice, thus drawing attention from the outset to the subject of food. Moreover, the speaker is no novice but one who has enjoyed imperial favor in the past and hopes to win it back, for his previous verses in the same style were well received, despite their lowly form.[101] His affliction (πόνον . . . πάθος, 16–17) is real enough, but this time it is no disease, only a wife whose cruelty emboldens him to try a new kind of writing/speaking on his patron. In the epilogue, he describes her crowning insult: he was at last allowed to taste "chunks of meat" (metonymically suggesting sex and coins?) from a recent family hot pot, but only in the guise of a Slavic mendicant! Then he launches into a closing appeal calculated to win his patron's sympathy—and munificence—in a masterstroke of the "politics of hunger":

> Τοιαῦτα πέπονθα δεινά, κρατάρχα στεφηφόρε,
> παρὰ μαχίμου γυναικὸς καὶ τρισαλιτηρίας,
270   ὡς εἶδέ με κενώτατα ἐλθόντα πρὸς τὸν οἶκον.
> Ἂν οὖν μὴ φθάσῃ με τὸ σὸν φιλεύσπλαγνον, αὐτάναξ,
> καὶ δώροις καὶ χαρίσμασι τὴν ἄπληστον ἐμπλήσῃς,

τρέμω, πτοοῦμαι, δέδοικα μὴ φονευθῶ πρὸ ὥρας,
καὶ χάσῃς σου τὸν Πρόδρομον, τὸν κάλλιστον εὐχέτην.

Such were my dread sufferings, almighty crowned lord,
my sore tribulations caused by a warring wife,
270   when she caught me coming home with empty hands.
Unless your loving mercy reaches me, sole ruler,
unless you satisfy her lust for gifts and favors,
I tremble, terror-stricken, lest untimely murder
deprive you of your Prodromos, your best congratulator!

With equal playfulness but boldly connecting politics, economy, and state with literary style and penury, the narrator introduces himself in Poem II "from the same, to the Sebastokrator," as a paterfamilias who, like his patron, the emperor, and Christ himself, needs to keep order in his household.[102] His opening address to a *sebastokrator* from one encircled and entrapped by penury wittily prepares the way for the narrator's plea for money, based on a detailed inventory of his income and expenditure as a careful *oikonómos* (comptroller/householder) with thirteen mouths to feed. Plain speaking is linked with plain living, yet even in his suffering he can offer his patron some benefits in the form of a new—if deviant— "pleasure of words, joy of letters" (ῥημάτων χαρμονήν, γραμμάτων τερποσύνην). Why the elusive references to sitting down with his superior and to his enforced perambulations between palace and church? The motif of unequals sitting together to discuss serious matters has a precedent in the *Odyssey*, where Odysseus' strategies depends on his beggar's disguise as he prepares to sit down to eat his fill, face-to-face with the lowly swineherd, Eumaios (13.429–35; cf. 14. 55–79). The perambulations indicate both the status of one forced to seek alms and the obligations of Christian charity.[103] The closing plea to Poem II follows a complaint that his folks are so hungry that they are forced to eat their own clothes, reminding his patron that he too is dependent—like all mortals—on Christ's continued munificence as *oikonómos* of the universe (101–17).

Poem III is the longest and most discursive, surviving in six manuscripts bearing diverse titles.[104] Now a lowly and abused monk, the narrator, "Hilarion," petitions Manuel I with a long list of complaints about the misdemeanors of those in charge of the Philothei monastery to which he belongs, drawing attention to his own miserable state. In the course of this poem, monastic life—especially its hierarchy—is mercilessly satirized. In the proem, metaphor and metonym playfully disturb the categories of

powerful/powerless, truth/flattery, abundance/deprivation, and inclusion/
exclusion. At the same time they provide a link with the theme of account-
ing, outlined in Poem II: you had better listen carefully to my tale because
I am the first to render you *lógos* "account" of how they are cheating you!
the narrator goes on to specify his complaints against the habits of abbot
and *oikonómos* (too much eating, drinking, and bathing), emphasizing his
own confinement, starvation, and exclusion. He ends with an ambivalent
hint that the emperor of the *Oikouménē* "inhabited world" is no less dependent on the mercy of his own intermediary, Saint George (champion in
battle), before his ultimate lord, Christ himself.

Poem IV is also addressed to the Emperor Manuel.[105] The proem (absent
from G, but transmitted in short form by g and at greater length by CSA),
recalls Proem III in the oppositions evoked between power and powerless-
ness, abundance and deprivation, truth and flattery, inclusion and exclusion,
but this time in three manuscripts (CSA) there is explicit reference to three
historical figures—"Nouradenos," "Melias," and "Neeman,"—who did indeed challenge Manuel's "quadruply august" imperial rule, and, by implication, the emperor's share in the four parts of the Holy Cross, in terms
which cannot be dismissed as post-twelfth-century interpolations. The four
proems to Poem IV are unusual: each manuscript transmits a different version, ranging from none (G), eight lines (g, replicating almost word for
word the proems to III in H and g), to no less than fifty-five lines in the
later manuscripts (CSA). Unlike the other three proems, none here points
us to the narrative content of the fourth poem—the plight of the starving
scholar. Were they set pieces, composed between 1172 and 1181 and
adapted as proems to the fourth poem in the early 1170's (around the time
of Prodromos' death)?[106] If so, that would give us a *terminus ante quem* of
1181 for the compilation of the four Ptochoprodromic Poems in their extant forms.

The narrating persona of Poem IV is a scholar or teacher (*gram-
matikós*), whose education and learning have earned him nothing but
starvation and exclusion, in contrast to the craftsmen and common artisans, workmen and street women of Constantinople who eat and drink,
have sex and leisure, in better style than he does, in contrast to his own
father's promises of wealth in return for "learning his letters". He closes
his story of street encounters and humiliations with an appeal, first to his
"cloak of penury", purple with the blood of his own lice-bitten state
(g), then to his emperor, "born in the purple", with pleas for money in a
parody of the Lord's Prayer. Denied his "daily bread" by all his fathers, he
now demands succor, just as the emperor needs to be rescued from his

foes in battle by the four patron saints of war, who also happen to figure on the obverse of Manuel's coins.[107]

In all proems, the addresses to imperial personages seem direct, yet prove ambivalent: Is the narrator speaking or writing? Serious or playful? Flamboyant use is made of the rhetoric of hesitation (How can an inferior dare to address his superior?) in terms of praise (*épainos*); yet this rhetorical device, common to the *enkōmion* "praise" and *epitaphios logos* "funeral oration," serves to mask his boldness in introducing the *psógos* "blame" implicit in the narrated dialogues. Interventions to his patron remind us of the inequality of status between addresser and addressee, while epilogues repeat, often with an anecdote, the gist of the complaint in order to clinch demands for favors, with a veiled threat of the consequences of refusal.

So much for the frames. In the main part of the poems, the narrator invents episodes, themes, and encounters as appropriate to the persona he has adopted. In Poem I his major confrontation is with his wife, so he starts by giving us a taste of her tongue; in twelve years of marriage, he has brought her no new dresses, ornaments, or jewelry, only imperial castoffs. In the meantime he has squandered her dowry, leaving their children destitute, apart from some old pots and pans he brought from his parents' household.

> ἔχεις με χρόνους δώδεκα ψυχροὺς καὶ ἀσβολωμένους,
> οὐκ ἔβαλα ἀπὸ κόπου σου τατίκιν εἰς ποδάριν,
> 50 οὐκ ἔβαλα εἰς τὸ ράχιν μου μεταξωτὸν ἱμάτιν,
> οὐκ εἶδα εἰς τὸ δακτύλιν μου κρικέλιν δακτυλίδιν,
> οὐδὲ βραχιόλιν με ἔφερες ποτὲ νὰ τὸ φορέσω.
> Οἱ ξένοι κατακόπτουσι τὰ γονικά μου ροῦχα,
> καὶ ἐγὼ καθέζομαι γυμνὴ καὶ παραπονεμένη.
> 55 Ποτὲ οὐκ ἐλούθην εἰς λουτρὸν νὰ μὴ στραφῶ θλιμμένη,
> ἡμέραν οὐκ ἐχόρτασα, νὰ μὴ πεινάσω δύο,
> στενάζω πάντοτε, θρηνῶ καὶ κόπτομαι καὶ κλαίω.
> Τὴν θάλασσαν τὴν μὲ ἔφερες, γνωρίζεις, ἔπαρέ την·
> τὸ διβλαντάριν τὸ κουτνίν, καὶ τὸ ὑψηλὸν διβίκιν,
> 60 καὶ τὸ μεγαλογράμματον ἱμάτιν τὸ κνηκᾶτον,
> ἢ χάρισον, ἢ πώλησον, ἢ δὸς ὁποῦ κελεύεις·
> τὰ λουτρικὰ τὰ μὲ ἔποικες καὶ τὸ κραββατοστρῶσιν
> εἰς κλῆρον νὰ τὰ δέξονται οἱ παῖδες σου πατρῷον·
> τὰ γονικά σου πράγματα καὶ ἡ οἰκοσκευή σου
> 65 ἀρκοῦν τὰς θυγατέρας σου νὰ τὰς ἐξωπροικίσῃς·
> καὶ σὺ ἃς εἶσαι σιγηρὸς καὶ ἀσπομεριμνημένος.
> Ἐπεντρανίζεις, ἄνθρωπε, κἂν ὅλως θεωρεῖς με;

ἐγὼ ἤμην ὑποληπτικὴ καὶ σὺ ἤσουν ματζουκᾶτος·
ἐγὼ ἤμην εὐγενικὴ καὶ σὺ πτωχὸς πολίτης,
70   σὺ εἶσαι Πτωχοπρόδρομος καὶ ἐγὼ ἤμην Ματζουκίνη,
σὺ ἐκοιμῶ εἰς τὸ ψιαθὶν καὶ ἐγὼ εἰς τὸ κλινάριν·
ἐγὼ εἶχον προῖκα περισσήν, καὶ σὺ εἶχες ποδο[.....]
καὶ σκάφην τοῦ ζυμώματος καὶ μέγαν πυροστάτην.

—You've kept me twelve long years—and all were cold and dreary:
not a single sandal to wear upon my feet,
50   not once a silken gown to drape around my shoulders,
I've never seen a fine knurled ring to set upon my finger,
not once did you bring home a bracelet for my arm.
Strangers have made shreds of the clothes my parents gave me,
while I sit here complaining, with nothing to put on.
55   Not one visit to the bathhouse, but I get back depressed;
not a decent meal on one day, but then I starve for two,
All day I moan and groan, weep and wail and beat my breast!
Now, that court robe you brought me—guess what—take it back!
and the woolen silk robe with double fringes, and that long thing too,
60   and the cloak that's dyed, with large emblazoned figures,
give them away, sell them off, or hand on where you like!
Those bath wraps you had made for me, the bed cover as well,
why not give them to your sons as their father's portion?
All those goods and utensils you brought here from your parents,
65   they'll do nicely for your daughters when you dower them off,
so long as you keep safe with not a care to vex you!
Why gaze so into space—can't you look me in the eye?
I was of good household, you just a common soldier;
I was of noble stock, you were just a pauper;
70   you are poor old Prodromos, I came from Matsouka,
you used to sleep on mats of straw, I slept on a bed;
I brought dowry gifts in plenty, you just errand [tips;]
I brought gold and silverware, you your scrubbing boards,
one board for kneading dough and one big cooking pot.

Beneath the comic topoi, we may glimpse some fascinating insights into
Komnene society, with some double-edged ironies: Women now scoff at
the rich garments, given out as favors by imperial patrons to their retainers;
they demand instead luxury items which can be bought only for cash, as
appropriate to their (alleged) superior economic status.[108]

What is worse, he just sits around, waiting to be fed, letting the house fall
into disrepair.

75   Καθέζεσαι εἰς τὸ ὁσπίτιν μου, καὶ ἐνοίκιον οὐ φροντίζεις,
     τὰ μάρμαρα ἠφανίσθησαν, ὁ πάτος συνεπτώθη,
     τὰ κεραμίδια ἐλύθησαν, τὸ στέγος ἐσαπρώθη,
     οἱ τοῖχοι καταπίπτουσιν, ἐξεχερσώθη ὁ κῆπος,
     κοσμήτης οὐκ ἀπέμεινεν οὐ γύψος, οὐδὲ σπέτλον,
80   οὐδὲ ρηγλὶν μαρμάρινον, οὐ συγκοπὴ μετρία,
     αἱ θύραι συνεστράφησαν ἐξ ὁλοκλήρου πᾶσαι,
     τὰ κάγκελα ἐξηλώθησαν ἀπ' ἄκρας ἕως ἄκραν,
     καὶ τὰ στηθαῖα ἔπεσον τὰ πρὸς τὸ περιβόλιν.
     Θύραν οὐκ ἤλλαξάς ποτε, σανίδιν οὐκ εὐψύχει,
85   ποτὲ οὐκ ἐξεκεράμωσας, οὐδὲ ἀνερράψω τοῖχον,
     οὐ τέκτονα ἐκάλεσας ἵνα τὸν περιρράψῃ,
     οὔτε καρφὶν ἠγόρασας νὰ ἐμπήξῃς εἰς σανίδιν.

75   You sit in my house, but pay no heed to upkeep:
     the marbles are worn and faded, the floor has sagged,
     the tiles are dangling loose, the roof's completely rotten,
     nothing is left of all the lettering, plaster, glass,
80   nor of marble cornices nor finely-wrought mosaics,
     the walls are tumbling down, the garden has run wild,
     while the doors have all turned inside out from warping,
     the banisters are hanging loose from end to end,
     the outside parapets have fallen inward to the garden.
     You've never changed a door, there isn't a sound floorboard,
85   you've never changed a tile, nor yet repaired a wall;
     you haven't even called a builder in to fix it,
     nor bought a single nail to knock into a floorboard!

She claims she does all the chores and runs the household and estate as well;
she makes linen, cotton, and woolen garments from raw materials to finished product and attends to the family's religious duties (90–101), doing a
man's job as well as a wife's, insinuating his impotence, laziness, and homosexuality.

At this point, he reminds his patron that this is only a brief excerpt from
her insults, not the whole tale (113–22), never losing sight of his main
ploy—to use his wife's treatment of him to get a pay increase. He describes
the incident that caused her latest outrage: one night he came home (somewhat the worse for drink) from the palace with a crowd of riotous friends,

demanding to be fed, and what did she do?—locked him out of pantry and bedroom! (123–54). What follows is pure slapstick, with sexual innuendos: powerless as he is to give her a thrashing, he battles through the bedroom keyhole with a broomstick, only to get hurled down onto the pavement when she suddenly releases her hold on her end.

'Ὡς δ' οὐδὲ ῥάβδον ἐφευρεῖν ὁ τάλας ἠδυνήθην,
ἀπαίρω τὸ σκουπόρραβδον γοργὸν ἀπὸ τὴν χρείαν,
παρακαλῶν, εὐχόμενος, καὶ δυσωπῶν καὶ λέγων·
175   —Πανάχραντέ μου, κράτει την, ἐμπόδιζε, Χριστέ μου,
μὴ παίξῃ κοντογύρισμα καὶ ἐπάρῃ τὸ ῥαβδίν μου,
καὶ δώσῃ καὶ ποιήσῃ με στραβὸν παρὰ διαβόλου.
Ὡς δὴ αὐτή, θεόστεπτε, πρὸ τῶν λοιπῶν ἁπάντων,
καὶ τὸ ψωμὶν ἐκλείδωσε καὶ τὸ κρασὶν ἐντάμα,
180   φεύγει, λανθάνει, κρύπτεται, καὶ κλείσασα τὴν θύραν,
ἐκάθισεν ἀμέριμνος καὶ ἐμὲ ἀφέκεν ἔξω.
Κρατῶν δὲ τὸ σκουπόρραβδον, τὴν θύραν ἀπηρξάμην·
ὡς δ' ἠγανανάκτησα λοιπὸν κρούων σφοδρῶς τὴν θύραν
εὑρὼν ὁπὴν ἐσέβασα τ' ἄκρον τοῦ σκουπορράβδου·
185   ἐκείνη δὲ πηδήσασα καὶ τούτου δραξαμένη
ἐταύριζεν ἀπέσωθεν, ἐγὼ δὲ πάλιν ἔξω·
ὡς δ' ἔγνω ὅτι δύναμαι καὶ στερεὰ τὴν σύρω,
χαυνίζει τὸ σκουπόρραβδον, τὴν θύραν παρανοίγει,
καὶ παρ' ἐλπίδα κατὰ γῆς καταπεσὼν ἡπλώθην.
190   'Ὡς δ' εἶδεν ὅτι ἔπεσον, ἤρξατο τοῦ γελᾶν με,
ἐκβαίνει καὶ σηκώνει με γοργὸν ἀπὸ τοῦ πάτου,
καὶ τάχα κολακεύουσα τοιαῦτα προσεφώνει·
—'Ἐντρέπου, κύρι, νὰ σωθῇς - ἐντρέπου κἂν ὀλίγον,
οὐκ εἶσαι χωρικούτσικον, οὐδὲ μικρὸν νινίτσιν·
195   κατάλειψον τὴν δύναμιν, τὴν περισσὴν ἀνδρείαν.
καὶ φρόνει—καλοκαίριν ἕν, τίμα τοὺς κρείττονάς σου,
καὶ μὴ παλλικαρεύεσαι, μηδὲ λαξοφαρδεύῃς.

Well—as I couldn't even find a staff, poor wretch,
I quickly grabbed the broomstick from the privy,
pleading, beseeching, and crying out in misery:
175   —All-immaculate one, control her, stop the bitch, my Christ,
or else she'll turn around and take my stick away,
then use it to beat me more crooked than the Devil!
As for herself, God-crowned one, before what next transpired,
she had placed all the bread and wine under lock and key;

180   sneaking furtively away, she closed the door behind her,
       and, leaving me outside, she just sat there regardless.
       With the broomstick in my hands, I stole behind her door;
       just as I got tired of banging hard upon the door,
       I found a little hole, and slipped inside my stick end:
185   In quick response she got up and held fast onto my stick;
       we kept on shafting, she from inside, me from outside.
       Just as I knew my potency and I had her firmly grasped,
       she came, loosened on the broomstick, set the door ajar,
       and there I was, quite suddenly, stretched out on the ground.
190   When she saw I'd fallen down, she started mocking me,
       as she came to help me up from the ground where I was lying;
       feigning loving care, here is what she said:
       —Shame on you, husband, on your life! Have you no pride?
       You are no village tomboy, nor no whining baby.
195   Leave off your potency, your excessive manliness,
       and have the sense—it's summer time!—to respect your betters,
       stop trying to play the hero, stop your bellowing howls!

At this point, one of their sons falls "from on high," giving our narrator the
chance to sneak into the pantry and steal food, while street women ped-
dling in magic (μανδραγούραι) put him to shame by restoring his son to
life, an insult crowned only by his wife's exclusion of him from her bedroom (204–22). His children turn on him, give him a thrashing, and offer
him a place at the evening meal as a barely comprehensible Slavic beggar
(253–67).[109]

   These extracts from Poem I show how cleverly the narrator interweaves
abusive dialogue, episodic diversion, and slapstick comedy with interjections to his addressee. It may be surmised that many of the comic topoi
here derive from the popular genre of "verses against women." If so, the
misogyny is double-edged, since even this biased perspective allows us to
note the contrast between the competent, ambitious housewife and her
lazy, drunken husband, an imperial hanger-on, with more care for his belly
than for the safety of his own child, who might not have fallen had the roof
not been rotten.

   Tactics in Poem II are similar, but the narrator addresses dialogue to his
patron in terms suggesting as model genre a last testament in its itemization
of incoming funds and outgoing expenditures, as well as a closing intima-
tion of his death. The narrator appropriates discourse used against him by
the impossible wife of Poem I and directs it—albeit more politely—to his
patron. The irony of this inventory lies in the fact that many of the desider-

ata, listed as basic to family subsistence, were not only prized luxuries in the twelfth century but also include some commodities that the nagging wife of Poem I so unjustifiably demanded: goods available for ready cash. Just as Poem I ends with the tall story of the child who fell from on high to be miraculously resurrected by street women, so we close with the starvation symptoms displayed by his own children. A paterfamilias unable even to provide his family with food is ungendered, and once again, the dangerous magic of astrology and drugs is implicated (Poem II, Lines, 83–94).[110]

Poems III and IV are the longest, but their rhetorical strategies are similar. The humor of III lies in the narrator's juxtaposition of opposites—luxury and want—in matters of bathing, eating, and caring, with connotations of his masters' homosexuality in the bathtub and gluttony at table and of his own lack of freedom of speech and action. First, he is told to stop stealing food so that he can bathe his superiors:

Κομμάτιν, βλέπω, ἀπέδειρας τρανὸν καὶ γωνιδᾶτον
καὶ μαγειρίαν τριπίνακον καὶ τρία κομμάτια θύνναν,
105   καὶ πλύσιμον οὐ δέχεται κἄν ὅλως τὸ πινάκιν,
καὶ ἄφες τρώγειν τὰ πολλά. ν' ἀλέθης πασπαλᾶτα·
ἄπελθε, εὐθείασε θερμὸν καὶ νίψον τοὺς πατέρας.
σπούδασον, φθάσον, πέτασον γοργὸν ἐπὶ τὸν μύλον·
ἐρώτησε εἰς τὸ διάβα σου ἐπὶ τοὺς Βενετίκους
110   τὸ πῶς πωλεῖται τὸ τυρίν, τί ἔχει τὸ κεντηνάριν·
ὕπαγε, λοῦσε σύντομον τὸν μέγαν οἰκονόμον,
λοῦσε καὶ τὸν ἡγούμενον, παράστα καὶ τοὺς δύο.
Ἐν μέρει κράζει ὁ ἡγούμενος, ἐν μέρει ὁ οἰκονόμος,
ὁ μὲν προστάττει·-Τρίψε με καὶ τάρασσε τὸ σκάμμα·
115   ὁ δ' ἄλλος πάλιν·-Γέμισε, περίχυσέ με, ἃς ἔβγω·
καὶ σὺν ἐκείνους ἔρχεται τρίτος ὁ ἐκκλησιάρχης.

—You have sliced off, I see, a huge corner piece
and a three-plate meal and three slices of tuna,
105   so the dish doesn't even need a rinsing,
stop eating so much, go and grind fine flour;
off with you, prepare hot water and wash the fathers,
hurry now, get on with it, fast to the mill;
and just ask on your way there in the Venetian quarter
110   —what's the price of cheese, how much the hundredweight?
go bath the great bursar [oikonómos] instantly,
and bath the abbot too, attend to both at once.
On one side shouts the abbot, on the other the bursar;

one orders—Rub me up and stir the suds,
115   the other again—Fill up, pour over me, I'm getting out!
—and along with them here comes the third, the ecclesiarch.

Food and sex are interlinked; while the monastic hierarchy indulges on a grand scale, the poor narrator and his likes are deprived even of the sick monk's diet. Their respective dishes are described with a precision tantamount to recipes. First comes the rich *bourride*:

Μετὰ γοῦν τὴν παράθεσιν ὧν εἴρηκα βρωμάτων
175   εἰσῆλθεν, ὦ τοῦ θαύματος, καὶ τὸ μονοκυθρίτσιν.
ὑπεραχλίζον ὁ λίγον καὶ πέμπον εὐωδίαν.
Εἰ βούλει, πάλιν μάνθανε καὶ τὰ τοῦ μονοκύθρου·
κραμβὶν καρδίας τέσσαρας, χοντρὰς καὶ χιονάτας,
καὶ ξιφοτράχηλον παστόν, κυπριναρίου μέσην,
180   γλαύκους καλούς κἂν εἴκοσι, ἀπάκια βερζιτίκου,
ὠὰ κἂν δεκατέσαρα καὶ κρητικὸν τυρίτσιν,
ἀπότυρα κἂν τέσσαρα καὶ βλάχικον ὀλίγον,
καὶ λίτραν τὸ χριστέλαιον, πεπέριν φοῦκταν μίαν,
σκόρδα κεφάλια δώδεκα καὶ τσίρους δεκαπέντε,
185   καὶ ἀπαλαρέα μουχρούτινον γλυκὺν κρασὶν ἐπάνω,
καὶ ἀνακομπώματα τρανά, καὶ βλέπε τότε βούκκας.
Αἴ, τσοῦκκα ὁποῦ τὰ ἐβάστασεν! πῶς οὐκ ἐσχίσθη μέσα;
ἐκείνη βαπτιστῆρα ἦτον, ἐκείνη τσοῦκκα οὐκ ἦτον.
Ἐκίνησαν τὰ σάλια μου· χριστέ, νὰ τὴν ἐπιάσα.
190   Χριστέ, νὰ τὴν ἐπέπεσα καθὰ ἦτον φουσκωμένη,
νὰ ἐκάθισα εἰς τὸ πλάγιν της, νὰ ἠρξάμην ρουκανίζειν,
νὰ ἐχρίσθη τὸ μουστάκιν μου, νὰ ἐχόρταοα λιγδίτσαν,
καὶ τότε νὰ εἶδες, δέσποτα, πηδήματα νεωτέρου,
καὶ καλογέρου ταπεινοῦ γυρίσματα καὶ κρότους.

So then, after the array of foods I've spoken of
175   there enters, o what a miracle, the stewpot,
gently steaming and sending out a lovely smell.
If you will, learn also now about the stew:
four cabbage hearts, thick and snowy white,
with salted swordfish, ?inner part of bream?/?cleaned cuttlefish,
180   up to twenty grey mullet, best smoked back bacon from Vertzidikia,
around fourteen eggs and some Cretan cheese,
a good four soft fresh cheeses and a bit of Vlach cheese,
a liter of refined [anointing] oil and a handful of pepper,

185
twelve whole bulbs of garlic and fifteen salted spring mackerel,
and a platter with a jug of sweet wine on top of it,
then great girding of the loins for action, just see their mouths
    agape!
Ai, what a dish it was that held them! How did it not break inside?
That was a baptismal font, that was no cooking pot.
My mouth was watering: Christ, if I could have seized it,

190
Christ, if I could have fallen on it, swelling as it was,
and sat down by its side, begun to dig my teeth in,
get my beard anointed, have my fill of grease,
then you would have seen, lord, the leapings of a novice,
the dance turns and rumbles of a humble monk.

Then comes the "viral swill."

290
Ἡμεῖς δὲ νῦν ἐσθίομεν καθόλου τὸ ἁγιοζοῦμιν,
καὶ σκόπει τοῦ ὀνόματος αὐτοῦ τὴν ποικιλίαν·
κακκάβιν ἔνι δίωτον, ὡσεὶ μετρῶν τεσσάρων,
καὶ ἕως ἄνω οἱ μάγειροι γεμίζουσι τὸ ὕδωρ.
καὶ πῦρ ἐξάπτουσι πολὺ κατὰ τοῦ κακκαβίου.

295
καὶ βάλλουσι κρομμύδια κἂν εἴκοσι καλολέοντας.
καὶ τότε, βλέπε, δέσποτα, καλὴν φιλοτιμίαν·
εἰς κλῆσιν γὰρ βαπτίζονται τριάδος τῆς ἁγίας.
στάζει γὰρ τρεῖς τὸ ἔλαιον ὁ μάγειρος ἀπέσω,
καὶ βάλλει καὶ θρυμβόξυλα τινὰ πρὸς μυρωδίαν

300
καὶ τὸν ζωμὸν ἐκχέει τον ἐπάνω τῶν ψωμίων.
καὶ δίδουν μας καὶ τρώγομεν καὶ λέγεται ἁγιοζοῦμιν.
Νεύω τὸν συψωμίτην μου, σύρω τον ἐκ τὸ ἱμάτιν.
λέγω τον.—τί ἔν τὸ τρώγομεν· καὶ λέγει με—ιοζούμιν·
καὶ πίστευσον, οὐ ψεύδεται, μᾶλλον εὐστόχως λέγει.

305
τῶν γὰρ κρομμύων δάκνει με συντόμως ἡ δριμύτης.
καὶ ὁ ἰὸς τοῦ λέβητος ἐπάνω πρασινίζει.

290
Meanwhile we get nothing but fasting broth to eat,
—just think of the diversity in that name:
a two-handled pot, four meters wide,
filled to the brim with water by the cooks,
then the pot is fiercely heated from beneath,

295
and they add onions—up to twenty rings of them,
then just see, lord, their good generosity;
for they do their baptisms in the name of the Holy Trinity:

the cook sprinkles in three drops of oil,
adding savory bits and pieces just for flavor,
300   then he pours the liquid over breaded slices,
—that's what they give us to eat for fasting broth.
I nudge my fellow eater, I tug his robe,
asking—What are we eating? He tells me—viral swill!
Believe you me, he tells no lie, he's got it spot on,
305   for the sour taste of onions bites into me at once
while the rust on the saucepan turns to verdigris on top.

The thinly veiled blasphemy inherent in the narrator's comparison between cooking pot and baptismal font to indicate the huge size of the hi-
erarchs' rich repast, on the one hand, and the watery, rusting contents of his
own, on the other, is offset by his constant reminders to the emperor that
his superiors violate the rules of the monastic typika, and therefore
he urges Manuel to act at once (33–35, 129–30, 164–66, 225–33, 234–50,
251–62, 273–89, 367–84, 401–19). The poem's structure may appear discursive, but it bears close resemblance to the typika: "Hilarion" appropriates
the discourse of his oppressors to convince his patron of the rightness of
his cause.[111]

As in Poem I, things are not so simple: in a lengthy episode, Hilarion
complains that he and his fellow novices are obliged to tell blatant lies to
get permission to leave the monastery (326–44). Beaton has argued on
the basis of this passage that the poem can be read as a character study
(ēthopoiēia) of the "naughty monk", who always wants to go off "downtown" when he should be in his cell, contemplating God. Beaton has a
point; but he fails to measure this "peccadillo" against the monstrous transgressions of Hilarion's superiors nor does he take account of the relative
freedom accorded to cenobitic monks in the twelfth century both by the
typika and by the casual monastic plan, which sometimes afforded direct
access from cell to street. What the poem does show is the urgent need
for monastic reform, particularly in matters relating to the inequalities of
status (348–65).[112]

Having dealt elsewhere with Poem IV, I shall try here to summarize
some of the ways in which traditional comic personae and topoi—familiar from Aristophanes, Menander, and Roman comedy to the twelfth
century—have been recombined to produce a new, vernacular version of
the "starving scholar." The narrator's presentation of his station as gram-
matikós is ambivalent. Had he been required to provide no more than
rudimentary literacy and knowledge of basic scriptures and religious

texts, his complaints of poverty would have aroused little surprise or sympathy.[113] However, he claims knowledge of secular learning—such as ancient myths (1bbb), learned verse and meter (71–77, 82), Homer, Libanios, Oppian, and the classics (213–23), as well as philosophy (255)—and would thereby qualify as a teacher of the second cycle of Byzantine education (esōthen paideia and enkyklios paideia, internal or encyclical learning). At the same time, references to the priesthood (137–40, 173) are consistent with the teacher of the highest stage (exōthen paideia, or hiera grammata, external learning, or holy letters). In this way our narrator's plight draws attention to the poverty not just of the lowliest teaching or professions but also of all those forced to earn a living from their education.[114]

Comic topoi can be deceptive, traditional in form but contemporary in target. We have noted from the proems our author's strategy of blurring the boundaries between high and low. Although Byzantinists have no trouble identifying classical allusions in such texts as the Timarion, the learned romances, or even the satirical poems (composed in elevated meter), there is an unspoken presupposition that anyone who employs the vulgar style cannot have known Homer or Aristophanes, despite the fact that Eustathios' commentaries on the former and Tzetzes' scholia on the latter were widely discussed and Plato was read (if upside down!) by the man in the street. Comic topoi in our four poems are dismissed, either as "universal" (even when they have a textual history stretching back to Homer) or as "later interpolations" by scribes influenced by popular tradition.[115] May they not suggest simultaneous exploitation of learned and popular elements in a newly "coined" vernacular?

How are these topoi integrated into the structure of the four poems; and what are the resonances in literary and popular tradition?[116] First, language, style, and learning: In the proems, the myths of the ancients and the rhetoric of learning are linked with lies and flattery, in contrast to the "plain fare" that is all our impoverished narrators can offer as the "main course" of the poems. Plainness not only promises truth but also constitutes the pleasure of writing, if not of living, because baseness and ugliness are more concretely depicted in the vernacular than in the learned language. Learning brings poverty and distress; the "craftsman of letters" is unable to earn even his daily bread. Many words for everyday items have disappeared from "common modern Greek", but live on in dialect usage.

Second, as for crafts, in Poem IV our scholar emphasizes his role as "craftsman of the word" (τεχνίτης τοῦ λόγου), then goes on to compare his lot with other sedentary craftsmen (gold embroiderer, cobbler, and tailor) who, like him, use hand and implement (pen and ink; awl, strigil, and thread; needle and scissors) to work on processed material (paper, cloth and gold, leather, fabric). But they make things to wear, whereas he weaves empty verses. Their mouths, pockets, and cupboards are "stuffed" (γέμειν); his are empty. Excluded from their lifestyle, he takes to the streets, where he meets local vendors: a yogurt seller, porter, baker's wife, and butcher's wife. They sell their wares and fill their bellies but keep him away. Three grades of goods are implied—first, middle, and third, in descending order of merit—with clear links between the three categories and social prestige: our scholar is at the bottom (IV.21). [117] All four poems invert the "natural" order, as husband and courtier, respectable family man, humble monk, and impoverished scholar each prove that the baser craftsmen and street vendors live better than a writer, whose implements and rhetoric become the instruments of abasement and self-abuse (I, IV).

Writing, clothes, and food. The narrator's appeal to his *kappa* (cloak/chapel/tenth letter of the Greek alphabet) at the close of Poem IV sums up the scholar's dilemma and is worth citing in full as an example of the interaction between learned and popular traditions. Transmitted in only one of the later manuscripts (g), it has been dismissed as an interpolation:

Κάππα μου, πάλιν κάππα μου, παλαιοχαρβαλωμένη,
κάππα μου, ὄνταν σ' ἔθεκεν ἡ Βλάχα νὰ σὲ φάνη,
260   πολλὰ δάκρυα σὲ γέμισεν καὶ στεναγμοὺς μεγάλους.
'Εσέν' ἔχω καὶ πάπλωμαν, κάππα, καὶ ἀπανωφόριν,
ἐσέναν καὶ ποκάμισον, ἐσέν' καὶ ἐπιβαλτάριν.
Καὶ τὴν λαμπρὴν τὴν κυριακὴν στὴν ἐκκλησιὰν ἂν πάγω,
ὅλους χωρεῖ ἡ ἐκκλησιὰ καὶ μὲν οὐδὲν ἐχώρει.
265   καὶ ἀπὸ τὸ σεῖσμαν τὸ πολὺν καὶ τὸ πολὺ τὸ διῶμαν.
ἐπαίρνω, πάγω, βασιλεῦ, στὸ σπίτιν ὑπαγαίνω,
τὸ σπίτιν, τὸ παλαιόσπιτον, τὸ καινουργιοχαλασμένον.
Νυστάζω, πέφτω τάχατε, τυλίγομαι τὴν κάππαν,
κοιμοῦμαι ὡς τὸ μεσάνυκτον, καὶ ἄκου' τί παθαίνω·
270   ἐμπλέκουνται μ' οἱ ψεῖρες μου ἄνωθεν ἕως κάτω,
καὶ βάνω τὸ χερίτσιν μου, συντρίβω καὶ τσακίζω,
ἐβγάνω τ' ὁλοκόκκινον, νᾶπες βαφέαν ὁμοιάζω.
Κάππα μου, ὅπου δύναται, κάππα μου, ἅς σὲ ἀγοράση,
κάππα μου ἠγανάκτησα, κάππα, τὰς χάριτάς σου.

Cloak, again my cloak, my shabby old ruin,
my cloak, when the Vlach woman set you up to weave you,
260   she filled you with many tears and with deep groans besides.
You are all I have for rug, for cloak, for jacket.
And on an Easter Sunday, if I go to church,

265
the church has room for everyone, but none at all for me,
and from much swaying and from much swaggering
I take my leave, I depart, emperor, I make for home,
to my home, my old house, which recently collapsed.
I feel drowsy, go to lie down, snug in my rug,
sleeping till midnight—then listen to what I suffer:
270
I am crawling with lice from head to foot,
so I put in my hand, I scratch and I scrunch,
I pull it out all red, as though I were a fuller.
Cloak, whoever has the means, my cloak, let him buy you,
my cloak, I am worn out by your charms.

Formulaic structures here can be paralleled in folk songs and vernacular literature. The following folk song provides an exact *contextual* parallel with our passage: a poor man or woman in debt addresses a barren vineyard and threatens to sell it off; the vineyard replies that the owner need only cultivate it properly for it to bear fruit.[118]

—'Αμπέλι μου πλατύφυλλο καὶ κοντοκλαδεμένο,
τί δὲν καρπεῖς, τί δὲν ἀνθεῖς, τί δὲν κάνεις σταφύλια;
'Αμπέλι μου μ' ἐχρέωσες καὶ θέλα σε πουλήσω.
—Μή με πουλεῖς, ἀφέντη μου, καὶ μή με παζαρεύεις.
Μόν' βάλε νιοὺς στὸ σκάψιμο, γερόντους εἰς τὸν κλάδο,
βάλε κορίτσια ἀπάρθενα νὰ με κεφαλοδέσουν,
νὰ βάλεις καὶ μικρὰ παιδιὰ νὰ με βλαστολογήσουν,
τότε να ἰδεῖς, ἀφέντη μου, σταφύλια ποὺ θὰ κάνω.
                              (Politis, *Laog.*1 (1909):1, 274 no.70, cf. 60–72)

My vineyard, broad-leaved and close-pruned,
why don't you bear fruit or blossom, why don't you make grapes?
My vineyard, you have brought me into debt, so I will sell you off.
—Don't sell me off, my master, and don't barter me.
Just set young men to digging, old men to pruning,
and put young virgin girls to bind up my head,
and small children to gather my blooms,
then just see, my master, the grapes I'll make for you!

The lice-infested cloak of Poverty, Poetry, and Prophecy as interchangeable with the purple cloak of Power can be traced back to Aristophanes' *Ploutos* (537–47) and to Homer's *Odyssey*, where Odysseus depends on his beggar's disguise to plot with his swineherd Eumaios, as they sit on thick rugs (ῥώπας...δασείας), the downfall of the haughty purple-cloaked suitors.[119] There are good historical reasons for attributing the origins, if not the precise form, of this passage to the later twelfth century, when the figure four, so prominent in the proems, was associated both with tetraugust metaphors of imperial power and with the prophecy—current since the birth of Alexios II in 1169—that the Komnene dynasty would rule so long as the first letter of the emperors' names spelled the four-letter word, A-I-M-A (= "blood"). The sequence runs Alexios I (1081–1118); Ioannes II (1118–43); Manuel I (1143–80); Alexios II (1180–83); Andronikos I (1183–85). The figure four is developed in the closing address, which is a parody of the Lord's Prayer.[120] It refers to the four soldier saints, and is taken up from the proem, where the tetraugust metaphor is linked with the motif of the Cross, which is particularly relevant to Manuel's porphyrogenital state: he is the fourth son, while "Kappa" is the fourth letter of a five-part Cross monogram on the obverse of Manuel I's coins that our poet so much covets:

M[anue-]
D[espotes Porphyrogennetos] K[omnenos]
L
M[ανουη-]
Δ[εσπότης -Πορφυρογέννητος ο] Κ[ομνηνός]
Λ

275   'Αλλ' ὦ κομνηνοβλάστητον ἀπὸ πορφύρας ῥόδον,
βασιλευόντων βασιλεῦ, καὶ τῶν ἀνάκτων ἄναξ,
καὶ κράτος τὸ τρισκράτιστον μητρόθεν καὶ πατρόθεν,
εἰσάκουσόν μου τῆς φωνῆς καὶ τῆς δεήσεώς μου,
θύραν ἐλέους ἄνοιξον καὶ χεῖρα πάρασχέ με,
280   ἀνάγουσαν ἐκ βόθρου με, λάκκου τοῦ τῆς πενίας.
Σὺ γὰρ ἐλέους οἰκτιρμῶν μετὰ θεὸν ἡ θύρα,
σὺ μόνος ὑπερασπιστὴς τῶν ἐν ἀνάγκαις βίου,
σὺ καὶ τὸ καταφύγιον πάντων τῶν χριστωνύμων,
285   ῥῦσαί με τῆς στερήσεως, ῥῦσαί με τῆς πενίας,
τῶν δανειστῶν μου, βασιλεῦ, λῦσον τὰς ἀπαιτήσεις,
οὐδὲ γὰρ φέρειν δύναμαι τὰς τούτων κατακρίσεις.
Τοὺς τέσσαρας προβάλλομαι, θεόστεπτε μεσίτας,
τοὺς μαρτηρήσαντες στερρῶς ὑπὲρ Χριστοῦ τοῦ λόγου,
290   Γεώργιον, Δημήτριον, Τύρωνα, Στρατηλάτην,
οἳ καὶ συνταξειδεύσωσιν ἐν πᾶσι ταξειδίοις
καὶ συνοδοιπορήσωσιν τῇ σῇ θεοστεφίᾳ.

275   But, o rose from the purple offshoot of the Komnenes,
emperor of all who reign, and ruler of rulers,

and might thrice-mighty on mother and father's sides,
hear my voice and heed my prayer,
open unto me the gate of mercy, lend me your hand,
280   lead me out of the cesspit and the sewer of penury.
For you, after God, are the gate to sympathy and mercy,
you are the only protector of those who live in need,
you are the shelter of all Christians,
you are the Emperor of Emperors and Lord of all,
285   deliver me from want, deliver me from penury,
resolve, Emperor, the demands of my creditors,
for I cannot withstand their accusations.
O divinely crowned one, I call on the four mediators,
who were bravely martyred for Christ the Word,
290   Georgios, Demetrios, Tyron, Stratelates,
that they may travel with you on all your journeys,
and accompany the path of your God-crowned grace.

It is impossible to prove allusion to the texts I have mentioned, although the coins can be dated.[121] If Theodore Prodromos is our author, there is no difficulty in accepting his use of Homeric and Aristophanic nuances to back up his plea for bread and money in a parody of the Lord's Prayer. As for folk songs, they did not exist in the twelfth century as now recorded, but contextual association of debt with the threat to sell off nonproductive assets is consistent both with the close of Poem II and with themes and forms of address in the folk tradition. Interpolation is well integrated with performative context.

As for metonyms of food, clothes, and sex, the verbs *roukanízo* "gnaw at" and *klōthō* "weave" are used of the craftsmen's activities of eating and weaving in contrast to a diet of iambs and anapests and are proverbial for a voracious sexual appetite. Meat and fish, grilled on red-hot charcoals, signify gastronomic and sexual enjoyment, while chewing at entrails/tripe (ἄντερα) indicates entry to inner female parts. The baker's wife, who saucily nibbles the crusty end of a long white loaf (*aphratítsin*), like the yogurt seller hawking his "frothy white stuff" (*oxygalo*) and the City's good lady handworkers (*cheiromáchisses*), suggests the promise of sexual reward for manual labor. Our narrator is denied food, clothes, and sex. The nagging wife of Poem I locks up food and wine in her larder as firmly as she locks him out of her bedroom, leaving him to steal or beg for food. The impoverished father of II begs his patron not to leave him to starve on an unmanly diet of mountain greens and locusts, while complaining that his folks are forced to eat their own clothes. In III the abused monk is denied his due portion of food and wine (even when ill and entitled to extra quality) and watches the abbot and his ilk gorge themselves on meat and fish on fast days, while he and his mates are fed with viral swill consisting of stinking onions boiled in water.[122] The ultimate outrage is reserved for the teacher-scholar of IV, who is invited by the butcher's wife to sit down for a bite of belly meat, only to find it stuffed with shit.

Throughout the four poems, the only food our narrator enjoys is either begged for (I, II, IV) or stolen (I, IV). A further irony here is that stolen food is proverbially tastier than any other, much as his verse is all the spicier for transgressing the normal conventions of writing/speaking to his emperor of the nefarious activities of his inferiors and superiors. Hunger and poverty are unenviable states, leading their victim to dizziness (I–IV); beatings and thrashings (I, III, IV); blasphemy and damnation (III, IV); lying and envy (III, IV); and disease resulting from starvation or consumption of inappropriate substances (I–IV). When all pleas to his patron for alms appear to have failed, he is driven as a last resort to appeal to Hunger (Peina) and his lice-infested Cloak of Poverty (Kappa) as an excuse for his own transgressions and self-destruction.

The humor of these beggar poems is not straightforward. Learned and vernacular modes converge to emphasize the alienated plight of the court jester in the midst of plenty for others, at a time of socioeconomic change in the later twelfth century, when aristocrats complained of the upwardly mobile urban classes, bourgeois and artisan.[123] Nuances of metaphor invite comparison with texts widely distanced in time. Whether these similarities are coincidental or interpolated does not really matter; they are embedded in figurative codes of the Greek language, both *of* their times, yet speaking *from* and *to* others. Types of humor range from slapstick to literary allusion, with the use of hyperbole, abuse, insinuation, and wordplay, and are rendered in multiple registers. They belong to the "politics of hunger," encoded in the Greek language.

To sum up on the twelfth century, I have tried to draw attention to the diversity of language, style, and theme and to indicate the wisdom, combined with subversive humor, in three literary texts. Byzantine diversity, inherited from antiquity, has afforded modern Greek writers models different from those of the West: allegory and rhetoric, with revisionist appropriations of a multifaceted past. The modern Greek novel is not a direct descendant of its Byzantine or ancient precedents, any more than is the modern wondertale (*paramythi*) of ancient myth. Two key features of representation and style—antithesis and ekphrasis—perfected in the twelfth century, have been integrated into modern prose fiction without overt imitation. The linguistic registers available in the twelfth century and the humor inherent in their interconnections have proved remarkably productive.

PART II

MYTH

—Get on with it! I said to him. Are we through with anecdotes? Begin the story now!

—Wait a bit! he answered, cut to the quick. D'you think we're in Europe, where they sell meat without bones? I'm telling you the story as it happened. If you don't like it, leave it. We'll go and see the Turkish *hanim* lady!

G. M. VIZYENOS, *Who Was My Brother's Killer*

CHAPTER 5

The Diversity of Mythical Genres

In Part I, I indicated that language, if studied as *parole*, or utterance, rather than as *langue*, or structure, is neither transparent nor to be satisfactorily understood in isolation from its performative context. Utterance provides the clues necessary to define both the nature of the speech genre and the range of its significations. Neither the *Timarion* nor the Ptochoprodromic Poems derive meaning from fixed and literal truth; specific modes of writing/speaking invite the reader to explore ever-shifting layers of meaning. In Part II, I wish to examine how Bakhtin's concept of "speech genres" might be made more specifically relevant to the rich and varied Greek oral traditions, as recorded since the early nineteenth century and still vibrant today. To that end, I shall explore what I call "mythical genres" by way of working definition. Just as speech genres are determined by dialogic interaction (both within a given text and between speaker and author and between audience and readers), so are mythical genres determined not merely by form, structure, or theme but also by context, audience participation, and response. There are many ways of "telling the story."

1. From Speech Genres to Mythical Genres?

Recent studies of Greek speech genres at the level of everyday discourse call into question the validity of J. L. Austin's "speech-act theory."[1] Do speakers "mean what they say" or "say what they mean," or does language provide a way of playing with meanings? Michael Herzfeld has demonstrated the importance of language games (both sung and spoken) in

the everyday struggle for power–and survival—in a Cretan mountain village; and he has since extended his analysis to include urban rhetoric and
politics.[2] Renée Hirschon has drawn attention to the vivacity, duplicity, and
violence inherent in the speech of impoverished Asia Minor refugees con-
centrated in the urban slums of Kokkinia between Athens and Piraeus.[3]
Her examples are instructive: she was shocked to hear mothers and grandmothers shrieking at their offspring, Θὰ σὲ ξεσκίσω, θὰ σὲ σουβλίσω, θὰ
σὲ κολλήσω στὸν τοῖχο! "I'll rip you open, I'll roast you on the spit, I'll
stick you on the wall!" only to realize later that such talk was a kind of game,
not unlike some folk genres, such as the parodic-tragic songs "Mother
Murderess" and "Evil Mother-in-Law." In a more severe case of testing, a
young mother, holding her nine-year-old son by the hand, strolled across to
the local kiosk to chat with the owner. They enacted a dramatic dialogue in
deadpan tones about how the boy's father was hit by a truck on his way to
work that morning and now lay in pools of blood on the operating table of
the local hospital. The boy, by this time visibly anxious, received no reassur-
ance either by word or gesture that this was only a game! Such behavior
would be unthinkable to many mothers; but the intended lesson for the
Greek child was that adult speech should not be taken at face value and that
agonistic stances must be developed from an early age. Hirschon's examples
resonate well with everyday encounters in Greece today.

What these cases indicate and what I shall explore in my treatment of
myth is that violent utterance may not result in violent action. Indeed, it
may well avert it, by allowing verbal license: similar tactics have been observed in the magic spells of late antiquity[4] and will be found in Epirot
curse songs (Chapter 10). As for "telling the truth," Greek storytellers have
always delighted in ψέμματα καὶ παραμύθια "lies and tales," and such
games are evident not just in writing or literature but also in everyday discourse.[5] What difference does it make when words are not *meant* to be
taken literally? Violence, rape, and incest are current in all societies; myth
provides the means of projecting, through fantasy, social experience onto
another plane, to be shared and debated among all members of a community. These themes will be examined in narrative songs (Chapter 6), in
wondertales (Chapter 7), in prose fiction (Chapter 8), and in ritual songs
(Chapters 9 and 10).

2. What Is Myth?

"Myth" is arguably an outworn term, so overused and appropriated to
our own concepts of ancient and exotic cultures that anthropologists and

folklorists have been inclined to restrict it to narrow (if divergent) definitions or to discard it altogether. And yet the ancient verb *mythéō* means, according to ritual context, both to "initiate speech" and to "silence speech,"
by putting the finger on the lips and making the sound "mmm."[6] The root
mu is still productive in the Greek language. Etymology and usage therefore
invite us to approach the question "What is myth?" in ways specifically relevant to Greek oral tradition. In the course of this chapter, genres will be
surveyed and scrutinized to distinguish scholarly taxonomies from performative practice. In this way, Procrustean pitfalls of universalizing and reductionist definitions can perhaps be avoided.[7]

There are three major problems to be addressed. First, definitions tend to
rest on the polarizations primitive/civilized, oral/literate, superstitious/
rational, and urban/rural, as if these were mutually exclusive states or evolutionary stages in the ascent of man, rather than useful labels for divergent
aspects of the complex interaction between orality and literacy. All societies
need, and cultivate in diverse ways, their own myths; and if the word
"myth" has become a pejorative "lie" in the common usage of many languages, including Greek, that does not mean that tall stories touching on
matters national, political, and religious are not circulated by word of
mouth, whether channeled through oral tradition, literature, or the mass
media or by a mixture of all three. The second problem is that taxonomies
are made according to textual rather than contextual and performative criteria, hence they are hard to apply to the rich output of Greek literature,
which, from antiquity to the present day, has passed to and fro between
orality and literacy. Third, to recapitulate my discussion in the Introduction,
classical scholars have tried to define mythology so as to distinguish it from
folklore, regarding the latter as a derivative adaptation of the former to the
needs of rural or mixed societies. Despite assiduous work on structural/
compositional building blocks, the cosmological systems and moral values
of the folklore have been consistently underestimated or misunderstood
according to modern criteria of belief and rationality.[8]

It may be more fruitful to think in terms of a diversity of *mythical genres*,
oral and literary, where historical, legendary, uncanny, fantastic, and marvelous elements constantly intertwine.[9] My own use of "myth" is open, designed to include categories which in other cultures might be regarded as
discrete. Myth is a story, often involving supernatural or nonnatural elements, which may be told, sung, or implicit, whether by word of mouth or
in writing (or a combination of both). It draws on a shared yet not undisputed fund of beliefs, experiences, and memories, rather than on an officially or scientifically determined consensus imposed from outside. It serves
to link the past with the present, the known with the unknown worlds.

Thus, myth is defined not just by form (song, poetry, prose tale, biomythography, novel) or by thematic content (birth of a god, founding of a city, genealogy of a people) or even by a readily definable treatment of the heroic and supernatural but also by the responses and resonances it evokes through dialogic exchange between teller and audience and between author and readership. The creation of myth is, above all, an interactive process. Cynthia Ward, in her study of the novelist Buchi Emecheta, has pointed out how Western academic approaches to African orality have attempted to constitute the oral as the meaning-producing equivalent of a European literary tradition by constructing textualized counterparts of genre and canon, whereas, she argues, "the value of the oral tale to the oral culture lies not entirely in the tale itself, but, perhaps more significantly, in the discussion it generates after it is told, discussion that allows each participant to respond, whether by taking the center, presenting another illustrative fiction, or displaying his or her individual style. . . . Attention to the crucial importance of the resulting response, rather than of the tale itself, elicits a judgment different from the standard opinion of African tradition as conservative, fixed, and intransigent, as repressive of individuality, or as something to be preserved before it is 'lost.'"[10] Ward's observations are valid not only for African oral tradition but also for Greek, where the interpenetration of sung, spoken, and written forms of utterance has long been operative within the same language (she emphasizes the distinction characteristic of most West Africans, who "speak" with their native vernaculars and "write" with European languages [1990, 87]). First, examples from my own fieldwork confirm the importance of audience participation. During the early 1960s in the village of Sklithron Ayias (Thessaly), I recorded many songs and tales at the main café (and only shop), appropriately known as Kathotis (τοῦ Καθότη) from the proprietor's predilection for the katharevousa expression "inasmuch as" (καθότι). At one session, Kathotis, then in his forties, sang a melancholy and fragmented Kleftic lament: not a spectacular performance, but it triggered a flood of stories and recollections among fellow villagers about the Turkish occupation, the German occupation, and the civil war, in the course of which heroic feats and tales of endurance were recounted. The text as recorded cannot be defined as myth; yet the performance resonated with past myths and generated the response necessary for the creation of new ones.

In Greece, people love to dispute what they hear, read, or watch, from novels and newspapers to televised serializations: they are not passive consumers. My mother-in-law, Aspasia, with no formal education beyond the first grades of village primary school in Sklithron and with minimal chance to read during her active years of production and reproduction in the village, died, aged ninety-nine, at home in Volos where she lived with her third daughter and her husband. After recovering from cataract surgery, and with "second sight" following eight years of near blindness, she would, until four years before her death, read as avidly as she embroidered and could finish Greek translations of Gorki's *Mother* or Toni Morrison's *Beloved* in a day and a half. She also entered into voluble debate with the television set, correcting newscasters on errors of fact and disputing dramatizations of works she had read for omissions and changes of characters and episodes. As she talked, she relived and revisualized her past. In defining "orality" and "literacy" and the many shades between them, we need to think not only in quantitative terms (How much can—and do—people read and write?) or even in abstract cognitive terms (How is knowledge processed?) but also in terms of everyday attitudes, interaction, and discourse. Reading need not be a silent or solitary process.

Attitudes to authority, power, and knowledge are differently shaped. It is a paradox that, whereas expert opinion has dominated the media in Anglo-American societies despite popular skepticism, Greeks from all backgrounds contest the voice of authority with at least as many empirically and anecdotally based counterarguments as there are discussants. The quality of good discussion depends not so much on logical coherence or conclusiveness, let alone amicability, but rather on the degree of enjoyment afforded to participants in airing discordant views from all possible perspectives.[11] The experience can be discomforting for the outsider, who tends to misinterpret discussion as argument. Similarly, the categories of private and public are differently constructed: Greek has no word for private ownership (ιδιωτικός, ιδιαίτερος, δικός μου imply "special"), without connotations of aloneness (μόνος, μοναδικός, μοναξιά); while its opposite, δημόσιος, refers to "public" in the sense of "pertaining to the state." In Greek these terms are less inclusive than in English. Κοινός is more inclusive than its English equivalents, "common, shared." In other words, Greek invests moral value not in the dichotomy private/public but in the problematization over the category of "what is shared," and how it gets transmitted across generations and how the disemia of public and private self is displayed.

To sum up, myth is a special kind of utterance whose performative context determines genres ranged across the historical, allegorical, and fantastic axes. Bearing in mind the ambivalence inherent in Greek speech genres and in their underlying attitudes to truth, we may now ask, How do mythical genres explore dangerous subjects in order to challenge authority, while strengthening a sense of community?

3. Linking Past and Present: Myth and History

Two key words, *parádosis* "tradition" and *istoría* "history, story" will serve to illustrate some crucial contextual differences between scholarly taxonomies and live meanings. Paradosis means "handing down / over." Folklorists use it as a term to define short prose legends, generally believed to be true, which relate to (a) historical events and figures (Fall of Constantinople, Asia Minor catastrophe, Alexander the Great, Jesus Christ, Digenes Akrites, Klefts); (b) geographical locations and toponyms (rivers, mountains, caves, village sites); and (c) supernatural events and figures, such as Death, Fates, Nereids, the Panagia, saints, and the Devil. All share a blend of historical or topographical fact with legendary fiction. However, as told by ordinary people from different walks of life, such narratives are inserted casually into everyday conversation to illustrate a point or to justify an argument, and they are named—if at all—not paradoseis but istories, sometimes prefaced with the comment, "We have a custom/tradition [paradosi]—I'll tell you a story [istoria]." In addition to those mentioned above, topics may include unusual encounters, diseases and cures, and dreams and dream interpretations—in other words, they are less formal and solemn in content and context than the fossilized taxonomy would suggest. As for whether they are "believed to be true," it is worth pointing out that Greek does not distinguish between "story" and "history," just as the AG verb *historéō* meant "to enquire; observe; tell a story through pictures." The point is not that the tales must be *believed* but that they should be *well told*. The best rendering for this mythical genre is perhaps "stories" and "sayings" (as in older meanings of μῦθος / ἱστορία) relating to the known or knowable world in all its diversity but integrated into an informal performative context.

The outsider-empiricist draws a distinction between historical fact, which is "real," and any story related and debated about the event ever since, which is "myth"; for the nonempiricist insider, all is myth and history in a positive sense. The Fall of Constantinople is a case in point. It happened in 1453, but what do we make of the numerous legends about the miraculous disappearance of the Emperor Constantine during the last siege and his predicted return?[12] Constantine XI Palaiologos was no longer ruling emperor in Constantinople when the City fell, but legend has it that he was there, in the Church of Holy Wisdom during the last liturgy: he escaped by a secret door behind the rood screen, and he will come out of the same door ὅταν θὰ ξαναπάρουμε τὴν Πόλη "when we take back the City." Another legend tells that he was seen near the gates of the City frying dried fish which leapt live from the pan, signaling his own return from the dead and his power to exact retribution.[13] Such legends are powerful not because they are historically "true" but because they reach back to the distant past of Greek-Persian conflict and because their widespread diffusion during the centuries of Ottoman rule helped shape Greek national consciousness and foreign policy during the late nineteenth and early twentieth centuries. The Asia Minor campaign (1919–22) to regain the lost territories of Byzantium was led in the name of the king of the realm, also named Constantine: he would fulfill the popular prophecy.[14] Without some basis in popular mythology, manipulated but not invented by nationalist politicians, official propaganda could not have been formulated in these terms.

Stories about the re-siting of a village from seacoast to mountain terrain "in the time of our great-grandfathers" are common currency in everyday conversations of many mountain villagers, with additional detail on what caused the ensuing population shifts: Turkish incursions, natural disaster, famine. Opinions will vary, and truth cannot always be documented from local archives. Such stories and the debate they arouse serve a vital function in creating a mythology, or "oral archive," which bonds village communities of heterogeneous origins in the face of past and possible future change.[15]

On an equally local but more mythical level, legends from Arachova (a village on Mount Parnassós overlooking Delphi) include "*Katevatós*, or Lord North Wind" (cf. AG Καταιβάτης): an old monk from the Monastery of Blessed Luke once dared to challenge Katevatos' might by inhabiting his cave on the windswept peaks of Parnassos throughout the treacherous month of March to spy on the great "Wrestling of the Winds"; Katevatos burned him to a cinder.[16] This little story tells a great deal about Greek concepts of power: a monk from a renowned monastery was punished for his audacity to quarrel with Nature, here personified as Katevatos ("he who comes down"). At the same time, it neatly absolves ordinary mortals from transgression during the most capricious month of the year.

This mythical genre presupposes past story/event, around which similar and more recent narratives may be built: it is accretive;[17] it can be integrated into everyday conversation; and above all, it links the present with a collectively remembered (if disputed) past, both local and religious. It is fixed only when it dies on the spoken tongue.

4. Averting Danger: Myth, Ritual, and Religion

Myth, ritual, and religion cannot be rigidly separated. Songs and tales "telling a story" may be accorded a quasi-ritual function by virtue of their performative context, while those accompanying a rite of passage may still depend on a common fund of stories. Since these will form the major focus of Chapters 6, 7, 9, and 10, this section will be brief, in an attempt to link the informal stories of the last section with similar ones concerning ritual and religion. As Charles Stewart has demonstrated, stories about Christ, the Virgin Mary, the Devil, and other demons (Charos, Fates, Nereids) cannot be relegated to the spheres of either religion (Christian) or mythology (pagan).[18] The overlap in legendary content underlying biblical, hagiographical, and mythological stories is too great; details in each case tend to get adapted to local needs—for example, to prove that this village is older than the next.[19] In stories and songs told during Holy Week, Mary may be interrupted with news of her son's imminent Crucifixion either by Mary Magdalene or by Κυρὰ-Καλώ, Queen of the Nereids, at the wrong moment, when she is inappropriately in a silver bathtub or combing her hair with a golden comb.[20] Christ may change into different shapes of bread in a peasant girl's basket to escape capture by the guards in the Garden of Gethsemane; or Mary, pregnant with Jesus, may be granted the cherries she desires not by Joseph but by the tree itself.[21] Divinities, like humans and demons, can lust, trick, and err, with the advantage of immortality.

In stories from Cyprus and Asia Minor, Charos (Death) is chosen by a poor man as "the most just" godfather, in preference to God and Wealth (Θεός and Πλοῦτος), to bestow a name and blessing on his newborn son, expressing, as in "Katevatos," an anticlericalism which subverts the two "gods" of the modern world, Religion and Materialism: the boy prospers into manhood until the moment of his death arrives, which he tries to evade by trickery. Sometimes, he succeeds.[22] Death and God can both be cheated, as in the humorous tale "Card-Player in Paradise," in which the protagonist tricks Christ into opening the Gates of Paradise to himself, and his eleven thieving companions, on the analogy of the Twelve Apostles, even though he has made a pact with the Devil.[23] Humor, as in the Ptochoprodromic Poems, provides a favorite means of coping with disease, poverty, and death.

The Nereids, female demons of pre-Christian origin as they may be, bother and tease not only Alexander the Great when tossed on high seas but any handsome shepherd caught napping under the trees beneath the noonday sun. Sometimes, they snatch the offspring of a woman in labor in exchange for a changeling of their own, who fares better than humankind until recaptured into the "other world"; they may even submit to temporary domesticity by marrying handsome young shepherds adept at the flute, but after bearing fine sons to mortal husbands, they win back their freedom by retrieving through guile the kerchief stolen from them by their bridegrooms in the nuptial dance. The transforming power of dance is another key motif to be found in almost all mythical genres.[24]

As for the Fates (*Moíres*), stories and legends abound: whether in the form of a single old haridan from the ends of the earth who intervenes to save a young mortal in return for a favor or as three beautiful young women, dressed in white nuptial garb with pearl necklaces and bracelets to "fate" a newborn child, one to spin, the second to wind, and the third and eldest to cut the thread. The first two Fates may decree a good life for a newborn child, only to be overruled by the third, who drank too much wine at the "fating," fell downstairs, and blocked the child's fate at the crucial point.[25] The ritual lessons to be learned from such tales are that you should be kind to strangers, however unprepossessing, and that you should serve just the right amount of delicacies, sweetmeats, and wine during the "fating" (*moírama*) of a newborn child. Too little will provoke the Fates' anger; too much will cloud their sense. As we shall see in Chapter 7, Fate and the Fates play a crucial role in the tales.

Such stories are among the most flexible—and most enduring—of mythical genres, depending on formal and informal transmission and adaptation of stories transmitted from one generation to the next and on a developed and shared sense of self and other within a localized context. They have been defined as aetiological stories told as if true—that is, they relate to observable phenomena or personal experience, despite recourse to magic and metamorphosis. The question of belief is more complex: tales remind us that codes of behavior exist for mortals and divinities. They need not be politically correct, so long as you win.

5. Dialogic Ethics: Parables and Fables, Proverbs and Riddles

Oral tales and rhymes, known to scholars as parables, proverbs, and riddles, are still current. They incorporate fabulous and supernatural elements, often with an explicit or implicit moral which may be contradictory or open to question. Animal fables belong to this mythical genre and are generally termed by scholars as allegorical, drawing a direct comparison or contrast between human and bestial worlds. Yet, for the people who tell these tales, interpretation depends on shifting metaphorical/metonymical associations. Snake and eagle, frogs and mice may act for good or evil depending on how you treat them: a shepherd nurtures with milk in his backyard a snake which yields him three gold coins a day, until his small son accidentally treads on its tail and gets fatally bitten. Neither father nor snake can bear to see each other again, because the one thinks always of his dead son, the other of his wounded tail.[26]

Such oral tales cannot be reduced to symbols or allegories with a simple equation between signifier and signified, although many literary re-creations and redactions from the fourteenth century to the present day have tended to emphasize more explicitly their moral–didactic potential. A case in point is the well-known and widely diffused Aesopian fable "The Ass, the Wolf, and the Fox," in which power games between the three beasts are played out with satire and humor but the Ass wins out in the end because Wolf (the Church?) and Fox (the bureaucracy?) underestimate the cunning of the lower classes.[27] Such tales remind us of the fragility of boundaries between the human, animal, and vegetal worlds. Metamorphosis across these boundaries is fundamental to mythical genres of birth, marriage, and death, in tale and song alike, as we shall see in Chapters 6, 7, and 10.

Proverbs (παροιμίες) encapsulate collective wisdom from conflicting perspectives, often with a tripartite structure indicating thesis, antithesis, and synthesis in some kind of euphonic or rhyming jingle. They are used to clinch an argument or to score points against an opponent, who may respond with a conflicting example. Despite their mnemonic form, they are not easily interpreted without reference to wider mythical and metaphorical perspectives: the proverb χέρι, μαχαίρι καὶ τρεχούμενο νερό "hand, knife, and running water" does not signify, although the hand may stand metonymically for friendship; the knife, for a fight and blood; and running water, for time's cleansing oblivion and the passage of generations.[28] Semantically and syntactically they are three disconnected images, hence the proverb resembles an unusual picture, each part linked by sound and rhythm. These images at once evoke a host of contrary proverbs: ξένα χέρια μαχαίρια "foreign hands knives" (don't trust nonkin); αἷμα νερὸ δὲ γίνεται (blood can never become water), "once kin, always kin"; "salt water will never be sweet"; "your relatives are your worst enemies."[29] Does our first proverb mean that quarrels can be mended or that they cannot? The proverb θάλασσα καὶ πῦρ καὶ γυνὴ κακὸν τρίτον "sea, fire, woman, threefold evil" is attested from Aeschylus to the present day and is normally interpreted as meaning "woman is as evil and treacherous as sea and fire."[30] Viewed from a different perspective, fire, woman, and sea are the three productive and reproductive forces—as in *Hysmine*. Another example, τάχ' ἡ Μοῖρα στὸ χαρτί, πελέκι δὲν τὰ κόβει "What Fate has on paper, an axe cannot cut" is a metonymic fusion of weaving and writing with a long history in the language.[31]

Proverbs may be more equivocal in ellipsis than declarative in their synthesis, and in any case, their meaning is determined not by the literal sense of words but by shared associations and active interpretation, thereby disturbing the literalism of discourse. If studied as utterances, rather than as isolated texts, one proverb can always be found to contradict another, as in our "Too many cooks spoil the broth" and "Many hands make light work." The Cretan dramatists exploited the rich resources of Greek proverbs to lend color and vibrancy to the speech of their characters, especially that of the older women, from the wily matchmakers, pimps, and prostitutes of comedy to Sara in religious drama and the nurses in tragedy and romance. These women are each defined as characters by their proverbial language, used to scold, cajole, console, lament, and amuse.[32]

Proverbs and riddles, formulated in rhythmic sets (sometimes in a fifteen-syllable line), depend on wit and ready response. As we shall see in Chapter 7, proverbs lie at the core of many tales, while the ability to solve riddles requires arcane wisdom rather than rationality or linear logic. Perhaps because they communicate indirectly, often through pictures, they hold a particular fascination for autistics. In a culture with a long literary past, like Greek, there is considerable continuity, variation, and oral-literary interaction in their transmission.[33]

6. Songs and Tales: Myth and Fantasy

Problems of classification are nowhere so apparent as in the narrative songs and tales, and detailed discussion will be deferred until Chapters 6 and 7. For the moment, I wish to draw attention to the fantastic dimensions in these two genres. First, songs: scholars have divided them into two broad categories: those with historical and those with mythical frames of reference.[34] This distinction is easier to draw in theory than to observe in practice; fabulous elements predominate in almost all narrative songs, while alleged historical elements often amount to no more than passing reference to a name or place, sometimes inferred rather than actual. The term applied by scholars to the mythical song, of *paralogē*, is no less problematic than our "ballad," as the Greek is rendered.[35] Although *paralogē* has dropped out of common usage, it is attested in former dialects, while its associations with the paralogic ("strange," "against reason") are nevertheless appropriate to theme and content.

If the categories "historical" and "mythical" are less clear-cut than has been implied, different "moods" of time and place are nevertheless apparent. Some stories are sung as if they took place at a particular time and place, linking present with past as in the *paradoseis* (indicative); others are sung as if they might happen at any time or place, thus projecting onto the future on the basis of past perceived experience (subjunctive). Two examples will make the point. The Cretan song "Death of Digenis" celebrates the death of a hero in mythic proportions: he could catch birds on the wing, stags as they ran, and pluck boulders from their roots and toss them like kites. He was so brave the whole world was not room enough for him (one is reminded here of liturgical praises of Christ); yet he could not escape that trickster Death (Charos), who waylaid him in ambush.[36] Similar verses sung on Crete and elsewhere refer not to Digenis but to a "shepherd." If even the bravest hero could not escape Death, today it is no shame to die with honor.[37] The same principle, "if then, so now," also applies to Kleftic songs about heroic battles and defeats in the struggle for independence: they commemorate, but also lament, past collective losses, and so they tend to be repeated and adapted in songs for new losses.

By contrast, the mythical—almost dreamlike—quality of songs defined as *paralogés* derives not merely from their inclusion of the supernatural, the sinister, and marvelous, but rather from the timelessness of place and character. Where a location is specified, it is legendary rather than historical, as in "The Bridge of Arta," where the myth of the walled-up wife is attached to specific but differently localized bridges, monasteries, or castles in songs known throughout the Balkans.[38] The setting may appear more domestic than mythical, but the tragic conflict takes place within and between families or between human and supernatural forces, giving objectivized expression in mythical form to the same fears and anxieties to be found in three overlapping categories of ritual songs: the wedding songs, laments for departure, and dirges.[39] They provide a means of exploring, through fantasy, such subjects as the overpossessive mother, the interfering mother-in-law, adultery, incest, filicide, even necrophilia. While not all end in death for the protagonists (although many do), tragedy and violence are paramount, sometimes tinged with parody.[40]

Turning to the tales, or paramythia (cf. παραμυθέομαι, "to comfort, console, talk on the side"), we can rely on live usage to infer meanings ranging from tall story to our fairy tale. *Paramythi* is best rendered as "wondertale": "folktale" is a scholarly term, restrictive in its reference to the rural peasantry, whereas paramythia have traditionally been told across a wide cross section of the population, urban and rural. As for "fairy tale," quite apart from its derivation from the seventeenth-century English translation of the French *conte de fées* for literary reworkings of oral tales, there are no "fairies" as we understand them in Greek mythology. Vladimir Propp's term "wondertale," as he applies it to a specific type of Russian folktale, captures both the cosmology and the fictitious narrative strategies of all Greek paramythia, whether or not they contain supernatural elements.[41]

As I suggested in the Introduction, "There was and there was not" is a common incipit, while "I wasn't there then, and nor were you, so don't believe a word I've said, but let's eat, drink, and be merry if you've enjoyed my story" is a common conclusion. Just to complicate matters, expert tellers of spine-chilling ghost stories like to enhance their effects by insisting that this tale is "true," witnessed by myself or so-and-so, and see, here is food and drink from the festivities to prove it. The emphasis is on verbal art as performance; as in the Ptochoprodromic Poems, fictionality and veracity are rhetorical devices. Folklorists have been at pains to classify tales into neat categories: animal fables, tales of fate, humorous tales, tales of wonder and magic, and so on. But once again, if we listen to the voice of experienced tellers, no such distinction can be made.[42]

Beneath the narrator's formulaic emphasis on the successful resolution of family conflicts, tales involve human protagonists and demonic powers alike in horror and violence, while some have ritual dimensions, whereby sacrificial violence leads to metamorphosis (Chapter 7). Wondertales of this kind are not so different from the tragic legend, defined as a paradosis by N. G. Politis, recorded by Vizyenos from his native Thrace, "The Nightingale, the Swallow, and the Hoopoe" (Τὸ ἀηδόνι, τὸ χελιδόνι κι ὁ πούπουτας), in which two sisters are tricked by turns into marrying the same wicked king; they exchange stories by tying letters or pictures round a cat's neck and in revenge cause the king to devour his children, their own offspring. All three adults are transformed into birds, as in the ancient myth of Prokne and Tereus.[43]

Myth passes easily from one tale and genre to another and can always be retold from a different perspective. Greek tales have little in common with "fairy tales" as preserved in the sanitized canons from Charles Perrault to the Grimm brothers and thereafter, perhaps because they have been so often repeated and depend on audience participation.[44] Their durability is owed to the fact that they explore, and sometimes fill, the "site of a loss." As if a mirror image of mythical songs ending in human death, tales defer mortality by transferring it to another cycle.

Of all mythical genres, the paramythia are most comparable with ancient myths. They differ not so much generically or thematically but rather in relation to the religion of their time: the heroes and gods of antiquity were held to be immortal, whereas the protagonists of modern tales and songs are mortal, even when they live out their happy lives, and we more happily. A more productive distinction between myth and paramyth might be that myth, however polysemic, belongs to dominant beliefs and practices, whereas paramythia exploit elements with little overt reference to official Orthodox dogma. That is why they provide an invaluable—and largely un-researched—source for the study of popular forms of religion, coexisting and overlapping with the dominant one but frequently escaping censorship because they are only para-mythia.

7. From Myth to Literature

Interactions between present and past, performer and audience, can take place at the level of composition in diverse ways to create the means for reappropriating myths to new contexts. The distinction conventionally drawn between "oral myth" and "literary fiction" remains broadly valid for our culture, but it may not be applicable to others, such as Greek and Irish, where orality and literacy overlap synchronically and diachronically, thanks to a long literary tradition. Myths do not die with the passage from orality to literacy; like Proteus, they change shape and form. Ancient myths are literary in quality and in means of transmission; medieval literature harked back to the mythical past to question and comment on the present, as we saw from Timarion's ventures into the Underworld.

What of modern literature? Surely we must distinguish between oral variation of literary texts, such as paramythia derived from popular romances, and literary exploitation of mythical themes, especially when inspired by nostalgic hellenism, as would seem to be the case with so many Greek poets? The answer is not so simple. George Seferis, in his poem "Helen" (*Logbook III*), weaves a complex but unifying thread between mythical past (the Trojan War, Euripides' Helen) and writing present (1953), where Helen becomes an eternal, almost apocalyptic symbol for the cause of war and failure. Despite Seferis' indebtedness to T. S. Eliot in his concept of "tradition" and "mythical method," the Greek case differs from the Anglo-American one, partly because, for reasons outside his control (indeed, against his express wishes), Seferis' poems have been set to music by popular composers such as Mikis Theodorakis in songs to be heard, sung, and talked about by a far more diverse audience than the readership of, say, *The Waste Land* or *The Four Quartets*. Seferis' texts, like those of other leading Greek poets of the twentieth century, have been reinterpreted by discourses not restricted to the cultivated elites.[45]

As for prose fiction, although it lacks the bardic dimension of the Greek poetic voice, it has absorbed many themes and techniques from mythical genres, such as the legends, tales, and songs we have just reviewed, and above all a tendency to engage the reader in direct, second-person dialogue and to tell a story not in straight lines (as Kydion wanted Timarion to do) but by telling tales within tales in different voices.

From our postmodernist perspective, such reversion to the past and insistence on orality may seem naïve, at times nationalistic. What matters is not whether but how those voices from the past are appropriated. The time for visionary dreams of a unified and integrated Hellenism may have passed, in literature if not in politics; but the diversity and plurality of Greek mythical genres continues to inspire the present generation of writers, just as they always have done. I shall return to this question in Chapter 8.

8. How Do Myths Mean?

Constant features of Greek mythical genres include both a tenacious connection with the past and an active present function, often associated with ritual, and the suspension of disbelief: their meaning lies precisely in the gap between "true" and "not-true"—that is, between past experience and potential future—and is therefore constantly *deferred*. The question, "Did the Greeks believe in their myths?" has been addressed by Paul Veyne with regard to the corpus of ancient myths, but his premise is disconcertingly rational, and his evidence comes mainly from the intellectual elites of late antiquity. It needs to be broadened into a problematization of what constitutes the belief system of a heterogeneous culture, like Greek, poised between orality and literacy, superstition and rationalism.[46] The Greek word δέος, "fear, wonderment, doubt" indicates ambivalence, as is inherent in the English word *awe*.

So far as literature is concerned, Tzvetan Todorov has defined the "fantastic," as opposed to the "uncanny" or "marvelous," on the basis of whether the characters in or readers of a given text accept, deny, or doubt a rational explanation of supernatural events.[47] For him, tales belong to the "marvelous" and fables to "allegory," whereas the truly fantastic is found only in literary prose. But what happens when beliefs in the fantastic belong to a whole community rather than to individual characters or readers? Is Toni Morrison's "Beloved" a ghost? A memory of the enslaved black past? A psychological projection of the burden from that past and the need to exorcise it? Does Gloria Naylor's George in *Mama Day* die as a result of a congenital heart condition, precipitated by the shock experienced by an urban and successful black businessman when confronted with his wife's Southern and African roots, or is he the victim of Ruby's "black magic"? Is Stratis Myrivilis' Smaragdi in *Mermaid Madonna* a mortal woman or born of mixed human and Gorgon parentage?

There is no answer to these questions. As to the Greek-speaking world, it did not experience a reformation but rather a resurgence of Orthodoxy as a cultural and linguistic rallying point for people of all stations during the period when Rum (Greece) was a *millet* of the Ottoman Empire (1453–1828); hence the categories of reason and superstition are not easily separated, even in terms of Orthodox dogma, which to this day recognizes within the term "demonic" its particular manifestations and is therefore prepared to sanction or acquiesce in exorcisms against the evil eye (τὸ μάτι) and enchantment (τὰ μάγια), while still tolerant of popular figurations of the Fates and Death.[48]

Attempts to translate mythical genres into a single meaning are flawed. Formalists and structuralists have tended to reduce myth and folktale to a set of incomprehensible—and joyless—algebraic formulas. Marxists have argued for a more historical perspective, often from a simplistic assumption that myth reflects reality at a determinable historical level. Psychoanalysts have pointed to Oedipal and other complexes at the core of every myth. Feminist studies have exposed gender bias in tellers and collectors. Post-structuralists have queried the concept of meaning. These different approaches will be examined with reference to specific stories, songs, and novels in the next three chapters. But if we give up the notion of "what myth means" in favor of the question, "In how many ways can myth mean?" following Sperber's lead, then neither the questions nor the answers posed by these diverse critical theorists need prove mutually exclusive. Myth is multidimensional, just as the meaning of metonyms and metaphors alike can always be deferred/transferred.[49]

It cannot have escaped notice that many Greek mythical genres bear the prefix *para*, with a wide range of meanings: παρά-δοση "down / across-giving," "tradition"; παρα-βολή "juxtaposition," parable; παρ-οιμία "side road," "by word," "proverb"; παρα-μύθι "lying tale," comfort; παρα-λογή "ballad," sung story with dramatic and paralogic elements. Παρ-ωδία "parody, cross-song" and παράδοξος/παράξενος "strange, contrary to expectation," are related terms. All share the concept of boundaries transgressed. In ancient Greek, *para* functions both as a preposition followed by genitive and dative cases, meaning "aside from, at the hands of, besides, beyond the norm," and as verbal prefix, signifying "beside or beyond the norm". In modern Greek, the preposition takes the accusative, in the sense of "despite" or "all but", as in παρὰ τὴ θέλησή μου, "against my will," παρὰ τρίχα, "by a hair's breadth," δέκα παρὰ πέντε, "five to ten." As a verbal prefix, it signifies "going beyond the boundaries," as in the common sayings τὰ παραλές "you exaggerate," μὲ παρεξήγησες "you have mis-understood me." In an adverbial phrase, it may denote both excess παρὰ πολύ, "very / too much" and deficiency παρ' ὀλίγο, "by a little." *Para-* signifies going outside the normal frontiers, as if no distinction is possible between "very much" and "too much." Beyond the frontiers, anything is possible, and incommensurable.[50]

9. The Nereid "Kalypso"

To illustrate the power of myth and the narrow line between myth and reality, orality and literacy, I will cite in conclusion to this chapter a story I recorded in 1963 from Maria Gourioti of Sklithron Ayias, sister-in-law to my former husband's mother, Aspasia, about her dead husband's encounters with the Nereid Kalypso. The events must have taken place at least twenty to thirty years earlier, between the two world wars. She encapsulates, within a single narrative, the tensions and contradictions between belief and disbelief, tradition and modernity, orality and literacy which are so characteristic of the past five decades.

Αὐτὴ τὴ νεράιδα ποὺ θέλετε νὰ μάθετε καὶ ν' ἀκούσετε τὴν βρῆκαν πολλοὶ ἀλλὰ τὴν ἐβρῆκαν διαφορετική. Ὁ ἄντρας μου ὅμως τὴν ἐβρῆκε γυναῖκα, ὡραία, τὰ μαλλιὰ ξέπλεγα, πολὺ μακρυά, καὶ τοῦ προσέφερε τσιγάρο. Πήγαινε ἔξω, εἴχαμε τὰ ζωντανά, τὴν ἐβρῆκε, τὸν εἶπε πολλὰ καὶ διάφορα λόγια γιὰ τὸ σπίτι του, πῶς λεν τὴ γυναίκα του, πῶς λεν τὰ γυναικαδέρφια ποὺ τὰ εἶχε, ποὺ ἦταν στὴν Ἀμερική, καὶ τὸν εἶπε ὅτι—Ἐγὼ προσπαθῶ γιὰ τὸ καλό σου. Ἔχω καὶ σπίτι ποὺ θα σοῦ τὸ παρουσιάσω ἀμέσως νὰ τὸ ἰδῆς. Καὶ τὸ παρουσίασε, ποὺ εἶχε μέσα διάφορα καὶ πολλὰ πράγματα.

—Λοιπόν, τοῦ εἶπε, ὅτι ἐγώ, λέει, εἶμαι νεράιδα. Ἂν ἔχεις διαβάσει Ὀδύσσεια, ἡ Θιὰ ἡ Καλυψὼ ποὺ βάσταξε τὸν Ὀδυσσέα ἐπὶ ὀχτὼ χρόνια καὶ δὲν τὸν ἄφησε νὰ πάει στὴν πατρίδα του. Μὴ φοβᾶσαι, δέ σε κάμω τίποτα. Σ' ἔχω ἀπὸ μικρὸ παιδὶ ποὺ σε παρακουληθῶ. Θυμᾶσαι μιὰ φορὰ ποὺ πήγαινες μὲ τὴν ἀδερφή σου στὸ μαντρί, καὶ ἔπεσες ἀπὸ τὸ ζῶο, κι ἐγὼ σ' ἀνάβασα καβάλα, ἀλλὰ δὲν τὸ κατάλαβες.... Προσπαθῶ πάντα γιὰ τὸ καλό σου.

Ξανὰ τὴν ἐβρῆκε πάλι, καὶ τὸν παρουσίασε πολλὰ πράγματα, ποὺ ἦταν ἀκόμα ἀξύριστος καὶ ἤθελε νὰ τὸν ξυρίσει. Τὸν παρουσίασε μιὰ φορὰ ἕνα βουνὸ μπροστά του πολὺ πυκνό, ποὺ δὲν μποροῦσε νὰ περάσει οὔτε ζουλάπι ἀπομέσα. Ἀφοῦ τὸν εἶδε καὶ στεναχωρέθηκε τόσο πολύ, ἄνοιξε τὸ δρόμο πάλι καὶ τοῦ λέει - Πήγαινε, τώρα δὲν ἔχω δικαίωμα ἀπὸ κεῖ νὰ σε παρακολουθήσω.

Ξανὰ ἄλλη φορὰ ποὺ ἦρθε ἐδῶ στὸ χωριὸ τὸν ἔβαζαν διάφορα φυλαχτικὰ ἀπάνω του. Ἀλλὰ αὐτὴ πάλι δὲ φοβήθηκε, καὶ τοῦ εἶπε,

—Δέν με φοβίζουν αὐτά. Δὲ πήγαινε κοντὰ ὅμως. Τὸν πάει σε ὡρισμένο μέρος μόνο, καὶ τὸν εἶπε—᾽Εσὺ σκάζεις ἄνθρωπο ὄχι. . . . Δὲ μιλᾶς. Μιὰ κουβέντα θέλω ν᾽ ἀκούσω μονάχα, τίποτ᾽ ἄλλο. Κι ὅταν ἦρθε, ἦρθε ἐλεεινὸς καὶ τρισάθλιος ἀπὸ φόβο. Δὲν μποροῦσε νὰ σύρει οὔτε τὰ πόδια του.

Τὴν πρώτη φορὰ ἦταν στὰς δώδεκα ἡ ὥρα, τὴν δεύτερη φορὰ ἦταν στὰς τρεῖς ἡ ὥρα τὴ νύχτα, τὴν τελευταῖα φορὰ τὸ πρωὶ ἦταν ἢ πάλι τὸ βράδυ δὲν θυμᾶμαι, ἀλλὰ ἦταν ἄρρωστος, ἄρρωστος, πεθαμένος ἀπὸ φόβο. ᾽Αφοῦ τον εἶπα—Τί ἔπαθες στὸ δρόμο καὶ γιατί ἄργησες; καὶ μοῦ λέει—Μὴ μοῦ μιλᾶς τώρα, ἄφησέ με, αὔριο θὰ σοῦ πῶ.

῏Ηταν μέσα σε ρὸζ φόρεμα, τὰ μαλλιά της τἄχε στὶς πλάτες της ριγμένα ποὺ κρέμονταν ὡς κάτω. ῾Η μορφή της ἦταν, δὲν λέγεται, πολὺ ἔμμορφη. Σὰν γυναῖκα. Γυναῖκα, ἀλλὰ τὰ πόδια της ἦταν σὰν πάπια. ᾽Απὸ κεῖ φοβήθηκε, κατάλαβε ὅτι δὲν ἦταν ἄνθρωπος καὶ δὲν μίλησε, ἀπὸ τὰ πόδια.

Αὐτὴ εἶπε ὅτι ἔχει ὡρισμένα μέρη. . . . Χαρὰ στὴν ὑπομονή της. Φαίνεται ὅτι πήγαινε ὅπου εἶναι νερό, στὴ ρεματιά. . . . Μάλιστα ἔβγαλε καὶ ταμπακιέρα καὶ τὸν πρόσφερνε τσιγάρο, τσιγάρο με φελλό. ῞Οτι ἔχουν τσιγάρα δὲν ἔχουν, ἀλλὰ ἡ φαντασία. . . . Μὰ αὐτὸς τὴν ἔβλεπε, νά, ὅπως βλέπεις ἕναν ἄνθρωπο καὶ μιλᾶς μπροστά.

Τρεῖς φορὲς τὴν ἐβρῆκε. Τελευταῖα φορά, χτύπησε τὰ παλαμάκια, εἶπε—᾽Εσὺ σκάζεις γάιδαρο, ὄχι ἄνθρωπο. ῞Αμα θέλεις, χτύπησε τὰ παλαμάκια καὶ θὰ με βρεῖς, ἐγὼ ἐδῶ θὰ εἶμαι. ᾽Αλλὰ κουτὸς ἦταν νὰ κάνει τίποτα; ῎Επαθε πολλὲς φορὲς ὁ Γιάννης. Φαίνεται εἴτε ἀλαφρωΐσκιωτος ἦταν, εἴτε ἀγαθὸς ἦταν, εἶχε καλὴ ψυχή καὶ τὸν κυνηγοῦσαν πολύ.

This Nereid you want to learn and hear about, many people have found her but they found her different. My husband though, he found her a woman, beautiful, hair loose, very long, and she offered him a cigarette. He used to go out, we had the animals, he found her, she told him many different words about his house, what his wife was called, what his children were called, what his wife's brothers and sisters who were in America were called, and she told him that "I try for your good. I've got a house too. I'll show you right now for you to see." And she showed it; it had many different things inside.

"Well," she said to him, that "I," she says, "am a Nereid, if you've read the Odyssey, the goddess Kalypso who kept Odysseus for eight years and wouldn't let him go to his homeland . . . Don't be afraid, I won't do anything to you . . . I've been watching over you since you were a little boy. Do you remember once when you

were going with your sister to the sheep pen, and you fell off the animal, it was me that put you back again, but you didn't realize it . . . I always try for your good."

Another time he found her again, and she showed him many things, when he was still unshaven and she wanted to shave him. She showed him a mountain so dense not even the tiniest mite could pass through. When she saw him so worried she opened the road again, and she says to him, *"Go, I don't have the right to follow you from there."*

Again another time when she came here to the village they put different charms on him. But she still wasn't afraid, and she said to him, *"Those things don't scare me."* She wouldn't go near though. She took him to only up to a certain place, and she said to him, *"You'd drive a mortal crazy, let alone . . . You don't speak. Just one word I want to hear, that's all."* And when he came back, he came wretched and miserable with fear. He couldn't even drag his feet.

The first time it was at twelve o'clock, the second time it was at three o'clock at night, the last time whether it was the morning or then again evening, I can't remember, but he was sick, sick, dead from fear. Because I said to him, *"What happened to you on the road, and why are you so late?"* and he says to me, *"Don't speak to me now, leave me alone, I'll tell you tomorrow."*

She was in a pink dress, her hair she wore loose down her back hanging to the ground. Her form was, well it can't be described, very well shaped. Like a woman. A woman, but the feet were like a duck's. That's why he was afraid, he realized she wasn't mortal and he didn't speak, from the feet.

She told him she has certain places. Good luck to her patience! It seems she used to go where there is water, in the ravine. Yes, she even got out a tobacco pouch and offered him a cigarette, a cigarette with a cork in it. Do they have cigarettes, well they don't, but the imagination . . . But he saw her, you see, just like you see someone and talk to them.

Three times he found her. The last time, she clapped her hands, she said, *"You'd drive a donkey crazy, let alone a human! If you like, clap your hands and you'll find me, I'll be there."* But was he so stupid as to do anything? Many times Yiannis suffered. It seems whether he was "light-shadowed" [clairvoyant], or good-hearted, or whatever, he had a good soul and they chased him a lot.

The narrative is not told straight, but repetitions, breaks, and inconsistencies vividly reflect both the process of recollection and the immediacy with which she relives the past and sees it again before her. There are abrupt changes of subject, unfinished sentences and thoughts. Does her "You'd drive a mortal crazy, let alone . . ." imply "a Nereid," as suggested by her reiteration, "You'd drive a donkey crazy, let alone a human"? There are several curious katharevousa expressions for time (ἐπὶ ὀκτὼ χρόνια, στὰς δώδεκα, στὰς τρεῖς) when she wants to convey documentary precision.

Yet her Greek has rhythm, while her story, however informal, contains elements of many mythical genres.

Most relevant to the question of meaning is the prevalance of stories about Nereids and other female tree and water spirits in Sklithron, the most remote village on Mavrovouni, the "back side" situated between Pelion and Kissavo, and until the 1980s without electricity, running water, or even a decent road. It is generally held that demonic creatures rarely enter a village that is protected by the church and four outlying shrines forming the sign of the Cross in a "magic circle" to ward off evil.[51] Instead, they inhabit outlying areas near water or trees, where shepherds graze flocks and play the flute (φλογέρα) or where women tend their "orchards, vineyards" (μποστάνια) and dance. Yiannis was among the most accomplished flute players in Sklithron, although Maria does not mention this. Mavrovouni is exceptionally dense with fig, scrub chestnut, and oak on its higher reaches, with thick pine forests on the lower and outer edges, while mountainous terrain causes dangerous torrents and treacherous streams. Before felling trees for timber and barter, Sklithriots used to propitiate the female tree spirit with a sacrificial ritual; otherwise she would take her revenge. What was once ritual passed into story. Crossing a bridge over a gully outside the village entailed similar hazards: Maria's nephew (my former husband, Christos) describes his terror when, aged thirteen, he had to cross over it to deliver messages for the local ἀντάρτες "resistance fighters," because he believed the female water spirit might change him into a dog or a horse, as happens frequently in the paramythia. If you so much as spoke to a demonic creature, let alone allowed her to cut your hair or shave you, you might be deprived of λόγος "speech, reason" or maimed for life. As to time, Maria's narrative reminds us that Nereids waylay their victims during the "dangerous hours" between noon and early evening or during the night and early morning, when most people are safely asleep.[52] Flowing hair, pink dresses, and cigarettes—not to mention a duck's feet—bespeak loose women malingering around villages. My former student Sophia Emmanuel ingeniously conjectured that Yiannis' encounters were with a lone and long-haired Western female tourist wearing beach flippers!

What do we make of Maria's reference to Kalypso in the Odyssey? Obviously, it is not a case of oral transmission from Homeric times, but rather one of village school-lore, picked up by Maria or more probably by Yiannis and inserted—with relevance, it must be noted—into her narrative to me, a classical scholar. And does she believe her husband's stories? Not entirely—she doesn't think that Nereids really have tobacco pouches or smoke filter cigarettes—but ultimately she acclaims faith in what her husband saw. As for her closing comments, they have the gnomic quality of a proverb: "light-shadowed" people, born on Saturdays, are prone to see demons, yet at the same time they are protected from demonic harm. Yiannis, in other words, could get away with a great deal. Myth provides a means of dealing with his possible infidelity.

Returning to Sklithron in the summer of 1991, I was struck by the relevance of Maria's story of almost three decades ago as a comment on social and cultural change. Then, the village was suffering from depopulation and decay; now, its houses and gardens have been renovated by former residents retiring from Athens and elsewhere to accommodate the summer flow of family and visitors. It looks thriving and prosperous, with good asphalt roads, running water, and electricity. What was missing? I saw only one elderly man cultivating his orchard on the upper reaches of the village. Villagers now depend on fundings from outside. Yet despite the fact that most residents have television, they still pay calls throughout the day to exchange news and gossip, sometimes malicious but always engaged, about disputed properties and folks married, departed, or deceased, named not conventionally but as "Dimitris, son of Yiannis."

Meaning and belief are elusive concepts and can be determined only by context. Mythical genres play dangerous but satisfying games in exploring the gaps between known and unknown worlds.[53]

CHAPTER 6

Myth in Song

In the last chapter, I suggested how myth functions in general terms, emphasizing interactions between speech genres and mythical genres. In the first part of this chapter I situate the early song collections in their European context. As it emerged in the 1880s, the Greek folklore canon was shaped by generic boundaries and hierarchies within European folklore, where the ballad enjoyed a privileged position as a distinct species of oral poetry, even as a kind of yardstick by which the vitality of a folk tradition might be judged.[1] In the second part I shall analyze examples in order to explore new approaches to account for such pervasive concerns as family conflicts, kinship ties, and "life beyond the grave," each of which might be subsumed under the theme of death and marriage, so paradoxically interwoven in Greek culture and thought.[2] Although analysis of music and dance lies beyond the scope of this chapter, I describe some features of performance to suggest how future studies might enhance our appreciation of the ambivalence of Greek "tales told in song" and of their ritual dimensions.

1. Ideology and Folklore: Greek Songs and European Models

As we saw in Chapter 3, Greek "ditties" (ἀσμάτια) have been recorded ever since the period of Roman domination. Despite the disdain they affect for their vulgar language, Byzantine historians cite the songs as potentially useful items of evidence, more often to blame and ridicule than to praise the powerful. No attempt was made to collect or record the songs for their intrinsic value; but the casual manner of reference suggests that they were regarded as an integral part of a common culture. From the late sixteenth century onward, Greek songs began to attract the attention of European scholars and travelers intent on comparing "ancients" and "moderns."[3] Nowhere else in Europe was the comparative model imposed, from the outset and from outside, as the major criterion validating the recording of popular traditions, two centuries before Greece became a nation-state. The European origins of this model—by which the modern Greeks could not fail to come off the worse—explain why the Greeks, once they had achieved independence in the nineteenth century, redefined it in terms of incipient nationalism: the comparison of ancients and moderns was replaced with notions of "continuity" (συνέχεια / ἐπιβίωσις / διάρκεια), while the songs of the unlettered folk were mined to prove direct links with antiquity through oral tradition.[4]

In Europe before the eighteenth century, aristocracies still shared in the production and performance of popular culture, much as remains the case with Greek elites today.[5] During the Enlightenment, resistance to popular culture as irrational coincided in western Europe with the struggle against witchcraft.[6] Romantic nationalism, as opposed to the liberal nationalism of western Europe and America, began to develop in central and eastern Europe, leading to what may be termed the first theoretical discussion of folklore by the German scholar Johann Gottfried von Herder (1744–1803), who formulated the equation of nation with language, Volk with moral virtue, and introduced the terms Volkslied, Volksseele, and Volksgeist ("folk song, folk soul, folk spirit"). For Herder, "the most natural state is one people with one national character," and the most unnatural, "the wild mixtures of various breeds and nations under one sceptre."[7] Woe betide the scattered Greek-speaking peoples of the late Roman, Byzantine, and Ottoman Empires as perhaps the ultimate, and longest-documented, examples of the "unnatural" state! In Germany were present all the factors relevant to the creation of folklore as theory and praxis: nascent romanticism, aspiring nationalism, and the search for an identity within itself, both in the rural folk and in its medieval past. Western romanticism and its appropriation of popular culture excluded the urban populace. In Herder's words, "Das Volk heisst nicht der Pöbel auf den Gassen, der singt und dichtet niemals, sondern schreit und verstümmelt" ("The folk are not the people on the streets, who never sing or compose, only screech and garble") (cited by Burke 1978, 8).

The first decades of the nineteenth century saw a growing emphasis in Europe on songs collected in the field, as opposed to reliance on manuscripts, printed texts, and fabrications. In developed European nations, the collections served literary rather than ideological interests. But among those peoples still aspiring to nationhood, songs and indigenous traditions formed part of the search for identity and the struggle for national independence. By 1840, collections of Finnish, Dalmatian, Serbian, Croatian, Slovenian, Romanian, Polish, and Bohemian songs were in circulation, mostly compiled by native researchers.[8]

Was Greece an exception to this general pattern, and if so, why? The first efforts to produce systematic collections were undertaken neither by Greeks nor in Greece but by philhellenes from Switzerland, Germany, France, and Italy, in collaboration with educated Greeks resident abroad. The story of their efforts has been researched with philological detective zeal and careful documentation of sources by Alexis Politis, culminating with the publication of Claude Fauriel's *Chants populaires de la Grèce moderne* (Paris, 1824–25). Greek folk songs were discovered in the literary circles of European philhellenes, for whom these songs held particular appeal, partly because they provided live clues to antiquity and partly because those selected celebrated the feats of heroes in the struggle for independence. Paris was, after all, one of the major centers of European philhellenism.

Once published, Fauriel's collection was rapidly translated into German by the poet and philhellene Wilhelm Müller (1825), into English (1825), and into Russian (Petrograd, 1826).[9] The literary market to which other projected collections might have appealed was therefore satisfied, and the next collections, those of Theodor Kind (1834) and Niccolò Tommaseo (1842–43), were published after the Greek War of Independence (1821–28). As for the Greeks, it has been said that they are perhaps unique in Europe in having had folklore "thrust upon them."[10] Fauriel and other European philhellenes complained—no doubt with good reason—of the apathy of their Greek informants. The reasons for Greek apathy should not be sought in simplistic arguments, such as Greek preoccupation with the War of Independence, or the conflicting aspirations of French and German romanticism, which they inherited. National struggle might have acted as a spur, as it did elsewhere; it was precisely from the interaction between French and German scholars and poets that the activities of the European philhellenes were generated.[11] The songs, proverbs, and vocabulary of the common people were invoked by diaspora Greek elites only at random, mainly to support differing positions in the "language question." Korais, whose intervention in the language dispute we have already discussed, rejected folk culture outright as superstitious, irrational, and backward. A contemporary of his, writing in Λόγιος Ἑρμῆς ("Learned Hermes") on 15 August 1817, exhorts his fellow Greeks as follows, with the clear implication that "base ditties" signified enslavement to Ottoman rule: "Whence

I, beloved countrymen, have translated this verse enkomion on Homer, desiring from the depth of my soul that the youth of Greece, genuine servants [θεράποντες] of the Helikonian Muses, the bright hopes of the race [τοῦ γένους] should at all costs avoid reading those wretched and base ditties [ἀσμάτια], the most patent tokens [τεκμήρια] of our common misfortune" (Politis 1984, 141–42; my translation).

Greek folk songs were discovered not in Greece but in the literary salons of Europe, in response to the tastes of European poets and philhellenes, whose informants were expatriate Greeks educated in the same circles and whose principles derived from centuries of preoccupation with the comparison of ancients and moderns. One year before publication of his collection, Fauriel declared in his preface a determination to demonstrate through it that "the spirit of the ancients, the breath of poetry, lived there yet" (1824). His Greek contemporaries might not have disapproved of his sentiment, but few were ready at that time to concede that this spirit lived on the lips of the "vulgar" (χυδαῖοι), especially since they despised popular songs as "Oriental" and "Turkish." Literary recognition of the folk songs was inspired by romantic Hellenism and divorced from the country, culture, and people that produced them. The interconnections between Goethe, German neo-Hellenism (the rediscovery of ancient Greece), and Greek intellectuals are treated with poignant irony in Vizyenos' "Consequences" (1885), as will be seen in Chapter 8. As for the impact of the songs, it is tempting to see in Wilhelm Müller's "Die schöne Müllerin" and "Die Winterreise," so memorably set to music by Schubert, some of the lyrical impulse in Greek song so admired by Goethe and made known to him through Müller's circle.

If the discovery of Greek folk songs was a phenomenon of European romanticism, the emergence of folklore as a discipline was the product of Greek demoticist nationism, as it developed in the last decades of the nineteenth century, shaped not only by internal factors but also by complex and interacting forces operating in Greece and Europe. Around the time of the creation of the Greek state, literary interest in the folk songs began to develop, but in rather restricted ways.[12] Songs were useful for poetic inspiration but as yet neither idealized as the spontaneous expression of the nation's soul nor upheld as a model for linguistic imitation, as happened later in the century.

Fallmerayer's role in effecting a shift of emphasis from the folk songs as literary to national texts has been demonstrated by Herzfeld. Fallmerayer's thesis (that the modern Greeks shared no pure blood with the ancients) sparked off intense activities among Greek scholars, who began collecting ἐθνικὰ ἄσματα "national songs" and studying their affinities with ancient

Greek tradition, in folklorist Michael Lelekos' case with the stated intention of "demolishing the rotten edifice of that crazy historian from Germany [*sic*]."[13] In Europe, classical scholars turned their attention to the affinities between ancient Greek religion and modern Greek folklore.[14] Yet Fallmerayerism, and reactions to it, should be viewed within the context of ideological and political wrangles over the "site of Greece" since the sixteenth century. The intensity of the reaction to Fallmerayer kept Greek folklorists locked within a closed model of their culture in relation to its past and encouraged European classicists to value folklore only insofar as it could illuminate antiquity. The marginalization of modern Greek culture as a contemporary culture in its own right is at least as much the result of European attitudes as of Greek ethnocentrism.[15] Meanwhile, the debate had repercussions for the formation of a Greek canon of folklore in the 1880s.

2. The Greek Canon, the Ballad, and the Muses

N. G. Politis, in his classic taxonomies (1909), divides the canon of Greek folklore (λαογραφία) into two categories: "monuments of the word" and "traditional activities and practices," both of which have been summarized and commented on by Herzfeld (1982, 145–48). Textual items are separated from and privileged over nontextual items, hence they are viewed as verbal monuments divorced from ritual functions and from social and material contexts. "Music and musical instruments" is included as an afterthought (under item II.19), despite the fact that, to this day, the songs are always sung or danced, never recited (except by academics and poets). The taxonomy thus frees the folklorist from the need to study performative context or ritual function, in order to concentrate on ancient origins and genres. As Herzfeld has noted, the textual category lists all sung items under one heading, while dividing the spoken items into no less than nine groups along lines which seem arbitrary but in fact once again facilitate the derivation of modern from ancient. Folklore is therefore an amalgam of separable units rather than a coherent system. Politis' taxonomy, which has remained a model for subsequent collections and studies, is based on criteria more appropriate to the study of archaeology or philology, privileging the search for origins over synchronic analysis of function, context, and system.[16]

In Politis' anthology of 1914, the songs are grouped as follows: Historical; Kleftic; Akritic; Ballads; Love Songs; Wedding Songs; Lullabies; Songs of Exile; Laments; Songs of the Lower World; Gnomic Songs; Work Songs; Songs of the Middle Ages; and Songs in Greek Dialects (from areas outside Greece). They are presented in *logical* and *chronological* order, as we move

from historical through mythical to ritual songs; but it is an order designed
to emphasize linearity and national oneness rather than diversity and interpenetration. It ignores the shifting boundaries determined by performative
speech genres and mythic genres, and it privileges narrative over ritual
songs. Thus, wedding songs and laments with supposed Akritic elements
are regarded as "conflations" (*symphyrmoí*) of a lost epic tradition to clinch
connections with antiquity. Politis' editorial methodology is no less philological in orientation than his taxonomy. Some thirty years after new editorial principles for the collection of folk ballads had been pioneered by F. J.
Child (1884), who published all known variants of each song, Politis defined his editorial task in terms borrowed from the methods of textual criticism current in his day (1914, vii). The underlying assumption is that each
song is the fragmented remains of a text-in-itself, with its own history to
be traced independently of related songs, detached from region, performative context, and music and restored as a text (κείμενον) by conflation of
different and incomplete variants according to the scholar's conception of
what constitutes an ordered and beautiful whole.[17] In folklore, as perhaps in
no other discipline, the researcher quite literally selects and creates the materials. Reconstituted songs are fed back to the people—via schoolroom
and the media—as authoritative texts, undermining the element of variation considered essential to live oral tradition; yet such philological appropriation was itself a part of the its time. We cannot study the songs in pris-
tine isolation from literary and scholarly hegemonies.[18]

Despite the range and precision of Politis' scholarship, the search for origins and continuity is no less evident in his studies of songs, tales, and legends. A song or story type is identified, given a specific or generic name
(such as "The Dead Brother" or "cosmogonic myths"), while variants are
collected and examined with a view to reconstructing the Urtext and its
historical and geographical diffusion. He makes comparison with other
Balkan examples; but his major thrust is to link the hypothetical archetype
with an ancient Greek myth, which in turn is used to assert the anteriority
of Greek over other Balkan types by its origins in ancient Greek. It is a circular argument. In the preface to his early study of folk traditions, significantly subtitled Νεοελληνικὴ Μυθολογία ("Modern Greek Mythology"),
Politis states: "Towards the compilation of this study . . . I have gathered the
remains [λείψανα] scattered here and there within it, whether in legends
[παραμύθια], synaxaria of the middle ages, or in different regional traditions [παραδόσεις], observing with joy that in this so constituted *mosaic*,
many parts of *ancient mythology* are reflected" (1871, 4; emphases added).
The archaeological metaphor views tradition not as a dynamic structure
with an internal system of its own but as mythology, from which remains

("corpses") can be isolated to reconstruct a mosaic that is then triumphantly shown to mirror ancient Greece!

My critique is not intended to undermine Politis' contribution to Greek folklore—to him is owed not only the creation of the discipline but above all the collection and study of a wealth of material—but to indicate some of the premises, conscious and unconscious, which lie at its roots, many unchallenged to this day. These were shaped by the intellectual horizons of both Greece and Europe; meanwhile, his position as Professor of Folklore at the University of Athens was exploited by nationalist demoticists to establish the hegemony of "the demotic songs" as the major component of the new literary canon.[19]

The distorting effects of European romanticism and demotic nationalism on the collection and study of Greek folk songs can be summarized under the following headings:

1. Textualization and compartmentalization. Detached from context and function, shorn of music and dance, diverse songs are reduced to the single category "demotic poetry," compartmentalized according to criteria designed to facilitate comparison with the "high" ancient genres (historical/Kleftic/Akritic = epic; ballads = myth/tragedy; love/marriage/birth/exile/death = ritual). Humorous, satirical, and risqué erotic songs are marginalized or suppressed to conform to certain ideals about Hellenism.[20]

2. Texts as mirrors. Demotic poetry reflects an image of the collective and national soul. It can be read in and of itself, as a mirror of reality, with minimal reference to craft of composition. Poetic genres are fixed and therefore better mirrors than prose tales.

3. Idealization of the "folk." The concept of the "folk" is never closely defined but is implicitly linked with the rural peasantry, untainted by literary and vulgar urban influences. At the same time, texts are separated from actions and beliefs, perhaps because the Christian context of performance disturbed the model of pure Hellenism (Herzfeld 1982). Such premises were shared by many other European folklorists, particularly during the latter part of the nineteenth century, but in Greece their impact has proved more enduring than elsewhere: Politis' canon of laographia in general and of songs in particular remains intact, despite the shift over the past two decades from diachronic to synchronic analysis.

In the course of the nineteenth century, songs—especially ballads—became the site where rival claims to the ancient Muses were staked. It was Goethe, in a letter to his (1814), who first drew attention to the mythic-dramatic qualities of Greek songs, made known to him through Werner von Haxthausen's manuscripts: (not published until 1935). Goethe wrote:

"All features, lyric, dramatic and epic, appear united in a single form. Theirs is a synthesis of the northern, Scottish spirit with the southern, mythological spirit of antiquity." By contrast, as the German philologist Gustav Meyer pointed out some seventy years later, the Serbian songs resemble "broad canvases painted in bright colours" or "a grand river flowing through monotonous wide plains," whereas Greek songs are "pellucid as the southern breeze."[21] While we may smile today at such conceits (especially links between songs unheard and landscapes unvisited), they testify to an assumption that Greek songs must be somehow different by virtue of their associations with Greek soil.

Not long after Child had commenced publication of his monumental collection *English and Scottish Popular Ballads* (1882–98), Politis chose to resurrect the archaic dialect word *paralogē* "ballad" to distinguish narrative songs on *mythical* themes from historical, Akritic, and Kleftic songs, on the basis of a statement by M. Kambouroglou that in the Old Athenian dialect, "the poetic products of the epic or short epic type used to be called παρ- αλογαί" (1889). How valid is the term "ballad" for Greek songs, and would Politis have reintroduced an obsolete word were it not for the preeminence of the ballad in Western scholarship? The Old Athenian term was generic and stylistic rather than specific and inclusive of Akritic, erotic, and other songs in which the melodic element was subservient to recitation. Some decades later, the folklorist Stilpon Kyriakidis argued that παραλογή can be related both to the Cypriot περιλοή, attested in the narrative "Song of Zographou," and to the more widespread καταλόγι "proverbial song; love song," and that it derives by haplology from the ancient Greek παρακατα- λογή. He cites ancient sources to argue that it was a form of delivery distinct from song, used for melodramatic recitations of mythico-tragic stories declaimed to instrumental and sometimes danced accompaniment in catalectic iambic tetrameter, one of the postulated antecedents of the fifteen-syllable politikos stichos. Kyriakidis concludes with a review of testimonies for the pantomime in the Greco-Roman period, when he believes the modern song tradition began to take shape.[22]

The thesis is supported by a considerable body of evidence. Comparable suffixes occur in μοιρολόγι, "lament, fate song" (widespread in current usage), and ἐπιλογή "narrative song" (limited to the northern Greek mainland), while modern τραγούδι "song" derives from ancient τραγῳδία "tragedy." As for modes of performance, στιχοπλοκία "verse weaving" is used for rhymes chanted to instrumental accompaniment (Pontos), in the manner of rhymes improvised on historical and melodramatic events by the Cypriot *poiētárides* or the Cretan *rimadóroi* "professional poets; minstrels." Yet the temptations of such linear argumentation lie in reaching the conclusion, by lines a little too straight, that "all roads of folk song lead back to ancient tragedy" (Ioannou 1975, 10). The antiquity and complexity of generic terms still in current usage are not disputed; but words—even etymologies—can be misleading in the absence of contextual evidence: the suffixes -λογή, -λόγι do not necessarily prove a declamatory as opposed to sung performance, any more than the common expression νὰ σοῦ πῶ ἕνα τραγούδι "let me tell you a song" literally means what it says or indeed than the term "ballad" indicates danced performance, now as then.

At least one voice dared to challenge the exclusivity of Greek claims on the ancient Muses, and at the height of nationalism. In a lucid and wide-ranging essay, playfully entitled "Up Mount Helikon: *Ballísmata*," the poet and prose writer Georgios Vizyenos (1893) asks, Where did the Muses go after they deserted the slopes of Mount Helikon? His answer takes us not to Greece but across centuries and continents to danced ballad rhythms and verses in medieval and Renaissance Italy, Spain, France, and northern Europe; to the major European poets, from Dante and Petrarch to Schiller and Heine; and to German Lieder. He closes the Muses' journey with a poignant lyric by Ludwig Uhland about two star-crossed lovers: the girl was secluded in a monastery, the boy shut up in a deep prison. As for Greek ballads, he links them with Roman satire and ceremonial (anticipating Kyriakidis' thesis on pantomime); but the only Greek examples he cites are parodic versions of ballads designated as "tragic" by the canon of his day, such as "The Poisoned Bride" or "The Uncaring Wife" (who dances her husband into the grave!), and rendered in Greek heavily tinged with Bulgarian phonology and syntax.

The essay was published in March 1893, one year after Vizyenos was confined to an insane asylum near Daphni and three years before his premature death in 1896. His choice of the word *bállisma* (as opposed to *paralogē*) for "ballad" underscores his insistence on defining genre according to context: "bállos" is a solo dance, so named from the dancer's habit of slapping the hand on the knee and leaping into the air. Did Vizyenos, coming from ethnically unclean regions of eastern Thrace, wish to challenge the prevailing orthodoxy on the purity of Greek folk songs? His concluding comment that "such songs [as Uhland's] unfortunately do not exist in Greece" is perceptive and casts tragic light on *Consequences of the Old Story* (1885), in which a German girl locked up in an insane asylum plays the harp and sings, with the ironic twist that her favorite lyrics are Vizyenos' own verses.[23]

3. Toward New Approaches?

Following Vizyenos' lead, let us try to reevaluate Greek songs. As Alan Bold has shown, attempts to define the ballad in universal terms are notoriously imprecise: "a folk song that tells a story" and "any sort of traditional narrative poem sung with or without accompaniment or dance in assemblies of the people"; or else specificities from one culture are extrapolated even when not applicable to others.[24] Songs telling stories have existed and traversed ethnic boundaries since time immemorial: the question is, How are similar stories adapted to diverse regional traditions, narrative and musical? From the twelfth century onward, a common fund of narrative songs, originating as dances (English "ballet," French "ballade"), spread rapidly across Europe, thanks to increased opportunities for travel and exchange of literary tastes. These songs interacted with literary genres, both indigenous and other, such as epic, romance, and prose tale, which led to the predominance of tragic themes of love or war.

At the margins of Europe, especially where native musical traditions persisted alongside pre-Christian mythologies, as in northern Scotland, Ireland, or the Balkans, the picture is by no means homogeneous. Paradoxically, Scotland is perceived as one of the major sources of the classic tragic ballad ("the mickle sangs"); yet the genre is restricted to the Scots dialect of English and is not found in Gaelic, even though ballad themes such as "The Twa Sisters" have been adapted to the different context of women's "waulking songs" performed at the pulling and dyeing of the cloth. In Ireland, only four ballads have entered the song tradition from Scotland, and in each case the story is treated differently from its donor culture. Even in France, ballad forms have taken humorous and parodic directions which do not conform to literary stereotypes of the ballad.[25] As for Greek songs, melody and dance predominate over story. In the course of the nineteenth century, literary appropriation of the ballad (especially by British and German poets) and scholarly emphasis on common European origins in the Middle Ages led to the privileging of the ballad over other genres and to the enhancement of romantic love at the expense of older ritual/mythic elements.

Over the past decades, several new approaches to Greek songs have been explored. In 1935, Swiss musicologist Samuel Baud-Bovy published his collection of Dodekanesian songs, with musical notation and analysis. In 1968, folklorist G. K. Spyridakis and musicologist S. A. Peristeris followed suit, publishing songs from the Folklore Archives of Athens, with extensive musicological commentary. Greek songs from many regions became accessible for the first time and are now available on authenticated disks, although few scholars have used either music or dance to assist their interpretive strategies or analyses of formula systems.[26] The French scholar Guy Saunier, in his study of concepts of justice and injustice in Greek popular song, has contributed an extensive analysis of narrative songs, with careful documentation of variants. He extrapolates from the songs a case for an overall moral system of good and evil, based on close analysis of the significations of the formulaic phrase δὲν εἶναι κρῖμα κι ἄδικο; "isn't it a shame and wrong?" His approach is a welcome departure into ethicosocial perspectives, although he says nothing about music, while excluding the paramythia from analysis on the grounds that they are "impure," subject to "nonpopular" influences (1979, 25).

Beaton's *Folk Poetry of Modern Greece* (1980) draws attention to the structural composition of oral formulas and examines the mythical system of song genres. Despite incisive analysis, he fails to challenge the limitations of established generic boundaries and sometimes falls into the trap of literalist readings.[27] My own analysis (1983) draws on anthropological studies in order to highlight the nature of family conflicts, in particular the interrelated themes of marriage and death; but adherence to structuralist models privileges plot analysis over technique, imagery, context—and music. G. Sifakis, drawing on earlier studies of Kyriakidis and Baud-Bovy, attempts a detailed analysis of the poetics of Greek folk song, laying the foundations for extending formulaic analysis to musical as well as verbal units (1988). But he fails to apply his model for the oral–compositional basis of the decapentasyllable to the octosyllabic and heptasyllabic verses, although Baud-Bovy's evidence suggests that these meters antedate the decapentasyllable, at least in song. L. M. Danforth's study of fire-walking rituals (1989) reminds us of the crucial importance of performative context: the four "narrative songs" he recorded are integrated with distinct stages of the Anastenaria ritual. He is careful to cite comments of singers and participants, thereby affording rare insights into how the songs mean for them, functioning not merely as *narratives* about distant events and figures but also as *myths* which give expression on multiple levels to their own domestic conflicts and historical experience, contributing significantly to the healing powers of *ritual* as well.

Greek songs as narratives can be analyzed productively only if the boundaries between myth and ritual are dissolved. Such songs as "Mikrokostandinos," "The Mother Murderess," and "The Bridge of Arta," may accompany dances at fire walking and weddings. Ritual songs constantly include and encode narrative/mythical elements: a well-known story needs only the barest reference for the allusion to be caught. Maniot laments are narrative in form but ritual in performance, referring to specific killings (history) and their relevance for the present (myth). Song categories used by performers are: χορευτά "danced songs"; καθιστά or τῆς τάβλας "seated songs"; μοιρολόγια "funeral laments"; and μαντινάδες "improvised couplets." Even these categories are not fixed: not only may the same song take more than one of the above forms, but singers will often also draw attention to their interchangeability. Τὸ λες μοιρολόγι, τὸ λες καὶ νυφικό "you can sing it as a dirge, you can also sing it as a bridal song," as informants told Danforth (1982, 174). Women from Cyprus, Crete, and Nisyros will practice laments as they do their household chores or bake their daily bread.[28] What changes is manner of performance, timbre, and pitch: dirges are sung unaccompanied, at high pitch in rapid tempo, with a narrow tonal range; songs lamenting the bride's departure are sung at normal pitch, with instrumental accompaniment.

My field archives (1963; 1966) include performances of two well-known Epirot laments: Σήκω Μαριώ, "Get Up, Mario," and Πέντε μέρες παντρεμένη, "Five Days Married." Both songs take the form of a dialogue between mother and daughter: in the first, a mother begs Mario to rise from the grave, but she replies that she cannot because she has no legs, hands, or heart; in the second, a bride of five days returns a widow "with ritual tokens in her apron" to her mother, who bids her wed again; she refuses. One performance (1963) was recorded in a dentist's waiting room in Larisa from a dental nurse, Alexandra Tsipi, who sang in the high-pitched tone of a dirge, with intricate melismata. The second performance, by a group of itinerant musicians, was recorded in the main square of the mountain village of Samarina, in western Macedonia (1966) and marked the opening of the Feast of the Dormition on 15 August, a joyous occasion when Samariniots from as far afield as North America and Australia, as well as from Greece, gather together to feast, sing, and dance for several days and nights. The lead klarino-player makes his instrument his voice as he wails out the tune in loud complaint to the accompaniment of the violinist, occasionally interjecting the odd key phrase in semirecitative as he pauses to take breath.[29] His performance of the two songs is no less than a celebration of *pónos* "pain," particularly striking because there is no apparent connection between song themes and auspicious occasion. Or can we be so sure? Might not a virgin mother who gave birth to Christ, her son and God, perhaps be moved to pity, on the Feast of the Dormition, by songs of mothers and brides who likewise suffered pain and loss? It reflects the same paradox underlying the ritual contexts for "The Mother Murderess" and "Mikrokostandinos."

4. Form and Structure: Melody and Narrative

Greek traditional singers do not recite words as verse and may be unable to do so, for reasons I shall suggest. Greek music, with its regional diversity, complex modalities, irregular rhythmic patterns, and close affinities with Byzantine chant and Near Eastern music, constitutes a "language" different from that of northern and western European music. Perhaps the most striking difference concerns the apparent asymmetry of words and music in many songs, especially those in fifteen-syllable verse. Except on Crete, Cyprus, and in former Greek-speaking parts of Asia Minor, where narrative songs may extend to over one hundred lines, songs rarely exceed fifty nonstanzaic, usually nonrhyming lines. Read as verse, they are iambic, with a regular number of syllables throughout, oxytonic in the first hemistich, paroxytonic in the second. However, the musical phrase, often covering one and a half lines of verse, may not correspond to the spoken meter. Musicologists distinguish three main categories of rhythmic structure. First, "rhythmic" (ἔρρυθμα), with regular meter, simple or compound, divisible into the same bar lines throughout: such are "danced songs" (χορευτά), performed on festive, ritual, and informal occasions, either solo or with lead singer and antiphonal choral refrain, usually to instrumental accompaniment; *mantinádes* (rhyming couplets), improvised on erotic and topical themes on Crete and other islands; rhyming and nonrhyming octosyllabic and heptasyllabic ritual songs and children's quête songs, especially common in the Dodecanese and other Aegean islands. Second, "semirhythmic" (ρυθμοειδῆ), or songs with no regular melodic rhythm but with fixed units of stress, divisible into variable bar lines: such are laments and narrative songs. Third, songs in "free meter" (ἐλευθέρου ρυθμοῦ), are sung either in recitative or in melismatic vocal and instrumental performance, with frequent *tsakísmata* ("breaks") and *gyrísmata* ("turns"): such are most "table songs" (historical and Kleftic).[30] The categories used by the singers (dances, table songs, laments) begin to make sense when related to the music.

Two examples will illustrate the general principle. The first is a version from the Sporades islands of the well-known ballad "The Bridge of Arta," to be analyzed below.[31] Although it tells the tragic story of how the master craftsman's wife was lured into the foundations of a mythic bridge to make it secure, it is sung to a jaunty dance and performed by a male lead with female responses and instrumental accompaniment:

Example 1

(Violin plays melody throughout)

Leader: Σαράντα‑πέ‑, σαράντα‑πέ‑, σαράντα‑πέντε μάστοροι
           (chorus repeats)
           κι ἑξῆντα μαθητάδες (chorus repeats + instrumental and vocal
           variation)
           γιοφύρι χτί‑, γιοφύρι χτί‑, γιοφύρι χτίζαν στὸ γιαλό
           (chorus repeats)

           Forty-fi-, forty-, forty-five craftsmen
           and sixty apprentices were a-bui-, bui-, building a bridge on the
           shore. . . .

Words are split and syllables repeated according to the device known as
"hocket," as in the medieval carol "Personent hodie" (*Oxford Book of Carols,*
no. 78, *Piae Cantiones* [1582]).

My second example, a wedding aubade from the Peloponnese in semirhythmic form, refers allusively through bird song to a cypress tree in whose
arms the battle-weary warrior will return to find rest (Spyridakis and Peristeris, 3–5). (See next page.)

In the first example (without *tsakísmata*), "hocket" interrupts the narrative
flow but underscores its danced structure. In the second (with *tsakísmata*),
the singer lengthens words and syllables—semantically unmarked but emo-

Example 2

Peloponnese

Τώ-ρα τὰ που - - λιά_____ τω · ρα_τὰ χε - - λι -

δό - - - - νια, τω - ρα - - - αοὶ πέ - τώ - ραοί πέρ - - δι - - - - κες.

Του

Macedonia

Τώ-ρα τὰ που - - - - - - - - - - λιά_____ τώ

- ρα - τὰ χε - - - - - - - - - λι - - -

tionally charged—against the spoken rhythm. Such features have been attributed to the tendency to adapt recent songs to older melodic patterns, a plausible hypothesis perhaps in the case of table songs in free rhythm in which the musical phrase covers one and a half lines of verse. The asymmetry between words and melody in rhythmic and semirhythmic songs alike points, however, to the particular delight Greek singers take in pitting music against words: old tunes have always been adapted to new words but without the same "jouissance" in the variance between them. Baud–Bovy's characterization of Kleftic song is appropriate to many other types:

> Ainsi la strophe d'un vers et demi nous apparaît comme une étape dans l'évolution du vers politique chanté. Le traitement qu'elle lui impose détruit son unité poétique, et c'est peut-être une des raisons pour lesquelles les *textes* des chansons cleftiques sont loin d'avoir la valeur des textes des chants épiques antérieurs. Mais, du point de vue *musical*, cette asymétrie du texte et de la musique s'est révélée une source d'enrichissement, et a conféré à la chanson "cleftique" un intérêt bien supérieur à celui

des chansons, plus régulières, où la musique se contente, humblement, de porter les paroles. (1958, 33)

Turning now to the ways stories are told in song, if we set aside the special cases of the songs composed on Crete and Cyprus by professional bards,[32] we may define the structure as dramatic. The singer likes to begin by combining graphic visual detail with unmediated second-person address *to the protagonist* to draw us right into the *scene*, rather than into the *story*. In most versions of "The Dead Brother," the singer focuses on the chief cause of the tragic myth, a mother jealously guarding her only daughter:

Μάνα μὲ τοὺς ἐννιά σου γιοὺς καὶ μὲ τῇ μιά σου κόρη!
(Politis 1914, 92.1)

Mother with your nine sons and with your only daughter!

In "The Poisoned Bride," the listener is told to look at a poor orphan girl in what seems to be a wondertale wedding, with no apparent hint of the impending disaster:

Θωρεῖς τὴν κείνη τὴν κορφή, τὴν πράσινη μαδάρα;
'Εκεῖ ἀπὸ πίσω κάνουνε μιᾶς ὀρφανούλας γάμο.
Χίλιοι τσῇ πῆγαν τὰ προυκιά, χίλιοι τ' ἀπανωπρούκια
καὶ τοῦ γαμπροῦ τὸ κάλεσμα ἦσαν ἐννιὰ χιλιάδες.

You see that peak, that green mountain clearing?
Just beyond they are holding the wedding of an orphan girl.
A thousand bear her dowry, a thousand her wedding gifts,
and the groom has guests of nine more thousands.
(Acad. Ath. 1962: 348–49, 1–4)

Frequently, the singer may indulge in apparently needless repetition before "getting on with the story," as in "Mikrokostandinos" and "Monoyiannes":

'Ο Κωσταδίνος ὁ μικρός κι ὁ μικροΚωσταδίνος
μικρό dον εἶχ' ἡ μάννα dου, μικρό δ' ἀρραβωνιάζει,
μικρό dον ἦρτε μήνυμα νὰ πάῃ στὸ σεφέρι.
(Megas 1961, 488–90.1–3)

Kostadinos the Little, Little Kostadinos
was his mother's little one, little when she betrothed him,
and little when the summons came for him to go to war.

'Ο Γιάννες ὁ Μονόγιαννες κι ὁ μοναχόν ὁ Γιάννες,
ὁ Γιάννες ἐτοιμάσκεται νὰ φτάγ' χαρὰν καὶ γάμους.
Χάρος ς' σήμ' πόρταν ἔστεκεν κι ἀτόναν φοβερίζει.

(Ioannou 1975, 73–75.1–3)

Yiannes, Lone Yiannes, Yiannes alone,
Yiannes is preparing to go to his joy and wedding.
Charos stands at the door and threatens him.

These repetitions do not engage us in events, but serve a mythic-dramatic
purpose by indicating a critical paradox: Kostandinos is "little" at the beginning, dominated by his mother, only to grow to maturity through war and
to kill her with his own sword at the end in revenge for her harsh treatment
of his wronged bride (Beaton 1980, 132–34). Yiannes is marked as "alone" at
the outset to highlight his bride's successful rescue of him. In all these open-
ings, the listener is attuned—but not told—to expect a paradoxical outcome.
As for endings, Greek songs close starkly, without emotional comment:

῾Ώσπου νὰ βγῆ στὴν πόρτα της, ἐβγῆκε ἡ ψυχή της.

She had not reached the door when her soul departed.

("The Dead Brother," [Thrace] Ioannou 1975, 38, Line 7)

Στὴ μέση τὴν ἔσκισε, στὸ μῦλο τὴν πηγαίνει.

He ripped her through the middle, he takes her to the mill.

("Evil Mother-in-Law," [Thrace] Megas 1961: 490, Line 59)

'Ο Γιάννες κάμει τὴν χαράν, ὁ Γιάννες κάμν' τὸν γάμον.

Yiannes prepares for joy, Yiannes goes to wed.

("Monoyiannes," [Pontos] Ioannou 1975, 75, Line 48)

However, in performance the singer can choose to stop at any point: narrative closure does not seem to matter, provided the ending is rendered in appropriate dramatic fashion. Verbal expression is suppressed, although it may
come out passionately in the music, as in the song Τώρα τὰ πουλιά, "Now
the Birds," to which I shall return in Chapter 10.

These features may be related to the treatment of time, place, and person. In the classic Scottish ballad, story is located, as in "Andrew Lammie,"
at a particular mill of Fyvie, with the denouement occurring in "Edinburgh town" (Child 4:233, 300–308). Time is not specified, but the event is

assumed to have taken place, and some scholars have pointed to incidents in Scottish history to explicate a significant number of ballads.[33] The tense is indicative. Greek songs move closer to the subjunctive, opening with an address, such as "Mother with your nine sons!" or "Do you see that peak?" Even when named, places are indeterminate (as in the laments for the fall of cities), hence "Babylonia" can easily pass into "Romania" or simply στὰ ξένα μακρυά "in foreign parts"; and the "Bridge of Arta" becomes the mythic "Bridge of Hair," situated somewhere between life and death. Persons are defined by kinship/status (daughter, mother-in-law, sister, brother) or by an epithet or name so recurrent as to decenter reference to individuals (Areti, Rinoula, Mikrokostandinos, Monoyiannes). In the next section I shall attempt to explain these structural features in terms of the mythical, rather than historical/individual, perceptions of life and death.

5. Focal Conflicts: Life beyond the Grave

Theme and character can be best appreciated contextually, by asking, what are the areas of focal conflict? I shall analyze two songs widely diffused throughout the Balkans, "The Bridge of Arta" and "The Dead Brother," to show the importance of conflicts revolving around kinship and marriage. First, "The Bridge of Arta," already encountered as a dance song from the Sporades. Here is a version from Mytilini (1947).[34]

> Σαρανταπέντε μάστοροι κι ἑξήντα μαθητάδες
> γεφύρι θεμελιώνανε στῆς Ἄρτας τὸ ποτάμι.
> Ὁλημερὶς ἐχτίζανε, τὸ βράδυ γκρεμιζόταν.
> Μοιρολογοῦνε μάστοροι καὶ κλαῖνε μαθητάδες.
> 5   —Ἀλίμονο στοὺς κόπους μας, κρίμα στὴ δούλεψή μας,
> ὁλημερὶς νὰ χτίζομε, τὸ βράδυ νὰ γκρεμιέται.
> Καὶ τὸ στοιχειὸ ποκρίθηκε ἀπ' τὴ δεξιὰ καμάρα·
> —Ἄ δὲ στοιχειώσετ' ἄνθρωπο, τοῖχος δὲ θεμελιώνει.
> Καὶ μὴ στοιχειώσετε ὀρφανό, μὴ ξένο, μὴ διαβάτη,
> 10   παρὰ τοῦ πρωτομάστορα τὴν ὄμορφη γυναῖκα.
> Τ' ἀκούει ὁ πρωτομάστορας, ραγίζει ἡ καρδιά του.
> Μὲ τὸ πουλὶ παρήγγειλε, μὲ τὸ πουλὶ τ' ἀηδόνι·
> —Ἀργὰ ντυθεῖ, ἀργὰ 'λλαχτεῖ, ἀργὰ να πά τὸ γιόμα,
> ἀργὰ νὰ πά' καὶ νὰ διαβεῖ τῆς Ἄρτας τὸ γεφύρι.
> 15   Καὶ τὸ πουλὶ παράκουσε κι ἀλλοιῶς ἐπῆγε κι εἶπε·
> —Γοργὰ ντυθεῖς, γοργὰ 'λλαχτεῖς, γοργὰ νὰ πᾶς τὸ
> γιόμα,
> γοργὰ νὰ πᾶς καὶ νὰ διαβεῖς τῆς Ἄρτας τὸ γεφύρι.

Νά την καὶ ἐξεφάνηκε ἀπὸ τὴν ἄσπρη στράτα.
Τὴν εἶδε ὁ πρωτομάστορας, ραγίζεται ἡ καρδιά του.
20 —Ὥρα καλή σας, μάστορες κι ἐσεῖς οἱ μαθητάδες·
μὰ τί ἔχει ὁ πρωτομάτορας κι εἶν᾽ ἔτσι χολιασμένος;
—Τὸ δαχτυλίδι τοῦ 'πεσε στὴν πρώτη τὴν καμάρα,
καὶ ποιὸς νὰ μπεῖ, καὶ ποιὸς νὰ βγεῖ τὸ δαχτυλίδι νὰ 'βρει;
—Ἐγὼ νὰ μπῶ, ἐγὼ νὰ βγῶ, τὸ δαχτυλίδι νὰ 'βρω.
25 Μηδὲ καλὰ κατέβηκε, μηδὲ στὴ μέση μπῆκε·
—Τράβα, καλέ, τὴν ἄλυσο, τράβα τὴν ἀλυσίδα,
ὅλο τὸν κόσμο γύρισα καὶ τίποτα δὲν ἦβρα.
Ἕνας πιχάει μὲ τὸ μυστρὶ κι ἄλλος μὲ τὸν ἀσβέστη,
πιάνει κι ὁ πρωτομάστορας καὶ ρίχτει μέγα λίθο.
30 —Τρεῖς ἀδερφάδες ἤμαστε κι οἱ τρεῖς κακογραμμένες·
ἡ μιά 'χτισε τὸ Δούναβη κι ἡ ἄλλη τὸν Αὐλώνα,
κι ἐγὼ ἡ πιὸ μικρότερη τῆς Ἄρτας τὸ γεφύρι.
Ὡς τρέμει ἡ καρδούλα μου, ἄς τρέμει τὸ γεφύρι·
ὡς πέφτουν τὰ μαλλάκια μου, νὰ πέφτουν οἱ διαβάτες.
35 —Κόρη, τὸν λόγο ἄλλαξε κι ἄλλη κατάρα δῶσε,
κι ἔχεις ἀδερφὸ στὴν ξενιτιά, μὴ λάχει καὶ περάσει.
—Σίδερο ἡ καρδούλα μου, σίδερο τὸ γεφύρι·
σίδερο τὰ μαλλάκια μου, σίδερο κι οἱ διαβάτες.

(Ioannou 1975, 46–47)

Forty-five craftsmen and sixty apprentices
were building a bridge on the river of Arta.
All day they kept building, at night it fell down.
The craftsmen lamented, the apprentices wept.
5 —Alas for our labors, a pity for our toil,
all day we build, at night it falls down!
And the spirit responded from the right-hand arch,
—If you don't sacrifice a human, the wall will not stand firm.
Do not sacrifice an orphan, nor stranger, nor passerby,
10 but only the master builder's beautiful wife.
The master builder heard this, his heart is shattered.
He sent word with the bird, with the nightingale bird.
—Dress slowly, change slowly, bring the food slowly,
come slowly to cross the Bridge of Arta.
15 The bird misheard and told the words wrong,
—Dress quickly, change quickly, bring the food quickly,
come quickly to cross the Bridge of Arta.
Here she comes and appears on the white road.
The master builder saw her, his heart is shattered.

20   —Good hour to you, craftsmen and you, apprentices.
           But what ails the master builder that he is so angry?
           —He dropped his ring into the first arch,
           who will go in, who will come out to find the ring?
           —I will go in, I will come out and find the ring.
25   She did not reach right down, not even halfway down:
           —Draw up the chain, good man, draw the chain up,
           I've searched the whole world and nothing have I found.
           One digs with the pick, another piles on lime,
           the master builder heaves, hurls in a huge boulder.
30   —We were three sisters, each of us ill-fated:
           One built the Danube, the other the Avlon,
           I, the youngest, have built the Bridge of Arta.
           As my heart trembles, so shall the bridge;
           as my hair falls, so shall the passersby.
35   —Girl, change your tune and give another curse,
           your brother from strange lands may pass this way.
           —Iron be my heart, iron be the bridge;
           iron be my hair, iron the passersby.

This song, widely diffused across the Balkans (Albania, Yugoslavia, Romania, Hungary, Bulgaria; and among Vlach and Gypsy peoples) and in the Greek-speaking world (Asia Minor, Black Sea, Cyprus, Crete, mainland Greece, Ionian Isles) is not easy to interpret. The structure is dramatic-episodic, with everything pared down so as to focus on the awesome nature of the supernatural command and its inexorable execution, rather than on sentiment. Of the master builder, we are twice told ραγίζει ἡ καρδιά του "his heart is shattered"; but he doesn't hesitate to throw in, third and last, the greatest boulder to seal his wife's fate! Of her feelings, we know only that her ties to male kin (her brothers) force her to cancel her initial destructive curse. So volatile is human sentiment that in other versions the craftsmen lament but the apprentices rejoice when the bridge falls down every night, because they are paid as pieceworkers (Dodekanese); or the master craftsman rejoices when he hears the command, because now he can find a better, prettier wife (Rhodes); or the wife tells the master builder to go down himself and find the ring, because she can always buy another, thus obliging the menfolk to use force to push her in (Cyprus). The only constant is kinship. In the minority of versions, where the sacrificial victim is specified as female in the supernatural command, the master builder chooses wife over mother or sisters because she is replaceable, they are not; in the majority of versions where the immured wife is made to undo her curse, she does so for the sake of her only brother.

Narrative impetus is achieved throughout by stylistic and thematic juxtaposition of opposites, whether within one or two musical phrases ("all day they kept building, at night it fell down") or across several (bird miscarries message, wife gives another curse). The "habit of thinking in balances, antitheses and parallelisms" operates not only conceptually and verbally, as David Buchan has said of the Scottish ballads (1972, 88), but extends to the moral and emotional planes, hence it is easy to explain how the variations of rejoicing apprentices and master craftsman arose. The possibility of changing one thing into another so readily disturbs our preconceptions of seriousness and complicates interpretation. That is why Beaton's argument (1980, 124)—that the versions naming the bridge as the mythical "Bridge of Hair" separating the world of the living from the world of the dead, together with the "snakes and vipers" the wife finds in the arch, "are a sure indication that the world of the dead is being described"—is a deceptively simple solution, because it does not account for the majority of versions and misses the ambivalence. The bridge signifies any liminal, and therefore dangerous, passage from one state to another (birth, marriage, death), while "snakes and vipers" connote both death and fertility in Greek tradition. Is the song playing with these variable oppositions? That would explain how the bridge came to be located "on the shore" in the Sporades, a paradox dismissed as "improbable" by Beaton (1980, 121), but consistent with its survival today as a dance, much as death is laughed at and the earth trodden upon in the dance song Χαρῆτε νιές, χαρῆτε νιοί "Rejoice, young women, rejoice young men!", in which mortals triumphantly trample on death in song and dance: death conquers death, as in the Orthodox liturgy.[35]

Stories of the need to sacrifice human life in order to secure an edifice, whether bridge, castle, or monastery, are known the world over, from as far afield as India and China. But only in the Balkans is the victim invariably the *wife* of the master builder: it is her sacrifice that secures the possibility of future life, so that on another level the edifice is the artifice of life itself. Ritual killing, whether by immuring or by slaughter and consumption of human, animal, and bird flesh, followed by burial of the bones, is a constant theme in the tales that leads to regeneration, as we shall see in the next chapter, and can help to explain here how our song functions as myth. Human sacrifice occurs only in the fantasy world; but it is still customary in Greece, as elsewhere in the Balkans, to slaughter a cock and let the blood run into the foundations of a new building, as it is among Orthodox Christians to roast and eat the Paschal lamb to celebrate Christ's rebirth. The community's life triumphs over individual death, on spatial and temporal levels, therefore the most precious being must be sacrificed in a reciprocal pact with God/nature. And who is more precious than the master builder's beautiful young wife? Meaning does not lie at the level of "story."

The mini–Balkan War that has been fought over the origins of the "Song of the Walled-up Wife" has proved inconclusive. Rather than attempt to trace origins and interconnections through similarities, why not look at some divergences? Romanian versions of "Manole" are longer and more complex than the Greek. They focus on the dramatic lead-up to the beautiful Anna's arrival on the scene: it was agreed among the builders that whichever wife appeared first on the following day must be sacrificed. All except Manole, the master builder, cheat by telling their wives to come late. When Manole sees his fair Anna approaching with his midday meal, he exhorts all supernatural powers—mountains, forests, rains—to obstruct her passage. They do their best, but Anna overcomes all obstacles to reach him, implying that she is stronger than nature or that Fate is strongest of all. She is not tricked into the arch by the ruse of the ring but immured from the ground up as if in play, and she realizes the masons' deadly intent only when the mortar reaches her breasts. The focus is on hyperbole of a kind encountered in Greek wondertales but not in song. Albanian versions stress the fertilizing properties of the milk flowing from the two little holes the wife begged the masons to drill into the wall so she could feed her children for the last time. Ever since, infertile women drink her milk and become pregnant. Hungarian, Serbian, and Croatian versions sometimes end in tragedy, as the commanding spirit destroys the edifice in envious spite, demanding a new one.[36] Greek versions closing with the wife's two curses draw attention to the primacy of kinship over marital ties, reinforced by the master craftsman's active role in her deception. Whether or not cultural differences explain these textual ones—and the question is too large to be decided on the basis of a single song—throughout the Balkans the focus is on the fate of the young wife as the innocent victim whom death takes unfairly, and it is precisely the inevitability of living a life predicated on death that the song insists we celebrate: she is important not as particular wife cruelly put to death at a particular time but as a symbol of woman's eternal power to secure generational continuity. Maybe it is not so inappropriate to a wedding dance, after all? But we are worlds away from romantic ballads!

Let us turn now to another pan-Balkan song, known to scholars as Τοῦ νεκροῦ ἀδερφοῦ, "The Dead Brother," although referred to by singers as "Areti" or "Kostandinos and Areti." Here is a version from eastern Thrace:[37]

Μάνα μὲ τοὺς ἐννιὰ τοὺς γιοὺς καὶ μὲ τὴ μιά σου κόρη,
τὴν κόρη τὴ μονάκριβη, τὴν πολυαγαπημένη,
τὴν εἶχες δώδεκα χρονῶ κι ὁ ἥλιος δὲν τὴν εἶδε·
στὰ σκοτεινὰ τὴν ἔλουζες, στ' ἄφεγγα τὴν ἐπλέκας,
5   στ' ἄστρα καὶ στὸν αὐγερινὸν ἔφκιανες τὰ σγουρά της.
᾽Οποὺ σὲ φέραν προξενιὰ ἀπ' τὴ Βαβυλώνα

νὰ τὴν παντρέψεις στὰ μακριά, πολὺ μακριὰ στὰ ξένα.
Ὀχτὼ ἀδερφοὶ δὲ θέλουνε κι Κωσταντῖνος θέλει.

—Δῶσ' τηνε, μάνα, δῶσ' τηνε τὴν Ἀρετὴ στὰ ξένα,
10   στὰ ξένα κεῖ ποὺ περπατῶ, στὰ ξένα ποὺ πηγαίνω,
νά 'χω κι ἐγὼ παρηγοριά, νά 'χω κι ἐγὼ κονάκι.
—Φρόνιμος εἶσαι, Κωσταντή, κι ἄσχημ' ἀπελογήθης·
κι ἂν μ' ἔρθει, γιέ μου, θάνατος, κι ἂν μ' ἔρθει, γιέ μ',
    ἀρρώστια,
κι ἂν τύχει πίκρα γιὰ χαρά, ποιὸς θὰ μὲ τὴν φέρει;
15   Τὸν Θεὸ τῆς ἔβαλ' ἐγγυτὴ καὶ τοὺς ἁγιοὺς μαρτύρους,
ἂν τύχει κι ἔρθει θάνατος, ἂν τύχει κι ἔρθει ἀρρώστια,
κι ἂν τύχει πίκρα γιὰ χαρά, νὰ πάει νὰ τὴν φέρει,
Καὶ σὰν τὴν ἐπαντρέψανε τὴν Ἀρετὴ στὰ ξένα,
καὶ μπῆκε χρόνος δίσεκτος καὶ μῆνες ὀργισμένοι,
20   κι ἔπεσε τὸ θανατικὸ κι οἱ ἐννιὰ ἀδελφοὶ πεθάναν,
βρέθηκ' ἡ μάνα μοναχή, σὰν καλαμιὰ στὸν κάμπο.
Παιδάκια κοιλοπόνεσε, παιδιὰ δὲν ἔχ' κοντά της·
χορτάριασε ἡ πόρτα της, πρασίνισε κι ἡ αὐλή της.
Στὰ ὀχτὼ μνήματα δέρνεται, στὰ ὀχτὼ μοιρολογάει,
25   στοῦ Κωνσταντίνου τὸ θαφτὸ τὶς πλάκες ἀνασηκώνει.
—Σήκω, Κωνσταντινάκη μου, τὴν Ἀρετή μου θέλω·
τὸν Θεὸ μοῦ 'βαλες ἐγγυτὴ καὶ τοὺς ἁγιοὺς μαρτύρους,
ἂν τύχει πίκρα γιὰ χαρά, νὰ πᾶς νὰ μὲ τὴν φέρεις.
Ὁ Κωσταντὴς ταράχθηκε 'πὸ μέσα τὸ μνημόρι·
30   κάνει τὸ σύγνεφ' ἄλογο καὶ τ' ἄστρο σαλιβάρι,
καὶ τὸ φεγγάρι ουντροφιὰ καὶ πάγει νὰ τὴ φέρει.
Παίρνει τὰ ὄρη πίσω του καὶ τὰ βουνὰ μπροστά του,
βρίσκει την καὶ χτενίζουνταν ἔξω στὸ φεγγαράκι.
Ἀπὸ μακριὰ τὴ χαιρετᾶ κι ἀπὸ μακριὰ τῆς λέγει·
35   —Περπάτησ', Ἀρετοῦλα μου, κι ἡ μάνα μας σὲ θέλει.
—Ἀλίμονο, ἀδελφάκι μου, καὶ τί εἶν' τοῦτ' ἡ ὥρα;
Ἂν εἶναι ἴσως γιὰ χαρά, νὰ βάλω τὰ χρυσά μου,
κι ἂν εἶναι πίκρα, πές με το, νὰ 'ρθω καταπῶς εἶμαι.
—Περπάτησ', Ἀρετοῦλα μου, κι ἔλα καταπῶς εἶσαι.
40   Στῆ στράτα ποὺ διαβαίνανε, στῆ στράτα ποὺ πηγαίναν,
ἀκοῦν πουλιὰ νὰ κελαηδοῦν, ἀκοῦν πουλιὰ νὰ λένε·
—Ποιὸς εἶδε κόρην ὄμορφη νὰ σέρν' ἀποθαμένος!
—Ἄκουσες, Κωσταντάκη μου, τί λένε τὰ πουλάκια;
'Ποιὸς εἶδε κόρην ὄμορφη νὰ σέρν' ἀποθαμένος!'
45   —Λωλὰ πουλιὰ κι ἂς κελαηδοῦν, λωλὰ πουλιὰ κι ἂς λένε.
—Τί βλέπουμε τὰ θλιβερά, τὰ παραπονεμένα,

νὰ περπατοῦν οἱ ζωντανοὶ μὲ τοὺς ἀποθαμένους!
—Ἄκουσες, Κωσταντάκη μου, τί λένε τὰ πουλάκια·
Πῶς περπατοῦν οἱ ζωντανοὶ μὲ τοὺς ἀποθαμένους;
50   —Πουλάκια εἶν' κι ἃς κελαηδοῦν, πουλάκια εἶν' κι ἃς λένε.
—Φοβοῦμαι σε, ἀδελφάκι μου, καὶ λιβανιὲς μυρίζεις.
—Ἐχτὲς βραδὺ ἐπήγαμε πέρα στὸν Ἄϊ-Γιάννη,
καὶ θύμιασέ μας ὁ παπᾶς μὲ περισσὸ λιβάνι.
Καὶ παραμπρὸς ποὺ πήγαιναν κι ἄλλα πουλιὰ τοὺς λένε·
55   Θεέ μεγαλοδύναμε, μεγάλο θάμα κάνεις
τέτοια πανώρια λυγερὴ νὰ σέρν' ἀποθαμένος.
Τ' ἄκουσε πάλ' ἡ λυγερὴ καὶ ράγισ' ἡ καρδιά της.
—Ἄκουσες, Κωσταντάκη μου, τί λένε τὰ πουλάκια;
Πές με ποῦ ν' τὰ μαλλάκια σου, τὸ πηγουρὸ μουστάκι;
60   —Μεγάλ' ἀρρώστια μ' ἔβρηκε, μ' ἔριξε τοῦ θανάτου,
μὲ πέσαν τὰ ξανθὰ μαλλιά, τὸ πηγουρὸ μουστάκι.
Βρίσκουν τὸ σπίτι κλειδωτό, κλειδομανταλωμένο,
καὶ τὰ σπιτοπαράθυρα ποῦ ταν ἀραχνιασμένα.
—Ἄνοιξε, μάνα μ', ἄνοιξε καὶ νά την Ἀρετή σου.
65   —Ἂν εἶσαι Χάρος διάβαινε κι ἄλλα παιδιὰ δὲν ἔχω·
καὶ μέν' ἡ Ἀρετούλα μου λείπ' μακριὰ στὰ ξένα.
—Ἄνοιξε, μάνα μ'. ἄνοιξε κι ἐγὼ εἶμ' ὁ Κωσταντής σου·
ἐγγυτὴ σοῦ 'βαλα τὸν Θεὸ καὶ τοὺς ἁγιοὺς μαρτύρους
ἂν τύχει πίκρα γιὰ χαρά, νὰ πάω νὰ σὲ τὴν φέρω.
70   Ὥσπου νὰ βγεῖ στὴν πόρτα της, ἐβγῆκε ἡ ψυχή της.
(Ioannou 1975, 36–38)

Mother with those nine sons and with your only daughter,
your cherished only daughter, much beloved,
for twelve years you kept her, and the sun never saw her:
you washed her hair in darkness, combed it on moonless nights,
5   you braided it by starlight and by the morning star.
But then they sent from Babylon with offers for her hand
to marry her in foreign parts, in distant alien lands.
Eight brothers will not have it, but Kostandis insists.
—Give her hand in marriage, mother, let her go abroad,
10   then when I'm on my travels in distant alien lands
I shall have some comfort and a resting place.
—You are shrewd, my Kostandis, yet you answer foolishly.
If death comes to me, my son, if sickness should befall,
if there is grief or joy, who will bring her to me?
15   He called on God as guarantee, and on the saints as witness,

if death should come, if sickness should befall,
if there were grief or joy, he would go and fetch her.
And when they married Areti in distant alien lands
a leap year came to pass and months of wrath.

20 The plague struck, and all nine brothers died.
Their mother was alone, like stubble on a plain.
So many labor pains, and yet no children near her.
Her door was overgrown, her courtyard full of weeds.
At eight tombs she beat her breast, at eight she sang laments,

25 and at Kostandis's grave she raised up the tombstone:
—Get up, my Kostandis, I want my Areti!
You called on God as guarantee, and on the saints as witness
if there was grief or joy, you would go and fetch her.
Kostandis heaved from within his grave.

30 He makes the cloud his horse, the star his clothes,
and with the moon as company rides off to fetch her.
On and on he goes, mountains behind and others still before,
he finds her as she combs her hair outside in the moonlight.
He greets her from afar, and calls out to her:

35 —Come, my Areti, our mother wants you.
—Alas, my brother, at such an hour as this?
If there is joy, I'll wear my gold,
if grief, I'll come just as I am.
—Come, my Areti, come just as you are.

40 On the road they travel, make their way
and hear the birds sing, hear birds speak:
—Whoever saw so fair a girl led by the dead?
—Did you hear, my Kostandis, what the birds are saying?
"whoever saw so fair a girl led by the dead!"

45 —They are foolish birds that sing, let them say what they will.
—What a sad and grievous sight
for the living to be walking together with the dead!
—Did you hear, my Kostandis, what the birds are saying?
that the living are walking together with the dead?

50 —They are only birds that sing, let them say what they will.
—I fear you, my brother, you smell of incense.
—Last evening we went to the Church of Saint John,
the priest used too much incense in his censing.
Still further on they went, yet other birds speak out:

55 —Almighty God, what miracle is this
for maid so fair to be led by the dead!

Again the girl heard, it struck her to the heart.
—Did you hear, my Kostandis, what the birds are saying?
Tell me, where is your hair, where is your thick mustache?
60   —I have fallen sick, I have come near to death,
my blonde hair has fallen out, my thick mustache is gone.
They find the house shut up, locked with bolts and bars,
the shutters on the windows thick with cobwebs.
—Open, mother, open, your Areti is here.
65   —If you are Charos, go away, I have no more sons,
my Areti is far away in distant alien lands.
—Open, mother, open, here is your Kostandis.
I called on God as guarantee and on the saints as witness
if there was grief or joy, I would bring her to you.
70   She had not reached the door when her soul departed.

Widely diffused throughout the Greek-speaking world and attested in ap-
proximately 262 versions (Saunier 1979, 128), it is tightly structured, dramatic rather than narrative in mode, each episode underlining a linked series of oppositions. A mother with nine sons jealously guards her only
daughter, washing her hair by night so she should never be seen by the sun.
These precautions precipitate offers for her hand from far afield (ξένα
μακρυά). Eight brothers support their mother in refusing such a distant
match; but Kostandis, the youngest, insists, on the grounds that he wants
kinsfolk at hand on his travels abroad. To silence his mother's objections, he
swears a solemn oath that come what may he will bring his sister home
should "sickness or joy" arise in the family. The words πίκρα and χαρά, repeated by mother, son, and daughter, connote death and marriage (Vlastos
1931, s.v.v.). A leap year strikes: all nine brothers die of the plague, and their
mother is left barren, "like stubble on the plain," a simile allusively associated in Greek song with a girl who curses her unfaithful lover (Politis 1914,
128a; Alexiou 1974, 194). The mother laments, curses Kostandis at his
gravestone, and invokes him to fulfill his vow. He becomes a revenant: with
the cloud his horse, the star as clothes or reins, and the moon for company,
he rides swiftly over mountains to find his sister outside, combing her hair
by moonlight (or dancing or otherwise inappropriately occupied). He demands instant departure, but she demurs—is it for joy or grief? (marriage or
death?). Without explanation, he seats her behind him. During the macabre
ride home, three times the birds sing warnings of her unnatural ride with
the dead. Three times she questions her brother on his sinister appearance;
but his replies are evasive. In some variants, he disappears with the horse as
soon as they reach the village churchyard, where he returns to his grave and

his body dissolves now that his vow has been fulfilled, leaving Areti to complete her journey home alone and on foot. She finds the garden overgrown with weeds, windows and doors barred and bolted, the house hung with cobwebs. Three times she knocks, demanding entry and calling out her name. Twice her mother refuses, calling her a revenant or Χάρος "Death." The third time, she opens; but as soon as the girl crosses the threshold, both embrace and die, or in variants from Crete and Mani, the girl is transformed into a lamenting owl.[38]

For the past 160 years or so, scholars have debated the mythical, historical, and ethnic origins of this tragic song, usually in an attempt to trace the possible process of its diffusion in Greece. On the question of links with ancient myths, I disagree with the view that the song is a direct descendant of the Demeter-Persephone myth or of any single ancient myth, although there are some significant oppositions and areas of focalization common to both. The most relevant link is the theme of mother and daughter refusing to accept separation through marriage. But whereas Demeter and Persephone achieve a compromise open to immortals (Persephone is both maid and wife, alive and dead), for mortals such as Areti and her family, there is no such option: they must be alive or dead. More general oppositions common to ancient myth and modern song include living world/other world; marriage/death; fertility/sterility; marital ties/kinship ties, but these suggest no more than a tenuous connecting thread.[39] A more promising approach might be to isolate specific mythical features—and their interrelated signification—common to both traditions: the force of a mother's lament and curse; the girl's metamorphosis into a lamenting owl (Crete, Mani) or lamb (Crete); the impossibility of the soul's release before the fulfillment of a vow; and the particular attributes of the personification of Death. The fact that some of these features are incidental while others are restricted to a few regional variants, and that all recur in different contexts in the paramythia, demonstrates the futility of attempting to disentangle the historical and geographic diffusion of a particular song or song type in a tradition as long and complex as the Greek (Beaton 1980, 112–20).

Judging from the number of versions, this song, like the "Bridge of Arta," held particular relevance for Balkan societies, becoming gradually absorbed into the distinct cultural patterns of each group. No comparative analysis, however intensive and extensive, can solve the question of ethnic origins; yet the differences between Greek and other Balkan versions can be revealing. In the Serbian song "Yovan and Yelitsa," the mother is opposed only to her daughter's marriage in a distant village, not to marriage itself, while all Yelitsa's brothers support the match because the groom is rich. It is the isolated Yelitsa, not her mother, who raises Yovan from the dead, re-

minding him of his promise to visit her.⁴⁰ Tension in the Greek versions revolves around a series of conflicts both within the family (mother / son,
brother / sister, daughter / mother) and between the house / family (σπίτι)
and the outside world (ξένα). The constant overemphasis or underempha-
sis of family ties, exceeding all norms of moderation, leads to a series of
unnatural events in the worlds of living and dead and ultimately to the finale, a tragic reversal from a close-knit family (embodying the ideal of
many sons and one daughter) to the elimination of the whole line.

These oppositions may be closely related to the context of Greek rural
society, as described by John Campbell (1964), Juliet du Boulay and others.
The house is the economic focus of village life and socially pivotal (du
Boulay 1974, 15–40, 140–41). It acquires symbolic meaning in village gossip, traditional expressions, and proverbs and is therefore directly translatable
from speech genre to mythical genre, as we saw in Chapter 5. Absolute loyalty between members of the same household should be displayed to the
outside world, even when this is not the case. Of a house that is not lived in
owing to the emigration or death of father and/or sons, it is said τὸ σπίτι
δὲν καπνίζεται, "the house is not smoked," an evocative expression based
on actuality, for without a constant fire the house rapidly deteriorates, and
there is an abundance of weeds in the abandoned courtyard (du Boulay
1974, 32). This adds a realistic dimension to the formula, common to both
wedding and funeral laments, when the departure of a member of the
house is mourned in similar terms: σκοτείνιασε τὸ σπίτι σου! "your
house has darkened!" χορτάριασ' ἡ αὐλή σου! "your courtyard is overgrown with weeds!" Its universality in rural societies is aptly illustrated by
the Irish curse, "May grass grow over your doorway!"

These dimensions heighten the dramatic effect of the moment in the
song when the mother is left alone, with all her children dead or departed,
and prepares us for the final scene, when her daughter returns to find doors
and windows barred and bolted the garden overgrown with weeds; we do
not need to be told that it is the house of death. Tales of misfortune afflict-
ing particular families are concluded with expressions such as σκόρπισε τὸ
σπίτι "the house has scattered" or καταστράφη / ξερριζώθη / ξεκληρώθη
"the house has been destroyed / uprooted / disinherited," used frequently
in the funeral laments (du Boulay 1974, 20; Alexiou 1974, 194–95). "Blood"
should not return backward in on itself but must move spirally upward and
outward, hence the necessity of "scattering the daughters." In the song,
whose central theme is the destruction of a household, the opening line,
"Mother with your nine sons and with your only daughter," and the concluding line, "She went in, they both embraced, and died," express this tragic
reversal in terse antithesis, all the more effective in their contrast between

the initial triumphant second-person address and the finality of three finite, third-person verbs.

Some incidental details, contradictions, and omissions can also be explained in terms of Greek society. Why is Areti so anxious to know what dress to wear when she receives her brother's unexpected summons? It is a common motif in the songs, occurring in versions of "The Bridge of Arta" when the master builder's wife is called to the bridge; yet I never appreciated its significance until reading Danforth's arresting account of Eleni's death (1982, 9–23). Eleni, one of the most gifted young girls from Potamia, was studying to become a teacher in Thessaloniki when she was killed in a hit-and-run accident. On hearing the news, her relatives in Thessaloniki put on festive clothes, packed mourning garments into a suitcase, and took a taxi to her native village. Then they summoned her family from the fields to the best room of the house, "to hear joyful news." When all were gathered, they changed into mourning, put a photograph of Eleni in the center of the room, and lamented her "marriage to death." Some days later, Eleni's mangled body arrived and was buried in full bridal attire, thereby completing the necessary ritual sequence from birth and baptism to marriage and death (Hart 1992, 121–45). Cruel and unnatural? Rather, a different means of coping with death, where clothes act as signifiers and transform people into actors. Kostandis has only to tell Areti to "come just as she is" for us to know the end will be death, much as Eleni's relatives use the dramatic fiction of marriage in death to lend the occasion an appropriate solemnity and to alleviate her family's shock.

In the song, no mention is made of Areti's father or husband, even in versions where Kostandis finds her nursing a child when he rides to fetch her. The focus is starkly upon an introverted family, where none of the brothers is married and only Kostandis is prepared to break out of the family circle. Even after marriage, Areti is tied by unnatural loyalty to her family of origin. As youngest son, Kostandis had least right to insist on her marriage, in view of the obligation usually associated with the youngest son to support his parents; yet his insistence is primarily for selfish reasons. The family is a closed circle, inevitably doomed. The song presents yet another angle on the conflicting values inherent in a society where extended families coexisted under one roof, with autocratic mothers-in-law, squabbling—or overintimacy—between brothers and sisters-in-law, disputes over land and property, and allocation of dowries. Examples of such cases of family strife in the songs readily spring to mind, such as "The Mother Murderess" and "Two Loving Brothers and the Evil Wife," in which a wife's adultery leads to death—even when she is more sinned against than sinning. In the songs, family crimes are directed by parents/parents-in-law against children, never the reverse (Saunier 1979, 133–233), although as we shall see in the next chapter the theme of wanton matricide is not unknown in the tales. In those songs where the husband commits adultery, it is his illicit concubine who pays with her life, killed by the wife. The song material could usefully be compared and contrasted with anthropological studies of how such conflicts and tensions are dealt with according to varying patterns of virilocal and uxorilocal residence, inheritance, and kin relationships. Even where women are socially empowered, as on some islands of the Cyclades, myth perceives them as subservient to male authority.

How are myths expressed in song? Events are never presented realistically; nor can they be related to recorded incidents, although the *paradóseis* reviewed in the last chapter suggest known analogies. Nor is there any explicit social or moral message. In order to find the answer, other dimensions must be explored: ritual and fantastic content. In this song, the mother's oppressive behavior to her daughter is foregrounded in the opening and closing lines. She opposes not only this marriage but any kind of marriage. In most villages on mainland Greece, residence after marriage is virilocal—that is, a bride leaves her parental home on marriage and transfers her loyalties to the house of her in-laws (du Boulay 1974, 136–37). Here, the use of the word ξένα, "foreign parts" in the context of the wedding is instructive: as Saunier has shown, marriage is termed ξενητειά, the in-laws are ξένοι, while the bride is given στὰ ξένα καὶ στὰ μακρυὰ καί στοῦ γαμπροῦ τὰ χέρια "to foreign parts and distant lands and to the bridegroom's hands" (Samos: Saunier 1968, 85). Distance is metaphorical rather than literal, symbolizing the girl's passage from her own home, where she has known protection, affection, and comfort, to her in-laws, where, as the songs state explicitly, she must learn to face hard work, hostility, and physical deprivation. The importance of the bride's brothers in offering protection, which motivates Kostandis' vow and his mother's curse, is aptly illustrated by the following Macedonian wedding song, a dialogue between bride and mother:

—Τί σ' ἔκαμα μανίτσα μου / καὶ μ' ἔδωσες τόσο μακριά;
Γυρίζω ράχες καὶ βουνά / βρίσκω ποτάμια ἀπέρατα.
—Μὴ τὰ φοβᾶσαι, κόρη μου. / Ἐσύ ἔχεις ἀδέρφια σ' ἀπερνοῦν,
ξαδέρφια ποὺ σε καρτεροῦν. . . .

—What did I do to you mother / that you gave me away so far?
I traverse gulleys and mountains / I find rivers unpassable.
—Don't be afraid, my daughter! / You have brothers who will reach you,
cousins to await you. . . .

(*Laog.* 19. 202 [Saunier 1968, 56])

The laments of bride and mother—frequently sung by others on their behalf—reflect what she *ought* to say or think, not necessarily her actual feelings, as Saunier stresses. The reluctance is more ritual than real: she must depart, if the family line is to continue, as in the mother's exhortations which abruptly close the lamentations at the bride's departure in a wedding song from Crete:

—Σήκω κι ἀποχαιρέτησε, μὴν κάνεις πὼς δὲ θέλεις,
τὰ ροῦχα τοῦ γαμπροῦ φορεῖς, καὶ νὰ μισέψεις θέλεις.

—Get up and take leave, don't pretend you don't want to.
You wear the bridegroom's clothes, and you want to depart.

(MS 1775: 1952 [Saunier 1968,86])

The links between wedding laments, funeral songs, and laments for kinsfolk going abroad confirm the significance in ritual song of the identification of departure, marriage, and death, as well as the duality of assumed reluctance/final acceptance.[41] These links will be analyzed more fully in Chapter 10.

Seen against this metaphorical code of the ritual songs, the song seems to warn of the terrible consequences of ignoring the proper balance between these oppositions. In other words, there is inherent danger in trying to block the ritual passage from girlhood to marriage. Such an interpretation is further strengthened by the allusive associations of some striking but apparently arbitrary details in the song. The sun, from which the girl has been so unnaturally hidden, is suggestive of fertility, marriage, and life, on the one hand, but of burning and withering, on the other. The starlit or moonlit night which predominates over so many actions is also inauspicious and ambivalent. The grotesque marriage-in-death is presented on several levels during the macabre ride (Beaton 1980, 60–64), and Kostandis' lack of teeth, mustache, and hair indicates infertility and impotence (Durham 1924, 301–4). His last excuse in the variants where he leaves her at the churchyard provides the final clue, with cryptic grimness: like the master builder in "The Bridge of Arta," he must find his wedding ring (Academy of Athens 1962: 312.43, Sarakatsani); or he owes a wax taper and candle (*lambáda*) tall as himself to the saint (ibid., 314, 14 Cyprus). It is the ring, taper, and candle of *his* ultimate marriage to death, which can at last be consummated now that his body is allowed to dissolve. He accompanies his sister on *her* last journey from marriage to death in the clutches of her oppressive mother. The sinister tone of the whole episode is further enhanced by the motif of the birds' threefold warning, discounted as an illogical intrusion by L. Politis and as a later contamination by Saunier (Politis 1956, 271–80; Saunier 1979, 128–30). Its function in the variants where it occurs is nevertheless poetically consistent: to underline with triple emphasis the danger of her situation and the irony of his excuses by means of nonhuman mediators who speak with human voice, since we know from other songs that it is men who make the fatal mistake of dismissing "birdsong" as trivial, while women invoke it in magic and lamentation.[42]

To sum up, a mother's refusal to give her daughter in marriage—that is, to allow the inevitable transfer of loyalties from parental to marital home—leads to the loss of her daughter in marriage and her nine sons in death, especially as there is no active father or husband to lead and name the household or to ward off the dangers of a "leap year" in which all nine sons died of the plague. It is a mythical song of sterility as opposed to fertility, in terms outlined by Detienne for the ancient myth of Adonis (1977, 99–122), and as such must be viewed in the context of its converse, "Mikrokostandinos." It is not a tragic or romantic ballad about an individual's life, love, or death.

In a fascinating study, Peter Dronke (1976) surveys testimonies relevant to the common European ballad theme of "the ghost's return." With subtlety and erudition, he traces the complex web of interactions between learned lyric and popular ballad, literary and oral traditions, including the ancient myth of Protesilaos and Laodamia, the Eddic lay of Helgi and Sigrun, medieval Latin love poetry, and the modern ballad tradition. On the Greek and other Balkan songs of the "dead brother" type, he concludes that they are only indirectly related to the romantic legend of the "lover's ghost," although traces of the theme can be found in other narrative songs and in the wondertales.[43] How and why should the power of the dead to return be attached, with more or less consistency, to the girl's lover in the one tradition or to her brother (invoked by his mother's curse) in the other?

The answer lies in divergent linear and cyclical concepts of life and death, love and kinship. The linear concept, which has gained ascendance throughout most of Europe since the Renaissance, views individual progress and personal fulfillment as paramount: death is therefore final and linked to tragic failure in love. Thanatos and Eros are romantically counterposed, whereas kin play peripheral roles, except when they intervene to block a marriage. The cyclical concept—still strong in European cultures which were once shifting parts of the Byzantine and Ottoman Empires—emphasizes kinship and cross-generational ties rather than the individual ties: it is not that death is not tragic, but its significance transcends the romantic. These differences are reflected in the songs. Whereas chief actors in European ballads are lovers who "die of broken hearts," in the Greek songs the focal point of action is conflict within or between families, where characters never just pine away but tend to be violently done to death. Death in one generation can lead to fertility in the next, where collateral kin play a crucial role, however tragic the individual's death.

Death does not bring an end to communication between the living and dead. Contact is maintained through graveside conversations, which spell out just how the living may affect the quality of their dead ones' existence in Hades. In a song of the Underworld, a dead daughter responds to her mother's lament, begging her not to weep at sundown:

Παρακαλῶ σε, μάννα μου, μιὰ χάρη νὰ μοῦ κάμης,
ποτέ σου γέρμα τοῦ γηλιοῦ μὴν πιάνης μοιρολόγι,
γιατὶ δειπνάει ὁ Χάροντας, μὲ τὴ Χαρόντισσά του.
Κρατῶ κερὶ καὶ φέγγω τους, γυαλὶ καὶ τοὺς κερνάω,
κι ἄκουσα τὴ φωνοῦλα σου κι ἐσπάραξε ἡ καρδιά μου,
καὶ μοῦ ραγίστη τὸ γυαλὶ καὶ τὸ κερί μου σβήστη,
καὶ στάζει ἡ στάλα τοῦ κεριοῦ μεσ' στοὺς ἀποθαμένους,
καίει τῶν νυφάδων τὰ χρυσά, τοῦ νιῶνε τὰ στολίδια.
Θυμώνει ὁ Χάρος μὲ τὰ μέ, στὴ μαύρη γῆς μὲ ρήχνει,
τὸ στόμα μ' αἷμα γιόμισε, τ' ἀχείλι μου φαρμάκι.

(Politis, 220)

I beg you, my mother, to do me just one favor,
never to take up your lament at the turning of the sun,
for that is when Charontas [Death] dines with his Charontissa [wife].
I hold the candle, give them light, and a glass to drink from,
just then I heard your voice and my heart was shattered,
and the candle drips, drips down to the dead,
burning young brides' gold and young men's adornments.
Charos is angry with me, into black earth he thrusts me,
my mouth is filled with blood, my lips with poison.

How, then, can we summarize the differences between the European "dead lover" and the Balkan "dead brother"? Both belong to the broader theme, the "return of the dead," whether on hostile or friendly missions. In the ballads, the ghostly return is motivated by the power of mutual love beyond the grave between man and wife, whereas in Greek and Balkan songs the pull of kinship prevails. Where the man returns, as in "The Dead Brother," it is to fulfill an obligation to his mother; where a woman returns, it is often to suckle her neglected baby, as in Greek paramythia to be discussed in the next chapter. A Gypsy storyteller from Liebach in the former Yugoslavia (1951) tells the tale of Vana, a girl from "one of the Serbian

Gypsy tribes" married to Niglo, the narrator's cousin (Tong 1989, 22–25). Niglo and Vana were deeply in love, but as Vana grew heavy with child the strength sapped out of her, and she died soon after childbirth in Niglo's loving embrace. Niglo was heartbroken, half-hating the child for taking his beloved Vana's life but caring for it as best he could. One moonlit night, he saw Vana at the crib, feeding the baby and crooning to it all night long. Next night, he dressed the child as usual but put the clothes on inside out and back to front, with a necklace of garlic around its neck. When she came, Vana was both confused and repelled. Forced to confront Niglo, she asked him, "Niglo, dear Niglo, why do you keep a mother from her child? Is your love so shallow that it cannot reach as deep as the grave?" This story, told as true—Vana's grave was shown as proof—ends with Niglo following the local priest's advice: he tries to grasp Vana in his embrace, but mother and baby are reunited in death. Vana returns no more. The tale has more in common with "The Dead Brother" (and Irish tales of the other world) than with European balladry, despite the presence of the "dead lover" theme. It suggests that the dead are compelled by some higher force, predicated on care for a child or a vow to a mother, to return. The outcome is not predetermined but contingent upon the loved ones' response. Excessive eroticism between man and wife may also prove detrimental to the procreation of healthy offspring.

Let us now turn briefly to the theme of heroic death in order to explore key *differences*, as well as interactions, between literary and oral renderings. In the Grottaferrata version of *Digenes Akrites* (twelfth century: henceforth GRO), Digenes ("Born of two races") rises rapidly from an infancy and childhood as prodigious as Alexander's to the years of maturity, when he defeats his enemies, abducts his bride (previously betrothed elsewhere), and deflowers first a captive maiden and then an Amazon warrior. Eventually, he meets his death not as a result of mortal combat but from a common cold caught in the bath (VIII:1–50). His demise is contingent on his choice to take up a sedentary life with his spouse in a splendid palace, rather than continue his roving, warriorlike existence in a tent.[44] Grief-stricken at his imminent death, his wife, Eudokia, expires in his arms of a broken heart rather than face the prospect of widowhood (GRO VIII); he dies immediately afterward. The same story of heroic life culminating in romantic death is repeated, with slight variations, in other versions of the romance. It is consistent with the predominantly heroic-lyric mode of much medieval poetry and of European balladry (Dronke 1976). But it does not accord well with the harsher code of strife between martial/marital ties evident in the Greek song tradition as a whole, including those of the so-called Akritic cycle.

As Herzfeld (1980) has argued, the category "Akritic songs" is largely of the folklorists' invention, postdating the discovery of the versions of the

Byzantine epic romance (Sathas 1873) and inclusive of a wide range of songs, not all relating to the hero Digenes or (in the Pontos) Akritas. The songs come from all parts of the Greek-speaking world, the longest and—it is sometimes argued—the most "ancient" from Cyprus, Asia Minor, and the Pontos. If there is a common theme, it is attached not to a name (Digenis, Yiannis, Kostandis) or to any occupation (warrior, shepherd, hunstman) but rather to the theme of the premature death of a young man whose parentage (mother or father of foreign birth; mother a nun or a virgin) may point to his ambivalent—and therefore both strong and vulnerable—position as "social borderer." The name "Monoyiannes" in the song, one of the very few cases of successful confrontation with Death, not only recalls μονογενὴς υἱός "Only-begotten Son," or Christ, the Virgin's son, but suggests semantic opposition to Διγενής "born of two races," "of double birth" (Beaton 1980: 82; Ekdawi, Fann, Philokyprou 1993, 25–42). Semantic play on such names is not uncommon: my father-in-law was known as μονογενήσιος "Onlybegotten" from the frequency with which he declaimed the words μονογενὴς υἱός "Only begotten Son" as cantor in the village church. Here and elsewhere, religious discourse is the invisible interlocutor of song and tale.

How do young men—social borderers or otherwise—confront death in Greek songs? First, death is violent, the result of supernatural intervention, trickery, or force; hence "death" is personified in diverse forms (Charos the huntsman, rider, or vintner). Second, in the predominantly men's songs from Cyprus and Asia Minor, the young man gathers his comrades when he knows death is at hand to relate his past heroic exploits: the onset of death precipitates recapitulation of life in celebration of his *kléos*. ("fame, glory"). Third, where a wife is mentioned, the deathbed scene is by no means so tender as in the Byzantine epic romance. He asks three times whom she will marry after his death. Twice she replies, "Black clothes shall eat me just as the earth eats you"; but the third time she says, "I'll marry the noble chief / for he was my first joy, he was my heart's delight." / He seized her by the hair and swung her round three times" (Crete). Or, when he hears from the birds that he must die—they have seen the Lord write his name among the dead—he concludes, "If it is true, my bird, that I will never reap / I will cut up my wife, that no one else shall wed her, / I will cut up my oxen, that no one else shall yoke them" (Macedonia). Nor is violence a male prerogative in these songs. In a version from Thebes, Digenis' coveted bride gets the better of him, with the acquiescence of her father (first two lines only are cited in Greek to reflect normal practice in performance):

Τρίτη ἐσπάρθη ὁ Διγενὴς καὶ τρίτην ἐγεννήθη,
τρίτην ἐκαβαλλίκευσε τ' ἀπαίδευτο μουλάρι....

Digenis was conceived on Tuesday, and on Tuesday he was born,
and it was on a Tuesday too he set out on untamed mule,
he tamed it and went off to fight in cruel wars.
On Tuesday came a message to go at last to battle.
As he went in he slew a thousand, as he went out two thousand more,
and as he went round again he slew three thousand others.
A princess looked out from her lofty palace,
and Digenis decided he wanted her as wife.
She was the daughter of a king, the daughter of a prince,
she had a skilled nurse, and was the praise of all.
He sent forth his great army to stand outside her door.
When the girl caught sight of him, she went to see her father.
—Welcome, welcome to Anneta, to my daughter fair.
–My lord, it is Digenis, the youth of great renown,
who goes into battle like a dragon, like a lion;
now his army spend the night in my own courtyard.
—My daughter, go and take him, for my throne is now in danger,
and when I am dead and gone, you'll be without a lord.
All night Anneta sat as though weaving at her loom,
but in the morning she rose up and acted like a witch.
She took her golden dagger from its golden case,
and she cut off Digenis' head like a ripe young cucumber.
She crossed her arms and went back to her father.
—Welcome, my daughter, welcome to my dear one.
Why have you come back so soon to see me?
—I have cut off his head like a ripe young cucumber
and nailed it to his spear. His army ran away.
The sun has set at last upon his wretched eyes.
—My daughter, you are worthy of my throne, you deserve my crown,
for you have saved our Babylonian land and villages.

(*Laog.* I. 59, 265–66)

It would be futile to try to pin down this extraordinary song to a specific historical epoch, let alone event; but it signifies woman's ambivalent power to triumph over death, by sangfroid and absence of sentiment, as in the biblical myth of Judith and Holofernes.

To sum up on themes and characters. Scholars have divided *paralogés* into those related to popular tradition and belief, family life, social life, national life, nautical life (Ioannou 1975). The model works in descriptive terms, but tells us little about how mythical themes may be incorporated into song and what their focus is. Buchan (1972, 83–85) characterizes the Scottish

ballad cast as a central triangle of three characters (hero/ine, villain, media-
tor). Does this pattern fit? Who is the hero/ine / villain / mediator in "The
Dead brother"? Kostandinos, Areti, or their mother? In "The Bridge of
Arta," in what sense is the master builder a villain? Even in songs where a
mother's wanton cruelty is justly punished, as in "Mikrokostandinos" or
"The Mother Murderess," it is hard to say whether characters are protagonists or mediators. Who is to blame for the tragic outcome of "Lamkin" or
"The Gypsie Laddie"—the laird who neglects his house and land, or those
that claim their due, or perhaps the highborn ladies? We shall pursue this
question as it relates to tales in the next chapter, but in songs it has to do
with an underlying ambivalence.

Finally, some comments on myth, magic, and parody. Among the oldest
Scottish ballads, Buchan cites as "mythical and magical" "The Elfin
Knight," "Hind Horn," "King Henry," "Allison Gross," and "Tam Lin"
(Child 2, 17, 32, 35, 39). He claims that while ballads may lack the similes
and images of written literature, they possess a symbolic imagery rooted in
what he calls a "now fragmented mythology" (1972, 171), in terms that recall nineteenth-century views of folklore as the "debris of mythology." Yet
magic is absorbed into the ballad in lyric-romantic ways that may occur in
Greek tales, as shall see in the next chapter, but rarely in song without a
touch of parody. Examples include the witch in "Allison Gross" (Child 35),
compared by Child with the Nereid of a Greek tale;[45] and the metamorphoses of the fairy bridegroom in "Tam Lin" (Child 39), compared with an
early-nineteenth-century Cretan tale about a young man who secures his
Nereid bride, on the advice of a wise old woman, by stealing her kerchief
and seizing her by the hair until cockcrow, but then loses her at the birth of
their child, when he follows the same old woman's advice to break his
wife's silence by putting their child in the oven to roast.[46]

Supernatural elements have been differently integrated. Whereas Scottish ballads have adapted motifs and figures from a wide range of genres in
a manner that suggests the uncanny, marvelous, and grotesque, it is arguable
that Greek songs take only Charos the soul snatcher seriously, although he
appears (if at all) in the tales as a benevolent godfather. The three Fates, the
Nereids, and other shape-shifting *exotika*, so graphically depicted in the
tales, are barely mentioned in songs. As for man-eating Lamia and Drakos,
those seductive and voracious demons who lure young men and women to
destruction or triumph, they are found in song and tale alike, but often with
a hint of parody. Why these differences? Greek genres have remained discrete, songs being concerned with the human life cycle, tales with interactions between human and other worlds. Scottish ballads, in common with
those of northern and western Europe, Spain, and Latin-America cultures,
have absorbed diverse mythic and magic elements into a romantic mould.

As my concluding example, let us look at Drakos in "Lightning's Daughter" (Spyridakis and Peristeris 1968, 25–28, no. 7), recorded from Kromnos (Pontos, 1950) from G. Petridis, who accompanies himself on the lyre. After a lengthy musical prelude, the singer commences as follows, although he does not get beyond the third line. The text is completed from a version recorded in 1910, also from the Pontos:

"Ωχ, ὁ Γιάννες, ὁ Μονόγιαννες καὶ ν‐ὁ μαναχὸν ὁ Γιάννες (δὶς)
ὤχ, ὁ Γιάννες ἐπεπέρνιξεν καὶ στὸ πεγάδ' ἐπῆγεν. (δὶς)
Ἐξέβαινε ὁ δράκος ἄγγελος καὶ θέλ' νὰ τρώῃ Γιάννη . . .

Ohh, Yiannes, Lone Yiannes, Yiannes alone (twice),
ohh Yiannes woke up and he went down to the well. (twice)
The drakos came out as messenger and wants to eat Yiannes.
—Welcome, welcome to my breakfast, to my supper;
welcome to my food and wakefulness, and to my rest and sleep.
—Let me go, drakos, let me go, leave me for five days;
I'll go and see my father, then come back so you can eat me.
Yiannes went back, he was late, the drakos was enraged:
—Let me go, drakos, let me go, wild beast, for five more days;
I'll go and see my mother; when I come back, you'll eat me.
Yiannes went back, he was late, the drakos was enraged
and when he sees what lies beneath, Yiannes goes right down.
—Welcome, welcome to my breakfast, welcome to my supper,
welcome to my food and wakefulness, and to my rest and sleep.
—I beg you, my drakos, give me five days more,
I'll go and see my brothers, come back, drakos, and you can eat me.
Yiannes went back, he was late, the drakos was angry
when he sees Yiannes opposite coming again toward him.
—Let me go, drakos, let me go, only five more days.
I beg you, my drakos, by the will of God.
I want to see my babies, settle my affairs;
I'll go back there, come back here, and quickly you can eat me.
Yiannes went, he was late, the drakos wild with fury,
then he saw him over there, Yiannes coming down.
His arms were crossed, hanging from the neck
behind him came his father plucking at his beard,
and behind him was his mother red with blood,
and behind them all his wife in gold on horseback,
playing and tossing a golden apple in her hand.
She puts heart into Yiannes, sows fear into the drakos.
—Welcome, welcome to my breakfast, welcome to my supper,

welcome to food and wakefulness, and to my rest and sleep.
—Drakos, a bow shall be your breakfast, a knife your evening meal.
—In God's name, by God, my girl, where was your father from?
—My father's from the heavens, my mother from the clouds,
my brothers make lightning and thunder, and I hunt down drakous.
—If you say so, girl, and if that is where you're from,
then Yiannes shall be my brother, his wife my sister-in-law,
and Yiannes' little children are my nephews.

Whether or not the song can be classified as Akritic, the motif of out-witting Drakos belongs to the realm of myth. It illustrates how themes and characters can be adapted from one song type to another: exchange Drakos for Charos, and there is little difference between the theme of postpone-ment in this song and the Pontic version of "Death before Marriage," in which the hero is also "Monoyiannes." Instead of ghoulish demons, we have a greedy but essentially comic and impotent Drakos, who does not lack a sense of family honor when his victim's wife dares to say "boo" to a snake! Monsters can be made fun of, and we are reminded of the dragon in the shadow play "Karaghiozis, King Alexander, and the Dragon." Ties are determined not by romance but by kinship, marriage, and death.

There remains the enigma of the music. How can a song as tragic as "The Bridge of Arta" be performed as a dance, while the parodic "Light-ning's Daughter" sounds like a lament? And, given the evidence for recita-tion and declamation indicated by many older terms for "song," why has melody predominated over story in songs, especially those recorded over the past forty years or so? Can the ambivalences of myth be transposed into song and dance more easily than into spoken words? Both my autistic sons, Dimitri and Pavlos, fail to understand stories from words alone, yet each re-sponds well when pictures, music, and dance are present, although compre-hension of logical and temporal order may be deficient. Vizyenos, insane as he may have been, understood the European ballad's contribution to *Lieder* and modern prose fiction and used Greek songs and tales in his own fiction to explore paradox in a manner that is almost operatic. Nor are operatic features absent from the songs—indeed, our Pontic dragon is not unlike the Snake so easily slain by the Three Ladies in Mozart's *Die Zauberflöte*. Yet there is still no explanation as to why, despite their commonalities of struc-ture, composition, and cultural heritage, south Slavic and Greek song tradi-tions should have developed along such different lines—the former epic and narrative, the latter tersely mythic and lyrical.[47]

We shall see in the next chapter how song and dance, magic and meta-morphosis, life on this earth and beyond are interwoven in the tales.

CHAPTER 7

Magic Cycles in the Wondertales

In this chapter I shall explore the magic of the Greek wondertales (paramythia). It is often assumed that tales are all alike, with predictable plots and happy endings, stereotyped protagonists, naïvely polarized conceptions of good and evil, and, of course, a good measure of gender and racial bias.[1] I shall challenge these assumptions by addressing four general questions: What are wondertales? Why are they important? How should we approach them? And what is special about the Greek tales? Then I shall illustrate some characteristic features of narrative and performance, themes and images, magic and metamorphosis. Finally, I shall draw some conclusions about morality and cosmology.

Because I cannot assume that Greek tales will be as familiar as "Little Red Riding-hood" or "Snow White and the Seven Dwarfs," I shall depart from the accepted convention of providing brief summaries and try to convey their flavor through the familiar Greek skill of paraphrase. The art of narration lies not just in plot but in the spinning of yarns and weaving of pictures. Wondertales owe their appeal to the tension the narrator creates between the reassuring predictability of structural, functional, and compositional elements, on the one hand, and the endless variation of symbolic images, on the other. These two strategies contribute to that essential paradox of the wondertales which makes them true and not-true at the same time. Greek tellers avoid making explicit moral judgments, preferring to leave it to the audience to debate and interpret the boundaries of known and unknown worlds.[2]

I have already stated my reasons for preferring Vladimir Propp's term "wondertale" to "fairy tale" or "folktale" as a rough translation of paramythi

(Chapter 5). Unlike Propp, I use it for all oral tales where suspension of belief is involved, as in tales of talking birds and beasts; descents to and returns from the Underworld; impossible quests and cunning tricks, tests of endurance, torture, and poverty; and, above all, every conceivable metamorphosis between human, natural, and otherworldly planes. If this usage seems unscholarly to some, it is supported by story-tellers. At the turn of the century, an expert from Tinos commented to archaeologist and folklorist Adamandios Adamandiou:

> Yes, there are paramythia with ogres [δράκοι], magicians [μάοι] and witches [μά̈ϊσσες] . . . and others about thieves and priests and priests' wives and love affairs. . . . First we'll tell quite a few of those with ogres and all that, then we'll start the shorter ones on love affairs and so on. . . . Oh yes, I know plenty of stories about priests and priests' wives! (1900, 290)

Pressed by Adamandiou to draw closer distinctions, he continued:

> Those paramythia with ogres and magicians, well they're not more beautiful . . . These others are tasty too [κάνιν γοῦστο], because you see they are teasers [ἔχιν περίεργα], what became of (him), how (he) pulled it off. (1900, 291)

His observations accord well with Diane Tong's experiences with Greek Gypsy story-tellers, who like to vary an evening's session with as many different kinds of tales as possible, rather in the manner of a diversified concert.[3]

In Chapter 5, wondertales were compared with dreams in their metaphorical/metonymical associations. Although they cannot be pinned down to a single meaning, they can prove a powerful force in shaping the imaginative horizons of a culture, drawing the listener into the realm of magic: "they lived well, we even better" is a more open closure than our own "and they lived happily ever after." We saw that paramythi is used for any tall story told to amuse, deceive or console and that the word is closely related to paramythiá, "consolation," also known as parēgoriá "funeral feast." Surprising as it may seem to us, wondertales are to this day told among Greek Gypsies during the all-night vigil at the wake to give comfort to the bereaved. In this sense, "tales of comfort" are the exact and necessary converse to the "songs of fate" (moirológia).[4]

Wondertales are fantastic stories, orally told, which explore the boundaries between known and unknown worlds. Why are they important? Because they are make-believe, they act out our wildest fantasies—"What if . . . ?"—allaying fears of disease and death while dealing with such dangerous themes as sex and violence, family strife, fate, and demonic powers, as in the mythical songs. Because they seem to end "happily ever after," they appeal to utopian instincts to find, through conflict and suffering, an ideal resolution to the human predicament. Paradoxically, just because they do not have to be believed literally, wondertales can be a subversive force: the tale may not involve a change in actual social conditions and relations, rather a reversal of the protagonist's fortunes. What changes is our perception of self and others in relation to established social conventions. Tales create a heightened self-image among the downtrodden and oppressed. Perhaps that is why Greek tales survive today most strongly among the Gypsies.

Turning to modes of collection, interpretation, and analysis, the collections of most European tales have been cited, until quite recently, from literary collections rather than from oral tradition.[5] In the process, the teller's tone of voice and gesture, the humorous, bawdy and ironical asides, and above all the vital performative interaction with the audience have been lost. Adamandiou commented to one of his informants that his mode of delivery was more subdued when telling a story for dictation. His informant replied:

> You see, you'll say it different when you tell it for writing than when you tell it with people. You see, when you tell the story you have to put the accents/sharps [oxeiés] in, you know. It has to have accents . . . it's beautiful with accents. Yes, the tale's lovely when you can take it fast. (1900, 281 n. 2)

In the light of such comments, how are we to interpret the tales when they have come down to us shorn of their "accents"? A musical analogy is implied, rather as if songs were to be studied as texts without tunes. Various approaches have been explored: historical–diffusionist, formalist, structuralist, historicist, psychoanalytic and feminist; but despite useful strategies and insights, all suffer from a Procrustean desire to pare the tale down to its supposed core. The historical–diffusionist legacy of the Finnish school, although no longer in vogue, has left us with monumental indexes of worldwide motifs and tale types, of considerable value for comparative purposes: quick reference will show where to find parallels to unusual themes in the Greek tales, although even the most assiduous research can never prove the connections, such are the vagaries of tale transmission.[6] Tong's collection *Gypsy Folktales* (1989) is a reminder that to this day, tales travel fast in ways not easily recoverable by scholarly deduction.

Formalist analysis begins with Propp ([1929] 1968). In an attempt to break away from questions of origin and diffusion and to analyze narrative form, he provides a comparative analysis of some one hundred Russian tales and concludes that they can be reduced to thirty-one functions of plot and character, despite infinite variability of detail: as a result of an initial lack, the protagonist sets out on quest, meets hostile forces, and, thanks to donors/ helpers, finally succeeds in vanquishing foes. The ending is a resolution, marked mostly by "happy marriage for ever after." It is useful to have the rules of telling tales so neatly set out, but I doubt if a literary critic who concluded that novels—or detective stories—begin with a problematic situation and end with an apparent resolution would be credited with much insight. Why should we assume that those vital "accents" matter less in oral than in literary fiction? In his critique of Propp, Claude Lévi-Strauss seeks relationships not at temporal or linear levels but in terms of binary oppositions (wet/dry, raw/cooked, inside/outside, up/down). His analysis glosses over the tales' narrative force and wealth of imagery and privileges myth over tale in terms of cosmological and religious signification.[7]

Psychoanalytic and psychological approaches have been explored by Sigmund Freud, Carl Jung, and their followers. Freud pointed to Oedipal and other key complexes in dream and joke, myth and tale, emphasizing the concept of repressed memories and fantasies in the creation of symbols. Thus, for his followers, "Bluebeard" is a tale warning us of the dangers of female curiosity and sexuality: you give your wife the keys to 101 rooms, tell her she can open one hundred but not the hundred and first—and what does she do when your back is turned? She opens that forbidden door and deserves all she gets![8] No reference is made to the varied strata of such tales worldwide, where woman's disobedience leads to her discovery of filth and sexuality and ultimately to her own and her husband's salvation, as in several Greek tales to be discussed below. I do not deny the existence of sexual symbolism, but the focus seems to me to be on fertility and ritual. Greek dream theory and interpretation rest not on sexual repression but on the predictive or prognostic nature of the dream, sent by divine or demonic forces. As we shall see, tellers draw an explicit parallel between tales and dreams.

Jung argued, from the perspective of "depth psychology," that the unconscious has a collective as well as personal component: the mind, like the body, develops according to a plan, creating images and dreams which become symbols. Common to the structure of mind and tales is a fourfold archetype: lack, search, meeting, and integration. Jung has inspired more open-ended interpretations of myth and tale than Freud, although his hypothesis for a universal archetype as the origin of the human mind has been challenged.[9]

Feminist critics have shown a healthy reaction against gender bias in interpretation. Following the lead of the post-Freudian French psychoanalyst, Jacques Lacan, Hélène Cixous and Julia Kristeva explore the dimensions of bisexuality and creativity, the multiplicity and diversity of women's voices, and questions of women and power in the "third world." Although French feminists have paid scant attention to tales, their insights into bisexuality and creativity can usefully be applied to the Greek tales, particularly those involving cross-dressing or an actual sex change.[10] Among American feminists, Carol Gilligan and Susan Gordon offer valuable analyses of gender differences in myth and tale.[11] Yet there has been a contrary tendency to reduce tale types and protagonists to stereotyped paradigms and to give literalist readings of themes and images. A prince who falls in love with a poor girl so beautiful that her tears shed pearls and her laughter gold coins is seen as "acquisitive of material goods"; reference to evildoers as black and/or female is both racist and sexist! Stereotypes for "otherness" and humor surely exist in *all* forms of fiction, or else there would be no plot, character—or fun. Beauty is "fair and white" in European tales, and "dark and curly" in Gypsy tales, whereas white people are without skin, blood, or face in African American fiction, as in Toni Morrison's *Sula* and *Beloved*. Are David Lodge's depictions of Philip Swallow and Morris Zapp, in *Changing Places* and *Small World*, to be censured as anti-British, anti-American, or perhaps for poking fun at academics? As for feminist retellings of old tales by Angela Carter and others, they are ingenious responses to sexist interpretations of familiar fairy tales, but their moral is too obvious and the closure too final. The best traditional tales avoid explicit judgment, despite the occasional stereotype, often encoding—as do jokes—a built-in irony against the social or kin group to whom they are addressed, as well as against others.[12]

Historicist analysis of the kind represented by Jack Zipes (1979) avoids some of these reductive pitfalls in that it seeks interpretation through particularities, not universals, but there are problems. First, there is no evidence to support the thesis he adopts from A. Nitschke that tales, in something like the form we have them now, can be dated back to the Ice Age. Second, in most cases it is impossible to substantiate the precise relationship between tale and sociohistorical context without making simplistic connections. Zipes cites only one convincing example of a tale from the Grimms' collection where conditions in the army at the time may be relevant; but even that example does not take us far, since any good teller would simply change the details when those conditions ceased to prevail (1979, 30–33). Third, Zipes' thesis that folktales carry the message "might makes right" simply does not fit the Greek tales, where the protagonist never wins by power or strength alone; rather she or he must undergo a process of maturation and self-empowerment through wit, cunning, or suffering. Fourth, how are tales situated in time and place? As make-believe, they cannot easily be located in specific sociohistorical contexts. Tales, like myths, use "zooming" and "distancing" techniques, drawing us into the present by topical allusion and distancing us to mythical time when taboo topics, such as cannibalism, rape, and incest, are involved.[13]

What Zipes does succeed in showing is that the general trend in Europe from the sixteenth century was toward the appropriation of oral texts by literate elites: in Italy and France by the aristocracy during the seventeenth and eighteenth centuries, and in Germany by the rising nationalist bourgeoisie in the nineteenth century. By the later nineteenth century, he argues, the increasing technologization of the mass media homogenized and sanitized tales into ready-made artifacts designed to reconcile people with their lot or to provide outlets through fantasy. Thus we observe a gradual transformation of European tales originally *told among adults* into mass-produced educative and moralizing *written or filmed fables for children.* Those cultures where tale-telling has remained part of oral tradition, such as Greek and Irish, have resisted the overall trend outlined by Zipes.[14]

One invaluable resource for the study of tales which has not been fully exploited is ethnography. Curious details or recurrent themes and images in the tales can be contextualized by reference to the many fine ethnographies now available. "Bread" *functions* not just on the level of plot and theme but also metaphorically. Here, the insights of du Boulay (1974), Hirschon (1989), Stewart (1991), and Hart (1992) on the symbolic and religious dimensions of bread in four regions of Greece can help us understand how bread *signifies.* In other cultures, its place might be occupied by rice, potatoes, or pasta. Herzfeld (1985b) demonstrates the agonistic context of tale-telling on Crete, where women are not always losers. Ethnographic approaches escape the pitfalls of historicist analysis by contextualizing the tales culturally as well as historically.

1. The Cinderella of Greek Folklore?

How do Greek tales differ from ones we know in the West? The *paramythi* is the Cinderella of Greek folklore, relegated to a lowly corner by the hearth, as if inferior to her older sisters, Song and Myth. The earliest collectors were interested primarily in songs, especially those which could be argued to demonstrate the heroic spirit of the Greek people. Paramythia were not collected until the 1860s onward and even then were published either outside Greece or in scattered form in regional or scholarly folklore journals.[15] They were not standardized or anthologized as in the West from a much earlier date, partly perhaps because they are still known and told among a wide cross section of the population, by no means restricted to children or to rural areas, but, more importantly, because they lacked the privileged status enjoyed by song in the canon of Greek folklore. As we saw, N. G. Politis, in his classic taxonomy (1909), lists myths separately, valued primarily as "corpses" of ancient mythology. The vitality and diversity of the tales, their narrative ingenuity, and their live place in the mythical tradition have been largely ignored.

Wondertales have always been Protean, subject to retelling and remolding. All oral genres are prone to variation; but in the wondertale, there is no fixed ritual occasion to dictate parameters, as in the laments and wedding songs, and no metrical or musical structure to preserve even the vestige of a text, as in the narrative songs. No good teller will repeat a tale in exactly the same form but will adapt, curtail, and elaborate as appropriate to audience and occasion. Because dependent on context, tales interact with other cultures, greedily assimilating contemporary urban and literary elements, not to mention the continual "modernization of props," whereby transportation is now by jet rather than by magic carpet, and metamorphosis by transplant technology (Tong 1989, 29–34). It is well-nigh impossible to reconstruct the national origins and diffusion of a particular tale or tale type.

This may explain why the genre has been neglected. Paramythia do not offer an easy paradigm of Greekness: they share more common features with Gypsy, Turkish, Arabic, Persian, and Indian wondertales than with those of northern and western Europe. Common features include the prominence of cosmic and vegetal imagery (metamorphosis into stars and planets, trees, fruit, and flowers) and incidental details such as the hero falling in love with the heroine through contemplation of her portrait. How these Eastern elements got into Greek oral tales is not easily determined. From the eleventh century or earlier, translations from Arabic and older Indian and Egyptian tales and myths fed into learned and vernacular romances. Judging from the diffusion of Aesop's fables and of legends about Alexander the Great, tale traffic between Greek speakers and neighbors goes back at least to late antiquity. Interaction with the East and the Balkans was facilitated by the shifting frontiers, yet regular trade routes, throughout the Roman, Byzantine, and Ottoman Empires.[16]

If some Greek tales have Eastern connections, others contain mythical elements which seem to spring straight from ancient mythology, such as the labors of Herakles, many-headed monsters, the water of life, and clashing rocks. Many such motifs derive not from "pure" oral tradition but from compilations of ancient mythology. As we saw in Chapter 1, chapbooks from the Greek presses of Venice enjoyed wide circulation in towns and villages from the sixteenth to nineteenth centuries, popularizing the feats of Alexander and Apollonios of Tyre, the tales of Halima (Shahrazad), and the romances of Voskopoula, Erofili, and Rotokritos. Literary material was absorbed into popular consciousness, as into the wondertales: in my archives is a three-hour version of the "Tale of Rotokritos," told by a sixty-year-old farmer, Papayiannis, from the Thessalian plain, and without reference to the famous romance *Erotokritos* by the Cretan poet Vitzentzos Kornaros. By no means all tellers were illiterate, and the more educated introduced elements from all available sources, including ancient mythology. Once part of the oral tradition, details were remembered by subsequent generations. Tales are in no way inferior by virtue of possible "contamination" by foreign or literary elements: what matters is the degree of their assimilation into local narrative tradition.[17] Here is how a much-traveled shoemaker, again from Tinos, responds to accusations that he had "stolen" his stories from "Halima": "No, these tales aren't Halima's—what do I know of Halima? [He] went down to the sea and found treasure. They're Halima's little ones [*mikrákia*], nothing more. They are *paramythia*, that's it!" (Adamandiou 1900, 282–83). The sense that paramythia are neither purely Greek nor purely oral explains why to this day there is no canon of Greek tales, only collections and anthologies (the best in obscure regional periodicals) and little serious criticism. Early collectors and scholars, influenced by E. B. Tylor's survivalist thesis, focus on plots, names, and themes believed to derive from ancient mythology and pay scant regard to narrative form and imagery. Dialect is standardized, inconsistencies inherent in all oral narratives ironed out, and details arbitrarily omitted or changed.[18]

Since the mid–twentieth century, a more systematic and comparative approach to the Greek tales has prevailed, pioneered by two scholars from different backgrounds: R. M. Dawkins and Georgios Megas. Dawkins, Professor of Greek at the University of Oxford, had an abiding interest in the dialects of the Dodecanese and the Greek-speaking peoples of Asia Minor. His collections of tales from these areas, with commentary and translation, remain a model of scholarly accuracy, documentation of sources, and retention of dialect features. Not wedded to the Hellenist hypothesis, Dawkins points out parallels between Greek and other tale types. Megas, Professor of Folklore at the University of Athens, compiled the first pan-Hellenic collection, with comparative annotation. Unlike Dawkins, his overriding concern was to establish connections with ancient myths through oral transmission. Several popular anthologies and collections have appeared since then, both regional and national, but their scholarship is uneven.[19]

Despite their lowly status in the Greek folklore canon, paramythia have shown remarkable resilience. Indeed, the lack of canonization, anthologization, and critical analysis has probably contributed to continuing diversity, at least until the advent of elecricity and television, common in even the remotest villages since the 1980s. It is a fitting irony that the Greek demand for commercialized and sanitized tales has been met from Western films and publications, leaving the Greek tales unaffected: Cinderella's disadvantage turns out to be a bonus. While adequate information on context of performance may be absent in the case of texts recorded last century, much evidence lies within living memory. Once again, let us listen to Adamandiou's careful notes from the turn of this century, as he vividly recaptures contexts of performance from Tinos. Tale sessions in town and country took place above all in winter, to make up for inadequate heating. The teller with the best repertoire was known as "the one with forty days of paramythia," much as the South Slavic *guslar* claimed to know thirty stories, enough for each night of Ramazan. Everyone knew the tales, but the most skilled tellers were in demand outside their immediate locality. Held in honor, they were often summoned to entertain the local grandees (*proúchontes*):

So each with a lantern, all would go to the evening session [*sperokáthisma*], as they called these evenings, and there they invite the village storyteller and listen to the tale with religious attention. There they forget their poverty, they forget the cold and their nakedness, all crowded together, women pressing babies in their arms. The story teller begins: the audience warms up and individual comments interrupt the narration. "Did you ever see such a faithless woman [ἄπιστ']!—Oh the poor thing!"—"Just wait to see what happens." But the teller too interrupts his narration, turning to someone seated nearby and speaking out his own opinion on an event in the tale in a very teasing way. (1900, 279–80)

Public performances, when a single tale might last several evenings, were held at a local house or at the bakery, where people could keep warm and women usually gathered. One woman told Adamandiou, "Last year we gathered at a painter's house, he got someone to read out 'Halima' and the rest of us listened—old women, women and children." More private sessions included nurses and grandmothers, mothers and aunts telling tales to children to kill time till fathers got home. Another important locus was at sea: as fishermen waited at night to trawl in their nets, they would drink strong liquor (*strophliá*) and vie with each other: who could tell the longest, bawdiest tale? Every profession—fisherfolk, sailors, cobblers, bakers—had their own repertoires, which came into their own on the night shift.

Times like that seem to have passed. Or have they? Some sixty years later, in the village of Sklithron Ayias in Thessaly, the café proprietor "Kathótis," so named for his predilection for the puristic conjunction καθότι ("inasmuch as"), with a possible pun on his fondness for sitting down to tell stories, seized the opportunity of my presence with a tape recorder to regale an impromptu audience of up to fifteen people with a repertoire of several paramythia, including one about a poor village boy who married a foreign princess after many tribulations—his references to fashion and modern modes of transport within and outside Greece were included for my benefit, but they also served to invite general comment on modern ways of life. Tales were still remembered and enjoyed, even if no longer told as regularly as in the prewar period, when as the local gendarme, Kathótis would go on his evening rounds of households whose goats and sheep had trespassed into neighboring orchards. Having made his complaint, over a glass or so of wine and a slice of pie he would entertain the family round the hearthside with tales so enthralling that many a young lad sent out to tend animals would let them stray deliberately so as to ensure another visit! That was in the 1930s: Kathótis is long gone, and his shop is now a disco-grill for tourists in the summer season. But have the tales been forgotten? Maroula Kliapha's collection of Thessalian tales from mothers, aunts, and grandmothers she has known suggests that live storytelling still engenders new versions of old tales.[20]

If storytelling traditions are moribund among the native Greek population, they still form a vital part of Greek Gypsy lore. Tong's collection includes several tales she recorded since 1982, mainly from northern Greece. They are not substantially different from those recorded since the nineteenth century, but the quality of her fieldwork affords new testimony to context of performance: men and women, professional and lay storytellers, will use their repertoire to while away the time washing dishes or on a train journey or to entertain neighborhood families not necessarily too poor to afford television (on the contrary, she was instructed to bring them the latest videos from America) but so fond of the lively discussion generated at every session of tale-telling that they still gather in one another's houses in the evening to exchange news, gossip, and tales. Here is how Lazaros Harisiadis, Greek Gypsy musician resident in New York for the past twenty years, describes storytelling in his family of musicians in northern Greece, where he goes back to perform during summer festivals:

> My mother and father went around to all the villages and knew a lot of people. Whenever we would all meet up, the women would leave and the men would sit alone. In those days there weren't any radios, TV, phonographs, and so on, but everyone knew one or two hours' worth of folk-

tales, and so the time went by until dawn. We didn't have blankets and we were cold, but we warmed ourselves telling the folktales that I'm telling you now and other old stories. The old men told them so we, the younger ones, could learn them, and this is the wealth that stays with us today. And so our riches are in these stories, not in our pockets. (Tong 1989, 66)

2. Spinning Yarns and Narrative Contingency

Since its inception, folklore has been plagued with apocalyptic pronouncements of decline. "The remains of all living folk (or national) thought are rolling with an accelerated final plunge into the abyss of oblivion," warned Herder, father of European folklore, well over two hundred years ago.[21] To this day it is assumed that both the quality and the quantity of folklore are rapidly diminishing. While not denying the decline of paramythia since the advent of television, I argue that the best Greek examples of the genre are not the oldest but those in which the collector has kept the narrator's "accents." As Adamandiou's storyteller perceived, a good story depends not just on plot but on narrative skill as well, on moving with dexterity from narration to dialogue and back again and including those familiar intrusions and refrains which remind us of the narrating instance, where the teller is free to develop an individual style appropriate to the occasion, "to cut a long story short, for the hour is late and the children are sleepy" or to interject, "oh yes, and I forgot to mention that he had put a sleeping potion in the ogre's wine" or "one-two and he goes inside." More curious are such direct addresses as "my good woman" and "madam" (kyrá mou) at crucial moments, although we may recall Adamandiou's observation that expert tellers address the closest individual to make a good point. Unusual forms of direct address are similarly inserted into everyday discourse, much as my mother-in-law Aspasia peppers her speech with "my son" (yié m'), whoever she is talking to.[22]

It is time to analyze some characteristic tales. I begin by comparing one of the earliest to be published (1843) with one of the most recent (1977), of a type well known throughout the Greek-speaking world for at least a century and a half. My concern is with narrative strategy rather than plot.

Τὸ ἀθάνατο νερό ("The Immortal Water")

Beginning of the story, good evening to you. There was once a virtuous and god-fearing king, who always won wars and was loved by the people. But the time came when he got old and sick, and not all the doctors in the world could find a cure. One day an old man came early to the palace: —Last night I lay awake thinking about you, and I saw a dream. I was in a green meadow, not a soul in sight, and I lay down to rest. A young boy like an angel tapped me on the shoulder and said "Get up, go tell the king to find a trusted person to fetch him the immortal water, then he'll be cured!" So here I am. Your people love you so choose the best and he can reach the ends of the earth. The king gave him a new set of clothes and told the news to the queen and their son, who wept for joy and said he must be the one to go. He said goodbye to his friends and was about to mount his horse when he remembered his mother's words of long ago—My child! Take your parents' blessing and you'll climb mountains. So he went back and bade them farewell, taking their blessing.

On his journey he passed mountains, plains, meadows, forests, gullies, deserts, villages, cities and kingdoms until he reached his mother's brother's palace. O my child, said the king when the prince told him his quest, you must pass through all seven of my kingdoms and travel seven days on a road of poisonous beasts before you reach the end of the world, where two tall mountains reach the sky, opening and closing every minute. You'll find a tree which looks like our pomegranate trees, and through its golden blossoms runs the immortal water in thousands of springs. Take care, for many a brave lad has gone there and never come back. One hero of old— as my grandfather told me—managed to get the water but lost it on the way back in the dark through the clashing mountains.

The prince left with a heavy heart. He traveled on and on, stopping for neither food nor sleep, until he came to the road with the poisonous beasts—he could see their eyes glinting in the darkness. Through forests he went, until his horse stumbled against sun rays and sprang free into a vast open plain. Suddenly the prince sees a palace, with a beautiful girl seated at an upper window. He goes in, and her father tells him his story: he was once a poor hunter who lived with his wife, struggling to make ends meet, but always sharing his spoils with the hungry. Three years pass before God gave them a daughter, and on the third day after the three Fates came to tell her fate, so his wife sits up to see what happens. The Fates taste the wine, so sweet that the first decrees her angelic beauty, the second that roses shall fall from her cheeks when she laughs, and the third that pearls shall fall from her eyes when she weeps. They leave her a jeweled ring to protect her. In time the hunter became rich with all the pearls and built this palace. The prince then tells his own story over a banquet, and the girl's heart is stirred to love and pity for his fate. That night her tears shed so many pearls in bed they awaken her mother, who suggests the prince be loaned the magic ring to protect him on his quest. Early next morning he sets out.

Such was the power of the ring and the joy in his heart that his horse sped through roads with wild beasts and reached in three not seven days the two mountains just as they were opening. In fly horse and hero, and reach the water. The mountains close, but lit by the ring the prince fills the bowl with immortal water and waits till the rocks open. Back he speeds on his horse and would have gone straight to his father had his heart not pounded for the girl waiting for him in the palace by the meadow, so he passes by. Torn by conflict between his love for the girl and his duty to his father, he leaves her asleep in the garden with many rings as his token: on waking, she weeps, cursing her roses and rings in song for "stealing my priceless eagle." The prince rides back to his father's kingdom, taking care to hold the bowl with the water steady. Crowds of mourners block his way, lamenting the death of the king, but they make room. He reaches his father fighting for his soul. As soon as he puts immortal water on his father's lips, the old king raises himself up, takes the bowl, and drinks his fill of it. . . . Joy and celebrations, feasting for all as they rush to church to give thanks to God. The prince would never have stopped talking about his journey, about the beauty and generosity of his beloved had his father not inter-rupted—My son! from today I hand over to you my kingdom, and the girl whose love or whose ring saved you from danger to give life to your father shall be your wife, the queen. So the prince is sent off with two golden carriages laden with three preciously embroidered dresses to fetch his bride, by now in the depths of despair at losing her loved one. Wasting no time to hear her complaints, he puts her with her father in one carriage, and seats her mother in his own. They ride back through twelve kingdoms, strewing the roads with the pearls of her tears shed in grief at his absence and the roses of her laughter as they go. The girl shone like the sun in a golden chariot. The whole kingdom turned out to welcome them, and the king and queen couldn't believe their eyes at her beauty. Next day was set for the wedding. The girl wore the best of the three dresses the queen had sent, embroidered with the sky and the stars, and she put on all the rings the prince had left her in the garden. As she smiled two red roses so fresh you have just picked them fell from her cheeks, and she sang a new song, thanking her roses and rings for "bringing me to the arms of my eagle."

(Kafandaris 1: Athens 1843 [Evlambios])

This charming tale, artfully told, resembles a blissful dream. Neither prince nor girl suffers serious obstacle; there are no threatening supernatu-ral creatures or weird metamorphoses; even the beasts keep their distance; and there is never any doubt about the successful outcome. There is no moral judgment, but the values of loyalty and love, trust and endurance, are indicated. If the king had not been virtuous, his meanest subject would not have confided his prophetic dream to him, nor would the king have be-lieved it and rewarded him with gifts. If the prince had not remembered his mother's words on the need for parental blessing, his quest would not have prospered. If the queen had not maintained good relations with her brother, who ruled the neighboring kingdoms, the prince would not have received instructions for the journey. If the hunter had not been generous with his spoils to those needier than himself, he would not have been blessed with a daughter. If his wife had not given the Fates the choicest food and wine and sat up to hear the results of her offerings, she would have been unaware of her daughter's gifts, and the magic ring could not have protected the prince. If the prince had forgotten to call back at the palace after securing the immortal water, he would have lost the girl. If he had succumbed to her wishes and stayed on, he would have lost his father and a kingdom. And so on.

G. Evlambios' version is linguistically and conceptually closer to the salon than to rural reality, where good fortune is hard won; but it has its charms, above all in the concrete images of the roses of laughter and the pearls of tears, in the thousand springs of immortal water welling up through the branches of a wondrous tree, in the dresses of the sky and stars, and in the comparison of the girl in her chariot with the sun. The hero of olden times who failed to bring back the immortal water would appear to refer to Herakles. In terms of plot, these images seem fortuitous or decorative, and their functions could have been performed by any other magic object/donor. Yet in the symbolic web of paramythia, they are interlinked, revealing new dimensions of meaning. Laughter and tears are not just expressions of joy and sorrow but, provided they are performed appropriately, also become ritual gestures with life-giving force, linked with the fertilizing powers of sun and rain.[23] It is the girl, blessed by the Moires (Fates) to shed tears of pearls and roses of laughter, who provides the prince with the means of access to the immortal water, defying the laws of nature and turning death to life. We shall see in other tales what happens in cases of inappropriate, mocking laughter. For the present, the importance of symbolic imagery, as opposed to plot and function of character, is apparent: analysed according to Propp's model, the tale can be reduced to the following eight moves: a (Initial situation); Ib (Absentation- death); VIII A (Lack); XI (Departure); XIV F (Magical Agent); XIX K (Initial Lack Liquidated); XX (Return); XXXI W (Hero married, ascends throne).

Now let us turn to one of Kliapha's tales from Thessaly. Here is how ninety-year-old Mati Agoritsa from Farsala tunes a traditional tale of violence and metamorphosis to her audience of young children in the 1970s.

'Ο "Ηλιος, ὁ Αὐγερινὸς καὶ ἡ Πούλια ("The Sun, the Morning Star, and the Pleiad")

A king once decreed that no one in his realm should light lamps after dusk. Three poor sisters—orphans, each one more beautiful than the next—lived in the forest and had to make ends meet. They blocked out the light with curtains and hangings and worked the night at weaving and sewing. They tried to keep awake by telling each other their dreams.—I, said the eldest, dreamed I married the king and bore him three beautiful children, the Sun, the Morning Star and the Pleiad.—I, said the second, dreamed I married the baker and the house was filled with bread.— And I, said the third, dreamed I married the coalman and my little bone was warmed. At that moment, the king passed by. When he heard what the eldest said, one-twos and he goes inside.—I want you as my wife to make me three children, he said, just like you said. The wedding was held. Nine months later the queen was about to give birth, but the king had to go to war. He tells the midwife to take good care of his wife, and she says to him,—Don't you worry, I'll see to her like my own two eyes. One-two and off he goes. The queen gave birth to the Sun, the Morning Star and the Pleiad, just as she had seen in her dream—the room shone from their beauty. But the midwife, one-two she takes the children and she buries them in the sunless basements of the palace. Time came for the queen to feed her children, the midwife gave her a puppy. —You're a bitch, you've given birth to puppies. She was upset, but what could she say? The king came back and heard the midwife's lying news—the queen was a bitch and had given birth to puppies! He got a bit worried, so he set the queen to mind the turkeys, and married the midwife. At evening he would close the curtains and say —Where are you, my Sun, where are you my Pleiad, and you, my Morning Star? —Here we are, father! answered the children with one voice. The midwife was on hot coals, and began to wail —Let's pull down this palace and build a new one! When the palace was pulled down, the evil queen found the three children's bones so she puts them in the yard and shit. Three cypress trees grew up—what cypress trees! But the evil midwife (a witch) realized the trees were the three children and went complaining to the king, and the trees are felled. Soon after, three beautiful flowers grow up—what flowers, what scent! The evil queen goes out of her mind and sets her lamb to eat the flowers. The lamb got pregnant. One-two, the queen goes to the king, —Let's slay the lamb! —Why? he says, she's pregnant; let her give birth, then we'll see. —No, at once! she says. A servant girl takes the ewe and slays it. As she washed out the stomach in a river, three children come out. —How did you get here? asked the slave girl. They tell their story. She let them go free, saying nothing to anyone. Many years passed. The three children walked along the shores and reached the kingdom next to their father's. A childless old fisherman takes them in and brings them up until the fame of their beauty and wit spread to the king, who recognized them as his own and summoned them to his palace. They tell him their story and get their real mother reinstated in the palace. As for the evil midwife, she is sent out to tend the turkeys . . .

(Kliapha 13: Thessaly 1977)

This tale conforms to a familiar type, recorded in many versions since the 1870s, but it has all the freshness of a live tradition, with playful variations on the key motif of metamorphosis between human, vegetal, animal, and cosmic beings. The action is set in motion by three girls sharing their dreams in order to keep awake. Dreams play a major role in Greek tales, just as they do in everyday discourse, imparting vital information from other worlds and frequently determining plot and resolution.[24] Here, the strangeness of the eldest girl's dream transports us at once into a world of fantasy and dream logic—or paralogic. It is she who looks toward the future, whereas the younger two think only of gratifying their bodily needs: warmth and food.[25] No explanation is offered as to why the king had banned lights in his realm after dusk, but it is presented as an unnatural injunction, and it is because his lowliest subjects disobey that he is ultimately blest with three children whose brightness protects them from death and spans the universe: death rituals close, birth rituals open. There is something compelling and deeply reassuring about the will of the three beautiful children to live against all odds. Apart from the girl's initial dream, the adults are relevant only as instruments or obstacles to the children's survival.

The earliest recorded version of a similar tale opens nonchalantly, pointing in a different direction: to the consumption of human flesh and incestuous cannibalism.

Ἀστερνὸς καὶ Πούλιω ("Star and Pleiad")

Once there was a poor woman whose husband went hunting and brought back a dove [περιστέρι] to eat. She roasts it on the spit and leaves it to cool, then goes out to chat with neighbors, so the cat gets it. What can she give her husband when he gets home? She cuts off one of her breasts and roasts it. —What wonderful meat! won't you have some? he asks her. —Oh, I've eaten already—What flesh is this? —I've never tasted anything so good. She shows him her cut-off breast, and he persuades her that human flesh is so succulent they should kill their two children and eat them tomorrow. A little puppy hears them plotting and warns brother and sister to leave home at once. . . . In their wanderings, Asternos is turned into a lamb by his mother's curse, but Poulio refuses to forsake him even after she is tricked into marriage by a foreign prince. In the end, her wicked mother-in-law kills the lamb and serves up his flesh at a family meal, but Poulio refuses to eat, and buries the bones in the garden. From the bones there grows a wondrous golden apple tree whose topmost branches transport sister and brother to the skies as eternal stars.

(Kafandaris 2: Epiros 1850 [von Hahn in German], 1879 [Pio in Greek])

Here, the serving, eating, and refusing of family flesh provide the frame for a version of the story substantially different in form and meaning from its modern Thessalian counterpart, in which the three children seem protected from evil throughout, rather like the protagonists of "The Immortal Water." Both versions focus on parent-child and sibling relations rather than on marriage; and in both, parental figures try to block the children's passage to adulthood. But the later version ends happily, whereas the earlier one has a tragic-mythic dimension, since brother and sister, forced into an unnaturally close bond during their lifetime, are literally ejected from the world, albeit as stars. I was tempted to speculate on the declining appeal today of the theme of incestuous cannibalism, until reminded by Diane Tong that she recorded a tale with the same opening motif (mother cuts off breast to feed family): it was told with great gusto by an eleven-year-old Gypsy girl who was fascinated by the growth of her own breasts and their possible source of food and interest for others! (Tong 1989, 179–83).

As a reminder of the importance of performative context in the craft of "spinning yarns," let us listen again to one of Adamandiou's informants from Tinos:

> Soon as I hear it, master, I get a hold of [*paírno*] the tale. Eh! if it's short, I stick a bit on myself [*kat' kollô ki egó*], like side branches [*parakládia*] so it gets long . . .
>
>   That story now can go on two hours, then you'd see *da capo* (*synanastrophê*).
>
>   (Adamandiou 1900, 288)

Such practices did not meet with universal approval. Another teller comments, "He makes his stories long because he adds from others": "he sticks them" (*ta kollâ*), folks will say." Adamandiou notes that this technique of synanastrophe is not a sign of poverty or lack of inspiration but of the teller's infinite ability to adapt and draw out the tale, as do Odysseus or Shahrazad. A favorite device is to have the protagonist build a palace or garden, find inside the loved one, who then tells his or her own tale, as in the Byzantine vernacular romances.[26] At this point the protagonist or teller can begin again from the beginning, saying "Shall I tell you a tale? I am a tale!" Episodes may be repeated twice or three times, as each new character begins with "I am the one who . . ."

Tales are variations on a limited number of units, like letters of the alphabet or musical notes, and as infinitely variable. Beginnings and endings seem peripheral, but subtly they signpost the course of the tale. Once launched, it gives the impression of inexorability, yet it is the contingency of details and images (vocabulary) rather than function of character and plot (morphology and syntax) that decide the course and meanings of the tale. The protagonist, male or female, leaves home and meets other creatures, whether human, animal, or supernatural. In each encounter there is a ritualized form of exchange, where the hero/ine must get both words and actions right in order to prosper. Let us consider the principle of contingency in a beautiful tale where the hero's quest is to win the fair Trisevgeni ("Thrice noble"), inherently no more difficult a quest than for the immortal water. But here our prince has a much harder time of it. Why?

Ἡ Τρισεύγενη ἤ τὰ τρία κίτρα ("Trisevgeni, or The Three Citrons")

A king and queen pledge to God to open three fountains to run for three days each with oil, honey, and butter for everyone to share, if only their many years of childlessness are rewarded with an heir. A son is born. They forget to honor the pledge. He grows up, and the queen is reminded by an old woman in a dream. A poor old woman gets to the fountains only after they dry up. When she tries to scrape what butter is left around the third fountain, the young prince from an upstairs window laughs at her efforts and throws down a stone, smashing her dish and spilling her butter. She curses him to long for Trisevgeni just as she has longed for her butter cake. On his quest he meets three lamies. He greets them kindly, and in return the eldest tells him how to win Trisevgeni. He obeys instructions and accomplishes what seems the greatest peril of his quest: to secure the three golden citrons from a tree guarded by Nereids and lions. But his curiosity gets the better of him, and he ignores the third lamia's injunction not to open the citrons except in plentiful water. He opens the first on dry land—a beautiful girl comes out, crying "Water, water!" She dies. He goes on, and upon reaching a ditch with a little water in it, tries the second. She dies too. He opens the third in a full cistern, and out comes Trisevgeni. She asks after her sisters, but he says he left them behind on the magic citron tree. Wrapping her in his cloak he sets her atop a cypress tree by a well and goes home to fetch clothes and carriage for their wedding. An arapina *["Moorish girl"] comes by to draw water, sees Trisevgeni's reflection in the well, and thinks it her own. From her treetop, Trisevgeni laughs. The arapina topples her from the tree, pushes her into the well and takes her place, telling the prince on his return that she has gone black from grief at his delay and will turn white again when he proves his love for her. He is tricked into thralldom to her.*

Trisevgeni is restored to him only after three further metamorphoses. A poor girl finds a golden eel in the well where Trisevgeni was drowned and takes it to the prince to cheer him up. The wicked queen is so jealous of the eel's seductive dance that she has it cooked for dinner—the prince buries the bones of his portion in the garden. There grows a beautiful lemon tree—what scent! what foliage!—but the evil queen has it hacked into pieces and left on the roadside for firewood—only the stump is left by the well. A poor old man takes it home for firewood, but just as he raises his axe a voice sings out "Strike the top and strike the bottom, but in the middle do not strike, for there's a girl inside whose head is hurting her." His son gets home and obeys the stump's instructions: out comes Trisevgeni. She asks him for clothes to cover her nakedness and a fine white kerchief with some gold and silk thread. Then she embroiders her whole story and the boy takes the story cloth to the prince, who recognizes the truth about the Moorish girl. First he rewards the boy, then he gives her a fair trial in which she condemns herself, and finally he wins Trisevgeni: "he took her as wife, and they lived well, we even better."

(Kafandaris 41: Athens, 1883)

The prince succeeds in his quest only at the end, after he has learned wisdom from suffering. The internal logic of the tale is not spelled out but implicit in incidental narrative cues which may change the course of the plot at any point, and therefore contingency keeps up suspense to the end. If the king and queen had opened up the fountains of honey, oil, and butter for all their subjects as soon as their son was born, his path could have been as smooth as that of the prince in "The Immortal Water." If he had not dashed the last hopes of a poor old woman, there would have been no quest. If he had not squandered the first two citrons, he would have won Trisevgeni sooner; but then the narrator would have given him two elder brothers who could have married her sisters.[27] If Trisevgeni had not laughed inappropriately at the arapina, like the prince at the old woman, she could not have been forced down from her treetop; but then, as in "Asternos and Poulia," someone else might have lured her down by guile, though her sufferings would have been less. At each point the trials of the two protagonists are unpredictably balanced: a broken pledge and taunt lead into the first quest: the prince has three encounters, follows the rules, and wins three citrons. There follow three transgressions—impatience, a lie, and a taunt—leading to loss of the heroine and the second quest: the heroine is metamorphosed three times (eel, lemon tree, tree trunk) and rescued by three poor subjects (girl, old man, and young boy), after which the hero is regained.

There is no simple moral of good rewarded and evil punished. Unlike the bland hero of "The Immortal Water," the prince does not always behave well, almost deserving to lose Trisevgeni for having destroyed her sisters and lied to her, and is therefore rendered impotent (like the king in "Sun, Morning Star, and Pleiad") to counter the black queen's cruelty. Rather, the tale underlines the value of *reciprocity* inherent in the success of all relationships, human and nonhuman: if you learn from past mistakes, you may be saved by others, including those of different gender, status, or species. The prince prospers so long as he shows respect to the three lamies, but it takes Trisevgeni's endurance *and* the generosity, wit, and forbearance of three poor subjects to secure a happy ending. Good and evil are not fixed opposites, and it is within everyone's power to turn the one into the other. As for gender, again, the emphasis is on reciprocity: the hero may be a prince, but he is confronted throughout by female powers. His parents' pledge was made to God, but God assumes an old woman's form to warn his mother in a dream to fulfill it, just in the nick of time; he insults a poor old woman (from his mother's dream?), but it is the three female lamies who guide the way to his beloved: he has to treat them kindly, and she has to undergo trials and metamorphoses by water and fire for his sake. In the end it is a poor old forester and his son with nothing to owe and nothing to own who guide the way to salvation. Such qualities of magic and economy have inspired art from *The Winter's Tale* to *Die Zauberflöte*.

How can "spinning yarns" be linked to what I have called "narrative contingency"? The link between telling and spinning is made explicit by a rhyming jingle used as incipit:

Once upon a time zaman	Green thread a-threaded
Turks were holding ramazan	twined around the reel,
Jews were having bariam	push the reel and kick it
Greeks were having Easter.	let it turn just where it will

not a care your mind to fill.

Beginning of the story good evening to you, welcome one and all, and please don't shilly-shally.

Once started, the reel has its own momentum, spinning out thread without waiting for stragglers. As for "contingency," I have borrowed the term from Stephen Jay Gould, who demonstrates its centrality to the story of the Creation he spellbindingly tells from the time of the Burgess shale some 540 million years ago to present forms of life on earth: replay that tape of evolution once more with the same initial species, and the rules of contingency will produce different results. Species could be grotesquely remingled, as indeed is the case in the Belgian Gypsy tale "The Mosquito," in which an audacious young mosquito engages in battle with a candle, negotiates the exchange of his charred wings with six chicken legs and three chicken wings thanks to hospital transplants, then uses his native cunning to swap these accoutrements with the outfit of a gullible gajo mayor. The mayor ends up as looking as strange as Gould's Opabinia, Anomalokaris, and Pikaia, except that Mosquito and his friends can enjoy chicken flesh afterward over the telling of a tale! "Contingency" in biological evolutionary narrative is not a whimsical comparison; rather, it suggests that wonder-tales may know more than they say. The principle has been overlooked by critics.[28]

3. Teasers, Twisters, and Movers: Metanarrative and Paranarrative

A wondertale is rarely told "in plain stitch." The teller loves to surprise and tease listeners with unexpected knots and dropped stitches: "Did I say 300?" "What did I say the first *máissa* ("witch") did?" "What is here? Black," "What is there? White." Woe betide whoever had nodded off and failed to respond appropriately! Adamandiou recalls how he was tested by informants, especially sailors, who repeated whole episodes word for word up to four or five times, curious to see if his writing could keep up with their spinning. When they found that he did, they commented with approval, "He's a good man to tell tales to: he hurries to keep track, you don't have to chase after him!" Women on Tinos preferred a more elaborative style in fast, high-toned delivery and intricate "back stitching," with glosses such as "And he went in, the *siízis*, the *siyézis*, that is the stall-boy, the one in the stable." By such tactics women not only enrich the vocabulary of the tales but increase the suspense. Most curiously, they play with all available registers between dialect and puristic words until they hit upon just the right "needlepoint," rather as Maria Gourioti availed herself of puristic phrases in telling her husband's story.[29]

As teller and audience enjoy teasing strategies (Tiniot *períerga*), so communication between protagonists takes place not only in normal dialogue but through dreams, songs, dance, and embroidery. Dreams play a key role in the three tales discussed so far, imparting information from other worlds and frequently determining plot as well as resolution.[30] Songs express the heroine's mood and signal her final path to happiness in "The Immortal Water" and "The Three Citrons." Through gesture and dance, Trisevgeni as golden eel demonstrates her devotion to the king, while embroidery provides the only means at her disposal to write her tale, crucial to resolution.[31] These nonverbal strategies are not just effective on the level of plot, because they elude or subvert hostile forces; they also illustrate the more profound truth that communication can operate outside the verbal level.

Verbal discourse includes metanarrative and interpretive skills to encode a "story within story" and to decode riddles, as in Τὸ φτωχόπαιδο προκομμένο, "The Poor Boy Made Good" (Kafandaris 3, 1873),[32] in which wit and cunning are vital strategies of telling and interpreting, hence riddling questions figure as a means of testing. Κορακίστικα, "Crow Language" (Kafandaris 4), tells of a prince who refuses to marry until he can find a girl to speak in a kind of code language only he can understand: one of the poorest girls in the kingdom meets his requirements and becomes queen. Βασιλοπούλα καὶ τσοπάνης, "Princess and Shepherd" (Kafandaris 5, 1870), tells the same story with reversed gender roles: a princess insists on marrying the man who can set her a riddle she cannot solve; many fail, but a poor shepherd succeeds through adventure, wit, and cunning. Αἰνίγματα, "Riddles" (Kafandaris 6, 1870), concerns a princess whose father is unjustly deposed by his brother and imprisoned without food or drink: she saves her father, first by offering him her breast to suck through a hole in the dungeon wall, then by making a wager with the usurper-uncle to solve a riddle he cannot answer (again, she shows both physical and mental powers). But the prize for wit surely goes to a miller's daughter, superior to the above in that her skills depend not on incidents unknown to the other party but on wisdom and judgment alone.[33]

Ἡ μυλωνοῦ ("Miller's Daughter")

A king promises a tray of golden coins to anyone who can solve three riddles— What are the two that stand [στεκούμενα], the two that walk [περπατούμενα] and the two that inhabit [κατοικούμενα]? Not even the most learned man in the kingdom knows the answer, but a poor miller's daughter insists her father go to the palace and tell the king "heaven and earth; sun and moon; life and death." He wins, but only after he admits to the king that it was his daughter who solved the riddles. Intrigued, the king sends him back with a single strand of cotton for her to weave him a set of white clothes without adding any thread: she responds by sending the king a single matchstick from which he must build a bed without adding any wood before she can start weaving. The king marries her, but warns her that if she interferes in affairs of state, he will send her straight back to the mill with only one prized possession to take from the palace. In the interests of justice, she disobeys over a court case, and the king tells her to get out by next morning. So she puts a sleeping potion in his drink, packs him fast asleep on the back of a mule, and goes home:—Well, she says, when he wakes up a bit dazed next morning at the mill, you told me I could take whatever I liked best from the palace, so here you are! I like money and jewels, but I like you best of all. They go back to the palace and rule as equals.

(Kafandaris 70: Naxos 1890)

Examples could be multiplied, but Greek wondertale winners come from every class and each gender if they have the wit to tell and interpret on all communicative levels—and wisdom and compassion too. Conversely, losers are not only the wicked or even the ill fated, since you can manipulate your personal fate (*moíra*) even *after* her birth decree has been issued with the requisite cunning and initiative.[34] If the prize winner is the miller's daughter, the dunce cap goes to the sackmaker in a humorous tale from Lesbos:

Στούπωσε! ("It's Stopped Up!")

Once there was a sackmaker so poor he has no bread to eat, so he goes out to seek his fate, and comes upon three fountains. One trickled, one flowed, and in between was a river.—Those are the three fates, a passerby tells him, yours is the one that trickles, and the king's is the river. So the sackmaker pokes a stick into the trickle to unblock the hole but he jams it up. "It's stopped up!" he wails until the king passes by and hears him. Next day the king sends him a roast goose stuffed with gold coins, just as two hungry strangers pass by, and so he exchanges the goose for a small coin. Again the king hears him wailing "It's stopped up!", so next day he sends a pie half stuffed with gold coins, but a beggarwoman comes by and he gives her the better half. The third day the king says—Take this golden apple and as many houses as you can throw it over will be yours. The apple hits a wall and rebounds on the sackmaker's head—and so the wail "It's stopped up!" was stopped for ever.

(Kafandaris 79: Lesbos 1905 [Kretschmer])

Greeks do not suffer fools lightly![35]

Such tales of wit and fate give some idea of diverse modes of telling in the paramythia, by no means concerned with Proppian "victims and seekers, heroes and villains, dispatchers and receivers." Narrative outcome may be predictable, but incidental versatility and humor are boundless. The hero of Ἡ βασίλισσα τῶν γοργόνων, "Queen of the Gorgons" (Kafandaris 42: Athens 1883), is not the prince—an effete, idle, and malicious youth—but his inferior, the vezir's son. One of his tasks is to fetch for the prince the jeweled eagle, so he takes a quantity of wine to the well frequented by the eagle, empties out the water, and fills it up with wine. The eagle swoops down to drink, finds it difficult to lift his wings, and so is caught. In Τῆς ἐλιᾶς τὸ δάκρυ "Olive Tear" (Kafandaris 53,: Samos 1887), the young hero surpasses in physical prowess a band of forty drakoi "ogres" so big and strong that when their leader's daughter pisses, seven windmills are set in motion! A clever mouse in Σταχτοπουτάκι, "Cinderello" (Kafandaris 78,: Lesbos 1905), contrives to retrieve the ring that will rescue the lowborn hero—who had earlier saved a dog, a cat, and a snake from death by vandal youths—by first dipping its tail in honey, then twisting it in pepper, and finally by stuffing it up the nose of the wicked Moor who sneezes out the magic ring.[36] In Τὸ βασιλόπουλο καὶ τ' ἀδέρφια του, "The Prince and His Brothers," the prince three times flouts the helpful instructions given him by monsters and demons in his quest to retrieve his father's silver bowl, but each time he wins their chiding forgiveness by his generosity (food), kindness (favors), and undaunted determination to win (Kafandaris 51).

The best ruse comes from Skyros (Kafandaris 146): on his way to bring back the singing nightingale, a poor boy takes shelter in the cave of a huge blind drakos who has just finished eating: *He cowers in a far corner of the cave, but then Drakos lets out a most gigantic* FART: PFFFFFFF . . . . *The reverberations send the boy whizzing across to the other side of the cave, where he lands with a thud. Running to Drakos' rear quarters, he calls out—Here I am, master, what can I do for you?—Who are you, and how did you get here?—Master, you've just birthed me with that great fart!* Even Odysseus would have been proud of that one! What follows is poignant: Drakos adopts him as his son, takes him onto his lap, and lets him climb up onto his shoulders, where he can just reach up to Drakos' one eye, all clogged up with eyebrows and facial hair. He trims the hairs and restores his sight. Drakos then gives him the information he needs to win his quest.[37]

Such details indicate the inadequacies of formalist/structuralist approaches, which focus on functions of characters, distribution of post-Proppian "motifemes" and "ecotypes," and binary oppositions. Should Drakos' fart be classified as "magical agent" alongside magic wand, or is it "future donor accosts hero"? The point is that the boy cunningly turns a potentially hostile force into a friendly one by inverting the normal course of events, in which a human groan of despair can call up an otherworldly being, as in "Lord of the Lower World."

Since the wondertale is a performative genre, any narratological analysis must include not only plot, story, and character but what I term *metanarrative* and *paranarrative* features. Metanarrative may be defined as story about story, or tale within tale. Insofar as they comment symbolically on the story, dreams, riddles, proverbs, and nonsense rhymes can be classified as metanarrative. Paranarrative includes those features that forward narrative not just as story but also in terms of perception, emotion, and teller-audience interaction, such as wit and humor, songs, dances, and ekphrastic passages. The best tales contain what may be called "key lines," dear to tellers and audience alike. Examples in tales to be reviewed in the next section will be cited in roman type, but of those analysed so far, *I like fine clothes, jewels and riches, but I like you best of all* ("Miller's Daughter") surely qualifies. Through these paranarrative devices, the teller can live out his or her fantasies and realities symbolically: the oral tales become "fictionalised metaphors of the teller's own life-drama."[38] Metanarrative and paranarrative function as *movers* and *shifters*—the "accents" of Adamandiou's informant?

It is possible to reduce tales to their barest thread and outline, but it is the narrator's loving attention to detail that gives them color, vibrancy and ethos, humor and irony. Viewed in this way, heroes/heroines and villains, monsters and demons—even animal, vegetal, and cosmic beings—cease to be stereotypes and gain an individuality of their own. We cannot talk of character in the sense of a novel's classic realism; but beneath the apparently flat exterior we glimpse a variegated composition of personified character-istics which span human emotions and experience, and integrate them with the universe. How this is achieved will be considered in the following section.

4. Weaving Pictures: The Interpenetration of Themes and Images

The late Albert Lord defined theme in oral narrative as a repeated pas-sage, emphasizing the importance of exact verbal repetition, as in the de-scription of a piece of armor or the preparation of a horse for battle.[39] In the paramythia, what counts is not the fact of repetition; where, when, and how it is placed in the fabric of the story gives rise to associative allusions which determine the value of the next repetition, so that each theme forms a strand in a complex web of interlinking patterns: hero mounts horse to start quest; protagonist greets / rescues / assists passersby; protagonist turns into tree / snake / marble; hostile force goes up in smoke / to smithereens; and so on. Exact repetition may occur within the same tale through the tech-nique of synanastrophe and across different tales through common formu-laic passages for beginnings and endings and for the exchange of greetings; for the description of beauty / ugliness; and for the passage of time / travel across distances. Themes can also be repeated incrementally, so that the ef-fect is cumulative rather than merely replicated: the hero in "The Three Citrons" gives one greeting to the first lamia, another to the second, and performs a good deed for the third, as appropriate to age and status.

In applying Lord's definition of theme as repeated passage to Greek wondertales, I should like to reverse Propp's methodology of conflating agents and objects according to function (eagle / dragon / witch pursues hero; hero hides in river / cave / chest / tree / well), and ask instead, How do these differences operate in terms of imagery? Do wells / trees / fruit or bread / water / meat acquire cumulative symbolic meaning? If analyzed in their totality both within and across tales, themes can be shown to signify in a manner akin to images. Many themes in tales are like images in ritual songs *literally acted out*. A mourner in laments may express grief for husband or son in the cries Στύλο τοῦ σπιτιοῦ μου! Ἥλιε μου! "Pillar of my house!" "My sun!", or a bride in wedding-songs may be addressed as Φουντωτή μου νεραντζιά! "My leafy bitter-orange tree!" In wondertales, men are actually turned into marble or metamorphosed into planets, and women may turn into fruit and fruit trees. What functions as compressed

metaphor in the songs ("straight and strong as a pillar," "bright and warm-
ing as the sun") is filled out into metonymic chains in the wondertales—
girl turns into an eel when pushed into well, or into a lemon tree when
buried in garden—as the axis shifts from paradigmatic (similarity / selection / substitution) to syntagmatic (contiguity / combination / contexture).
Perfect metaphorical distillation of theme occurs in the proverb (cited in
Chapter 5) "hand, knife, running water," in which only disjunct images remain; yet their juxtaposition implies a story of friendship, quarrel, and reconciliation. Conversely, some tales are structured around the explanation of
a proverb and are referred to by Adamandiou's Tiniots as *paroimíes*
"proverbs," *xómblia, esémpia* "examples," "patterns," as in tales and in embroideries, *lógoi palaioí* "old sayings."[40] Metaphor and metonym are not
polar opposites, but slip into each other according to context of utterance.

It is hard to know where to open up a seam in the intricate web of
themes and images, but the most frequently repeated passages are the endings: "The wedding took place with feastings and rejoicings, and they lived
well, we even better"; "I wasn't there and nor were you, so don't believe a
word I've said"; "and I was there at the feast, and here is some of the food
and drink so let's all enjoy it." Closure is neither final nor uniform in the
Greek formulations, as in our familiar "they lived happily ever after," but
draws attention to the variable narrating instant, as well as to love of food.
"Happy marriage" is a device for joining past to present, them and us, for
marking the close of one cycle of conflicts with festivities while not pre-
cluding the seeds of another. It is of less narrative interest than death and
dismemberment, eating and drinking, defecation and urination, engorge-
ment and disgorgement, travel to other lands and worlds, intercourse with
other bodies, metamorphosis, and so on. And while wedding festivities
close the majority of wondertales, they are not universal: a significant number close with the isolation, even death, of the hero or heroine for example,
in "Myrsinió" (Kafandaris 88), without the intervention of "villains."

What of beginnings? Most tales open with a transition, whether at
childbirth, sexual maturation, or death; once again, bodily functions connected with food and drink figure prominently. To take childbirth first, a
couple, royal or humble, may be unable to bear children without supernatural intervention; the queen in "The Three Citrons" was granted an heir
only after pledging sustenance to all in the kingdom, while the prince's
tribulations resulted from her failure to do so at the proper time and from
his two willful squanderings of food and fruit. Impregnation is frequently
effected by the consumption of food or drink in response to a higher or supernatural command: the hero's virgin mother in "Olive Tear" gets pregnant
by licking an olive and letting its sap trickle down to her belly; a childless

wife conceives by eating a fish, pear, or apple. Parents pledge potential off-spring to whichever elemental force offers to get them with child, such as the sun, sea, rivers, and trees. In Ὁ Γιάγκος "Yiankos," an elderly fisher-man sighs and groans as he gathers in his empty nets, barely able to scrape a living for himself and his wife. The sea mother rises to the foamy surface and offers them a son on condition he is returned to the sea at the age of eighteen to wed her youngest daughter. The fisherman and his wife bear a son and honor their pledge, but the boy escapes and falls in love with a princess while working as a shepherd. After their marriage, the sea reclaims him, but his wife wins him back through resourcefulness and courage (Kafandaris 16, Naxos, 1895). Tales of this type depend on a pact between supernatural agents and human parents involving the consumption of food and the repayment of debts. Only if the initial pledge is honored and the sacrifice is made can the outcome be positive.

Second, sexual maturation may involve the consumption of unusual substances, a theme especially common in tales of the lower world, as in the following tale, where it is linked with clothes, washing, and weaving.

Τῆς κάτω γῆς ὁ ἀφέντης ("Lord of the Lower Earth")

A poor old man groans in despair "from the leaves of his heart" as he rests by the wayside on his way home from the forest. —How can I feed my daughters, let alone get them married? At once an arapis [Moor] appears. —Bring each of your three daughters on three successive days. The first goes and is taken to a beautiful palace. The arapis brings her a worm-eaten human foot to eat! If you eat this foot, he says, you'll marry the lord of the lower earth. Otherwise I'll send you back to your father. She throws it in the privy, pretending she has eaten it. When the arapis asks the foot where it is, the foot tells the truth. Next day the second sister goes and is served a worm-eaten human hand—she does the same as the first and is sent home. The third sister is offered a filthy stinking human belly to eat. I'd love to, she says, just bring me two cloves and a little cinnamon to spice it first. So she spices it and straps it onto her belly. When the arapis asks the belly where it is, it replies, In my mis-tress's belly. In this way she becomes the bride of the lord of the lower earth, but she never sees him because he comes to her only at night, and the arapis always puts a sleeping draught in her coffee before bedtime. Then one day her two sisters pay her a visit and reveal the truth: her husband is not the arapis, but a handsome youth, and if she throws away the coffee that night, she will see him. —On his navel is a key, just turn it round once and you'll see the whole world! the "bad" sisters tempt her. She does as they suggest, and what did she see? Constantinople, Smyrna—every-thing, then an old woman bleaching her thread of cotton in a river whose strong cur-rent keeps snatching it away. —Old woman, she cries out, the river has stolen your thread! At once her lord screams —Bitch, turn back the key, you're killing me. Next morning he tells the arapis to turn the girl out with a crust of bread, but first he must cut two hairs from her head, put them in a bowl of water, and let his master know at once if either sinks. . . . She travels, changes clothes with a shepherd boy, and works as "Yiannis," a gardener's boy for a king and queen. The queen tries to seduce the fair Yiannis and on failing to do so accuses him of rape, demanding his death by hanging. Just as everyone is gathered to watch the spectacle, the arapis warns the lord of the lower world that the two hairs are sinking in the bowl of water: he arrives on the scene. —What crime has this person committed? —He tried to rape me, lies the queen. —And if he turns out to be a woman? —Then let them hang me instead! The lord of the lower world rips off Yiannis' clothes to reveal her breasts. —Look! he says. —Do you want me to tear further down? —Enough, cries the king. So the lord carried Yiannis back to the lower world as his wife and the wicked queen was hanged. —Neither was I there, nor are you to believe me, but they lived well, we even better.

(Kafandaris 2: Melos 1870)

The tale contains themes common to others worldwide, such as "Cupid and Psyche," "Bluebeard," and "Potiphar's Wife," not to mention Byzantine hagiographies, but my concern is to show how themes and images interact as metonymic signifiers rather than to trace connections or origins. First, food, drink, and the body. All three sisters are given rotting human flesh to eat, but only the youngest is given the belly, the most disgusting yet at the same time the seat of the body's digestive and procreative organs. Her ruse of strapping it to her own belly, rather than eating it or destroying it as her sisters had done with their morsels, suggests incomplete carnal knowledge, hence she lives for some time in ignorance of her true marital state, thanks to the sleeping potion she unwittingly drinks every night before bedtime. And so would her life have gone on, had not her sisters aroused her curiosity to explore her husband's body. The narrator is careful to explain how they got down to the lower world (their father tells them to sigh and groan at the same place where the arapis had appeared to him) but seems unconcerned with how they knew of the secret key on her lord's navel. Other versions say "they were witches," but here we are simply told "they were bad": their badness leads her to prove her worth.

When the girl turns the forbidden key, she sees not carnage but bustling city life and an old woman whose white threads (νήματα) are swept away by a strong current (rivers in Greek are masculine in gender)—things she never dreamed of! From this point, images shift from food to thread, hair, and clothes, with sexual connotations. A woman washing threads suggests menstruation, the piercing of the hymen, even childbirth. The saying ἔχω τὰ ροῦχα μου "I have my clothes" is used by women to mean "I have my period," referring to the cotton swabs worn during menstruation. And in a slightly different version of the tale recorded by Dawkins (1953, 91–95), when the girl turns the key she sees a woman washing baby clothes. Her curiosity is a necessary part of her maturation, but because she acquires her knowledge illicitly, or prematurely, her lord sends her away not so much to punish her as to let her learn from experience and labor; her two hairs kept in water to signal danger connote his continuing share in her sexuality. When dressed and working as a man in the service of the king, she is dragged into a bed fight with the queen, who seizes her (ἁρπάζει) and scratches her face, drawing blood. Here and elsewhere, transvestism, a man's work, and bleeding flesh signify passage from girlhood to fertility. The closing theme of disrobing completes her sexual initiation and averts execution. In the paramythia, as in ancient myth, dangling females are associated with sexual ripeness (compare the prince's encounter with the first two swinging lamies in "The Three Citrons" and the sexual innuendos of eating and cutting in the dialogue). She had seen in stealth the woman's swab swept away by the river; in the final scene everyone looks on as her true lord rips the clothes from her body, thereby reclaiming her from her false accuser. The happy ending does not operate on the superficial level of "man gets woman in the end." Other tales tell of protagonists who marry outside this world, do not disobey injunctions, but get so bored with luxury that a bargain is struck: after some time, they return to earth (Dawkins 1953, 270–87). Themes and images explore the complementarity of the universe.

Stinking human flesh and blood lead the girl to intimate knowledge of self and others. The belly is not what it seems, for it leads the girl to the lower earth and its handsome young lord. The lower earth figures in Greek tales as a place through which the protagonist must pass to acquire wisdom and understanding, but it is never designated as the land of the dead, as in the *moirológia* (laments of the dead). Indeed, one woman gets back from a forty-day sojourn to tell her incredulous husband she was transported by an arapis in a magic chandelier to "the world below—not where the dead are, but a quite different place" (Dawkins 1953, 259–62). Following bodily clues, let us consider a tale where the prince's quest is to find the secret of the cosmos itself, the navel of the earth.

ʽΟ ἀφαλὸς τῆς γῆς ("The Navel of the Earth")

An old king on his deathbed summons his three sons and instructs them to give his three daughters to whomsoever should ask their hand in marriage, however unpre-

possessing his appearance. A lame man, a one-eyed man and a ragged beggar present themselves but are turned away by the two elder brothers. Only the youngest consents, giving each of his sisters in turn. Then he sets out to win the Beauty of the World. But the Beauty sets her own test: whoever seeks her hand must find the secret of the navel of the earth, otherwise she will cut off his head to complete the tower of human heads she is trying to build—only one more head is needed! Our hero succeeds, first by meditation in the underground dungeon, and from there by finding his way by chance (an unexpected window) to the Underworld, where he finds his three sisters married to Underworld drakoi (lame man, one-eyed man and beggar). With their assistance, and from the top of the highest tower in the Underworld, the secret of the navel of the earth is eventually revealed by a mangy old eagle: it is a wondrous old tree at the center of the earth, and at its roots are three fountains flowing with gold, silver and pearls. The eagle gives the prince samples wrapped in gold cloth to take back as proof of the verity of his tale. The princess thanks him for rescuing her from her cruel habit of tower building, and their wedding feast lasts forty days.

(Megas 34: Ainos 1883)

Here, the search for the navel of the earth signifies neither carnal knowledge nor death but the need to plumb the depths and soar to the heights of the cosmos, at once a *káthodos* "descent" and *ánodos* "ascent." The lame, one-eyed and ragged suitors are not what they seem, and the prince's respect for his father is rewarded and balanced by an old eagle who also heeded his dying father's advice on a cure for the mange. The prince needs seclusion to discover himself (the open window in the underground prison) and the secrets of the cosmos, climbing downward (forty steps from dungeon to the Underworld) and upward (from the Underworld to the top of its highest tower), inside and outside of himself. The Beauty of the World can only then be rescued from her compulsive building of a tower of human heads. The other world of the paramythia suggests the innermost parts of body and cosmos, the Underworld, where all dead matter must go, yet from which new life springs. As in the "Dead Brother" (Chapter 6), it is good to have sisters married elsewhere. There is magic realism in the suggestion that untold riches and jewels lie buried in the bowels of the earth, if only we have the patience and compassion to find them. Vizyenos exploits the images and themes of this tale type in his short story, Αἱ συνέπειαι τῆς παλαιᾶς ἱστορίας, "The Consequences of an Old Story" (1884).

Exposure (giving sisters in marriage abroad) and seclusion (forty days underground) are equally necessary to the prince's success, but they have to occur at the right time. What happens when this order is upset, as in a blood-curdling tale from Cyprus?

Τρίμματος "("Three Eyes")

A poor woodcutter despairs of making ends meet, let alone dowering his three daughters, so he sits the eldest at the attic window with a pretty kerchief. A peddlar comes by and makes a bid for her, so she goes off with him. He takes her to a palace and gives her a hundred and one keys, telling her she can open one hundred rooms, but not the one hundred and first. After a while she feels cooped up, so she unlocks the last room to find nothing but four walls, a big chest—and then a little window, the only one in the whole palace facing outward. She looks out, but what does she see? A funeral cortege—she bursts out crying, thinking of her family she isn't allowed to see. Then her husband turns into a monster and goes into the tomb—his head as big as a sieve, with three eyes, hands so long they want to grip the earth and nails a whole cubit long. He digs out the corpse and gobbles it up. Shivering, she goes to bed, frigid with fear. He comes home in human form to find the forbidden room unlocked. . . . When she sees him, she is wild with terror, curling herself into a ball buried under the covers.—What's the matter? he asks. You are ill, would you like me to fetch your mother to see you?—Oh yes, she replies. So he goes out, changes [μεταμορφώνεται] into her very own mother, and comes back.—What's the matter? What's he done to you, you look so ill?—Nothing, the girl replies, I'm just ill,—With all the money you have, can't you give us a few coins so we can get by?—Oh no, I couldn't do that, my husband is out at the moment and you'll have to ask him. After some time, "mother" leaves and her husband comes back to hear what happened.—You should have given her the money, he chides. Aren't you mistress of the house? Seeing his bride is no better, he offers to fetch her granny. Out he goes, turns into her granny [στετοῦλα], and comes back.—I'm so happy to see you, granny, I've been so wretched.—Tell me, my little one, what's he done to you? She tells all. "Granny" turns back into Trimmatos and screams—Filth! [βρόμα]. I wasn't going to eat you, but you've given away my secret, so I'm going to eat you! He prepares a huge fire whose tongue came out and reached halfway up the sky, then he lights a spit stake [σούβλα], and when it's red-hot he calls her.—I'm ready, do you want to be eaten roast on the spit or raw, swallowed whole?—I need two hours to say my prayers, then eat me. She seizes the key, opens the secret room, and leaps out of the window onto the street.

She runs for her life until she reaches a cart driver and begs him to save her from Trimmatos, offering him coins.—Oh no, he'll catch up with us and eat me and my horse as well as you. But run on, you'll reach a caravan of camels on the way to the king. She runs on; the caravan leader hides her in a bale of cotton. Trimmatos with his red-hot stake finds his bride gone and begins the chase. He catches up with the cart driver, then with the caravan leader, still he's got his red-hot stake so huge you had to close your eyes for shame, madam. He unloads the sacks from the camels, then pokes his stake through each one, and takes it out again, looking for blood.

Finding no trace, he goes off.—Didn't you bleed? the caravan leader asks the girl.—Only on my ankle, and I wiped his stake with cotton so it wouldn't show. The caravan reaches the king's palace. The driver delivers his goods, keeping back the sack with the girl inside. Slave girls notice and tell the king. The girl is unsewn from her sack, and such is her beauty and skill in embroidery that they want her for a daughter-in-law. She tells her story and marries their son, the prince.

News of her wedding reached Trimmatos, so he turns into a peddlar and goes to the king with a load of sacks, crying "Pistachios, dried apricots and chestnuts, all from Aleppo!" The girl sees the peddlar is Trimmatos but feigns longing for his goods and gives orders for the sacks to be opened next morning "when it's time." The court jester overhears Trimmatos' plot: his sacks are filled with blacks, who are to come out and kill everyone at the words "it's time now." Girl and jester approach the sacks at night: "Time now," they say. Out come the blacks, and their heads are chopped off, but Trimmatos remains. He sneaks into the girl's bedchamber, throws death dust on her groom, and says—The spit is waiting, I'm ready to swallow you. They start downstairs, and she says,—You go down first, I'm afraid. When he gets to the bottom she hits him with the banister rail, and he slips on grain seeds and falls into a well, where a lion eats him all up. She faints on the stairs. Next morning king and queen find prince and princess at death's door and fetch a doctor to bring them back to life. The girl tells their story, all make sure that Trimmatos has really been eaten, then the wedding goes on for forty days and forty nights—how they feasted!—we left them there then and find you now, and here is food to prove it.

(Kafandaris 66: Cyprus 1891)

This tale indicates the metonymies of eating people, roasting meat on red-hot spits, and sexuality. Prematurely exposed to the outside world by her father's poverty, the girl is seized by her vampire husband but finds her own way to maturity in the end. Trimmatos, like Bluebeard, seems to belong to the world of the dead, but he also provides the means of initiating his bride to womanhood, having first tempted her to explore the one hundred and first room with her key, then poked through her ankle with his red-hot stake (a blatantly sexual gesture), and finally fallen victim to her violent push down to the bottom of a well, where he is eaten by a lion. She wins out. Is he really so evil? A close look at narrative style and images reveals an ambivalence. The narrator delights in describing Trimmatos in hyperbolic terms, punctuating blood-curdling bits with the odd interjection *kyrá mou*, "madam," apparently addressed to a particular woman present, so that the effect—hard to convey in a paraphrase—is that we find him funny, laugh in fascinated horror, and almost feel sorry for him at the end as he is battered down the stairs with a loose banister rail in true Ptochoprodromic style (pages 137-38). Is the girl so innocent? Her initial self-exposure leads to her enforced seclusion in her husband's palace. "Death" frequently poses as a peddlar, and she—or her father—should have demonstrated more caution, despite the constraints of poverty.[41] No wonder she gets bored in her palace without windows! When she decides to explore, she finds more than she reckoned for: Trimmatos is a hypersexed monster, who eats corpses and once aroused will have his way. Like the corpse in the graveyard, she turns frigid, rolling herself into a ball and hiding under the bedclothes. Her responses to mother and grandmother are tight and loose in the wrong ways, as Trimmatos points out: she won't give her needy mother a few coins, but she will tell her grandmother the secrets of her husband's body (rather as she offered her own body to the first passerby). The granddaughter—grandmother relationship is important in Greek culture, since both share the same name, but too close a dependency is incompatible with marital status. Her initiation into sexuality inside the sack is violent, but—unlike her earlier confinement in house/bed—it is productive: by the time she is let out, she has learned how to staunch her wound with swabs and impresses the king and queen with her sewing and embroidery, as well as with her beauty. Only then does she attain the cunning and initiative necessary to reverse Trimmatos' ruse and to "kill" her familial and sexual past in order to win her prince. "Trimmatos" is different from "Lord of the Lower Earth," but action and plot are advanced through a comparable sequence of themes and images.

Children, like food, may lead to trouble when they are the object of greed. We have seen what befell Asternos and Poulio, whose parents wanted to cook and eat them. But what happens when parents are not satisfied with the children they have or when brother is jealous of sister? Here is a tale recorded in Old Athenian dialect.

Ἡ στρίγλα ("The Witch")

An old man and his wife had fine grown-up sons but longed for a daughter, and after many years of prayer a daughter was born. The youngest son notices that his baby sister's eyes shine "like stars." At night a whistling noise is heard in the stables, and next morning a horse is found strangled and half-eaten. He steals down on the third night, catches his sister with eyes glinting and fingers outstretched as she makes for the best stallion's throat, so he cuts off her little finger. His family accuse him of jealousy, and turn him away. On his travels he encounters by turn two weird but beautiful women. The first is a lamia in league with a hunter, who seek to destroy him; the second a Nereid queen. After many quests he is hacked into pieces, but revived by the Nereid's dog and the water of life, and decides to check up on his family before marriage to the Nereid. He finds the legless, armless trunk of his father's body at the entrance—at once it summons his strigla sister to avenge her fingerless hand. She pursues him with relentless cruelty, but thanks to the aid of a mouse, three dogs and three fruit-stones, he escapes and marries the Nereid queen.

(Kambouroglou: Athens 1883; cf. Garnett 1896: 245–60 [English])

A psychoanalytic approach might point to sibling rivalry and the Oedipus complex as "keys," but the tale also warns of the known physiological dangers of begetting monsters instead of children in old age (refusal to hand over to the next generation) and of the consequences of wanting more than you have: children can eat parents, just as parents may desire children's flesh.[42] Suspense is maintained because we are not sure until the end whether the second female is acting for the hero.

Themes and images suggest that a proper balance between consumption (food and drink) and production/cultivation (weaving, gardening) is necessary to a successful outcome. Let us now explore marriage not as closure but as theme/image. Many tales involve a double marriage, the first when hero or heroine's falling in love leads to wedlock and the second only after trials, tribulation, and sacrifice of one or both partners. Sometimes, as in the case of the tales "Trimmatos" or "Trisevgeni," the first consort is evil and must be destroyed. A more common theme involves a loved one who must be released from a spell. Just as the girl in "Lord of the Lower Earth" has to be coaxed by her sisters and taught to act for herself in order to mature sexually, so in tale types in which the beloved is entrapped in an alien form (groom as frog or crab, bride as fruit or bird), the lover has to endure humiliation and hardship—metamorphosis, intercourse with monsters—for the sake of the other before the story can end happily. Ἡ ἀνεράιδα, "The Nereid," tells of a poor young girl who rescues a prince from a depression that renders him incapable of speaking to any woman, let alone contemplating marriage, first by making him speak with the help of a singing bird and then by her brave penetration into his underworld, where she discovers he has been enchanted and blinded by a Nereid queen (Kafandaris 40: Athens 1883). While wit and patience are most commonly demanded of the woman and bravery and activity of the man, neither gender has a monopoly of mental, emotional, or physical qualities: a woman may become a man—through disguise in "Lord of the Lower Earth," but in physical reality in "The Girl Who Went to War" (Kafandaris 24)—and a man may undergo imprisonment, as in "Navel of the Earth," before the "other" (which also lies within the self) can be rescued. Happy marriage is not so easily achieved, and seldom the first time round. Secondary marriage in the paramythia parallels the secondary burial of funerary ritual, where the soul's passage is completed not at burial but at the exhumation ceremony some years later. The girl's emergence from the sack in "Trimmatos" resembles exhumation, bringing to successful completion the cycle of themes (confinement/burial/hiding/running), while underscoring the significance of observing the proper balance between seclusion and exposure in rites of passage. Ritual dimensions do not exclude psychoanalytic interpretation: partners may be a projection or splitting of a single person, just as the good mother/wicked stepmother/midwife can be seen as the child's perception of the mother. Ritual aspects of images and themes enrich our understanding by means of contextualization.

As a profound comment on "double marriage," let us explore the tragic fate of "The Girl with Two Husbands."

Τουρόγλες ("Tsyrógles")

Once lived a man and wife very much in love. Neither too rich nor too poor, blest with a small daughter as clever as she was beautiful, they sent her to school. Teacher falls in love with child's father. He had eyes only for his wife. Teacher works on child, giving her must-cakes and promising her everything she wanted. She tells child to ask mother for nuts from marble chest in the courtyard and to kill her by dropping the heavy lid down on her neck: child does so, and mother's head was sliced off. Child persuades father to marry teacher through ruse of peeing on slippers he hangs on wall with vow never to remarry till they fall from nail. All goes well until stepmother gives birth to ugly daughter. Every day stepmother sends girl out with a load of washing and a crust of bread, and only scoldings and beatings on her return. Time goes by, and the girl thinks of her mother. One day, burdened with a load of dirty linen, she goes to her mother's grave, tends it with flowers, and weeps. A voice speaks out: —Daughter, great was your sin, and great will be your suffering. But endure all in silence, and God may forgive you, as I have already forgiven you! *That evening, as the girl finishes her task, she sits on a stone by the well to eat her crust. A beggar comes by*—Won't you give me some bread? I'm starving. *She takes the crust out of her mouth, and offers it to him.* —Now I need water! *She takes her flask, fills it with fresh water, and gives it to him.* —And now I need delousing! *Setting his filthy head in her lap, she takes out the lice. Well pleased, he gets up and touches her hair with a blessing.* —For the good you have done me, may God reward you. *As she touches her hair, it turns to gold. She folds up the clothes—they turn to gold. By the time she got back to her village she was radiant with gold, everyone came out to admire her beauty. Her stepmother? Mad with jealousy, next day she sent her own daughter to the same spot. What do you think? Stepmother's daughter sent the beggar off with an insult, and he gave her* such a blessing she got back with horns and prickles all over her, a veritable porcupine she was! Stepmother determines to get rid of the girl.

Meantime the king and queen in that realm were childless, so the queen prayed—God, give me a child, even if it has to be a snake. She gave birth to a snake. Who would suckle it? She sends out town criers to find a suitable person, and stepmother sends word to the king to take girl by force. Girl begs permission to go to her mother's grave, where she weeps. —Have no fear, my child. Ask the king to make two golden cups with a hole at their point, put these over your breasts and you will feed the snake-child without harm. She does as instructed, and the snake-child (called Ophis) grows big and strong, following his nurse-mother everywhere. Time comes for him to get married. Who will marry the Snake-prince? Stepmother goes to king and says she who suckled the prince should also marry him, and again the girl goes weeping to her mother's grave.—This time, her mother tells her, take seven loads of firewood, seven garments for yourself, and one clean shirt. When you get to the bedchamber, light seven ovens. He will tell you to undress. Take off your first layer, tell him to take off his first skin, then throw them on the fire. When you get to the seventh garment—well, then you'll see. The girl did as bidden—out of the seventh snakeskin came a handsome prince "like cold water." What a night they had together! Next morning the servants came to clear up the girl's remains and found her in the arms of a young man who looked exactly like his mother! Weddings, rejoicings all over again, no one was happier than Ophis and his bride. Before long she gave birth to a handsome son. . . .

War broke out, and Ophis was called to serve. The stepmother saw her chance, so she forges letters from the king and queen to the prince on the front, saying his wife is unfaithful and he must order her banishment. King and queen are puzzled, but what can they do? They turn the girl out with nothing but her child, not even a crust of bread. On and on she goes, until she reaches the next kingdom. Seeing a little church near a big black palace, she goes into the church and weeps floods of tears, lamenting her fate. . . . WHOOSSSS! —Have no fear, girl, I have heard your tale and have taken pity on you, says a voice. I am Tsyrógles, and if you do as I say you will be saved. Take your child, go to the palace, and say—Let me in, for the love of Tsyrógles! My mother will treat you well, but do not tell her you have seen me. I will come to you at night, but must be gone every morning. And so it turned out: the queen treated the girl and her child with kindness. One day she so pestered the girl to tell about Tsyrógles, her only son who had been changed into a ghost by a wicked spell, that the girl revealed the secret. The queen has three hangings woven, one embroidered with the moon, one with the stars, one all black, and drapes them across the windows of the girl's bedchamber to block out the light. Next morning, Tsyrógles wakes up late. At that moment, his mother (waiting behind the door) bursts in and opens one of the drapes—in floods the sunlight and WHOOSSSS! . . . The spell is broken, and Tsyrógles turns back into a handsome young prince. He marries the girl, and they live and reign very happily together for many years to come.

What of Ophis? The war ended, and he got home to find the stories about his wife were slander. He found the culprit and had her duly punished. But where was his wife—and child? All the town criers were sent out, and after years came a rumor that she was now wife of Tsyrógles in the next kingdom. Ophis gathers his army and marches to the frontiers, declaring war. Tsyrógles is summoned, and a bitter exchange follows, as each claims her as his own. They were just about to fight when a wise old man intervenes—Why go to war? The girl is here, tell her to give her pitcher to the one she likes best, he can fill it with water and the other can depart in silence, taking his army. When she heard this, the girl sat on a stone and wept. How to make up her mind? She looked at Ophis —she had nursed him, she had made a man of him, she had born his child, he was her first husband—but he fed her poison and turned her out. She looked at Tsyrógles who loved her and became man again for her sake, who rescued her and made her queen. Her eyes ran fountains of tears. With a sigh so heavy it shattered her heart, she sang:

I love my Ophis and Tsyrógles I desire.

Tsyrógles, give me water and let my soul expire!

Before Tsyrógles came back with water, her soul departed.

(Kafandaris 152: Skyros 1943)

What are the recurrent themes and images in this tale of matricide, maturation, and atonement? Let us begin with food, water, and bodily fluids. The teacher seduces the child with promises of sweetmeats. Without any sense of guilt, the child obeys instructions, decapitating her mother and using her daily piss to rot her father's vow. Through forced labor (washing dirty linen), she realizes her terrible deed, and her tears of remorse arouse her mother's voice of pity from the grave. The first turning point is her kindness to the old beggar (Christ?) as she takes the crust moistened by her own saliva to feed him, gives him fresh water, and extracts the vermin that feed on his head. The second comes when she suckles the snake-child with the milk of her breasts, then marries him (through burning clothes and skins) and bears his child. Both are effected through ties with her mother. Once she is driven out of the kingdom, she is on her own; but again tears of remorse move powers from beyond the grave. She reaches a state of happiness, but her first husband still has claims on her as father of her child. Her final choice is to be determined by a request for fresh water, yet she responds only with tears and a song to release her soul. The ending is neither happy nor tragic, but mythic: the girl has atoned for matricide by nursing and marrying a snake and by bringing a ghost back to life.

This tale is known in at least four versions from different parts of Greece, and each begins and ends differently. In "Yavrouda" (Dodekanese, in Dawkins 1950, 369–93), perhaps the most complex of all in its use of psychology, ekphrastic passages, and song, the seductress is not a teacher but a skilled embroideress whose motivation for stealing Yavrouda's father is clearly stated: "she was passed by and not sought in marriage by anyone" (369). It is appropriate to her craft that she splits open at the end from her own wickedness, rather than from receiving punishment at the hands of the Snake-prince, named "Ophis," AG and K word for Snake. The incident with the marble chest is similar, except that Yavrouda drops the lid by accident. Yavrouda gives birth to Snake's child not before her banishment but in her second husband's home, aided by his mother. He is not named Tsyrógles (derived from the name of the seventeenth-century Turkish bandit-hero Köroglu), but Neros, recalling Eros, as Dawkins points out. The reasons for his bewitchment are spelled out by means of the "story within story" device: when alive, Neros had been a serial rapist and killer, strangling and eating as many female victims he could lay hands on, until punished by twelve Nereids. His transgression matches Yavrouda's, yet his mother's care of her and her child (whom she names, in the belief that it is her son's child) gives him a stronger claim to Yavrouda. In this version, Yavrouda does not die but is obliged by chance, not choice, to go with Snake, the real father of her child. In no extant version of this tale is she allowed to go with her second husband, as our Skyros version suggests she would have preferred.

A few examples illustrate how this extraordinary tale connects with other genres, both mythical and ritual. The same line—"before he came back with water, her soul departed"—ends the song "The Poisoned Bride," in which a bride, poisoned by her mother-in-law with a dish of snake heads at the wedding feast, asks father-in-law and brothers-in-law in turn for water and is refused: the groom goes to fetch it but comes back to find her dead. (Ioannou 1975, 65–68). Further, the girl's song in the tale is a tragic variation of the well-known erotic song in which a young married woman of uncertain repute is asked,—"Whom do you love best, your husband or the stranger?" Playfully, she compares her husband to marble, her stranger to a cypress tree, declaring her preference for the latter, as in the popular song "Maria Dressed in Yellow." Finally, suspense is created and maintained in the tale just because prohibitions are broken. When the girl disobeys Tsyrógles' interdiction and tells his mother she sleeps with him every night, the spell is broken just as we expect catastrophe. As in "Sun, Pleiad, and Morning-Star," failure to observe interdictions on light leads to new birth. Both apparently arbitrary narrative details have ritual dimensions: at childbirth, doors and windows are flung open, creating noise and light to assist the birthing process.[43]

The conclusion to be drawn from our review of themes is that they function not merely on the level of plot but allegorically as well, in accordance with the same signifying system that underlies Greek mythical thought and, as we shall see in Part III, ritual practice. Let us turn now to metamorphosis as a means of linking body and cosmos, nature and culture.

5. Metamorphosis: Cyclical Images of Body and Cosmos

Metamorphosis has always played a prominent role in Greek myth and religion, legend and tale, however many transformations its forms and functions have undergone since the transition from paganism to Christianity.[44] We may start with a paradox. If official religion separates the boundaries between human and other species, tales explore—even celebrate—their transgression. The Orthodox Church associates metamorphosis with the demonic and the devil: God is wholly good and unchanging, but the Devil is unstable, shifting shape and substance.[45] Local legend and practice allow flexibility: there is danger in mixed species, such as beautiful Nereids with a duck's feet; but the Panagia, the saints, or Christ himself also have power to change their own or another person's shape. Shape shifting is ambivalent— a means of explaining perceived dangers, such as sickness or death, through shared experience and belief.[46] In tales, metamorphosis is more varied than in legends, frequently positive rather than negative in outcome. Why these differences?

In the tales, shape shifting occurs back and forth across species (animal, vegetable, mineral) and between spheres (earth, sea, sky, lower earth), implying a reciprocal concept of divine, human, and demonic beings. People may become animals, insects, birds, fish, and sea creatures; trees, plants, and flowers; stones and stars. They may also change gender or assume grotesque and demonic forms. Even demons can be rescued and made human. The nature and causes, occasions, and functions of shape shifting are no less varied and complex. If caused by witchcraft or magic, the spell can be broken by the intervention of a "helper," as in "The Twins" (Kafandaris 25), in which the first twin, petrified by an old witch, is rescued by the second. If caused by a curse, the change may be permanent, as in the case of Asternos and Poulió. Serious transgression brings similar results. In "Myrsinió" (Kafandaris 88), the girl first forfeits the protection of the myrtle tree she inhabits by offering her virginity one night to a passerby; she then loses human status by attempting to intervene on the third day after his wedding to another and is turned into a myrtle tree. We may contrast the happier outcome in "Girl in the Bay Tree," in which the heroine, cast out by her bay tree when "kissed and cuddled" by a prince as she sleeps on its branches, succeeds, through fortitude and monkish disguise, in reclaiming him just as he is about to marry another (Dawkins 1950, 207–12). Metamorphosis is not just a matter of magic and witchcraft: it is contingent on and negotiable by humankind.

This manipulative aspect becomes more apparent when we consider certain forms of shape shifts. By performing acts of kindness to animal species, the human protagonist may be given a hair, feather, or wing, thanks to which she or he may either summon its owner's aid to perform impossible tasks, and/or borrow its form for limited periods. My favorite example is from "Yiankos," whose birth, and subsequent flight from the Sea mother has already been described:

> *Yiankos settles a dispute between an eagle and a lion over an ass' carcass by assigning the rotting flesh to the eagle, the bones to the lion. In recompense, each gives him a feather and a hair, which he need only rub to transform himself into their shapes or summon their aid. Thanks to the eagle's feather, he is able to fly hot frothy sheep's milk every morning to the local princess, just as she desires! The princess takes a fancy to him. What to do? He pours a sack of grain onto an ants' nest, and asks the King of the Ants for one of his wings in return. "Ant," he cries, and creeps into the princess's bedroom. "Man," he says, on seeing her beauty. He turns out the lights and caresses her. She screams out—There's a man is in my bedroom! but just as her father comes in to check, Yiankos says "Ant." This comic episode is repeated twice: the third time, her father tells her on no account to disturb him again. "Man," says Yiankos, and sports with the delighted princess for the rest of the night! Next day they are married. . . . Trials and tribulations remain: with aid of the lion's hair, Yiankos vanquishes king's foes in battle, but is reclaimed by Sea mother as he washes his wounds on the shore. The princess recovers him by outwitting Sea mother with magic fruit and music. He finally escapes her waves of wrath in the form of an eagle.*
>
> (Kafandaris 16: Naxos 1874)

Yiankos, himself of double birth, has learned to manipulate shape shifting to his own advantage once the girl's sexual interest is aroused (presaged by her predilection for "hot frothy milk" every morning?), but his rescue is effected by species of earth, land, and sky, from lowliest ant to lion and eagle. Here, as in other tales where metamorphosis is positive, cosmic reciprocity must be respected.[47]

Paramythia do not conform to the categories of good/evil, beautiful/ugly, hero or heroine/villain, as some have maintained is the case in wondertales the world over. Demons abound alongside cunning humans, but few are inherently evil, with the exception of the *strígla* ("witch"). If properly greeted, they may be placated with food or money and turned from hostile force to friendly helper. Indeed, they sometimes behave according to a code of honor. Finding the hero asleep by a fountain in their tower, the forty drakoi in the Cypriot tale "Fiakas" (Kafandaris 69) decide not to eat him right away—it wouldn't be fair for forty drakoi to fight a lone weak human, the eldest argues—but to engage him on equitable terms with tests of strength, wit, and endurance. Like Herakles, Fiakas proves himself through multiple labors and ends up king of the drakos kingdom. The source of evil lies within as well as outside the self, hence characters cannot be reduced to heroes/heroines and villains.[48]

Greek demons are sexually potent and often *grotesque*, although our word distorts nuances of *geloîos* "ridiculous", *paráxenos* "strange," *parálogos* "par-alogic". Consider the prince's encounter with the third lamia in "The Three Citrons": *He pushes in the rotten old door of a hovel high up on the rocks and finds her inside. Tall and wild, with a mass of hair standing on end, she is try-ing to clean out her oven with her huge breasts. He cuts off a piece of his cloak, moist-ens it in water, ties it on a stick, and pokes round the oven till it is cleared of embers. He puts in her loaves, bakes them, takes them out and places them in a row beside her.* (Kafandaris 41, see pages 228–29 above) Senile hag she may be, but hair, breasts, cloak, stick, oven, and bread are images of fecundity and childbirth. Before he can win Trisevgeni, he must come to terms with sexuality in all its pungency and potency. Similarly, the drakontissa's daughter in "Olive Tear" who turns seven windmills when she pisses suggests hyperbolic synecdoche to indicate size; but she is an environmentally friendly demon, charged with life-giving forces of food, procreation, and childbirth by turning windmills and grinding grain. The flow of body fluids (urine, tears, sweat, rheum, blood, semen) brings wealth and reproduction—as do the tears that turn into pearls in "The Immortal Water." By contrast, unnatural thirst suggests infertility and death, as in "Asternos and Poulio."[49]

According to Greek aesthetic criteria, beautiful *ómorfos* < *eúmorfos* means "well formed," whereas ugly is *áschēmos*, "shapeless." All heroes/heroines are beautiful, but that is about all there is to say. As Maria Gourioti put it so well in her account of Yiannis' encounter with Kalypso, "she was—*it can't be told/described [de légetai]*—very beautiful." The category is closed.[50] By contrast, ugliness or shapelessness is open, shifting, and sexual; it can also be described in devastating detail. In a three-generational tale of two king-doms, "Myrmidonia and Pharaonia" (from Kos, in Dawkins 1950, 334–49), the king's son is pursued in a dream by the female demon *Peina* "Hunger" for his crime of hacking down a grove of sacred trees. She makes straight for his belly:

Then suddenly he sees something afar off moving very slowly and coming towards him. Presently it came near him, and what does he see? It was an old woman, hunchbacked as a hook, and her hair in its filth hung disordered on her scabby head;

her forehead was all wrinkled, her eyebrows had half fallen out and were hardly to be seen for pimples and pustules; her eyes were sunken deep as though in basins; her nose was eaten away—far and away may this be from us!—by gnawing ulcers; her mug was as yellow as a sulphur candle; her lips were white and black, covered with slaver; her teeth were like axes hung up in a row, dirty black and all rotted into holes; her body was skin and bone; her ribs you could count, so lean was she; inside her you could see her entrails; the bones of her hips in broken array stuck out like dugs; where the joints should fit they were coming apart, she was so decrepit; the cap-bones of her knees seemed to stand out like the pulleys in wells; she was altogether a terrible old maumet (δείωλο "false image'") [Dawkins, 339].

It has been suggested that this ekphrastic passage may be indirectly inspired by Ovid's description of Ravening Hunger in *Metamorphoses*, 8.[51] Yet both graphic detail and function are consistent with the concept of the body in the modern tradition: ugliness is open and protuberous, exuding unwanted fluids. Hunger as a hideous old hag is a familiar figure in medieval vernacular poetry (Prodromos wanted her banished from the city to the peasantry), and old harridans are made fun of in Cypriot children's songs of more recent times in similar terms.[52] In this tale, she is the necessary counterpart to the fertile and beautiful tree spirit, whose wrath the king has provoked by wanton destruction of her sacred grove. Her ugliness matches his evil. Moreover, protagonists may need to pass through all shapes if they are to be reproductive, while it is often ugly, ill-formed humans and demons, with their open and grotesque bodies, who assist them in this process.

If tales open with birth from mixed species and end with second marriage, the center tends to include metamorphosis of bride or groom and encounters with demons. She or he may have to shift many shapes between beauty and deformity before the right balance, or maturation, can be achieved. Granted the possibility of infinite changes of shape, young men tend to turn into marble, cypress trees, lions, lambs, eagles, frogs, and crabs, and young women, into fruit, trees, doves, eels, deer, and dogs. Both may become snakes, tortoises, stars, or planets. Demonic creatures are often humans "gone wrong" or "fixed," without a loving partner to rescue them. Birth, marriage, and death, as transitional points in a cosmic cycle of fertility, include badness and ugliness because absolute beauty and goodness cannot be achieved within one species on this earth. The body, if it is to prove fertile, must be at once open and closed, reaching downward and upward, inward and outward.

Metamorphosis provides the symbolic means by which the transition from a state of dependence to a state of maturation can be effected. Its surreal and erotic qualities appeal to our imaginations as a playful entry into the unknown, the taboo.[53] At the same time, it is not "just a metaphor," as some scholars have maintained, since we know from legends that people did believe that saints and demons alike could maim and deform.[54] If paramythia allow protagonists more control in guiding shape shifts toward a happy outcome, can it be because human fantasy, operating outside the bounds of established religion, is our ultimate source of consolation when confronted with what lies beyond death? Evidence for tale performance during the night vigil at the wake is scanty in the case of Greek paramythia, but the possibility is suggested by etymological and comparative data.[55] Whereas in moirologia women lament during the day the finality of death, in paramythia men and women can laugh at the other world with children during the night.

6. Cosmology and Morality

The cosmology of the paramythia can best be summed up not by a list of binary oppositions but rather by a series of concentric circles, or a spiral, centered on the bodily concept of the navel. The "navel of the earth" is the inner hub of all creation, while stars, planets, sun, and moon constitute the outer circle, determining both the seasons of the year and day and night on the middle circle, earth. The earth's physical features are conceived and described in terms of human organs and bodily functions: apertures from the inside are wet (wells, springs) or dry (burrows, caves); land surfaces are smooth (plains, pastures, deserts) or hairy/dense (thickets, forests), indented (valleys, gullies), or protuberous (hills, crags, mountains); waters are salt and moving (tears, seas), fresh and moving (springs, fountains, rivers, rain), fresh and still (wells, lakes), or stale and dirty (puddles, ditches). These physiognomical features shelter all known species of land, sea, and air—men and women, mammals tame and wild, reptiles, fish and crustaceans, birds and insects, trees and shrubs, flowers and fruit—which depend on mutual intercourse with each other as well as with the inner/outer spheres (lower earth/heaven).

For humankind, the earth contains both known and unknown, inhabited and desert parts (*oikouménē /erēmiá*). To the former belong cultivation and domesticated creatures; to the latter, untamed beasts and demons. Yet the two are interdependent, and therefore need natural and supernatural mediators, as well as stable structures. If the hearth is to earth as navel is to body and kosmos (innermost center of warmth and food), then the house is its immediate covering. Dwellings are grouped in communities of varying size and degree of social hierarchy: cottage, mansion, palace; village, town, kingdom. Frontiers must be penetrated as well as guarded, hence roads, bridges, and towers are liminal but productive. The resources of earth, land, and water require cultivation and restraint if they are to yield their riches and feed a whole people, from wealthiest to poorest. Human powers—even in the best of kingdoms with the mightiest of armies—are inadequate, as in "The Immortal Water." All species of fauna and flora can help or hinder, but they too are mediated by powers that may be divine and demonic *at the same time*. This cosmic paradox lies at the core of our paramythia: God is perfect, whereas the Devil is always changing shape. Humankind has a share in both: singularity and plurality, male and female, life and death, right and left.[56] I therefore propose the following:

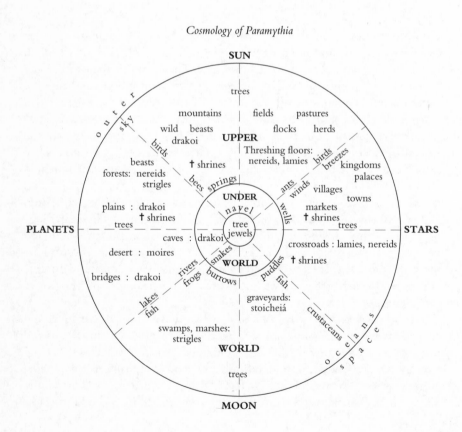

Cosmology of Paramythia

The idea of cosmic reciprocity is beautifully expressed in two tales from the Dodekanese. The first is a tale of seasonality:

Οἱ δώδεκα Μῆνες "The Twelve Months"

Two sisters are married to two cripples, one rich, the other a pauper. Poor sister helps rich one on baking days but gets no money for her labors, only the scourings of flour on her fingers and clothes she scrapes off to bake for her children. Rich sister wonders why poor one leaves without washing and dusting herself, so one day she follows her home and spies. Furious, she won't let her cross her threshold ever again, sending her off in tears to her crippled husband, also reduced to tears of despair because dismissed from his job as laborer by rich brother-in-law for answering back to taunts about his hunchback. He disappears. Poor sister goes out to seek bread and finds twelve men feasting in a garden. They invite her to join them, but she asks—My children are hungry, how can I eat? Might I take home just one portion of leftovers for them? They promise her food for them too, but first she must eat herself. She does so, but the food won't go down well because she thinks of her starving children. —Tell us, they ask, which is the best of the months? —Each and every one, she replies, is gold and silver, silver and gold. Summer months keep us warm, winter months nurture seeds sown in the earth. The twelve are well pleased and fill her sack. She gets home to find inside not food but so many gold coins she borrows rich sister's scales to weigh them. Suspicious, rich sister sneaks after her again and spies through a hole, to find her weighing coins. Mad with jealousy, she asks where so much gold can be found and next day sets off to the garden, carrying a huge sack. The twelve men invite her to eat. She declines.—I've eaten, I want my sack filled with gold.—Which is the best of the months? they ask her.—Every one is cold and black, black and cold. In winter you shiver with cold, in summer you burn. They fill her sack, and she goes home, shuts the door and blocks all holes and gaps so no one can spy on her, but when she opens the sack, out come poisonous snakes. Finding no way out, they eat her alive.

Meanwhile, poor sister's crippled husband naps under a tree in a forest at midnight. Twelve naked black men appear, dancing a wild, demonic dance. Seizing him into their circle, they tell him to dance and sing like them "Tonight is Thursday, tomorrow's Friday," although in fact it was the turn of Saturday evening and Sunday morning. But he did as they said. Well pleased, they take away his hunchback and disappear. He goes home to find his wife happily cooking round a fire. Next morning rich brother-in-law asks how he lost his hunchback. That night he goes to the forest, but does he sing and dance with the black men? They give him his brother's hunchback as well, so with a double burden he goes home to find it seething with poisonous snakes. He blew up from fear [eplántaxen], before he even set eyes on his wife's snake-eaten body. Sure as we live, that would have split him a second time [tha éskaen] from sorrow. All this the two of them suffered because of their evil and pitilessness [kakiá ki asplachniá].

(Dawkins = Kafandaris 92; Megas 39: Ainos 1892; cf. Tong 65)

A tale of good rewarded and evil punished? Beneath the story level, ambivalence is conveyed by shifting metonyms for the consumption and expulsion of matter. First, food and coins, tears and poison: The rich sister denies the poor one scourings from her own hands' labor, sending her away with pain and tears (*pónos* and *dákrya*) as at death. She refuses the twelve months' repast (an insult according to Greek rules of hospitality), accuses them of sterility, and gets her sackful of bodily fruits—venomous snakes, ambivalent mediators between life and death who emit either coins or venom. Twice she trespasses on her sister's inner space, sealing up her own: the snakes have no choice but to eat her. Poor sister labors for others, turns scourings to bread, tears to travel. She ensures food for her children before accepting the twelve months' repast, then affirms the principle of seasonal reciprocity and productive labor, as in *Hysmine*. Her bodily fruits? A sackful of coins.

Second, form and formlessness, blackness and whiteness: The poor cripple, lost in forest and crazed with despair, understands the demand to dance and sing according to a different tune and offloads his hunchback. Rich cripple thinks he knows better and gets a double burden. Months and blacks share a sense of justice in apportioning good and evil, since handicaps of body or station may be reversed and "black" is evil only if perceived so. According to this model, oppositions are equal: summer/winter, black/white, Friday night/Saturday night (holy days for Muslims and Christians, respectively).[57] Third, the ending is consistent with this bodily logic: we leave the poor couple with food and money at the family hearth surrounded by children, but the rich couple destroyed, one devoured by snakes, the other burst open from fear with no room even for grieving. The verbs "he blew up" and "he split open," common in the paramythia to describe the end of the wicked, are also used in exorcisms to signify the total destruction of vampires and the devil.[58] Splitting open marks the end of life in any form, with no possibility of metamorphosis into another shape. As a metaphor of explosion, it equals bulimia and autophagy in our next tale. If there is a moral, it is that everyone can make good, despite handicap or past crime, provided goodness resides in your soul. Your body gives back what you expend and put into it, in accordance with your treatment of the other, in human, divine, or demonic form.

My second tale is unusual in that it concerns not a mortal quest but the forces of nature and humanity locked in a conflict engulfing two kingdoms and three generations. The trigger in the cycle of evil is an act of sacrilege so enormous that two generations must be destroyed before the third can restore equilibrium, by further sacrifices and by movement outside the doomed kingdom. A brief summary of this complex tale must suffice to indicate the major stages in the cycle of destruction, self-destruction, and regeneration.

"Myrmidonia and Pharaonia," or "The Nereid's Revenge"

Stage 1. *The king of Myrmidonia falls in love with Dimitroula, daughter of a Nereid (tree spirit), but she is betrothed to a brave and handsome young plough-man. The king has the ploughman treacherously put to death, and in revenge the Nereid has him and his men drowned in a hidden well.* Stage 2. *Enraged by his fa-ther's death, the king's son, with his men, viciously hacks down the Nereid's sacred grove: a mighty oak tree bleeds, and Dimitroula's voice is heard cursing him. In a dream he is first consumed by flames, then visited by Ravening Hunger, who afflicts him with insatiable hunger. Having consumed all the resources of his kingdom, he tries to sell his own son and daughter to buy food, but they escape. He turns on himself and dies with his nails clawing at his mouth.* Stage 3. *At the funeral feast, his daughter smashes an old woman's plate of butter and bursts out laughing. The old woman curses her to fall in love with the prince of the kingdom of Pharaonia. Her brother arranges the match, but a jealous arapis gets him to wager his life for her chastity, then obtains false tokens. Condemned to die, the prince goes home to settle his affairs. Believing his sister unchaste, he puts her out to sea in a chest. She is res-cued by a fisherman in the kingdom of Pharaonia. As her brother is led out to exe-cution, she devises a means of publicly exposing the arapis' treachery. He is put to death, and she marries the prince of Pharaonia.*

(Dawkins 33: Kos 1890s)

In his commentary on this tale, recorded in the 1890s on the island of Kos by the antiquarian Iakovos Zarraftis from informant Hadzi-Yavrouda, Dawkins singles out three features. First, for the motivating theme of tree sacrilege he finds "no parallels at all in modern folklore" (1950, 347). Sec-ond, punishment by Ravening Hunger is the major theme of the myth of Erysichthon and his daughter Mestra, treated by Kallimachos in his *Hymn to Demeter* (6.24–117) and by Ovid in *Metamorphoses* (8.738–878). Hadzi-Yavrouda's tale contains some details close to Kallimachos (manifestation of divine presence in tree; axes/sword embedded in trunk) and others close to Ovid (tree sheds blood, prophesies retribution; description of Ravening Hunger), none of which is common to both (Dawkins 1950, 347–48).

Dawkins offers two possible explanations: isolated survival in Kos of an ancient legend or, "almost impossible," a double literary contact. Third, since the final episode centers on the widespread theme of a brother's wager on a sister's chastity (as in the song "Mavrianos and His Sister," in Politis 1914, 81), Dawkins sees the first part, up to the death of the second king, as "a real survival, an appearance in Modern Greek folklore of a story which was known in the classical age and located in the region of the Dodekanese," and the final episode as a later accretion (348).

Dawkins' conclusion is consistent with the premise that links between tales can be determined only by common plot, never by use of one incident. Although classifying myths and tales according to plot can be useful, it can also be reductive and misleading. While tree sacrilege rarely provides the motivation for *plot* in the paramythia, it is a pervasive *theme/image*, often triggering the next step in the story, as in "Poulia and Avgerinos," when the prince and his men hack viciously at the tree to bring down the shining Poulia from its peak: she is saved by her lamb-brother, who licks hard at the trunk and makes it grow twice as big as fast as they cut it down. Nothing in the symbolic system of "Myrmidonia and Pharaonia" contravenes modern tale tradition.

At the same time, literary influences appear evident in several incidental but significant features of style and presentation. First, names: In most cases, as in the songs, characters and places are designated by generic or descriptive names (Poulia, Avgerinos, Trisevgeni, Trimmatos, i.e., Pleiad, Morning Star, Thrice Noble, Three Eyes), while specified locations lend color to indicate size and function (Constantinople and Smyrna signify "big city," Aleppo "big market"). The concurrence of three names with classical associations—Myrmidonia, Pharaonia, and Dimitroula—invites skepticism as to direct *oral* transmission from antiquity, because in other tales where names are specified, interaction with literary tradition can be demonstrated. "Doltsetta," a tale of comparable complexity spanning two generations and two kingdoms, survives in several versions which derive from *Dolcetta and Fiorentino*, a chapbook romance of the Frankish period.[59] Furthermore, the name *hellēnópoulo* "young Hellene," is used three times in "Myrmidonia and Pharaonia" to describe the bravery of the ploughman and—somewhat incongruously—the fate of the trees. Reference to heroic Hellenes suggests the mediation of reawakened Hellenism rather than direct oral transmission of a local legend.

Second, idiosyncratic use of simile: Similes are not unknown in the paramythia, but they tend to be undeveloped, designed to emphasize a sudden transformation. Trimmatos "made his head as big as a sieve," and the girl in "Tsyrógles" finds her snake-prince "like cold water." Similes in

"Myrmidonia" are unusually frequent, introduced in adverbial phrases comparing present with classical antiquity or with the Orthodox Church: "he came forward like the angel"; "he lay stretched on the ground like the fair cypress tree" (as in the famous Homeric tree simile μέγας μεγαλωστί, *Il.* 16.775–76, *Od.* 24.39–40); "he . . . lays the axe to the poor silent trees, which were like beautiful maidens and like young Hellenes"; "and he stayed there like a dry trunk"; "she breathes on it three times like a priest."

Third, sources: Whereas Dawkins reduces the problem to "*either* double literary contact *or* direct oral transmission," the reality may be more complex. The three other tales in his collection probably taken from the same informant, Hadzi-Yavrouda (whose name indicates a woman who had been on a pilgrimage to the Holy Land and therefore of more than average means and education), are all exceptional for complexity of plot, psychological detail, use of developed similes and ekphrastic passages, and, above all, strong religious coloring.[60] In one, "Yiannakis," literary elements can be demonstrated unequivocally. Her tale resembles only loosely the ancient romance, extant in Latin translation, which served as one of the sources for Shakespeare's *Pericles, Prince of Tyre.* In most points it follows more faithfully the popular *Rhymed Poem of Apollonios,* first printed in Venice in 1534, with frequent later editions.[61] Clearly, the narrator had access, either directly or—more probable—through her predecessors, to literary tradition. As for Kallimachos and Ovid, unlikely as it is that any single narrator on the island of Kos knew either in the original, Kallimachos' *Hymns* had always been familiar to the literate Greek world, while Ovid's *Metamorphoses,* current in Planoudes' Greek translation since the thirteenth century, had been available in printed form since 1822 in the edition of J. F. Boissonade.[62] The complexity of "Myrmidonia and Pharaonia," as in "Doltsetta," suggests condensation from a longer text. The most plausible explanation is that it derives in part from a popular compilation of Greek mythology circulating during Frankish or Ottoman periods. As Gareth Morgan observed, "lost romances of the Frankish period may underlie many present-day folksongs."[63] The same is no less true of the tales. I see such a process not as one of "contamination" but rather as an example of *ars combinatoria* on the part of a skillful and not unlettered teller: Hadzi-Yavrouda's stories are neither simple "folktales" nor yet fully fledged novellas, but they testify to a community where narrative talents were enjoyed at all social levels.

Despite possible literary influence on "Myrmidonia and Pharaonia," narrative threads are well integrated into the symbolic and cosmological system of the paramythia. Wondertale logic and fantasy never allow an entirely negative closure. There must be some hope of renewal in another form of life, therefore the second king's self-destruction brought on by his father's sacrilege has to be followed by the possibility of regeneration. This is brought about by mutual assistance and transgression between brother and sister in the third generation: he is sold into slavery by his father to buy food but happens to be in the right place at the right time to save his sister from the same fate. Condemned by inappropriate laughter to seek love and marriage in another kingdom, she is deceived by a servant's guile. Reborn into a family of humble fisherfolk in the new kingdom of her future in-laws, she hears her brother's cry for help as he is led off to execution. He utters the key line, -"Αχ, Δημητρούλα! Τί σοῦ φταίξαμεν ἐμεῖς τὰ βαρυορρίζικα, καὶ μᾶς ἤφταξεν ἡ ἁμαρτία σου; [*Ah, Dimitroula, what harm have we unfortunates done you that your wrong has reached us?*]. Proof of her chastity frees him from death and wins her a husband. Viewed in this way, "Myrmidonia and Pharaonia" and "Poulia and Avgerinos" are mirror images of the same theme. In the former, brother and sister atone for their father's and grandfather's sacrilege against cosmic powers and win a fertile role in this world. In the latter, brother and half-sister are hounded by mother/stepmother, forced into mutual dependency, and threatened with destruction by the mother-in-law. Poulia cries out in another key line: Ἔχε γειά, καλέ μου πεθερὲ καὶ καλέ μου βασιλόπουλο. Ἐγὼ στὸν κόσμο αὐτὸ δὲν μπορῶ νὰ ζήσω· ἀπὸ τὰ χέρια τῆς κακιᾶς μητρυιᾶς ἔπεσα στὰ χέρια τῆς κακιᾶς πεθερᾶς [*Farewell, my good father-in-law and my good prince. I cannot live in this world: from the hands of a wicked stepmother I fell into the hands of a wicked mother-in-law*]. (They are accorded cosmic powers.)

7. The Tree of Life and the Cosmic Cycle

"Myrmidonia and Pharaonia" shows how a skilled narrator can reintegrate a tale of mixed parentage into oral tradition by means of a set of images best subsumed under the general heading "the tree of life." Throughout Greek culture, there is scarcely a more powerful symbol of the sanctity of life, death, and rebirth than the tree. The tree is bisexual, self-engendering, and polysemic. While its inner spirit may be female, its juice is sperm. Its roots lie buried underground, nurturing snakes which yield gold coins to those that deserve them and poison to transgressors. Its many branches are of silver and gold, harboring fruits to be released in plentiful waters as beautiful women, feeding birds of the air, or spurting forth immortal waters. Its topmost peak shelters liminal women, sometimes shooting them to the heavens as constellations. Sap gets virgins pregnant; the trunk protects the soul of life, as in a womb, tomb, or chest. Magical instruments are made from its bark, and enchanted dances are performed beneath its branches. Nuts and dried fruits have regenerative and protective powers; yet it depends on human cultivation to give forth its produce: girls lick sap and bring forth heroes, boys lick the trunk to double its size.

Variable yet concrete images add new dimensions to sustained analogies between tree and human cycles in the ritual songs. Detailed analysis will be deferred to Part III, but key points of contact between the two genres may be suggested. First, the tree as a symbol of love. Love "is caught from the eyes, goes down to the lips, and takes root in the leaves of the heart no more to depart" (Politis 1914, 93). Uprooted love causes irreparable damage and blood loss not just to the human heart but also to the tree by metonymy, as the consequences of a broken pledge are transferred: an apple tree in an orchard withers at the parting of a young boy and girl who had sworn at its roots an oath of eternal love (Politis 1914, 127). Second, marriage and fertility. The bride is addressed as a bushy cotton plant, a dense-leaved citrus tree, while the groom is as tall and straight as a cypress. The sexual act may be expressed in wedding songs in terms of tree images. A brave young soldier finds shelter neither in fortress nor village (heroic exploits), only in a tall shady tree, who bids him tie his horse at her roots, hang his weapons on her branches, lie down in her shade, and leave a drop of water at her root in payment (Politis 1914, 147B). Or the bride may be greeted as purest water and brightest moon as she crosses the threshold of the groom, then blessed to stand upright as a cypress, take root as a holm oak, blossom forth as an apple tree, so she may be granted nine sons and one sweet apple tree/daughter (Politis 1914, 145B). Third, at death the tree becomes a cosmic symbol: the world is a tree, and we are its fruit; Charos is the vintager who garners our fruit. In the lower world, Charos makes his own garden, plucking young girls as lemon trees, young men as cypresses, and small children as carnations and gillyflowers and implanting old men as gateposts.[64] The tree of life goes on after death in another form, provided there is a sufficiency of running water.

Such a cosmological system seems remote from Christianity. But in the hymns and liturgy of the Orthodox Church, the Cross signifies not merely the instrument of Christ's torture, martyrdom, and death but also the means by which "the whole of creation," can be renewed and "dance together". Hence the Cross is "the tree of life," as in Romanos' hymns on the Nativity, Crucifixion, and Resurrection (Chapter 2 and appendix). The miracle of the virgin birth is expressed through tree imagery: Mary holds the uncultivated grape cluster (that is, Christ) "on her arms as on branches," while the issue of fruit (karpós) from her body has broken no seal (On the Nativity 2, 1–2). The image is no more nor less powerful than that of "Olive's Tear," where a poor virgin licks olive sap and brings forth a hero; at his birth, the olive grove and its drakos inhabitants clash with thunder as her

virginity is sealed up again. As we have seen, the central feast of the Orthodox calendar is not Christmas but Easter, when death and rebirth become
one. Liturgies and rituals continue throughout the forty days of Lent, while
the most crucial take place between Holy Thursday/Good Friday (*epi-
táphios thrēnos*) and Easter Saturday / Sunday (*anástasis*). Here lies a possible
clue to why the black dancers in "The Twelve Months" insist that their
mortal guest acknowledge the paradox of the reversibility of these turns of
day: death is life, life is death; both are a kind of rebirth.

In Orthodox Christian symbolism, the tree of life is also the Paschal
Lamb, who must be literally as well as figuratively slaughtered and eaten before he can be reborn in each of us. Once again, "Poulia and Avgerinos"
offers a similar cluster of images differently put together. Disregarding Poulia's warning, Avgerinos turns into a lamb; but her loyal protection of him
after his metamorphosis gives him the power to save from destruction the
tree on whose peaks she is perched. Pushed to the bottom of a well by her
mother-in-law, she is powerless to save her lamb from slaughter; but by
gathering up the bones and burying them, she ensures their mutual transition to eternity. Sacrifice, according to Orthodox and wondertale perceptions, imparts new life when a reciprocal source of communal food. There
are times when "eating people" is *right*!

The theme of sacrifice, enacted in tales as killing and eating another's
flesh, is one of many indications of the unexplored ritual dimensions in the
paramythia. Birth, marriage, and death are perceived as interactive processes:
birth may be the progeny of different species; secondary marriage ensures
fertility on earth; secondary burial affords the possibility of the soul's renewal in another life. The tripartite narrative structure implicit in all Greek
wondertales—natal home / foreign parts / new life—plays out a complementary ritual pattern, signifying not just departure from the natal hearth,
encounter with the outside world, and reintegration into marital home but
also the possibility of infinite cosmic renewal.

8. Concluding Comments

By way of conclusion to this chapter, I shall summarize some of the
distinctive features of the paramythia in the light of other mythical genres
surveyed in the last chapters. Legends belong to the world as observed, describing natural features, local heroes, or actual experiences, and it is therefore not surprising to find their cosmic and moral categories polarized between good and evil. Songs, when narrative or mythical, are projections
through fantasy of dangers attendant upon the human condition, especially

if caused by family conflict and marriage. Predominantly tragic, they polarize good and evil in surprising ways, not without a touch of parody. Songs for death and departure, marriage and courtship, in one sense cast each stage in the life cycle as an occasion for a separate performance, yet the interpenetration of imagery suggests ambivalence. In the paramythia, time and space operate outside, as well as inside, the human cycle of birth, marriage, and death, and therefore the parameters of good and evil are at once more open, shifting, and complex. A negative ending in the ballads (girl sacrificed, hair taken by bulrushes, dust turned to flour) may be viewed more positively in the tales, where life unjustly taken may assume another form. Final death is by explosion or the destruction of all living particles.

From romanticism until postmodernism, there has been a tendency to privilege the tragic genres as "high," the comic genres as "low," and those which fit neither as beneath contempt. Greek tragedy—separated from trilogy and satyr play—has been regarded as the pinnacle of literary achievement; hence Aeschylus' *Agamemnon* and Sophokles' *Oedipus* have received more acclaim than Euripides' *Alkestis* or *Helen*. It was not always so. The healing and restorative qualities of comedy were explored in medieval and Renaissance literature. At the turn of the Enlightenment to romanticism, Mozart perfected the Italian *opera buffa* style with his Italian operas, yet he turned to the world of magic and German *Singspiel* for his most profound musical expression, *Die Zauberflöte*. All the faults and inconsistencies in this opera have been blamed on his librettist, Emanuel Schikaneder: beautiful music, but what a silly story! judged the critics, who derided the ridiculous serpent, the confusion between good and evil (Queen of Night and her Three Ladies appear good to Tamino at the beginning of act 1, only to be revealed as evil in act 2), the liminal bird-human status of Papageno and Papagena, and above all the mixture of magic and Masonic, comic and serious elements. Yet Mozart's music reaches its most sublime heights and mysterious depths precisely at those moments when magical paradox is explored, as in the duet between Pamina and Papageno ("Bei Männern"), in which captive princess and birdman sing together of the joys of love in a strange kingdom, reaching "an die Gottheit" ("to the Deity"); or in Pamina's prelude to the trials by fire and water she and Tamino must undergo in the finale of act 2, where the bassoon plays the haunting tune of how her father carved the magic flute from the bark of a tree, amidst thunder and lightning. Wondertale elements have been expressed more perfectly in opera than in the novel; music *includes* the strange and dramatic, whereas classic prose fiction *separates* realism from fantasy, tragedy from comedy, didacticism from entertainment, according to a false Cartesian dualism. Nor is it fortuitous that the libretto of *The Magic Flute* derives from Eastern wondertales.[65]

The all-embracing cosmology and morality of the wondertales find unexpected support in recently popular scientific paradigms. Stephen Hawking's *A Brief History of Time* has demonstrated the impossibility of separating beginning and end, our world and others, cosmic time and space, explosion and implosion. James Watson's *The Double Helix* and Francis Crick's *What Mad Pursuit* document the quirky and spiral process of biochemical development which provides the key to genetic coding (DNA). Stephen Jay Gould's *Wonderful Life* celebrates the proliferation of biological species at the dawn of creation and the many other possible outcomes, were the tape to be replayed according to different contingencies. Oliver Sacks' *The Man Who Mistook His Wife for a Hat* and *An Anthropologist on Mars* explore the neurological mysteries of the human brain. Two of Sacks' studies have been made into opera and film, perhaps because both genres give expression to the synesthetic properties he emphasizes. Song and music are integral to wondertales, as themes and in performance. Song can be crucial to plot, character, and mood; music also aids memory. Spanish Gypsies, for example, "use music as an adjunct to storytelling. Ask them to tell you a *paramish* [folktale, pan-Romany for paramythi] and they will first of all clear their throats and hum a tune, and then fit the words to the story of the tune. One of the women recited a long poem for me about a ship that had been wrecked and described the adventures of the passengers, repeating over and over again a musical phrase, occasionally changing it into the minor key" (Tong 1989, 9).

Tales are not derived from or inferior to myth and song. Their meanings and endurance over time are re-created and transmitted by tellers who continue to perform and exchange stories with other peoples of diverse faiths. The verb *múō* from which mythos and paramythi derive, signified in ancient Greek the act of putting a finger on the lips both to initiate speech and to seal the mouth when speech is sacred.[66] Paramythia are comforting, everyday versions of the more solemn myths. In Greece they have flourished ever since literacy first recorded the Homeric poems: the spoken word—the interaction between "I" and "you," teller and audience, has not been silenced. Their appeal to people of all ages and abilities lies in their narrative ingenuity, moral wisdom, and performative flexibility: they permit tellers to act out life drama through assumed personae in fictionalized form, which does not compromise their sense of self in the eyes of the community.[67] Thus, tales may be related to the experiences of tellers and audiences in ways less direct but more vital than those envisaged by Zipes. Persecutions and pursuits, exploits and escapes, disguises and hiding places, fantastic as they may seem to us, have all been lived out at one time or another by the local communities that produced the corpus of tales here reviewed, from the Greek War of Independence (1821–28) to the turbulent aftermaths of World Wars I and II (Asia Minor Catastrophe; Metaxas' dictatorship; Civil War; Junta years).[68]

In the next chapter, we shall see how one of the greatest Greek prose writers, Georgios Vizyenos, exploited the tales, myths, and songs he inherited in ways other than those of the Cartesian legacies of the West. Meantime, if story is subservient to mood and paradox in the mythical songs, the narrative ingenuity of the tales is boundless, blended with snatches of sung stories and laments where words and actions alone are inadequate to express human emotion.

CHAPTER 8

Between Worlds:
From Myth to Fiction

In the past three chapters, I have tried to indicate the diversity of mythical genres in Greek folk tradition, to trace the development of folklore studies and the impact of demotic nationalism, and to analyze how myth functions. In the concluding chapter of Part II, I wish to address a different set of questions. What forces shaped the emergence of Greek prose fiction after the establishment of the nation-state, and how do they differ from those prevalent elsewhere in Europe? Which mythical and literary features from past textual traditions have been absorbed into modern fiction, and how has this heritage affected its nature and quality? In what ways have writers incorporated oral techniques and themes from songs and tales into their works? These are large questions and cannot be answered with reference to the whole of modern Greek prose fiction. I shall begin by outlining the emergence of the novel, with a résumé of the historical and literary context of four novellas; then I shall proceed to detailed discussion of Georgios Vizyenos (1849–96); finally, I shall comment on subsequent developments, with brief reference to four novelists of the twentieth century. In this way I hope to illustrate the distinctive features of modern Greek fiction, particularly those relevant to character and plot, narrative techniques, and imagery. Since my concern here is historical and cultural rather than purely literary, I have refrained from adopting the cumbersome panoply of narratological terminology and have tried instead to adapt some Greek terms inherited from a long rhetorical tradition.[1]

Why Vizyenos? First, his stories—five of the major six written in the 1880s—coincide with the interrelated movements of nationalism, demoticism, and folklore; yet their originality lies precisely in their refusal to conform to the rules laid down by the new literary establishment. Second, coming as he did from Ottoman Thrace, Vizyenos' perspectives on ethnicity and gender, language and rationality are richer than those of his compatriots within the new nation-state of Greece: reaching back through the Ottoman present to the Byzantine past, he succeeds in integrating oral with literary narrative strategies in ways relevant not only to the 1880s, but also to the splintering nationalisms of the 1990s. Third, although he has enjoyed less literary acclaim than his near contemporary, Alexandros Papadiamandis (1851–1911), and has therefore exercised less *influence* on subsequent writers, his revitalisation of some nonnarrative qualities of earlier modes of perception and representation, as realized through his multitoned use of the Greek language, have been insufficiently appreciated. Vizyenos—like Cavafy—was an outsider who saw more than usual in the Hellenic looking glass. In subtle ways, his presence can be remarked in subsequent Greek poetry and prose up to the present day.

1. The Greek Novel, c. 1830–1880

At first sight, the political, social, and intellectual climate in the new Greek state could scarcely seem less favorable to the rise of the modern novel, traditionally linked with developing economic and social structures within the nation-state, increased literacy, and an emergent bourgeoisie with its printing presses.[2] The Greek population in the 1820s was overwhelmingly rural, without formal education, and traditional in outlook, with only ten thousand people (5 percent) resident in Athens, many of whom still spoke Arvanitika (a form of Albanian). Even Athens was not a "city"— the major urban centers of Greek commerce, such as Istanbul, Izmir, Alexandria, and Thessaloniki, were multiethnic, and lay outside the new realm. Between 1828 and 1833, Greece was torn by civil strife, attributable to local rivalries as well as to the machinations of foreign powers.

By 1834, Greeks of the diaspora—intellectuals and merchants—had begun to settle in Athens, hence from a provincial settlement it had rapidly to assume the functions of a metropolis. Veterans from the War of Independence, such as Makryiannis, were dismissed with promises never to be fulfilled. Turkish domination was replaced by subservience to foreign powers (Britain, Russia, and France). The first monarch, Bavarian Otho, was powerless to solve economic and social problems. Brigandage was rife, even ideologized by the invented opposition *kléftis/listís* "bandit-hero"/"robber" with no recourse to law courts and little conception of institutional justice. In the course of this national crisis, Otho's Prime Minister, Ioannis Kolettis, first formulated in 1844 the *Megálē Idéa* "the Great Idea" as the solution to Greece's internal problems: the dream to recover the Greek-speaking territories in Asia Minor ruled by the Byzantine Empire, including Constantinople.[3] As Richard Clogg puts it; "It was [the] grafting of the forms, but not the substance, of Western constitutional government onto an essentially traditional society, with a very different value system from that prevailing in the West, that was to create within Greece a fundamental political tension that has continued for much of its post-independence history" (1979, 61).

Clogg's assumptions of essentially traditional and therefore corruptible societies in contrast to our own, assumed to be inherently upright, may be open to question, but the tensions he highlights have been cultural as well as political in Greece. On the political plane, how democratic could Greece be, given that the new national egalitarian policies were grafted onto a clientelistic system? On the sociocultural plane, how could conflicting forces of familism and individualism be reconciled? Alongside Greek irredentism and nascent European racial theories of Aryanism were sown the seeds of a dichotomy, or rather a sense of fragmented identity, divided on the one hand between Europe and Asia, West and East, and on the other between Greeks living within the narrow boundaries of the nation-state (mainland Greece south of the Arta-Volos line and some islands) and the more numerous "Tourkomerítes' (or Greeks resident in areas still under Ottoman rule), often more thriving and intellectually cosmopolitan.[4] In Greece, the desire to appear European was combined with small-nation chauvinism to quell suspicions among European powers that [modern] Greece was not so European after all. These issues, confronted both in politics and literature during the 1880s, have their relevance to this day, and not only for Greece.

The first literary writers were members of the new Athenian elite, former expatriates who had been educated in Europe. Their Europeanizing tendencies led them to appeal to the Byzantine and ancient past to define Greekness in terms of purity of language, lofty themes, and national ideals. To that end, in 1850 a prize was instituted for National Poetry which would hymn the present by reference to its glorious past.[5] As for prose fiction, Beaton claims that "the precedents available to Greek writers were essentially only four: older Greek narrative in verse; the quasi-philosophical dialogue cultivated by Phanariot exponents of the Enlightenment; the eighteenth- and early nineteenth-century European novel, which began to be translated into Greek in the second half of the eighteenth century; and the Greek novels . . . of late antiquity." To these may be added the numer-

ous translations from Arabic and Persian fiction, shown by Georgios Kehayioglou to have been in circulation between the eleventh and nineteenth
centuries.[6] Despite Kehayioglou's accumulation of bibliographical data,
neither he nor Beaton gives sufficient weight to the popular demand for
diverse fictional forms of an order different from those conventionally regarded as precursors to the modern novel. These may be grouped in the
following categories: narrative verse on erotic or marvelous themes; histor-
ical-legendary tales; humorous and satirical verse fables; prose compilations
of saints' lives and legendary events, rooted in local traditions; translations
from Arabic and Persian tales; and the ancient novel and its Byzantine se-
quels. Last but not least, there has been the rich fund of paramythia reviewed in the last chapter.

The late-antique and Byzantine novels, the former reedited by Korais in
an attempt to lay Hellenic claim to the origin of the genre (1804), appealed
to the literary elite; but many features continued to be exploited in Greek
fiction long after they had been discarded in Europe. Popular precedents
circulated in provincial towns and villages under Ottoman rule, where they
were recited at local gatherings. This was not just a passive, one-way
process: as we saw in the last chapter, tales of literary origin were assimilated
into the live tradition of paramythia, hence the age-old tradition of telling
tales was reinvigorated by contact with literary texts of West and East, more
especially the latter. *Mutatis mutandis*, prose writers from Vizyenos to
Zyranna Zateli (1993) have drawn on wondertales to create distinctive
forms of modern —and modernist—fiction.

What Greece lacked was not novelistic precedents—these were exceptionally diverse, including genres ranging from oral to literary, religious to
secular, serious to humorous, prose to verse—but rather the centripetal
forces of an established national identity and a homogeneous reading public, female and male. If some of the first modern Greek novelists wrote
close and often unispired imitations of Western genres, with a predilection
for the adaptation of European historical, romantic, and epistolary novels to
the patriotic context of the recent Greek War of Independence, composed
in katharevousa, it was because they chose to do so, preferring to follow established models rather than to explore the "distant contexts" of indigenous traditions.[7]

It was not a promising beginning: critics write of the historical novel
that "throughout the whole of the first stage of its development, it was
characterised by shallow, false patriotism, commonplace rhetoric and unattractive romanticism."[8] Nevertheless, the exceptions are worth noting, because they suggest that Greek fiction might mark out a path somewhat dif-

ferent from that of the historical-romantic or classic realist novel. Just as Greek song and tale diverge from their European counterparts (Chapters 6 and 7), modern Greek fiction excels in difference.

These modes arise from different perceptions of the individual in relation to society and from a more diversified ethnic, religious, and linguistic identity. They include the paradoxical juxtaposition of documentary and fantasy, formal description and narration, and show comparatively little attempt to integrate plot and character. Indeed, character is viewed not vertically or in depth but may be split horizontally across other personas, rather in the manner of Orhan Pamuk's novella *The White Castle* (1979, trans. 1991), in which the sophisticated seventeenth-century Venetian narrator is captured by Turkish brigands, captivated by Turkish ways, only to become captive to a Turkish "other self." In surprising ways, Vizyenos' stories anticipate modernist and postmodernist techniques in their dexterous combination of irony and parody with serious purpose.[9]

Gregory Jusdanis has analyzed the difficulties confronting Greek writers in terms of what he calls "belated modernity," pointing to antinomies in Greek culture, especially an ambivalence toward the past (ancient and medieval) and the present (Europe versus the East). On the one hand, dependence on the West inclined the intelligentsia to exploit the Hellenic past. On the other, the need to negotiate a space as a latecomer to Europe led to assertions of Eastern otherness, in diverse forms of resistance to Western hegemony traceable from the 1880s to the present day.[10] Yet if Greek literature was to be dissociated from its legacy of four centuries of Ottoman rule, popular culture had to be discarded, and the misfit between European literary forms and underlying political structures ignored.

Among the earliest departures in Greek fiction was the novella *Thanos Vlekas* (1855), published serially in the periodical *Pandora* by the lawyer and historian Pavlos Kalligas, who, after studies in Germany, became actively engaged in politics during the 1840s. Short, unpretentious and without obvious foreign models, it claims in its prologue to be no more than ἐν σμικρογραφία σκιαγράφημα τῶν καθ' ἡμᾶς "in microcosm a sketch of our times," and that is precisely what it is. Instead of reverting to the Byzantine past as a model for the heroic struggles of the Greeks, as did his contemporary Alexandros Rizos Rangavis, Kalligas confronts the reader with the least pleasant facts of liberated Greece, choosing as his central theme the inflammatory topic of local brigands.

Kalligas addresses, through fiction, the most contentious issue of the day: the interdependency of brigand chiefs in rural Greece (Thessaly and the Peloponnese) and political circles in the new metropolis of Athens. Here is the kind of tension referred to by Clogg. The novella provides a wealth of information on how injustices were corroborated, at local and governmental level; on the ineffectual nature of the judicial system; and on the division of land, which cheated the peasants of hopes for a fair distribution after the departure of the Turks. Written in response to Edouard About's exposure of brigandage in his *La Grèce contemporaine* (1854), partially translated in Romilly Jenkins' *The Dilessi Murders* (1961), Kalligas succeeds by virtue of dispassionate social critique. Many of his ironical asides have been cited as a refrain by Vassilis Vassilikos throughout his satirical vignettes in Ἐκτὸς τῶν τειχῶν ("Outside the Walls," 1966), as an oblique means of commenting, over a century later, on the stifling atmosphere of "la Grèce contemporaine."

Despite its social relevance, *Thanos Vlekas* is, for our tastes at least, naïvely couched within the conventions of ballad or wondertale plot and character. Of the two brothers, the good Thanos is imprisoned and finally killed unjustly in the course of a rebellion by the villagers with whom he lives and works, after they have been cheated of their land; the bad Tasos—his mother's darling—goes unpunished, despite his guilt, because he is protected by the authorities of the metropolis. There is also a love theme: Thanos falls in love with the daughter of his benefactor, but although her intervention secures his release from jail, they do not confess their love; after he is killed, she dies of a broken heart. Sentimental? Perhaps. If we take the case of British fiction, such melodramatic and romantic elements are not lacking in the nineteenth century, but they are given fullest expression in the genre of popular and traditional ballads, to be tempered with historicism and realism in the maturing genre of the novel. In Greece, where narrative songs are more heroic-mythic than romantic (Chapter 6), the taste for sentiment was accommodated in prose fiction simultaneously with documentary biography and folkloric features. A further point: Thanos' "heroism" derives not from male assertiveness but from his inability to "stand up for himself as a man." Thanos' erotic abstinence may owe something to the asceticism so prominent in the saints' lives; it can also be seen as a precedent for Vizyenos' Paschalis, for Papadiamandis' reticent heroes, and for Myrivilis' problematization of gender. It is a fictional reversal of the dominant male values of Greek society and stands in contrast to the polarization of gender roles noted in the emergence of Anglo-American modernist fiction.[11]

Mario Vitti (1991: 15–36) contrasts Kalligas' exposure of the evils of brigandage (and state complicity) with Rangavis' Αὐθέντης τοῦ Μορέως ("Lord of the Morea," 1850) and Ὁ συμβολαιογράφος ("The Notary," 1851), two more ambitious novels of the decade. The former invokes Walter Scott's *Ivanhoe* and the medieval Greek *Chronicle of the Morea* to glorify Byzantine struggles against the Franks; the latter "conceals the view of a turbulent and uneasy society . . . by distracting the reader with screens to satisfy and reassure him" (Vitti 1991, 29). Where Kalligas questions the status quo, Rangavis affirms it.

An interesting example of "naïve" writing which scored an immediate and lasting success was Iakovos Pitsipios' Ἡ ὀρφανὴ τῆς Χίου, ἢ ὁ θρίαμβος τῆς ἀρετῆς ("The Orphan Girl of Chios, or the Triumph of Virtue," 1839). Based on the tragic events of 1821–23, when the island of Chios was destroyed by the Turks in the course of the War of Independence, it tells of a poor but virtuous orphan girl, brought up by cruel relations, who falls in love with a handsome young hero from the same village but of higher social rank. Crammed with adventure and coincidence, it relates kidnappings, attempted violations, captures and escapes, supposed deaths and suicides—even Platonic loves—in the manner of late-antique and Byzantine learned novels, while the thwarted hero's rhetorical lamentations and protestations against *Tyche* (Fortune) seem to come straight out of the vernacular verse romances of the thirteenth to fifteenth centuries. Despite the lack of depth in characterization and plot, from the viewpoint of the reader unacquainted with Greek or equivalent concepts of the self, Pitsipios' novella was an immediate success. It was widely circulated and later dramatized. I. A. Panagiotopoulos describes a performance by shadow theater players on the island of Skyros, which held all spectators spellbound and reduced many older people to tears. Such has been its appeal that this literary work has reentered oral tradition in the form of a romantic ballad, still performed on the island of Cyprus by *poiētárides* (professional poets).[12]

It is easy to deride the naïveté of popular Greek responses to literature and art in the nineteenth century; but rural audiences still flock to the theater of Dodoni in Epiros to watch and comment on ancient tragedy. Leslie Brubaker, in her recent studies of Byzantine icons, notes that modern and medieval reactions to art differ precisely in the manner and extent to which the viewer identifies with the viewed, although she draws analogies between medieval icons and modern commercial advertisements in their direct appeal through image and logo.[13] These analogies apply equally to fiction and spectacle as manifested in the illustrated chapbooks, popular theater, and prose stories current in premodernized Greece, and in the media of our contemporary world. Whereas high and low art were separated in the West (until the advent of postmodernism), Greek perceptions during the nineteenth century were shaped by different historical and cultural experiences.

In the genre of documentary biography, Dimitris Vikelas' *Loukis Laras* (1879) has been acclaimed as one of the earliest successful attempts to write biomythography in a realistic narrative mode. Written in simple puristic Greek from the perspective of the ego-narrator, Loukis Laras, the novella purports to describe the actual experiences of an elderly and not very handsome, brave, or well-educated man from the island of Syra. Despite some melodramatic episodes, the emphasis is on first-person authenticity: Δὲν τὰ εἶδα καὶ δὲν θέλω νὰ γράφω εἰμὴ μόνον ὅσα εἶδα "I didn't see [such things], and I don't want to write except what I saw" (20), mediated by frequent second-person address to his readers.[14] The narrator's emphasis on events as he witnessed them arises not merely from Vikelas' reaction against romanticism but also from that reluctance to reveal inner emotional states which characterizes the transition from orality to literacy.[15] As we saw in the last chapter, oral tales are full of invention and fantasy, but they are never overtly about the self. To *write a life story* is to suppress the self and write only what is "true"—that is, to report what you have seen and heard and how these events are evaluated by others. Biomythography flourishes when boundaries between spoken and written word are not clearly drawn.

If *The orphan* was the popular hit, Emmanuel Roidis' Ἡ Πάπισσα Ἰωάννα (*Pope Joan*, 1866) was the learned one. Roidis, educated in Italy and Germany, remains to this day a controversial figure who played a crucial role in Greek letters during the latter part of the nineteenth century, when profound changes were taking place in attitudes to society, religion, language, and culture. In his critical essays, he takes a consistent stand against provincialism and parochialism, most notably in his extended controversy with Angelos Vlachos.[16] His novella, which he later dismissed as νεανίσκον ἁμάρτημα, "a juvenile transgression," expresses the full paradox of "contemporary Greece" (ἡ σημερινὴ Ἑλλάς). It is a deviant and subversive text, banned by the Orthodox Church (which Roidis does not attack, at least overtly), but not by the Vatican, although Catholicism is its ostensible target. Available in the readable, if not always full and accurate, translation by Lawrence Durrell (1960), it has also been made into a film after Shaw's version. In its intertextuality and self-referentiality it presages Umberto Eco's *Name of the Rose* (1980 [trans 1983]), another novel which, despite its erudition, progressed from best-seller to film.

Roidis is careful to call *Pope Joan* not a novel but a *mesaionikē melétē*, or "medieval study." As Maria Kakavoulia has shown, appearances are deceptive; while posing as a scholarly tract, complete with footnotes and endnotes, with no concessions made to the reader either in its chosen linguistic register (elegant katharevousa) or in assumed learning (abstruse references in similes and notes to a wide range of literary, philosophical, religious, historical, and political figures of cultures from antiquity to the present day, including America), the text proves as "readerly" as it is "writerly," entertaining despite the difficult Greek, not just because it is scandalous, but because it demythologizes classical narrative.[17] Even before it was banned by the Orthodox Church, Greek critics were "deeply shocked." How does Roidis succeed?

First, the story ("histoire"): a beautiful, sexy, and intelligent girl, born of humble Anglo-Germanic parentage in the ninth century, has amorous affairs (as a transvestite) in monasteries which lead her to the pinnacle of male sacred power (the papacy), then to her equally spectacular demise when she prematurely aborts the child—conceived during her papacy as a result of a passionate affair with her predecessor's son!—in the course of a public ceremony. In fact, the story is an ironic comment on medieval legends of male prowess, humorously inverting many stock episodes and motifs familiar from the lives of Alexander the Great, Constantine I, Digenes Akrites, and even the saints. At the same time, the amorality of the heroine and the scandalous intrigues of the monks undermine both our preconceptions of appropriate character and plot and our romantic idealization of the past, all the more so since the story—which Roidis claims to have documented with painstaking research—takes the outward form of a hagiography. Second, if narrative ("récit") is understood as the totality of the text, then it must include the learned introduction, footnotes, endnotes, digressions, similes, and asides, which impede the flow of the story and add nothing to characterization but suggest a strategy of engaging the implied reader in constant dialogue on a wide range of questions, past and present. Third, narrating instant ("narration"): dialogue takes place not between the characters, who rarely converse, but between author and implied reader through frequent, stylized asides addressed separately to male and female readers, who are never allowed to forget that they are reading a fictional text, in which medieval past (ninth century) and contemporary present (nineteenth century) are ironically juxtaposed.

As Dimitris Dimiroulis has noted (1985), it is as if Roidis decided to dress up just once as a novelist to conduct a polemic against all those conventions, both Greek and European, which he continued to attack as a critic throughout his life. It is not coincidental that the most successful prose fiction in this early period was produced not by those who tried to write European-style novels on patriotic themes but almost accidentally by those who were motivated, by circumstances and experience, to challenge the sociopolitical and intellectual institutions of the emergent Greek state. Satire, documentary, and romance are differently combined in the form of the novella, with emphasis on ironic dialogue—direct and indirect—between author and narrator, addresser and addressee, and with minimal attention to complex plot or "rounded" characterization.

In terms of Greek literary tradition, the nineteenth-century novella shares many features with twelfth-century narrative modes examined in Chapter 4. The *Timarion* is a learned prose text which grafts onto a fantastic narrative a subversive juxtaposition of past and present, much as Roidis is dependent on a past learned scholastic traidition. In the Ptochoprodromic Poems, slapstick comedy and sheer fantasy belie the serious critical intent, "clowning wisely" by engaging in dialogue, actual and intertextual. The difference between European and Greek modes of narration lies perhaps in the European predilection for neat oppositions, with each emotional state, character, and plot motif viewed separately and in depth, and the Greek love of paradoxical juxtaposition. If character and plot seem reducible to Proppian functions, complexity lies in antithesis, ekphrasis, dialogue, and imagery.

2. Paralogic Fiction: The Case of Georgios Vizyenos

Vizyenos was born of humble parentage in the village of Vizye (Vize) in Ottoman Thrace (hence his name). By dint of his talent and thanks to the generous private sponsorship of Georgios Zarifis, he studied first in Cyprus and Athens, then in Göttingen and Leipzig, where he completed a doctoral dissertation in psychology. After spending crucial years between the ages of thirty-four and thirty-six in London, he was appointed in 1885 as Lecturer in Philology at the University of Athens, eking out his salary by giving lessons in psychology and logic at a girls' gymnasium. His poetry was derided during his lifetime; his prose stories largely ignored or misconstrued. His death at the age of forty-seven in the mental asylum of Daphni, where he was consigned as insane, attracted prurient critics to read and praise his stories, regarded as autobiographical, claiming him posthumously as the "father of the Greek genre story."[18] His unorthodox views on issues such as ethnicity and language may have contributed to his consignment to Dromokaïteion, much as dissident writers in the former Soviet Union also ended their days in psychiatric units.

Like Roidis, Vizyenos is a writer with few parallels in his day. But Vizyenos was writing almost two decades after *Pope Joan*, at a time when the interrelated movements of literary realism and nationalist demoticism were in the ascendant. A powerful challenge to romanticism came in 1879—the year Vikelas' *Loukis Laras* appeared—with the publication of a Greek translation of Emile Zola's *Nana* (with τολμηρὸ ἐξώφυλλο "provocative dust-jacket"), prefaced by an exhortation from A. G. Epirotis for a shift away from insular romanticism toward Western realism. In 1883,

Roidis' adversary Angelos Vlachos published his translation of Balzac's *Eugénie Grandet* to counter what he regarded as Zola's immorality, but looking once again toward different circles in Europe (cited in Vitti 1991, 62–63).

Greek reaction to such "foreign influences," whether realist or not, came the same year when the periodical *Estia* instituted a contest, at the instigation of N. G. Politis, πρὸς συγγραφὴν ἑλληνικοῦ διηγήματος "toward the writing of a Greek story." On the purpose of the contest, he notes that "The Greek people [*laós*], if indeed any other, has noble mores [*ēthē*], varied customs, manners, myths, and legends for all representations of its historic life [*bíos*]; while Greek history, ancient, medieval, and modern, is brimming with scenes able to provide plots for the composition of the finest stories and novels." The message was clear: authors should steer clear of imported prototypes and turn to pure Greek themes, folkloric and historical. The resurgence during the 1880s of Greek nationalism brought intensified propaganda for the "Great Idea" and a politically motivated interest in Greek folklore.[19]

In Greece, literary realism, folklore studies and demoticism were interlinked, each defining the other. The terms *logotechnía* "literature" and *laographía* "folklore" were coined in 1883–84 as the equivalents of *Nationalliteratur* and *Volkskunde* to replace *grammateía* "lettres."[20] Greek realism was fine in theory, so long as it contributed in practice to patriotic aspirations and to the idealization of the Greek "folk." *Ethographía* (genre story), as this kind of fiction became known, took the form of *diēgēma* (short story) rather than the full-length novel. The best and most enduring examples break out of the restrictions of their theoretical model: Andreas Karkavitsas' stories, from Ἡ Λυγερή ("The Young Girl," 1890) to Ὁ ζητιάνος ("The Beggar," 1896) reveal the harsh truths of Greek rural life with a good deal of psychological insight. Both girl and beggar are coarsened through their experiences: she loses her innocence when she succumbs to family pressures to marry for money rather than love; he plays the game of masculine cunning (*poniriá*) to the destruction of all. Yet Karkavitsas and his contemporary Georgios Drosinis differ from Vizyenos in their journalistic assimilation of folkloric material into fiction.[21]

Let us now examine how the "Tourkomeritis" Vizyenos challenged, through his stories, the new realism, nationalism and demoticism, much as that other outsider, Cavafy the "Hellēnikos," was to do in poetry in the following decades. There is no doubt that he intended to do so: in 1895, one year before his death and two years after his consignment to Dromokaïteion, he noted in an interview with two psychiatrists that "I was the first to open up the new road of modern Greek fiction [*logographía*], and I managed to show through my stories [*diēgēmata*] in *Estia*, by contrast with Rangavis and the rest, just what a story is." And again: "So, despised little 'Tourkomerites' as we are, let's get in there with our love of beauty [*philokalían*] and sharpness of wit, right up the nostrils of the blind pedants [*muiocháphtēdon*] of Athens.[22] Four (possibly five) stories were written between December 1882 and February 1885 when the author was in London; the sixth appeared in 1895, a year before his death, but may have been drafted as early as 1886 and deliberately held back because the hero is a Turk. There is no unifying theme, hence the stories do not constitute a novel in the conventional sense, yet themes and characters in each story are so closely interwoven that together they can be read as different perspectives on a series of interrelated oppositions—or six stories in search of a novel.[23]

Major themes include guilt and innocence; sanity and insanity; rationality and irrationality; modernity and tradition; literacy and orality; and ambivalences of ethnicity, religion, and gender. Conventional perceptions of these oppositions are probed, even reversed, so that sanity, ethnicity, and gender are seen as shifting rather than fixed categories. As Michalis Chryssanthopoulos has noted, the odd-numbered stories (1, 3, and 5) are set between Ottoman Thrace and Constantinople; the even-numbered ones take place on board ship (2), in Germany (4), and in Thrace (6), with wider reference to Piraeus, Naples, Calcutta; Athens; Istanbul, Crimea, Bosnia / Herzogovina / Serbia. All are narrated in the first person: Georgis in 1, 3, and 5, and an unnamed person in 2, 4, and 6 (henceforth N).[24] I shall consider how Vizyenos problematizes ethnic conflict in 3 and 6 and then move to a close analysis of 4 and 5 to analyze two distinctive modes of perception and representation, antithesis and ekphrasis.

3. Ethnicity and Sanity

Ποῖος ἦτον ὁ φονεὺς τοῦ ἀδελφοῦ μου ("Who Was My Brother's Killer") concerns violent death within the narrator's own family, from an unknown and apparently outside source. Three years before Georgis's narration commences, his brother Christakis was found killed near the bridge of Lüleburgaz, just twelve days after he had taken over the job of postman from his fellow villager Lambis and one day before the Russian occupation of the same bridge ended the Russo-Turkish War. The search for the killer takes place in Istanbul (1880). It involves two families, Greek and Turkish, each a mirror image of the other, whose misfortunes over many years have brought them together: two mothers, two living brothers, and two "dead brothers." Investigations lead nowhere, but a complex web of dramatic contingencies and narrations within narrations leads Georgis to the truth: the killer was none other than Kiamil, one of the two Turkish brothers, in revenge for his own blood brother, murdered some years before by Lambis, the former Greek postman from Vizye. It was a case of mistaken identities and kinship vendetta. Yet Georgis does not tell his mother the truth about Kiamil and leaves for studies abroad. He returns to his village three years later (1883), and in a brief epilogue finds his mother caring lovingly for the now crazed, and devoutly Muslim, Kiamil. She will not hear of turning him out, to "go back to his own people," as Georgis demands—after all, she argues, he's like my own flesh and blood, he runs errands, he even tends the flowers and candle on Christakis' grave! How can I turn him out? All these years, and they still haven't found the killer. Georgis still cannot tell her the truth. Who *was* the real killer? he asks himself at the close—Kiamil, who performed the act? Or the former Greek postman, Lambis, who exploited his resemblance to Christakis to lure him to his death?

At the end of the story, the reader is left to work out what the narrator's role was in the affair—a question he conspicuously fails to consider. As Chryssanthopoulos has shown, there are some teasing ironies in these two family tragedies, one Greek, the other Turkish, set against the background of the Russo-Turkish Wars and ferment in the Balkans. It is implied, but never stated, that the killings might have been averted if the men in both families were less opinionated and hostile to one another. The closest ties are between the two mothers, united by common suffering and concern for their sons, and the story is framed by two parallel situations: at the beginning, the Greek mother cares for the Turkish Kiamil as her son, who at the beginning suffers physical distress, and at the end, mental derangement. These two edges are separated by six years of narrative time and by three killings: the first in late April 1877, when the Greek postman Lambis killed Kiamil's Turkish blood brother and prospective brother-in-law; the second on 17 January 1878, when Kiamil killed the Greek postman (now Christakis) in revenge; and the third in 1880, when Kiamil killed Lambis in a fit of madness. The first two killings coincide with Russo-Turkish hostilities, which commenced with Russia's declaration of war on 24 April 1877 and concluded with the occupation of the Lüleburgaz bridge on 18 January 1878. The nine-month duration coincides with a full-term pregnancy, and the reader is reminded several times that during this war, the Greek mother nursed Kiamil from sickness to health in the absent Georgis' own bed for seven months, the minimum time for successful birthing.[25]

After the mothers, it is the two educated sons in each family who have the most in common, but they detest each other: the Greek Georgis, whose absence triggered his mother's adoption of Kiamil, and the Turkish Efendi, Kiamil's elder brother, who as public prosecutor leads the investigation for Christakis' killer. Both are Westernized in dress, education, and manners and contemptuous of their mothers' superstition; both are professionals, Georgis at narrating / interpreting, Efendi at investigating / punishing. Neither contributes anything substantial to the discovery of the killer: Georgis sits around in his Istanbul hotel, having declined to take up the Turkish mother's exceptional invitation to the Greek family to stay in her home in the Turkish quarter (where his mother and his brother Michailos stay). Efendi goes in punitive chase of the killer from Istanbul to Vizye and back, failing to find the culprit but killing and imprisoning many innocent suspects on the way. The two uneducated brothers, Michailos and Kiamil, are well disposed to each other, but Michailos is ineffectual and Kiamil becomes crazed. As for the two dead brothers, the Greek Christakis was a victim of mistaken identity, killed by the Turk Kiamil in an act of revenge for his blood brother, butchered in cold blood by the Greek Lambis. The two mothers share common interests in magic, tales, and the care of children, even visiting together the historic sites of the City (which mark the triumph of Turk over Greek); the four living brothers are divided by hostility or misunderstanding.

Our enlightened Georgis likes neither Turks nor Gypsies. He steals upon the two mothers consorting in the garden with a Greek-speaking Turkish Gypsy woman just as she declares, through bean divination, that the killer is "hard by . . . close as you and me . . . no one is as close to you as he is." Taken metaphorically, her words could mean "within the family"; but at that moment, the garden door through which Georgis has been spying opens with a creak, "and I was caught red-handed standing behind it" (Greek p. 83; English p. 76). Such is his mistrust of Gypsies that he thinks nothing further of the incident; but the reader notes with a *frisson* that no other member of either family was near the house at the time. Later that evening—the only occasion on which Georgis stays at the Turkish home—he meets Efendi face to face for the first time and learns his secret: as an enlightened member of the New Turk movement (Neótourkoi), he indulges his devotion to the spirit in the form of *oinópneuma* (alcohol) and ends up slouched over the dinner table as his mother tells the story of Kiamil's earlier life, which provides vital clues to the earlier killings (Greek p. 90; English p. 82).

One is left with a series of questions, "What if . . . ?" according to the principle of contingency reviewed in the last chapter. If Christakis had not chosen to sleep away from home while his mother was nursing the sick Kiamil in 1877, Kiamil could not so easily have mistaken him for the guilty Lambis, whom he resembled in stature and dress. If Georgis had not been absent from home for so long, his mother would not have adopted a Turkish son in his stead. If the father of Kiamil's Turkish blood brother had not rejected Kiamil after the Greek postman killed his son, Kiamil would not have got sick and taken revenge. If Georgis had not refused to stay in the Turkish home during the investigations, he would have learned sooner a vital clue to Kiamil's life story in time to avert the final catastrophe (slaying the "ghost of the past," the real Lambis) that drives Kiamil insane.

Vizyenos has done more than compose a masterful detective story, among the earliest Greek examples of the genre after the manner of Edgar Allan Poe. He has imbued plot and character with deeper layers of signification through his subtle exploitation of themes, images, and techniques drawn from the Greek mythical genres. The ghost in the song "The Dead Brother" seems to haunt this story, as in "The Only Journey of His Life," but at the end its presence is almost palpable. As Georgis enters Vizye for the first time since he left it as a child, his coach passes a collapsing, abandoned house, where he finds deathly silence instead of a once bustling life, ruin and abandon instead of prosperity and ease. But "the closed windows, the yawning walls, the courtyard overgrown with weeds, the fenceless garden laid on its back for any pillager" (motifs from songs) provoke in him not sadness but "strangely" (paradóxōs) a sense of satisfaction: it was the house of Mitakos, whose son Lambis had lured Christakis to death; and Lambis, he concludes at this point, *was* his brother's real killer, not Kiamil. His satisfaction is short-lived. Turning into his own house, he is accosted in Turkish by a filthy dervish whose voice seems to come "from some deep grave": it is Kiamil, who now lives with his mother and tends their once neglected garden, cultivating roses on his dead brother's grave (Greek pp. 102–3, English pp. 93–94). His most stern rhetoric is powerless to persuade his mother to turn Kiamil out, while his revulsion blinds him to the more profound truth which his mother (in her ignorance) and Kiamil (in his derangement) seem to have grasped: reconciliation through atonement.

Vizyenos also draws on oral modes of narration encountered in the wondertale, encoding one story within another. The solution is not spelled out by an omniscient narrator, as in most detective stories, but ambivalently implied through dialogue, the significance of which N (Narrator) seems unaware. On arrival at an Istanbul hotel, Georgis, and his brother and mother go over the events which led to Christakis' killing. After his long absence, N is impatient to get down to facts, but their conversation is interrupted by the arrival of the Turks, Kiamil and his mother, of whom N till then knew nothing. His displeasure is matched by his brother Michailos' amusement at the reunion: the two women and Kiamil are left to their coffee, N and brother adjourn next door to continue their dialogue:

—A Turk mother healed in our house for seven months! And since when has mother been a nurse to Turks? I asked, scowling with indignation. I should note that Michailos was in the habit of making jokes about our mother's excesses, the more gladly as he paid for them readily and without complaint from his own purse. Nothing gave him more pleasure than to mimic our mother acting under the influence of some excess of affection, the elements of which he would twist comically in a way altogether his own. The forbearance of our good mother, who laughed herself as often as she heard him, implanted this bad habit in him all the more. That is why, when he saw me so indignant at the news,

—Listen to what I'm saying, he said. If you mean to take everything so crossly, I won't tell you anything. *You'll spoil my story.* Better leave it for another day, so you can have a good laugh, so mother can laugh a bit,—*all these days and she hasn't had a really good laugh, poor thing.*

—Come on! I said then. Mother seems very happy with the visit, and she's totally preoccupied with her Turks, *while I can't stand them.* So till they drink up their coffee and we're rid of them, tell me the story.

—Listen then, he said to me. You know how worried mother was when you left. And it's not just that she was worried, she wouldn't leave anyone else in peace. Someone passes by, she stops him in the street. Someone turns up from some place, she'd go ask him: had they seen you, had they heard of you. You know her. Early one morning we were picking melons out in the field. Suddenly she sees a traveller pass by. She won't let him go about his business, off she runs to the fence.

—May the hour be good, uncle!

—Many years to you, ma'am!

—You come from Europe?

—No, ma'am, from my village. Where is this Europe?

—How should I know? It's where my son is. You heard folks tell of my son?

—No, ma'am. And what's your son's name?

—As if I knew myself! His godfather baptised him Georgis, and his father was Michailos the tradesman, my husband. But see, he's moved up in the world and got himself one of those *eddicated* [*sic*: ἀπὸ τοῦ περιγραμμάτου] names; and now, if they write about him in the newspapers, I don't know, like, if it's my boy they mean or some European!

—*The story, Michailos! The story about the Turk!* I cut in impatiently.

—Wait a minute! he said. The story came after the conversation. After the conversation, you see our mother go and cut the best and biggest melon.

—Won't you take some fruit from our garden, uncle?

—No thankyou, I've nowhere to put it.

—No matter, uncle, I'll cut it so you can eat it here.

—No thankyou, ma'am, I have a stomach ache.

—Please do me the favour. You see, I have a boy in foreign parts, and I have an aching heart. And as I can't send it to my boy, eat some yourself, as you're a foreigner. Perhaps he'll find one too from someone else.

The man lost his patience. —*Canin*, my good woman, you're a Christian! You may have a son abroad, but how am I to blame, I'm fasting, why stuff all that cholera into my stomach? D'you think I'm tired of life? I've a wife waiting for me, kids to feed. But if you really want to make use of that melon, send it off to old Mourtos' inn. There's a foreigner near there wrestling with death, he's been in a fever three weeks now. Once he tastes this cholera, believe you me, he'll be rid of his fever and his fever will be rid of him.

—*Get on with it! I said to him. Are we through with anecdotes? Begin the story now!*

—*Wait a bit! he answered, cut to the quick. D'you think we're in Europe where they sell meat without bones? I'm telling you the story as it happened. If you don't like it, leave it.* We'll go and see the Turkish *hanim* lady!

—I just wish you could have been there, he continued, so as to see mother when she heard that. —Christ and Panagia, all-holy mother, *it's my boy!* And the melon dropped from her hands, fell flat as a pancake it did. She straightened her scarf and took to the road.

(Greek pp.70–72, cf. English 91–93,
with added modifications and emphases)

N does not want to know his own role in the story, how his uneducated brother paid out of his own pocket for his mother's indulgences, why his mother was driven to distraction by his own absence to adopt Kiamil in his stead. One is reminded of the *Timarion*, in which Kydion's interjections to the narrator to tell the story in proper order interrupt the narrative flow but highlight the narrating instant. Here, it is the narrator's *interlocutor* who affords the reader clues to the mystery. Anecdotal digression may be despised in literary discourse, but men of letters are often slow to grasp what is important in a real-life story!

Vizyenos' use of myth and oral discourse is not decorative folklorism, as with Drosinis; it problematizes and probes a more urgent question relevant to his time—are such killings the result of familial or ethnic conflict? Both: familial because motivated by personal greed and kinship vendettas, not the direct result of war; but ethnic too because the story unfolds against the backdrop of war, which dictates the depersonalization of the enemy.[26] Despite her loss, the Greek mother understands this and continues to care for Kiamil not as a Turk but as her son. As in "My Mother's Sin," the adult narrator cannot accept his mother's need to adopt another in place of a child that has been killed.

Μοσκὸβ-Σελήμ ("Moskov-Selim," story 6, 1895) is about an elderly and gentle Turk, generally believed to be crazy, who lives in Kaynarca (Kainardza), a village near Vizye. Known as Moskov-Selim because of his obsession with everything Russian, Selim discloses to N the story of his life and how he came to reject his Turkish ethnicity and adopt in its place a Russian identity. Born the third son to a well-to-do bey's family in Istanbul, as a child Selim was dressed as a girl and brought up in the harem by his mother in her desire for a daughter, and was thereafter rejected by his father. At the outbreak of the Crimean War (1854), his elder brother Hasan (father's favorite) was called up, but his nerve failed him and eighteen-year-old Selim went in his place, thereby hoping at last to gain his father's respect. He served for seven years, participating heroically in the battle of Silistria only to be cheated of his medals and posted to menial labors in the Romanian Carpathians. He returned to Istanbul to face a chain of catastrophes: Hasan put to death as a deserter; his mother dead from grief; his father a drunk; and a prison sentence for his own complicity in Hasan's desertion. When Herzegovina revolted against the Sultan in 1862, he enlisted and served for two years, returning home to marry the girl his mother had chosen for him on her deathbed. When Herzegovina revolted again in 1875, once more Selim joined up, fighting the Serbs in the battle of Alexinac (1876) and defending Plevna against the Russians (1877), only to find himself abandoned as dead by fellow Turks near the battlefield and a Russian prisoner of war. It was his first encounter with the "hereditary enemy" of the Ottomans outside a military uniform—and what did he find? Not the bestial cruelty he had been brought up to believe he would face, but compassion and kindness. After deportation to Russia, he was offered hospitality by an elderly veteran whose widowed daughter he lived with as wife until repatriated in 1879 to face yet more cruelty at the hands of the Turkish authorities. Small wonder he grew to hate the cruel Turks and admire Russians, setting up a Russian-style log cabin at Kaynarca to end his days in solitude, fed by an inner faith that one day, the Russians will come!

As usual in Vizyenos' stories, there is an ambivalent coda. Following the coup against the Sultan in Bulgaria (1886), local folk tell Selim "the Russians have come". He suffers a stroke, assumed to be from elation, but in fact, as he reveals on his sickbed, from the realization that his renunciation of Turkish ethnicity and religion was an illusion. N assures him that the Russians have not come and never will; Selim suffers a fatal stroke.

The story is presented by its Narrator in the form of a "documented bi-ography" (Greek, p. 202, English, pp. 186–7), and it is therefore not surpris-ing to find a wealth of authenticated detail in Selim's account of his mili-tary experiences. As in "Killer," the historical references—both actual and implied—have a symbolic dimension as well. As one who fought in the Crimean War and its aftermath (1854–61), in Herzegovina (1862–64), and in Herzegovina and Serbia (1875–76), Selim was actively engaged between the ages of eighteen and forty-three in all the major Ottoman campaigns against the Russians. Furthermore, he tells his story and eventually ends his life in Kaynarca, renowned not only for the purity of its springs (described by the narrator at some length (Greek p. 203, English pp. 187–88)) but also as the scene where the Treaty of Küçük-Kaynarca (1774) marked Russian victory in the great Russo-Turkish War (1768–74) with terms intended to halt further Ottoman advances west and north, and at the same time to pre-clude Russian interference on the side of the Balkan peoples' revolt. The story implies not just Selim's activities but 118 years of Russians and Turks as "hereditary enemies" that involved several chapters of Greek history. In the later eighteenth century, the Greeks pinned their hopes on the belief that "one day the Russians will come," as in the song θὰ ἔρθει ὁ Μόσκοβος ("Moskovos will come"), hopes fed by belief in a prophecy at-tributed to the Byzantine emperor, Leo the Wise, that the city would be liberated 320 years after its fall, that is, in 1773. In fact, the terms of Küçük-Kaynarca turned Greek hopes for liberation from Russia to France.

These details are relevant to the ambivalent close of Vizyenos' last story. From the moment Selim talks of his "conversion," N begins to take over Selim's story, summarizing and interpreting his feelings with ingenious guesswork and psychological analysis, allowing Selim to make only the odd interjection on his personal life thereafter (Greek pp. 238–39, English pp. 217–18). N then spends the journey from Kaynarca back to Athens recon-structing Selim's experiences in accordance (the reader notices) with his own desires:[27] many Turks today *want* the Sultan to relinquish claims on Europe and remove his throne to Damascus or Baghdad where it belongs (Greek pp. 246–49, English pp. 224–26). After Montenegro, Serbia, Roma-nia, Bosnia, and Herzegovina had fallen away from the Ottoman Empire, news of the Bulgarian coup (1886) found N back in Vizye: like everyone else, he assumes Selim's stroke when told "the Russians have come" was from joy. Visiting his bedside, N and a Greek doctor find his condition se-rious but not terminal; with rest and peace of mind, he will recover, the doctor affirms. After Selim's disclosure that his attack was not from joy but from painful realization that "blood can never become water," N's assurance that the Russians have not come and never will provokes a second seizure.

Doctor pushes N away, telling Selim to look after himself and never mind the Russians. After a prolonged convulsion, Selim dies. "He died from joy," diagnoses the doctor. Κι ὁ Τοῦρκος ἔμεινε Τοῦρκος "And the Turk remained a Turk," concludes the narrator of this sixth and last of Vizyenos' stories (Greek pp. 249–52, English pp. 226–29).

It is not possible to reconstruct Selim's feelings at the end, beyond his own broken comments on the conflicting emotions that seized him on hearing the "good news." What is certain is that N's final revelation, intended to improve Selim's condition, actually killed him and that as Selim concluded his story (told for the first time), N felt increasingly obliged to fill in the details. Did Selim die not from joy but from the accumulation of painful memories stirred up by conversation with a well-meaning but opinionated Greek, whose concluding comment has just a hint of dismissive contempt?

Ethnicity and sanity: both Turks, Kiamil and Selim, are driven insane by conflict between their ethnic duty to kill familial / hereditary foes and by their personal dependence on the nurture of the "other" mother / wife / country. If the Greek narrators end with ambivalence on the question of guilt, but with conviction on ethnic difference, the prologue to "Moskov-Selim" differs from the other stories in that it is addressed in an *authorial* voice to "you good, strange Turk," fearing the displeasure of Turkish and Greek readers: "I do not doubt that the fanatics of your race will curse the memory of a 'believer' for opening up the secrets of his heart before the defiled eyes of an 'infidel.' I fear lest the fanatics of my race will revile a Greek author (*syngraphéa*), because he did not conceal your virtue (*aretē*), or did not substitute a Christian hero in the telling of your tale" (Greek 202, English 187) Less than one year after the story's publication, Vizyenos suffered a stroke in the asylum to which his fellow Greeks had consigned him and died. Kiamil and Selim, like Klara and Paschalis in another of Vizyenos' stories to be discussed below, presage in fiction what was to be his lot in life.

What is Vizyenos trying to tell us? Not the story of his life, despite the first-person narration and the splitting / doubling of narrators and characters. Nor does he choose to depict pure Greek mores. Rather, he explores paradoxical relations within and between families, genders, generations, and ethnicities, above all the paralogic dimensions of the mind. Each story can be read as a different novelistic "genre exercise": autobiography; travelogue; detective story; romance; wondertale; documented biography.[28] As with Roidis, however, appearances are deceptive: each story undermines in its own way the very genre it seems to adopt as model. Unlike Roidis, but rather in the manner of Cavafy, Vizyenos distances reader from text, subject from object, while at the same time expressing and evoking strong emotion by probing the difference between the two. He achieves this by exploring the processes that render problematic the decoding of messages between sender and receiver.[29] At the same time, his juxtaposition of different novelistic and literary genres has the variety and musicality of a symphony. Let us look more closely at how he achieves this in "Consequences" and "Journey" through use of two quintessentially Byzantine features of narrative craft: antithesis and ekphrasis.

4. Antithesis as a Strategy of Reading / Writing

Henry Maguire (1981, 53) has demonstrated the interconnections between art and literature in Byzantium through antithesis and ekphrasis: "in the Byzantine church, antithesis was more than a figure of speech; it was a habit of thought." Antithesis entails not just the rhetorical juxtaposition of opposites but also the paradoxical ways in which every theme, event, character, or state of mind can be experienced and perceived in terms of its opposite or defined as what it is not. It is more than the binary oppositions of structuralism, in that it explores positives as well as negatives, similarities as well as differences. Antithesis is imbued with greater feeling than is implied by the deconstuctionist terms of Derrida; the closest approximation in modern literary theory is Bakhtin's concept of "the dialogic imagination."[30]

In Vizyenos' stories, antithesis becomes the major means of defining character, plot, and genre. If his characters seem to a Western eye a series of one-dimensional re-presentations of endlessly similar figures,[31] they can be interpreted more subtly as infinite splittings or doublings of self and other—a poignant expression of the impossibility of a perfect whole and of the difficulties inherent in all forms of human communication. In Vizyenos, plot is unfolded not by an omniscient narrator, but through antithetical dialogue between narrator (henceforth N) and interlocutors, dialogues within dialogue, and —most subtly—dialogue between reader and text, the truth of which is a matter of interpretation. Antithetical modes of narration are not readily compatible with a linear or rational ordering of events: it is as if we are moving in a realm of mood rather than of tense and across space as well as time.

Αἰ συνέπειαι τῆς παλαιᾶς ἱστορίας ("Consequences of the Old Story," story 4: 1884) describes N's experiences as a Greek graduate student of psychology at the University of Göttingen in Germany, in the course of which his friend Paschalis, Greek graduate student of metallurgy, dies of a heart attack during a mining accident in Klausthal, at precisely the same instant as does the mad German girl whom N has earlier visited in a mental asylum, assumed to be the beautiful Klara, object of Paschalis' hopeless passion.

How does antithesis function on the level of character? The Greek word *ēthopoiēía*, as we saw in Chapter 4, has resonances other than "characterisation." Less the stamping of a figure (*charaktēr*), more a process of re-presenting moral qualities, as on stage. It is therefore not surprising to find that each of the protagonists in "Consequences" seems to impersonate antithetical aspects of the author's own sense of self and other. N and Paschalis are closest friends, yet mirror images. Where N provides rational explanations for *sanitas* (physical and mental), Paschalis is romantic and mystical. Where N claims authority to interpret as "formidable philologist," Paschalis puts his faith in poetry and mythology. In their everday lives, N leads an unsullied intellectual existence, while Paschalis goes down the mine every day and comes back physically dirtied, yet with a stern sense of moral and aesthetic purity. Both are complementary opposites of the Greek abroad and likewise of the author's own experience as a graduate student of psychology in Germany, who also happened to engage in mining activites in Thrace. In contrast to the German poet Goethe's successful mining activities during the Weimar period in the 1770s, Vizyenos' ventures ended in failure.[32]

Paschalis and Klara are—according to Paschalis' narrations within N's story—perfect "soul mates," one destined for the other but separated in life by cultural and class differences, as their names—Greek and German counterparts—suggest.[33] He is an impecunious Greek studying abroad; she is the only daughter of his eminent and wealthy German professor. He is dark, morose, and introvert; she is blonde, flirtatious, and extrovert. Both love music, opera, and skating on frozen lakes. She has the advantage of wealth and leisure to indulge these pleasures; he pays dearly with health and life by excavating gems from "the navel of the earth" in order to purify his soul.

There are two other shadowy figures in the background. The first is the mad German girl in the mental asylum near Göttingen, witnessed by N before his meeting with Paschalis. Suffering from a rare psychiatric disorder, thought to be from a broken heart, the girl sings to her own harp, then smashes the harp and thrashes about the blue velvet of her padded, dome-shaped cell. Is she Klara? N assumes so only when he hears Paschalis' vision of himself and Klara united in heaven; but the evidence for this assumption is purely circumstantial. N is so certain that the girl in the asylum *is* Klara that he fails to ask Paschalis the simplest question which could have clinched the identification, thereby forcing us, as readers, to query his motives for concealment.[34]

The second shadowy figure is the ostensible originator of the old story,

Evlalia, who had seduced then jilted Paschalis in Athens: he was a virgin; she wanted men with experience. Evlalia, whose name means "the eloquent one" (*eu-lalos*, although her voice is never heard), was a washerwoman's daughter to whom Paschalis gave lessons gratis in exchange for free laundering of dirty clothes as he worked his way through university.[35] As a consequence, he feels his soul is sullied, its inner gems trampled by swine, and proves unable to respond to Klara's passion; yet he is fiercely eloquent in his denouncement of Evlalia in language redolent with images from Christ's Sermon on the Mount and Plotinus' essay *On the Beautiful* (p. 140; cf. Matt. 7:6)

Ethopoieia is not "stamp" or "character," but rather the scrutinization of every persona under the antithetical twists of the narrative lens. "Plot" is equally recalcitrant to conventional analysis. The Greek word *plokē* "web" implies the weaving together of different strands. That is precisely what "Consequences" is. There is no straight story line, only an exploration into shifting categories of language, sanity, gender, ethnicity, and artistic and scientific discourses, antithetically intertwined through imagery and wordplay and by intertextual allusion to Greek and German poetry and mythology across the ages.

To unpick the web, let us start with beginning and end. The story commences with a pedantic excursus on the rigors of the German winter, which, as N confides to his Athenian readers, have afflicted him with a vexatious cough, a common enough ailment which nevertheless prevented him attending public lectures for more than two semesters because his coughing bothered his otherwise hospitable German fellow students (104–5; Eng. 99–100). Climatology is a recurrent theme throughout the story, connected with mineralogy but also metaphorically with ethics and art and by wordplay with psychology (*psycho-logía*). N's professor, Herr H★★★, an adherent of the neuropathologist R. H. Lotze, if not Lotze himself, insists that his cough is not the result of German cold (*psýchos*) but of a weakness of the soul (*psychē*), or the Psi factor.[36] The story concludes with N's citation in Greek of Goethe's poem "Über allen Gipfeln ist Ruh" (1780), best known to English readers in Schubert's rendering as "Wanderers Nachtlied": "warte nur, [warte nur,] balde ruhest du auch" [o wait, wait, soon you too will find peace] are the last words he whispers on the death of Paschalis, in Vizyenos' Greek translation (Greek 167; English 162).

The intervening narration takes us from the confined spaces of a mental asylum near Göttingen to a miner's cottage in Klausthal. After his exclusion from class, N is persuaded by Herr H★★★ to receive treatment for his "nervous weakness" (*nevrikē asthéneia*), the cause of his persistent cough. Their interview is rescheduled, on the excuse of a sudden emergency, at the asylum where Herr H★★★ has a serious case of a girl suffering from an incurable psychotic disorder, brought on by an unhappy love affair. Fearful of his own incarceration in the institution, N arrives to witness, first, a crazed warder preaching to pigs and chickens (a parodic aside on Saints Francis and Antony?), then a young German girl confined to her cell: she sings of abandoned love, then suffers a hysterical seizure, shattering her harp. Herr H★★★ and N leave. Back in the professor's office, N announces his decision to go for a brief vacation in the mining village of Klausthal in the Harz mountains to see his friend Paschalis, who is engaged in metallurgical research. Herr H★★★ objects: the altitude is too great, the climate treacherous, and Greeks abroad are too fond of one another's company, thereby avoiding salutary practice in their deficient German!

Disregarding sound advice (as do ballad and wondertale protagonists), N goes to Klausthal, where he arrives on a clear day to find Paschalis thin and nervous. Confident that he will prove his professor wrong about the climate, he looks forward to mountain walks to improve their health. But next day the weather turns, and the two are confined indoors for days on end by the kind of torrential rains that occur at high altitudes. Paschalis enters a deep depression, which N tries to cheer him out of by reminding him of the old story of Evlalia from their student days at Athens University. Sure that Paschalis has fully recovered from this old story, he mentions it as a joke, only to provoke his friend's violent reaction and Paschalis' account of the story's unhappy consequences.

On one level, the story seems to concern illness—physical and mental—and its various causes and effects, including love and death. But psychology and medicine are intertwined with other discourses, from science (metallurgy and climatology) to art (opera, song, and dance; mythology and literature; philology and language) and ethical (chastity, morality, honesty). Let us begin with Greek and German poetry, where Vizyenos seems to be playing a game of literary paradox—amusing and at the same time serious. As a German philhellene, Herr H★★★ regales N with Homeric citations, delivered in impeccable ancient Greek, yet rendered incomprehensible to the reader by the author's mercilessly accurate transcription of the German professor's Erasmian pronunciation into modern Greek, as in his exhortation to his pupil, Ἀϊὲν ἀριστοϊαϊν καϊ γιουπέεροκον ἔμεναϊ πάντοον Τοϊτόνοον (Greek 105–6; English 101); or in his wish Ἀϊ γκὰρ Τσόυ τε πάτερ, καϊ Ἀτεενάϊεε καϊ Ἄπολλον / τοϊοῦτοϊ ντέκα μοϊ ζουμφράντμονες ἀϊεν Ἀχαϊῶν (Greek 110; English 104). The effect can perhaps be rendered as "alvegs alle Toytowns besser und tsourpass tsu" and "Ach, Faater Dzoys und Ateenayee und Applon, / zat tzen coonslers of Achayoy var immer mine!" My pseudo-Germanic rendering is meant to convey what the Homeric tags might have sounded like to N: "always to do better than and surpass the Teutons" and "Father Zeus, Apollo and Athena, would that the Achaeans always have ten such councilors." But our Greek author gets his own back on his fictitious German professor by putting into Greek the mad German girl's rendering of Goethe's "Kennst du das Land / wo die Zitronen blühn?" (sung by the mysterious minstrel-harpist's daughter in *Wilhelm Meister*), then making her curse all great epic and national poets (implicitly Homer and Goethe) for their inability to express suffering, only to break out into her own stunningly beautiful lyrics and melody. There follows an extended ekphrasis on the impossibility of describing music in words. Her own song, presumably sung in German but rendered in Greek, is in fact the author's own lyric poem Ἀνεμόνη "Anemone," and it is the intensity of passion it arouses that causes her hysterical reaction.

The German professor's appropriation of Homer, N's of Goethe, and the mad girl's rejection of both in favor of Vizyenos suggest something more than a literary game. For Beaton, citations from *Faust* are "characteristic of Vizyenos' treatment of realism" because the story is "an extended commentary on "Gretchen" and 'Walpürgisnacht' "; and for Chryssanthopoulos, the text "desire[s] to show a debt to Goethe and the German romantic movement."[37] Is it so simple? Goethe's "Über allen Gipfeln ist Ruh," the poem which frames the Klausthal part of the narrative, was inspired at the height of the German romantic movement of neo-Hellenism by Alkman's beautiful lyric fragment (frag. 34 Page): εὕδουσι δ᾽ ὀρέων κορυφαί τε καὶ φάραγγες / εὕδουσι δ᾽ οἰωνῶν φῦλα τανυπτερύγων. There is irony and pathos for the contemporary Greek in the German poet's assimilation of Alkman at a time when neo-Hellenism was introduced to refer only to ancient Greece, and in N's reappropriation of Alkman, through Goethe, as a lament for exile and death.[38] *Xenitiá* ("Exile") is a familiar theme in Greek folklore, frequently exploited by Vizyenos, but it was also a condition of Greek rural life, experienced by author, narrator, and interlocutor. At the same time, the concept of exile, especially when associated with unhappy love, was a favorite theme of such German romantic poets as Goethe, Schiller, Müller, and Heine, whose lyrics have been immortalized in the Lieder of Beethoven, Schubert, Schumann, Wolf, and Brahms. What can be sublimated in German as romantic lyric is experienced as grim reality by contemporary Greeks: textual clues lead us to associate sickness, both mental and physical, with Greek-German connections—and the Greek psychē, not German psŷchos, "cold," gets the blame!

Another target of Vizyenos' elusive ironies seems to be Philology. Toward the end of his narration, Paschalis discloses a series of five letters: one received from Klara; one he wrote to her but destroyed; another he sent [to

Klara] too late; one he received from Klara's female companion, Mrs. B.; and another from her father. The last contains—for him—incontrovertible proof of Klara's death. N seizes the letter and, "formidable philologist" (*deinós philólogos*) as he claims to be, reinterprets it: Professor M. is not saying that an unexpected evil (death) has deprived him of his only consolation (his daughter) but that an unexpected evil (Paschalis) threatens to steal away his daughter to the other ends of the earth, and that he, Paschalis, should therefore keep away. They argue about shifting moods and tenses in German and Greek; but, since the letter is cited only partially in Greek, the reader has nothing but N's renderings to rely on. (As Herr H★★★ had noted, N's German was not beyond reproach). Paschalis then reveals his certainty about Klara's death from his vision of her in Heaven the previous night. Only then does N connect Klara with the girl in the asylum. Remarkably, he says nothing to Paschalis of the incident. Why not? The reader is left wondering whether Paschalis would not have preferred to be told that Klara, if she was indeed the girl in the asylum, was waiting only for his return from the navel of the earth for them to live happily ever after, as in the wondertale, than that her father despised him as an impecunious Greek abroad who had stolen her heart and mind. N's credentials as clever philologist may be an open question, but he has learned precious little psychology! Can N be concealing his own infatuation with the girl and his suppressed jealousy of Paschalis? And why did N's impulsive decision to visit Paschalis follow immediately after the scene in the girl's cell? Did he feel a potential victim as a Greek, diagnosed as suffering from "nervous weakness" in an insane asylum by his German professor, and instinctively drawn to his compatriot, Paschalis, whom he torments, wittingly or unwittingly?

By not disclosing his thesis, N forces the reader into the role of detective. It is not an easy one. Try as we might, we can neither prove nor disprove his identification of Klara with the girl in the asylum. Yet on the last morning, he cheerfully lets Paschalis go down the mine, although Paschalis has just told him it will be a veritable death trap after the storms! When he receives Herr H★★★'s letter after Paschalis' funeral, he glosses over the "good old man's chiding" for having disregarded his advice, noting only of the postscript: the girl we visited in the asylum died three days ago at midnight (precisely the moment Paschalis had his vision of Klara in heaven). N congratulates himself for having disobeyed—at least he has been able to bury his closest friend. Would Paschalis have died had N not visited him? is only one of the unanswerable questions we are left with at the end of the story. And are Psychology and Philology not as ambivalently invoked as Folklore?

To turn now to mythology and the wondertale, the girl in the asylum asks N, "My lover went down there to dig for diamonds, big ones! That's why he hasn't come back yet. He's got a good hammer, he'll go to the center of the earth and find them, then come back. . . . How hot is the center of the earth?" (112; my paraphase). The oblique reference recalls both the miner-dwarf of German folklore and the Greek wondertale "Navel of the Earth," in which the princess is rescued from her obsession of building towers out of human heads by the youth who dares to enter the Underworld and return with jewels as proof of the earth's secret. Vizyenos plays with Greek and German gender stereotypes to produce an apparently romantic-tragic end, but he undermines romantic closure through antithetical juxtaposition of artistic and scientific discourses. The wondertale theme provides the only tenuous but textual link between the girl N saw in the asylum and Paschalis' Klara.[39]

The link operates through literal and metaphorical associations of jewels and mining: the girl's belief that her lover has gone to the center of the earth to bring back diamonds transfers to the realm of myth Paschalis' actual mining activities in Klausthal: every day, weather permitting, he goes down the mine, and by the time of N's visit his collection of specimens inspires N to consult Karl Vogt's geological treatise, in a train of thought that leads to the question of purity and triggers the old story of Evlalia. Whereas the girl in the asylum understood jewels literally as precious stones to be brought back from the center of the earth to adorn her wedding ring, Paschalis sees them metonymically, as crystalizations of the purest and innermost human emotions. The washerwoman's daughter sullied him, rendering him unworthy and impotent to respond to Klara's passion—*psychrós* "cold," as the girl in the asylum says of her lover, in yet another inversion of conventional expectations (it is Germans who are supposed to be cold, while Greeks are hot). "She wallowed in swinish fashion in the most tender emotions, the most divine feelings of my heart," Paschalis says of Evlalia, who stole his virginity, "and when she had had her fill, she polluted it with her poison, she muddied it . . . ! She rolled around in it like a filthy pig! . . . She rendered it an unworthy seat of the noble, the beautiful, the sublime, for which it had been destined!" (Greek 137; English 127) In vain N remonstrates—how can a cheap woman's behavior damage the worth of a pure heart? "Diamonds and pearls," Paschalis retorts, "when once they are set before swine and chewed and trampled by them, become unsuitable to adorn even the most humble head, let alone to be raised to the height of a queen's diadem." Then can't they be washed? the narrator asks with somewhat tactless jocularity. "You can wash 'physical' jewels and clean them," he replies sternly. "But 'moral' ones? What about feelings and thoughts, the heart's only treasures? With what acid with what soap will you wash away that moral filth . . . ? Their stains are indelible" (Greek 139–40; English 129–30).

Something curious is going on here. It is true that Greek men from backgrounds like Paschalis', sensitized by self-privations, may develop stern moral standards for men and women alike. Paschalis' revulsion for Evlalia is in conformity with ethnographic evidence.[40] What is different is Paschalis' insistence that he has been *permanently* sullied by the affair: even holy men had youthful lapses only to be cleansed so as to give greater glory to the grace of God.[41] Had N taken a religious, rather than rationalist, stance toward his friend, he might have initiated a healing process. Had N taken a socially aware moral stance, questioning Paschalis' reasons for despising a poor Greek girl's sexuality while aspiring to unattainably high standards of purity in himself for a relationship with Klara (whose chastity he never questions), the outcome could have been different.

Paschalis confides at one point how the sentiment between himself and Klara, only daughter of his professor, arose. Klara was surrounded by admirers, with whom she liked to flirt. Paschalis frequented her father's home and enjoyed hospitality at dinner over academic conversations, without flirting with Klara, as did most other guests. His apparent indifference fired her passion. Some days after they attended together a performance of Wagner's *The Flying Dutchman*, in which the lead part was played by an actor "dressed in black, with black eyes, black hair and beard, and so pale and mournful that many thought they recognized me on stage" (Paschalis as a kind of Charos or, as in Wagner's plot, as one who is cursed to roam the world until rescued by the sacrifice of pure love), Klara confided in him her love of the Flying Dutchman—every German girl's ideal of the dark foreigner, as N points out! (Greek 142; English 131–32). Opera is just one of the media through which passion is conceived, declared and played out in this story. Another is on literal ice but in metaphorical dance: on a nearby frozen lake, Klara—like a Nereid—skates beautifully and guides Paschalis' unpracticed steps, moving hand in hand heavenward to sublimity as "two flying as one."[42] Klara and Paschalis are German and Greek mirror images of each other, in soul and name (ice is to lake as heat to flooded mine). And both appear to meet their death at the same instant.

Two fly as one: first, when love is conceived at the performance of *The Flying Dutchman*; second, when romantic passion reaches its height on the frozen lake; third, and most mysteriously, when Paschalis evokes, from his depression during a sleepless night at the height of the fearful howlings of mountain wind and rain, his vision of Klara in heaven, not long after the Feast of the Assumption on 15 August: "As I longed for her . . . , so she appeared: beneath the azure sky; under the sweet light of Paradise; in her white angel's dress; with her blonde hair flowing down her back; holding her golden harp in her tiny hands. . . . And the sounds of her harp, the music of her voice . . ." (Greek 160; English 146). He breaks off, visibly shaken by his own emotion and by the effect of his words on N, who recalls in a flash that he had seen this very same "vision" only a few days before in the asylum at Göttingen. While N is mentally engaged in fitting his recollection of the girl to Paschalis' vision of Klara, his friend's mind soars out of this world: "But my heart tells me . . . that she did not die entirely. Our souls still communicate with each other. You see, they were predestined one for the other. My own, in the frenzy of an untimely passion, risked its destiny and lost it. In this way our early union was frustrated. But up there . . . oh, up there I shall bring her a heart cleansed in my tears, purified through penitence. And we shall be united forever, forever!—What is life?—Besides, I feel it. My soul is impatient. . . . Its wings have grown large, and strong" (Greek 161–62; English 147).[43]

The next day, the weather clears, and Paschalis wakes up in an excellent mood: they will go to Caroline. To Caroline? asks N. Who is she? A mine thousands of feet below the Harz mountains, to be reached only from the snow-capped peak above Klausthal, answers Paschalis. Swallowing down his cold coffee, N declares himself ready to leave at once. The way you're dressed? Paschalis asks, commenting on his casual attire. You don't expect me to have brought my Sunday best to go down a mine! N retorts. Oh no, but you will need a miner's outfit, otherwise you'll end up like poor old Heine in a mess. And what happened to Heine? He visited Caroline with the clothes he was wearing, says Paschalis, and came back a laughingstock, with his best suit dirtied up. Heine quipped, "I've known many Carolines in my life, but not one of them was this filthy!" Paschalis and N chuckle over Heine's joke, then Paschalis goes off to a morning's routine checkup at his usual mine. But if you know how Greek myth works, you realize that change of status at marriage and death may hinge on change of dress: "Tell me, my Kostandis, is it for joy or grief? Shall I put on my gold, or come just as I am? Come, Aretoula, come just as you are" ("Dead Brother": see above, pages 193–205). By midday Paschalis is brought back dead from a heart seizure suffered during an accident resulting from underground flooding.

Dirt and washing, clothes and jewels are shifting metaphors of exchange: Paschalis worked his way through Athens University by exchanging his dirty clothes for lessons to the washerwoman's daughter, only to have his purity of soul stained in his own eyes. The mad girl is expecting her lover to bring back diamonds from the navel of the earth, while Paschalis seeks them in vain from the depths of his soul without questioning Klara's purity—that is his and her tragedy. N is reluctant to climb Snow-cap in order to reach Caroline on the Harz peaks because he thinks it will be wet, only to be reminded that after such storms water never stays on the peaks, or even in the gullies, but rushes straight down into the navel of the earth. Whereas Heine makes a joke of dirty Caroline, Paschalis pays with his life for Evlalia's filth. One thinks of the beautiful but bitter Greek song of death in xenitiá:

I'm thinking once, I'm thinking twice, three times, five times over,
I'll go to live abroad in a distant foreign land.
As many mountains as I cross, to all I give my orders:
—Mountains, don't let it snow, nor you, plains, be frozen,
until I've been and gone and then come home again.
I find snow on the mountains and frost on the plains,
and I turned back again to desolate foreign parts.
I take foreigners as brothers, foreigners as nurse-mothers,
and I take a foreign foster sister so she can wash my clothes.
She washes them once, twice, three times, five times over,
but at the fifth time over she throws them on the streets.
—Foreigner, take your clothes, take your dirty clothes.
I don't want foreigners here, nor do I bury them.

(Danforth 1982, 92; my translation)

As in the song, images of climate are entwined with the themes of exile and mining, in a manner at once mythic and scientific, ethical and cosmological. Paschalis is anxious to take N to Harz's snow-capped peak, where Goethe had imagined "the most magical and extravagant scenes" of *Faust*, the Walpürgisnacht, or frenzied nocturnal dance of witches and goblins (Greek 129–30; English 121). Once again, there are some incongruous cross-renderings of German demonic forms into their modern Greek counterparts.[44] The howling gales and lashing storms that break out the next day and continue unabated are described in mythical terms which convey the intensity of terror and turmoil, at once physical and mental, as the two friends, confined indoors, unfold the consequences of old stories. As for mining, Vizyenos exploits Greek and German mythology as a backdrop to the girl's madness and Paschalis' death; yet there is also a connection between technical expertise in mining and the art of poetry, which escapes the notice of N, if not the reader. Paschalis is the more poetic of the two friends, despite his manual occupation, which makes him look like one of those homely figures of German folklore, as N notes. Paschalis also knows his Goethe and Heine better, reminding N that the best scenes of *Faust* were inspired on the Harz mountains and that Heine made a sexual joke out of his humiliating acquaintance with filthy Caroline. The Klausthal part of the narrative is framed both by Goethe's poem in poetic discourse and by the miners' strange everyday greeting "Glück auf," rendered into Greek as ἔσο τυχερός, "be lucky," which underlines the closed nature of the German mining community, warning outsiders against mocking local superstitions in a profession in which death is always at hand. Goethe's involvement with this same mining region proved productive both politically and artistically; Vizyenos' Thracian project led to failure. According to Vizyenos' perception of aesthetics, art and poetry are gems, excavated from the navel of the earth and elevated to mountain peaks by the Muses, to be cultivated by the pure in soul: "verses στίχοι . . . are diamonds and pearls most bright, with the difference that they enrich and adorn breasts and heads not from the outside, but from inside" (1893, 361). It is a perception which accords well with the morality and cosmology of the wondertale; but it is even closer to the Neoplatonist doctrines of Plotinus, whose treatise Περὶ τοῦ καλοῦ (*On the Beautiful*) was the subject of Vizyenos' inaugural presentation at Athens University. "Consequences" was published one year before his appointment was confirmed. He was working on the dissertation at the same time as composing this story of the consequences of the old story (P. Kaligas 1995, 17–24).

Mythical and scientific approaches are juxtaposed, calling into question the objectivity of truth and, as in other stories, N's single-minded rationalism. Can Vizyenos' antithetical modes, combining literary citation and parody and dialogic interaction between characters and discourses with rigorous control of myth and history, be judged according to criteria of European romanticism and realism? Are his stories deficient in characterization and plot? Whether or not the author is aware of the connection, his aesthetic modes of perception develop, in a modern literary context, those of Byzantine literature and art. And what *was* the old story? *Istoría* means not only "tale, narrative, and history" but also "process of enquiry, story told in a work of art." Re-read across time and space, the title can be interpreted as the consequences of the dialogue between Greek and German Hellenism from Homer and Alkman to Goethe and Heine, which proved paradoxical for the modern Greek. Vizyenos' aesthetics are closer to those of the Ottoman and Byzantine worlds than they are to those of the Greek nation-state.

5. Ekphrasis: Between Time and Place

In Τὸ μόνον τῆς ζωῆς του ταξείδιον, "The Only Journey of His Life" (story 5: 1885), Georgis tells of childhood fantasies, fed by a grandfather's tales of travel and adventure; of youthful aspirations as a tailor's apprentice in Istanbul; and of his dreamlike ride back to Thrace to visit his dying grandfather, who shatters his illusions by revealing that his only travels were in wondertales. "Journey" is no less enigmatic than "Consequences." But the level of narration appears to be that of a ten-year-old child who cannot tell the difference between reality and fantasy, not that of a graduate student of psychology. Perhaps that is why it lends itself to ekphrasis rather than antithesis as a key to unlocking the narrative modes? Ekphrasis is a set description, rhetorical in style, in which words (*léxeis*) and images (*eikónes*) are analogically counterposed to paint a word picture. The object of description may vary: painting, sculpture, or landscape, especially viewed from an akropolis.

The story, aptly described by Kostis Palamas as *oneiródrama*, "dream drama" (cited in Moullas 1980, 261), is in four parts, or symphonic movements, each in a different key and tempo, rounded off with a coda. It begins in the wondertale world of grandfather's stories and ends with the death of grandfather and wonderland. We know that the narrator's grandfather died at the age of ninety-eight and that the action takes place between Istanbul and Vizye, but there are few clues as to story time and none as to its narrating instant, except that in the interval between the end of the story and its narration, N has learned to write (Greek 175; English 162). We may surmise that he was apprenticed to a tailor's establishment in Istanbul some time between the ages of twelve and fifteen, at the time of his grandfather's death in the early to mid-1860s.

First movement (Greek 168–70; English 155–57: wondertale). *Georgis always knew* [ἐγνώριζον] *that princesses fall so deeply in love with young tailors who can sing and sew that even kings have to agree to such marriages in the end. Tailors can count on the magic assistance of Nereids to sew in a single night the forty bridal dresses "without seam or thread" demanded by the king as a condition for betrothal by next morning. He knew this because his grandfather, whose name he bears—the most widely traveled and worldly-wise man in the world—had always told him so. And where is one more likely to find princesses than in Istanbul?*

Second movement (Greek 170–78; English 157–64: apprenticeship). *Apprenticed to a tailors' guild in the City, young Georgis is often sent to deliver bundles of finished garments and handiworks to the Sultan's mother in the Topkapı Palace: along perfumed corridors and suites, lined with precious carpets and hangings, he is sometimes conducted by ugly Moorish eunuchs to a magic little cupboard, which revolves by itself and asks him in the sweetest tones (assuredly those of his princess), will he taste my* börek *and* baklavás? *—oh so delicious they seemed to cry out "Eat me!" But no sooner does he pluck up courage to speak to his princess* *than he is whisked away by nasty Moors, two in front and two behind.*[45] *Back at the guild, his more experienced mates tell him they used to get treated to sweetmeats by the eldest and ugliest Moorish eunuch behind the hatch in the palace kitchen. He won't speak to them ever again! And he lives in misery until one day his grandfather's servant Thymios arrives with an urgent summons: his grandfather "is fighting with the angel"; his last request is to see his grandson, otherwise "he'll die with his eyes open"—that is, he'll turn into a revenant to plague the living, especially the one who bears his name.*

Third movement (Greek 178–84; English 164–69: the macabre ride). *A more adult narrator's voice interjects a folkloristic discourse on the power of death to heal feuds. Mounted on his grandfather's tall white horse, swiftly and wordlessly he and Thymios ride back home over an unspecified number of days and nights. Grandfather fighting with the angel! Only he can save him from dying with his eyes open—yes, when he was small he wrestled in play with his grandfather on the threshold and always won. Any angel could knock him flat. Would the fight this time be on the threshold or on a marble threshing floor? The moonlight, the uneven road surface, and the rapidity of the horse play tricks with clouds and trees. He falls asleep. In the front parlor, grandfather is lying in state: he sees every detail of the room, furnishings and embroideries; he hears the women's laments. Next scene: a tomb, grandfather seated on top of it, eyes staring wildly ahead—lunging at him on horseback with such violence he can hear and feel the hoofs pounding inside his skull. He wakes up.*[46]

Fourth movement (Greek 184–87; English 169–72: scherzo). *Back home, grandfather's shoes are gone from the threshold, grandmother is screaming at everything within earshot, like a wound-up, clockwork machine. —Off with you this minute and fetch some water! she tells him. —Where's grandfather? Georgis stammers. —Gone and left me, the lazy good-for-nothing, sunning himself as usual, the idle bastard! Even in the next world she spies on him and knows what he's up to, he thinks. Poor grandfather, no peace even after death. He goes out to find grandfather calmly darning her sock, just as he always used to, seated on his favorite crag high above the village, the only place his arthritic wife can't reach him. What joy— he won't die with his eyes open after all!*

Fifth movement (Greek 187–200; English 172–83: journeys in counterpoint). *After a rapturous reunion, news is exchanged. Grandfather interrupts grandson's attempts to describe what he saw with questions on mythical encounters. Grandson asks grandfather to relate what he saw on his journeys: at birth he had been named, dressed, and treated as a girl to escape conscription, then at ten years old declared a boy in order to marry a girl, his childhood playmate (again to avoid conscription), who turned out to be more man than woman. Thereafter, every time he set out on a journey, she went in his stead. —And the stories? asks the boy. —My grandmother used to tell tales as she taught me to sew and embroider, sighs the old man, when I was a girl. —The princess who marries the tailor? Where can I find her? —My grandmother's story —So where have you been, grandfather? asks the boy on the verge of tears. —See that peak in the distance that reaches to heaven? That's where I always wanted to go, and I got my chance after I'd been declared a boy again, just before the wedding. But the further I went, the further it moved, so I came home and married your grandmother . . . The boy scans the grandeur of the horizon, seized by nostalgia for a way of life now almost vanished, in yet another flash of adult insight into the threshold between childhood and adolescence. —It's getting cold, the old man concludes—let's go home!*

Coda. (Greek 200–201; English 183) *next morning, after a clear but cold night, grandson finds grandfather dead, a peaceful smile on his face. What would his wife not have given to stop him from this journey. Now he had completed "the only journey of his life."*

What is the journey, and whose is it? Grandfather had passed his life in the fantasy world of his grandmother's wondertales, without ever having left his native village. What he lacks horizontally in experience of the outside world is compensated by vertical depth in space and time. His imaginative world can be traced back in the female line to the early eighteenth century. If he was ninety-eight at the time of his grandson's return in the early to mid-1860s, then he would have been born soon after 1760. His claim to have been at risk of conscription to the Janissaries is the only, possibly deliberate, example of historical anachronism in Vizyenos' stories. While it is true that *paidomázōma* (*devşirme* lit. "child-gathering," or "recruitment to janissaries") was discontinued from the last decades of the seventeenth century, it was not officially revoked, and the practice continued sporadically, especially in the provinces: Greek memories, fears, and myths of its execution survived into the nineteenth century.[47] His grandmother's stories take us back to the early 1700s; his grandson, on the other hand, was brought up in golden times, with access to travel and education. Yet the boy's awakening to reality is neither easy nor painless and brings with it first rage at the thought that his princess in the palace really was a hideous old Moorish eunuch and then a sense of impending loss, expressed through ekphrasis:

But then, the hardships and the torments that I endured and I was destined to endure in the sweet hope of returning to my village one day with a princess at my side, had they been wasted, had they gone for naught? Very well, Grandfather! If you ever see me pick up a needle again, say I'm a girl and I don't know it! And I was getting ready to pronounce that inward thought, at the same time reproaching Grandfather because he had been responsible for my going to the City to suffer in vain. *But when I looked up*

and saw Grandfather with his dreamy gaze still fixed far away on the top of that
conical mound from which he had once hoped to enter heaven, some inexplicable,
mysterious force made my tongue stick to the roof of my mouth.

The sun had sunk much lower in the west. Every creature, every sign of life was
withdrawing silently and slowly toward the interior of the village. The face of the
landscape appeared more melancholy to me now, sadder. My heart shuddered once
again. Between the appearance of the scene and the expression on Grandfather's
pale and withered face as it was illumined by the sun, there existed such a similar-
ity, such a close affinity!

Poor Grandfather! I thought to myself. He wrestled with the angel and
beat him without my help, but he's so worn out and weak that if he has
another bout in the shape he's in, no one can save him.

—It's begun to get cold, my [soul], the old man said suddenly. —Come on,
let's go.

Silently, I gave him my arm and, supporting him as best I could, I accompanied him to his house.

(Greek 200; English 182–83: emphasis added)

This ekphrasis, with its untranslatably rich variegations of Greek, conveys a sense of imminent loss at the passing of not only a beloved grandfather but also a way of life, unchanged for centuries—where life may have
been restricted and certainly not free of violence but somehow integral
with nature, with an inner peace unattainable in the modern world, despite
the advantages of travel and education. The gap that threatens to separate N
from grandfather is far greater—and more confusing because irreversible—
than that between grandfather and grandfather's grandmother, who passed
on her stories as she taught him, as a girl, to sew and embroider. It is a gap
expressed with equal poignancy by other writers who have witnessed or
experienced society's transition from orality to literacy, whether in England's "Wessex" or Ireland's Blasket Isles. In Thomas Hardy's poems "One
We Knew" and "In the Time of the Breaking of Nations," just as in Maurice O'Sullivan's biomythography *Twenty Years A-Growing*, one senses that
grandfather's peaceful end to the longest and most important journey—
life itself—will prove beyond N's reach, as indeed was the case for both
O'Sullivan and Vizyenos, leaving only poetic yearning, as expressed in
Goethe's verses:

Und wenn der Mensch in seiner Qual verstummt,
Gab mir ein Gott, zu sagen, wie ich leide.

(*Tasso* 3432–3)

And when man in his agony is dumb,
God gave me the gift to speak my pain.

There is a hint of Goethe's "Über allen Gipfeln ist Ruh" in the elegaic tones of the two ekphraseis which mark N's initiation into the grown-up world of contemporary life (Greek 196–97, 200). Which Georgis is the child and which the old man?

By the end of the story, Georgis has decided to give up the needle. Yet he has not forgotten the stitcher's craft or the magic attributed by legend to the skill of sewing χωρὶς ραφὴ καὶ ράμμα "without seam or stitch." Throughout, Vizyenos has exploited with exquisite subtlety the metonym of writing as sewing, as old in Greek as the rhapsode, or Homer himself; for the narration is, indeed, "without seam or stitch," just like the bridal garments sewn by the Nereids in the wondertales or Vizyenos' poem Ἡ τέχνη μου.

The separation between worlds of grandfather and grandson is rendered more poignant by the closeness of their personal relationship: both share the same name, and whereas the boy mentions his mother only once (175), his grandfather addresses him tenderly as "my soul." The merging of souls—like those of Klara and Paschalis—is further effected through the double image of the journey, both as metaphor for life and as nocturnal fantasy reuniting "home" and "foreign parts," but here it takes place before and not after death. Throughout, use of imperfective moods conveys a sense of timelessness, concealing the seams and stitches of the narrating act—even though grandson's last image of grandfather is that he was darning his wife's sock!

It is not only grandson and grandfather who merge into each other: orality and literacy, writing and sewing, words and pictures are interwoven, not least through the multiple registers of the Greek language, shifting from dialect for exchanges between grandfather and grandson—and grandmother's squawking reproaches to all and sundry (including the cat!)—to moderate katharevousa for the narrator's narration and high katharevousa for the intricately embroidered ekphraseis. First, grandfather and grandson exchange stories, with grandfather using his hands to knit and gesticulate for emphasis at the same time in the mode of oral narrative:

—Καὶ πῶς εἶναι ἡ Φώκια, παππού;
—Νὰ ἔτσι—εἶπεν ὁ παπποῦς χειρονομῶν οὕτως, ὡς ἐὰν εἶχε τὴν Φώκιαν ἐνώπιόν του καὶ μοὶ ὥριζεν ἀνατομικῶς τὰ μέλη της. —Ἀπὸ τὸν ἀφαλὸ καὶ πάνου εἶναι ἡ ἐμορφότερη γυναῖκα, ἀπὸ τὸν ἀφαλὸ καὶ κάτω εἶναι τὸ φοβερώτερο ψάρι. Κάθεται στὸν πάτο τῆς θάλασσας. Μὰ κεῖ ποὺ σκιαχθῆ κανένα καράβι ποὺ περνᾶ ἀπὸ πάνω, κάμνει μία χόπ! καὶ βγαίνει στὴν ἐπιφάνεια· κάμνει μιὰ χάπ! καὶ ἁρπάζει τὸ καράβι μὲ τὸ χέρι της καὶ τὸ σταματᾶ. Ἀπαί, φωνάζει τὸν καπετάνο καὶ τὸν ἐρωτᾶ· Ἀλέξανδρος ὁ Βασιλεὺς ζῆ καὶ βασιλεύει; Τρεῖς φορὲς τὸν ἐρωτᾶ, ψυχή μου, καὶ τρεῖς φορὲς ὁ καπετάνος σὰν

τῆς εἴπῃ πῶς ζῇ καὶ βασιλεύει, τὸν ἀφήνει καὶ πάγει στὴν δουλειά του. Σὰν τῆς εἴπῃ πῶς δὲν ζῇ, τὸν βουλᾷ καὶ τὸν πνίγει!

Καὶ ἀναποδίσας τὴν κάλτσαν τῆς γιαγιᾶς καὶ σείσας αὐτὴν οὕτως, ὥστε νὰ πέσῃ τὸ ἐντὸς αὐτῆς κουβάριον, μοὶ ἔδειξε πῶς ναυαγοῦν τὰ πλοῖα ὁ παπποῦς, καὶ—Γι᾽ αὐτὸ ἐπρόσθεσε —καλλίτερα, ψυχή μου, ποὺ δὲν τὴν εἶδες.

—᾽Ω βέβαια καλλίτερα, παπποῦ! Γιατί, διές, πῶς θὰ ἐπήγαινα στὴν Πόλη σὰν ἐπνίγομουν; Νὰ ἰδῆς δὰ παπποῦ, τί μεγάλη ποὺ εἶναι ἡ Πόλη, καὶ τί λογῆς λογῆς ἄνθρωποι ποὺ εἶν᾽ αὐτοῦ καὶ χανούμισσαις καὶ βασιλόπουλ᾽....

—῎Ας τ᾽ αὐτά!!! διέκοψεν ὁ παπποῦς πάλιν, ὡς ἐὰν ὡμίλουν περὶ πραγμάτων κοινῶν καὶ τετριμμένων. Εἶδες τὸν τόπο, ποὺ εἶναι οἱ ἄνθρωποι οἱ μαρμαρωμένοι;

—῎Οχι, παπποῦ! Δὲν τὸν εἶδα!

—᾽Αάχ, ψυχή μου. Τίποτε δὲν εἶδες, στὴν ζωή σου, τίποτε!

—What's she like, Grandpa, the Seal?

—Like this, Grandfather said, rapidly moving his hands in such a way as if he had the Seal in front of him and was marking out the shape of her limbs for me.—From the navel up she's the most beautiful woman, from the navel down she's the most terrifying fish. She lives on the sea's bottom. But when she senses a boat's shadow passing over, she goes hip-hop! and she's up on top. Then she goes hop-hip! and she grabs the boat in her hand and stops it. Well, then she yells at the cap'n, asking: King Alexander, does he live and is he ruling? Three times she asks him, my soul, and three times if the cap'n says he lives and rules, she lets him go. If he says he's not alive, she sinks and drowns him!

And, turning over Grandma's stocking with a shake just so as to make the ball of wool fall out from inside it, Grandfather showed me how ships are sunk,—and—That's just why, he added, it's better, my soul, you didn't see her.—

Oh of course it was better, grandpa! Because, look, how'd I have gone to the City if I'd drownded? You should just see, grandpa, how big the City is, and how many, many folks are there, high-born women and princesse. . . .

—Forget them!!! Grandfather interrupted once more, as though I were speaking of things common and outworn.—Did you see the place with the marble people?

—No, grandpa, I didn't see it!

—Aah! my soul. You've seen nothing in your life, nothing at all.

(Greek 189–90; English 173–74: my translation)

This passage has the same qualities of humor and tenderness, tinged with sadness for a vanishing world of tales and beliefs as do Maurice's talks with his grandfather, "Daddo," in *Twenty Years A-Growing*. Vizyenos and O'Sullivan alike use the spiritual bond between grandfather and grandson to underline the cultural gap that lies between them. The ekphrasis that follows Vizyenos' dialogue is among the best in the course of the tale. In contrast to N's informal tone when talking to his grandfather (including the dialect form ἰπνίγομουν that I have rendered "drownded"), the language is high katharevousa, appropriate to the mythical—almost mystical—quality of the scene. His grandfather has just told him about his "girlhood," early marriage, and failure even to set out on a single journey—except for one, although that too remained unfinished. "How, grandpa? When?":

The old man put his handiwork aside on the ground, and extending his gaze toward the horizon, he seemed silently to busy his eyes with the sight of the townscape unfolding [ἐκτεινομένης χωριογραφίας] before us.

The sky was cloudless; the sun low on the horizon; and the height of the position we were in afforded the spectator [θεατήν] a view from above [πανόραμα] at once boundless and commensurable.

Around the borders [κράσπεδα] of the hilltop settlement [ἀκροπόλεως] immediately beneath our gaze lay town houses in huddled confusion; in the courtyards one could discern men, women, children, busily garnering in their autumn produce. In the immediate environs of the town could be seen vegetable gardens with aging trees shedding leaves around decrepit fences; and straggling harvesters, loading the last fruits onto their wagons. Nearby, smoke was still rising from the burning chaff of now deserted threshing floors. Just beyond, stretching out crescent-shaped in a huge arc, came the land's most fruit-yielding fields, wherein, however, ears of Demeter's grain no longer swayed heavy with produce like the surface of the golden-waved sea; instead, freely grazing sheep and cattle fed on the last blade of green as they were slowly herded back to town. At the furthest sweep of the horizon the local vineyards, likewise deserted after the harvest and now abandoned, closed round this immense picture like a tall frame. The brilliant variegation of the last autumn colors, the streams ribboning across the land in regular strips, the trees and houses vividly gathering in clusters around their banks, the Odryssean [= ancient Thracian, not "Odyssean"] tombs raised up like huge, cone-shaped mounds here and there, not only breaking up the usual monotony of flat land and townscapes but also lending to that boundless picture an exquisite, wondrous unity and variety.

And yet in front of this most entrancing spectacle [θεάματος]—I still recall it—some hidden anxiety, some kind of foreboding was stealing over my heart. You would think that life, that once so vigorously blossomed forth in that land, was now seeping slowly yet steadily down inward into nature's innermost recesses; the smile on her face was but the last, ultimate smile on the lips of one in the throes of death.

(Greek 181–82; English 179–80: my translation)

This is a set piece, with no direct relevance to the story but with a deeper allegorical signification well attested in traditions, like Greek and Irish, with a dual literary and oral heritage. Images of sewing and painting are exploited to frame the miniature, looking both inward and outward. Wondertale themes of the lower world and human dependence on nature are called to mind with new significations. As in dreams, images of enclosed spaces coincide with feelings of anxiety and foreboding.[48]

What is the nature and function of ekphrasis? In the ancient and Byzantine novels of love and adventure, it takes the form of a stylized description of landscape, akropolis, fair, garden, statue, and painting, often immediately preceding the hero or heroine's falling in love, thus signaling a change of direction or mood in plot or character. Makrembolites' *Hysmine* has the greatest concentration of ekphraseis (on gardens, statues, and paintings) in books 2–4, when Hysminias responds through dreams and contemplation of pictures to Hysmine's love. But the closest thematic parallel to Vizyenos' passage is from the *Timarion,* when Timarion, perched on the akropolis high above Thessaloniki, describes the bustling scene of the fair below in graphic—and minutely accurate—historical detail (Chapter 4).

Yet it would be a mistake to attribute Vizyenos' use of ekphrasis only to the learned Byzantine and ancient past, even if a direct connection could be proved. Rather, it stems from a tradition at once oral and literary, as in the west of Ireland, where the medieval bardic *aisling* (vision) was not only cultivated by peasant poets of the eighteenth century but incorporated into the biomythographies of the Blasket Islands within living memory. O'Sullivan, in *Twenty Years*, again perhaps comes closest to Vizyenos in combining intimate conversation with descriptive reverie. Like the narrator of "Journey," Maurice has a close relationship with his grandfather. Together they visit Pierce's Cave:

My grandfather and I were lying on the Castle Summit. It was a fine sunny day in July. The sun was splitting the stones with its heat and the grass burnt to its roots. I could see Iveragh painted in many colours by the sun. South-west were the Skelligs glistening white and the sea around them dotted with fishing-boats from England.

—Isn't it a fine healthy life those fishermen have, daddo? said I. I got no answer. Turning round I saw that the old man was asleep. I looked at him, thinking. You were one day in the flower of youth, said I in my own mind, but, my sorrow, the skin of your brow is wrinkled now and the hair on your head is grey. You are without suppleness in your limbs and without pleasure in the grand view to be seen from this hill. But alas, if I live, some day I will be as you are now. The heat was very great, and so I thought of waking him for fear the sun would kill him. I caught him by his grey beard and gave it a pull. He opened his eyes and looked around.

—Oh Muirisheen [liitle Maurice], said he, I fell asleep. Am I long in it?

—Not long, said I, but I thought I had better wake you on account of the sun. Do you see those trawlers out on the horizon? I was just saying that it's a fine healthy life they have!

—Musha, my heart, said my grandfather, a man of the sea never had a good life and never will, as I know well, having spent my days on it, and I have gone through as many perils on it as there are grey hairs in my head, and I am telling you now, wherever God may guide you, keep away from the sea.

—Musha, it seems to me there is no man on earth so contented as a seaman.

I looked south-east to the Macgillicuddy Reeks. They looked as if they were touching the sky.

—Musha, aren't those high mountains?

—They are indeed, if you were down at their foot.

                    (O'Sullivan 1953, 82–88; trans. Thomson)

Or again, consider O'Sullivan's set piece on "Nightfall": "It was growing late. The sun was sinking on the horizon, the dew falling heavily as the air cooled, the dock leaves closing up for the night, the birds crying as they came back to their young, rabbits rushing through the fern as they left the warrens, the sparkle gone out of the Kerry diamonds, and a lonesome look coming over the ravines. —It is night, Tomás."[49]

These word pictures express a profound harmony between human and natural life in terms of the eternal cycle of day and night, summer and winter, life and death (Thomson 1988, 43). Signs are described apparently at random, as if in the process of being seen and heard, with no logical pattern, in a series of paradoxical juxtapositions. As in the lament or the wondertale, what was in the past is no longer present, what is here now was not there then. Just as ekphraseis punctuate Byzantine learned and vernacular romances, in medieval Irish bardic tradition narrative poems such as *The Midnight Court* are introduced by the hero with a reflective aisling: "It gladdened my heart to set eyes on Lough Graney, the lake and the landscape, and on the sunlit horizon the mountains set in a huddle together, nodding their heads from behind one another."[50] Not so different, after all, from Goethe's "Wanderer's Nachtlied"?

Can ekphrasis be integrated with narrative? According to the conventional view, prevalent in Europe from Gotthold E. Lessing to the present day, ekphrasis interrupts the narrative flow, it pays obsessive attention to irrelevant detail, and it focuses on outmoded rhetoric while adding nothing to action or character.[51] Yet writers such as Vizyenos and O'Sullivan use ekphrasis as retarding pauses to provide a horizontal, rather than linear, dimension to time and space, almost as if wishing to insert such pauses into the process of history itself. Ekphrasis probes not only the inner world of narrators and characters but explores the mediating cognitive processes through the senses of sight and sound. Georgis, strapped round the middle by Thymios' broad red sash, nods off to sleep on the macabre ride home from the City to Vizye. There follows this dream ekphrasis:

> It was autumn, and already night was beginning to draw in; the wind, by now chill, was whistling through the sparse trees of the forest, shaking the shivering sleep from half-nude branches whose countless leaves were whirled groundwards, groaning tears of grief. On such nights as this, the moon, as she appears from behind dim clouds to enlarge Nature's wild blackness with her colorless shades "pale as death," instead of affording comfort, fills the traveler's heart with ill-defined fears and constant tremors. The wildness of our journey was rendered greater by the uneven speed with which our tall horse ploughed objects to each side of the road ahead, before I even had chance to discern their ambivalent shapes [ἀμφίβολα σχήματα] in order to restore quiet to my doubting heart. Thymios' enduring and solemn silence, the unexpectedness of the journey and the goal towards which it was aimed, the manner of that fantastic ride, during which one half of me was hanging from Thymios' sash while the other half was being cradled on the horse's haunches—all these things held my child's heart in the grip of enduring anxiety, at the same time kindling my imagination to the point of hallucination.
>
> I do not think that I fixed my gaze in the course of that night on weird cloud formations, some above the wind and others swept along by it, without filling them in with the aid of the moonlight and predisposed imagination into a huge, tangled pair of wrestlers risking all in combat. The one with his white and many-pleated bloomers blowing in the breeze, with the broad embroidered sleeves of his shirt, was without doubt my grandfather. The other with his long hair flowing loose, with the white wings on his

shoulders, with the scale-armored breastplate on his chest and the fiery sword in his bare right hand, he was surely the angel. I had seen him so many times on the left-hand door of the sanctuary in our village church. (Greek 181–82; my translation)

The visual imagery in this passage is carefully wrought on complex spatiotemporal levels. Everything the boy sees is in motion, and his blurred sensations are made palpable to the reader by use of imperfective tenses and moods for all verbal forms except two, both encased in negative phrases with reference to the boy's state of mind and intense watchfulness, usually conveyed in Greek by the imperfective: ἀντὶ νὰ μὲ παρηγορήσῃ, "instead of affording comfort" and Δὲν νομίζω νὰ ἠτένισα . . . χωρὶς νά "I do not think that I fixed my gaze . . . without". Thus, normal temporal usage is reversed: what happens is imperfective, what is felt is (negated) perfective. The terrifying instability of the boy's visual world stands in stark contrast to the fixity of both his physical state, strapped by a sash like a peasant's soulless bundle to the rider's waist (ὡς ἐὰν ἤμην κανὲν ἄψυχον παράρτημα) and his emotional state of enduring anxiety (διαρκῆ ἀνησυχίαν). His nightmare is further intensified by enduring and solemn silence (ἡ διαρκὴς καὶ ἐπίσημος σιγή) throughout the "journey." As N reminds us, had Thymios not thought to strap him in, there would have been no one seated behind to talk to anyway!

On another level, the scene evokes the macabre ride in "The Dead Brother" where, after an equally ambivalent and peremptory summons, Arete is alerted by birdsong to her rider's sinister appearance. Her terrified questions receive ambivalent answers; Georgis' terror is unspoken. Thymios and the tall white horse disappear before they reach home, just as mysteriously as do Kostandinos and horse in the song. Grandmother was not expecting Georgis and tells him he looks "pale as death": is Thymios (not a common forename) a throwback from past memories (thymízo "remind"), like Toni Morrison's Beloved? Other details suggest those songs of xenitiá in which the girl awakens in her lover's arms in a panic as from a dream: she saw his horse without a rider, his saddle broken, his sword split in two, and his fine kerchief dirtied on the ground; he reassures her that the dream signifies not death but xenitiá. Rider and saddle, sword and sash, and dreamlike state are equally significant in this ekphrasis, but their order and function are changed. The point is that the passage, despite its apparent literariness, has deep resonances in songs of death and exile which intensify our sense of the boy's terrifying hallucinations and make them more convincing: illiterate as he then was, his imagination fed on songs and tales.

But our educated narrator has injected notes of boyhood terror from Goethe's "Erlkönig," set to music by Schubert at the age of seventeen.[52] This passage also bears remarkable thematic, stylistic, and verbal affinities with Timarion's nightmarish ride from Thessaloniki back to Constantinople, when, immediately preceding the onslaught of the two demons who carry him down to Hades, "one of the pack horses carried me towards Constantinople strapped across its back like a parcel" [ἱππάριόν τι φορτηγὸν ὡς τι τῶν ἐπισαττομένων ἐπισαχθέντα ἦγε πρὸς τὸ Βυζάντιον: Baldwin 1984, 12.320]. Although a direct connection cannot be proved, it is possible that Vizyenos came across the first modern edition of the twelfth-century dialogue, published in 1860 by the German scholar A. Ellissen in Leipzig.

Vizyenos' tendency to define positives in terms of negatives, presence as absence, and action as inaction can be found in all his stories, especially at their conclusion. Yet in this ekphrasis, the absence of normal modes of cognition allows him to complete, through imagination and memory, the verbal picture of the night ride. He fills in the fragmented and distorted images of nature with an icon of the Archangel Michael remembered from childhood. Trees and clouds, wind and moon become animate; only humanity is silenced, frozen in fear. The contemplation of Nature leads not to romantic peace, as in Goethe's song, but to madness, as in "Consequences." Whether or not Vizyenos really was insane at the end of his life, he has left us an indelible word-picture of what it might feel like.

Ekphrasis explores cognitive processes and inner emotion, dialogue and antithesis, to challenge normal modes of communication and representation. N's journey is marked by enduring silence; the only meaningful dialogue in the story takes place between grandson and grandfather on the threshold of life and death, since the boy's few conversations in the first two movements are in reported speech, while brief exchanges with grandmother in the fourth are fraught with misunderstanding. Vizyenos, through his interweaving of narrative and descriptive modes and through intertextual allusion brings together diverse traditions—oral and literary; modern, medieval, and ancient—to produce a distinctive form of prose fiction which reintegrates poetry and prose, music and song, nature and art. What he may lack in diversification of character and plot is compensated by richness and depth of texture, as well as by musical structure of composition. He encapsulates in artistic form the difference between modern realist and premodern modes of fiction. In the former, there is a clear distinction between subject and object, beholder and beheld; in the latter, the beholder provides the emotional bridge between image and mind. The force of images is subjective, so that the beholder—and reader—completes and becomes part of the picture or reality. In that space myths and metaphors can be creatively explored and developed.

For Vizyenos, fiction needs more than the written word, more than mere *histoire, récit, narration*. It needs bones along with the meat, as well as images and music (sight and sound), to fill in the tones and colors of human emotion, as N in "Consequences" reminds us as he listens to the mad girl singing Vizyenos's own poem in German:

> And now, dear reader, don't expect from mortal pen that I can represent to you the deeply moving scene of which we were the mournful, astonished witnesses. Perhaps some perfected form of phonograph could manage instantaneously to transcribe one by one and preserve the individual notes of that sad music in such a way that it could be read by others as well. But read only, not sung. The demonic force that engulfed us like a magic spirit of life and that inspired the imaginative and improvised arrangements of those notes that were at the same time so simple and yet so inexpressible, the melodic and yet dramatic nuances of each individual line, of each word—yes, of each individual syllable through which she made us see before us with a shudder, alive and moving, those scenes only faintly, only figuratively hinted at in her composition—these things no machine manufactured by mortal hand, no musical genius can repeat or imitate even remotely.
>
> But the sad frailty of her posture, the indefinably desperate expression on her face, and at the same time the special facial movements with which she accompanied the sounds of her voice and the tones of her instrument—what camera, or what superhuman painter's skill could transcribe them! I say nothing about genius in writing because the fact that even in this most feeble recounting I am forced to separate the elements of music and physiognomy, things that in nature are so inseparably united, reveals, I think, most clearly, the descriptive imperfection of any written account. (Greek 114; English 107–8)

The power of music and image to inspire love is a favorite theme of Greek and Oriental tales, as expressed in Mozart's *Magic Flute*, as Tamino beholds the portrait of Pamina. It may not be possible to transcribe feeling into words, but loss is marked by allusion to opera, song, and dance ("Consequences") and to darning, weaving, and embroidery ("Journey"). By "writing against silence," he re-creates in fiction the kind of synesthesia implicit in premodern artistic modes, including those of Byzantium and Ireland.

To return to O'Sullivan to highlight differences between Ireland and Ottoman Thrace, E. M. Forster points out in his introduction to *Twenty Years* that the reader is attracted by two features, "the gaiety of youth and the magic of the old Gaelic world, one blooming, the other in decay, juxtaposed throughout in counterpoint."[53] In Vizyenos, gaiety is given an ironic—even tragic—twist: Masinga's enchantingly musical laugh in "Between Piraeus and Naples" reminds us of the tones behind the revolving cupboard in "Journey," which the narrator takes to be the voice of his princess but which in fact proved to be that of the oldest and ugliest Moorish eunuch in the Topkapı Palace!

It has been said that O'Sullivan might seem to have "had only to abandon the first person in order to produce a novel. The novel is a story of a new type. The oral and collective elements have been completely eliminated and the subject is the personal relations between individuals in modern society. All this lay beyond Muiris' experience."[54] But not beyond that of Vizyenos: the socioeconomic conditions of Ottoman Thrace, more complex than those of the Blasket Islanders' pre-cash community, and his own education in Europe, allowed him to write a form of fiction more probing of the ambiguities of gender, ethnicity, and language. Both Vizyenos and O'Sullivan died at the age of forty-seven, the former from insanity, the latter from drowning.

The difference between Vizyenos' sense of topos and tropos and that of his contemporaries in the new Greek state is unspoken yet profound. His City is not the idealized Constantinople of the past, as in Palamas or Psicharis, but the Ottoman Istanbul of the present, albeit portrayed as "dream drama," with reference to busy Turkish households, hans, bazaars, and guilds; to swirling dervishes and New Turks; and the tomb of Constantine and Topkapı Palace, rich with eunuchs and silk hangings. His language is *not* the demotic of Palamas and Psicharis, a choice he justifies obliquely by paying tribute to Ibsen's antinationalist stance in his critical essay; its range includes words resurrected from Homeric and Byzantine Greek as well as from the Thracian dialect and Turkish.[55] Literary allusions bring under scrutiny not just the medieval, Renaissance, and romantic West but the Balkan and Ottoman East as well, while problematizing notions of the literary canon and the appropriation of Hellenism by nationalism and aestheticism. It is the inner code rather than the external packaging that is both oral and literary, modern and Byzantine.

6. Coda: After Vizyenos

Vizyenos stands at the crossroads between old and new, between the multi-ethnic, polyglot Ottoman world and the assertive nationalism of the Greek state. After 1923, the intellectual horizons of Greece changed. The ideal of a greater Greece was shattered. In literature, the impact of the Asia Minor catastrophe was apparent in poetry, in the visionary nostalgia of Angelos Sikelianos and George Seferis and in the Marxism of Kostas Varnalis and Yiannis Ritsos. Poets turned to the past in order to create a myth of Hellenism, from Sikelianos' attempt to revive the Delphic Idea in poems such as Ἱερὰ Ὁδός ("The Sacred Way," 1935) to Seferis' innovative collection Στροφή (*Turning point*, 1935), and to the exuberant lyricism of

Odysseas Elytis' *Axion Esti* (1959), which incorporates Byzantine chant to celebrate "this world, small and great."

After the 1920s, three major developments can be discerned in Greek prose fiction, in accordance with the movement to synchronize Greek literature with that of Europe:[56] in language, a decisive shift from katharevousa to demotic; in form, a preference for the full-length novel; and a diversification of thematic range to include contemporary urban life. Without entering the futile debate on whether modernism or postmodernism is possible in Greece,[57] I will allude to four novels in order to suggest that Greek fiction continues to excel in narrative and structural ingenuity. Two novels have received worldwide acclaim: Nikos Kazantzakis' *Life and Times of Alexis Zorbas* (1943), filmed by Michael Cacoyannis as *Zorba the Greek*; and Kostas Takhtsis' *The Third Wedding* (1961). The other two, Stratis Myrivilis' *Mermaid Madonna* (1949) and Evgenia Fakinou's *The Great Green* (1987), adopt painterly modes to depict the power of the Aegean Sea against a backdrop that is both mythical and historical.

What do these novels have in common? First, cyclical structure situates action against seasonal changes on the thematic level, underscoring a reversal (*peripeteia*) on the symbolic level. *Zorbas* opens at the port of Piraeus, as Kazantzakis' narrator (henceforth N), bound for Crete on a mission to build a lignite mine, bids farewell to his aristocratic friend, Stavridakis, bound for the Caucasus to repatriate exiled Greeks (chapter 1). On the voyage to Crete, where the central action takes place, N meets Zorbas, a working-class man whose assertion of earthy values and rejection of patriotism change N's attitudes to life and death, religion and philosophy (chapters 2–25). It closes as N receives letters informing him of the deaths of Stavridakis and Zorbas (chapter 26). Despite the fiasco of his attempt to construct a mine (largely the fault of Zorbas), N has gained the power to write the portrait of Zorbas, with metaphors of mining and writing for material and spiritual dimensions.[58]

Takhtsis begins and ends his novel with his narrator, Nina, fulminating against her daughter, offspring of her first marriage to Fotis, whom she divorced some time after finding him on the third night after their wedding in bed with her brother. The time span covered by the reminiscences of two adult women, Nina and her interlocutor, Ekavi, takes us from present (aftermath of World War II) to past (aftermath of World War I) and back to the present, reviewing history from the perspective of family relationships. On the textual level, readers are invited to question the reliability of oral narrators and the relationship of contemporary Greece to its ancient past. After the deaths of Ekavi, her second husband Antonis, and her aunt Katingo, Nina contemplates yet a fourth marriage in the event of the death of her third husband, Thodoros (Ekavi's son)—just to spite her daughter![59]

Myrivilis' *Mermaid Madonna* opens with a description of how a seaman of unknown origins paints an icon of Our Lady in nonrealist colors (still worshipped on the island of Mytilini) and closes with the dedication of Smaragdi (a foundling from the sea), to the icon's shrine, with a vow of perpetual virginity. Action covers roughly eighteen years (Smaragdi's life on the island); yet through the perspectives of older characters, the novel has a reach of one hundred or so years, back to Ayvali in 1830, coeval with the modern nation state. Changes of seasons are marked, with a focus on Aegean summers. Spatially, the novel ranges from Anatolia to America through the reminiscences and tales centered around the *kafeneion* "coffeehouse." Island life is painted so as to view it from wide perspectives.[60]

Like Myrivilis, Fakinou opens her novel with a mysterious entry and closes with a symbolic return. Between these frames, Ioanna, an icon restorer, rejects the boredom of bourgeois Athens to explore the sites of Greece as a vagrant, questioning her identity and going in search of dreams. Her vagrancy is most notably marked when, as in the songs of xenitiá, she washes her only set of clothes in unfavorable circumstances (94). Ioanna's entry into the village on the backwoods of Mount Pelion is matched by her dreamed departure from its shores. Ioanna, like Smaragdi, is a woman from outside who refuses to conform to local values and is therefore branded as a *xotikó* "demon."

In each of these novels, time and space are perceived in cyclical, seasonal terms, with specific reference to history, landscapes, and townscapes and with mythic reference to the past. As for character, it could be argued that not a single persona is depicted in depth or in the round, as is recommended by E. M. Forster (1927, 73–81). *Zorbas* is a study in the attraction and identity of opposites within the Hellenic self or the paradoxical presentation of Zorbas as reverse hagiography in the manner of *Pope Joan*. N is revealed less through his actions than from his conversations with Zorbas and from his correspondence with Stavridakis and his mis-Hellene obverse in Africa, Karayiannis. Myrivilis' protagonist is no less inscrutable: who is Smaragdi, and what is she? Her identity is defined not from the perspective of an omniscient narrator (the novel is narrated in the third person) but from the diverse focalization of all the islanders, indigenes and refugees. The voices of Nina and Ekavi are audible throughout Takhtsis' novel, but they are fragmented by their very inconsistencies and ambivalences, while oral discourse is complicated by their uses of learned and religious expressions. By contrast, Fakinou's novel is enacted in ghostly silence: the few speaking voices we hear are the villagers' opening deprecations of Ioanna's refusal to speak (p. 10) and their closing imprecations "that the earth may not eat you" (p. 162); the longest utterance in direct speech is that of the mysterious Nikolaos K., called Doukas (himself a ghost from the Komnene

Doukas past?), who demands to know the reason of her night prowl on the ruins of Mistra (34–35). She responds with her single utterance to another being in the course of the novel, with the words, "I am seeking to find my dreams" ψάχνω νὰ βρῶ τὰ ὄνειρά μου, 36. Otherwise she speaks only twice, once as she sings to herself snatches of a children's song, involuntarily remembered from the past (87–88), and once to the firewood, asking it to kindle (95). Her final refuge is the great green of the sea, where she encounters, in her recovered power to dream, the Homeric and Egyptian past. Voice neither elucidates nor concludes in these novels but creates an ironic distance between speaker and interlocutor, writer and reader, rather in the manner of an ancient Greek chorus, whose function is not to speak with one voice but to engage in disputation: "their eyes were watching God."[61]

Plot, in our sense, may be absent, yet the four novels are packed with scenic performance, local anecdote, and vivid description: table feasts, exchanges in the local coffeehouse, frenetic activities, mock weddings, and deaths are set against religious festivals of the Orthodox calendar. In *Zorbas*, the widow is stoned to death on Easter Day during the festive dance (chapter 22). Nothing seems integrated. Plot is secondary to dialogue, correspondence, and debate. N's conversations with Zorbas range over topics of freedom, ethics, and society. Is man beast or God or both? Are death and immortality one and the same thing? How do women affect our lives, and can we believe in anything outside the self? Is patriotism a substitute for religion and morality? What is the meaning of life, death, and sacrifice? On all these questions, the two hold opposing views, but Zorbas' cultivation of folly (*trélla*) and enjoyment of life wins out. Minor characters lend incidental color rather than depth to plot. French-born Hortense, stranded on Crete since girlhood by the allied fleet, dies just as she thinks she is about to realize her dream of marriage to Zorbas. Local women do not mourn her but tear apart her clothes and possessions at the wake. The village widow—never named—is killed by local men. It is Zorbas, not N, who intervenes in her stoning, although N has been partially responsible for the men's hostility. Characters are stereotypes, plot a concatenation of stock themes, conforming to principles of *ēthopoieía* and *plokē*. Unlike Vizyenos or Papadiamandis in the previous generation, both Kazantzakis and Myrivilis were ardent demoticists, yet their language is enriched by the Cretan and Mytilenean dialects and by a strong sense of antithetical style, juxtaposing everday dialogue with lyrical expositions expressed in a vocabulary entirely their own. Takhtsis, a transvestite homosexual assassinated in mysterious circumstances in 1990, captures the linguistic nuances of female conversation in semiurbanized Athens and Thessaloniki, as well as pinpointing ironic differences of gender. Fakinou explores the difficulties of being female, educated, and artistic in Greece today.

In conclusion, let me try to answer some of the questions I raised at the beginning of this chapter. In contrast to the European novel, Greek fiction has eschewed the ideal of romantic love leading to marriage as the (implied) ending of the domesticated and usually middle-class female. Love is erotic rather than romantic, tinged with violence and death; death may be a renewal, not an end. Often illicit, love comes into conflict with traditional values, according to which marriage is a matter of duty and convenience, not of bourgeois individualism. Focal areas of conflict tend to be intrafamilial, their resolution paradoxical, as in the mythical songs. Wars, civil strife, and ethnic conflict have impinged so deeply on Greek consciousness that attention is on the fragmentation of the individual within the social and historical context of upheaval and displacement, rather than on personal fulfillment: hence the splitting of character in response to historical experience. Myth and fantasy are allowed a special space: themes and names are drawn from the past, not just as nostalgia but from a need to explore the reciprocal other.

But perhaps the most striking feature is the multiplicity and diversity of languages. It is as if the lack of a standard language, spoken and literary, established elsewhere in western Europe since the late eighteenth century or before, goaded Greek writers to find their own voice amid the plethora of oral and literary texts. The result is that their linguistic range is polyphonic and multitextured, suggesting the synesthesia encountered in the paramythia. Greek fiction is perhaps at its best in the form of the short story rather than the full-length novel. The transition to demotic may have put an end to the polyglossia of Vizyenos and Papadiamandis, although exceptions can be found in Pendzikis, Takhtsis, and Galanaki. Diversity and verve characterize the Greek of even the most ardent demoticists and of this century's fiction as a whole, as evidenced in the remarkable novel *Kyrano* (1990) by my friend and cofieldworker from Larisa, Vasiliki Papagianni, who fuses her own experiences into those of her mother, grandmother, and family, rather in the manner of Vizyenos. To return to Bachtin's question considered at the end of Chapter 1 ("Why have most of the resources of the past been kept outside the pale of contemporary usage?"), we may respond that it is the precepts of demoticism, not the practices of creative writers, that have proved restrictive. One must also note the debt acknowledged by so many writers to the songs and tales of oral tradition, familiar not merely from textbooks but from grandmothers and mothers as well.[62]

If Greek fiction challenges our norms of modernism and postmodernism, is it not time to take a more global view of literature and culture and to listen more carefully to dissenting voices? It remains in Part Three to examine how metaphoric dimensions of the Greek language have been constantly revitalized through ritual.

PART III

METAPHOR

Toute une magie est deposée dans notre langage
Imaginer veut dire imaginer une forme de vie

—LUDWIG WITTGENSTEIN, trans. Jacques Bouveresse

CHAPTER 9

The Resources of Ritual

In this chapter I wish to demonstrate the ritual underpinnings of the Greek metaphorical system, first synchronically, by drawing attention to some significant features of ritual, such as analogical modes of action and perception, and the continuum between rituals as practiced on levels ranging from everyday life and discourse to times of crisis and songs of the life cycle; and second, diachronically, with brief reference to texts already examined in detail in Parts I (Language) and II (Myth). The chapter is therefore pivotal to the central argument of this book: that language, myth, and metaphor can best be understood in their interconnectedness and in relation to "things done," whether with or without words.

1. Ritual and Metaphor

"Les mots et les choses": two issues are raised here. First, how are words and things related in ritual, and what are their metaphorical dimensions? The question will be addressed with reference to specific rituals, such as the smashing of a vessel of water over the threshold, and the different significations of this act when performed at funerals, weddings, and emigration rites. Second, how do our uses of words affect our conceptualization and interpretation of them? Here, Greek usage may provide a valuable corrective to our own tendency to reify concepts such as "ritual" and "metaphor"— abstract terms derived from dead languages—and to seek reductive or universalizing definitions and interpretations. "The Greeks have a word for it, but they don't have *it*," quipped Greek novelist Vassilis Vassilikos on a BBC television program, in an attempt to convey the Greek tendency to carry old words for obsolete categories.[1] In the case of ritual, the reverse is true: the "word for it" (*teletē*) is rarely used except to denote church baptisms, weddings, and funerals, as on formal invitation cards to official ceremonies.[2] Arguably, no current word exists because ritual is so much a part of everyday life that the concept is expressed by such phrases as "this is how we do things" (ἔτσι κάνουμε) or "this is what must be (done)" (ἔτσι πρέπει). The lack of a Greek word for once does not suggest the absence of concept or practice but rather the implicit recognition that ritual activities cross sacred and profane, civil and religious, and individual and social categories. By contrast, we have invested the word "ritual" with intellectual baggages inherited from the nineteenth century, while reluctant to acknowledge that we have "it." If we define ritual as an attempt to control the outside world in relation to the self by symbolic means, as will be argued, then perhaps we should begin with everyday activities and only then proceed to strategies for coping with crisis and the more formalized activities associated with the life cycle, such as birth, marriage, and death.

In the Introduction I indicated my intention to treat metaphor as an overarching category for all kinds of symbolic representation, inclusive of both syntagmatic and paradigmatic axes of figurative thought, rather than to follow Jakobson and Halle's model of metaphor and metonym as discrete poles of linguistic usage.[3] My reasons for doing so are not to deny the relevance of their distinctions but to suggest that it works better to think in terms of a general system of transferring images from one mode of utterance or performance to another. *Metaphorés* in Greek retains the concrete meaning of "movers, shifters" (as in the logo on Greek removal vans), as well as the abstract sense of metaphor. Metonym exists only in the less common literary term *metonymía*, defined as "replacing literal word with another name, e.g., *Themis* for *justice*" (Proïas, s.v.). If a distinction is to be made between metaphor and metonym, it lies not in the images themselves but in how they are combined and presented. Metaphor remains the overriding category. My working premise is that Greek symbolic modes of expression cannot be viewed as separate from performative modes of representation, hence ritual can illuminate the processes by which metaphor signifies and renews itself. Just as metaphor is embedded in everyday speech, so ritual is embedded in everyday life: ritual systems carry metaphorical systems, each forming a treasury of associations transmitted over time.

I shall try in this chapter to indicate the synesthetic nature of ritual and metaphor through a tour of common experiences encountered in Greece both in everyday life and at times of crisis. Metaphor shapes ritual (conventional action), just as ritual gives body to metaphor. First I shall situate

Greek ritual not just as a corpus of activities and practices undertaken by rural folk at times of crisis or ceremony but also as a profoundly analogical way of seeing, thinking, and acting which has inspired many of the finest writers, while at the same time informing ethical codes on the level of everyday actions and utterances.[4]

Second, I shall take the unusual step of drawing both on field studies and from the ritualistic behavior of autistics. Autism can provide an illuminating example of how ritual may be based not in communicative strategies but in the need to organize the self where language and social structures are deficient or absent. It can also form an excellent testing ground for my contention that ritual and metaphor are inherently connected, since the speech of even the most advanced autistics has been characterized by its literal mindedness, as lacking in imaginative and symbolic dimensions. I shall use my Greek family's experiences over eighteen years of bringing up my non-speaking autistic son in the provincial urban environment of Volos to illustrate the concept and practice of reciprocity, which includes both binding and loosing strategies, negative and positive for relations between individual, family, and wider community.

Third, I shall link the results with rituals and songs of the life cycle, in preparation for my analysis of their metaphorical codes in the next chapter. Here I shall be concerned primarily with symbolic systems, not with the origins and development of particular practices, which have varied considerably in different parts of Greece and over different historical periods. My reference to rites and practices, drawn from a wide chronological and geographical range, can be justified as an attempt to show that Greek ritual structures have been sustained across a remarkable number of texts. They can therefore help us to reconstruct some enduring cultural resources—or a treasury of associations that has continued to be used—where we might have expected secularization and pragmatization.

Finally, I shall suggest that genres discussed so far in this book (oral and literary, religious and secular) may also be performative and therefore possess metaphorical and ritual dimensions which may be overlooked by an exclusively textual approach.[5]

2. Contextualizing Ritual: Everyday Life

In the later nineteenth and early twentieth centuries, ritual was associated with procedures and activities, sometimes entailing the use of magic, undertaken by one group or more within traditional, preindustrial, or small-scale societies in order to avert danger, procure fertility, promote group solidarity, and so on—that is, as something remote from our own everyday life. We tend to think that ritual has been taken over by individualism, by state religions or ideologies, by improved technology and medical care, and by national or local activities promoted by the media, although S. J. Tambiah has shown that this is not necessarily the case.[6] Ritual is not limited to mediation at times of crisis—for example, to the *rites de passage* which accompany birth, marriage, and death or to rites of healing.[7]

False assumptions, both popular and scholarly, have grown up partly as a result of the separate emergence of the disciplines of folklore and anthropology since the nineteenth century and partly because we like to distinguish traditional prescientific from modern science-oriented societies.[8] The consequences have proved detrimental to the study of the "verbal products" of folklore—the myths, tales, and songs. Vladimir Propp, in an attempt to define a historicist theory of folklore, makes a clear distinction between lyric and ritual poetry in terms of origin and function. "Ritual poetry," he claims, "whose purpose was to accompany rituals and dances and promote by magic all kinds of luck, *existed from time immemorial quite independently of lyric poetry*" (added emphases).[9] In another essay, he divides culture into two separate spheres, the spiritual and the material, believing that only the former is the proper domain of folklore (1984, 4). Such rigid distinctions—the legacy of taxonomies such as that of Politis (discussed in Chapter 6)—have only recently been challenged. In the Greek case, spiritual and material domains overlap. Granted that love songs and lullabies might be described as lyrical, their specific metaphors are determined by mythical and ritual dimensions found in all songs of the life cycle. If myth is predominantly verbal, involving some kind of narrative, ritual is synesthetic, with a complex if underestimated role in all cultures, including our own.[10]

Let us try now to contextualize ritual as it may be applied to Greek culture today and situate it not from the perspective of belief, as did J. G. Frazer, but from the perspective of language, according to the game model posited by Ludwig Wittgenstein.[11] If Frazer approached ritual through the tenuous notion of belief, Wittgenstein saw language itself as a ritual system that structures forms of life. Metaphor is embedded in the language of ritual.

In the broadest possible terms, ritual may be defined as an attempt by a group or by an individual to control the perceived outside world in relation to the self and to organize that outside world by symbolic means, involving repetition of actions, gestures, and utterances. Anthropologists have therefore talked of ritual as communicative or performative: communicative in the constitutive, rather than in the propositional, sense; and performative because it involves shared actions. Interaction rituals—or games people play—have been analyzed by sociologists and psychologists of modern Western societies.[12] The rules of the game, however, are less predictable because they are determined by a wider network of individual and group factors.

Greek rituals cannot be relegated to discrete spheres of private/public, secular/religious life. Rather, they comprise a continuum of flexible rules for confronting the human condition on three levels: (1) everyday life: activities within the household and in relation to community/outside world; (2) adversity: illness and poverty, distress and hardship; (3) the life cycle: birth, marriage, and death. These levels are often experienced concurrently, but the mechanisms for coping share the same material concerns and verbal images (food and drink, clothes and washing) and are governed by the same moral principles (sense of propriety and reciprocity), both private and public, secular and sacred.

How does ritual operate on the level of everyday life? Renée Hirschon has pointed out that the worldview of the Asia Minor refugees she studied in the district of Kokkinia (Piraeus) "can be characterized as religious for it is based on the notion of continuous interaction between the human and divine realms."[13] I would take this one step further and suggest that there is a strong sense of what is or is not proper, what will and will not do, what is or is not beautiful (*prépei / den prépei, kánei / den kánei, eínai / den eínai oraío*), which operates in synthesis with the sphere of religion, but independently of it, providing an unwritten set of rules for *all* human activities, especially those to do with the aesthetic ordering of the household and its contacts with others. There are also historical and literary dimensions: how are present utterances shaped by past experiences and texts?

First, clothes and food. One does not have to be religious to know that clothes must never be washed in the same basin used for food, even if there is only a single tap in the household; that is something only dirty foreigners do. The prohibition is based on the notion that "contact must be prevented between that which goes into the body and that which comes out and between things associated with cleaner and dirtier areas of the body," [14] itself part of the Greek cyclical, left-right concept of body and cosmos.[15] Such themes are elaborated in the imagery of songs of *xenitiá* "exile," in which the foreign woman's refusal to wash the stranger's clothes is equated with her refusal to bury him.[16] Food, likewise, is a mediating bond between members of a household and between household and outside, therefore both its preparation and its consumption require special care, however humble the ingredients. The simplest family meal has a spiritual dimension and will commence only when all expected members are present, usually with an informal exchange of wishes on taking the first sip of water.[17] Eating is a communal activity, hence even teenagers are discouraged from eating a snack from the fridge standing up!

An unwritten set of rules likewise governs the choice of clothes deemed appropriate for wear inside/outside the house, with importance attached not so much to ostentation as to propriety in accordance with age and occasion (Hirschon 1989, 229–31). Great pride is taken in the clean, neat appearance of all clothes and household linen, even when stored in chests and cupboards, as if they too, like food, signify inner states of cleanliness and orderliness: old clothes are not discarded but, where possible, washed, unraveled, and made into colorful rag rugs (*koureloúdes*) for a stone floor or garden shed, or for use as ground cover at the beach or on picnics. Before leaving her house in Volos for a brief visit to the family home in Sklithron in the summer of 1991, my sister-in-law Katina took out a set of perfectly clean but slightly yellowed, lace-edged white cotton curtains, beautifully handwoven and embroidered by her mother, Aspasia, some sixty years ago for the village house and kept in careful storage in Volos since that house ceased to be occupied: she spent two days soaking, washing, starching, and ironing them, allowing only minimal assistance from myself—"Eh! she said, these things have their ways [*ta períerga*], you must have the knack!" Why did she do it? "They are beautiful [*ómorphes*], and who knows? One day Pavlos or Dimitri [my sons] might live there," was her comment. On arriving in Sklithron late in the evening, laying the beds entailed going through two large chests (*baoúlia*) filled with lace-edged sheets, woven coverlets (*veléntzes*), and pillowcases (*maxillarothēkes*), all handmade by Aspasia, who reminisced as we took each one out on the story of its making. Handicrafts too can map the memory: setting up the washed curtains in the village house was a symbolic act linking present to past (Aspasia's labors) and present to future (Katina's hopes). There was probably another, unspoken calculation on Katina's part: since my father-in-law, Dimitris, died without bequeathing by testament the village house to my sons, as he had intended, its ownership is still a matter of family dispute. Setting up the curtains in the proper manner was Katina's symbolic way of staking her side of the family's claim to the property.[18]

As a consequence of this revisitation to the past, Aspasia (then ninety-one) asked me to send the exact measurements of my son Dimitri's bedroom window back in England, so she could make him similar curtains; by the time I left for England five days later, she had already begun the lacework "so he can have something of me to remember over there." He still treasures them. Lace, whiteness, and pure cloth are associated with artwork and memory: they link past and present, here and there, life and death. It is no accident that I caught Katina (who rarely leaves Volos), at 3:00 A.M. preceding our departure for Sklithron, noiselessly scrubbing her virtually immaculate floors: any departure, however brief, signals the possibility of no return, therefore no labors (*pónoi*) on the house should be spared now in order that her past labors (she dug its very foundations when her husband, Thanasis, was in prison during the Junta years) should be remembered by the neighborhood if she failed to return. Πόνεσα γι' αὐτὸ τὸ σπίτι ("I *pained/labored* for this house"), she had frequently said of those difficult years, creatively adapting a metaphor for childbirth (her physical handicap had rendered her childless). Needless to say, I did not need to put these thoughts into words but simply assisted her in what tasks remained to be done until I could persuade her to take some rest.

Second, visits and gifts: Occasions vary from casual, neighborly calls among women, usually inside the house in late morning when chores, shopping, and cooking will have been completed and gossip can be exchanged over coffee, perhaps with a take-home gift of an odd, tasty tidbit or sweetmeat, put on one of the good dishes and covered with a fair linen cloth. Dish and cloth will be returned the next day or so, probably with a reciprocal offering. Evening visits (from six to nine o'clock) take place in the courtyard (*avlí*) and tend to be intrafamilial, cross-gendered, and cross-generational: chairs will be brought out to accommodate all over coffee and iced water as news, gossip, and jokes are exchanged. Unlike the women's morning visits, evening occasions tend to be prearranged, although they do not normally involve gift exchange. Men may talk politics, women may exchange news on children and grandchildren (the latter usually present); but women intervene in political discussions rather more forcefully than do men in family affairs.

Formal visits occur on name days, when home-cooked or bought delicacies are offered by the household of the celebrant to all comers, who bring wrapped gifts not necessarily to be opened immediately. Such visits cut across social boundaries in urban and rural Greece alike: even in bourgeois settings, hosts may be insulted by guests who bring gifts of wine or basic foodstuffs to dinner at their home, because to do so implies failure to provide the necessities of a meal: as luxuries, flowers, dessert, and chocolates are acceptable.[19]

Shopping at luxury stores is a pleasure to be indulged. My simple gifts of nonutility clothes for the infant granddaughter of Katina's sister, Elpiniki (who occupies the house on the opposite side of the same courtyard), were received with especial pleasure because Elpiniki's only son's daughter by a second marriage was conceived and birthed with difficulty and because Elpiniki had saved herself and her newborn son by diving with him under the iron bed in a Volos hospital when the town was the epicenter of a major earthquake in 1954. Aged about sixteen, she had been the victim of ear slashing during the Civil War (1946–49) by Rightist gangs, an event witnessed in the village square. Such things are not easily talked of, but my small gift was an indirect means of acknowledging the importance that the birth against hope of a grandchild might have for her. Similarly, I bought— with Elpiniki's guidance—a pretty set of clothes at the neighborhood shop for my former husband's three-year-old daughter Aspasia (named after her paternal grandmother) by his second marriage: some days later, Katina told me it was a fitting token of reconciliation, showing that I was not jealous of (δέν ζήλευες) his remarriage and, more important, the birth to him of a "normal" daughter. Some years later, the local shop closed, or else neighborhood rules of reciprocity would have inhibited us from going outside without deception (πονηριά); but Elpiniki and I still enjoyed our forays into downtown fashion shops when looking for appropriate gifts. As we walked through the Volos neighborhoods, she told me her associations with them, as on Sophokleous Street, where she cared for her family in a shack without running water or sewage for fifteen years while maintaining utmost cleanliness and meticulous cooking in her corner of that courtyard. Gift exchange is a process of negotiation determined by rules of reciprocity which cannot be measured in material values or expressed in words.[20]

Third, high days and holidays in the Orthodox calendar: On New Year's Eve, kin and friends are invited to share in good food, drink, and game playing, hoping that luck in cards and dice will determine prosperity throughout the following year. At Easter, candles lit from the church lamp after the midnight Saturday service ("Light has scattered the darkness, Christ is risen!") must be taken home unquenched untill the threshold is crossed and marked with the sign of the Cross by the flame. On Sunday, ceremonial red eggs, decorated with different flower patterns by the women, are shared out before the festive meal commences. Women may have fasted for forty days before partaking of the *mageirítsa* "entrails" of Sunday morning (cooked by women) and Paschal Lamb of Sunday afternoon (roasted by men, who may thereby excuse themselves from attendance at the early morning church service). These things are done not because people "believe" they can change the course of events but because they mean fun, dance, and song to be enjoyed with others. Ritual is not just a solemn affair: it involves shared control and indulgence of the senses, while leaving room to express individual creativity. As one of Hirschon's informants exclaimed after her labors for a religious festival, ή θρησκεία μας είναι ώραία! (Our religion is beautiful!).[21]

3. Autistic Rituals

As Sally Falk Moore and Barbara Myerhoff have emphasized, ritual should not be romanticized: it may be destructive of social norms or just boring and ineffective.[22] Ritual is a protean concept. The syndrome of autism is characterized above all by perseverative gestures, postures, and actions; by fetishism; and, in the case of many verbal autistics, by repetitive, stereotyped speech. Obsessive ritualism is the major behavioral and diagnostic trait common to all autistics, providing their way of ordering the self. In the absence of social skills, the sense of self is fragile, requiring constant and idiosyncratic ordering and patterning of a kind only intermittently externalized by most non-autistic people.[23] Their goal is self-control, not world control, hence the endearing innocence and inability to deceive, however maddening their bad habits. Psychiatrists have characterized autistics' need for ritual as physiological and psychological, in compensation for their lack of communicative and social skills.[24]

What is certain is that rituals, autistic and other, share common characteristics, especially in relation to grief and loss. First, physiological actions: speaking and nonspeaking autistics alike express grief or anxiety by rocking incessantly to and fro; by head banging and self-mutilation; by perseverative manipulation, tapping, and sniffing of fetishistic objects; by dropping, throwing, or smashing prized articles; by smearing feces; by rapid eye movements accompanied by switching lights on and off; and by swinging and spinning. By these means, autistics alternate between hyperactive and catatonic states. Violence is directed primarily against the self, but may be extended toward objects and other persons. The testimony of two partially recovered autistic women suggests that the basis for these actions lies not in the desire to communicate but, on the contrary, to shut out the outside world by stimulating and regulating by turns the sensorimotor system.

As for speaking autistics, they love to map the memory by repeating names of people and places in an endless chant (getting on everyone's nerves!) and defining "what is" in terms of "what is not": "what was there then is not here now, what is here now was not there then." My son Dimitri feels irremediable loss at the death of close ones of all ages but finds relief in repetitive chantings through negative statements, which he then types onto his computer and prints out in bold type with a litany of names and places—a process not disanalogous to Orthodox memorials (*mnēmósyna*).[25]

What of metaphor? Granted the well-known autistic tendency to what we consider "literal mindedness" in verbal expression and comprehension (as in the clinical anecdote of a boy who, when told to "stick his coat somewhere," asked for glue!), there is evidence to challenge our own verbal preconceptions in terms of a process of "thinking in pictures."[26] Since the age of three, my nonspeaking son, Pavlos, has carried in his head mental pictures of houses, streets, and whole districts or cities with such a degree of accuracy that, after the briefest of visits, he is able to find his way around unaided years later. Nor is visual recall limited to the concrete: attachment to fetishistic objects, such as twiddling and lining up toothbrushes, screws, and pebbles or traveling on buses and amassing timetables (some of my sons' obsessions over the years) can be explained by analogical association, signifying ability to control the connectedness of one thing, person, or place to another.[27] Moreover, a preliminary study of self-report of inner experience by three able people with autism found that they described their mental contents in terms of pictures in the head, as opposed to a control group of normal subjects who described a mixture of inner speech, pictures, and pure thought.[28] I doubt whether this ability to think in pictures is limited only to the ablest autistics: aged fourteen, when mildly reprimanded by his maternal grandmother for a sight-reading error in a music lesson, my son Dimitri exclaimed, "Brain lights gone out—all black!" Many of us have shared this experience at some time in our lives, but few can have condensed it so vividly into metaphor.

What is impaired among autistics is the ability to infer meaning from context *when confronted by spoken words alone*. Eddy, twenty-six-year-old Anglo-Caribbean friend of my son Dimitri, may have a temper tantrum and even break windows if reprimanded verbally for piling the contents of the sugar bowl into his tea, but he does not demur if a written note, "Nice young men take only two lumps of sugar," is pinned to the bowl. Eddy will not talk, but he can sing beautifully and be taught to hold a part, as can Ruth, who does not speak but chants her requests, "I want to go home now" or "Let's take the bus now," to the same pentatonic tune. Autistics can best be taught to communicate through bodily movement and representation—painting, dance, song, and play—in short, through ritual, not verbal, language. It is as if they *know* that language is a game and refuse to play it except on their own terms.[29]

Most of these habits and mannerisms of autistics can be paralleled in mourning laments and rituals, with the difference that the mourner's pattern of disturbed behavior is ultimately socially controllable and can be channeled into creative forms of expression. Two examples will make the point. First, when confronted with her husband's dead body during the civil war, a woman from the Peloponnese exclaimed, "My pine tree!," a condensed image not dissimilar to Dimitri's "brain lights," except that it had resonances with past texts associating Christ - Cross - tree - shade - shelter—or even with the felled Homeric hero.[30] The woman was able to find in metaphor a given form for her grief. Yet—and herein lies a critical paradox—the felling of a tree is powerful image: when Oakfield House Autistic Music and Drama Group staged a performance of the Greek tale "The Twins" (Birmingham, July 1995: adapted from Pio 1879), our narrator, Barry King, had to speak the lines "And so it happened. The young hero felled the massive oak tree with a single sword-stroke." During a break in rehearsal, he asked, "But how did the tree sound as it was being felled?" then brilliantly improvised his own music on a small Yamaha. "And this is how the tree fell!" he added, putting the instrument aside to perform a perfect, acrobatic dive in slow perpendicular. The point is, the mourner attunes the image of the felled tree to her dead husband, but the autistic person wants to know what the tree felt like! Time did not permit Barry's improvisation to be incorporated into the performance: the director, Sara Clithero, judiciously emphasized group collaboration (not easily achieved with autistics) and gently chastized him, "Barry, you can't play all the parts—you're the narrator!"[31]

Second, in 1968 the folklorist Mary Vouras documented, with camera and tape recorder, a remarkable sequence of events during Holy Week in the village of Olymbos, Karpathos. On the morning of Good Friday, during a small service when men were largely absent, the priest was perfunctorily conducting the liturgy for the Deposition of the Cross (Kathēlosis). At the moment when the icon was brought down, a woman in the congregation let out a piercing shriek, like an ancient *ololygē*: she had suffered four family bereavements over the previous year. Her inarticulate and hysterical wailings went on for fifteen minutes; yet gradually she found herself supported by other women who held her upright while they wept for their own dead. Imperceptibly, as the priest withdrew into the background, they helped her to channel her grief into the time-honored form of a traditional lament of the All-Holy Mother of God's lament for Christ:

Σήμερα μαύρος ουρανός, σήμερα μαύρη μέρα·
σήμερα ἐσταυρώσανε τὸν Βασιλιὰ τῶν πάντων.

(Baud-Bovy 2.248–49)

Today the sky is black, today the day is black,
today they crucified the King of All.

Through her religion and sense of personal identity with the Panagia, she was able to find in the lament a given form for her grief. Social milieu provides the means for sustaining structures lacked by autistics, who fail to articulate griefs no less deeply felt.[32]

Ritual derives its power from all the senses and emotions that can be harnessed to map out the memory of self and others.[33] After a death in Greece, feelings of anger, grief and guilt are assuaged not just at the public wake and funeral by prescribed actions (the smashing of vessels, washing and dressing the corpse, positions of kin and nonkin, lament performance) but by physiological acts performed in private, such as laceration of the flesh, the tearing of clothes, dancing in front of the household icon, smelling and caressing the dead person's clothes or hair, and talking to the dead at the graveside or in dreams.[34] Smell is closely linked to memory, hence a mourner takes comfort from sniffing a piece of the dead person's clothes, a detail which finds its way into Syriac religious laments in *memre* (metrical sermons) on "The Binding of Isaac" from the fifth to sixteenth centuries A.D.[35] Smashing vessels over the threshold is an important part of Greek funeral rites, while possessions associated with the deceased may be annihilated on the day before the funeral.[36] As for violence against other persons, head hunting among the Illongots of Southeast Asia is an expression of grief as well as anger.[37]

The means by which ritual signals is symbolic: it performs functions and conceptualizes phenomena not directly related to the perceptual level of experience. It includes nonverbal as well as verbal activities and selection across paradigmatic and syntagmatic axes (metaphor and metonym) through juxtaposition of similarity/difference and contiguity/synecdoche. The sadness of autistics' ritualism lies in the burden placed on the individual to compensate for the fragility of social and communicative structures by means of compulsive actions. Yet does not their experience have something to teach us about the importance of ritual in coping with all forms of difficult behavior?

4. Ritual and Reciprocity

Let us turn now to mechanisms for coping with adversity: sickness and poverty, accident and distress. Notions of right and wrong guide moral as well as practical behavior, operating outside as well as inside the religious sphere. In contrast to the emphasis placed on self-dependence by the Protestant ethic, the frailty of human nature is accepted in Orthodox practice, hence actions tend to be judged conditionally and contextually rather than in absolute terms, often after lively debate.[38] The overriding importance of securing the future of the family has been emphasized in recent anthropological studies; but a family which looks only to its own interests will be subjected to adverse criticism by friends and neighbors. Hirschon has noted that "people's dependence on one another is recognised and allowed expression. This notion tempers the values of self-regard (*egoismós*) and independence characteristic of Greek life, which would otherwise take on an absolute character. The strength of neighbourhood expectations in the locality is undoubtedly also related to this recognition of human limitations and need" (1989, 139–40). The worst offense is to ignore goodwill and favors, built up by years of everyday interaction with neighbors, and to fail to help others in their hour of crisis and need.

Lest it be thought that Hirschon's subjects of study are atypical because bound by the common experience of *prosphygiá* "refugeeness," I will cite the experience of Katina and Thanasis in bringing up my son Pavlos in a suburb of Volos. He is not easy to deal with, and his antisocial behavior cannot be confined within the household. Over eighteen years, he has willfully smashed prized *glástres* (ornamental pots) with flowering shrubs in the courtyard of the family across the street, whom he dearly loves (the suburb, by no means affluent, prides itself on the cleanliness of its side streets and the beauty of its small gardens and courtyards). He has thrown stones at people and property; he has gone on night rampages, leaping from one roof terrace to another and descending via the outer staircase into other people's houses to investigate and consume the contents of their refrigerators and steal their toothbrushes. His latest ploy was to jump out of his bedroom window (the only one facing onto the street, out of sight from living room and kitchen occupied by Aspasia and Katina) and to plunder the local kiosk for goodies he is not supposed to eat. In societies more familiar to the Anglo-American West, the neighborhood would refuse to tolerate him. And yet, while a few voices (mainly from outside the immediate *geitoniá* "neighborhood") can be heard to mutter that he "ought to be locked up in an institution," most neighbors are unstinting in their admiration for the courage and self-sacrifice of Katina and Thanasis (γιὰ δές, τί κουράγιο, τί ἀγάπη, πῶς θυσιάζονται αὐτοὶ οἱ ἄνθρωποι! "See! what courage, what love and look at how they *sacrifice themselves!*") and in their sympathy for Pavlos himself (τί κρῖμα, τί ὅμορφο κι ἔξυπνο παιδί "what a shame, what a beautiful and clever child!"), or (ὁ Παῦλος δὲν πρέπει νὰ τρώγει τέτοια πράγματα· δὲν σᾶς τὸ λέω ἐπειδὶς τὰ παίρνει ἀπὸ δῶ, ἀλλὰ δὲν τὸν κάνουν καλό! "Pavlos oughtn't to eat such food: I don't say this because he takes from here [Pavlos' rampages at the local kiosk were always meticulously reimbursed], but because they aren't good for him!"). How to explain this different level of tolerance? It is not simply because in Greece, institutional care for those with mental disorders is still regarded as state intervention into family affairs or equated with subhuman conditions on the island of Leros,[39] but because Katina and Thanasis unstintingly share their neighbors' tribulations at times of crisis and joy and also because ἄνθρωποι εἴμαστε, θὰ μποροῦσε νὰ συμβεῖ καὶ σὲ μᾶς "we are human, it could have happened to us." People are valued in relative, moral terms, not in absolute and materialistic ones, yet the system of binding oneself to another can itself become a curse, as expressed by the meaning of δένω "bind" = "curse."[40]

This sense of reciprocity operates at a level deeper than that of Orthodox observance: Katina and Thanasis, known for their sufferings as left-wing victims of the Civil War (1946–49), are not regular church attenders, although they are on friendly terms with the local priest. When he visited my ailing mother-in-law, Aspasia (summer 1995), Katina apologized to him for her failure to attend church regularly. He gestured to Aspasia, then to Pavlos, saying Νά, ἡ ἐκκλησία σου! "Here is your church!" If anyone criticizes Katina for her devotion to Pavlos, she will say, speaking from the perspective of a "lame woman" (ἡ κουτσή) with a dislocated hip and one leg seven inches shorter than the other: Τί μὲ νοιάζει τί θὰ πεῖ ὁ κόσμος; Κάνω αὐτὸ ποὺ πρέπει! "What do I care what people say? I do what is right!" Such a statement might seem to conflict with our notions of reciprocity, but it was intended to affirm communal judgment, as opposed to individual interest (egoismós). Thanasis, a political prisoner from the age of eighteen to thirty-six and then again during the Junta (1967–74) for a further four-year term, is disillusioned with politics but has lost none of his humanity (anthropiá, a key concept in Greek culture): "If they shut up Pavlos, Margaret, I will follow him, wherever he is, even to England and America, to take care of him and others like him. Even if they don't pay me!" No doubt Pavlos might have been accommodated elsewhere; but he was accepted as part of neighborhood life, along with every other difficult household situation, according to principles of reciprocity and a strong sense of self, rather different from the absolute ethics of Protestant brotherliness.[41] He could not have been so accommodated had Katina and Thanasis failed to reciprocate the needs of others.

Two more examples will illustrate how crisis may call for a more urgent form of ritual action operating both inside and outside the religious sphere. The first concerns Pavlos at the crucial time of his baptism in April 1971. Times were hard (the Junta years); but it was Easter, Thanasis had just been released from jail on Yioura, and it was the first time my boys had visited Greece. No expense or labor was begrudged by the family in preparing for Easter and the double baptism at the local church. It was widely said among family and neighbors that Pavlos, then aged four and still not talking, would have the gift of speech once he was baptized: this did not happen. Eight days later at the confirmation liturgy, they persisted: he would speak. Not only did he fail to do so, but he threw his Communion bread onto the church floor and dashed the chalice from the priest's hands, probably because the priest's assistant had tried to force the wine down Pavlos' throat by holding his nose. The sacred drink was spilled! Clearly, something had to be done—but what? A few days later, with no recriminations and a minimum of fuss, a pilgrimage was made: my two four-year olds, their two grandmothers (Aspasia and Katharine), their two aunts (Katina and Elpiniki) and myself walked some six miles to the shrine of Panagia Gouritsa in Ano Volos. I doubt if any of us believed a miracle would happen, but then, who knows? My father-in-law, Dimitris (who was deeply religious), was satisfied, and other people concluded we had done everything we could. More than that, our long trek up the mountain at sunset brought an inner peace, because the scenery was beautiful and our anxiety shared. The walk against the sunset over the sea inspired one of Dimitri's most striking uses of metaphor; "Red knife cuts sky." What more can be asked of ritual? Our belief systems were so different—two British agnostics, three Greek Orthodox women, and two autistic sons—yet had we not participated, we would have risked people's saying, "They didn't consult the saint!" Saints mediate and negotiate between human and divine realms: if you do your part, they may (or may not) do theirs, but you have to try, and you can always blame the saint afterward if disappointed.[42]

My second example concerns an emigration ritual from Epiros. In Monolithi, one of those villages around Ioannina aptly known as *nekrokhória* "corpse villages" on account of the high rate of emigration, it is customary for mothers to place a coin in a *misiokára* (half-measure vessel) of water, set it on the threshold for their departing sons to upset as they leave the house, and to utter the words ὅπως τρέχει τὸ νερὸ νὰ κυλᾶ καὶ τὸ χρῆμα μέσα στὸ πουγγὶ τοῦ μετανάστη "As the water flows, so may the money flow in the purse of the emigrant."[43] As in many other rituals, both verbal and nonverbal elements are metaphorical, words reinforcing and explaining the symbolism of actions. In other cases, such as *mágia* "enchantment," rites of healing and exorcism, and funeral rites for those whose bodies cannot be recovered, the efficacy of ritual depends on the inclusion of a small physical item which represents the whole of the person concerned—for example, hair and nails, clothes, or intimate belongings, even a photograph. Synecdoche is a part of metaphor.

Redefined in this way, ritual can be demystified, no longer remote, but an indispensable physiological, psychological, and synesthetic part of our daily interactions and transactions, although its particular manifestations

may vary across histories and cultures. The interconnections between ritual
and metaphor provide valuable clues as to the complex nonverbal, as well as
verbal, processes of cultural transmission.

5. Rituals of the Life Cycle: Separation, Transition, and Integration

Rituals of the life cycle, associated with childbirth and baptism,
courtship and marriage, and sickness and death, can be shown to have interacted with the metaphorical system, which has, in common with other
cultures, drawn continuous analogies between the cycles of human and
natural life. Their pre-eminence is due to many factors which cannot be
ranged in any order of priority. Is it because birth, marriage, and death are
the most formative events in human life? How and why have they resisted
the kind of secularization that occurred in the West from the time of the
Reformation? Is it because the Orthodox Church, however condemnatory
of women's rites and superstitions, has proved tolerant in practice? It is true
that despite continuous prohibitions, the church has learned to coexist with
and even assimilate beliefs and practices not sanctioned by official theology,
thus giving rise to a symbiosis between church, state, and family, but surely
this is as much a symptom as a cause?[44] In *Ritual Lament* (1974, 51) I proposed that a key factor in the long tradition of the Greek lament lay in "the
vital unity of poetry and ritual." Let us extend and develop this suggestion
by reviewing some interactions between ritual and metaphor at each stage
of the life cycle, with some reference in footnotes to earlier formative texts.

Following Leach's tripartite system, based on van Gennep and Hertz, I
propose to summarize the major parallels and differences between rituals of
the life cycle (Table 1) under three headings: rites of separation, rites of
transition, and rites of integration.[45] These will be illustrated by specific examples, which, although not restricted to a single region or period, have
been documented over the past 180 years and are therefore contemporary
with the narrative songs and tales discussed in Part II, and with the ritual
songs to be presented in Chapter 10. The tripartite system is a convenient
framework around which to organize ritual as *structure*; if adhered to over-
rigidly, the complexity of ritual as *story/drama* will be masked. As in the
tales and songs, people have to do and say the right things at the right time
and in the right place, although the sequence is not absolute and will vary
from one ritual occasion to another.[46] It would seem logical to review the
three major passages in the linear order in which they occur in life: birth,
marriage and death; but since the metaphorical quality of ritual is to interpret one in terms of the other, I propose to treat them concurrently ac-

cording to Leach's three states. Marriage and death rituals share the most common features, while birth and courtship rituals move in contrary flow. It is arguable that marriage is the pivotal sequence, lent as it were to death and adapted for birth; but, since death rituals have been more fully recorded and have proved more tenacious, I shall follow the order death/marriage/birth in my discussion of each state:

Table 3

Initial State	Liminal State	Final State
Rites of separation	*Rites of transition: exposure/seclusion*	*Rites of integration*

Separation

At death and marriage, rites of separation commence with initial preparations in the house and culminate when the threshold of the house is crossed for funeral and nuptial rites at church. Death comes uninvited and unannounced. Where it can be predicted, as in the case of the sick and elderly, kinsfolk from far afield and neighbors are encouraged to gather round the departing one, so that the past can be remembered, enjoyed, and forgiven and last wishes—whether testamentary or alimentary—can be indulged. Whenever possible, a terminally sick and hospitalized person will be brought home for the final rites.[47] It remains a matter of utmost importance to observe silence and to avoid cries of grief during the actual death throes, still known in popular speech as *psychorrhágēma* (soul rupturing) and *charopálema* (death wrestling), because the dying person is *angelophoreménos* (dressed in angels) and would only be distracted by mundane conversation.[48]

Following the initial snatching of the soul by Charos, personified as male and violent, the soul is said to be exposed to the intervention of angels and demons literally fighting over its possession. Premature lamentation provokes *angelókomma* (angel cutting), or the prevention of access to the soul by benevolent forces.[49] Once the soul has departed, ritual silence gives way to informal cries of grief, which is freely vented as the body is prepared for the wake and for the long journey ahead: eyes and mouth are sealed, often with a coin; and the body is washed with water or water and wine and then dressed in new clothes and shoes, with nuptial attire for the unmarried and for newlyweds. Fruits and flowers, evergreens and herbs, and coins and other ring-shaped objects are placed around the body in preparation for the formal wake.[50] These acts are performed by elderly relatives and neighbors as the house is dramatically opened to all comers.[51]

The following laments, for son and daughter respectively, testify to the importance of providing the right clothes for the journey in the ritual dressing of the dead:

Τόνε καλοσυγύρισα,
τοῦ χτένισα τὴ γ κάπα του,
καὶ τόνε στόλισα γαμπρό,
μὲ τὸ στεφάνι τὸ μονό.
῏Ηρθασι καὶ τὸ πάρασι,
ἡ νεκροφόρα κι ὁ παπᾶς,
καρότσες κι αὐτοκίνητα.

I have made him tidy,
I have combed his cloak,
and I have decked him out as bridegroom
with the single wedding crown.
They came to take him off,
funeral procession and priest,
carts and cars.

(Kassis 3.47–48: Mani)

᾽Ελλάξα σε, στόλισα σε, λουλούδια πουπουλούδια
τσαὶ στὶς δικές μας τὶς καρδιές ἀφτούμενα καρβούνια.

I changed you, I dressed you, in flowers and downy blooms;
and in our own hearts burning coals.

(Komninos 55: Kastellorizo)[52]

The actions narrated in these two short laments signify both ritually and metaphorically, because the dressing of the dead is both performative and symbolic of a change in status, while the dressing theme allows the mourner to draw a poetic contrast between her dead child's beauty and her own inner grief.

The wake, which forms the climax of the first stage in the funeral ritual, combines different media in a drama of the utmost efficacy if the roles are well played. There is a formal *positioning* around the body of kin and non-kinsfolk, as intending mourners arouse themselves to the pitch of tension required for lament performance by rapid, heavy *breathing* (hyperventilation).[53] The occasion to lament (in forms at once conventional and improvised) is then ritually passed from left to right in a circular movement,[54] to the accompaniment of strong *gesture and posture*, as mourners pull at hair and scarves and lacerate cheeks and breasts. Antagonisms between kin and non-kin are fought out, lost or won, especially where the widow's status is concerned, according to the skill of the players. That ritual can be actively manipulative is aptly illustrated in the following case recorded from the Mani. At the funeral of Pavlos Tsitsiris, a young teacher who died of tuberculosis in 1926, his fiancée, Kalliope (also a teacher), began the lament in rhetorical style. His mother took it up, expressing not only grief for her son but also addressing sympathy for her *nýphē* (daughter-in-law) and *koronítsa* "little bride." Deftly, Kalliope avoided the "widow trap" by rejecting these terms of address on the grounds that she was educated and—implicitly—that no sexual relationship was ever realized between them:[55]

> Ἄκος, μαννοῦλα μου γλυκειά,
> μὴ γ κλαίεις τ' γ κορονίτσα ζου.
> Νὰ κλαίεις τὸ γ καθηγητή
> ποὺ δὲν ἔχεις ἄλλο παιδί.
> Τὸ δὲ ἐγὼ θὰ παντρευτοῦ
> κι ἄλλο γ καθηγητὴ θὰ βροῦ.
> Τι ἐγὼ ἀπὸ τοῦ λόγου μου
> δὲν ἔχου ἀνάγκη τίποτα.
> Ἔχου πατέρα δάσκαλο
> καὶ ἀδερφό ἔχου γιατρό
> καὶ σπουδασμένη εἶμαι καὶ 'γώ.
> Καὶ θὲ νὰ ξαναπαντρευτοῦ
> κι ἄλλο γ καθηγητὴ θὰ βροῦ.
> Ἐγὼ ἀπὸ τοῦ λόγου μου
> δὲν τόνε κλαίου γι' ἄντρα μου,
> οὔτε γι' ἀρρεβωνιαστικό
> μόν' τόνε κλαίου γι' ἀδερφό
> ποὺ ἔσπουδάζαμε μαζί
> πέρα στὴν Ἀρεόπολη
> Ἐσύ, ἒ μάννα καψερή,
> ἀμπῶς θὰ παρηγορηθεῖς
> καὶ ποῦ θὰ βρεῖς ἄλλο παιδί;

(Kassis 3.53)

Listen, my sweet mother,
don't mourn for me, your little bride.
Mourn for the teacher,
for you have no other son.
As for me, I'll get married,
I can find another teacher.

So far as I'm concerned,
I have no need of anything.
My father is a teacher,
my brother is a doctor,
and I've had an education.
I'll get wed again,
I'll find another teacher.
So far as I'm concerned
I mourn him not as husband,
nor even as betrothed,
but only as my brother,
for we studied together
over in Areopolis.
But you, eh grief-stricken mother,
how will you be comforted,
where will you find another son?

As Dimitra Scavdi has observed, the public context of the lament perform-ance provided Kalliope with the opportunity she needed to avoid the dreaded status of widowhood: members of the audience were witnesses to her disavowal of further obligations.[56] Had she followed normal practice for fiancées and kept silent at the funeral, tongues would have wagged, and she might have found it hard to marry. Despite the beauty of her opening lament, many conflicting sentiments were involved in her calculations!

During the all-night vigil, lamentation ceases. Jokes and tales may be ex-changed to help stay awake; *pónos* "pain" gives way to *paramythiá* "comfort." Intensity of grief recurs next day, when the church bell tolls to summon people to the house of the bereaved to witness the farewells, lamentations, and offerings. The first ritual stage draws to a close as the body, placed in an open coffin with head uncovered, is carried over the threshold by four male bearers, preferably neither kinsmen nor newlyweds.[57]

Unlike death, marriage is carefully prepared for by the families of bride and groom. It used not to be uncommon for a betrothal to be planned even before birth of the individuals if the match between two families was con-sidered desirable.[58] In Sklithron at the turn of the century, Aspasia's family owned the greatest number of flocks, whereas Dimitris' family owned the most vineyards and produced the best wine. Their mothers reached an agreement that their children should eventually marry, and so Aspasia and Dimitris grew up as informally betrothed. Trouble came later, when Aspa-sia's family lost the lead as pastoralists and Dimitris' family tried to break off the agreement, which had no binding force. But by this time the young couple had developed a genuine affection for each other and would not hear of marrying elsewhere: with the help of friends, Dimitris "stole her" (τὴν ἔκλεψε).

This is a story of dialectics between heart and head or of how marriage may be negotiated. First, as a social contract that affects not just the future of the two families concerned but the balance of power within the village, marriage is thought of in association with and from the time of childbirth. Second, whereas in theory the parents have the right to dictate or forbid a match, in practice the community can exercise constraints. If Aspasia and Dimitris had developed a purely individual emotional attachment to each other, the theft would not have been condoned. But because it was known that their parents had agreed, however informally, to betroth their offspring, Sklithriots were predisposed in favor of the young couple's wishes. Dimitris' family risked accusations of improper lust for power and property, hence his "theft" was condoned by village opinion. Nor can it have escaped Sklithriot calculations that it was probably better that a match between the two prominent families of the day not take place. This kind of tension between individual and group and between fixity and improvisation forms the sine qua non of effective ritual, as in the case of Kalliope's lament and of social life in general.[59]

Death and marriage both involve the crucial transfer of property through inheritance and dowry, although details of how and what vary throughout Greece. Traditionally, a girl's dowry was prepared from infancy, whereas betrothal between couples is formally and publicly marked by an exchange of gifts and feasts. The occasion for nuptials is arranged in advance, preference being given to a Sunday in the winter season; Lent, May, leap years, full moon, Mondays, Tuesdays, and Wednesdays are best avoided.[60] Intensive preparations commence some five days before the wedding, as bread is baked, food and clothes are prepared, and bride and bridegroom are ritually washed, combed or shaved, and dressed, each in their separate households, to the accompaniment of special songs. For the washing of the bridal pair, as for the corpse, all water must be brought from outside the house, sometimes from special springs, while clay vessels are broken over the threshold, as after a death, metaphorically signifying the impossibility of return to former status.[61]

Meanwhile, the bride has been carefully secluded within the household. Her confrontation with the outside world commences when the groom's group (men) greets her own group (women) in the courtyard of her house with an exchange of antiphonal songs, often overtly hostile in tone, as in the following song from Macedonia, where the men's firing of guns that accompanies the song reinforces the vocal tones and images of conflict, resonant with aggression and male sexuality:

Νιὸς γαμπρὸς στὴν πόρτα,
θρῆνος, πόλεμος.
Τριακόσια παλλικάρια,
ὅλα μὲ σπαθιά,
ρίχνουν τὰ τουφέκια.
Νιὸς γαμπρὸς στὴν πόρτα,
θρῆνος, πόλεμος.

(Saunier 1968, 55)

Young bridegroom at the door,
lamentation, war.
Three hundred young warriors,
all with spears,
fire their guns.
Young bridegroom at the door,
lamentation, war.

Before the bride departs, there is an exchange of lamentation between bride and mother (each supported by antiphonal women's groups), one expressing reluctance and the other threatening force. Sometimes, the bride has to be physically carried over the threshold by the groom's group.[62] The groom's violence in the wedding songs is couched in terms parallel to Charos' violence in the laments, as the two following examples illustrate:

—Κρύψε με, μάνα, κρύψε με, ὁ ξένος μὴ μὲ πάρει.
—Τί νὰ σὲ κρύψω, μάτια μου, ποὺ σὺ τοῦ ξένου εῖσαι.
Τοῦ ξένου φόρια φόρεσε, τοῦ ξένου δαχτυλίδια,
γιατὶ τοῦ ξένου εῖσαι καὶ σύ, κι ὁ ξένος θὰ σὲ πάρει.

—Hide me, mother, hide me, lest the stranger take me.
—Why should I hide you, dear one, for you are the stranger's.
Wear the stranger's clothes, [put on] the stranger's rings,
for you too are the stranger's, and the stranger will take you.

(L.S. 3.281)

—Κρύψε με, μάνα, κρύψε με, νὰ μὴ μὲ πάρει ὁ Χάρος.
—Ποὺ νὰ σὲ κρύψω, Χάιδω μου, ποὺ ὁ Χάρος θὰ σὲ πάρει.
—Κρύψε με στὰ βασιλικά, καὶ μέσ' στὶς μαντζουράνες, . . .
—Ὅπ' νὰ σὲ κρύβω, Χάιδω μου, ὁ Χάρος θὰ σὲ πάρει.

—Hide me, mother, hide me, so Charos cannot take me.
—Where can I hide you, my Cháido, for Charos is going to take you.

—Hide me in the basil and in the marjoram. . . .
—Wherever I hide you, my Cháido, Charos is going to take you.

(L.A. 2.401)

The formulaic and thematic structure is common to both songs: details differ as appropriate to the rituals, for the departing bride is about to have the
crown and ring of marriage set upon her, whereas the dead daughter is already placed in the coffin amid herbs and greenery. Ritual reinforces
metaphor: the clothes and rings of the first song signify ties to the human
cycle, while the herbs of the second suggest reintegration with the plant
cycle. As the bride joins the groom's group after crossing the threshold, the
separation rites come to a close, and the music suddenly changes from
lamentation to jubilation.[63] The separation rites at death and marriage are
parallel, especially in the sequence from silence and seclusion to song and
exposure. In both, antiphonal groupings play out contesting roles on behalf
of groom, groom's group, bride, and bride's mother and on behalf of
Charos, the dead person, and mourners.

At childbirth, the sequence is inverted. As with marriage, birth is carefully prepared for in advance by rituals designed to secure a male heir, the
only means by which a young wife can ensure her position as an adult
where residence is virilocal.[64] And if at death the greatest danger is marked
by silence at the moment of the soul's departure from the body, at birth the
infant's emergence from the mother's womb is marked by loud opening
noises. Not long ago, before the institution of modern birth clinics, women
from the villages of Kyriaki and Stiri in Boiotia would go up Mount Helikon and shout to assist a woman in travail.[65] Spells may be whispered into
the mother's right ear to ease delivery; hair is loosened to avoid knots
which "bind" (*desmoún*) the child to the womb; doors, drawers, and cupboards all over the house may be banged open to assist the process in ritual
and metaphorical simulation; ring-shaped objects (both open and closed)
may be placed on the *lechóna* "woman-giving-birth." The separation rituals
end with the birth of the child.

Death, marriage, and birth entail an initial rupture, thus marking the
emergence from one state to the next and providing the occasion for similar ritual precautions differently arranged.

Transition

After the rites of separation come the rites of transition or passage.
Corpse, bridal pair, and infant are all liminal in that although the previous
state—mortal, premarital, embryological—has been left behind, the new

state is not fully secured. Two keynotes in the case of death and marriage are the long, symbolic journey and the juxtaposition of rites of exposure with rites of seclusion ("open" and "closed").[66] Similar objects, foods, fruits, and clothes are commonly supplied to ensure safe ritual passage from one stage to the next: tall torches and candles provide light; wine, honey, and spices promise sensual gratification; evergreens, flowers, and fruit point to another life; ring-shaped articles suggest the unending cycles of human and natural existence. The rituals are similar but with a crucial difference: objects are provided singly in the case of death, doubly at marriage.

The corpse, wrapped in a *sábbanon* "shroud" and placed in an open coffin decked with flowers, is escorted in public procession from house to cemetery, traditionally via streets and marketplace to Church and graveyard, sometimes to the accompaniment of instrumental music. The bride, hitherto secluded in the parental home, is similarly escorted from parental home via church to her in-laws, as her dowry items are displayed for public scrutiny to the accompaniment of songs and dances. This exposure is followed by seven days of further seclusion, before the process of integration with her in-laws can begin. After childbirth, popularly known as *locheía* "after-birth," for seven days the household is considered unclean and polluted, a source of potential danger to others as well as to mother and infant. It is prone to visitation not only from the capricious Moires, "Fates," who come on the third or seventh day after birth to determine the infant's fate,[67] but also from the dangerous Nereids, who may destroy or enchant the infant, and then replace it with a changeling of their own.[68] At this time, mother and infant are closely confined, the infant in older times (before World War II) in *spárgana* (swaddling bands) wrapped around him/her in the shape of the Cross, because, according to one of the church fathers, κατὰ πᾶσαν τὴν ἑβδοματικὴν αὐτοῦ ζωὴν ὀφείλει περιφέρειν ἐν ἑαυτῷ τὴν νέκρωσιν "for the whole first week of his life he must carry deathness with him" (Migne 79, 1493). The parallel seclusion of new bride and new mother is still alluded to: "How can the bride 'go out'?" expostulated an elderly woman from Kokkinia in the 1970s, recalling her early years in Smyrna. "She was inside for the first days, like the new mother (λεχώνα). Νύφη 'bride' and λεχώνα 'new mother' are alike—they must take care."[69] As at death and marriage, evil spirits can be warded off by anointing the door lintels with oil and by breaking clay vessels over the threshold or by pinning a blue-stoned round gem onto the baby's garments to avert the evil eye.

Seclusion rituals occur at different stages of the three passages. For the dead, eyes and mouth are sealed immediately after death, frequently by the covering of an aperture by a coin (*kalúptein*). For the bride, the mouth may be ritually sealed by her mother-in-law, who places a silver coin on her tongue at the commencement of the ceremony, enjoining her symbolically to a silence which in some cases cannot be broken until the seventh day afterward, when the groom proffers a gift to her with the words νὰ μιλήσω τὴ νύφη "I'll get the bride to speak."[70] In the past, seclusion preceded the consummation of the marriage even after the wedding day, the bride customarily spending the first night in chastity with a female relative. Sexual abstinence is not a manifestation of peasant prudishness but a ritual precaution to bind the marriage, with many echoes in the songs.[71]

Only at birth, following the open rituals of the initial separation, are mother and infant confined completely to the household, the infant in tight swaddling bands, the mother excluded from contacts with the outside world. Silence is enjoined, as at death and marriage, and a mother sings her child to sleep with the reminder of the *moírama* "fating" to come:

> Ἔχε τὴν ἔννοια τοῦ παιδιοῦ καθόλου νὰ μὴν κλάψει
> γιατὶ θὲ νἄρτ' ἡ Μοῖρα του ἀπόψε νὰ τὸ γράψει.

Watch out for the child that he not cry at all,
for tonight his Fate is coming round to write him.

(Laog. 14.185: Thrace)

Yet even if she cannot go out, the new mother still has the wings of song and metaphor:

> Γιόκα μ', ὅταν σ' ἔκανα,
> πῶς δὲν ἐξαπέτησα,
> πῶς δὲν ἔκανα φτερά,
> σὰν τοῦ παγονιοῦ χρυσά,
> νὰ πετάξω στὰ βουνά,

(Politis 151: Athens)

My little son, when I made you,
how is it I did not fly off,
how is it I did not grow wings,
gold as the peacock's own,
to fly up onto mountains?

Integration

At the final stages of death, marriage, and birth rituals, the long process of reintegration begins, to be completed when the next passage is em-

barked upon. Common practices, some associated also with rites of separation, include the cutting of hair, the breaking of vessels, and the fetching of
fresh water from outside the house, followed by offerings, libations, and gift
exchange (jewelry, property, money), all concluded in a communal feast,
with food, music, and dance.

First, the *parēgoriá*, the funeral feast or consolation, normally held on the
evening of the funeral, closes the burial but begins the new passage of the soul
to its eternal life, secured only by the mourners' regular visits to the tomb
with offerings and lamentations and by memorial services and liturgies held
on the third, ninth, and fortieth days after death.[72] Despite church disapproval, women often keep up their graveside vigils for much longer. Only
at the exhumation ritual, held during the third, fifth, or seventh years after
death, is the soul believed to be freed from mortal contamination and to
rest in peace as formal obligations of mourning kinswomen are brought to
an end. At the Orthodox liturgy which precedes the occasion, *koímēsis*
"sleep" has been granted to the dead and new life ensured for all. One reason for the tenacity of mortuary rituals surely lies in the belief that they
can make a perceptible difference not only to the salvation of the soul but
also to the physical comfort of the dead in the "lower world."[73]

Second, the wedding feast seals the bond between man and wife through
formalized praise of their physical and spiritual qualities, but above all
through wishes for healthy male offspring. Wedding festivities may continue for seven days, even a year, by which time the bride is expected to
produce an heir, thereby securing full status within her new household. Mὲ
ἔναν γιό! "With a son!" is one of the commonest bridal blessings, while all
kinds of spells, charms, and rituals are applied to secure the birth of a son,
many of which, with their left/right cyclical pattern, underline the fe-
male/male system of oppositions in Greek culture, as in the anti-clockwise
movement of the dance.[74] Failure to produce an heir is regarded as the fault
of the woman; her husband may exercise the right to seek a new wife.
Marriage is satisfactorily sealed only by the birth of the next generation,
preferably in the male line, hence the birth of sons is a means of denying
mortality, as can be illustrated by the proverb *ákleros átheos*, "heirless, god-
less," whereby childlessness, the result of purely biological factors, is socially
equated with godlessness.[75] The importance of sons in securing the marriage bond provides a clear example of how folk practices and church
teachings interact and reinforce one another, despite official disapproval of
"women's ritual and superstition."

Third, just as death and marriage look forward to the next generation
while consoling the previous one on loss, so birth rituals (*genésia*) contain
the seeds of the next cycle—marriage. The feasting and gift exchange,

which customarily ended the first seven days of pollution after childbirth, sealed the infant's entry into the world and helped to determine its marriage and death. Yet the infant's future is not secure until given a name, normally around the first year of life. The bestowal of name, made at baptism not by parents but by godparents, remains a matter of crucial importance and of frequent dispute, since it is believed that the spirit of a dead parent, grandparent and great-grandparent, or a relative prematurely deceased can be appeased and reborn by way of *paramythiá* "consolation," the same concept as is evident in the term *parēgoriá*, "comfort," at the funeral feast.

In such cases, the name is chosen ν' ἀκουστεῖ τὸ ὄνομα, νὰ μὴ σβυστεῖ "so the name is heard, not quenched." As Saint Basil put it, βάπτισμα ὀφλημάτων ἄφεσις, θάνατος ἁμαρτίας, παλιγγενεσία τῆς ψυχῆς "baptism [is] the remission of debts, the death of sin, the rebirth of the soul."[76] Or, as a modern mother mourns her son:

Γιούλη μου, πάει τ' ὄνομά σου· θὰ σβυστεῖς ἀπὸ τὰ χαρτιά·
μόνο στὰ χαρτιὰ τοῦ παπᾶ γιὰ τὰ τρισάγια θὰ σὲ γράψουμε.

(Scavdi 1984, 102: Distomo)

My little son, your name is gone. You'll be erased from papers!
Only in the priest's papers for the "thrice holy" shall we inscribe you!

Baptism links present with past and present with future both spiritually, through naming, and materially, through transfer of gifts and coins. It is therefore not surprising to find that the lullabies, although not strictly ritual according to standard definitions, frequently look forward to maturity for a son and marriage for a daughter:

Ύπνε, ποὺ παίρνεις τὰ μικρά, ἔλα, πάρε καὶ τοῦτο·
μικρὸ μικρὸ σὲ τό 'φερα, μεγάλο φέρε μοῦ το·
μεγάλο σὰν ψηλὸ βουνό, ψηλὸ σὰν κυπαρίσσι,
οἱ κλῶνοι του νὰ φτάνουνε σ' Ἀνατολὴ καὶ Δύση.

(Akad. Ath. 3.388)

Sleep, you who take the small ones, come take this one too.
I brought him to you very small, bring him back full-grown,
great as a high mountain, tall as a cypress tree,
his branches reaching out to East and West.

Κοιμήσου ἀστρί, κοιμήσου αὐγή, κοιμήσου νιὸ φεγγάρι,
κοιμήσου, ποὺ νὰ σὲ χαρῇ ὁ νιὸς ποὺ θὰ σὲ πάρῃ.

(Politis 153)

Go to sleep, star; sleep, dawn; sleep, new moon;
sleep, so the young man who'll take you may enjoy you.

Viewed in relation to one another and in their entirety from rites of separation to rites of transition and rites of incorporation, the passages of
death, marriage, and rebirth merge to form an unending process, in which
linear and cyclical elements are combined. Death marks the end of the individual's existence in this world, but it leads to a double rebirth, that of the
soul in its new journey toward the immortal light (φῶς) and that of the
body through male heirs, who relive the past through names and in parallel
with female lines on the islands of the Dodekanese. Marriage entails for the
bride, especially in virilocal communities predominant on the mainland
and some islands, the severance of old family ties and the creation of new
ones, forging regeneration. Birth, initially enclosed as in death to secure a
safe passage, is celebrated at baptism as a means of achieving continuity between present, past, and future. The sustained parallels between the three
occasions provide a ritual and metaphorical means of confronting the limits of human mortality.

The past five decades or so have seen a marked attenuation of rituals, especially at marriage and birth, with Western fashions and modern clinics having
removed the desire and need for many of the older traditional practices. Yet
fierce quarrels still break out at weddings over which guests should be asked to
dance by the bride and in which order, and at baptisms, if any party feels that
the infant has been named after the wrong relative.[77] Here, as indicated in my
earlier discussion, gift giving, with all its complex messages of memory and
reciprocity, seems to be replacing the older and more traditional observances.

Death rituals have proved more resilient in urban and rural communities
alike, perhaps because death is unpredictable but certain, while the older
generation exercises its own constraints and controls. Greek rituals outlined
so far "fit neatly enough into van Gennep's scheme," as has been noted by
Robert Parker of ancient mortuary rituals; so there is nothing surprisising
about interconnections which belong to a general pattern inherent in many
preindustrial cultures.[78] At the same time, as Huntington and Metcalf have
shown in their wide-ranging survey *Celebrations of Death* (1979), there are
divergencies in the specific cultural forms by which rituals are expressed. It
is at this point that metaphor becomes relevant. Greek folk songs show remarkable coherence and interdependence in their use of metaphor, permitting us to reconstruct a common system, with a particular dependence
on the analogy between human and vegetal life cycles.

Meantime, we can now fill in the tripartite system with the narrative details:

Table 4

	Initial state rites of separation rupture, violence	Liminal state rites of exposure and seclusion transition, passage	Final state rites of integration feasting, gift exchange
Death	Soul leaves body	Corpse paraded Soul on last journey	Burial: 3 days; Exhumation: 3–7 years
Marriage	Bride leaves home	Couple paraded	Bride integrated: 7 days birth of heir: 1 year
Birth	Infant leaves womb binding/loosing	Close confinement binding/loosing	Moírama/genésia: 3–7 days; Baptism: 1 year

6. Greek Texts: Resources of the Past

I have chosen to close my survey of Greek ritual with a summary of past texts not out of a predilection for what anthropologists have termed "eclectic redundancy" but because each group of texts has, in different but significant ways, informed present perceptions and practices, in literature as in life. First, religious tradition. As we saw in Chapter 2, the hymns of Romanos the Melodist, composed for performance in the late fifth and early sixth centuries, present the Nativity, Crucifixion, and Resurrection of Christ not only on the horizontal plane of "story" but also on the vertical planes of time and space (Bakhtin's chronotopes). This is achieved through intricate and interlinked systems of imagery, often drawn from the life cycle: the effect is multidimensional and transgressive of realist modes of representation, as in much Byzantine art.[79] Romanos' tree symbolism for Christ's Nativity, Crucifixion, and Resurrection (seed, shoot, tree, blossom, fruit, kernel, seed), a potentially universal cognitive system, draws also on the culturally specific associative chain of tree, shade, water, spring, tears, cross, rebirth, heaven (*On the Nativity II*), which in turn is linked to the redemptive chain of tears, perfume, water, tongue, language, flame, fire, dance (*On the Resurrection V*: see Appendix for texts and translation). These images, far from being merely decorative, are imbued with symbolism drawn from the liturgy and rituals of Orthodox celebrations of the Nativity, Crucifixion, and Resurrection, as also from the rites of baptism and inauguration (ἐγκαίνια), hence they have profound resonances in the ways people perceive and observe Orthodox fasts and feasts to this day.[80] As we shall see in the next chapter, folk traditions have fed on the resources of religious language and ritual to endow laments and love songs with inner qualities of meaning.

If we turn to the texts of the twelfth century (Chapter 4), we find that even the *Timarion*, the most secular in its satirical appropriation of Lucianic dialogue and the classic theme of the descent to the Underworld, depends for its denouement on the ritual belief, still widely held, that the soul cannot be released from the body until all particles of flesh have been shown to be cleanly severed.[81] Contemporary medical practices, rather than folk beliefs, were no doubt uppermost in the author's mind, but the fact remains that the text may be juxtaposed with later poems on the same theme, such as Bergadis' disturbing poem *Apokopos* (c. 1400), in which the dead want to be told that they are remembered by the living, only to learn what they least desire—that the living have forgotten the dead and now jump over their graves! We may also look to the Underworld dialogues of modern folk laments, where the latest comer, laden with messages from the world of the living, is faced with a barrage of questions from the souls of the dead not dissimilar from those of Timarion's interlocutors, who demand to know the price of food and whether it can be conveyed down to Hades.[82] On another level, the *Timarion* is a tale of safe return to the body and this world, after a series of adventures in the other world, with all the ritual dimensions such a story line entails.

Makrembolites' learned romance *Hysmine and Hysminias* is one of the earliest examples of the Byzantine revival of the late antique novel to explore the awakening of individual sexuality, both female and male, and at the same time to celebrate the sanctity of Eros Basileus. As in Romanos, ritual dimensions are expressed through the warring images of fire and water, elaborated in extended ekphraseis which juxtapose the drives of human sexuality with the constraints both of the twelve laboring young men (the months) during the calendar year, depicted on the garden frieze, and of the four female figures who precede them: Phronēsis, Ischys, Sophrosyne, and Themis (Wisdom, Strength, Chastity, and Justice), a noble quartet followed by Eros Basileus. It scarcely matters that none of these allegorical figures is canonized in the Orthodox Church; rather, the Platonic concepts have been kept alive through artistic representation and Christian precepts of virtue throughout the Byzantine period. Hero and heroine are subjected to trials and tests and triumph at the end through art. These metaphorical and ritual elements add quasi-religious dimensions to the text as story, much as was the case in Heliodoros' *Aithiopika*. Such texts proved formative, albeit indirectly, to the rise of the modern Greek novel (Chapter 8).

The four Ptochoprodromic Poems incorporate, through games and play, ritual as well as rhetorical modes of discourse as the learned client assumes diverse personae in his begging ploys addressed to imperial patrons in the

Komnene court.[83] Links with earlier and later texts lie in comic topoi associated with food, sex, and money, which can be traced back to Aristophanes (the learned thread) and forward through the Cretan playwright Georgios Chortatsis (sixteenth century) to modern shadow theater and folk song (literary and popular threads).[84] While such topoi may be regarded as common currency, the connections between particular edible items and sexual parts are specific to the Greek language.

As we saw in Chapters 5 to 7, mythical genres are no less performative, often combining narrative modes with dramatic use of voice and dance. Greek narrative songs juxtapose marriage and death, often in dance form on the occasion of a wedding: they do not tell a romantic story; rather, they explore ambiguities of words and melody. Sometimes the tune is wailed out by male performers on the *klaríno* at the festival of the local saint with few, if any, words at all; at other times, tragic words may be danced out in wedding festivities (Chapter 6). In the songs performed on the occasions of birth, marriage, and death, a common fund of images is not aligned in narrative sequence but presented in what strikes us as a disjointed and fragmented manner (Chapter 10). It is ritual, rather than story, which provides the narrative framework for these songs, as we have seen in this chapter; in the next, I shall illustrate how Greek metaphorical and ritual systems have reinvigorated each other through utterances and performances pertaining to the life cycle.

Likewise, the tales are live performances, with teller-audience interaction. Neither the performative occasion nor the origins of the genre may be strictly defined as "ritual," although there is some evidence for their performance during the all-night vigil after a death and before the funeral: they are "tales of comfort" (*paramýthia, paramythiâ*), in contrast to the ritual "songs of pain" (*moirológia*) performed during the day. Tales, ever since they were first recorded in the nineteenth century, "act out" in traditional forms the drama of life as imagined by diverse communities, while the teller lends particular weight to "key lines" uttered by male or female protagonist. The tripartite structure of most tales (departure, adventure, integration) has analogies in ritual, and serves to explore dimensions beyond human experience in this world. What is more tales address key issues of speech and silence not unrelated to mutism and autism (Chapter 7).

As for modern prose fiction, although nonperformative, it has retained some of the metaphorical qualities associated with ritual and religious genres. Here, Vizyenos has perhaps come closest to imbuing the short story with nonlinear levels of meaning: his ekphraseis add nothing to plot or character but create a pause and space to transpose, through imagery, the narrative process onto other discourses, interconnecting experience and perception, aesthetics and ethics. "Journey" ends with a tale within a tale of a pilgrimage to a mountaintop which never took place. The story may not itself be ritual, but its interpretation demands a knowledge of ritual and metaphor (Chapter 8).

In view of the richness of postclassical Greek tradition, both literary and oral, I make no excuses for drawing on earlier texts to elucidate the present where the relevance of the past can be demonstrated. Ritual and metaphor cannot be separated from language, but language alone cannot explain the synesthetic power of rituals, surely among the most profoundly sensual strategies for survival, as the example of autistics has demonstrated. In the next chapter, we shall use the narrative structures of ritual to interpret the metaphorical ellipses in songs of the life cycle.

CHAPTER 10

Metaphors in Songs of the Life Cycle

In this chapter, I wish to explore songs of the life cycle in order to demonstrate the flexibility and coherence of Greek metaphors. The notion is not a new one. Over fifty years ago, George Thomson remarked on what he called "the consistency and interdependence of Greek poets in their use of metaphor" (1938, 2:44). Following Walter Headlam's pioneering work on Aeschylus, Thomson demonstrated in his commentary on the *Oresteia* the extent to which ancient literary, philosophical, and medical writers drew on a traditional fund of images linked to the life cycle, creatively adapted to different contexts. These images did not disappear with the collapse of the ancient world but were revitalized in later Byzantine and modern Greek literature and folk song. In my *Ritual Lament* (1974) I suggested the importance of ritual in keeping the metaphorical system alive (chapters 1–3) and illustrated the consistent analogies between the human and natural life cycle in the themes and images of Greek laments from antiquity to the present day (chapters 8–9). Since then, other scholars have contributed extensive and in-depth studies of Greek funerary ritual and lamentation from different disciplinary perspectives and from antiquity to the present day.[1]

Why so much emphasis on death? Studies of funerary customs in Greek culture are part of a wider resurgence of interest in death and sacrificial violence which has developed in the West over the past few decades.[2] While this trend has enriched our understanding of death in relation to the family and state and, above all, of the fundamental changes in attitudes to death since the Middle Ages, there is a danger of succumbing to fin de siècle obsession with death, disease, and violence or at least of implying that death is somehow more significant than birth, love, and marriage. We need to re-

349

dress the balance and look at how images of death are inextricably linked with images of coition and fruition. The fullest study of metaphor in the laments published since my own is L. M. Danforth's: in his chapter on "metaphor and mediation in Greek funerary laments," he demonstrates, with captivating examples from his fieldwork in a Thessalian village as well as from secondary sources, the interconnectedness of imagery in bridal songs of departure, in the songs of exile, and in the funerary laments (1982, 78–129). Guy Saunier (1968, 1985) has documented, with meticulous reference to archival sources, the links between laments for the departure of the dead, the bride, and the traveler to foreign lands.

The same metaphorical system permeates the imagery of lullabies (*nanourísmata*), play songs (*tachtarísmata*), songs of love and courtship (*erotiká*), no less than songs of loss and departure. Wedding songs may indeed lament the departure of the bride or express fears of potential conflict between families of bride and groom, particularly between bride and mother-in-law; but they also celebrate, through music and dance, the promise of joy and strength from new unions. If, as Danforth says, Greek metaphors "mediat[e] the oppositions between life and death," they also reintegrate human and vegetal life cycles in terms of a journey or passage from one state to the next.[3] The fact that in many cases the words alone give no clear indication of the occasion for which a song is intended makes it all the more essential to examine the imagery as an integrated but highly variable system.

For these reasons, although my analysis relies on collections, both general and regional, I have drawn on my own and other scholars' fieldwork, where performance can afford valuable clues, and on the fine musical recordings available on disk.[4] Music may add nothing to what is said, but it does convey the the singer's mood and therefore adds a new dimension to our interpretation of how song means. In the case of texts published up to a century or so ago, recent musical archives lend both immediacy and authenticity: we can hear the voice and feel the feet behind the text! No analysis of this kind can claim to be exhaustive, but I have included songs from as many regions as possible with the intention of demonstrating not so much the homogeneity of the tradition as its infinite versatility.

The allusive and cumulative quality of imagery in the Greek folk songs poses formidable methodological and organizational problems. Images merge into one another; they simply refuse to be neatly separated into categories. I shall not follow a logical order but will adopt an approach suggested by the major sequences, objects, and actions of the rituals themselves, as outlined in the previous chapter.

If I devote undue space to love songs, celebratory wedding songs, and lullabies, it is because these have received the least critical appreciation.

Folklorists have tended to regard them as corruptions, conflations, and abridgements of a once integrated narrative-heroic tradition, especially where the motifs, images, and themes are common to both. The evidence suggests otherwise; most songs cited in historiographies and preserved on manuscripts from the seventh to the seventeenth century are short and allusive, erotic, satirical or plaintive (Chapter 3). Erotic songs have always been the target of official condemnation and repression, especially by the church. Even in our own century, demotic poets of the literary establishment have turned more to mythical songs, while love songs have been exploited mainly by popular singers and composers. Songs live through ritual, music, and dance, and dance songs are the most indelible owing to Greeks' love of dancing.

There is another reason for devoting special attention to the love songs and wedding songs. Ethnographies have, with good reason, emphasized the seclusion of young girls before marriage and the determinative role of the families of bride and groom in negotiating a suitable match and an appropriate dowry.[5] It might be inferred by uninformed outsiders that marriage in Greece has little room for individual emotion and even less for love. These songs, many still danced all over Greece, provide a different perspective. If the mythical songs discussed in Chapter 6 suggest the severity of punishments meted out to unfaithful wives and disobedient daughters, the love songs are more playful, indicating how an ostensibly repressive system can be manipulated to the advantage of the female, much as women can turn the lament into a form of social protest.[6] Anyone equating social ideals of female chastity with puritanical prudishness will be surprised by the bold eroticism of many love songs. And it isn't only men who have the fun! Love lyrics, from antiquity to the present day, have been studied by J. C. B. Petropoulos.[7] What I attempt here is to present a selection of modern examples alongside other songs of the ritual cycle.

As for lullabies and knee songs, they are inconspicuous in published collections, but they testify to the vital role played by mothers in handing down the love of music and poetry from one generation to the next. In a remarkable collection of songs from Western Thrace, Pandelis Kavakopoulos presents 145 texts with full musical notation and dance-step instruction, nearly all recorded from a single source, the talented Chronis Aedonidis, son of Christos the priest from Karoti, but also of his mother, Chryssanthi, who inculcated in him from infancy a refined sense of musicality and rhythm with her lullabies and knee songs (1981: 13). Such was her fame as a singer and dancer that her son was renowned in the village as son of "Papachrístaina [wife of Christos the priest]," a nickname that pays tribute to his mother's reputation.

My aim is to demonstrate the cohesiveness of imagery in the modern song tradition. The songs provide evidence for links with earlier texts considered so far, but they are not merely fragmented remnants of a once flourishing literary and religious tradition. They have generated their own allusive system, rooted in the Greek language.

1. Journey

Metaphors of travel over lands and seas mirror the ritual process already examined by means of a complex interweaving of images which link death and marriage with departure for distant lands, where new family ties are forged. In a beautiful lament from the Pontos sung at a wake, a widow repeatedly addresses her dead husband as "my sun," a metaphor which suggests the sun's daily course from east to west, providing day and night, seasons and vegetation in her cosmos. Now eclipsed, like Christ in the tomb, he deprives his whole family of their life course, leaving them "at the five roads," as another mourner at the same wake put it, and his widow of all movement, with her knees cut off, her wings broken.[8] The black boat at the door evokes the funeral cortege, come to take him not to foreign parts but to Hades, the land of no return. In a final gesture of protest against his determination to keep company with Charos, she threatens to enter a monastery, leaving his children in the care of his dying mother. Her epithet "half-souled" implies an antinomy with the Pontic *dípsychos*, "two-souled," used for a pregnant woman:[9]

Ήλε μ', π' έχπαστες καὶ θὰ πᾶς καὶ ποῦ θ ἀφίντς τὴ χόρα σ';
καὶ ποῦ θ' ἀφίντς τὴ μάννα σου γραῖαν μὲ τ' ἤμ' σον ψήν-ι;
καὶ ποῦ θ' ἀφίντς τὰ ὄρφανά σ' μικρὰ καὶ μουτζιρούμ' κα;
Ήλε μ', ἤλε μ', ἤλε μ', ἤλε μ', ἤλε μ', καὶ ξαν' ἤλε μ'.
Ήλε μ', ἀτζάπα π' έχπαστες ἐσὺ 'ς σὴν ξενιτείαν;
Ντό έν' τὸ μαῦρον τὸ καράβ' ντὸ έρθεν καὶ 'ς σὴν πόρταν;
Μαῦρα πανιά έχ' ἀτό, 'ς σὴν ξενιτὰν κι πάει,
ἀπὸ ξενιτείας κι ὁμάζ', ἀτὸ σὸν Ἄδην πάει,
ἀτ' ὄσ' νομάτ' 'ς ποὺ παίρ' καὶ πάει, κανεὶς ὀπίσ' κ' ἐγύρισεν.
Ἀτοῦ 'ς σὸ μαῦρον τὸ καράβ' ἐγὼ ἐσέν' κι βάλλω,
ἀτό ὀπίσ' ἂς κλώσκεται κι ἂς πάη ἀπόθεν έρθεν.
Ήλε μ', ἤλε μ', ἤλε μ', ἤλε μ', καὶ ἤλε μ' καὶ ἡμέρα μ',
έκοψες καὶ τὰ γόνατά μ' κ' έσπασες τὰ γάνατά μ',
κ' ἐσυντρόφαες, νε ἤλε μ', τὸν ἀσπλαχνόν τὸν Χάρον.
Ἐφέκες μὲ παντέρημον, ποῖον στράταν νὰ παίρω,
καὶ κάτ ἂν πάω, έν' κρεμός, καὶ ἄν' ἂν πάω, φούρκα.

Θὰ πάω 'γὼ 'ς τὸ Μαναστήρ καὶ θὰ φορῶ τὰ μαῦρα,
θ' ἀφίνω τὰ πουλλόπα σου τῆ μάννα σου τῆ γραίαν.
"Αχ ἦλε μ', ἦλε μ', ἦλε μ', ἦλε μ', ἦλε μ', ἦλε μ', καὶ ξαν' ἦλε μ'.
                                                        (*Archeion Pontou* 16. 189)

My sun, where have you set off for, where will you leave your widow?
Where will you leave your mother, aged, with half a soul?
and where will you leave your orphans, small and weak?
My sun, my sun, my sun, my sun, my sun, and again my sun!
My sun, do you really think you have set off for foreign lands?
What is that black boat standing at the very door?
It has black sails, it is going not to foreign lands,
nor does it come from foreign lands, it is bound for Hades.
Of those it takes on board, not a single one returns.
I will not put you on that black boat out there,
let it turn round again and go back where it came from.
My sun, my sun, my sun, my sun, and my sun and my day,
you have cut my knees, and you have broken my wings.
You are keeping company, o my sun, with merciless Charos!
You have left me desolate, which road am I to take?
If I go downward, there's a precipice, if upward, gallows.
I'll go to the monastery, I'll put on black,
I'll leave your little fledglings to your aged mother!
Ahh! my sun, my sun, my sun, my sun, my sun, again my sun!

In a lament from Crete, recorded by Caraveli-Chaves in 1979, Katerina
Pateraki praises her dead mother's skills in housecraft, embroidery, medicine, midwifery, recalling her tireless night journeys to women in childbirth
and her unstinting generosity in visiting and curing the sick. Her control of
the cosmos was such that she knew "how to embroider the sky with stars"
(πού ἤξερες τσαὶ ξόμπλιαζες τὸν οὐρανὸ μὲ τ' ἄστρα), and she is acclaimed in the closing address as "a proud frigate" setting out on her own:

Oh slowly, oh mournfully I will begin lamenting
crying for all your sorrows, mother—one by one.
Ah mother, keeper of the home and mistress of embroidery,
you knew how to embroider the sky with all its stars.
Ah mother, keeper of the home, mother, weaver and spinner
even the night sky itself was woven in your loom.
Ah mother, your hard work could keep a village alive
and so could your orderliness—keeping all things in line.

Oh mother, I'm crying out to you! Oh mother—midwife!
You used to come home each night, I say each night;
you walked home from deliveries and made darkness scatter.
How many times wouldn't you come back from work—pale and tired
    out—
way past midnight, near dawn, after roosters had crowed!
Everyone is crying out to you, asking for you, my lady,
because you were the midwife and had a generous heart,
because you were needed, mother, known and praised by all.
Ah women of [Tzermiádon], weep, sing laments for her;
she too gave you her words to comfort and to soothe you.
Where are you women of [Tzermiádon], decked out in your best
    clothes?
The midwife is going who used to hold your children.
Give her your forgiveness now and give her your last word,
because she's travelling far away and won't return again.
Eh mother, mother, midwife, mother, proud frigate,
you were among the best; I'm crying out to you mother.

                    (Caraveli-Chaves 1980, 133, lines 1–8, 19–23, 29–39:
                                        no Greek text given)

As in the Pontic lament, metaphors of travel provide the mourner
with the means of exploring both concrete details and symbolic dimensions of past, present, and future. The imagery is traditional but not
stereotyped: it can be finely tuned to different situations. Whereas the
Pontic widow sees the black boat as Charos' violent means of transport-
ing her husband on the road to death, the Cretan daughter sees her
mother as one whose skills and standing in the village were so great as to
keep her integrated with life, even after her death: she now sets out in full
control, like a frigate on a maiden voyage of her own. The song is as
much a celebration as a lament. The differences between these laments
accurately reflect the status of the two mourners: the widow faces the
prospect of becoming a social outcast, her children made orphans,
whereas the daughter is subtly exploiting her mother's reputation in the
village to enhance her own.[10]
    That she could do so depends on the central miracle of childbirth in the
Orthodox faith. Mary's primary appellation is not "the Virgin," as in the
Catholic West, but *Panagiá*, "the All-Holy One," above all as mother. In a
delightful *kálando* (carol) from Thrace, sung at Christmas, her birth pangs
are described in imagery not unlike that used by the Cretan daughter, de-

signed to excite sympathy for her human predicament: no midwives were
there to assist her in labor, so Apostles and Archangels came down from
heaven to release her amid laurels and cypress trees, as she shone out like
the sun and moon:[11]

Σαράντα μέρες, σαράντα νύχτες
κι ἡ Παναγιά μας κοιλοπονοῦσι·
Κοιλοπονοῦσι, παρακαλοῦσι
τοὺς Ἀποστόλους, τοὺς Ἀρχαγγέλους.
Κι οἱ Ἀποστόλοι μαμὲς γυρεύουν
κι οἱ Ἀρχαγγέλοι γιὰ μύρο τρέχουν.
Κι ὡς που πα-πάνι κι ὡς που νὰ ἔρτουν
ἡ Παναγιά μας ξιλιφτιρώθ'κι.
Ξιλιφτιρώθ'κι κι φανερώθ'κι
μέσα στὶς δάφνες, στὰ κυπαρίσσια.
Σὰν ἥλιους λάμπει, σὰν φέγγους φέγγει.

(Romaios 151,11)

Forty days and forty nights
our Panagiá felt labor pains.
In her labor pains she begged
the Apostles, the Archangels.
And the Apostles seek midwives,
the Archangels run off for myrrh.
By the time they came back
the Panagiá freed herself from labor.
Freed and revealed she was
amidst laurels and cypress trees,
shining like the sun, giving light like the moon.

The Pontic widow, by contrast, links death with *xenitiá*. Literally rendered, the term means "foreign parts" or "exile." But *xenitiá* is a female figure, personified in songs of departure as an enchantress who *enjoys* (*chaíre-
tai*) the young men she entices away from their families and homeland with
"good things." The following example was recorded in 1963 from Alexandra Tsipi, an Epirot nurse then working in Larisa. Perhaps her rendering
derived some of its passion from the fact she too, like the dentist she
worked for and who accompanies the song with the *ison*, were themselves
xeneteména paidiá, "exiled children," from their native village, seeking advancement in a "foreign" town, as in versions sung by Greek immigrants in

America: ἀνάθεμά σε, 'Αμερική, μὲ τὰ πολλὰ τὰ ἀστέρια "A curse on you, America, with your many stars":

> "Άχ, ξενετεμένα μου παιδιά, αὐτοῦ στὰ ξένα ποὺ εἶστε.
> "Άχ, ἡ ξενετιὰ σᾶς χαίρεται τὰ νιάτα τὰ γραμμένα.
> "Όχ, ἀνάθεμά σε, ξενετιά, ἐσὺ καὶ τὰ καλά σου.
> "Άχ, μᾶς πῆρες ὅλα τὰ παιδιὰ μέσα στὴν ἀγκαλιά σου!

> (Alexiou archives, 1963)

> Ah, my exiled children, over there in foreign lands.
> Ah, xenitiá enjoys your allotted youth.
> Oh, a curse upon you, xenitiá, you and your good things.
> Ah, you've taken all my children into your embrace!

At death, it is the earth who performs the seduction, enjoying all forms of human fodder:

> Πρέπει ἡ γῆς νὰ χαίρεται, πρέπει νὰ καμαρώνει
> ποὺ τρώγει αἰτοὺς καὶ σταυραιτούς, καὶ νιὲς μὲ τὰ στολίδια,
> τρώγει τῶ μαννάδων τὰ παιδιά, τῶν ἀδερφιῶν τ' ἀδέρφια,
> ποὺ τρώγει καὶ τὰ ἀντρόγυνα τὰ πολυαγαπημένα .

> (Politis 175)

> The earth should be happy, she should be proud,
> for she eats eagles, brave eagles, young girls with ornaments,
> she eats children who have mothers, brothers and sisters,
> she even eats couples very much in love.

A grim set of new family ties is forged in preparation for the other world: for young women, the violent bridegroom is Charos himself, as we have seen; for men, the black earth becomes the new mother—or wife, in the case of young men; the heavy tombstone is—aptly—the new mother-in-law; stones are affines. We are reminded of the proximity of birth, marriage, and death and of how each impinges on our daily lives. A pan-Hellenic theme is that of the young man in the throes of death far from home who instructs his comrades to tell his mother he is not dead but married (Danforth 1982, 80). The same traditional formulas are included in the songs of *xenitiá* in which the young man dies a stranger in foreign lands. In a version from Thrace, he falls sick on the voyage, and in the absence of kinsfolk, three ladies in turn offer him cold water, bread, and a bed to lie on, bidding him to "get up so he can lie down." He replies, with the same formula as in the funeral laments, that he cannot, and requests ink and paper. The three ladies suggest the Fates:

Ἔπεσε καὶ ἀρώστησε στοῦ καραβιοῦ τὴ πλώρη.
Δὲν ἔχει μάνα νὰ τὸν δεῖ, ἀδέρφι νὰν τὸν κλάψει,
μόν' ἔχει τρεῖς γερόντισσες καὶ τρεῖς γιαρενοπούλες.
Ἡ μιὰ τὸν δίνει κρύο νερό, ἡ ἄλλ' ἀφράτο μῆλο,
ἡ ἄλλη ἡ μικρότερη τοῦ στρώνει νὰ πλάγιάσει.
—Σήκω, ψηλέ μ', σήκω, λιγνέ μ', σήκω γιὰ νὰ πλαγιάσεις.
—Ἐγὼ σοῦ λέω δὲν μπορῶ κι ἐσὺ μοῦ λέγεις, σήκω·
δῶστε μελάνι καὶ χαρτὶ νὰ κάτσω γιὰ νὰ γράψω,
νὰ στείλω στὴ μανοῦλα μου καὶ νὰ τὴν πῶ παντρεύτ'κα,
πῆρα τὴν πέτρα πεθερά, τὴ μαύρη γῆ γυναῖκα.

(Romaios 158,28)

He fell sick on the prow of the ship.
He has no mother to see him, no brother or sister to weep for him,
only three old women and three young friendly ones.[12]
One gives him cold water, the second a crisp juicy apple,
while the third and youngest makes up his bed.
—Get up, my tall one, get up, my handsome one, so you can lie abed.
—I tell you I cannot get up, and you tell me to rise!
Just give me ink and paper, and I'll sit down and write,
I'll send word to my mother that I have got married,
I have taken the stone as mother-in-law, the black earth as mother.

As Romaios has noted (1956, 204–5), there is playful assonance between *pétra / petherá*, "stone / mother-in-law" and *yí / yinéka* "earth / wife," as also found in the love song in which the girl promises her lover νὰ γίνω γῆς νὰ μὲ πατᾶς, γεφύρι νὰ περάσεις "I'll become earth for you to tread, a bridge for you to cross" (Yiankas 463, 4–5). Maybe this is another clue to "The Bridge of Arta," in which woman (*yinéka*) must be buried in earth (*yí*) to make firm a bridge *yefíri*.[13]

In the wedding songs, images of travel to new family contracts are evident in the farewells sung by the bride's group before her separation from the parental home. She has contracted an obligation with strangers in distant parts; she must deny her kin, and they must deny her, in an exchange of bitter ritual accusations: ἀρνήσου τοὺς δικούς σου, κι ἔλα ἀντάμα μου "Deny your kin and come with me," a groom from Patras peremptorily orders his bride (LA 1953: Saunier 1968, chap. 2). She will get a *xéni mánna* "foreign mother," and must learn to suffer slights with dignity until she

bears a son. The ambivalent metaphors of many bridal farewells express the
girl's ritual reluctance to leave maidenhood but also her sense of hostilities
to come. In one remarkable song the girl asks her mother to welcome the
in-laws to the house as to a funeral and suggest that they be served with
wine aged for three years and twice-distilled raki, calculated to make them
drunk. The green coverlets and black kilims connote mourning, whether in
death or in an unhappy marriage.[14]

Σὰν ἔρντι, καλῶς ἔρχονται, στρῶσε, μάνα μ', κι ἄς κάτσουν·
Δὲν μπορῶ μάνα μ', χάνομαι!
Στρῶστε βελέντζες πράσινες καὶ τὰ κιλίμια μαῦρα,
δῶς τους μάνα μ' παλιὸ κρασί, κρασὶ 'πὸ τρία χρόνια,
κέρνα τους, μάνα μ' καὶ ρακή, ρακή ματαβρασμένη!

(Laog. 19. 205: Macedonia)

When they come, mother, bid them welcome, bid them sit down!
—I can't, mother, I'm lost!
—Lay out green coverlets and black kilims,
give them old wine, mother, at least three years old,
serve them, mother, with raki boiled twice over.

It is hard to tell whether death or marriage is the occasion. Ambiguity between genres is an essential feature of meaning, as in the Greek pairs *már-
tys/martyriá, Cháros/chará, pónos/poniriá*. In a similar song from Epiros the
voice seems to be that of the dying bride. As her mother tries to rouse her
from her heavy sleep to greet the wedding guests, she asks that her sister
take her place, with less finery and ceremony than would normally be accorded to a bride:

Σὰν ἦρθαν καλῶς ὥρισαν καλῶς τοὺς νὰ κοπιάσουν,
στρῶστε τὶς τάβλες θλιβερὲς καὶ μαυροφορεμένες
δῶστε νὰ φᾶνε καὶ νὰ πιοῦν, κρασὶ γιὰ νὰ μεθύσουν
κι ἁπλῶστε στὴν τσεπούλα μου, τὴν βαρυορημαγμένη
καὶ πάρτε τὰ κλειδάκια μου κι ἀνοῖξτε τὴν κασσέλα
καὶ πάρτε τὰ ρημάδια μου, ντύστε τὴν ἀδερφή μου,
φορέστε της καλὰ σκουτιά, δάκρυα νὰ μὴ χύσει,
νὰ μὴ βαρέσουν τὰ βιολιά, ὅσο νὰ βγεῖ ἡ ψυχή μου,
καὶ πάρτε με καὶ θάψτε με στὸ Ἅγιο τὸ δήμα.

(Yiankas 361, lines 14–22)

If they have come, bid them welcome, bid them come in.
Lay the tables in mourning, clothed in black,

give them food and drink, wine to make them drunk,
and reach into my small pocket, sorely spoiled,
take out my keys and open up my chest,
take out my ruined clothes, dress up my sister,
dress her in good rough cloths, let her shed no tears;
let no violins strike up until my soul comes out,
and you take me and bury me at the holy altar.[15]

Rather than speculate on how this song type, "death before marriage" (including versions where it is the young man who dies on the way to fetch his bride), may be related to the "Akritic" song Τῆς Εὐγενούλας "Eugenoula," I prefer to see it as an ambivalent variation of the song Τῆς κακοπαντρεμένης "The Ill-married Wife," in which the young wife complains bitterly—sometimes to her absent lover—of being married to an aging, sick, or drunken husband. The music is searing, belying the apparent humor of the text. The following version is from Epiros:

Νὰ μὴ λυπᾶσαι ὀρφανή, νὰ μὴ λυπᾶσαι χήρα,
νὰ λυπηθεῖς μιὰν ὄμορφη, μιὰ κακοπαντρεμένη,
ἄντρας της πίνει καὶ μεθάει κι αὐτὴ κάνει χωράφι,
μὲ τὸ παιδὶ στὴν ἀγκαλιὰ τὰ βόδια της κεντοῦσε.
—Κάνετε, βόιδια μ', κάνετε, τ' ἄντρα μου τὸ χωράφι.
Τὸ βράδυ πάνει σπίτι της, τὴ δέρνει, τὴ μαλώνει.
—Κόρη μ', τὸ ποῦ εἶναι ὁ δεῖπνος σου, δεῖπνος γιὰ νὰ δειπνήσω;
—Μή με μαλώνεις, ἄντρα μου, καὶ μὴ παραπαίρεις
τὸ τί δεῖπνο νὰ φειάκ' ἐγώ π' ὁλημερὶς δουλεύω.

(Yiankas 479)

Have pity for no orphan, pity for no widow,
but have pity for a beautiful, ill-wed wife,
whose husband gets drunk while she works in the field,
goading the oxen with a child in her arms.
—Plough, my oxen, plough my husband's field.
In the evening she goes home, he beats and scolds her.
—My girl, where is supper, supper for me to eat?
—Don't scold me, husband, and don't take on so,
what kind of supper can I make when I'm out at work all day?

Songs such as this are a salutary reminder of the harsh realities of rural life, despite the beauty of images and melodies whose expressive powers derive from their ambivalence, as in the following lament from the Peloponnese:

Κάτω στὶς ἐλιὲς τὶς πολυανθούσες
γάμος γίνεται, νύφη ξεβγαίνει,
κι ἡ μάνα της δὲν ξέρει ποὺ τὴν στέλνει.
Κάτσε παιδάκι μου καὶ μή μου φεύγεις
τι εἶν' τὰ φίδια πλεχταριὲς οἱ ὀχιὲς ζωνάρια.

(Tarsouli 222)

Down in the olive groves with many blooms
there is a wedding, a bride comes out,
her mother knows not where she sends her.
—Stay, my child, don't leave me,
for snakes are plaited, vipers belts.

Probably the context is death, given the emphasis on "down under" and on the bride as single partner bound for an unknown destination knotted with snakes and vipers. Two formulas seem to have been joined together, at some expense to narrative consistency, but with terse, gnomic comparison. With equal ambivalence, a song from the island of Thasos, performed by the groom's group as the bride is about to take the irrevocable step of crossing the threshold of her in-laws, implies her impending loss of virginity:

Πουρπάτει, φιργαδούλα μου, μὴν ἀπομείνεις πίσω,
κι ἄλλες πολλὲς τὸ πάθανε, δὲν εἶσαι μοναχή σου.

(Spyridakis and Peristeris 298)

Walk on, my little frigate, don't stand back,
many other women have suffered it, you're not the only one.

But if marriage seems sterile at the outset, it promises to blossom forth again:

Εὐτοῦ ποὺ πᾶς νυφούλα μου εἶναι ξερὰ τὰ ξύλα,
κι ἀπ' τὴν πολλὴ τὴν ὀμορφιὰ βγαίνουν καινούργια φύλλα.

(Saunier 1968, chapter 3: Lefkas)

There where you set out for, little bride, the wood is dry,
yet from so much beauty will come forth new leaves.

In lullabies and love songs, metaphors of meeting in a garden, courtyard, or neighborhood predominate over those of journey. In the next lullaby from Thrace, the singer deftly adapts the images of journey to the context of her sleeping child:

Ξημέρωσε ἡ Ἀνατολή,
κούνιε, παραμάνα, τὸ παιδί,
κι ἡ Πούλια πάει στὴ Δύση,
κούνα τὸ νὰ μὴν ξυπνήσει.
Πᾶν τὰ πουλάκια στὴ βοσκή,
κούνιε, παραμάνα, τὸ παιδί,
κι ἡ ἀγαπῶ στὴ βρύση,
κούνα τὸ νὰ μὴ ξυπνήσει.

(Romaios 178, 79)

The East has awoken,
—rock the child, nurse—
and the Pleiad goes West,
—rock the child, don't let him wake.
The birds go off for food,
—rock the child, nurse—
my loved one to the spring,
—rock the child, don't let him wake.

Whereas Romaios can see in this song only a corruption of a version of Ὁ γυρισμὸς τοῦ ξενιτεμένου, "The Return of the Exile" (1956, 235; cf. 201–4), it illustrates the cyclical nature of the journey as expressed in imagery: while sun, stars, birds, and young girl prepare for a new day's travails, the small child is rocked asleep. The contrast between the child at rest and the outside world in motion has the delicate structure and utter simplicity of the short folk ekphrasis so successfully exploited by Vizyenos in his stories, with the difference that his examples are predominantly autumnal, on the threshold of evening and death, whereas here, as appropriate to the context of a lullaby, the world is just beginning to wake up. The child lulled to sleep at dawn is the counterpart of the bride summoned by the groom to come out with the shining of the sun (see below, pages 371–72).

2. Clothes and Gems

As we saw in Chapter 9, the ritual dressing of the dead and the bridal pair alike is accompanied by songs which draw attention to the elaborate preparation of clothes for a journey to mark the change of status: the unmarried or newly married dead are dressed *as if* about to embark on marriage, while the bride is blessed with as many good years as there are *ploumídia* "embroidered decorations" stitched onto her dress (Spyridakis and Peristeris 1968:289, 5-6), which may have been sewn by ten girls and eighteen tailors (290–91) with the blessing of the Panagia and Christ (288–89). Songs such as these can be related to the tales and legends of the tailor who marries the princess, so integral to Vizyenos' "Journey" (Chapter 8). Once the clothes of the next ritual stage are worn, there can be no return to former status ("wear the *xénos'* [stranger's] clothes, the *xénos'* rings, for you belong to the *xénos*, and the *xénos* will take you").

It is not only the bridal pair and the dead who must be appropriately dressed. Mourners too, especially widows, must divest themselves of bright apparel and wear a token of bereavement during the specified period of mourning. The custom of widows dressing in black for the rest of their lives has attracted much adverse comment as a barbaric imposition of an androcentric society. To quote Maurice Bloch, "Perhaps most striking is the way in which it is women who carry death around with them with their black dresses in the whole Mediterranean area. Again and again women are *given* death while the social order is affirmed elsewhere" (1982, 226; Bloch's emphasis). Several points need to be made in response to this insensitivity to different perceptions about mourning in particular and clothes more generally. If in the West there is an assumption that grief must be private ("don't wear grief on your sleeve"), Greeks may express a *desire* to wear black as a sign of mourning, usually a black armband or tie for men and a black scarf or clothes for women. They do so not just out of respect for the dead and certainly not as a display for others but also as a means of ritualizing their grief and keeping up contact and memory, as in the song formula "black clothes shall eat me, as the black earth eats you." Clothes worn in mourning should be viewed in the wider context of how dress signifies as an outer indication of an inner state. Black for death is balanced by red, purple, silver, and gold for marriage and childbirth. Nor does black unequivocally spell death; it can be erotic, as in the following song from Thrace, in which the young lover invites his girl to the dance by telling her to take off her sexy black so he can dress her in gold:

Αὐτὰ τὰ μαῦρα ποὺ φορεῖς (δὶς), Ἑλένη μου,
ἐγὼ θὰ σοῦ τὰ βγάλω,
καὶ θὰ σε βάλω στὰ χρυσά, Ἑλένη μου
κι ὕστερα θὰ σε πάρω.
Αὐτὰ τὰ μαῦρα ποὺ φορεῖς, Ἑλένη μου
δὲν τὰ φορεῖς γιὰ λύπη
μόν' τὰ φορεῖς γιὰ ἐμορφιά, Ἑλένη μου
καὶ γιὰ τὸ ζαριφλίκι.

(Romaios 158–59, 29)

That black you wear [*bis*], my Eleni,
I'll take it off you,
and I'll put you in gold, my Eleni,
and after that I'll take you. . . .
That black you wear, my Eleni,
you wear it not for grief,
you wear it for beauty, my Eleni,
and for sexy elegance.

In other versions of the same song, she may be told to take off black so he can dress her in purple and red or to take off her purple and put on gold.[16] These nuanced references to contemporary fashions lend a lighthearted touch to the theme of changing clothes as encountered in the mythical songs "Dead Brother" and "Bridge of Arta" (Chapter 6).

From birth, girl infants are lulled to sleep with promises that precious clothes and jewels have been ordered from Constantinople and Venice for their wedding:[17]

Κοιμήσου ἀστρί, κοιμήσου αὐγή, κοιμήσου νιὸ φεγγάρι,
κοιμήσου ποὺ νὰ σε χαρεῖ ὁ νιὸς ποὺ θὰ σε πάρει.
Κοιμήσου ποὺ παράγγειλα στὴν Πόλη τὰ χρυσά σου,
στὴ Βενετιὰ τὰ ροῦχα σου καὶ τὰ διαμαντικά σου.
Κοιμήσου ποὺ σοῦ ράβουνε τὸ πάπλωμα στὴν Πόλη,
καὶ σοῦ τὸ τελειώνουνε σαρανταδυό μαστόροι·
στὴν μέση βάνουν τὸν ἀετό, στὴν ἄκρη τὸ παγόνι.
Νάνι τοῦ ρήγα τὸ παιδί, τοῦ βασιλιᾶ τ' ἀγγόνι.
Κοιμήσου καὶ παράγγειλα παπούτσια στὸν τσαγγάρη,
νὰ σοῦ τὰ κάνει κόκκινα μὲ τὸ μαργαριτάρι.
Κοιμήσου μές στὴν κούνια σου καὶ στὰ παχιὰ παννιά σου,
ἡ Παναγιὰ ἡ δέσποινα νὰ εἶναι συντροφιά σου.

(Politis 187: Peloponnese)

Sleep star, sleep dawn, sleep new moon,
sleep, so the young man who'll marry you can enjoy you.
Sleep for I have ordered your gold in the City,
your clothes and diamonds in Venice.
Sleep for they are weaving your quilt in the City,
and forty-two craftsmen are completing it:
in the middle they put the eagle, on the edge the peacock.
Lullaby child of a prince, grandchild of a king
Sleep, for I have ordered your shoes from the cobbler;
he'll make them red with pearls for you.

Sleep in your cradle and in your thick cloths.
May the lady Panagia keep you company.

Fine new clothes signify status within the family at the three major stages in the life cycle: birth, marriage, and death. If the transition from one to another state is disrupted, whether by marriage elsewhere or travel abroad, the metaphor shifts from positive to negative. A deserted girl curses her lover to come in little pieces to her courtyard at her funeral, when her own hands will make his winding-sheet. Images of birth, marriage, and death are interlinked, equating his denial of her with denial of his own mother's milk. The following version from my archives is sung with great gusto and with a relish for imagined violence reminiscent of ancient love spells.[18] The second half of each line is repeated:

Ἔμαθα πῶς παντρεύεσαι, μὲ γειά σου μὲ χαρά σου.
Ὅλοι νάρθοῦν στὸ γάμο σου, κι ἐγὼ στὰ κόλλυβά σου.
Ἐσύ 'σουνα ποὺ μοῦ 'λέγες ἂν δὲν μὲ δεῖς πεθαίνεις,
τώρα γυρίζεις καὶ μοῦ λες ποῦ μ' εἶδες, ποῦ μὲ ξέρεις;
Μ' ἀρνήθηκες ποὺ ν' ἀρνηθεῖς τῆς μάννας σου τὴ γέννα.
Τὸ γάλα ποὺ σε πότιζε νὰ τὸ ξηράσεις αἷμα.
Μὴ παντρεφτεῖς προτοῦ νὰ εἰδεῖς παπᾶ στὴ γειτονιά σου
κι' ἡ μάνα μου στὰ ὁλόμαυρα νὰ κλαίει τὴ λεβεντιά μου.
Μὴ παντρεφτεῖς προτοῦ νὰ εἰδεῖς παπᾶ στὴ γειτονιά μου,
καὶ νεκροφόρος νάρχεται νὰ παίρνει το κορμί μου.
Ἔλα ποὺ νὰ σε φέρουνε κομμάτια στὴν ποδιά μου,
καὶ νὰ σε σαββανώσουνε τὰ χέρια τὰ δικά μου.

(Alexiou 1963, Alexandra Tsipi: Larisa)

I heard you're getting married—health and joy to you!
All will come to your wedding; I'll come to your *kóllyva* [burial grains].
You used to tell me if you didn't see me, you would die.
Now you turn round and tell me you don't know me, haven't seen me.
You have denied me as you would your mother's birthing.
The milk she fed you on may you spew out as blood.
May you not marry till you see a priest in your neighborhood,
my mother all in black weeping for my bravery.
May you not marry till you see priests in my courtyard
with corpse bearers coming to take up my body.
Come, may they bring you in little pieces to my apron,
and my own hands shall make your winding-sheets.

Her mode of expression is allusive and needs to be interpreted contextually: *kóllyva* are the mixed grains and dried fruits served at a funeral; "a priest in the courtyard" signifies death or bad luck; and reference to her own funeral suggests that she too must pay the price of love betrayed.[19]

By contrast, the girl left behind at home promises to cook for him, make his bed, wash his feet—even to drink the dirty water afterward!—if only he will take her with him (Saunier 1983, 37, lines 14–16.) If this suggests the self-humiliation of woman in an androcentric society, the motif goes back to ancient Egypt, and may be used by both sexes.[20] In the following love song from Thrace, it is the young man who has to bathe both himself and his clothes in tears before he can win his heartless bride:

''Όλ' οἱ λιγνοὶ ἀλλάξανε κι ὅλοι λαμπροφορέσαν,
μὰ 'γὼ λιγνὸς δὲν ἄλλαξα, δὲν ἐλαμπροφορέσα,
μόν' μιὰ Λαμπρή, μιὰ Κυριακή, μιὰν 'πίσημον ἡμέρα,
παίρνω τὰ ρουχαλάκια μου καὶ στὸ λουτρὸ παγαίνω,
καὶ βρίσκω τὸ λουτρὸ σβηστό, τὶς γοῦρνες σφαλισμένες.
Φυσῶ κι ἀνάβω τὸ λουτρό, κλαίγω, γεμίζω γοῦρνες,
καὶ λούνομαι, χτενίζομαι, σκουπίζομαι καὶ βγαίνω.

(Romaios 148, 4)

All lithe young men got changed and put on bright festive clothes,
only I did not get changed, I did not put on bright clothes;
but one Easter, one Sunday, one festive day
I take up my few clothes and go to the bathhouse.
I find the bath [fires] quenched, the cisterns all sealed up.
I blow and heat the bath, I weep and fill the cisterns,
I get washed and combed, dry myself and come out.

This short song continues as a courting song, in a game that can be lost as easily as won, and the young man draws attention to his emotional plight by indicating his bodily needs.

The most potent item of clothing in Greek folk songs is the *mandíli* "kerchief", perhaps because it is indispensable to the dance, where love ties are formed at courtship and sealed at marriage. A typical scenario in the love songs is for the young man to give a kerchief, or ribbon, to his loved one, seated on her porch or balcony, who may toss him an apple in return. When she wears the ornament at the next dance, her inquisitive mother (or neighbors) ask her where she got it from. If the young man meets with approval, marriage negotiations will begin; otherwise, her mother will scold or beat her. But even so, if the young couple are in love, they will get their way. Sometimes, the kerchief the girl is weaving serves as the only means of communication between the lovers, since direct contact between them would attract undesirable attention at this delicate stage of their relationship, and the physical symptoms of Eros would surely betray them:[21]

Τὸ μαντηλάκι ποὺ κεντᾶς καὶ χρυσομπιμπιλώνεις,
ἂν θὰ τὸ στείλεις χάρισμα στὸν ἀγαπητικό σου,
μὴ τοῦ τὸ στείλεις μοναχό, στείλ' τὸ μὲ τὴν ἀγάπη,
Ἡ κόρη τ' ἀλησμόνησε, καὶ τὄστειλε μονάχο.
Στὰ γόνατά του τὤβαλε καὶ τὸ συχνορωτάει·—
—Γιὰ πές μου, μαντηλάκι μου, πῶς μ' ἀγαπᾶ ἡ κόρη;
—Ὄντας σὲ συλλογίζεται, κι ὄντας σε βάν' ὁ νοῦς της
στηλώνονται τὰ μάτια της, δὲν εἶν' στὰ λογικά της·
ὄντας σε γλέπει καὶ περνᾶς, κι ἀκούει τὴ λαλιά σου
πηδάει ἀπὸ τὸν τόπο της καὶ ροδοκοκκινίζει·
ὄντας ἀργήσει νὰ σε ἰδεῖ στέκεται μαραμμένη
κι ὅπου κι ἂν στέκει μοναχή, κλαίει κι ἀναστενάζει.

(Yiankas 398)

The little kerchief you embroider and dot with gold,
if you send it as a gift for your lover,
don't send it to him on its own, send it with your love.
The girl forgot, and sent it on its own.
He spread it on his lap and asks it, time and time again:
—Tell me, my little kerchief, does she love me?
—When she thinks of you, when you cross her mind
her eyes light up, she's out of her senses.
When she sees you passing by and hears your voice
she leaps up on the spot and starts to blush.
When she hasn't seen you for some time she is withered up
and whenever she's alone she weeps and groans.

Once love is reciprocated, the kerchief becomes an indelible mark of the first kiss, capable of dyeing all it touches incarnadine, as in the following famous but untranslatable song:

Κόκκιν' ἀχείλι ἐφίλησα κι ἔβαψε τὸ δικό μου,
καὶ στὸ μαντήλι τό 'συρα κι ἔβαψε τὸ μαντήλι,
καὶ στὸ ποτάμι τό 'πλυνα κι ἔβαψε τὸ ποτάμι,
κι ἔβαψε ἡ ἄκρη τοῦ γιαλοῦ κι ἡ μέση τοῦ πελάγου.
Κατέβη ὁ ἀιτός νὰ πιεῖ νερὸ κι ἔβαψαν τὰ φτερά του,
κι ἔβαψε ὁ ἥλιος ὁ μισὸς καὶ τὸ φεγγάρι ἀκέριο.

(Politis 126)

I kissed red lips, my own were stained,
I drew my kerchief to my lips, the kerchief stained,
I washed it in the river, the river stained,
stained were the edges of the shore and the ocean depths.

An eagle came down to drink, his wings stained,
stained too were half the sun and the full moon.

The little kerchief is a potent symbol of the blood-colored bonds of love,
as Iago understood only too well when he arranged the theft of Desde-
mona's first gift from Othello. Its magic may be connected with the cyclical movement of the dance; but the motif can be adapted to the lament. A
mother asks her dead child:

Τί νὰ σοῦ στείλω, μάτια μου, αὐτοῦ στὸν κάτω κόσμο;
Νὰ στείλω μῆλο, σήπεται, κυδῶνι, μαραγκιάζει,
σταφύλι, ξερογίζεται, τριαντάφυλλο, μαδιέται.
Στέλνω κι ἐγὼ τὰ δάκρυα μου δεμένα στὸ μαντήλι.
Τὰ δάκρυα ἥτανε καφτερά, καὶ κάηκε τὸ μαντήλι,
καὶ τὸ ποτάμι τά 'ριξε σε χήρας περιβόλι,
ὅπου τὰ δέντρα δὲν ἀνθοῦν, τὰ μῆλα δὲ μυρίζουν,
τὰ κόκκινα τριαντάφυλλα ροδόσταμα δὲ χύνουν . . .

(Yiankas 911, 1-8)

What shall I send you, my loved one, down in the Underworld?
If I send an apple, it will rot, if a quince, it will shrivel,
if grapes, they will fall away, if a rose it will droop.
So let me send my tears, bound up in my kerchief.
But the tears were burning, the kerchief too was scorched,
so the river washed them up in a widow's garden
where trees have no blossom and apples no fragrance,
and where red roses give out no rose water.

Clothes provide a figurative means of communication and an indication
of status, but woman's weaving of them can be a subterfuge for a ruse as
old as Penelope's. Penelope undid her handiwork each night—supposedly a
shroud for her father-in-law—to avoid her unwanted suitors. A young
Epirot girl uses the excuse of weaving her dowry at her aunt's to spend the
night with her lover, where other things are woven:[22]

Ποῦ πᾶς, Λενίτσα μ', μοναχή, τώρα τὸ βράδυ βράδυ;
Πάνω στὴ θειὰ μου τὴ Γιαννοῦ, πάνω νὰ νυχτερέψω,
νὰ γνέψω τὰ σκουλάκια μου, νὰ φτειάσω τὰ προικιά μου,
βρακὶ νὰ φτιάσω κεντητὸ τ' ἀρραβωνιαστικοῦ μου,
νὰ φτιάσω κεντηστόμπολα γι' αὐτὴν τὴν πεθερά μου.
Κι ἡ 'Ελενίτσ' ἀντὶς νὰ πάει εἰς τὴ Γιαννοῦ τὴ θειά της,
ἐχτύπησε στοῦ φίλου της καὶ τ' ἀγαπητικοῦ της,

κι ἔγνεσ᾽ ἐκεῖ καὶ γύφανε φιλιὰ ὅλη τὴ νύχτα·
αὐτά ἦταν τὰ γνεσίματα, αὐτά ἦτανε τὰ προικιά της.

(Yiankas 447)

—Where are you going, my Lenitsa, alone, so late at night?
—I'm going to aunt Yiannou's, I'll spend the night there,
I'm going to weave my clothes and make my dowry,
I'll make embroidered trousers for my betrothed,
I'll make embroidered kerchiefs for my mother-in-law.
But Elenitsa did not go to her aunt Yiannou's,
she knocked on her lover's door, the door of her betrothed,
weaving and spinning kisses all night long together.
These were her weavings, these were her dowry too.

Nor is weaving only a woman's ploy: in a love song from Thrace, Yiannous goes in despair to his beloved Maidou's sister and grandmother for advice on how to win his loved one. He is told to dress as a girl, take up a spindle and distaff, and propose to Maidou and her friends an excursion to gather flowers: his ruse works (Kavakopoulos 1981, 41.7).

Care of clothes and gifts of gems are symbolic of affection and mutual obligation. They mark and consolidate new family bonds, ensuring the protection of Christ and the Panagia. A young mother calls on Hypnos "Sleep" to take her son, as she tenderly sings him to sleep with promises of gold and silver toys. Hypnos is the gentle counterpart to the violent male agents, Charos and the *gambrós* "groom" of the laments and wedding songs:

Ὕπνε, ποὺ παίρνεις τὰ μωρὰ καὶ πα-, *ἄχ καὶ πᾶς* τὰ στὸ Λιβάδι
ν-ἔλα, πάρε τὸ Φώτη μου καὶ φέ-, *καὶ φέ-* ρε μοῦ τὸν πάλι.
Τάσσω τῆς Παναγιᾶς κερί, καὶ τοῦ, *καὶ τοῦ* Χριστοῦ λιβάνι,
νὰ βλέπει τὸ παιδάκι μου νὰ-, *να 'χω* χαρὰ μεγάλη.
Φωτάκι, βέργα μάλαμα, Φωτάκι, βέργα ἀσήμι,
ποὺ σε δουλεύει ὁ χρυσοκὸς μὲ τὴν ταπεινοσύνη.
Νυστάζουν τὰ ματάκια σου, θέλουν νὰ κοιμηθοῦνε
μὰ 'γὼ γιὰ τὸ Φωτάκι μου τ᾽ ἀφήνω κι ἀγρυπνοῦνε.

(Spyridakis and Peristeris 384–85:
Dodekanese; repeated words and syllables in italics)

Sleep, you who take babies and take *ah take* them to Livadhi,
come, take my Fotis, and bring, *yes bring* him back again.
I promise a candle to the Virgin, incense to, *yes to* Christ,
to look after my child so I, *yes I* can have great joy.

Fotaki, a wand of gold, Fotaki, a wand of silver
for you the goldsmith is working on in all humility.
Your little eyes are drowsy, they want to go to sleep
but for my Fotakis' sake, I keep my own awake.

Gold and silver brooches and gems are to this day pinned onto babies' garments to protect them against the evil eye and other undesirable visitations.
In a wedding song from the Peloponnese, the bride is praised during the
dressing ceremony as one who has been protected—like precious gems in a
chest or pressed flowers—from the outside world:

Νυφοῦλα, ποιός σε στόλισε σ᾽ αὐτὸ τὸ νυφοστόλι;
ἀμάν, ἡ Παναγιὰ κι ὁ Χριστὸς κι οἱ δώδεκ᾽ Ἀποστόλοι.
Νύφη μου μὲ τὰ πλουμίδια, σένα πρέπουν τὰ τραγούδια
῎Οσα πλουμίδια, νύφη μου, ἔχει τὸ φόρεμά σου,
ν-ἀμάν, τόσα νὰ εἶν᾽ τὰ χρόνια σου καὶ τόσα τὰ καλά σου.
Νύφη μου μαλαματένια, βγήκες ἀπ᾽ αὐτὴ τὴν ἔννοια.
Τὴ νύφη μας τὴν εἴχαμε κασέλλα κλειδωμένη
ἀμάν, καὶ τώρα τὴν παντρεύουμε ἄξια καὶ τιμημένη.
Νύφη μου μαλαματένια, βγήκες ἀπ᾽ αὐτὴ τὴν ἔννοια.
Νύφη μου, γυαλί, κρυστάλλι, στὸ χωριὸ δὲν εἶναι ἄλλη.
Τὴν κόρη μας τὴν εἴχαμε στὴν κόλλα διπλωμένη
καὶ τώρα τὴν παντρεύουμε ἄξια καὶ παινεμένη.
Τὴν κόρη μας τὴν εἴχαμε σ᾽ ἕνα χρυσὸ γαστράκι
καὶ τώρα τὴν παντρεύουμε σ᾽ ἕνα παλληκαράκι.

(Ibid. 289–90; repeated words in italics)

My little bride, who decked you out in this bridal costume?
aman, the Virgin, Christ and the twelve Apostles.
My bride with stitched embroideries, you are worthy of songs.
As many are your embroideries, so many be your good years,
my golden bride, you'll be wed, have no fear.
Our bride we kept like a locked-up chest
and now we marry her in worth and honor,
my golden bride, you'll be wed, have no fear.
My bride, glass and crystal, there's none like her in the village.
We kept our daughter pressed in sheets of paper
and now we marry her in worth and praise.
We kept our daughter in a golden vessel,
and now we marry her to a fine young man.
My bride, golden one, you'll be wed, have no fear.

The same images of precious gems and metals may be adapted to express loss in the case of death, as a mother internalized her *pónos* into a finely wrought object of worship:

Ποῦ πᾶς, γαιτάνι, νὰ σαπεῖς, γκόλφι μου, ν' ἀραχνιάσεις,
γαρούφαλο βενέτικο, ν' ἀλλαξομουσουδιάσεις;
Παιδάκι μου, τὸν πόνο σου ποῦ νὰ τὸν ἀπιθώσω;
Νὰν τόνε ρίχνω τρίστρατα, τὸν παίρνουν οἱ διαβάτες,
νὰ τόνε ρίξω στὰ κλαριά, τὸν παίρνουν τὰ πουλάκια.
Θὰ τόνε βάλω στὴν καρδιά, νάν τὸν καταριζώσω,
νὰ περπατῶ, νὰ με πονεῖ, νὰ στέκω, νὰ με σφάζει.
Θὰν πάγω καὶ στὸ χρυσικό, γιὰ νάν τονε χρυσώσει,
νὰ φκιάσω να χρυσὸ σταυρὸ κι ἕν ἀσημένιο γκόλφι,
νὰ προσκυνάγω τὸ σταυρὸ καὶ νὰ φιλῶ τὸ γκόλφι.

(Petropoulos 2.235)

Where are you going, ribbon, to rot, my amulet, to gather cobwebs,
carnation from Venice to wither and die?
My child, where can I lay down the *pónos* I feel for you?
If I cast it at the crossroads, the passersby will take it.
If I toss it on the branches, the little birds will take it.
I will lay it in my heart, I will let it take root there,
so it will give *pónos* when I walk, slay me when I stand.
I will go to the goldsmith so he can plate it with gold,
I will make it into a cross of gold, an amulet of silver,
so I can worship the cross and kiss the amulet.

Such is the versatility of metaphor that the same image can be found in a humorous song about a man cursed with an ugly but faithful wife: he can't sell her, he mustn't kill her, so he decides to take her to the goldsmith and get her made into a ring, cross, and amulet!

Θὲ νὰ τὴν πάω στὸ χρυσικό, νὰ τὴν περιχρυσώσει,
νὰ φτειάσω γκόλφι καὶ σταυρό, σταυρὸ καὶ δαχτυλίδι,
τὸ δαχτυλίδι νὰ φορῶ, τὸ γκόλφι νὰ βασταίνω,
καὶ τὸ σταυρὸ νὰ προσκυνῶ, νὰ λέν νὰ ζεῖ ἡ ἀγάπη.

(Politis 237, lines 5–8)

I'll take her to the goldsmith and have her gold-plated,
I'll make an amulet and cross, a cross and a ring,
so I can wear the ring, carry the amulet,
and worship the cross, so they can say "long live love."

Here is a new and defamiliarizing twist, beloved of tale-tellers and singers alike. A gifted singer from Crete, much sought after to perform at local *glén-dia* "festivals" was asked why he repeated in love songs images he had just used in laments. He responded, ἀφοῦ ταιριάζει - δὲν ταιριάζει; "Well it fits, doesn't it?"[23]

Fine clothes and precious gems are not merely external ornaments. Their value is enhanced—or, rather, given an inner quality—through their associations with religion and music. Christ and the Panagia are invoked to assist in the craftsmanship, while *ploumídia* "embroideries" and *tragoúdia* "songs" are phonetically as well as figuratively linked. As for the bereaved mother, her *pónos* is at the same time grief for the death of her child and the birth pangs of song, a thing of beauty to be worshiped and cherished. The interconnection between gems and song made explicit by Vizyenos in his stories and essays has its basis in these diverse folk genres. The religious dimension lends additional magic.

Magic in these women's songs is not restricted to Orthodoxy in its literal sense, however important the roles of Christ, the Panagia and the saints may be. It includes the more elemental powers of the cosmos, such as sun and moon, sky and stars. Just as Katerina Pateraki praised her mother as one who could "embroider the sky with its stars," so the bride's relatives in western Epiros praise the beauty of the bridal pair as equal to the sun and moon at the arrival of the groom's group to take her to the crowning in church:

Λάμπει ν-ὁ ἥλιος λάμπει, λάμπει ν-ὁ ἥλιος λάμπει,
λάμπει ν-ὁ ἥλιος λαμπει στὰ παραθύρια σου,
'τοιμάσου, κυρὰ νύφη, βάλ' τὰ στολίδια σου.
Λάμπει ν-ὁ ἥλιος λάμπει κάτου στὰ ρέματα,
ἦρθα γιὰ νὰ σε πάρω, δὲν εἶναι ψέματα.

(Spyridakis and Peristeris 293)

The sun is shining, shining is the sun,
the sun is shining, shining on your windows,
make ready, mistress bride, put on your finery.
The sun is shining, shining down on gullies.
I have come to take you, make no mistake.

Or again:

Ἔβγα, μάννα, δές τὸν ἥλιο,
ἂν ἐνύχτωσε νὰ φύγω (δίς)
κι ἂν 'ναι γλήγορα, νὰ μείνω.

'Έβγα, ἰδές καὶ τὸ φεγγάρι,
ἦρθ' ὁ νιὸς γιὰ νὰ με πάρει.

Come out, mother, see the sun,
if it's night I'll take my leave (*bis*),
and if too soon, then let me stay.
Come out, see the moon now,
the young man has come to take me.

(Ibid. 296)

Metaphors of journey predominate in songs of departure, while metaphors of clothes and gems are common to all songs of the life cycle, from the swaddling bands of infancy through the filthy clothes of the *xénos* and the finery of marriage to the winding-sheet of death. Gems, often ring-shaped in form and decoration, reinforce the cyclical process, without *télos*.[24] Erotic and fertilizing, they assist the passage between birth, marriage, and death, in ritual and metaphor alike. In the tales, they are transformed into potent magical agents, used both to enchant and to undo enchantment. Witchcraft replays on the level of fictional narrative the potency of clothes and gems in ritual and song. The supernatural forces of good and evil in the tales are personifications of the power of love and hate in songs and curses.

3. Hair

In many cultures, hair signifies both power and vulnerability, male and female. Just as Delilah's clipping of Samson's headlock proved his—and his city's—downfall, so wondertales and ballads worlwide may situate the key point of combat between life and death on two or three single hairs.[25] What of the rituals and songs of the life cycle? Ritual prescriptions and proscriptions are clear enough. Woman's hair is loosened at childbirth to assist delivery, much as garments are eased, knots untied, doors and drawers banged open and shut. In mourning, the same gestures indicate her grief and ease the passage of the soul. Before marriage, care must be taken over the combing and washing of a girl's hair, because to reveal too much is to invite gossip and seduction. At marriage, as during courtship, beauty and good luck depend on how hair is braided and on her head adornments (ribbons, scarves, jewels). If hair is cut around the time of marriage or during mourning, danger or extreme grief is implied. For men, head hair is less important than facial and bodily hair: the "baldchin" (*spanós*) is far more sinister than the "bald head"(*falakrós*).[26]

The ritual code allows for considerable flexibility and ambivalence, since hair is powerfully alluring but linked with death. Seizing overweening heroes by the hair is a favorite ploy of Charos, while dying heroes in their turn may seize their wives by the hair, swing them round five times, and finally strangle them before giving up the ghost (Politis 1909, 242, no. 32). Girls, too, ensnare their future husbands by means of their own hair. A bride entwines and is entwined by plaited and knotted locks, often including snakes and magic. In the love songs, a girl's surest way of attracting a handsome young man is to sit on her porch or balcony, demurely carding her thread or combing her hair. If she likes the look of him, she may toss him an apple, which he immediately consumes, and he may offer her a ribbon to tie up her hair, which she wears to the next dance:

Τοῦ 'νιοῦ 'γὼ μῆλο τοῦ 'στειλα καὶ μοῦ 'δωκε γαιτάνι.
Κεῖνος το μῆλο τό 'φαγε, γὼ τὸ γαιτάνι τό 'χω,
καὶ στὰ μαλλιά μου τό 'πλεξα καὶ βγῆκα στὸ σιργιάνι
καὶ στὸ γιαλὸ κατέβηκα, κατου στὸ περιγιάλι,
ἐκεῖ γυναῖκες χόρευαν, μ ἐπιάσανε κι ἐμένα.

(Politis 103)

I sent the boy an apple, he gave me a ribbon.
He ate the apple, I have the ribbon,
I braided it in my hair and went out for a stroll
down to the shore, down to the coastline,
where women were dancing—they caught me in their dance.

Thanks to her braided hair, she remains in full control of the situation. If caught in bed before marriage with her loved one, a girl can plead that her own hair is so entwined with his fingers that she cannot possibly disentangle herself, and get up, as in laments and songs of death in foreign parts:

Πῶς νὰ σ'κωθῶ, λεβέντη μου, ἀπὸ τὴν ἀγκαλιά σου;
Πιαστήκαν τὰ μαλλάκια μου στὰ πέντε δάχτυλά σου.

(Spyridakis and Peristeris 219, 7–8)

How can I get up, my lord, from your embrace?
My hair is knotted into your five fingers.

When girls dress a bride and comb her hair, they will sing:

Χτενάκι μ' ἀλεφαντένιο
μὴν κόψεις τρίχα τῶμ μαλλιῶ
καὶ κόψω γὼ τὰ δόντια σου.

(Baud-Bovy 1.25–26; cf. *Laog.* 19.196)

My little ivory comb
don't tear a single hair
or else I'll cut your teeth.

One is reminded of the wondertale motif of throwing down a comb to escape hostile pursuers: the teeth sown in the ground grows an instant barrier of dense forests and thickets.

The power of the imagery stems from *breaking the ritual code*. A girl might not win the man of her choice if she did not reveal some hair. Conversely, the Panagia was inappropriately combing her hair with an ivory comb, or taking a bath in a silver bathtub—when news was brought to her of Christ's Crucifixion.[27]

4. The Garden of Love

The garden is an ideal space, where cultivation meets nature, where flowers and herbs lend scent and healing.[28] Songs of birth and courtship emphasize meeting points rather than travels abroad (as at marriage and death). The meeting may take place in a garden or orchard: the lover begs his girl to lend him the keys to her garden so he can cut citrons and cloves, offering in return a diamond ring for her finger and respects to her mother (Yiankas 392). Or he may enter her garden at dawn to cut basil, mint, and marjoram, together with citrus leaves, so he can beat his drum and wake her up at dawn (ibid. 397). If he chances to be out hunting, his hawk may stray into her garden. She has no dowry, but her beauty is such that, like the apple tree, she sheds pearls around her:[29]

Ὁ νιὸς μὲ τὰ λαγωνικὰ ἐβγῆκε στὸ κυνήγι
κι ἐκράτει καὶ στὸ χέρι του ἕνα μικρὸ γεράκι.
Τώφυγε, τ' ἀπολύθηκε, σε περιβόλι μπῆκε,
καὶ ἀφορμὴ τοῦ γερακιοῦ μπῆκε κι ὁ νιὸς κατόπιν.
'Εκ' ἠῦρε κόρ' ὁπώπλενε σε γούρνα μαραμαρένια,
κι ἦταν γεμάτη στὸ φλωρὶ καὶ στὸ μαργαριτάρι.
—Γιὰ μᾶστε τὰ σκυλλάκια σου καὶ δές τα σε δεντράκι,
νὰ μή με φᾶνε κυνηγέ, νὰ μὴ με κυνηγήσουν.
—'Εμένα τὰ σκυλλάκια μου λαγοὺς μονάχα πιάνουν
καὶ στὰ κορίτσια τὰ 'μορφα, ποτὲ κακὸ δὲν κάνουν.
Γιὰ πές μου, πές μου, κόρη μου, τί προίκα θὰ μοῦ δώσεις;
δὲ θέλω προίκα ἀπὸ φλωριά, δὲ θέλω ἀπὸ στολίδια.

—Δὲν θέλεις προῖκα ἀπὸ φλωριά, δὲν θέλεις καὶ στολίδια.
Σοῦ δίνω τούτη τὴ μηλιὰ πούναι γιομάτη μ' ἀνθία.
Ἔσεισ' ἡ κόρη τὴ μηλιά, ν' ἐπέφτανε τὰ μήλα
κι ἐσχίζονταν, κι ἐσκόρπαγαν φλωριά, μαραγαριτάρια.
—Μάζωξε, νιέ μου, μάζωξε, τὰ μήλα τῆς μηλιᾶς μου
καὶ πάλε ματαμάζωξε, καὶ πάλε ματαγύρνα.

(Yiankas 419)

The young man went off hunting with his hounds,
holding in his hand a little hawk.
The hawk escaped him, got away, flew into a garden,
so the young man found the chance to follow him.
There he found a girl washing clothes in a marble cistern,
full of florins and full of pearls.
—Call in your hounds and tie them to a tree,
lest they should eat me, hunter, lest they should hunt me down.
—My hounds catch hares and nothing else,
they'll never harm girls as fair as you.
Tell me, my girl, what dowry will you give me?
I don't want florins, I don't want pearls.
—If you don't want florins, if you don't want pearls,
I'll give you this apple tree, laden with blossoms.
She shook the apple tree, down fell the apples.
They shattered, scattering florins and pearls.
—Gather up, young man, gather the apples from my tree
and gather them again, then come back for more.

This allusive song suggests both the sensuality of courtship and the power of young love to overcome conventional demands for dowry, while the apple-tree symbolizes the regenerative powers of female sexuality, as in the Garden of Eden. As in *Hysmine* (Chapter 4), the garden is the ideal space for eroticism about to be sanctioned by marriage.

Most erotic of all are those love songs from Macedonia, Thrace, Epiros, and the Dodekanese where the young man finds the girl in the rose garden (γκιοὺλ-μπαχτσέ > Turkish *gül baçe*): he becomes so intoxicated by the merest glimpse of her slender ankles as she culls the blooms that he loses his mind (Yiankas 429); or he finds her asleep amid the roses and tries tossing first apples and then silver and gold to wake her up and make her greet him after a long absence from home:

Σέβ 'κα γιὰ νὰ σεργιανήσω (δίς) μέσ' στὸν Γκιοὺλ μπαξέ
δυό μου μάτια, μὲς στὸν Γκιοὺλ μπαξέ

βρίσκω κόρη πού κοιμούνταν (δίς) στά τριαντάφυλλα,
                    ἡ καημένη, στὰ τριαντάφυλλα,
ρίχνω μῆλο καὶ τὴν κρούγω (δίς) δὲν τὸ δέχεται
                    ἡ καημένη, δὲν τὸ δέχεται,
ρίχνω μάλαμα κι ἀσήμι (δίς) χαμογέλασε,
                    τὸ πουλί μου, χαμογέλασε.
Ποῦ 'σουν, ξένε μ', τὸ χειμώνα (δίς), ὅταν κρύωνα
                    ἡ καημένη, ὅταν κρύωνα
κι ἦρθες τώρα καλοκαίρι (δίς) πού θερμαίνουμαι
                    δυό μου μάτια, πού ζεσταίνουμαι.
—Ξένος ἤμουν ὁ καημένος, ξενοδούλευα
κι ὅ,τι ἤβγαζα ὁ καημένος σένα τά 'στελνα·
σόστειλα γυαλὶ καὶ χτένι νὰ γυαλίζεσαι.

                    (Spyridakis and Peristeris 222–124; repeated words in italics)

I went out for a stroll (bis) in the garden of roses,
                    my two eyes, in the garden of roses,
I find a girl asleep (bis) amid the roses—*alas, amid the roses,*
I hit her with an apple (bis), she will not have it—*alas, she will not have it,*
I throw her gold and silver (bis), she smiled—*my little bird smiled.*
Where have you been, stranger? All winter (bis) I have been cold—*alas, cold!*
and now you've come in summertime (bis) when I am warm—
                    yes, my two eyes, hot.
—I was in foreign lands, working for another,
what I earned, poor wretch, I sent to you.
I sent a mirror and a comb for you to shine.

The girl succumbs to silver and gold rather than to the apple not because she is mercenary but because the apple suggests sensuality, whereas silver and gold are associated with the Panagia and Christ, affording sanctification of their union. One is reminded of the Turkish wondertale "Girl of the Rosebush:" the girl takes shelter in the rosebush under which her mother is buried, until gently unearthed by the prince who will surely die unless he is married to the girl with the scent of roses (Merkelbach 1978, 1–15). The girl fast asleep amid roses, to be awakened by her lover, is a theme common to songs and tales, but condensed into metaphor in the songs, it becomes magic metonym in the tales, leading off into all kinds of narrative directions. The erotic imagery is enhanced by its parallel occurrence at birth and death. A mother asks Sleep to take her child to "the garden of May":

Ἔλα, ὕπνε, κι ἔπαρέ το,
καὶ γλυκαποκοίμησέ το,

σύρ' το μέσ' τοῦ Μάη τ' ἀμπέλι,
καὶ στοῦ Μάη τὸ περιβόλι,
νὰ τοῦ δώσ' ὁ Μάης λουλούδια
κι ὁ περιβολάρης μῆλα·
νάνι, νάνι τὸ παιδάκι
ποὺ κοιμᾶται σὰν ἀρνάκι.
Νάνι τὸ γλυκό τ ἀηδόνι,
τ' Ἀλεξαντρινό παγῶνι.

(Yiankas 681)

Come, sleep, and take him,
and put him to sweet sleep,
take him to May's vineyard,
and to the garden of May,
May will give him flowers
the gardener will give apples;
lullaby, lullaby, my child
sleeping like a lamb.
Lullaby, sweet nightingale,
peacock from Alexandria.

Mourning her small dead son, a mother sends him off to play in the garden of Paradise:

Πάννε καὶ σού, παιδάκι μου, μὲ τ' ἄλλα τὰ παιδάκια,
στοῦ παραδείσου τὸ πλατὺ μαγεύουλ λουλουδάκια.

(Politis 201)

Go, you too, my little child, with the other children,
they are gathering flowers on the plain of Paradise.

The garden or orchard, with an abundance of fruits and flowers and the tree in the center of the courtyard, signifies the space of lovemaking and fruition. The images of the love songs are not so distant from those expressed by ekphrasis in the learned and vernacular romances from the twelfth to fifteenth centuries or from the *flos florum* of medieval Western literature.[30]

5. Dangerous Spaces: Hunting and Hunted

If gardens and fountains provide the idyllic meeting place, women who frequent ridges, wells, plains, and seashores may present and be exposed to greater dangers. Just as the the young shepherd nonchalantly returning home from the sheepfold may be confronted by Charos lurking behind a ψηλή ραχούλα (high ridge) in versions of "Charos and the shepherd," so in the love songs a young man will lie in wait for the girl who comes down the mountain "spinning at her distaff, her spindle full, trailing dew in her feet and musk in her hair" (Yiankas 353.2-4). Young Malamo is warned by her lover that if her mother sends her to the spring for water, he will be waiting to smash her pitcher over a kiss and send her back empty-handed to her mother, who is sure to guess her guilty secret (Yiankas 357). Breaking vessels, as we saw in the last chapter, is a ritual gesture signifying no return to former status. In a Cypriot song, a young man boasts of his conquests, only to be outwitted by a black-eyed girl, who on the pretext of going to school, goes instead to the mountain, where she asks him to share apples, quinces, and marjoram in their jointly cultivated vineyard. She gets pregnant; after an exchange of subterfuge with her mother, she tells her father the truth. He makes the man marry her, and so this Cypriot Don Juan is caught in his own trap (Papadopoullos A26.78–80). Songs of this type form an interesting counterpart to those where it is the young man who is warned by his mother not to go up the mountain or stand by a tree and not to play his flute there: he does just that and is bewitched by the *lámia* of the well, who will not release him (Ioannou 52-53.5). Bewitchment by females at the well is both metaphorical and literal.

Spaces where music and dance are performed are particularly seductive. In the lively dance song "Zervopoula," young girls gather in the plains to build a monastery:

Κάτω στὸν κάμπο τὸν πλατύ, τὸν ὅμορφο τὸν τόπο,
μαζεύτηκαν οἱ γ' ἔμορφες νὰ χτίσουν μοναστήρι.
Τὰ περιστέρια κουβαλοῦν, τὰ χελιδόνια χτίζουν.
Σὰν χτίσαν κι ἀποχτίσανε, πιάνουν χορὸ χορεύουν.
Μπροστὰ χορεύουν οἱ ξανθές καὶ πίσω οἱ μαυρομμάτες,
καὶ μέσ' στὴ μέση τοῦ χοροῦ χορεύει ἡ Ζερβοπούλα,
καὶ λάμπαν τὰ μανίκια της, κι ἀστράφτ' ἡ τραχηλιά της.
Κι ὁ βασιλιὰς ἐξέβγαινε νὰ λαφοκυνηγήσει,
μὲ ἑξήντα δυὸ λαγωνικούς, σαρανταδυό ζαγάρια . . .

(Yiankas 378, 1-9)

Down in the broad plain, down in that fair space,
beautiful girls were gathered to build a monastery.
Doves fetch and carry, swallows do the building.
When they had finished building, they began the dance.
The blonde ones go in front, the black-eyed ones behind,
and in the middle of the band Zervopoula dances,

her sleeves are shining, her neck flashes lightning.
And the king came past to hunt for hares,
with sixty-two hounds, and forty-five hunting dogs . . .

Such is her beauty that he wishes away his kingdom so he might take her
by the hand and dance with her. We are not told whether he does so, but
the song sheds light on the "Bridge of Arta" (Chapter 6) and on the Byzantine swallow song (Chapter 3). Whereas the forty-five craftsmen and sixty-
two apprentices have a hard time building their bridge, and the master
craftsman is forced to immure his beautiful young wife to make it firm, in
this song the women make light work of their monastery, thanks to the
magical aid of doves and swallows. Are they Nereids? We do not know, but
the *incipit* "Down in the broad plain" suggests those curious versions of the
ballad which set the scene of the bridge building κάτω στὸ γιαλό "down
by the shore". To dismiss such versions as "improbable", as Beaton does, is to
miss the magic and mystery: the bridge, or monastery, is a not necessarily a
real edifice but any cultural artifact demanding labor, sacrifice, and beauty.[31]

Κάτω στὸ γιαλό "Down on the seashore," is the opening line of many
songs that deal with love and death, some tragic, others not. A mother up-
braids her daughter for going "down there" too often:

Δὲν σοῦ το εἶπα, σκύλλα κόρη, στὸ γιαλὸ μὴν κατεβεῖς,
τὶ ὁ γιαλὸς θὰ φουρτουνιάσει, κι ἄν σε πάρει θὰ πνιγεῖς.
—Ἄν μὲ πάρει, κι ἄν με βγάλει ὄξω στὰ βαθιὰ νερά,
τὸ κορμί μου κάνω βάρκα καὶ τὰ χέρια μου κουπιά
κολυμπῶντας θὰ περάσω στὸ ἀντίπερα νησί,
τὴν ἀγάπη μου γιὰ νἄβρω, γιὰ νὰ εἴμαστε μαζί.
Κάλλια τὥχω ν' ἀπεθάνω, καὶ τὸ κύμα νὰ με πιεῖ,
παρὰ νά 'μαι μέρα νύχτα ἔρημη καὶ μοναχή.

(Yiankas 388)

Didn't I tell you, bitch of a daughter, not to go down to the shore?
There will be a storm, and if it takes you, you will drown!
—If it takes me, if it sets me out in waters of the deep,
I'll make my body into a boat, my hands into oars;
I'll swim and cross over to the island opposite
to find my loved one, so we can be together.
I'd rather die, have the waves engulf me
than to be left so desolate, alone both day and night.

Is this a lament of a girl deserted by her lover, or an expression of her sexual longing? It is hard to say, but as in the wondertales, young people must

set out on a journey outside the family home, however hazardous it may be. The allusive imagery is equal to that of another love song, Κανελόρριζα "Cinnamon root", where it is not specified whether the girl's changed condition is due to lovesickness or pregnancy:[32]

Κάτου σε γιαλό, κάτου σε περιγιάλι
κόρην ἀγαπῶ ξανθὴ καὶ μαυρομάτα
δώδεκα χρονῶν κι ὁ ἥλιος δὲν τὴν εἶδε.
Μόν' ἡ μάνα της μονακριβή τὴν ἔχει,
ρόϊδο τὴν καλεῖ, τριάνταφυλλο τὴν κράζει
κανελλόριζα καὶ ἄνθη τῆς κανέλλας.
—Τ' ἐκιτρίνησες καὶ τί 'σαι χλωμιασμένη;
Μὴν ἀρρώστησες; μὴν ἐκρυφοθερμάνθεις;
—Δὲν ἀρρώστησα, κρυφὴ δὲν ἔχω θέρμη,
χθὲς τὸ δειλινό, ἐψὲς ἀργὰ τὸ βράδυ
πῆρα τὸ σταμνί, νερὸ νὰ πάω νὰ φέρω,
κι ηὖρα ἕνα παιδί, σὰν νὰ ἦταν ξαδερφός μου
καὶ μ' ἐφίλησε στὰ μάτια καὶ στὰ φρύδια
καὶ στὰ μάγουλα ποὖχα τὸ κοκκινάδι.   (Yiankas 438)

Down on the shore, on the seashore
was the fair black-eyed girl I love,
twelve years old, not seen by the sun.
Her mother kept her close to herself.
calling her quince, naming her rose,
root and blooms of cinnamon.
—Why so yellow, why so pale?
Are you ill? Have you a hidden fever?
—I am not ill, I have no hidden fever,
yesterday afternoon, late evening
I took the jug to bring back water,
I found a boy, like my cousin,
he kissed me on the eyes and brows
and on my reddened cheeks.

If rose gardens and orchards spell innocence, of all meeting places outside the house, the most erotic and dangerous is the public bathhouse. It is between the bathhouse and the barber's that illicit advances are made, as in the song "Two Loving Brothers and the Evil Wife" (Politis 1914, 80), in which one brother's wife pays with her life for being taken in by the promises of the other brother. Yet this song too has its converse: in Ἡ Βουλγάρα "The Bulgarian woman," it is between the bathhouse and the barber's that a young man, after an unspecified absence, confronts the Bulgarian mistress he had served for twelve years, without payment. Reminded of her debt, she offers any one of her female slaves instead; he wants her alone as his price (Yiankas 441). Some might want to claim this as yet another example of male exploitation of the female body; yet the song makes it clear that it is he who has been, and will remain, in her thrall:

θέλω τὴν ὄμορφη κυρὰ ποὺ με γλυκοκυττάζει
καὶ μ' ἔχει σκλάβο δουλευτῆ στὸν κῆπο τῆς αὐλῆς της.

(lines 17–18)

I want the beautiful mistress who casts me sweet glances,
and has me enslaved as labourer in her courtyard's garden.

These songs suggest a paradoxical dimension to the categories inside/ outside and open/closed.[33] On the one hand, a mother will seek to guard her daughter close until the time for marriage comes, sometimes punishing her cruelly—even beating her to death—if she ventures out so far as the courtyard to talk to a stranger (Ioannou 1975, 127–28). Despite the girl's apparently rigid seclusion, life offers the resourceful young couple opportunities to exchange tokens or glances, whether at the well, in the garden, on the dance floor, or "down by the shore." Quite often, although a girl's mother may express disapproval, such meetings take place with her connivance—even contrivance. "The Dead Brother" spells out the dire consequences of a mother guarding her daughter too closely, while a careful reading of the love songs suggests that the system of arranged marriages is neither as repressive nor as loveless as is often supposed. The allusive qualities of the imagery render the tone of the love songs erotic, sensual, and spiritual rather than romantic. Is supposed modern female promiscuity such a great departure from past practice?

6. Burning and Withering

The searing force of grief in love and death is conveyed by imagery of burning and thirst. Fire consumes, withers, and dries up not only the victim but all it touches as well. A river of fire, or grief at bereavement, can forge a passage to the Underworld so scorching that everything in its way will be burned up (Yiankas 911). In Καϋμός "Grief," a girl in love complains to her own heart:

—Καρδιὰ μὲ δεκοχτὼ κλειδιὰ βαριὰ εἶσαι κλειδωμένη,
γιατί δὲν παίζεις, δὲ γελᾶς πῶς ἦσουν μαθημένη;
—Τί νὰ γελάσω, τί νὰ εἰπῶ, πῶς ἤμουν μαθημένη,

τὰ χέρια ποὺ 'χαν τὰ κλειδιὰ εἶναι ξενητεμένα.
Νὰ στείλω μῆλο, σέπεται, κυδόνι, μαραγκιάζει,
νὰ στείλω μοσκοστάφυλο, στὸ δρόμο ξερωγιάζει,
νὰ στείλω καὶ τὸ δάκρυ μου σ' ἕνα χρυσὸ μαντήλι
τὸ δάκρυ μου εἶναι καυτερό, καὶ καίγει τὸ μαντήλι.
Φαρμάκι, νὰ φαρμακωθῶ, νὰ πέσω νὰ πεθάνω;
καὶ πάλε ἡ μαύρη σκέφτομαι τίνος κακὸ θὰ κάνω.
Ντέρντι δὲν εἶχα στὴν καρδιὰ κι ἀπόχτησα μαράζι,
τοῦ καραβιοῦ τὰ σίδερα νὰ ρίξω δὲν τὸ βγάζει.

(Yiankas 365)

—Heart with eighteen keys, you are heavily locked up,
why don't you play and laugh as you were always wont?
—How can I laugh, how can I speak as I was wont?
The hands that held my keys have gone to foreign lands.
If I send an apple, it rots; if a quince, it withers;
if I send muscat grapes, they shed their fruit.
Let me send my tear in a golden kerchief,
but my tear is searing, it burns the kerchief.
Poison, shall I take you, fall down and die myself?
In misery I take thought, to whom would I do hurt?
Not a care in my heart had I, now I have withering waste
—were I to cast a ship's iron grips, it would not lift it up.

Fires of passion give rise to thoughts of self-injury and violence, then to depression, heavy as lead, as the girl displaces her grief onto her metonymically severed heart, the only "other" she has left to address.

For Eleni, married to a rich but sick husband, grief has already consumed and withered up not only her husband and herself but also the trees, blossoms, and grasses, in poignant contrast to the promise of young life inside her untasted body. As in the song about the young man dying abroad, the paradoxical injunction, "Get up, so you may lie down," suggests impotence to rise up, whether for deathbed or marriage-bed. The coins refer not just to those attached to the bride's costume but also to those placed on her lips by her mother-in-law, enjoining silence:[34]

'Εμαραθῆκαν τὰ δεντριά, τ' ἄνθια καὶ τὰ χορτάρια,
γιὰ τῆς 'Ελένης τὸν καϋμὸ τῆς κακοπαντρεμμένης.
ποὺ 'χε ἀρραβῶνες δώδεκα καὶ δέκα δαχτυλίδια.
—Λένη, γιατί 'σαι κίτρινη; σὲ λένε μαραζαρά·
μή σε μαραίνουν τὰ φλωριὰ καὶ τὰ χρυσὰ στολίδια;

—Δὲ με μαραίνουν τὰ φλωριὰ καὶ τὰ χρυσὰ στολίδια,
μὰ με μαραίνει ὁ ἄντρας μου αὐτὸς ὁ μαραζάρης.
Σήκω, μαράζη, πλάγιασε, σήκω, μαράζη, πέσε,
κι ἄπλωσε τὰ ξεράδια σου στὸν ἀργυρό μου κόρφο,
νὰ βρεῖς δυὸ κιτρολέημονα ὅπου μοσχοβολᾶνε,
νὰ βρεῖς τοῦ Μάγη τὴ δροσιά, τ' Ἀπρίλη τὰ λουλούδια.
Ὁ μαραζάρης κείτεται στὴν ἄκρη πλαγιασμένος
κι ἐγὼ ἡ μαύρη μοναχὴ στὸ ἔρμο μου τὸ στρῶμα.

(Fauriel 2.160)

Shriveled are the trees, the blossoms and the grasses
for Eleni's grief, for her unhappy marriage,
though she wore twelve betrothal rings and ten for marriage.
—Leni, why so yellow? They call you shriveled one,
perhaps the coins have shriveled you, or the ornaments of gold?
—No, neither coins nor gold ornaments have shriveled me,
I am shriveled by my husband, he's sick and shriveled up.
Get up, shriveled man, come to bed, get up, withered one, lie here
and reach out your withered arms into my silver chest,
you'll find two citron lemons bursting with smell of musk,
you'll find May's coolness, April's blooms.
The withered man lies there stretched out in his corner
while I, alone and blackened, am on my desolate couch.

Metaphors of withering, shriveling, grief, and depression—expressed by cognates of the verb *maraíno* "wither"—evoke the young bride's desperation at
finding her husband, yellowed by his many coins, unable to consummate the
marriage. No wonder the bride tree in Τώρα τὰ πουλιά, "Now the Birds,"
demands that her groom repay his first night of rest in her arms/branches
by letting one drop of liquid fall onto her roots the next morning, before
he goes off to wars in distant parts! (see below, pages 403-4).

If women in their love songs and laments internalize the fires of grief
by turning their hearts and bodies into molten lead and dried-up wood,
men refer to passion as φλόγα "flames" or λάβρα "white heat" leaping out,
in need of quenching. In Τ' ἀφίλητο κορίτσι "The Unkissed Girl," an im-
petuous young man's determination to steal a kiss to preserve his self-
esteem is met with the girl's curses that his body may never dissolve! Her
curse (does she mean it seriously?) accords with exhumation rituals, when
careful attention is paid to the "clean white bones," while his excuse suggests that he too is acting under the constraints of an androcentric society
(other men would laugh at him):

Τρεῖς χρόνους ἐπερπάταγα μ' ἕνα γλυκὸ κορίτσι
κι ἀκόμα δὲν τὸν φίλησα, κι εἶχε ἡ καρδιά μου λάβρα,
νὰ τ' ἄφηνα ἀφίλητο θὰ γέλαγαν με ἐμένα.
Πεζεύω, δένω τ' ἄλογο, κρεμάω τ' ἄρματά μου,
φιλῶ τὴν κόρη τρεῖς φορές, στὰ μάτια καὶ στὸ στόμα
καὶ ἀνάμεσα στὰ δυὸ βυζιά, στὴ μέση ἀπὸ τὰ στήθη.
—Ξένε, μ' ἐγλυκοφίλησες, μοῦ πῆρες ὅ, τι εἶχα
καὶ τώρα πῶς με ἀπάριασες σὰν καλαμιὰ στὸ βάλτο;
Ξένε, νὰ σκάσει ὁ μαῦρος σου, ν' ἀστράψει νὰ σε κάψει
καὶ τὸ κορμί σου ἡ μαύρη γῆς ποτέ νὰ μὴ τὸ λυώσει.

(Yiankas 455)

For three years I went out with a sweet young girl,
I hadn't even kissed her, my heart held a volcano.
If I didn't steal a kiss, I'd be a laughingstock.
I dismount, bind my horse, and hang up my weapons.
I kiss the girl three times, on the eyes and mouth,
and in between her two breasts, right there in the middle.
—Stranger, you've sweetly kissed me, you've stolen all I had
and now you want to leave me like reed stubble on the marsh?
Stranger, may your horse burst open, lightning burn you up,
and may the black earth never dissolve your body!

A couplet (*mantináda*) from Kasos sums up the torment of "fire without water":

Πολλὴ φωτιὰ δίχως νερὸ πῶς ἠμπορεῖ νὰ σβήσει;
Μὲ βάσανα τήνε περνῶ τὴν ἔρημή μου ζήση.

(Baud-Bovy 2.45)

How can a great fire be quenched without water?
I spend this my desolate life in wretched torments.

7. Tears and Poison, Blood and Water

As Mary Douglas has shown (1966, 114–28), bodily fluids such as tears and blood are potent but ambivalent signifiers, indicating emotional as well as physiological states which can cross between negative and positive according to context and perspective. Liquids play an important part in rituals of the life cycle. As we saw in the last chapter, at marriage and death all water standing in the house must be thrown out, and the vessels smashed over the threshold; fresh water is then brought in from outside both for the ritual washing of the bridal pair or the corpse and for the cleansing of the household. At birth, cleansing rituals take place after the new mother's period of seclusion is over. Wine, signifying blood, is used to wash the dead and welcome guests.[35] Excessive admiration from strangers for an attractive child is believed to provoke the evil eye, which can be averted by spitting on the ground. Of bodily fluids, tears are the purest, perhaps because they are uncontaminated by digestive and procreative functions.[36] But of all the liquids used in folk rituals and symbolically referred to in the songs, the only unequivocally positive one is pure and fresh cold water, perhaps because it is a fluid the human body cannot produce but on which its survival depends.

Tears may be poison for the living, but they provide vital sustenance for the thirsty dead (*oi dipsasménoi*), burning their way down to the Underworld in a river of fire.[37] For the mourner, tears are a means of assuaging pain and are sometimes even said to be sweet (Alexiou 1974, 125), keeping open a channel of communication between living and dead, between our world and the unknown one, to which all must pass. Tears also have the power to transmute silent pain into songs or even gems. Shed by loving eyes, they work their way down to the heart, watering the roots of love. A young man from Karpathos tells the sky (*ouranós*) to stop raining, because his own eyes can water the meadows:

᾽Ω οὐρανέ, μὴ βρέξεις πιό, κάμε μ᾽ αὐτὴ τὴ χάρη,
κι ἐγὼ μὲ τὰ ματάκια μου ποτίζω τὸ χορτάρι.

(Baud-Bovy 2.272)

O sky, rain no more, do me that favour,
and I will water the grass with my own eyes.

Tears are potent because they spring from the eyes, where love is caught, descending to the lips and heart to water the tree of love which grows in the heart and cannot be uprooted without bloodshed:

᾽Εβγᾶτε ἀγόρια στὸ χορό, κοράσια στὰ τραγούδια,
πέστε καὶ τραγουδήσετε πῶς πιάνεται γὴ ἀγάπη.
᾽Απὸ τὰ μάτια πιάνεται, στὰ χείλια κατεβαίνει,
κι ἀπὸ τὰ χείλια στὴν καρδιὰ ριζώνει καὶ δὲ βγαίνει.

(Politis 93)

Come out boys to the dance, girls to the songs,
tell us and sing for us how love is caught.

It is caught in the eyes, it goes down to the lips,
and from the lips to the heart it takes root and never leaves.

In another song from Rhodes, a pine tree slashed to produce resin becomes
a symbol for unrequited, but not entirely hopeless, love, with further subtlety irony in the initial verb *chúnei* "pours," used here of the tree but also
suggesting metonymically ejaculation?

> Χύνει τὸ πεῦκο, σὰν κοπεῖ, σὰ δάκρυ τὸ ρετσίνι
> —Γιαννοῦλα μου, Γιαννοῦλα μου—
> ἔκαψες τὴν καρδοῦλα μου, κι ἡ ἐμορφιὰ σὰμ μαραθεῖ,
>   πάλι μορφάδα δείχνει.
> Δὲν ταγιαντῶ (δίς) τὸν ἐδικό σου τὸν καμό.
>
> (Baud-Bovy 1.164)

The pine tree, when cut, drips resin like tears
        —my Yiannoula, my Yiannoula—
you have burnt my heart; but even withered beauty
        can put out new bloom.
I cannot bear (bis) the pain you cause me.

Eyes can wound as well as burn, as a girl from Epiros complains. Or is her
plea to her lover to take out his sword, plunge it into her throat, and draw
blood erotic?[38]

> Αὐτὰ τὰ μάτια, Δῆμο μου, τὰ 'μορφα
> τὰ φρύδια τὰ γραμμένα.
> Αὐτὰ με κάνουν, Δῆμο μ', κι ἀρρωστῶ,
> με κάνουν κι ἀπεθαίνω.
> Γιὰ βγάλε, Δῆμο μ' τὸ σπαθάκι σου
> καὶ κόψε τὸν λαιμόν μου,
> καὶ μάσε, Δῆμο μ' καὶ τὸ αἷμα μου
> σ' ἕνα χρυσὸν μαντήλι.
> Καὶ σύρ' το, Δῆμο μ' στὰ ἐννιὰ χωριά,
> στὰ δέκα βιλαέτια.
> Κι ἂν σε ρωτήσουν, Δῆμο μ τί εἶν αὐτό;
> Τὸ αἷμα τῆς ἀγάπης.
>
> (Yiankas 347)

Those eyes, my Dimos, so handsome
and those penciled eyebrows,
Dimos, they make me languish,
they bring me close to death.
Take out your spear, my Dimos,

and cut my throat;
and gather up my blood, Dimos,
in a golden kerchief.
Take it, Dimos, to our nine villages,
to the ten *vilayets*.
If they ask you, Dimos, what is this?
The blood of love.

The eroticism is suggestive rather than explicit, as in the curses of the deserted girl.

In cases of a wife's adultery, her blood must be spilled to cleanse the dishonor. One night, Marousio accepts her lover into her house, assuring him that her husband has gone out levying poll tax (*charátsoma*) in the neighboring villages, a particularly nasty pursuit, reminding us of Byzantine songs in which the emperor "strikes the anvil, and strikes the neighbors too" (Chapter 3). Her lover asks her to spread pillows and light up the silver lamp and silver chandelier in the upstairs guest room, but her husband sees the blaze of light from a distant mountain ridge and at once suspects another man's presence:

Μήνα ἡ γυναῖκα μ' δὲ μπορεῖ, μήνα καὶ τὸ παιδί μας;
Δίνει βιτσιὰ τ' ἀλόγο του καὶ σὰν πουλὶ πετάει,
κρυφανεβαίνει στὸν ὀντᾶ, γλέπει τὴν ἀτιμιά του,
καὶ μὲ τὸ αἶμα δυὸ κορμιῶν τὴν πλένει σὰν λεβέντης.

(Yiankas 445,11–14)

Can it be my wife?—no,—can it be our child?
Spurring on his horse he flies back like a bird,
softly, softly he climbs up to see his honor stained,
and in two bodies' blood he washes it like a man.

He acts in accordance with prevalent codes of male honor. The song affirms Greek rural society as harshly androcentric. What may a wife do if similarly treated? She can lament, as in the many versions of Τῆς κακοπαντρεμένης "The Unhappy Wife"; she can curse, like the deserted girl; or she may do both and then decide to show him she can give as good as she gets, playfully varying the order of ritual offerings for the dead at the graveside by declaring her intention to wash herself on the second or third day, change on the fourth, and remarry on the fourteenth:

Ν' ὅλα τὰ δέντρα τῆς αὐγῆς δροσιά ειναι γιομισμένα,
κι ἐμένα τὰ ματάκια μου δάκρυγια εἶναι τὰ καημένα.
'Ανάθεμα ποιός μ' ὅρριξε τὰ μάγια στὸ πηγάδι,

νὰ με χωρίσ' ὁ ἄντρας μου γυναῖκ' ἄλλη νὰ πάρει.
Κι ἂν με χωρίσ' ὁ κερατᾶς πάλε θὰ μετανοιώσει,
στὶς δυό στὶς τρεῖς θὰ λούζωμαι, στὶς τέσσερις θ'ἀλλάξω
πάνω στὶς δεκατέσσαρες ἄλλον ἄντρα θὰ πάρω.

(Yiankas 482)

All trees at dawn brim with dew,
my own burned eyes brim with tears.
A curse on who cast on me that spell in the well
for my man to leave me for another woman.
If the cuckold leaves me he will be sorry,
in two or three days I'll wash, on the fourth I'll change
and on the fourteenth I'll find another man.

Songs such as these suggest that wronged women can and do get their own back, if not by killing, then by cursing and acting and above all by duplicity. In Θυσία "Sacrifice", young Georgis asks Lenitsa, whose husband is supposedly about to be hanged for an unspecified act, how she will reward him if he saves her man from death.

—Λενίτσα μου, τὸν ἄντρα σου πάνουν νὰ τὸν κρεμάσουν.
—Στὴ μπίστη σου Γιωργάκη μου, σύρε νὰ τὸν γλυτώσεις.
—Τὸ τί μοῦ τάζεις Λέγκω μου, κι ἂν πάω καὶ τὸν γλυτώσω;
—Τὸ Μάη θὰ πᾶς γιὰ πέρδικες, θἀρθῶ κι ἐγὼ κοντά σου,
θὰ σέρω τὸ ντουφέκι σου καὶ τὰ λάμπρ' ἄρματά σου.
—Λέγκω μου, κι ἂν πεινάσουμε, τὸ τί ψωμὶ θὰ φᾶμε;
—Τὸ χνῶτο σου, τὸ χνῶτο μου, ζεστὸ ψωμὶ θὰ φᾶμε.
—Λέγκω μου, κι ἂν διψάσουμε, τὸ τί νερὸ θὰ πιοῦμε;
—Τὸ δάκρυ σου, τὸ δάκρυ μου, κρυγιὸ νερὸ θὰ πιοῦμε.

(Yiankas 508)

—My Lenitsa, they are taking your husband out to hang him.
—On your faith, Georgakis, go out and save him!
—And if I do, my Lengo, what will you do for me?
—You'll shoot partridges in May, and I'll come with you,
carrying your gun and your bright weaponry.
—My Lengo, if we're hungry, what shall we eat for bread?
—Your breath, my breath, that will be our bread.
—My Lengo, if we're thirsty, what shall we drink for water?
—Your tear, my tear we shall drink as our cold water.

How are we to interpret this curious little dialogue? Not according to logic, for if Lenitsa believed Georgakis, she would not propose to reward him as she does. Rather, it is a love game enabling each partner to explore the other's feelings surreptitiously, hence Georgakis thinks up a contingency that would enable him to approach her directly but not illicitly and then puts a case to her as a fact to test her reaction. Her response is equally playful: she does not rush out to the scene of the sacrifice "just as she is"— like the Panagia on hearing of Christ's crucifixion—but puts the onus of action on Georgakis, by inviting him to seek her favors in return and by suggestive comments on his "bright weaponry." The final exchange is ambivalent. Does having only breath to eat and tears to drink indicate sexual play or starvation? Or perhaps both? The allusive imagery permits each to say one thing while meaning another, leaving a substantial area of indeterminate meaning. The scenario reminds us of the kind of dialogue reported by Hirschon as actually taking place in Kokkinia to test a child's reaction to his or her father's supposed accident (Chapter 5).[39]

These examples, while far from exhausting the full range of nuances in this cluster of images, are sufficient to indicate the ambivalence and paradox of the metaphorical system. Tears, poison, blood, and water can signify both seriously and playfully in laments and love songs, helping us to see the laments in a less one-dimensional light: not as less sincere but as more poignant because they draw on the same store of images as the love songs do. I conclude this section by citing a conversation, recorded by Richard Blum and Eva Blum in the 1960s, which sounds like blasphemy but takes to playful extremes the fertilizing power of God's bodily fluids:[40] "To earn the blessing of God one should not complain but always say 'Glory to God,' because if it is his wish we shall be better off or have more. It was wrong for my wife to complain about the drought we're having this summer by asking what happened to this cuckold God that he didn't piss this summer. I told her she shouldn't talk like that because God has ears, but she told me he is too old by now to listen to every word the people say" (1970, 106–7).

8. Plants and Fruits of the Earth

As with the fluids of the human body, the plants and fruits of the earth have multiple significations in ritual and metaphor. In funerary rituals, the use of herbs and flowers, fruits, and evergreens has been widely attested not just as a means of decorating the corpse or tombstone but, more indirectly, as a means of reminding the dead of nature's renewal and the promise of new life.[41] Similarly, at weddings and birth ceremonies, plants and fruit figure prominently in the ritual preparations of bride and groom and for the reception of guests. Images of planting, sowing, and reaping may be varied in accordance with the context of the songs.

Love is born in the eyes and drips down through the lips to the heart. If watered and nurtured, the seed of love can grow into a strong tree inside the heart, presaging the fertilization of the man's seed inside the woman's womb after marriage. Appropriately, the cultivation of potted plants is a female concern around which anxieties of love and sex are explored through imagery. A young man asks his girl, —What ails her that her lips are so dry? She replies that she saw herself in a dream watering and pruning her pot of basil when her fingers got caught on deadwood, so the pot fell and broke into pieces (Yiankas 416). Is this a way of intimating that her sexuality is now ripe and if not watered will shrivel up? A bride addresses her basil plant with forty leaves and forty girls who come to pay court; like the mourner with her tears, she decides not to cast the plant at the crossroads for passersby to take or even on the seashore, where it might grow cold. She concludes, θ' ἀνοίξω τὴν καρδούλα μου καὶ μέσα θὰ σὲ βάλω "I'll open up my heart and put you in there" (ibid., 524). Here, the basil plant suggests the groom, who must be planted securely in her heart if he is not to stray elsewhere or lose his ardor. The flower of their union is childbirth: a young mother from Karpathos sings a lullaby to her daughter on the first Sunday in Lent, addressing her as a precious blossom:

Σήμερο πρώτη Κυριακή, θε νὰ σοῦ πῶ τραγούδι,
Βενετικό μου γιασιμί κι ἀρκοντικὸ λουλούδι.

(Baud-Bovy 2.245)

Today on this first Sunday I'll sing you a song,
my jasmine from Venice, my noble blossom.

Songs and blooms are linked by rhyme and association in lullabies. When the time for marriage comes, girls ripen into fruits ready to be plucked and tasted. A young man chances upon the priest's daughter selling apples and lemons; he opens one of her fifteen lemons to find his love inside (Yiankas 375). He asks her to untie her hair so he can kiss her and then marry her. The imagery reminds us of the wondertale in which the prince finds Trisevgeni inside the third golden citron (Chapter 7).

If flowers and fruits are common images of birth and blossoming love, harvesting and reaping are invoked to suggest the ravages and labors of love, birth, and death. Most frequent is the dashing ploughman whose prowess attracts the prettiest young girl (Yiankas 440, 461); but a woman, too, can reap and bear fruit, as in "Garoufalia," or "Carnation Girl":

Τοῦτον τὸν Μάη μὲ τις δροσιές, τοῦτο τὸ καλοκαίρι
ἐκίνησ' ἡ Γαρουφαλιὰ νὰ πάει νὰ θερίσει·

εἶχε δρεπάνι δαμασκί, παλαμάρι ἀσημένια
καὶ στὰ δερβένια θέριζε, γοργὰ τὰ δεματίζει,
καὶ στὰ δεμάτι᾽ ἀκούμπησε κι ἔπιανε τὴν καρδιά της.
—Μάνα, ἡ καρδιά μου με πονεῖ, μάνα, με σφάζ᾽ ἡ μέση.
—Κόρη μ᾽, θαρρῶ κ᾽ ἐκρύωσες, θαρρῶ κ᾽ ἐπλευριτώθης.
—Μανοῦλα μου, δὲν κρύωσα, πλευρίτη δὲν ἐπῆρα,
τρέξε στὴ χώρα γιὰ μαμμή, γιατ᾽ εἶμ᾽ ἀγγαστρωμένη.
—Τί λες, μωρὴ κοψόχρονη κι ὀλιγοζωισμένη.
—Τί θέλεις, μάνα μ᾽, νὰ σοῦ εἰπῶ, τί νὰ σοῦ μολογήσω,
θὰ κάμω ἔναν χρυσὸν ἀητό, ἔναν χρυσὸν πετρίτη.

(Yiankas 446)

In the coolness of May, this last summer
Garoufalia went out reaping
with a sickle of damask, with bands of silver.
In the mountain passes she reaped, deftly she binds the sheaves,
and as she leaned on the sheaves her heart pierced through her.
—Mother, my heart aches, mother, my waist is killing me.
—Daughter, you must have caught a cold, you must have pleurisy.
—No, dear mother, I have caught neither cold nor pleurisy,
hurry to the town and bring a midwife, for I am with child!
—What do I hear, you wretch, your days are numbered!
—What can I say, mother, what can I tell you?
I'll bring forth a golden eagle, a hawk of gold.

Here, reaping operates both literally as the scene of action and allusively as a metaphor for sexuality and childbirth. The damask sickle and silver bands might be explained as "poetic license"; but reaping in the mountain passes (which often served as military stations) surely indicates that Garoufalia, whose name means "carnation," has been reaping more than ears of wheat! When applied to a young man, the same combination of intensive reaping and a red flower has the power to draw even nuns from their cells (Yiankas 435). Randy young Epirots do not roam the countryside raping innocent nuns, but the pull of the flesh can win out against that of the spirit! The girl's change of clothes reinforces her change of status. Just as the female protagonist of the wondertales may win back—by dressing as a shepherd boy or monk—the enchanted or otherworld lover she has inadvertently lost, so is the figure of the nun symbolic of the girl's virginity and seclusion. Or is she meant to be taken literally? In the light of other songs, the incongruity of her behavior makes her, like the priest and monk, a target of satire and sexual jokes.[42]

The well-known simile σὰν καλαμιὰ στὸν κάμπο "like stubble on the plain" has usually been associated with women's lamentation and curses, whether at the departure of a loved one in marriage, xenitia, or death.[43] Jilted young men may adapt the same simile to their own emotional state, as in Ντιλμπέρα "Woman with a lovely body". Here is a version sung by Aedonidis, son of a priest and of an accomplished mother-musician:

Πέντι χρόνοι, ντιλμπέρα μου,
πέντι χρόνοι σ' ἀγάπησα,
νερ δίκα σι καρτιροῦσα, σὰν τ' ἰσένα δὲν εἶν'ἄλλη (δίς).
Κι ὡς ἔγινες κι ἀξίνις, κι ἄλλουν καλόν πῶς παίρνεις
κι μένα μι παράτησις, σὰν καλαμιὰ στοὺν κάμπου.
Θηρίζουν παίρνουν τοὺν καρπό, κι ἀφήν'την καλαμνίτσα
βάνουν φουτιὰ τὴν καλαμνιά, κι κάικι οὐ κάμπους οὔλους.

(Kavakopoulos 52,36)

Five years, my lovely-bodied one,
for five whole years I loved you,
yes for ten I waited for you, none could match you (bis).
And then you took on airs, you had another man,
you left me here like stubble on the plain.
They reap the fruit and leave the stubble,
then set fire to it, the whole plain is scorched.

Men may apply the same concept to the ravages of winter's ice and summer's heat. All nature's ice melts, sings a young man to his lemon tree and rosebush, yet my own frozen heart cannot melt, because a love that could not be separated by Turkish swords has now been parted by village gossip. Old love can never rot nor be forgotten, and as the proverb says, "a tongue breaks bones" (Kavakopoulos 52, 37).

Highly allusive as the images in these songs are, we must not forget that they are linked not just with the rituals of the life cycle but more immediately with seasonal labors in the fields. In the following work song from the island of Kythnos, sung by men and women during the reaping season in May, reference is made both to the work in hand and to the approaching season of marriage and change of diet:

Ἦρθεν ὁ Μάης, μάτια μου, ἦρκε, ἦρκε το καλοκαίρι,
ἦρθε ὁ καιρός, πουλάκι μου, ποὺ θὰ γενοῦμε ταίρι.
Σοῦ 'φερα, σοῦ 'φερά, κυρά, τὸν Μάη
τὴν Πρώτο-, τὴν Πρώτο μαγιὰ τὸ βράδυ.
Παραστημό παραγλυμό μ' ἔβα-, μ' ἔβα- λαν νὰ θερίσω,

γιὰ νὰ μὲ δέρνει ὁ ἄνεμος κι ὁ ἥλιος νὰ μαυρίσω.
Κρίθινο, *κρίθινο* ψωμί καὶ λίγο
κι ὅλη μέ-, *κι ὅλη μέ-*ρα μεσ' στὸν ἥλιο.
"Οντας θὰ φύγω ἀπ' τὸ κελλί καὶ πα- *και πά-*ω σια ἀπ' τὴ σκάλα
μοῦ ἔρχεται, μωρέ παιδιά, να πα-, να πά-ω γιὰ κρεμάλα.
Κρίθινο, *κρίθινο* ψωμί καὶ γάλα
κι ὅλη μέ-, *κι ὅλη μέ-* ρα μέσ' στὴν σκάλα.
'Ανοῖξαν τὰ σπαρθόπουλα
φεύγουν τὰ Θερμιοτόπουλα.

                (Spyridakis and Peristeris 360–65; musical repetitions in italics)

May has come, my love ["my eyes"], summer has come, *yes come*,
the time has come, my little bird, when we shall be paired.
I have brought you, *yes brought,* my lady, May,
on the evening of the first, *yes first* of May.
I was put, *yes put* to reap from middle strip to edges,
so wind and sun beat down to turn me brown.
Barley, *barley* bread and not too much of that,
all day, *yes all day* in the sun I sweat.
When I leave the hut to go, *yes go* straight to my strip
I feel I'm going, lads, to the hanging post.
Barley, *barley* bread and milk
and all day, *yes all day* on the strip.
The brooms of May have opened,
the island's lads departing.

This seemingly inconsequential song sheds light on how the system of imagery functions to integrate human with agricultural and natural processes, as in *Hysmine*. Through human labor, nature's seasons—like men and women—change clothes and food at crucial stages. One is not necessarily *better* than another, because each part contributes to the completion of the cycle. In a shorter version of the same song from the island of Kea, a woman can't make up her mind which month she likes, January or May, because each seems to be dressed in appropriate garments:[44]

Τὸ Μάη δὲν τὸν ἀγαπῶ, γιατὶ φορεῖ καπέλλο
ἀγαπῶ, ἀγαπῶ, μόν' τὸ Γενάρη
ποὺ φορεῖ τὸ χιαλουβάρι.
Μάη μου μὲ τὰ λουλούδια,
σύ 'σαι ἀγάπη μου καινούργια.

                                        (Ibid. 365–66)

I don't like May, it wears a hat;
I love January, only that,
in his fine embroidered suit.
My May with all your blooms,
you are my new love fruit.

The hat, worn for protection against the sun's burning heat, detracts from May's charms; May also signals the lads' imminent departure. January's cold is compensated by the handsome traditional costume of waistcoat and breeches. As in the wondertale "The Twelve Months," all seasons of human and natural life cycles need to be appreciated if they are to be productive. According to this principle of reciprocity, old age and winter are valued no less than youth and spring.

Unbridled consumption, as opposed to controlled cultivation, of food and drink spells danger, not infrequently with a touch of humor. In a song from Epiros, a twelve-year-old girl decides to become a nun. Instead of crossing herself, she has an eye only for the boys and goes on the streets to sell them wine. Then follows this little dialogue:

—Καλή μέρα σου, καλόγρια, καὶ ἀμέ τι πουλεῖς;
—Καὶ κρασὶ πουλῶ, λεβέντη, καὶ καλὸ ρακί.
—Καλόγριά μου σὰν μεθύσω, πού θὰ κοιμηθῶ;
—Παλληκάρι μ' ἂν μεθύσεις ἔλα στὸ κελλί,
πόχω πέρδικα ψημένη καὶ γλυκὸ κρασί,
πόχω πάπλωμα στρωμένο καὶ χρυσό χαλί,
πού εἶμαι κόρη καὶ κοιμοῦμαι μον' καὶ μοναχή,
γιὰ νὰ φᾶμε καὶ νὰ πιοῦμε καὶ νὰ παίξουμε,
νὰ φιλήσεις, ν' ἀγκαλιάσεις καλογριᾶς κορμί.
—Τσώπα, τσώπα καλογριά μου κι εἶναι ἀντροπή.
—'Αντροπή 'ναι στὰ κορίτσια καὶ στὶς ὄμορφες,
καὶ σε μένα τὴν καλόγρια δὲν εἶν' ἐντροπή,
πού εἶμαι στὰ ράσα τυλιγμένη σὰ χλωρὸ τυρί.

(Yiankas 372)

—Good day to you, little nun, what is that you are selling?
—I sell wine, young man, and the best raki as well.
—Nun, if I get drunk, where can I go to sleep?
—Young man, if you get drunk, come into my cell,
for I have roast partridge and sweet wine to drink,
I have a mattress laid out and a golden carpet,
for I am a girl, I sleep all alone.
We can eat and drink and play,
and you can kiss and embrace the body of a nun.

—Be quiet, my nun, that is a disgrace!
—A disgrace, yes for young girls and fine women,
but no disgrace for me because I'm a nun
wrapped in my habit like a pale white cheese.

Here, as in the previous example, the nun's outrageous proposition, couched in double entendres on "pale white cheese," is in marked contrast to the behavior of most young lovers, who make explicit their preference for love and plain fare over an undesirable partner and rich food (Yiankas 386, 432). The only songs to make positive reference to lavish food and drink are the wedding songs, but the emphasis is on the labors of preparation rather than the delights of consumption. At traditional weddings on the island of Rhodes, a lyre or lute player assists in the baking of wedding breads by leading the songs sung at different stages before the feast, as in the following kneading song:

Γειὰ στὰ χέρια ποὺ ζυμώνουν
καὶ ταιριάζουν καὶ μαλλώνουν.
Ἔχου χέρια μαρμαρένα
καὶ δαχτύλια χρουσαφένα
καὶ ἀνύχια κρουσταλλένα.

Ζύμωσαν, ποζύμωσασι
τοῦ γάμου τὸ ζυμάρι,
μὲ ὑγειὲς καὶ μὲ χαρές,
μὲ τόσα κανακίσματα,
μὲ τόσες περιδιάβασες.

(Baud-Bovy 1.12–13, cf. 3)

Health to hands that knead
as they fit and fight.
I have fists of marble,
fingers made of gold,
and I have nails of crystal.

Kneading in and kneading fast
the wedding's yeast,
with health and joy,
so many caresses,
so many rejoicings.

The imagery operates on many levels. First, the binding of the yeast in the bread also binds, like braided hair, the imminent marriage. Second, women knead and pound the dough while musicians ply their instruments; both require a firm hand and light finger work, and both imply tough interaction to achieve the perfect balance. Third, making bread is an act of sacrament, reminiscent of Christ's miraculous loaves, the Last Supper, and, of course, communion. At each stage of the wedding, the musician leads in with the blessing.

> Νά ν' ὥρα καλή.
> Κι ὅλοι πῆτε το (δίς)
> Κι ὁ Χριστὸς περνᾶ.

(Ibid. 1.11, cf. 3–5)

> "May the hour be good."
> Say it after me (bis).
> Christ is passing by.

The consumption of food, like the cultivation of Earth's fruit and crops, needs to be controlled and shared to be productive. Overindulgence will prove detrimental for the individual man or woman or for the couple. But, as in the wondertales, if shared it can help bind a union when spread over the widest possible number of people. A *kalestís* (summoner) from Thrace, whose role is not unlike that of the Rhodian lutist and lyre player, boasts of his task of inviting wedding-guests (Romaios 1956, 150, 7). Cultivating the fruits of the earth is a complex process requiring frugality and caution. To squander the earth's resources is to invite destruction and impoverishment, much as the prince in "The Three Citrons," who opened the first two citrons without running water, was made to suffer. The imagery accords with traditional concepts of economy, whereby anything consumed has to be labored for and wealth is calculated in terms not of money but of goods stored up for the winter. As in the Ptochoprodromic Poems, profligate expenditure, sexuality, and gluttony are as undesirable as loneliness and beggary (Chapter 4).

9. Hunting Birds

Many of the songs cited so far make reference to birds of prey and birds as prey. Without repeating the same examples, I wish to sum up the role of birds as magic mediators between the two sexes, male and female, and between two worlds, ours and the other. The partridge (*pérdika*) and the dove (*trigóna*) are symbols of female sexuality that hesitates to be tamed, as in the following song from Epiros:

Πέρδικα, περκιδούλα μου, περδίκα μου γραμμένη,
σ' ὅλον τὸν κόσμον ἥμερη, σε μένα στέκεις ἄγρια. . . .
. . . .
Ρίξε τὴν ἀγριοσύνη σου κι ἔλα σιμά μου κάτσε,
νὰ σε κρατῶ στα γόνατα, νὰ σε βαστῶ στὰ χέρια,
νὰ σε ταΐζω ζάχαρη, νὰ σε ποτίζω μέλι,
νὰ σε φιλήσω σταυρωτὰ στὰ μάτια καὶ στὸ στόμα
νὰ σοῦ φιλήσω τὴν ἐλιά, πόχεις στὸ μάγουλό σου
κι ἀνάμεσα ἀπ' τὰ στήθια σου νὰ σε γλυκοφιλήσω . . .
. . . .
Δὲν ἔρχομαι λεβέντη μου, σιμά σου νὰ καθήσω,
ταχειὰ πᾶς καὶ παινεύεσαι, σ' ὅλα τὰ παλληκάρια,
πῶς πλάνεψες κι ἀγκάλιασες μιὰ πέρδικα γραμμένη.
Πῶς πλάνεψες καὶ φίλησες μιὰ Λαρσινὴ τρυγόνα.

(Yiankas 381)

—Partridge, my little partridge, so finely drawn,
tame to the whole wide world, but for me still wild . . .
Cast off your wildness, come and sit by me,
I'll hold you on my knees, tend you with my hands,
I'll feed you with sugar, give you honey to eat,
I'll kiss your eyes and lips crosswise,
kiss the mole you have there on your cheek
and between your two scented breasts the sweetest of them all . . .
—I will not come, young man, I will not sit near you,
for next you'll go and boast to all the fine young men
that you deceived and embraced a painted partridge.
You deceived and kissed a dove from Larisa.

Partridges, doves, and swallows are symbols of female grace and beauty, as
in the love song from Thrace in which the girl is endowed with the sacred
"signs of heaven":

Δὲν εἴδανε τὰ μάτια μου τέτοια μαυρομματοῦσα,
τέτοια σιγανομίλητη, καμαροπερπατοῦσα.
Σὰν πέρδικα πατεῖς τὴ γῆ, σὰ χελιδόνι τρέχεις,
καὶ τὰ σημεῖα τ' οὐρανοῦ ἀπάνω σου τὰ ἔχεις.

(Romaios 150.6, 3–6)

My eyes have never seen such a black-eyed beauty,
her voice is low, she has an arching step.
You tread the earth like a partridge, you run like a swallow,
you have the signs of heaven upon your person.

The eagle epitomizes male beauty and prowess. As a sign of marital consummation, it is also embroidered on the nuptial bed as a protective blessing. The bed is prepared on the island of Rhodes to the accompaniment of the following song:

'Εστέσαμέν τον τὸν παστό,
ποὺ πάν ὡς κάτω πλουμιστό
ποὺ πάνω 'χει χρυσὸν ἀϊτό
καὶ στὴν κορφὴ ζωγραφιστό

(Baud-Bovy 1.18–19)

We have made up the bed
plumaged from head to toe,
on top there is a golden eagle
emblazoned at the peak.

At the departure of the bride from her natal home, the groom's group hints at her fate. Unlike proud eagles and soft partridges, domesticated birds are a source of humor and obscenity in this wedding song from Rhodes, as in the song against Maurice (Chapter 3):

Ἕνας πετεινός (τί κακοπετεινός)
μᾶς ἐντρόπιασε τὴν κόττα
καὶ δὲν εἶναι σὰν καὶ πρῶτα.

(Ibid. 31–33)

A cock (what a naughty cock!)
has despoiled our hen
she isn't what she was before.

Birds are harbingers of tidings—usually evil—from the otherworld. In mythical songs, they mediate between heaven and earth and between divine and human realms; in the tales, young men and women may actually turn into eagles and doves. Birds may carry a message, but it is the woman's privilege to interpret it correctly, whereas men are inclined to dismiss it as "birdsong" and therefore meaningless. It is not coincidental that women's laments are often sung in a high-pitched, birdlike voice, thereby suggesting otherworldly powers so feared by men. In love songs, bird imagery is adapted to the game of courtship, itself regarded as a form of hunting.

10. The Tree of Love and Life

As we saw at the end of Chapter 7, the most powerful image of the paramythia centers on the tree. I have already examined tree symbolism in funerary rituals and laments (1974), and I have also indicated some religious and literary parallels. Here I wish to illustrate how tree imagery operates in the songs of love and marriage. First, apple, citrus, and cotton trees signify woman's fecundity with their bushy shape, juicy fruits, and edible produce (Yiankas 436). The lemon tree—like the rosebush or the apple tree in other songs—allusively suggests sexual intercourse, although the identification between girl and tree is rarely made explicit.[45] Sometimes the imagery darkens, as in the following ambivalent song from the Sarakatsani. Is it perhaps intended as a betrothal or prenuptial song for one sister about to be separated from another by marriage? It certainly gives added meaning to the tale of "The Three Citrons" (Chapter 7).

Οὖλες οἱ Πέφτες τοῦ Μαγιοῦ,
οὖλες φαρμακωμένες,
οὖλες φουρτοῦνα φέρνουν,
οὖλες κακὰ λογιάζουν,
ἡ πρώτη Πέφτη τοῦ Μαγιοῦ
φέρνει λιθάρια ριζικά,
δέντρα ξερριζωμένα
κι ὅλα ἀνακατωμένα.
Φέρνει καὶ μιὰ γλυκομηλιὰ
τὰ μῆλα φορτωμένη,
κι ἀπάνω στὰ κλωνάρια της
δυὸ ἀδέρφι' ἀγκαλιασμένα.
Γυρνάει τὸ μικρότερο
καὶ λέει στὸ μεγάλο·
Κρατήσου καλά, ἀδερφούλη μου,
νὰ μὴ ξεχωριστοῦμε,
γιατὶ σὰ χωριστοῦμε
δὲν θὰ ἀνταμωθοῦμε.

(Tziatzios 39, 94: Sarakatsani; cf. *Laog.* 5: 121.123, 139.9)

All Thursdays in May
all are poisoned
bringing storms
planning evil.
May's first Thursday

rips down grounded boulders,
trees uprooted
everything's amiss.
It brings down one sweet apple tree
laden with apples,
while on her branches
two sisters are embracing.
The young one turns
and says to the elder
—Hold tight, my sister
don't let us part,
for once we separate
we'll never meet again.

It is hard to pin down a meaning to this song, but it is worth pointing out in the light of others previously cited that May is a month of reaping and betrothal, looking forward to marriage with ambivalence. The same formula of separation occurs in funeral laments. If fruit trees symbolize female sexuality, cypresses and pines are predominantly male in reference. A young married woman of uncertain repute compares her husband to marble and her lover to a cypress, with a clear preference for the latter's prowess:

—Μωρή κυρὰ πολίτισσα, μωρή ξεπατωμένη,
ἂν ἀγαπᾶς τὸν ἄντρα σου, τὸν ξένον τί τὸν θέλεις·
—Ὁ ἄντρας μου εἶναι μάρμαρο, ὁ ξένος εἶναι δέντρο,
σὰν κυπαρίσσι φουντωτὸ ποὖναι στὴν Ἁγιὰ Μαύρα,
ποὺ πῆγαν καὶ τὸ φύτεψαν δυὸ ἄξια παλληκάρια.
Τὸν ἄντρα μου τὸν ἀγαπῶ, τὸν θέλω νὰ μοῦ φέρνει,
τὸν ξένον τὸν γλυκοφιλῶ γιατί ξενοδουλεύει.

(Yiankas 450)

—You, lady from the city, you, trampled one,
if you love your husband, why do you chase the stranger?
—My husband is marble, the stranger is a tree
like the full-leafed cypress down at Saint Mavra
planted there by two brave young lads.
I love my husband, I want him to bring me goods,
but I kiss the stranger sweetly because he works for others.

Songs such as this confirm the observations of Herzfeld and others that female chastity and marital fidelity is an ideal rather than a reality.[46] Transgressions are known to take place in practice and incur condemnation and punishment only when indiscretion gives rise to unseemly gossip that could "harm the family name." Songs provide a playful means of exploring what cannot easily be talked of in respect to specific cases. The song illustrates how the image of the tree, normally sacred, can be put to profane uses. Or is this woman perhaps finding her own solution to the tragic dilemma of the "unhappy bride," whose withered husband shrivels both her young body and the trees and grasses around them? Marble suggests not withering but the cold grip of the grave.

Paradoxically, this Epirot woman's apparent freedom of action and argumentation can be justified by reference to the imagery of the wedding songs. In the following example from Rhodes, sung at the baking of breads on the Thursday before the wedding day, each stage in the imminent celebration and consummation of marriage is spelled out by the musicians in an allegory of planting a cypress tree:

Πού τὴν Κεργιακή θ' ἀρκέψω
κυπαρίσσι νὰ φυτέψω
τὴ Δευτέρα σκάβγω λάκκο
καὶ τὴν Τρίτη τὸ φυτεύγω.
Τὴν Τετράδη τὸ ποτίζω
βγάζει κλώνους καὶ κλαδιά
καὶ γεμίζ' ἡ γειτονιά.

(Baud-Bovy 1.11–13)

On Sunday I'll begin
to plant a cypress tree,
on Monday I'll dig the hole
and on Tuesday I'll put it in.
On Wednesday I'll water it
so it can bear trunks and branches
and the neighborhood be filled.

It would be crude to interpret this song as an allegory for the sexual act. Nevertheless, the analogy between digging, planting, and bearing branches, on the one hand, and the consummation of marriage, on the other, is apparent. Any young wife whose husband fails to dig, plant, and water with due care or success is entitled to complain, at least in song.

A song from Thrace explores the same image of the cool cypress tree from a different perspective, possibly that of a groom's anxieties on the eve of his wedding. Romaios interprets it historically as a "remnant," still sung at weddings, of a lost oral-epic cycle of Akritic songs, whereas I regard it as the man's counterpart to the woman's song "Now the Birds." Having severed links with the parental home on that ambivalent "Saturday evening" and traveled abroad, he now longs for rest and shelter:

Σάββατο βραδύ με διώξαν οἱ γονιοί μου
ἀπὸ τὸ σπίτι μου κι ἀπὸ τὰ γόνικά μου.
Παίρνω τὸ δρομί, παίρνω τὸ μονοπάτι,
βρίσκω ἕνα δεντρί, βρίσκω 'να κυπαρίσσι.
—Δεῖξε μου, δεντρί, τόπο γιὰ νὰ πλαγιάσω.
—Νά, οἱ κλῶνοι μου καὶ κρέμασ' τ' ἄρματά σου,
νά, κι ἡ ρίζα μου καὶ δέσε τ' ἄλογό σου,
νά, κι ὁ ἴσκιος μου, πέσε, γλυκοκοιμήσου.

(Romaios 178, 81)

Saturday evening, my parents turned me out
from house and home and from my heritage.
I take the road, I take the path
and find a tree, yes a cypress tree.
—Show me, tree, a place to lie down upon.
—Here are my branches, so hang up your weapons,
here are my roots, so tie up your horse,
here is my shade for you to fall asleep.

The song may also be sung, with minute changes, as a lullaby (Romaios no. 81). The tree nourished in the courtyard, like the bird in a cage, is an allegory of love. A young man from Epiros asks himself, like many a female mourner, what is this magic tree?

Δέντρο εἶχα στὴν αὐλή μου, γιὰ παρηγοριὰ δική μου
καὶ δὲν ξέρω τί δεντρό εἶναι, τὸν καρπό του ἂν τὸν τρῶνε,
πῶχει ὁλόχρυσα τὰ φύλλα κι ἀσημένια τὰ κλωνάρια
καὶ στὴ ρίζα κρύα βρύση, ποιός θὰ πιεῖ, ποιός θὰ γιομίσει;
Κι ἔσκυψα νὰ πιῶ νερό, φιλῶ τὰ μάτια της τὰ δυό,
γιὰ νὰ πιῶ καὶ νὰ γιομίσω καὶ τὴν κόρη νὰ φιλήσω.

(Yiankas 358)

I had a tree in my own courtyard, I grew it for my comfort.
I do not know what tree it is, if you can eat its fruit,
with its golden leaves and silver branches
and cool water at the root, —who can drink and take his fill?
So I bent down to drink, I kiss two eyes
to quench my thirst and kiss the girl I love.

One is reminded both of the laments, where the tree and the cooling water at its roots reconcile living and dead to an inevitable state of forgetfulness and of the songs of love, marriage, and childbirth, where new seeds can be watered and fertilized.

My final example is an enchantingly enigmatic woman's song which brings together almost all the images discussed in this chapter. The melody and first five lines of this version were recorded in Macedonia in 1959, completed from a version from the Peloponnese, beautifully rendered on disk by Domna Samiou:

Τώρα τὰ πουλιά, τώρα τὰ χελιδόνια,
τώρα, *καλέ, τώρα* οἱ πέρδικες
ἄντι, *τώρα οἱ πέρδικες* συχνολαλοῦν καὶ λένε.
—Ξύπνα, ἀφέντη μου, ξύπνα, καλὲ ν-ἀφέντη
ξύπνα, ἀγκάλιασε κορμὶ κυπαρισσένιο
κι ἀσπρόνε λαιμό, βυζάκια σὰ λεϊμόνια.
—Ἄφ' σε μ', λυγερή, λίγον ὕπνο νὰ πάρω,
γιατ' ἀφέντη μου στὴ βάρδια μέ 'χε ἀπόψε,
γιὰ νὰ σκοτοθῶ ἢ σκλάβο νὰ μὲ πάρουν·
μά 'δωκε ὁ Θεὸς κ' ἡ Παναγιὰ Παρθένα
καὶ ξεσπάθωσα καὶ τὸ σπαθί μου βγάνω·
χίλιους ἔκοψα καὶ χίλιους λαβωμένους,
ἕνας μόφυγε κ' ἐκεῖνος λαβωμένος,
μά' χε ἀϊτοῦ φτερά, λαγοῦ γληγοροσύνη.
Πῆρα τὸ στρατί, στρατὶ τὸ μονοπάτι,
βρίσκω 'να δεντρί, ψηλὸ σὰν κυπαρίσσι.
—Δέξου με, δεντρί, δέξε με, κυπαρίσσι.
—Πῶς νὰ σὲ δεχτῶ, πῶς νὰ σὲ καρτερέσω·
νὰ ἡ ρίζα μου καὶ δέσε τ' ἄλογό σου·
νὰ οἱ κλῶνοι μου, κρέμασε τ' ἄρματά σου,
νὰ ὁ ἤσκιος μου, πέσε κι ἀποκοιμήσου
καὶ σὰ σηκωθῆς, τὸ νοίκι νὰ πλερώσης,
τρία σταμνιὰ νερὸ στὴ ρίζα νὰ μοῦ ρίξης.

(Spyridakis and Peristeris 3–6; musical repetitions in italics)

Now the birds, now the swallows,
now, *yes now* the partridges
adi now the partridges chatter and speak:
—Wake up, my lord, wake, my good lord,
wake, embrace a body like a cypress tree,
and a white throat, breasts like lemons.
—Leave me, girl, to take a little sleep,

for my master set me on the watch this night,
to go and be killed or be taken as a slave.
But God and the All-Holy Virgin granted me
to unsheathe my sword, and I take out my sword:
I cut down a thousand, a thousand I wounded.
Only one escaped me, and he too was wounded,
but he had an eagle's wings, the swiftness of a hare.
I took the road, road and path,
I find a tree, tall as a cypress.
—Receive me, tree, receive me, my cypress.
—How can I receive you, how can I wait for you.
Here is my root, so tether your horse.
Here are my branches, so hang up your weapons.
Here is my shade, so lie down and sleep
and when you arise, you are to pay your rent,
three pitchers of water to water my root.

Scholars have classified this song as a fragmented version of a heroic song
assumed to derive from the Akritic cycle, despite the fact that all versions
(recorded from many parts of Greece since 1860) have been sung by
women to the bride on the dawning of her wedding day. The song has to
be interpreted as metaphor, not as story: the bride speaks with the voice of
the awakening swallows and partridges to arouse her lord so he may embrace her cypress tree (her body) and taste her lemons (her breasts), but he
holds back, pleading war-weariness. Allusively, he recounts the cycle of
warfare from night vigil through battle to exhaustion and a plea for rest beneath a tall cypress tree. The tree demurs, but—like the young girl who
admitted her hunter-lover into her garden on condition he tethered his
hounds at her apple tree—she bids him divest himself of horse and weapons
(travel and warfare) if he would sleep in her shade, asking only that he
water her roots generously in return. The most testing moment for the
"wandering hero" in Greek epic and song alike is not success in battle but
harmonious reintegration with home and domesticity.[47]

Examples could be multiplied from many other regions of Greece, but
enough have been given to demonstrate the interconnectedness of imagery
in songs of the life cycle. It remains to draw some conclusions from the
wealth of songs and rituals presented.

11. What Is Love?

The cosmic tree can signify love's transcendental power and the beauty of the beloved on one level, and the sexual act and the procreation of children on a more concrete level. Transferred to the laments, it can be adapted as a figure of address to the dead one or as a magical feature of the Underworld landscape, with its silver leaves, golden branches, and cool fountain at the roots suggesting the separation of living from dead and the soul's reintegration into the next life. In the seasonal songs, sung at work or on religious festivals of the calendar, the associations of the tree are at once earthly and divine: Christ and the Panagia are invoked to bless human cultivation with their silver and golden presence, while the labor-pains and grief of the Panagia at the Nativity and Crucifixion are rendered in images of human suffering. At its most metaphysical, the tree is Christ / God, the branches are the Twelve Apostles, and the Panagia is the cool fountain at the root. The tree is both life and death, divine and human, a symbol of eternal reciprocity and renewal.

Can we extract a philosophy of love from the songs? It is often assumed that folk songs, however vividly they may convey the concrete and specific, are incapable of expressing abstract thought. Yet while never explicit, through the metaphorical system a profound metaphysical dimension is apparent. It is impossible to define a consistent or unified concept of love from the songs, hence the terms "morality" or "philosophy" seem inappropriate. But the images unite contrary qualities and express a profound truth about the nature of "love as the most powerful force in the whole of existence, earthly and heavenly" (Dronke 1968: I, 24). By comparing his beloved's grace to a partridge and her voice to a swallow, a lover endows her with the *sēmeia tou ouranoû*, "signs of heaven" (pages 397-98, above) and the "angelic power of knowledge traditionally attributed to birds" (ibid., 5). By addressing her as a rose or carnation, he alludes not only to the perfumes of her body but also to her divine grace and perfection of form. As a herb or spice, such as basil, marjoram, or cinnamon, she tastes good and has medicinal powers, while gems suggest blessed radiance crafted from the treasures of the innermost bowels of earth (ibid., 119), as in Vizyenos. Hair and clothes are outer indicators of her inner state—does she demurely comb her hair at the window or threshold, does she knot it with snakes and vipers, or is it neatly braided as at marriage? The lover endows his beloved with powers at once divine and demonic.

Are these codes of courtship to be censured as putting woman on a pedestal? Strictures of this feminist brand misconstrue the allusive magic of the imagery. If courtly love is predominantly male in medieval poetry, where the majority of extant texts are men's songs in praise of their mistresses, the Greek songs, preserved and revitalized to this day in many regional variations to celebrate and mourn the human condition at every stage in the life cycle, provide a different perspective by offering an example of how vernacular traditions, now vanished or fragmented, may once have functioned.

Greek songs give equal voice to the woman. She may lament, blame, and curse her man as well as praise and worship him, but through ritual and song she maintains control over birth, marriage, and death. This is not to deny the role of the male hierarchy in the Orthodox Church at baptisms, weddings, and funerals but rather to suggest that when "religion" passes from church to hearth, from liturgy to dance and song, from Communion to family meal, women do not only mediate—they take over. For her, as for the man, love is a divine and cosmic power, but it encompasses more than erotic passion. While he is out hunting, at war, or seeking a fortune in foreign parts, she must guard the household, tend the young and mourn the dead. The images used to praise the beloved are attuned by mothers who lament, or lull to sleep, their small children; by sweethearts and sisters who mourn departing menfolk; by men and women who celebrate betrothal and marriage in song and dance or mark the religious and seasonal festivals. It is through imagery that human and divine love are integrated, each lending a new dimension to the other. According to Greek metaphorical codes, men's part is to toil and travel, hunt and kill, to earn their families' livelihood and to safeguard territories. Women's part is to care for the present generation, bury the last, and give birth to the next. Through their laments they commemorate and immortalize in song "the deeds of famous men" and thereby contribute to the transmission of the heroic ethos to the younger generation.[48]

The violent and dangerous aspects of eroticism, so strong a feature of the ancient tradition (Carson 1986), are not absent from the modern love songs, but they are tempered with Christian thought, as in the following distich, which seems to borrow from Paul's Epistle to the Corinthians (1 Cor. 13:4–13):

Σὰν εἶν' ἡ ἀγάπη μπιστική, παλιώνει, μηδὲ λειώνει,
ἀνθεῖ καὶ δένει στὴν καρδιὰ καὶ ξανακαινουργώνει.

(Politis 135, ιβ')

When love is faithful, it grows old but does not melt,
it blooms and binds within the heart and renews itself again.

12. Who Is Speaking?

Oral genres we have considered so far depend on multilayered dialogues. In the mythical songs discussed in Chapter 6, the action unfolds through terse exchange between the major protagonists. Similarly, the successful storyteller holds our attention not only by interspersing narration with dialogue among protagonists but also by reminding us continually of the narrating instant (Chapter 7). Wedding songs and funeral laments are even more complex, as the antiphonal mode of performance gives voice to the bride and her kin, the groom and his kin, mourners and the dead, and the dead and Charos. Whether the genre is mythical or ritual, there is always an "other" voice. Who is speaking to whom, and *how* do these utterances mean? Are they personal statements, or do they belong to differently coded systems of communication? The case of the love songs is particularly relevant—are they individual or collective?

The answer, I think, is both. First, the common fund of images spread across songs of all types precludes a purely individual frame of reference. However much a singer wants to praise this hero's exploits or lament that loved one's passing, she or he can only do so by appropriation and variation of a traditional system. The "I" and "you" of the texts, named or unnamed, whether located in time or place or not, refer not just to the here and now. Use of first and second person in the songs indicates a social as well as individual voice. Traditional use of voice, as in ancient lyric poetry, is distinct from the individual "I" of romanticism and modernism: song and dance provide the individual with the ritual-dramatic means to act out possible dialogues and conflicts between all contestants.

Second, Greek tradition is exceptional in the wealth and diversity of women's songs, sung from cradle to grave. Some, such as the wedding songs and laments, are both public and private in that they express individual joy or grief at wedding or wake, adapting traditional imagery to a particular context, and even when mourners are brought in from outside to display their skills, they inject their own personal griefs into their songs for others (Alexiou 1974, 41). Are the love songs more individualized? Insofar as love songs are among the commonest dances, they too are shared by many groups. At a *gléndi*, each group takes its turn: first, the older men (including the priest) perform a slow, dignified dance; second, the older women do the same; then, in turn the younger men and women display their virtuosity and grace; and, finally, the whole gathering joins in, including small children.[49] Where dance songs express distinctively male or female perspectives on love and marriage, they do so in the presence of others. Gendered and generational differences are manifest and frequently agonistic, but they form reciprocal parts of a whole (Cowan 1990, 49–63).

What of those most secluded of songs sung by the young girl as she sits at her loom? Sometimes she seems to express a more private *pónos* as she splits her own image between body and heart, self and mirror image or woven text, as in the following song:

Μιὰν κόρην ὅμορφη καὶ χαϊδεμένη,
ἀπὸ τὸν κύρη της μισοδιωγμένη
κι ἀπὸ τὴ μάνα της βαργιωμισμένη,
μόνη, ὁλομόναχη, στέκει κλεισμένη.
Κλεισμέν' ἐκέντας εἰς τὸ γκεργκέφι
κι ὀμπρός της εἶχε χρυσὸν καθρέφτη·
Μὲ δάκρυα πότιζε τὸ κέντημά της
κι ἔλεγε παίζοντας τὰ δάχτυλά της·
—Καθρέφτη μου χρυσέ, καὶ πρόσωπό μου,
πότε θὰ βρῶ κι ἐγὼ τὸ σύντροφό μου;
πότε θὰ ἰδῶ τὸν νιόν, νὰ τὸν γνωρίσω,
καὶ χρυσομάντηλο νὰ τοῦ κεντήσω;
Γνοιά σου, μανοῦλα μου, συντρόφεψέ με,
ἢ κόψε σάβανα καὶ τύλιξέ με.

(Yiankas 409)

A girl, lovely and cherished,
half rejected by her father
weighed down by her mother,
alone, all alone, is shut away.
Shut at her embroidery frame
before a golden mirror
with tears she wet her handiwork
saying as she plied her fingers:
—My golden mirror, and my face,
when shall I too find my mate?
When shall I see my lad, know him,
embroider him a golden kerchief?
Mother, take heed, abide with me,
or cut winding-sheets to wrap me in.

The sentiment here is both private and collective, the voice both hers and others'. Private because sung by a solitary girl, secluded at her embroidery prior to marriage and with no other presence than her own reflection in the mirror to address. Collective, because her conflicting emotions of fear and desire at the prospect of moving out of girlhood are shared by others and expressed in traditional images. In the last two lines she wants to be reassured that her mother will stay by her at this critical time or else bury her.[50]

Weaving and embroidering are a woman's muted form of protest, for she can always unravel and begin anew. She also feels freed from constraints of self-expression as she works at her loom. One of my most memorable encounters in fieldwork was with a young married woman in a village on the lower slopes of Mount Olympos, whom I visited in the company of a distant kinswoman of hers, my friend, the writer Vassiliki Papayianni. We arrived unannounced at her house around midmorning, when we reckoned her husband would have left for the fields. She asked us in with the usual hospitality, but when we said we wanted her to sing for us, she became defensive: her husband would not approve of her singing to strangers. But, if we cared to step aside into the outhouse where she kept her *argaleió* "loom," maybe she could sing something. She banged on her treadle to muffle the sound of her voice as she gave us many invaluable songs. This was her refuge, where she could sing her pain and create: *pónos* is productive.

In a beautiful wedding lament from Arkadia, suffused with images of death and departure, the bride expresses her anxiety as she sings and signs at the loom, begging her mother to inscribe a silent bond between them by weaving her own likeness onto it:

Γράψε με, μάνα, γράψε με, στὸν ἀργαλειὸ ποὺ ὑφαίνω,
τὸν ἀργαλειό μου νὰ κοιτᾶς κι ἐμένα νὰ θυμᾶσαι
(*Laog.* 24.466, Lines 5–6)

Write me, mother, write me, on the loom I weave at,
stay looking at my loom and keep me in your mind.

In these songs, the singer is both the "I" and "other" of the text, because she indicates a predicament that was once her mother's and is now her own. The split between self and other is rendered through images which signify both literally, as in a mirror, and figuratively, as an embroidered bond between mothers and daughters.[51]

To sum up, what can the rituals and songs of the life cycle add to our appreciation of Greek language, myth, and metaphor? First, the Greek language, studied across time and space, provides the means to chart and explore the revitalization of myth and metaphor across horizontal and vertical lines of interaction and transmission. Through language, metaphor is carried across changing associations, told and acted out in myth and ritual. Second, the same metaphorical system underlies all mythical genres, however different its functions in each. How metaphor colors story in myth can illuminate the more allusive and elusive qualities in the ritual songs, al-though the narrative-mythical mode should not mislead us into supposing that it is anterior or superior. Conversely, how metaphor functions in the ritual songs uncovers new perspectives in narrative, halting and probing—like ekphrasis—the linear direction. It is this tension between horizontal and vertical levels that makes Greek songs and tales different from most European counterparts, in which the ritual dimension has virtually disap-peared. Third, how does metaphor operate in time and space? If mythical genres arrange themes and images from past indicative to potential future, the songs of the life cycle take place in the context of rituals which, as we saw in Chapter 9, form a single continuum from mundane/secular to eter-nal/sacred. They derive specific meaning—and artistic inspiration—from daily labors. Perhaps that is why ritual has proved so enduring in Greek tra-dition: stories and times may differ, but what is done and said may be trans-posed to other historical, social, and religious contexts.

CHAPTER 11

Conclusion: Backward to the Present

Κι ἄν πτωχικὴ τὴν βρεῖς, ἡ Ἰθάκη δέν σε γέλασε.
Ἔτσι σοφὸς ποὺ ἔγινες, μὲ τόση πεῖρα,
ἤδη θὰ τὸ κατάλαβες οἱ Ἰθάκες τί σημαίνουν

—C. P. CAVAFY, Ἰθάκη

So where has this journey across some two thousand years of Greek time and space brought us? What advantages are to be gained by juxtaposing Byzantine and modern Greek texts, sacred and secular, literary and oral? While there is, in some domains, linear development, the more important result of such an integrative approach is, in essence, to broaden our understanding of literature while giving precision to the concept of culture by means of close readings specific to performative contexts.

First, continuities, developments, and changes in the Greek language (Part I) are the easiest to show in linear sequence, although these too are the result of cultural as well as linguistic processes. The invention of the kontakion in the fifth and sixth centuries A.D. and the revitalization of ancient genres (novel, satirical dialogue, comic verse) in the twelfth are not remarkable just as Byzantine literary achievements. Each in its different way has fed both from past and into present linguistic, literary, and ethical perceptions, sometimes consciously, as in the exploitation by Elytis of Byzantine hymns, by Cavafy of Alexandrian epigram and mime, by Seferis of classical literature, but sometimes not, as in the liturgical imagery of women's ritual songs, the comic topoi of Prodromos, Cretan comedy and modern shadow theater, or the rich fund of proverbs, riddles, and legends that have passed into modern tales, anecdotes, and everyday conversation. The passing to and fro between texts past and present, literary and popular, has created a storehouse—or treasury—of key words and concepts in the Greek language, many of them emotionally charged and metaphorically enriched by virtue of past semantic associations with the New Testament.[1]

Second, what we see in focusing on the diversity and versatility of mythical genres, particularly in performance and through conversation (Part II) is the persuasive power of certain themes and concepts, such as the personifications of ambivalent and potentially hostile forces (Charos, Moires, Drakoi, Neraides, and other exotika). These figures have not remained static since antiquity, although all share ancient pedigrees; rather, their value is and always has been founded in dialogic interaction. In this sense, the present can illuminate the past, as much as the other way round. To take another example, metamorphosis, as treated in the modern tales, informs our readings of ancient myths and poetry not because it is "as now, so then" but because its enactment in live Greek narrative traditions and belief systems reveals the nature of its conceptual vitality. The threads here are contextual, not linear.

The role of women as mediators throughout Greek culture is an under-theme of the whole book. Indeed, it might have formed the topic of a separate, tidier book, were it not so central to my attempt to locate the conjunction of past texts with present precisely in the circumstances and constraints of transmission by women: integration of past and present, mediation between human and divine, belong to their sphere of activity. Through tales, songs, and dances, women have been at least equal partners in the transmission of Greek langugage, myth, and metaphor. Among modern prose writers, it is no coincidence that Vizyenos and Takhtsis achieved preeminence by crossing boundaries of gender and sanity, in literature as in life. Their stories, too, need writing in full, but not in this book.

Third, ritual performance, both male and female, sacred and secular, as in the songs and dances of the life cycle, demonstrates the "agonistic reciprocity" of gender and age in Greek culture. It also provides deeper dimensions of time and space, and that is why, in Part III, I depart most markedly from the linear model. The sheer beauty of music and imagery in the songs of the life cycle derives less from literary than from synesthetic and kinesthetic properties, both actual and symbolic. Here is where ritual practice may show the "meaning" of metaphor, as when women (who also tend vineyards and olive groves) may comment on another's son: Γιὰ κοίτα, πῶς δεντρίζει! ("See how he becomes a tree!").[2] Metaphor is not a literary figure of speech but live and therefore literal, much as Ruth Padel and others have argued was the case in pre-Aristotelian Greek thought.[3] Illuminating as deconstructionist approaches to oral and literary texts may have been for me in seeking multiple meanings, I part company with them when they regress into academic "newspeak."

Finally, such an approach to postclassical Greek literature and culture can contribute to other areas and disciplines by showing us *how to look*; both in the past, and in the present; both in literature, and in myth and ritual; and above all, at creative uses of language. What we find is the specific vitality of Greek tradition, a vitality rooted in the unusual diversity of its means and resources. If we have missed this in the past, it may be because our overly narrow views of literature can, in the long term, only impoverish literature. The reciprocal influences of creative traditions in different societies is to be found not just in masterworks but also in the regenerative powers of tales, songs, and dances, performed by women and men alike, and everything else that lies behind them.

Appendix: Romanos the Melodist
(circa Fifth to Sixth Centuries)

On the Nativity II

Προοίμιον

Ὁ πρὸ ἑωσφόρου   ἐκ Πατρὸς ἀμήτωρ γεννηθείς
   ἐπὶ γῆς ἀπάτωρ   ἐσαρκώθη σήμερον ἐκ σοῦ·
   ὅθεν ἀστὴρ   εὐαγγελίζεται μάγοις,
   ἄγγελοι δὲ   μετὰ ποιμένων ὑμνοῦσι
5   τὸν ἄσπορον τόκον σου,   ἡ κεχαριτωμένη.

α΄

Τὸν ἀγεώργητον βότρυν   βλαστήσασα ἡ ἄμπελος
   ὡς ἐπὶ κλάδων ἀγκάλαις   ἐβάσταζε καὶ ἔλεγεν·
   « Σὺ καρπός μου,   σὺ Ζωή μου,
   ⟨σὺ⟩ ἀφ' οὗ ἔγνων   ὅτι καὶ ὃ ἤμην εἰμί,   σύ μου Θεός,
5   τὴν σφραγῖδα τῆς παρθενίας μου   ὁρῶσα ἀκατάλυτον,
   κηρύττω σε ἄτρεπτον   Λόγον σάρκα γενόμενον.
Οὐκ οἶδα σποράν,   οἶδά σε λύτην τῆς φθορᾶς·
   ἀγνὴ γάρ εἰμι,   σοῦ προελθόντος ἐξ ἐμοῦ
   ὡς γὰρ εὗρες ἔλιπες   μήτραν ἐμήν,
10   φυλάξας σῶαν αὐτήν·   διὰ τοῦτο συγχορεύει
   πᾶσα κτίσις βοῶσά μοι·   Ἡ κεχαριτωμένη.

β΄

Οὐκ ἀθετῶ σου τὴν χάριν   ἧς ἔχω πεῖραν, δέσποτα·
   οὐκ ἀμαυρῶ τὴν ἀξίαν   ἧς ἔτυχον τεκοῦά σε·
   τοῦ γὰρ κόσμου   βασιλεύω·
   ἐπειδὴ κράτος   τὸ σὸν ἐβάστασα γαστρί,
         πάντων κρατῶ·

On the Nativity II

Proem

He who was born before dawn   from father without mother
    today without father   has been made flesh from you;
    whence the star   brings glad tidings to the magi,
    and angels   with shepherds praise in song
5   your seedless birth,   you "full of grace."

1.

The vine, sprouting forth   the grape without vintner
    in her arms as on branches,   held him, saying,
    —You, my fruit,   you, my life,
    you, from whom I know   I am what I was,   you my God,
5 as I behold intact   the seal of my virginity,
    I proclaim you   the immutable Word made flesh.
I know no seed   I know you as liberator from corruption;
    for I am pure   though you came forth from me.
    as you found my womb   so you have left it,
10   guarding it safe,   so the whole of creation
    can dance together, crying out to me,   "full of grace."

2.

I do not cast aside the grace   I took from you, lord,
    nor do I obscure the worth   I gained in bearing you,
    for I rule over   the world.
    Since I carried your might   in my womb   I have might over
    all things.

417

5   μετεποίησας τὴν πτωχείαν μου   τῇ συγκαταβάσει σου,
       σαυτὸν ἐταπείνωσας   καὶ τὸ γένος μου ὕψωσας.
       Εὐφράνθητέ μοι   νῦν ἅμα, γῆ καὶ οὐρανός·
       τὸν γὰρ ποιητὴν   ὑμῶν βαστάζω ἐν χερσί·
       γηγενεῖς, ἀπόθεσθε   τὰ λυπηρά,
10   θεώμενοι τὴν χαρὰν   ἣν ἐβλάστησα ἐκ κόλπων
       ἀμιάντων, καὶ ἤκουσα·   Ἡ κεχαριτωμένη. »

                              γ´

       Ὑμνολογούσης δὲ τότε   Μαρίας ὃν ἐγέννησε,
         κολακευούσης δὲ βρέφος   ὃ μόνη ἀπεκύησεν,
       ἤκουσεν ἡ   ἐν ὀδύναις
         τεκοῦσα τέκνα,   καὶ γηθομένη τῷ Ἀδάμ   Εὔα βοᾷ·
5   « Τίς ἐν τοῖς ὠσί μου νῦν ἤχησεν   ἐκεῖνο ὃ ἤλπιζον;
       Παρθένον τὴν τίκτουσαν   τῆς κατάρας τὴν λύτρωσιν,
       ἧς μόνη φωνὴ   ἔλυσέ μου τὰ δυσχερῆ
         καὶ ταύτης γονὴ   ἔτρωσε τὸν τρώσαντά με·
       ταύτην ἣν προέγραψεν   υἱὸς Ἀμώς,
10   ἡ ῥάβδος τοῦ Ἰεσσαὶ   ἡ βλαστήσασά μοι κλάδον
       οὗ φαγοῦσα οὐ θνήξομαι,   ἡ κεχαριτωμένη.

                              δ´

       Τῆς χελιδόνος ἀκούσας   κατ’ ὄρθρον κελαδούσης μοι,
         τὸν ἰσοθάνατον ὕπνον,   Ἀδάμ, ἀφεὶς ἀνάστηθι·
       ἄκουσόν μου   τῆς συζύγου·
         ἐγὼ ἡ πάλαι   πτῶμα προξενήσασα βροτοῖς   νῦν
                                                           ἀνιστῶ .
5   Κατανόησον τὰ θαυμάσια,   ἰδὲ τὴν ἀπείρανδρον
         διὰ τοῦ γεννήματος   ἰωμένην τοῦ τραύματος·
       ἐμὲ γάρ ποτε   εἷλεν ὁ ὄφις καὶ σκιρτᾷ,
         ἀλλ’ ἄρτι ὁρῶν   τοὺς ἐξ ἡμῶν φεύγει συρτῶς·
       κατ’ ἐμοῦ μὲν ὕψωσε   τὴν κεφαλήν,
10   νυνὶ δὲ ταπεινωθεὶς   κολακεύει, οὐ χλευάζει,
       δειλιῶν ὃν ἐγέννησεν   ἡ κεχαριτωμένη. »

                              ε´

       Ἀδὰμ ἀκούσας τοὺς λόγους   οὓς ὕφανεν ἡ σύζυγος,
         ἐκ τῶν βλεφάρων τὸ βάρος   εὐθέως ἀποθέμενος

5   You transformed my poverty   by your condescension,
        you humbled yourself,   you exalted my race.
    Rejoice with me at once,   earth and heaven:
        I hold your maker   in my arms.
        Earthborn creatures   cast griefs aside,
10   beholding the joy   I brought forth from my womb
        immaculate, who was called   "full of grace."

3.

Mary, as she sang praises to him she had borne,
    caressing the infant   she conceived on her own,
was heard by her   who bore children
    in pain—   rejoicing,   Eve cries out to Adam,
5   —Who has sounded in my ears   what I had hoped for?
    A virgin giving birth   to the curse's redemption,
whose voice alone   has freed me from travail,
    and whose childbirth   has wounded him who wounded me
                                        [= the Devil];
    she it is the son of Amos [= Isaiah]   prefigured,
10   the rod of Jesse   bringing forth a branch
        I can feed on without dying,   "full of grace."

4.

At the sound of the swallow   singing at dawn,
    you, Adam, leave your   deathlike slumber and arise!
    Listen to me,   your wife:
        I, who of old caused mortal fall,   I now rise up.
5   Let your mind take in wonders,   behold, the woman who knew not
                                man
        through childbirth   has healed your wound.
then, at that time,   the serpent struck me, and squirmed with
                                delight:
    but now, seeing   our descendants, he slinks away.
    He once raised his head   against me,
10   now humbled   he fawns, without mockery,
        afraid of him borne by the one   "full of grace."

5.

Adam hearing the words   his wife wove him
        at once shook off   the weight from his eyelids,

ἀνανεύει   ὡς ἐξ ὕπνου
καὶ οὖς ἀνοίξας   ὃ ἔφραξε παρακοῇ   οὕτως βοᾷˑ
5 « Γλυκεροῦ ἀκούω κελαδήματος, τερπνοῦ
μινυρίσματος,
ἀλλὰ τοῦ μελίζοντος   νῦν ὁ φθόγγος οὐ τέρπει μεˑ
γυνὴ γάρ ἐστιν,   ἧς καὶ φοβοῦμαι τὴν φωνήν ˑ
ἐν πείρᾳ εἰμί,   ὅθεν τὸ θῆλυ δειλιῶˑ
ὁ μὲν ἦχος θέλγει με   ὡς λιγυρός,
10   τὸ ὄργανον δὲ δονεῖ   μὴ ὡς πάλαι με πλανήσῃ
ἐπιφέρουσα ὄνειδος   ἡ κεχαριτωμένη.

ς´

—Πληροφορήθητι, ἄνερ,   τοῖς λόγοις τῆς συзύγου σουˑ
οὐ γὰρ εὑρήσεις με πάλιν   πικρά σοι συμβουλεύουσαν ˑ
τὰ ἀρχαῖα   γὰρ παρῆλθε
καὶ νέα πάντα   δείκνυσιν ὁ τῆς Μαριὰμ   γόνος
Χριστός.
5 Τούτου τῆς νοτίδος ὀσφράνθητι   καὶ εὐθέως ἐξάνθησον,
ὡς στάχυς ὀρθώθητι ˑ   τὸ γὰρ ἔαρ σε ἔφθασεν,
Ἰησοῦς Χριστὸς   πνέει ὡς αὔρα γλυκερά ˑ
τὸν καύσωνα ᾧ ἧς   ἀποφυγὼν τὸν αὐστηρόν,
δεῦρο ἀκολούθει μοι   πρὸς Μαριάμ,
10   καὶ αὐτῆς πρὸ τῶν ποδῶν   ἐρριμένους θεωροῦσα
εὐθέως σπλαγχνισθήσεται   ἡ κεχαριτωμένη.

ζ´

—Ἔγνων, ὦ γύναι, τὸ ἔαρ   καὶ τῆς τρυφῆς ὀσφραίνομαι
ἧς ἐξεπέσαμεν πάλαι ˑ   καὶ γὰρ ὁρῶ παράδεισον
νέον, ἄλλον,   τὴν παρθένον
φέρουσαν κόλποις   αὐτὸ τὸ ξύλον τῆς зωῆς   ὅπερ
ποτὲ
5 Χερουβὶμ ἐτήρει τὸ ἅγιον   πρὸς τὸ μὴ ψαῦσαι ⟨ἐ⟩μέˑ
τοῦτο τοίνυν ἄψαυστον   ἐγὼ βλέπων φυόμενον,
ᾐσθόμην πνοῆς,   σύзυγε, τῆς зωοποιοῦ
τῆς κόνιν ἐμὲ   ὄντα καὶ ἄψυχον πηλὸν
ποιησάσης ἔμψυχοˑνˑ   ταύτης νυνὶ
10   τῇ εὐοσμίᾳ ῥωσθείς,   πορευθῶ πρὸς τὴν ἀνθοῦσαν
τὸν καρπὸν τῆς зωῆς ἡμῶν,   τὴν κεχαριτωμένην.

lifting his head   as if from sleep
    opening the ear   blocked with deafness cried out:
5 —I hear sweet warbling   tones of delight
    but the melodist's   chant no longer enchants me.
It is a woman, and I fear her voice,
    for I have known   and shrink from the feminine sex.
    The sound draws me   it is clear
10 but the instrument fills me   with fear, lest as of old she lead me
                  astray
    bringing travail   she "full of grace."

6.

—Take heed, husband   of your wife's words:
    you will not find me again   a bitter counselor.
    Old ways   have passed away:
    Christ, son of Mary   shows all things   as new.
5 Sniff his moisture   and at once come forth
    like an ear of wheat erect,   spring has reached you!
Jesus Christ   breathes like a sweet breeze:
    having escaped from the scorching   severe as it was
    follow me now   to Mary
10 for beholding us prostrate   at her feet
    she will at once take pity,   she "full of grace."

7.

—I recognize spring, woman,   and I sense the delights
    we fell from of old;   yes, I see Paradise
    anew, another—   the virgin
    bearing in her arms   this tree of life once held
5 aloft by Cherubim in sanctity   to stop me touching it.
    Well then, beholding this untouchable   wood sprout forth
I have felt the breath of life,   wife, of the giver of life,
    dust as I am   and soulless clay,
    giving me soul;   for now
10 made strong by her perfume,   I'll make my way to her who brought
                  forth
    the fruit of our life,   "full of grace."

η΄

Ἰδού εἰμι πρὸ ποδῶν σου,   παρθένε, μῆτερ ἄμωμε,
καὶ δι' ἐμοῦ πᾶν τὸ γένος   τοῖς ἴχνεσί σου πρόσκειται.
Μὴ παρίδῃς   τοὺς τεκόντας,
ἐπειδὴ τόκος   ὁ σὸς ἀνεγέννησε νῦν   τοὺς ἐν φθορᾷ·
5   τον ἐν Ἅιδῃ παλαιωθέντα με,   Ἀδὰμ τὸν πρωτόπλαστον
οἰκτείρησον, θύγατερ,   τὸν πατέρα σου στένοντα ·
τὰ δάκρυά μου   βλέπουσα, σπλαγχνίσθητί μοι
καὶ τοῖς ὀδυρμοῖς   κλῖνον τὸ οὖς σου εὐμενῶς ·
τὰ δὲ ῥάκη βλέπεις μου   ἅπερ φορῶ,
10   ἃ ὄφις ὕφανέ μοι·   ἄμειψόν μου τὴν πενίαν
ἐνώπιον οὖ ἔτεκες,   ἡ κεχαριτωμένη.

θ΄

—Ναί, ἡ ἐλπὶς τῆς ψυχῆς μου,   κἀμοῦ   τῆς Εὔας ἄκουσον
καὶ τῆς ἐν λύπαις τεκούσης   τὸ αἶσχος ἀποσόβησον,
ὡς ἰδοῦσα   ὅτι πλέον
ἐγὼ ἡ τλήμων   τοῖς ὀδυρμοῖς τοῦ Ἀδὰμ   τήκω τὴν
ψυχήν ·
5   τῆς τρυφῆς γὰρ οὖτος μνησκόμενος   ἐμοὶ ἐπανίσταται
κραυγάζων ὡς· Εἴθε μὴ   τῆς πλευρᾶς μου ἐβλάστησας ·
καλὸν ἦν μή σε   λαβεῖν εἰς βοήθειάν μου·
οὐκ ἔπιπτον γὰρ   νυνὶ εἰς τοῦτον τὸν βυθόν.
Καὶ λοιπὸν μὴ φέρουσα   τοὺς ἐλεγμοὺς
10   μηδὲ τὸν ὀνειδισμόν,   κατακάμπτω τὸν αὐχένα
ἕως οὖ ἀνορθώσῃς με,   ἡ κεχαριτωμένη. »

ι΄

Οἱ ὀφθαλμοὶ δὲ Μαρίας   τὴν Εὔαν θεωρήσαντες
καὶ τὸν Ἀδὰμ κατιδόντες   δακρύειν κατηπείγοντο ·
ὅμως στέγει   καὶ σπουδάζει
νικᾶν τὴν φύσιν   ἡ παρὰ φύσιν τὸν Χριστὸν
σχοῦσα υἱόν ·
5   ἀλλὰ τὰ σπλάγχνα ἐταράττετο   γονεῦσι συμπάσχουσα ·
τῷ γὰρ ἐλεήμονι   μήτηρ ἔπρεπεν εὔσπλαγχνος.
Διὸ πρὸς αὐτούς ·   « Παύσασθε τῶν θρήνων ὑμῶν,
καὶ πρέσβις ὑμῖν   γίνομαι πρὸς τὸν ἐξ ἐμοῦ·

8.

—Behold, at your feet, here I am   Virgin, blameless mother,
    through me the whole race   lies at your feet.
Do not overlook   those who gave you birth,
    because your son   has now renewed those   born in
                      corruption.
5   Aged in Hades,   Adam, first-created as I am
    take pity on me, daughter,   your groaning father.
Behold my tears   and have mercy on me,
    lending kind ear   to my wailings.
You see these rags   I wear,
    —the serpent wove them for me;   so redeem my poverty
    for the sake of him you bore,   "full of grace."

9.

—Yes, hope of my soul,   listen to me, Eve, as well,
    and shake off the shame   of her who gave birth in sorrow,
for you see   how much more
    my soul is afflicted   in misery   because of Adam's weepings.
5   Whenever he recalls delectation   he turns against me
    crying out—Would you had not   sprung forth from my side;
better not   to have taken you as my aid,
    for I would not now have sunk   to these depths.
    And so, unable to bear the reproofs
10   and reproaches,   I bend down my neck
    till you raise me up,   you "full of grace."

10.

Mary's eyes   beholding Eve
    and looking down on Adam,   were impelled to tears;
but she stays them   and hastens
    to conquer nature   she who against nature   gave birth to Christ
                      her son.
5   Yet her entrails were stirred   in suffering with her parents
    —a compassionate mother   accorded with the Merciful one.
So she tells them   —Cease your lamentations,
    and I will be your ambassador   to him born from me.

ὑμεῖς δὲ ἀπώσασθε   τὴν συμφοράν,
10   τεκούσης μου τὴν χαράν ·   διὰ τοῦτο τὰ τῆς λύπης
ἐκπορθήσουσα ἥκω νῦν   ἡ κεχαριτωμένη.

ια΄

Υἱὸν οἰκτίρμονα ἔχω   καὶ λίαν ἐλεήμονα,
ἐξ ὧν τῇ πείρᾳ ἐπέγνων ·   προσέχω ὅπως φείδεται ·
πῦρ ὑπάρχων,   ᾤκησέ με
τὴν ἀκανθώδη   καὶ οὐ κατέφλεξεν ἐμὲ   τὴν
ταπεινήν ·
5   ὡς πατὴρ οἰκτείρει υἱοὺς αὐτοῦ,   οἰκτείρει ὁ γόνος μου
τοὺς φοβουμένους αὐτόν,   ὡς Δαυὶδ προεφήτευσε.
Τὰ δάκρυα οὖν   στείλαντες, ἐκδέξασθέ με
μεσῖτιν ὑμῶν   γενέσθαι πρὸς τὸν ἐξ ἐμοῦ ·
χαρᾶς γὰρ παραίτιος   ὁ γεννηθεὶς
10   ὁ πρὸ αἰώνων Θεός ·   ἡσυχάσατε ἀλύπως,
πρὸς αὐτὸν γὰρ εἰσέρχομαι   ἡ κεχαριτωμένη. »

ιβ΄

Ῥήμασι τούτοις Μαρία   καὶ ἄλλοις δὲ τοῖς πλείοσι
παρακαλέσασα Εὔαν   καὶ ταύτης τὸν ὁμόζυγα,
εἰσελθοῦσα   πρὸς τὴν φάτνην,
αὐχένα κάμπτει   καὶ δυσωποῦσα τὸν υἱὸν   οὕτω
φησί ·
5   « Ἐπειδή με, ὦ τέκνον, ὕψωσας   τῇ συγκαταβάσει σου,
τὸ πενιχρὸν γένος μου   δι᾽ ἐμοῦ νῦν σοῦ δέεται.
Ἀδὰμ γὰρ πρός με   ἤλυθε στενάζων πικρῶς ·
Εὔα δὲ αὐτῷ   ὀδυνωμένη συνθρηνεῖ ·
ὁ δὲ τούτων αἴτιος   ὄφις ἐστὶν
10   τιμῆς γυμνώσας αὐτούς ·   διὰ τοῦτο σκεπασθῆναι
ἐξαιτοῦσι βοῶντές μοι ·   Ἡ κεχαριτωμένη. »

ιγ΄

Ὡς δὲ τοιαύτας δεήσεις   προσήγαγεν ἡ ἄμωμος
Θεῷ κειμένῳ ἐν φάτνῃ,   λαβὼν εὐθὺς ὑπέγραφεν ·
ἑρμηνεύων   τὰ ἐσχάτως,
φησίν · « Ὦ μῆτερ,   καὶ διὰ σὲ καὶ διὰ σοῦ   σῴζω
αὐτούς.

As for you, drive away   suffering sorrow,
10   for I have given birth to joy;   that is why I have come now
to plunder anguish   I, "full of grace."

11.

I have a merciful son   full of compassion,
as I know from experience,   —I see how merciful he is:
fire though he is,   he dwelt in
my womb,   yet did not consume   my lowly self.
5 Just as the father pities his sons   so my son has mercy
on those who fear him   as David prophesied,
so dismiss your tears   and accept me
as your intermediary   to him who is from me,
for the cause of all joy   begotten
10   before the ages is God.   Rest quiet without grief,
for to him I shall turn,   "full of grace."

12.

Mary, with these words   and many others besides,
gave comfort to Eve   and her consort;
approaching   the crib,
she bends her head   and beseeches her son   with these
words:
5 —O my child, because you have exalted me   by your condescension
my impoverished race now   implores you through me.
Adam has come to me   groaning bitterly,
and with him Eve laments   in pain;
the cause of all this   is the serpent,
10   he stripped them of honor.   That's why they seek
to be clothed, crying out to me   "full of grace."

13.

As soon as the blameless one   presented her pleas
to God laid in the crib   he received and underwrote them;
expounding   the end,
he says:—O mother, both for you and through you   I save
them.

5   Εἰ μὴ σῶσαι τούτους ἠθέλησα,   οὐκ ἂν ἐν σοὶ ᾤκησα,
       οὐκ ἂν ἐκ σοῦ ἔλαμψα,   οὐκ ἂν μήτηρ μου ἤκουσας·
       τὴν φάτνην ἐγὼ   διὰ τὸ γένος σου οἰκῶ,
       μαζῶν δὲ τῶν σῶν   βουλόμενος νῦν γαλουχῶ,
       ἐν ἀγκάλαις φέρεις με   χάριν αὐτῶν·
10   ὃν οὐχ ὁρᾷ Χερουβὶμ   ἰδοὺ βλέπεις καὶ βαστάζεις
       καὶ ὡς υἱὸν κολακεύεις με,   ἡ κεχαριτωμένη.

                         ιδ΄

       Μητέρα σε ἐκτησάμην   ὁ πλαστουργὸς τῆς κτίσεως
       καὶ ὥσπερ βρέφος αὐξάνω   ὁ ἐκ τελείου τέλειος·
       τοῖς σπαργάνοις   ἐνειλοῦμαι
       διὰ τοὺς πάλαι   χιτῶνας δερματίνους   φορέσαντας,
5   καὶ τὸ σπήλαιόν μοι ἐράσμιον   διὰ τοὺς μισήσαντας
       τρυφὴν καὶ παράδεισον   καὶ φθορὰν ἀγαπήσαντας·
       παρέβησάν μου   τὴν ζωηφόρον ἐντολήν·
       κατέβην εἰς γῆν   ἵνα ἔχουσι τὴν ζωήν.
       Ἂν δὲ καὶ τὸ ἕτερον   μάθῃς, σεμνή,
10   ὃ μέλλω δρᾶν δι᾽ αὐτούς,   μετὰ πάντων τῶν στοιχείων
       σὲ δονεῖ τὸ γενόμενον,   ἡ κεχαριτωμένη. »

                         ιε΄

       Ἀλλὰ τοιαῦτα εἰπόντος   τοῦ πᾶσαν γλῶσσαν πλάσαντος
       καὶ τῆς μητρὸς τῇ δεήσει   ταχέως ὑπογράψαντος,
       ἔτι εἶπεν   ἡ Μαρία·
       « Ἐὰν λαλήσω,   μὴ ὀργισθῇς μοι τῇ πηλῷ,   ὦ
                                              πλαστουργέ·
5   ὡς πρὸς τέκνον παρρησιάσομαι·   θαρρῶ ὡς ὅ σὲ γεννήσασα·
       σύ μοι γὰρ τῷ τόκῳ σου   πᾶσαν καύχησιν δέδωκας.
       Ὁ μέλλεις τελεῖν   τί ἐστι θέλω νῦν μαθεῖν·
       μὴ κρύψῃς ἐμοὶ   τὴν ἀπ᾽ αἰῶνός σου βουλήν·
       ὅλον σε ἐγέννησα·   φράσον τὸν νοῦν
10   ὃν ἔχεις περὶ ἡμᾶς,   ἵνα μάθω καὶ ἐκ τούτου
       ὅσης ἔτυχον χάριτος   ἡ κεχαριτωμένη.

                         ις΄

       — Νικῶμαι διὰ τὸν πόθον   ὃν ἔχω πρὸς τὸν ἄνθρωπον »,
       ὁ ποιητὴς ἀπεκρίθη.   « Ἐγώ, δούλη καὶ μῆτερ μου,
       οὐ λυπῶ σε·   γνωριῶ σοι

5   If I had not desired to save them   I would not have dwelt in you,
          I would not have shone from you,   you would not be called
                                                                                        mother.
       I dwell in the crib   for the sake of your race,
              by my own will I now suck   at your breasts,
          it is for their sakes   you hold me in your arms.
10   The one unseen by Cherubim   behold, you see and hold,
          you caress me as son, you,   "full of grace."

                              14.

       I have taken you as mother   I, the Maker of Creation,
              and like an infant I grow   I, who am perfect from him who is
                                                                              perfect.
          I am wrapped   in swaddling bands
              because of them   that put on in the past cloaks of skin,
5   and the cave delights me   because of them that hated
              delectation and Paradise   and fell in love with corruption.
       They have transgressed   my life-bearing commandment.
              I have come down to earth   so they may have life.
          But if you learn, holy one,   what else
10   I must do for their sake,   the event will shake you
          with all the elements   you "full of grace."

                              15.

       But when he who shaped all tongues   had spoken thus,
              swiftly underwriting   his mother's prayer,
          Mary   spoke again.
              —If I speak out do not be wrathful, for I am of clay   o Creator;
5   I will speak my mind freely as to a son;   I have courage, for I gave
                                                                              you birth;
              by your birth you have granted me   all cause for triumph.
       I want to learn now what it is   you must bring to fulfillment.
              do not hide from me   your will from ages past.
          I gave birth to you wholly.   Tell the purpose
10   you have for us   that I may learn from this too
          what grace I enjoy   "full of grace."

                              16.

       —I am conquered by the longing   I have for humankind,
              the Maker replied.   —I, my servant and mother,
          will cause you no grief.   I will make known to you

ἃ θέλω πράττειν   καὶ θεραπεύσω σου ψυχήν,   ὦ Μαριάμ.
5   Τὸν ἐν ταῖς χερσί σου φερόμενον   τὰς χεῖρας ἡλούμενον
μετὰ μικρὸν ὄψει με,   ὅτι στέργω τὸ γένος σου·
ὃν σὺ γαλουχεῖς   ἄλλοι ποτίσουσι χολήν·
ὃν καταφιλεῖς   μέλλει πληροῦσθαι ἐμπτυσμῶν·
ὃν Ζωὴν ἐκάλεσας,   ἔχεις ἰδεῖν
10   κρεμάμενον ἐν σταυρῷ   καὶ δακρύσεις ὡς θανόντα,
ἀλλ᾽ ἀσπάσει με ἀναστάντα,   ἡ κεχαριτωμένη.

ιζ'

Ὅλων δὲ τούτων ἐν πείρᾳ   βουλήσει μου γενήσομαι,
καὶ πάντων τούτων αἰτία   διάθεσις γενήσεται
ἣν ἐκ πάλαι   ἕως ἄρτι
πρὸς τοὺς ἀνθρώπους   ἐπεδειξάμην ὡς Θεός,
σῶσαι Ζητῶν. »
5   Μαριὰμ δὲ τούτων ὡς ἤκουσεν   ἐκ βάθους ἐστέναξε
βοῶσα· « Ὦ βότρυς μου,   μὴ ἐκθλίψωσί σε ἄνομοι·
βλαστήσαντός σου   μὴ ὄψωμαι τέκνου σφαγήν. »
Ὁ δὲ πρὸς αὐτήν   ἔφησεν οὕτως εἰπών·
« Παῦσαι, μῆτερ, κλαίουσα   ὃ ἀγνοεῖς·
10   ἐὰν γὰρ μὴ τελεσθῇ,   ἀπολοῦνται οὗτοι πάντες
ὑπὲρ ὧν ἱκετεύεις με,   ἡ κεχαριτωμένη

ιη'

Ὕπνον δὲ νόμισον εἶναι   τὸν θάνατόν μου, μῆτερ μου·
τρεῖς γὰρ ἡμέρας τελέσας   ἐν μνήματι θελήματι,
μετὰ ταῦτα   σοὶ ὁρῶμαι
ἀναβιώσας   καὶ ἀνακαινίσας τὴν γῆν   καὶ τοὺς ἐκ γῆς.
5   Ταῦτα, μῆτερ, πᾶσιν ἀνάγγειλον,   ἐν τούτοις
πλουτίσθητι,
ἐκ τούτων βασίλευσον,   διὰ τούτων εὐφράνθητι. »
Ἐξῆλθεν εὐθὺς   ἡ Μαριὰμ πρὸς τὸν Ἀδάμ,
εὐαγγελισμὸν   φέρουσα τῇ Εὔᾳ φησί·
« Τέως ἡσυχάσατε   ὅσον μικρόν·
10   ἠκούσατε γὰρ αὐτοῦ   ἅπερ εἶπεν ὑπομεῖναι
δι᾽ ὑμᾶς τοὺς βοῶντάς μοι·   Ἡ κεχαριτωμένη. »

what I will do   to bring healing to your soul,   o Mary.
5   The child you hold in your arms   you will see before long
his arms nailed to the Cross   because I love your race;
the child you give milk to   others will give gall to drink;
the one you kiss   must be covered with spit;
the one you called life   you must behold
10   hanging on the Cross,   and you will lament as dead,
yet you will greet me raised up,   "full of grace."

17.

I will bring all this to pass   by my own volition,
and the cause of all   shall be the goodwill
that as of old   until now
I have shown as God to humankind seeking   to save them.
5   When Mary heard this,   she uttered a moan from the depths,
crying out,—O my grapevine,   they shall not crush you, the
lawless ones.
Now you have blossomed forth   may I not see the slaughter of my child!
But he spoke to her   with these words,
—Cease, mother, weeping   for what you do not understand.
10   Unless this comes to pass,   all those you plead for
will perish,   you, "full of grace."

18.

Think, then, of my death   as sleep, my mother.
I shall complete three days   in the tomb by my will,
and afterward you will   see me
bring new life and renewal to earth   to those on earth.
5   Announce this news to all, mother,   be enriched by it.
Mary went straightway   to Adam
and bearing glad tidings   she says to Eve:
—Be patient for yet a short while.
10   You have heard from him   what he must endure
for your sake, who cry out to me   "full of grace."

(Grosdidier de Matons 1965: 2, 88–111; my translation)

On the Resurrection I

Προοίμιον I

Εἰ καὶ ἐν τάφῳ   κατῆλθες, ἀθάνατε,
        ἀλλὰ τοῦ Ἅιδου   καθεῖλες τὴν δύναμιν
        καὶ ἀνέστης   ὡς νικητής,   Χριστὲ ὁ Θεός,
        γυναιξὶ μυροφόροις   τὸ χαῖρε φθεγξάμενος
5   καὶ τοῖς σοῖς ἀποστόλοις   εἰρήνην δωρούμενος,
        ὁ τοῖς πεσοῦσι   παρέχων ἀνάστασιν.

Προοίμιον II

Καταλαβοῦσαι   γυναῖκες τὸ μνῆμά σου
        καὶ μὴ εὑροῦσαι   τὸ ἄχραντον σῶμά σου
        ἐλεεινὰ   δακρύουσαι ἔλεγον ·
        «Ἄρα ἐκλάπη   ὁ συληθεὶς   ἐκ τῆς αἱμόρρου
                                τὴν ἴασιν ;
5   Ἄρα ἠγέρθη   ὁ προειπὼν   καὶ πρὸ τοῦ πάθους
                                τὴν ἔγερσιν ;
        Ἀληθῶς ἀνέστη Χριστὸς   ὁ τοῖς πεσοῦσι
παρέχων ἀνάστασιν»

α´

Τὸν πρὸ ἡλίου ἥλιον   δύναντά ποτε ἐν τάφῳ

On the Resurrection I

Proem I

Even though you have gone down to the tomb, immortal one,
  you have deprived Hades of power,
  and you have risen as conqueror, Christ God
  uttering the word "Hail" to the myrrh-bearing women
5 giving the gift of peace to your apostles,
  you who "offer raising-up to the fallen."

Proem II

The women, coming to your tomb
  and not finding your immaculate body,
  wept piteously saying
  —Can he be stolen, he who was robbed of healing by
      the woman with an issue of blood?
5 Can he be risen, he who predicted the rising even
        before his Passion?
  Indeed he is risen, Christ who "offers raising-up to the
    fallen."

I.

Toward the sun before the sun once sunk in the tomb

431

προέφθασαν πρὸς ὄρθρον   ἐκζητοῦσαι ὡς ἡμέραν,
μυροφόροι κόραι   καὶ πρὸς ἀλλήλας ἐβόων ·
«᾿Ὦ φίλαι, δεῦτε,   τοῖς ἀρώμασιν ὑπαλείψωμεν
5   σῶμα ζωηφόρον   καὶ τεθαμμένον,
σάρκα ἀνιστῶσαν   τὸν παραπεσόντα ᾿Αδὰμ
κειμένην ἐν τῷ μνήματι.
῎Αγωμεν,   σπεύσωμεν   ὥσπερ οἱ μάγοι,
καὶ προσκυνήσωμεν   καὶ προσκομίσωμεν
10   τὰ μύρα ὡς δῶρα   τῷ μὴ ἐν σπαργάνοις,
ἀλλ᾿ ἐν σινδόνι   ἐνειλημένῳ ·
καὶ κλαύσωμεν καὶ κράξωμεν ·   ᾿Ὦ δέσποτα,
                 ἐξεγέρθητι,
ὁ τοῖς πεσοῦσι   παρέχων ἀνάστασιν.᾿ »

β΄

῞Οτε δὲ ταῦτα ἑαυταῖς   ἔφησαν αἱ θεοφόροι,
ἐσκόπησαν καὶ ἄλλο   ὅ ἐστι σοφίας πλήρης
καί φησιν ἀλλήλαις ·   «Γυναῖκες, τί ἀπατᾶσθε;
Πάντως γάρ, ὅτι   ἐν τῷ τάφῳ πέλει ὁ Κύριος.
5   ῎Αρα ἕως ἄρτι   εἶχε κρατεῖσθαι
ὁ ἡνιοχεύων   τὴν τῶν κινουμένων πνοήν;
᾿Ακμὴν νεκρὸς κατάκειται;
῎Απιστον,   ἄστατον   τοῦτο τὸ ῥῆμα ·
διὸ συνήσωμεν   καὶ οὕτω πράξωμεν ·
10   ἀπέλθῃ Μαρία   καὶ ἴδῃ τὸν τάφον
καὶ οἷς ἂν εἴπῃ   ἀκολουθῶμεν ·
πολλάκις γάρ, ὡς προεῖπεν,   ἐγήγερται   ὁ ἀθάνατος,
ὁ τοῖς πεσοῦσι   παρέχων ἀνάστασιν. »

γ΄

῾Υπὸ δὲ τούτου τοῦ σκοποῦ   αἱ συνεταὶ ῥυθμηθεῖσαι
προέπεμψαν, ὡς οἶμαι,   τὴν Μαγδαληνὴν Μαρίαν
ἐπὶ τὸ μνημεῖον,   ὡς λέγει ὁ Θεολόγος.
᾿Ην δὲ σκοτία,   ἀλλ᾿ ἐκείνην πόθος κατέλαμπεν ·
5   ὅθεν καὶ κατεῖδε   τὸν μέγαν λίθον
ἐκκεκυλισμένον   ἀπὸ τῆς θύρας τῆς ταφῆς
καὶ εἶπεν ὑποστρέψασα ·
« Μαθηταί,   μάθετε   τοῦτο ὅ εἶδον
καὶ μή με κρύψητε,   ἐὰν νοήσητε ·

first came before dawn   in their search as for day
      the myrrh-bearing maidens,   and they cried out to each
                                    other
—Dear women,   come let us anoint with perfumes
5   the life-bearing body   here buried,
      the flesh to arouse   the first-fallen Adam,
            laid in the tomb.
Come,   let us make haste   like the wise men,
      and adore him   and offer him
10   the perfumes as gifts   to him not in swaddling bands,
      but bound   in a winding-sheet;
and let us weep and cry out   —O master,   be risen,
      you who "offer   raising-up to the fallen."

                              2.

When the god-bearing women   had spoken thus to each other,
      they had another thought   full of wisdom,
      and said one to another   —Women, why thus beguiled?
It is wrong, surely, [to say]   the Lord is in the tomb.
5   Can it be that till now   he has been constrained,
      he who reined in   the breath of moving creatures?
            Does he still lie dead?
Incredible,   unfounded   the utterance!
      so let us be prudent,   and act as follows:
10   Mary shall go   and look at the tomb,
      and we will obey   her bidding.
For it may be, as he foretold,   the immortal one   is arisen,
      he who "offers   raising-up to the fallen."

                              3.

By such purpose   the wise women were ruled,
      and sent on, I think,   Mary Magdalene
      to the sepulchre,   as the Theologian tells.
It was dark,   but longing lit her way;
5   whence she beheld   the great stone
      rolled away   from the door of the tomb,
            and came back to say
—Disciples,   hear   what I saw,
      and do not hide it from me,   if you understand:

10   ὁ λίθος οὐκέτι   καλύπτει τὸν τάφον ·
       μὴ ἄρα ἦραν   τὸν Κύριόν μου ;
       Οἱ φρουροὶ γὰρ οὐ φαίνονται,   ἀλλ᾽ ἔφυγον ·   μὴ
                                                            ἐγήγερται
       ὁ τοῖς πεσοῦσι   παρέχων ἀνάστασιν ; »

                            δ´

Τούτων ὡς ἤκουσε Κηφᾶς   καὶ ὁ υἱὸς Ζεβεδαίου,
       ἐξέδραμον εὐθέως   ὡς ἐρίζοντες ἀλλήλοις,
       καὶ τοῦ Πέτρου πρῶτος   εὑρέθη ὁ Ἰωάννης ·
       ὅμως καὶ φθάσας   οὐκ εἰσῆλθεν ἔνδον τοῦ μνήματος,
5   ἀλλὰ ἀναμένει   τὸν κορυφαῖον,
       ἵνα ὡς ποιμένι   ἀκολουθήσῃ ὁ ἀμνός ·
       καὶ ὄντως οὕτως ἔπρεπε.
       Πέτρῳ γὰρ   εἴρηται ·   « Πέτρε, φιλεῖς με;
       Καὶ τὰ ἀρνία μου   ὡς θέλεις ποίμαινε» ·
10   τῷ Πέτρῳ ἐρρέθη ·   « Μακάριε Σίμων,
       τὰς κλεῖς σοι δώσω   τῆς βασιλείας » ·
       Τῷ Πέτρῳ πρὶν ὑπέταξε   τὰ κύματα   ἃ ἐπέζευσεν
       ὁ τοῖς πεσοῦσι   παρέχων ἀνάστασιν.

                            ε´

Ἀλλ᾽ ὡς προεῖπον πρὸ μικροῦ,   Πέτρος τε καὶ Ἰωάννης
       κατέλαβον τὸ μνῆμα   δι᾽ ὃ εἶπεν ἡ Μαρία,
       καὶ εἰσῆλθον ἔνδον ·   τὸν Κύριον δὲ οὐχ εὗρον.
       Ὅθεν πρὸς ταῦτα   πτοηθέντες εἶπον οἱ ἅγιοι ·
5   « Ἄρα τίνος χάριν   ἡμῖν οὐκ ὤφθη;
       Μὴ τὴν παρρησίαν   ἡμῶν ἡγήσατο πολλήν ;
       Πολὺ γὰρ ἐτολμήσαμεν ·
       ἔδει γὰρ   ἔξωθεν   ἡμᾶς σταθῆναι
       καὶ περιβλέψασθαι   τὰ ἐν τῷ μνήματι ·
10   ὁ τάφος γὰρ οὗτος   οὐκέτι ὡς τάφος,
       ἀλλ᾽ ὄντως θρόνος   Θεοῦ ὑπάρχει ·
       ἐν τούτῳ γὰρ ἐγένετο   καὶ ᾤκησεν   ὡς εὐδόκησεν
       ὁ τοῖς πεσοῦσι   παρέχων ἀνάστασιν.

                            ς´

Περιετράπη οὖν ἡμῖν   ἡ παρρησία εἰς τόλμαν

10   the stone no longer   covers the tomb.
        Can it be   they have stolen my Lord?
The guards are not there,   they have fled.   Can it be he is risen,
        he who "offers   raising-up to the fallen"?

4.

At these words,   Kephas and the son of Zebedee
        ran off at once   as if in a race,
        and John got there first   before Peter;
yet when he arrived,   he did not go inside the sepulchre,
5   but awaited   the leader,
        so lamb   could follow shepherd.
              And indeed, that was right.
To Peter   it was said,   —Peter, do you love me?
        Then tend my lambs   as you will.
10   To Peter it was spoken,   —Blessed Simon,
        to you I give   the keys of the kingdom.
For Peter he once subdued   the waves   on which he walked,
        he who "offers   raising-up to the fallen."

5.

But, as I said just now,   Peter and John
        reached the tomb   because of Mary's news,
        and they went inside,   yet did not find the Lord.
At this the holy men,   fear-stricken, said,
5   —For what reason   has he not been seen by us?
        Perhaps he thought   our liberty too great?
              We acted too boldly:
we ought   to have stood   outside
        with a glance   inside the sepulchre,
10   for this tomb   is no longer a tomb,
        but the very throne   of God.
For in it he was,   and dwelt   as he saw fit,
        he who "offers   raising-up to the fallen."

6.

Our liberty   has turned to daring,

καὶ μᾶλλον ἐλογίσθη   καταφρόνησις τὸ θάρσος ·
   διὰ τοῦτο τάχα   οὐκ ὤφθη ὡς ἀναξίοις. »
Ταῦτα λαλούντων   τῶν γνησίων φίλων τοῦ πλάσαντος,
5 εἶπεν ἡ Μαρία   ἀκολουθοῦσα ·
   « Μύσται τοῦ Κυρίου   καὶ ὄντως θερμοὶ ἐρασταί,
     μὴ ὡς ὑπολαμβάνητε,
ἀλλ' ὑπομείνατε,   μὴ ἀθυμεῖτε ·
   τὸ γὰρ γενόμενον   οἰκονομία ἦν
10 ἵνα αἱ γυναῖκες   ὡς πρῶται πεσοῦσαι
   ἴδωσι πρῶται   τὸν ἀναστάντα ·
ἡμῖν θέλει χαρίσασθαι   τὸ 'χαίρετε'   ταῖς πενθήσασιν
   ὁ τοῖς πεσοῦσι   παρέχων ἀνάστασιν. »

ζ´

Ἐπειδὴ οὕτως ἑαυτὴν   ἐπληροφόρει Μαρία,
   παρέμεινε τῷ τάφῳ   ἀπελθόντων τῶν ἁγίων ·
   ἀκμὴν γὰρ ἐδόκει   ὅτι ἐπήρθη τὸ σῶμα ·
ὅθεν ἐβόα   οὐχὶ ῥήμασιν, ἀλλὰ δάκρυσιν ·
5 « Οἴμοι, Ἰησοῦ μου,   ποῦ σε μετῆραν ;
   Πῶς δὲ κατεδέξω   κεκηλιδωμέναις χερσὶν
     βαστάζεσθαι, ἀμώμητε ;
'Ἅγιος,   ἅγιος,   ἅγιος' κράζει
   τὰ ἑξαπτέρυγα   καὶ πολυόμματα ·
10 καὶ τούτων οἱ ὦμοι   μόλις φέρουσί σε,
   καὶ πλάνων χεῖρες   ἐβάστασάν σε ·
ὁ Πρόδρομος βαπτίζων σε   ἐκραύγαζε ·   Σύ με
                        βάπτισον,
   ὁ τοῖς πεσοῦσι   παρέχων ἀνάστασιν.'

η´

Ἰδού τριήμερος νεκρὸς   πέλεις, ὁ πάντα καινίζων ·
   ὁ Λάζαρον ἐγείρας   μετὰ τέσσαρας ἡμέρας
   καὶ δρομαῖον δείξας   τὸν κηρίαις δεδεμένον,
κεῖσαι ἐν τάφῳ,   καὶ ὡς εἴθε ᾔδειν ποῦ τέθαψαι,
5 ἵνα ὡς ἡ πόρνη   δάκρυσι βρέξω
   μὴ μόνον τοὺς πόδας,   ἀλλὰ καὶ ὅλον ἀληθῶς
     τὸ σῶμα καὶ τὸ μνῆμά σου,
λέγουσα ·   Δέσποτα,   ὡς τὸν τῆς χήρας
   υἱὸν ἀνέστησας,   σαυτὸν ἀνάστησον ·

our boldness   deemed contempt.
    Perhaps that is why   we have not seen him, for we are
               unworthy.
At these words   of the Creator's sincere friends,
5   Mary, following them,   said
    —Initiates of the Lord,   ardent lovers indeed,
      do not suppose such a thing,
but have patience,   do not lose heart.
    For what has come to pass   was divine disposition,
10   that the women   first to fall
    should be first to see   him resurrected.
On us in our mourning   he wished to bestow   the gift of the
            word "Hail,"
    he who "offers   raising-up to the fallen."

7.

Mary persuaded herself   in this way,
    but she lingered behind at the tomb   when the holy men had
            gone,
    for all the time she thought   the body was stolen,
and so she cried out,   with tears for words
5   —Alas, my Jesus,   where have they taken you?
    How could you endure   to be held
      by hands defiled, blameless one?
"Holy,   holy,   holy" cry
    the six-winged ones   with many eyes.
10   Their shoulders   can scarcely hold you,
    and deceivers' hands   have carried you off!
Prodromos baptising you   called out, "*You* should baptise me,
    you who offer   raising-up to the fallen."

8.

Behold, you are three days dead,   you, who make all things new.
    You, who raised Lazarus   after four days,
    you, who made a swift runner of him   bound with bandages,
you lie in the tomb   —if I only knew where you were buried,
5   so I might like the harlot   wet with my tears
    not only your feet,   but yes, your whole
      body and tomb,
saying,   "Lord,   as you raised up the
    widow's son,   so raise yourself;

10   ὁ τὴν Ἰαείρου   παιδίσκην Ζωώσας,
          τί ἔτι μένεις   ἐν τῷ μνημείῳ ;
        Ἀνάστηθι, ἐπίστηθι,   ἐμφάνηθι   τοῖς Ζητοῦσί σε,
        ὁ τοῖς πεσοῦσι   παρέχων ἀνάστασιν.' »

θ´

        Νενικημένην τῷ κλαυθμῷ   καὶ ἡττημένην τῷ πόθῳ
        ἰδὼν ὁ πάντα βλέπων   τὴν Μαγδαληνὴν Μαρίαν,
        ἐσπλαγχνίσθη τότε   καὶ ὤφθη λέγων τῇ κόρῃ·
        « Γύναι, τί κλαίεις ;   Τίνα θέλεις ἔνδον τοῦ μνήματος ; »
5   Εἶτα ἡ Μαρία   στραφεῖσα εἶπε·
        « Κλαίω ὅτι ἦραν   τὸν κύριόν μου τῆς ταφῆς
        καὶ οὐκ οἶδα ποῦ κατάκειται.
        Πάντως δέ ⌣ σόν ἐστι   τοῦτο τὸ ἔργον ·
        εἰ μὴ πλανῶμαι γάρ,   ὁ κηπουρὸς εἶ σύ ·
10   λοιπὸν εἰ ἐπῆρες   τὸ σῶμα, εἰπέ μοι,
        κἀγὼ λαμβάνω   τὸν λυτρωτήν μου ·
        ἐμὸς πέλει διδάσκαλος   καὶ κύριος   ὁ ἐμός ἐστιν
        ὁ τοῖς πεσοῦσι   παρέχων ἀνάστασιν. »

ι´

        Ὁ τὰς καρδίας ἐρευνῶν   καὶ τοὺς νεφροὺς ἐμβατεύων,
        εἰδὼς ὅτι γνωρίζει   τὴν φωνὴν αὐτοῦ Μαρία,
        ὡς ποιμὴν ἐφώνει   τὴν μηκωμένην ἀμνάδα
        λέγων· « Μαρία ».   Ἡ δ᾽ εὐθέως εἶπε γνωρίσασα ·
5   « Ὄντως ὁ καλός μου   ποιμὴν φωνεῖ με
        ἵνα τοῖς ἐννέα   καὶ ἐνενήκοντα ἀμνοῖς
        λοιπὸν συναριθμήσῃ με ·
        βλέπω γὰρ   ὄπισθεν   τοῦ με καλοῦντος
        ἁγίων σώματα,   δικαίων τάγματα ·
10   διὸ οὔτε λέγω·   'Τίς εἶ ὁ καλῶν με ;'·
        σαφῶς γὰρ ἔγνων   τίς ὁ καλῶν με ·
        αὐτός ἐστιν, ὡς πρόειπον,   ὁ κύριος   ὁ ἐμός, ἔστιν
        ὁ τοῖς πεσοῦσι   παρέχων ἀνάστασιν. »

ια´

        Ὑπὸ δὲ πόθου τοῦ θερμοῦ   καὶ τῆς ἐμπύρου ἀγάπης

10   you who brought to life   Jaeirus' daughter,
              why linger longer   in the tomb?
       Arise, stand by,   be manifest   to those who seek you,
              who "offer   raising-up to the fallen."

                              9.

       Vanquished by weeping,   overcome by longing
              was Mary Magdalene: beholding her, the all-seeing one
              was stirred to mercy,   and he appeared to her, saying
       —Woman, why do you weep?   Whom do you seek inside the
                                        sepulchre?
5   Then Mary turned,   and said,
                 —I weep because they have taken   my lord from the tomb,
                 and I know not where he lies.
       This deed   must be   your own,
                 for if I am not mistaken,   you are the gardener.
10   If you have removed   the body, tell me,
                 and I will take up   my redeemer.
       He is my teacher   and he is   my lord,
                 he who "offers   raising-up to the fallen."

                              10.

       He who examines hearts   and explores kidneys,
              knowing Mary   would know his voice,
              summoned as a shepherd   his bleating lamb,
       saying "Mary."   At once she knew his voice and said,
5   —Indeed my good shepherd   summons me
              so along with the nine   and ninety lambs
                 he can still count me.
       For I see   behind the summoner
              hosts of saints   and ranks of just,
10   and I do not ask   "Who are you that summons me?"
              For I know clearly   who my summoner is,
       it is he, as I said   my lord,   my own one,
              who "offers   raising-up to the fallen."

                              11.

       Seized with ardent longing   and burning love,

ἡ κόρη κατεπείχθη   καὶ κρατῆσαι ἠβουλήθη
τὸν ἀπεριγράπτως   τὴν κτίσιν πᾶσαν πληροῦντα ·
ὅμως ὁ πλάστης   τὴν σπουδὴν αὐτῆς οὐκ ἐμέμψατο,
5   ἀλλ' ἐπὶ τὰ θεῖα   αὐτὴν ἀνάγει
λέγων· «Μή μου ἅπτου·   ἦ μόνον βροτόν με νοεῖς ;
Θεός εἰμί, μὴ ἅπτου μου.
Ὦ σεμνή,   πέτασον   ἄνω τὸ ὄμμα
καὶ κατανόησον   τὰ ἐπουράνια ·
10   ἐκεῖ ζήτησόν με ·   καὶ γὰρ ἀναβαίνω
πρὸς τὸν πατέρα   ὃν οὐκ ἀφῆκα ·
αὐτοῦ πέλω ὁμόχρονος   καὶ σύνθρονος   καὶ ὁμότιμος,
ὁ τοῖς πεσοῦσι   παρέχων ἀνάστασιν.

ιβ΄

Ῥητορευέτω δὲ λοιπὸν   ταῦτα ἡ γλῶσσά σου, γύναι,
καὶ διερμηνευέτω   τοῖς υἱοῖς τῆς βασιλείας
τοῖς καραδοκοῦσι   τὴν ἔγερσίν μου τοῦ ζῶντος.
Σπεῦσον, Μαρία,   καὶ τοὺς μαθητάς μου συνάθροισον ·
5   σάλπιγγί σοι χρῶμαι   μεγαλοφώνῳ ·
ἤχησον εἰρήνην   εἰς τὰς ἐμφόβους ἀκοὰς
τῶν κεκρυμμένων φίλων μου,
ἔγειρον   ἅπαντας   ὥσπερ ἐξ ὕπνου,
ἵν' ὑπαντήσωσι   καὶ δᾷδας ἅψωσιν ·
10   εἰπέ· ''Ὁ νυμφίος   ἠγέρθη τοῦ τάφου
καὶ οὐδὲν ἀφῆκεν   ἐντὸς τοῦ τάφου·
ἀπώσασθε, ἀπόστολοι,   τὴν νέκρωσιν,   ὅτι ἐγήγερται
ὁ τοῖς πεσοῦσι   παρέχων ἀνάστασιν. ''»

ιγ΄

Ὡς οὖν ἀκήκοε σαφῶς   ὅλων τῶν λόγων τοῦ Λόγου,
ὑπέστρεψεν ἡ κόρη   καὶ φησι ταῖς ὁμοτρόποις ·
«Θαυμαστά, γυναῖκες,   ἃ εἶδον καὶ διηγοῦμαι ·
μή τις οὖν δόξῃ   ὡς ληρήματά μου τὰ ῥήματα ·
5   οὐ γὰρ ἐφαντάσθην,   ἀλλ' ἐνεπνεύσθην ·
πέπλησμαι τῆς θέας   καὶ τῆς ὁμιλίας Χριστοῦ,
καὶ πῶς καὶ πότε μάθετε.
Ὅτε με   ἔλιπον   οἱ περὶ Πέτρον,

the young girl felt urged   and willed to hold
    the uncircumscribed   filler of all creation.
Yet the creator   did not reproach her fervor,
5   but leads her upward   to things divine,
        saying—Do not touch me!   Do you think I am mortal?
            I am God—touch me not!
O seemly one, cast aloft   your eye,
    and contemplate   the heavens:
10   seek me there,   for I ascend
        to the father   I have not left.
With him I am coeval,   sharing throne and like honor,
    he who "offers   raising-up to the fallen."

                12.

So let your tongue, woman,   utter aloud these things,
    explaining them   to the sons of the kingdom
    who wait for me   to rise, the living one.
Make haste, Mary,   and gather the disciples.
5   For I shall use you   as a loud-voiced trumpet:
        ring out peace   to the fear-stricken ears
            of my friends in hiding,
wake   them all up   as if from slumber,
    so they may meet   and light torches.
10   Tell them, "The bridegroom   is risen from the tomb,
        he has left nothing   inside the tomb."
Shake off mortality,   apostles,   for he is risen,
    he who "offers   raising-up to the fallen!"

                13.

When she heard clearly   all the words of the Word,
    the young girl went back   to tell her companions
    —Wonderful, women,   are the things I have seen—I'll tell you,
so please don't think   my words are absurd!
5   Not by imagination,   but by divine inspiration,
        I am filled with the sight   and the voice of Christ
            —just listen how and when.
As soon as   Peter's group   was gone,

ἱστάμην κλαίουσα   ἐγγὺς τοῦ μνήματος ·
10   ἐδόκουν γὰρ ὅτι   ἐπήρθη τοῦ τάφου
τὸ θεῖον σῶμα   τοῦ ἀθανάτου ·
ἀλλ᾽ εὐθέως οἰκτείρας μου   τὰ δάκρυα,   ἐπεφάνη μοι
ὁ τοῖς πεσοῦσι   παρέχων ἀνάστασιν.

ιδ´

Μετεποιήθη ἄθροον   εἰς εὐφροσύνην ἡ λύπη
καὶ γέγονέ μοι πάντα   ἱλαρὰ καὶ γεγηθότα ·
οὐκ ὀκνῶ δὲ λέγειν·   ῞Ωσπερ Μωσῆς ἐδοξάσθην᾽ ·
εἶδον γάρ, εἶδον ,   οὐκ ἐν ὄρει, ἀλλ᾽ ἐν τῷ μνήματι,
5   οὐχ ὑπὸ νεφέλην,   ἀλλ᾽ ὑπὸ σῶμα,
τὸν τῶν ἀσωμάτων   δεσπότην καὶ τῶν νεφελῶν
τὸν πρὶν καὶ νῦν καὶ πάντοτε
λέγοντα·   ᾽Μαριάμ,   σπεῦσον καὶ φράσον
τοῖς ἀγαπῶσί με   ὅτι ἐγήγερμαι ·
10   ὡς κάρφος ἐλαίας   λαβοῦσά με γλώσσῃ,
τοῖς ἐκ τοῦ Νῶε   εὐαγγελίζου
σημαίνουσα ὡς πέπαυται   ὁ θάνατος   καὶ ἐγήγερται
ὁ τοῖς πεσοῦσι   παρέχων ἀνάστασιν. ᾽»

ιε´

᾽Ακούσας τούτων ὁ χορὸς   τῶν εὐσεβῶν νεανίδων
συμφώνως ἀπεκρίθη   τῇ Μαγδαληνῇ Μαρίᾳ ·
« ᾽Αληθὲς ὃ εἶπας   καὶ συναινοῦμέν σοι πᾶσαι ·
οὐκ ἀπιστοῦμεν,   ἀλλὰ τοῦτο μόνον θαυμάζομεν
5   ὅτι ἕως ἄρτι   ἦν ἐν τῷ τάφῳ
καὶ συναριθμεῖσθαι   τοῖς τεθνεῶσιν ἡ Ζωὴ
ἠνείχετο τριήμερον ·
ὅτι γὰρ   ἤμελλεν   ἐκ τῶν χθονίων
ἐλθεῖν ἠλπίζομεν ·   διὸ ἐλέγομεν ·
10   ᾽Τοῦ κήτους οἰκέτην   ἐξήγαγε τότε,
καὶ πῶς κρατεῖται   ὑπὸ θανάτου ;
Εἰ τοῦ θηρὸς ἀνήρπασεν,   ἀνίσταται   καὶ ἐκ μνήματος
ὁ τοῖς πεσοῦσι   παρέχων ἀνάστασιν. ᾽

I stood in tears   beside the sepulchre,
10   because I really thought   they had stolen from the tomb
the immortal one's   divine body.
But at once pitying   my tears,   he appeared to me,
who "offers   raising-up to the fallen."

14.

All at once my grief   was turned to gladness
and all things   became happy and joyful.
I hasten to add,   "Like Moses I am glorified!"
Because yes, I saw him,   not on the mount, but in the sepulchre,
5   not under a cloud,   but in the body,
the master of the bodiless   and clouds—
then, now and for ever—
saying—Mariam,   make haste and speak out
to those who love me   that I am risen.
10   Like an olive-branch,   put me on your tongue,
and spread the glad tidings   to Noah's descendants,
signaling forth the cessation   of death,   the arousal
of him who "offers   raising-up to the fallen."

15.

At these words,   the chorus of pious young girls
answered in one voice   to Mary Magdalene.
—What you've said is true,   we all agree,
we are not in doubt,   but wonder only this,
5   that till now   life was in the tomb,
reined in   numbered among the dead
for three whole days.
Of course   he was bound to come up from the dead
we knew it!   So we said
10   "He once delivered   the dweller from the whale,
so how can he be   prisoner of death?
If he freed the whale of its prey,   he can rise up,   even from the
tomb,
he who "offers   raising-up to the fallen."

ιϛ'

Νῦν οὖν μὴ νόμιƷε, σεμνή,   ὅτι χωλεύει ἃ λέγεις·
  ὀρθῶς ἡμῖν ἐφθέγξω   καὶ οὐδὲν ἐν τούτοις σκάƷον ·
  ἀληθὴς ὁ λόγος   καὶ προσηνής σου ὁ τρόπος ·
ὅμως, Μαρία,   κοινωνῆσαί σοι βουλευόμεθα
  ἵνα μὴ ἓν μέλος   ἡμῶν τρυφήσῃ,
  μείνῃ δὲ τὰ ἄλλα   νεκρὰ καὶ ἄγευστα Ʒωῆς
      ἐκείνης ἧς ἀπήλαυσας ·
γένωνται   ἄμα σοι   στόματα πλεῖστα
  ἐπισφραγίƷοντα   τὴν μαρτυρίαν σου ·
  ἀπέλθωμεν πᾶσαι   ἐπὶ τὸ μνημεῖον
  καὶ βεβαιοῦμεν   τὴν ὀπτασίαν ·
κοινὸν ἔστω, συνόμιλε,   τὸ καύχημα   ὃ παρέσχε σοι
  ὁ τοῖς πεσοῦσι   παρέχων ἀνάστασιν. »

ιƷ'

Ο ὕτω λαλῶν ὁ σύλλογος   τῶν θεοφόρων θηλείων
  ἐξήρχετο τὴν πόλιν   μετὰ τῆς διηγουμένης
  καὶ ἰδὼν τὸν τάφον   ἀπὸ μακρόθεν ἐβόα ·
« Ἴδε ὁ τόπος,   μᾶλλον δὲ ὁ κόλπος ὁ ἄχραντος·
  ἴδε ὁ βαστάσας   τὸν βασιλέα,
  ἴδε ὁ χωρήσας   ὃν οὐ χωροῦσιν οὐρανοί,
      χωροῦσι δὲ οἱ ἅγιοι.
Αἶνός σοι,   ὕμνος σοι,   ἅγιε τάφε,
  μικρὲ καὶ μέγιστε,   πτωχὲ καὶ πλούσιε,
  Ʒωῆς ταμιεῖον,   εἰρήνης δοχεῖον,
  χαρᾶς σημεῖον,   Χριστοῦ μνημεῖον·
ἑνὸς μνῆμα, τοῦ κόσμου δὲ   τὸ καύχημα,   ὡς ηὐδόκησεν
  ὁ τοῖς πεσοῦσι   παρέχων ἀνάστασιν. »

ιη'

Ὑμνολογήσασαι λοιπὸν   τοῦ Ʒωοδότου τὸν τάφον,
  ἐστράφησαν καὶ εἶδον   τὸν καθήμενον τῷ λίθῳ
  καὶ ἀπὸ τοῦ φόβου   εἰς τὰ ὀπίσω ἀπῆλθον,
εὐλαβηθεῖσαι,   κάτω κλίνασαι καὶ τὰ πρόσωπα
  καὶ μετὰ δειλίας   λαλοῦσαι ταῦτα ·
  « Τί τοῦτο τὸ εἶδος   ἐστίν, ἢ τίνος ἡ μορφή ;
      Τίς πέφυκεν ὃν βλέπομεν ;

16.

—Do not suppose, then, holy one,   your words to be faltering,
  for you have spoken to us uprightly   with no limp in all this.
  Your discourse is true,   your manner is gentle.
Yet, Mary,   we want to share it with you,
5   lest one of our members   tastes delight,
  while the rest stay dead,   without tasting that life
    you have enjoyed.
May most mouths   be with you
  placing the seal   upon your witness!
10 So let us all go   to the sepulchre
  to confirm   the vision,
  and let the vaunt   be common, friend, that was proffered
  by him who "offers   raising-up to the fallen."

17.

So speaking the band   of god-bearing women
  went out from the town   with the talebearer
  and, on seeing the tomb,   they cried out from afar.
—Behold the place,   or rather the immaculate bosom.
5   Behold the holder   of the king,
  behold the one who makes room   for whom the heavens have no
              room,
   but the holy may.
Praise to you,   hymns to you,   holy tomb,
  small and greatest,   poor and richest,
10 treasury of life,   vessel of peace,
  sign of joy   memorial of Christ.
One man's monument,   but the whole world's vaunting,   as was
              pleasing
  to the one who "offers   raising-up to the fallen."

18.

So singing praises   to the tomb of the life-giver,
  the women turned and saw   one seated on the stone,
  and recoiled backward   from fear,
stricken with piety,   casting downward their heads
5 and awestruck,   they spoke these words,
  —What kind of thing   is this? whence is its form?
  What is the nature of whom we behold?

ἄγγελος ; ἄνθρωπος ; ἄνωθεν ἦλθεν
ἢ τάχα κάτωθεν ἡμῖν ἀνέτειλεν ;
10 Πῦρ πέλει, φῶς πέμπει, ἀστράπτει, αὐγάζει ·
φύγωμεν, κόραι, μὴ φλογισθῶμεν ·
ὄμβρε θεῖε, οὐράνιε, ἐπίσταξον ταῖς διψῶσί σε,
ὁ τοῖς πεσοῦσι παρέχων ἀνάστασιν.

ιθ'

Ψυχαγωγήσουσιν ἡμᾶς νῦν ὡς σταγόνες οἱ λόγοι
τοῦ στόματός σου, Λόγε, ἡ χαρὰ τῶν θλιβομένων,
ἡ ζωὴ τῶν πάντων, μὴ νεκρωθῶμεν τῷ φόβῳ. »
Ταῦτα, ὡς οἶμαι, ἐλιτάνευον αἱ θεόπνευστοι ·
5 ὅθεν ἐμειλίχθη ὁ ἐν τῷ λίθῳ
καὶ πρὸς τὰς γυναῖκας φησί· « Μὴ φοβεῖσθε ὑμεῖς,
ἀλλ᾽ οὗτοι οἱ φυλάσσοντες ·
φρίξουσι, πτήξουσι καὶ νεκρωθῶσιν
ἀπὸ τοῦ φόβου μου, ἵνα καὶ μάθωσιν
10 ὅτι τῶν ἀγγέλων δεσπότης ὑπάρχει
ὃν νῦν φρουροῦσιν, ἀλλ᾽ οὐ κρατοῦσιν ·
ἀνέστη γὰρ ὁ Κύριος καὶ οὐκ ἔγνωσαν πῶς ἐγήγερται
ὁ τοῖς πεσοῦσι παρέχων ἀνάστασιν.

κ'

Ἀθανατίσθητε λοιπόν, θήλειαι, μὴ νεκρωθῆτε ·
τὸν κτίστην τῶν ἀγγέλων ἐζητεῖτε θεωρῆσαι,
καὶ ἑνὸς ἀγγέλου τὴν ὄψιν τί δειλιᾶτε ;
Δοῦλος ὑπάρχω τοῦ τὸν τάφον τοῦτον οἰκήσαντος,
5 τάξιν ὑπηρέτου καὶ φύσιν ἔχω ·
ἅπερ προσετάχθην ἐπέστην κηρῦξαι ὑμῖν ·
᾽ Ἐγήγερται ὁ Κύριος,
ἔτριψε τὰς χαλκᾶς πύλας τοῦ ᾅδου
καὶ σιδηροῦς μοχλοὺς αὐτοῦ συνέθλασε,
10 καὶ τῇ προφητείᾳ ἐπέθηκε πέρας,
καὶ τῶν ἁγίων ὕψωσε κέρας. ᾽
Δεῦτε, κόραι, καὶ ἴδετε ποῦ ἔκειτο ὁ ἀθάνατος,
ὁ τοῖς πεσοῦσι παρέχων ἀνάστασιν. »

An angel?   A human?   Has it come down from on high,
    or has it risen from below   for our sakes?
10   He is fire, he emits light,   he is lightning, he is dawning
    —Let us depart, young girls,   lest we be scorched.
Rain of God, rain of Heaven,   let your drops fall on us   who
                                    thirst for you,
    who offer   "raising-up to the fallen."

19.

Your words shall lead our souls forth   like raindrops
    from your mouth, Word,   joy of the grieving,
    life of all things,   lest we die from fear.
Such were the prayers, I think,   of the God-inspired women,
5   and at this the one   on the stone was softened,
    and said to the women,   —It is not you who should be afraid,
      but rather the guards here:
they shall be stricken with terror   and awe,   they shall be dead
    from fear of me,   so they may learn
10   he is master   of angels
    whom they now guard   but cannot contain.
The Lord is resurrected,   and they knew not   how he is risen,
    the one who   "offers raising-up to the fallen."

20.

Take on immortality, then,   women, not death:
    you who sought to behold   the Creator of angels,
    why be afraid   at the sight of an angel?
I am the slave   of him who dwelt in the tomb,
5   and my rank and nature   are those of a servant.
    I have come to proclaim to you   what I was bidden,
      "The Lord has arisen,
he has shattered   the bronze gates   of Hades,
    he has smattered   its bolts of iron,
10   he has brought to fulfillment   the prophecy,
    he has exalted the horn   of the holy ones."
Come and behold, young girls,   where he was laid,   the
                                    immortal one
    who "offers   raising-up to the fallen."

κα'

Λαβοῦσαι θάρσος ἄμεμπτον   ἐκ τῆς φωνῆς τοῦ ἀγγέλου,
φρονίμως αἱ γυναῖκες   ἀπεκρίθησαν πρὸς τοῦτον ·
«Ἀληθῶς ἀνέστη   ὁ Κύριος, καθὼς ἔφης ·
ἔδειξας ἡμῖν   καὶ τῷ ῥήματι καὶ τῷ σχήματι
5   ὅτιπερ ἀνέστη   ὁ ἐλεήμων ·
εἰ μὴ γὰρ ἀνέστη   καὶ ἐπορεύθη τῆς ταφῆς,
    οὐκ ἂν αὐτὸς ἐκάθισας ·
πότε γὰρ   στρατηγός,   τοῦ βασιλέως
παρόντος, κάθηται   ἢ διαλέγεται ;
10   Εἰ δὲ καὶ τελεῖται   ἐν γῇ τὰ τοιαῦτα,
ἀλλ᾿ ἐν ὑψίστοις   οὐκ ἔστι ταῦτα,
ὅπου θρόνος ἀθέατος   καὶ ἄφραστος   ὁ καθήμενος,
ὁ τοῖς πεσοῦσι   παρέχων ἀνάστασιν. »

κβ'

Μίξασαι φόβῳ τὴν χαρὰν   καὶ εὐφροσύνην τῇ λύπῃ
ὑπέστρεψαν τοῦ τάφου,   ὡς διδάσκει τὸ βιβλίον,
πρὸς τοὺς ἀποστόλους   καὶ ἔλεγον αἱ γυναῖκες ·
«Τί ἀθυμεῖτε ;   Τί τὰ πρόσωπα συγκαλύπτετε ;
5   Ἄνω τὰς καρδίας ·   Χριστὸς ἀνέστη.
Στήσατε χορείας   καὶ εἴπατε ἅμα ἡμῖν ·
   ᾿Εγήγερται ὁ Κύριος᾿·
ἔλαμψεν   ὁ τεχθεὶς   πρὸ ἑωσφόρου ·
μὴ οὖν στυγνάσητε,   ἀλλ᾿ ἀναθάλλετε ·
10   τὸ ἔαρ ἐφάνη ·   ἀνθήσατε, κλῶνες,
καρποφορίαν,   μὴ δυσφορίαν ·
πάντες χεῖρας κροτήσωμεν   καὶ εἴπωμεν ·
                              ᾿ Εξεγήγερται
ὁ τοῖς πεσοῦσι   παρέχων ἀνάστασιν.᾿ »·

κγ'

Οἱ δὲ ἀκούσαντες σαφῶς   καὶ εὐφρανθέντες τῷ λόγῳ
ἐξέστησαν εὐθέως   καί φησι πρὸς τὰς γυναῖκας ·
«Πόθεν τοῦτο, κόραι,   ἐμάθετε ὃ λαλεῖτε ;
Ἄγγελος εἶπεν ;   — Ναί, φησίν, καὶ εἶπε καὶ ἔδειξε,
5   καὶ ὁ τῶν ἀγγέλων   Θεὸς καὶ πλάστης
ὤφθη τῇ Μαρίᾳ   καὶ ἔφη· ᾿Λέξον τοῖς ἐμοῖς ·
ἐγήγερται ὁ Κύριος. ᾿

21.

Taking blameless courage   from the voice of the angel,
     the women answered him   with prudence,
     —In truth the Lord   is risen, as you said:
for you showed us   in both word and shape that yes,
5   the merciful one   is resurrected.
     If he were not,   and still dwelt in the tomb,
          you would not sit here.
When does   a general,   in the king's
     presence, sit down   to converse?
10   If such things came to pass   on earth,
     they do not happen   on high,
where the throne is unseen,   ineffable,   seated by
     him who "offers   raising-up to the fallen."

22.

Mingling joy with fear,   and gladness with grief
     the women turned back from the tomb,   as the Book teaches,
     toward the apostles,   saying,
—Why so downhearted?   Why cover your faces?
5   Lift up your hearts   —Christ is risen.
     Stand in line for the dance,   and say with us
          "The Lord is risen."
He who was born   before the dawn   has shone out,
     so cease glowering looks,   send forth new shoots.
10   Spring is here: blossom forth, branches,
     in fruitfulness,   not in vexation.
Let us all clap our hands   and say   "He is risen
     who offers   raising-up to the fallen."

23.

When the men had clearly heard   and rejoiced at the speech
     they stood up at once   and said to the women
     —Where did you learn this, young girls,   that you speak of?
Was it an angel?   —Yes, they said, he spoke and showed us too.
5   And the God and creator   of angels
     was seen by Mary,   saying "Tell my people:
          the Lord is risen."

Δεῦτε οὖν,   ὡς κριοὶ   καὶ ὡς ἀρνία
  προβάτων ἄπαντες   σκιρτῶντες εἴπωμεν ·
10   ' Ποιμὴν ἡμῶν, δεῦρο,   συνάγαγε ἡμᾶς
  τοὺς σκορπισθέντας   ὑπὸ δειλίας ·
ἐπάτησας τὸν θάνατον,   ἐπίστηθι   τοῖς ποθοῦσί σε,
  ὁ τοῖς πεσοῦσι   παρέχων ἀνάστασιν.' »

κδ΄

Συναναστήτω σοι, σωτήρ,   ἡ νεκρωθεῖσα ψυχή μου,
  μὴ φθείρῃ ταύτην λύπη   καὶ λοιπὸν εἰς λήθην ἔλθῃ
  τῶν ᾀσμάτων τούτων   τῶν ταύτην ἁγιαζόντων·
ναί, ἐλεήμων,   ἱκετεύω σε μὴ παρίδης με
5   τὸν ταῖς πλημμελείαις   κατεστιγμένον ·
  ἐν γὰρ ἀνομίαις   καὶ ⟨ἐν⟩ ἁμαρτίαις ἐμὲ
  ἐκίσσησεν ἡ μήτηρ μου,
Πάτερ μου   ἅγιε   καὶ φιλοικτίρμον,
  ἁγιασθήτω σου   ἀεὶ τὸ ὄνομα
10   ἐν τῷ στόματί μου   καὶ τοῖς χείλεσί μου,
  ἐν τῇ φωνῇ μου   καὶ τῇ ᾠδῇ μου ·
δός μοι χάριν κηρύττοντι   τοὺς ὕμνους σου,   ὅτι
             δύνασαι,
  ὁ τοῖς πεσοῦσι   παρέχων ἀνάστασιν.

Come then,   like rams,   and like lambs
    of sheep, let us say   as we frisk
10   "Come, our shepherd,   gather us in,
    scattered and scared   as we are.
You have trodden down death,   so stand by those   who long for
                        you,
    who "offer   raising-up to the fallen."

24.

Let my deadened soul   be raised with you, savior,
    or else grief will taint it   and it may come to forget
    these songs   which make it holy.
Yes, merciful one,   I beg you not to pass me by,
5   who am tainted   with error,
    for in lawlessness   and in sin
      my mother entwined me.
My Father,   holy   and compassionate,
    may your name   always be blessed
10   in my mouth   and on my lips,
    in my voice   and in my song.
Grant me grace as I proclaim   your hymns of praise,   for you have
                        the power,
    you who "offer   raising-up to the fallen."

(Grosdidier de Matons 1967: 4,380–420; my translation)

Notes

Introduction

1. Renfrew 1987, 60–62.
2. Bernal 1987. Neither Renfrew nor Bernal has escaped criticism, but their combined case against some assumptions of traditional Indo-European philology, coming from different political perspectives, has yet to be fully answered.
3. Ortony ed., 1979; Sperber and Wilson 1986.
4. Bakhtin 1981; Vološinov 1986; Bachtin 1935, 1938–39. It is now clear, as was long suspected, that Bakhtin was the author of many of Vološinov's studies (see Bocharov 1994, 1009–24).
5. Ong 1982; Havelock 1982; Stock 1984; Clanchy 1979; Fentress and Wickham 1992.
6. See Thomson 1974, 59–75. His thesis on the nature and origins of myth and ritual and the evolution of poetry and drama, first formulated in *Marxism and Poetry* (1945), is expanded and updated. Thomson's underlying argument on the differentiation between art and science as contingent on social evolution remains valid and refreshingly lucid. Sperber (1975, 1982) investigates the functions of myth from a comparably bold and interdisciplinary perspective.
7. On the transition from mythical to rational thought, see Thomson 1955 and Lloyd 1979. Although ideological perspectives and interpretations differ, both share the premise that the Greeks' contribution to science and philosophy should be related to social, economic, ideological, and political factors. On Aeschylus' uses of mythology, see Thomson 1938, 1–74; 1946.
8. Nagy 1979, 1990a; Havelock 1984, 175–97. Both Nagy and Havelock stress the importance of the oral-performative and sociohistorical context of ancient Greek literature. Among European scholars of the Italian school, see Gentili 1979, 1988, and Aloni 1981. Last but not least, Seaford 1994 provides a synthesis of anthropological, political, historical, and close literary analysis to shed new light on the ritual dimensions of Homeric epic and Attic tragedy.

9. See Hunger 1969–70, 17–38. For further bibliographic references, see below, Chapter 4.

10. Alexiou 1974; Stewart 1991. For the influence of evolutionism and survivalism (Charles Darwin and E. B. Tylor) on Karl Marx's understanding of religion, mythology, and folklore, see Bloch 1983, 34–35, 49, 98–102.

11. Kirk 1970, 37; see also 31–41, 242.

12. Burkert 1979, 22–24.

13. Stewart 1991.

14. In their seminal article, Jakobson and Halle (1956, 69–96) give neurological evidence, based on clinical studies of patients with brain disorders, for the fundamental distinction between the metaphoric and metonymic poles of expression. Their theory has formed the starting point for many subsequent critical studies in art, literature, and psychoanalysis: see Lodge 1977, and Lacan 1977. For critique, see Johnson 1987, 155–77. While I accept the usefulness to the literary critic of the distinction between these two poles, I do not think we have sufficient knowledge of how the brain works to view the two as oppositional. Above all I would reject any attempt, based on supposedly "scientific" evidence, to privilege either metaphor or metonym in literary discourse. On the complexity of brain chemistry and function, the inadequacy of the current state of research, and the need for more collaboration between the natural, social, and human sciences, see Crick 1988, 143–63.

15. For the earliest version of this tale to be published in Greek, see Pio 1879, 21–26.

16. My elder son, Dimitri, is aware of the rules of language as code and fluent in both Greek and English, but he finds it difficult to infer meaning from context, so that idioms and open-ended questions get misinterpreted, although he is capable of metaphorical expression. My younger son, Pavlos, is a mirror image of his twin brother: although he lacks effective expressive speech, he is expert at inferring meaning from context through nonverbal cues and conveys intentions through action signals. His rapt attention when watching television suggests decoding through pictures. Other autistics have problems with "shifters," hence statements such as "We always come this way *on Saturday*" are disturbing because for them, "on" must have an exclusively spatial reference. Alverson's discussion of prepositional and adverbial uses of "over" in English and German helps us to understand the conceptual basis of the autistic's dilemma (1991, 94–117, esp. 103–12).

17. For outstanding performances in drama, mathematics, mechanics, music, and sculpture by autistics and other persons with neurological impairments, see Sacks 1983, 1995. Selfe (1977, 98–109) documents her autistic daughter's loss of artistic ability on acquisition of rudimentary speech, while Luria (1987) explores the relation of mind and memory to synesthesia. Grandin (1989) and Williams (1992, 1993) both document their own slow and painful "emergence" from autism and discovery of self by means of complex synesthetic rituals and (in Williams' case) symbolic use of different personae. Rutter has conducted a long-term study of autism in twins (to which my sons contributed in 1973 and 1985–86) which suggests a genetic and chemically based deficiency as a probable cause of the disorder: see Rutter and Schopler 1977, 219–41. My personal experience of "clinical testing" on my sons makes me wary of basing any theory (let alone literary theory) on psychological tests applied to one disorder alone. Two examples must suffice: Dimitri, aged four, was tested for his need to attend a special school. Given a square to copy, he drew in windows, a door. and a chimney, concluding, "It's a house"; given a circle to copy, he drew in another appropriately spaced parallel circle, put a square on top, and triumphed, "It's a bus." Told to

copy a cross, he drew a square beneath it and stated, "It's a church." "Well," concluded the analyst, "I can see he needs special schooling: he just doesn't do what you tell him." And yet Dimitri was only trying to make concrete pictures out of abstract shapes! Maybe he just didn't understand what the word "copy" meant? My other son, Pavlos, proved even more recalcitrant to all attempts at testing. Instructed to follow simple commands by Michael Rutter and his assistants at the Maudsley Hospital, London, Pavlos, aged four, turned his back on the testers and twiddled his string of beads. At a follow-up interview, when asked to "put square pegs in the square holes and round pegs in the round holes," he hurled the puzzle across the floor in a fit of rage. "Pavlos cannot perform even these simple tasks," concluded the tester, as he turned his back to pack up his briefcase. Pavlos deftly picked up every peg and piece from the floor, slotted them into place, and had the puzzle ready on the table. I do not know to this day whether the tester believed Pavlos had performed this task without our aid. What is clear is that Pavlos was refusing to be tested by the standards of the "experts." For an overview on autism which challenges many shibboleths, see Sacks 1995, 233–82.

18. See Cohen 1979, 76; and contra, Rumelhart 1979, 78–90.

19. Cited in Alexiou 1974, 200.

20. Ortony 1979, 200; Broumas 1989. More generally, see essays by Quinn, Alverson, Turner in Fernandez 1991, 56–158.

21. The first to argue the anticontinuity case systematically and on racial-historical grounds, was Fallmerayer (1830–36, 1845), although as early as 1782, the Irish cleric and historian John Gast (1782, 708–9, cited in Spencer 1954, 295) expressed the view that the present Greeks "appear to be of mixed race, of whom few, if any, are of the ancient Grecian lineage. Most of them have been transplanted into this country from different parts, and at different periods, by those who were attracted by curiosity, or views of gain." Fallmerayer's systematization of the anticontinuity case coincides precisely with, on the one hand, the birth pangs of the Greek nation (War of Independence 1821–28; Constitution 1834) and, on the other, nascent racist theories such as Gobineau's *Essai sur l'inégalité des races humaines* (1853–55). Adverse Greek reaction to Fallmerayer, dating from the mid–nineteenth century, was relatively swift, but support came from strange quarters; see Karl Marx's laudatory reference to Fallmerayer and denigration of Greek expansionist designs in "Greek Insurrection," *New York Tribune*, 29 March 1854 (Marx and Engels 1980, 70–72). The anticontinuity case was taken up again in the West by Jenkins (1963): for "hard" support, see Mango 1965, 29–43; for a "centrist" position, see Nicol 1971; and for the opposition, see Vryonis 1978, 237–56. For an overview of the debate in Greece, see Herzfeld 1982 and Alexiou 1986a, 3–16; more generally, see Bernal 1987, 224–336.

22. Du Boulay 1974; Danforth 1982; Herzfeld 1983, 1985b, 1988; Dubisch 1986; Hirschon 1989; Cowan 1990. Anthropological studies which attempt to situate contemporary data in relation to the past, ancient and Byzantine, include Stewart 1991; Hart 1992; Seremetakis 1991.

23. Warburton 1970; Newton 1972; Mackridge 1985. An exception is Browning 1983.

24. The chief Greek exponent is Politis 1871, 1899–1902, 1904, 1914. Of the numerous studies by non-Greek scholars with a classical training, Lawson's book (1910; reprint, 1964) is among the most enduring; my *Ritual Lament* (1974) and this volume are among the most recent. For ideological assessments relevant to the "continuity case," see Danforth 1984, 53–85; Kyriakidou-Nestoros 1978; Herzfeld 1982; and Tziovas 1989a, 296–305.

25. Politis 1914, vi–vii. Among the finest studies from the historical-diffusionist school are Baud-Bovy 1935; Bouvier 1976; and Saunier 1972, 119–52, 335–70.

26. Goody 1968, 1987; Finnegan 1977; Ong 1984; Stock 1980; Havelock 1984.

27. Headlam 1910, 1922; Thomson 1938. Headlam's philology remains a model for scholarship, in that he pays close attention not only to the Greek language as a living continuum, showing an awareness of the difference between the language of the texts and that of its transmitters, but also to the creative variation of poetic *topoi* from an historical perspective. Bachtin published little beyond his monograph on the Greek language (1935), and his essays on Greek and English poetry ([1938–39] 1985, 333–56); and on Greek culture (1963); yet his insights on the significance of register in the Greek language and of Greek interaction with neighboring languages and cultures from Homer to the present day anticipate many current debates.

28. Marx (1857–58) 1973, 110; Mao 1961–65, 341; Lévi-Strauss 1966, 245–69. For a critique of structuralism's failure to address history and practice, see Bourdieu 1977.

29. Detienne 1977, 1979; Vernant 1974; essays by Gernet and Vidal-Naquet in: Gordon (ed.) 1981; Loraux 1987; Thomson 1946, 1949, 1955; Seaford 1994.

30. Eliade 1954, 1960, 1963; Geertz 1975. Dundes 1978 provides a welcome challenge to conventional definitions, yet his psychosexual interpretations of myth are often one-sided and based on dubious etymologies.

31. Bloch 1983, 124–40; Sperber 1975; Sperber and Wilson 1986.

32. Derrida 1976; Foucault 1970, 1972.

33. In the field of modern Greek studies, see Lambropoulos (1989, 1–39) and the responses elicited. The major issue is the need to find not a compromise between traditional empiricism and deconstructive skepticism but a means of exploiting and exploring new critical approaches and techniques without divorcing "literature" from "life," and without lapsing into technocratic "newspeak."

34. French feminist theories have centered on linguistics, philosophy, and psychoanalysis, rather than on literary criticism, under the influence of Derrida and Lacan; see: Kristeva in Moi 1986; Cixous 1986; and Irigaray 1987. American feminists, by contrast, have been more concerned with the politics of critical practice; see, for example, Johnson 1980 and Suleiman 1986. For analysis of the differences between French and American feminisms, see Jardine 1985. In the field of educational psychology, Gilligan (1982) poses a more fundamental challenge to Western male-orientated theory. For studies of women in non–first world cultures, see Spivak 1987 and Das 1983, 445–62.

35. For anthropological and literary studies on women in contemporary Greece, see Friedl 1975; du Boulay 1974; Dubisch ed. 1986; Hirschon 1989; Van Dyck 1998: the anthropological studies follow Friedl's lead in her pioneering study of the dowry system (1967: reprinted in Dubisch 1986, 42–52) in emphasising, from different social, economic, and cultural perspectives, the extent to which Greek women have played a stronger role than the overtly patriarchal organization of their society would seem, at face value, to allow. Stamiris (1986, 98–113) situates the nub of the problem in the isolation and commodification of woman in modern Athenian urban society; see also Fox-Genovese, 1982, 5–29, for an overview of the relevance of precapitalist societies to the problem of gender. As for antiquity, few studies make more than the most scant reference to postclassical Greece, even when aims are both diachronic and comparative: see Humphreys 1983. Rosaldo and Lamphere (1974) fail to address the adverse effects of modern capitalism on second world and

third world cultures. For critiques of Burkert 1983 and Girard 1977, see Traube 1979, 37–43, and Alexiou 1990c, 97–123.

36. Faubion 1993; Pollis 1992, 171–96.

37. Doumani 1983, appendix.

38. Gilbert and Gubar (1987) analyze the social, literary, and linguistic conflicts between the sexes that resulted from women's entry onto the literary scene from the late nineteenth century onward, indicating the extent to which the debate fueled much male misogyny and sexist fantasy associated with modernism. Their model does not fit the Greek case, and it is precisely such differences which deserve consideration. It is not simply that Greece had few women writers until much later; rather, Greek literature was shaped by different factors— above all by the force of its oral tradition—and therefore the literary conflicts took radically different forms, such as that between demoticism and purism, orality and literacy (see Tziovas 1986). Tziovas (1989b, 321–35) examines the significance of "phonocentrism" as a major factor in the absence from Greek literature of many features associated with modernism and postmodernism. Although Tziovas is careful to avoid simplistic value judgments, it is important to stress the *difference* (rather than "belatedness," with its connotations of inferiority) of Greek literature in this respect and to explore further the sociopolitical and cultural implications of gender. See Van Dyck 1994, 45–60.

39. Van Dyck 1998 situates the poetry of Rea Galanaki, Jenny Mastoraki, and Maria Laina (among others) in the broader social, political, and cultural context of Greek literature since World War II. She also points out that women prose-writers have been no less experimental. Their frequent blend of fantasy and documentary into a kind of biomythography forms an interesting parallel to African American women's prose writing (Alice Walker, Gloria Naylor, Toni Morrison), especially in their use of voice and of oral traditions. Hart (1996) demonstrates the force of women's oral histories from the Greek Resistance and Civil War; Greek singer Mariza Koch illustrates, through voice, a unique blend of poetry and song, often in her own lyrics. "Textuality" may prove more belated than "cantability"; and there is every reason why women should encourage cultures in which diversity and plurality of scripts and voices survive.

40. Eliade 1954. Du Boulay (1982) explores cyclical and spiral symbolism in Greek culture, while Seremetakis (1991) and Stewart (1991) are concerned with women's role in healing, death and divination. Sultan (1999) shows how man's individual death is presented in epic and heroic song as an irreversible catastrophe, mediated through woman's lamentation as commemoration. The influence of linearity on continuity proponents from the late nineteenth and early twentieth centuries can be judged from the attempts by Politis 1899–1902, 1904, Lawson 1910, and Kyriakidis 1934, to establish diachronic links in terms of story patterns, hero types, and names which often mask changes in function and structure.

41. On time and space in literature, see Bakhtin 1981, 84–256. Hawking (1988); Watson (1968); and Crick (1988) investigate the post-Einsteinian nuclear physical and microbiological models. Gould (1989) proposes a theory of biological evolution over space and time based on neither linear nor "tree" concepts of a single trunk reaching out to many branches but on a "bush" model, whereby bits fall away according to rules determined by biological lottery. Contingency games in tales will be examined below (Chapter 8).

Chapter 1

1. Cited from Bakhtin 1935, 71.

2. The historical summary that follows is based on my article "Diglossia in Greece" (1982, 156–92). Andriotis (1974, 5–13) traces the origins of dialect differentiation to the Hellenistic koine, emphasizing the significance of survivals on the peripheries of the Greek-speaking world today. Compare Andriotis 1976, 1:4–20, and Grosdidier de Matons 1976, 2:4–10.

3. Browning 1983 and Mackridge 1985.

4. Thomson 1966, 31; Palmer 1980, chap. 1.

5. The term "polyglossia" is adapted from Bakhtin (1981; 1986) to include the following subcategories in Greek: *heteroglossia* refers to use of a language by nonnative speakers, (e.g., *koine* Greek in the eastern Hellenistic kingdoms); *diglossia*, to the official coexistence of two forms of the same language, one of which may regarded as "high," the other as "low" (e.g., modern Greek—henceforth MG in notes and tables—from c. 1830 to 1976); *bilingualism*, to widespread use of two languages by the community (e.g., knowledge of Italian and Greek on Venetian Crete); *multilingualism*, to widespread use of more than two languages (e.g., Greek, Syriac, and Hebrew in the southeastern regions of the early Byzantine empire). Polyglossia therefore indicates multiple linguistic forms of diverse origins, sometimes referred to as *aglossia* (Alexiou 1982, 156).

6. Bachtin 1935, 11–15, 39–40.

7. Vološinov 1986, 71.

8. Bachtin 1935, 19–33.

9. Such tabulation of useful ancient perfective stems would have rendered Mackridge's otherwise invaluable treatment of the MG verb more comprehensible to all (1985, 167–70).

10. On grammatical borrowings in the Balkan linguistic area, see Bynon 1977, 246–48; and Joseph 1981, 139–54; 1983; 1985, 87–96.

11. Bachtin (1935, 65–76) emphasizes Greek "lexical greed" and the tendency of literary writers to "revivify" old words; yet he underestimates the number and significance of foreign loan words. Browning (1983, 12–18) points to the diversity and complexity of the Greek vocabulary at all periods, even though the categories of borrowings have changed (cf. Mackridge 1985, 307–18).

12. Parry 1971. The significance of Milman Parry's studies of Homeric language and style was first noted and developed by Thomson 1949, 501–82.

13. On ancient dialects, see Palmer 1980, chap. 1.

14. See Allen 1968. The vibrancy of registers in Attic Greek of the fifth and fourth centuries BC can be demonstrated both within and across genres. Tragedy, the most "elevated" genre, includes both the high level of choral odes and stichomythia, in which variable word order and significant use of particles can be conveyed in English by tone of voice, as when Orestes confronts Klytaimestra, having just dispatched Aigisthos, with the words σε καὶ ματεύω· τῷδε ἀρκούντως ἔχει, which is not "I'm looking for you as well—as for him, it's well enough", but "I've been *looking* for *you—he's* alright" (A. *Cho.* 892). The comedies of Aristophanes have an even wider range, from the colloquial level of comic repartee to the lyrical level of the choral odes. Perhaps the clearest examples of the essential difference between Greek and English in indicating "tone of voice" are to be found in the dialogues of Plato (composed in the language of everyday exchange), which cannot be conveyed com-

prehensibly in a literal English translation: in the *Crito*, early in the first exchange of greetings, Sokrates asks his visitor, Ἄρτι δὲ ἥκεις ἢ πάλαι;—·Ἐπιεικῶς πάλαι, which is not "Have you come just now, or [did you come] some time ago?—Moderately some time ago," but "Have you been waiting *long?*—Quite a long time." (Pl. *Cr.* I. 43B, 1.14) On translating Plato, see Cornford, 1941, Introduction. As Thomson has demonstrated in his translations from Greek into English and Irish, the more archaic languages, Greek and Irish, tend to amplify by means of antithesis, whereas the more modern English idiom tends to reduce. A fascinating feature of my autistic son Dimitri's speech is his aberrant insistence on "asking the same question twice over," hence never, "Are we going to *eat* now?" but, "Shall we be eating soon, or am I going to have to wait a long time?"

15. Writing in fairly high-style Greek of the second century A.D., Dio Chrysostom describes how he lost the road and became entangled in shepherd tracks in the environs of Olympia in the western Peloponnese, only to be rewarded by coming across an elderly but robust woman in charge of a rustic shrine to Herakles situated on a hillside grove of oak trees, who addressed him kindly "in Doric tones" (δωρίζουσα τῇ φωνῇ) and informed him of his whereabouts (*Or.* I, 60 R, cited in Thomson 1966, 48 no. 42). The modern Tsakonian dialect, still spoken in the more remote regions of Mount Parnon in the southern Peloponnese, is the only undisputed descendant of an ancient dialect (Doric), although claims have been made for ancient dialectal origins for the modern dialects of South Italy, Sicily, and the Pontos on the Black Sea coast. For bibliography, see Browning 1983, 124–25.

16. Norden 1898: Part I provides details of the dispute between Classicism and Neoterism and between Atticism and Asianism that took place around the time of the "second sophistic."

17. Browning 1983, 44–55.

18. For the most comprehensive study of MG dialect differentiation, see Newton 1972. Further evidence for the survival of late-Byzantine vocabulary in modern dialects will be provided in my study of the twelfth-century Ptochorodromic Poems (Chapter 4; see also my forthcoming edition and translation).

19. Thomson (1966, 47) and Browning (1978a, 105–9; 1983, 47–48) cite relevant examples, including the lexicographer Phrynichos (second century A.D.), who "corrects" non-Attic usages in a letter received from one of his pupils: the "wrong" forms are all attested in koine Greek, and most have survived to this day.

20. Mango 1980, 13–31; on heterogeneity of peoples and languages in the later Roman Empire, see Jones 1971; Hendy 1985; and Vryonis 1971.

21. Examples in MG include σπίτι (*hospitium*) = house (in contrast to derivatives from Latin *mansio* and *casa* in Romance languages); πόρτα (*porta*) = door; κάμαρα (*camera*) = room; κούπα (*cuppa*) = cup; φοῦρνος (*furnus*) = oven; κάγκελο (*cancellum*) = banister, railings; κάστρο (*castrum*) = fortress; κάμπος (*campus*) = plain; στράτα (*strata*) = road, path; τέντα (*tenta*) = canopy, tent; τεντώνω = to stretch; σέλλα (*sella*) = saddle; βάρκα (*barca*) = boat; βίγλα/βιγλίζω (*vigilium*) = watch; ἀκκουμπῶ (*accumbo*) = to lean.

22. Thomson 1966, 51–52; text from Triantafyllidis 1938, 195.

23. Browning 1978a, 103. See Ševčenko 1981, 289–312.

24. Jeffreys 1974, 176; emphasis added.

25. For interaction between Latin and the vernaculars in the medieval West, see Ong 1982, 93–116; 1977, 28–34; and Stock 1980. As Ong points out, the survival of Latin as the language of education and much oral conversation, long after it had ceased to be a spoken

language, can be explained by its being the only mutually intelligible language amidst the "swarming, oral vernaculars which often had different, mutually unintelligible forms among populations perhaps only 50 miles apart" (1982, 108). Where a more or less standardized form becomes established in writing, as a "grapholect," its rules for "correct" grammar and usage are popularly interpreted as the grammar and usage of other dialects (108). In the case of Byzantine Greek, interference between vernacular and learned registers is to be expected, especially during the early stages of developing the vernacular, because of the greater interpenetrations of learned and popular forms.

26. See below, Chapter 4, for discussion of *Timarion*, Eustathios Makrembolites' novel *Hysmine and Hysminias*, and the numerous works of Theodore Prodromos. The range and versatility of learned Greek are analyzed by Browning (1978).

27. Browning 1983, 82.

28. Hunger ed. 1973, 304. Tzetzes' passage is cited in translation, together with examples of conversation in the original Scythian, Persian, Latin, Alan, Arabic, Russian, and Hebrew, by Kazhdan and Epstein 1985, 259–60.

29. For Theodore Prodromos' challenge to Clement, see Kazhdan and Franklin 1984, 111. See below, Chapter 4, for my rendering of this passage.

30. Browning 1978a, 125–26.

31. Beck 1971, 3–6.

32. Beaton's analysis of the romances is more literary than philological, with the result that some of the finer linguistic and stylistic differences are missed (1989). See Agapitos and Smith 1992 for critique.

33. See Hörandner 1982; Jeffreys and Smith 1991.

34. Jeffreys 1977 (on Leo poems).

35. Baud-Bovy 1950, 53–78. For a select critical bibliography of the subject, see Alexiou and Holton 1976, 22–34.

36. Kontosopoulos 1981.

37. For the assizes, see Valetas ed. 1947: I,3; for the prose chronicle by Leontios Makhairas, see Dawkins ed. 1932, and for that by George Boustronios, Sathas ed. 1870, 411–543; for the love poems, see Siapkaras-Pitsillides ed., 1952.

38. On Naxiot archives, see Kasdagli 1988, 1997; for the text of the love poems, see Hesseling and Pernot edd. 1913 and Pernot 1931. On the possibly Cycladic provenance of other vernacular poems of the time, such as the *Dialogue between Man and Charon*, see Alexiou 1978, 226, 234.

39. Bakker and van Gemert 1977, 12–39.

40. On the historical and social background, see Alexiou 1965, 146–78; Maltezou 1991, 17–47. On the Jews of Crete, see Ankori 1968.

41. Zinkeisen 1856: 4, 658–59; compare sources cited in Maltezou 1991.

42. Foscarini, cited in Maltezou 1991, 33–34, from Spanakis 1969.

43. Zinkeisen 1856: 4, 659–60.

44. See Bancroft-Marcus 1983, 27–28.

45. Sofianos 1870. On other grammars from the early sixteenth to seventeenth centuries, see Browning, 1983, 93.

46. Tsourkas 1967.

47. Veloudis 1974; Politis 1982.

48. Balamoti (1984) notes that stories of Robin Hood and Maid Marion were often embroidered alongside Greek popular figures to decorate the textile borders (*bándes*) in

Epirot village houses. Jusdanis (1991, 13–41) provides a succinct summary of the literary and linguistic complexities during the Ottoman period.

49. *Atakta* 1833, 49ff. For a recent collection of papers on Korais' linguistic theories, see Korais 1984.

50. Mandilaras 1972, 61–66, 93.

51. Mackridge 1985, 7.

52. Herzfeld 1982, 75–122.

53. Thomson 1969, 1–24; cf. Thomson 1988 for Irish parallels.

54. Cited by Sareyiannis 1964, 41–43 (42).

55. For analysis and bibliography on Karyotakis (1896–1928), Nikos Kavadias (1910–74), and Andreas Embiricos (1901–), see Calotychos 1993; Katerina Anghelaki-Rooke (1939–), Maria Laina (1947–), and Jenny Mastoraki (1949–), see Van Dyck 1998.

56. Keller 1982, 70–93, 123–55. For the lack of standardization in the grammar of katharevousa, see Tzartzanos 1930).

57. Cited by Bien (1972, 152).

58. For denigrations of demotic as "vulgar," see relevant citations from Lambros Photiades (during the 1780s) in Mandilaras 1972, 60; for the awe of less educated people for forms of language they cannot understand, see comments from Nirvanas cited by Bien (1972, 161).

59. Frangoudaki 1973.

60. Mirambel 1937, fasc. 5, 19–53.

61. Mackridge 1985, 11–14.

62. Mirambel 1964, 405–36.

63. Mackridge 1985, 6; 11–14. Holton (1990, 23–33) stresses the diversity and complexity of SMG but does not consider the question of dialects.

64. On this term, see Mackridge 1985, 7.

65. Unlike English or French, Greek has tended to avoid homonyms and homophones among words of the same grammatical category, number, and gender. Thus AG nouns ὗς (pig) and οἶς (sheep) were replaced in KG by χοῖρος and πρόβατον; the adjective καινός (new) was modified to καινούργιος to avoid confusion with κενός (empty).

66. Exceptions include the poet Georgios Michaelides (1850–1917) and a few others of the "generation of the 1930s." My thanks to George Syrimis for advice on this matter.

67. My example is based on experience of teaching a course on Greek and black women's voices (1992), in which ethnicities and identities were diversely represented. On formal occasions, all used "good English." Informally, the groups did not readily mix, so that when I invited students to meet informally over dinner with African American sociologist Janet Hart after her talk, only those with Greek connections turned up. African American students were once more invited for a separate dinner occasion two weeks later, when Hart returned to Cambridge. I did not understand their vernacular, despite my familiarity with its literary forms. On similar habits of code switching in Greek, see Kazazis 1992, 57–70.

68. Some examples culled from slogans of the junta period (1973): τὸ πεπρωμένον τῆς Φυλῆς (the destiny of our race); λαμπρύνωμεν τὸ ἑλληνικὸν ὄνομα (let us brighten the Greek name); ὁ Θεός εἶναι φιλέλλην (God is Greek-loving). On K as *mentalité*, see Mirambel 1964, 405–36.

69. Georgios Vizyenos avails himself of all registers in his prose fiction but also sounds a cautionary approach to the identification of "fatherland" and "language" in his essay on Henrik Ibsen. Praising Ibsen for the richness and subtlety of his language, as well as for his dramatic talent and disregard for public acclaim, Vizyenos avails himself of the

opportunity to decry the simplistic attempts by Ibsen's predecessors to forge a national Norwegian literary language (the "language of the people," ὡς βάσις ἀληθοῦς δημοφιλοῦς φιλολογίας), purged of foreign (Danish and learned) elements; while he stops short of commenting directly on the Greek "language question," his remarks were clearly intended to sound a salutary warning for Greek letters: Ἐν τῷ ὑπερβολικῷ δηλαδὴ πόθῳ τοῦ νὰ εἰσδύσωσιν εἰς αὐτὴν τὴν καρδίαν τοῦ ἐθνικοῦ τῶν Νορβηγῶν βίου, ἀλωβητὰ τηροῦντες πάντα τὰ ἰδιάζοντ' αὐτῷ προσόντα, ἐνόμισαν ὅτι δὲν ἦρκει τὴν μορφὴν μόνον τῆς τέως αὐτῶν γλώσσης νὰ διαρρυθμίσωσιν ἐπὶ τὸ ἰθαγενέστερον, ἀλλ ἐπίστευσαν ὅτι ὤφειλον ν' ἀποπτύσωσιν ὁλοσχερῶς τὸ ἐκ δανικῶν καὶ νορβηγικῶν διαλέκτων κρᾶμα, νὰ δημιουργήσωσι δὲ νέαν ἀκραίφνως ἐθνικὴν γλῶσσαν ἐκ καθαρῶς νορβηγικῶν ἰδιωμάτων.... Ὁ αὐτοχθονισμὸς ἐν τούτῳ ὑπῆρξεν τόσον ἐμπαθής, ὅτι πᾶς ὁ ὑποστηρίζων τὴν τήρησιν τοῦ πρῴην γλωσσικοῦ καθεστῶτος ἐλογίζετο ὡς προδότης τῆς πατρίδος! Ἔρρικος Ἴψεν, in Γ. Βιζυηνός, ed. Panayiotopoulos 1954, 18:301–9; citation on 303). Cavafy, too, long before he had developed his own distinctive "poetic voice," indicated his dissatisfaction with the current demoticist trend in an article eulogizing the subtlety and sophistication of Byzantine learned poetry; see Οἱ Βυζαντινοί ποιηταί (1892) 1963a: 43–50.

70. Bien 1972; Psicharis (1888) 1971, 34.
71. Bachtin 1985, 333–56.

Chapter 2

1. Bakhtin 1986, 60–102.
2. Ibid., 103–31; Vološinov 1986, 109–40; Sperber and Wilson 1986.
3. At age four my son Dimitri would ask for a drink of milk or juice not with "I want" but with the question, "Do you want?" At age nine he proved a source of embarrassment following a visit to relatives where accommodation was limited by "stating," "Did you sleep with Mum?" meaning "I slept in the same bed as Mum did." At age fourteen he greeted me on returning from school with the news, conveyed with some excitement, "Mum, I got a Merit for reading in drama class today!" Since we were then operating a "star system," based on behavior modification, a Merit at school was worth a lot of points. "Oh no!" I said, facing him, in tones of pleased surprise. "Yes I did," he replied, crestfallen. "Was that bad, Mum?" Different ways of saying "Oh no!" to express surprise, shock, and horror have since been practiced and mastered, yet he still fails to detect nuances of anger, fear, and irony behind new utterances in everyday speech. Recently, thanks to a gifted teacher, he has learned to sing with control and feeling, perhaps because the emotion, being "displaced," is less threatening. For similar observations in two autobiographies by partially recovered autistic women, see Grandin 1989 and Williams 1992.
4. See Browning 1978a, 103–33, for a summary and analysis of relevant texts.
5. Browning 1983, 22–23.
6. Ibid. 6–7, 49.
7. Greek text cited from Hodges and Farstad 1985, 174–5, 285–87.
8. Bachtin 1935, 51–54; Thomson 1966, 83 n. 5; Browning 1983, 28–31, cf. 35–36 on the dearth of optatives in NT Greek.

9. Thomson 1966, 35–36; Browning 1983, 30. The process had already begun in the classical period; see Chantraine 1927.

10. Mandilaras 1972, 29–30.

11. Thomson 1966, 38.

12. The translation of Mark by A. Pallis (1901), which provoked riots in the streets of Athens, is perhaps misleading in its use of extreme "Psychariot" demoticisms.

13. Mark: ἐπί < + accusative (motion); ἐκ + genitive (place); ἀπό + genitive (motion); εἰς + accusative (motion after εἰσέρχομαι); ἐν τοῖς δεξιοῖς "on the right", cf. MG στὰ δεξιά. On ἐν + dative in NT to replace AG instrumental dative, see Browning 1983, 36–37.

14. On the restructuring of the personal pronoun, see Browning 1983, 62.

15. On the principle of analogy and its effects on the morphology and vocabulary of MG, see Thomson 1964, 204.

16. For a study of the religious significance of this word in antiquity, see the forthcoming study on pilgrimage by Rutherford.

17. Browning 1983, 49–50.

18. Ibid., 50.

19. Grosdidier de Matons 1977, 39. More generally, see also Trypanis in Maas and Trypanis 1963, xi–xv.

20. Wellesz 1961, chap. 7.

21. Grosdidier de Matons 1964, 1:20–24.

22. Trypanis in Maas and Trypanis (1963, xvi) suggests that he may have acted as one of the presbyters who read the lesson in Greek and translated it into Syriac for the benefit of the congregation.

23. Liturgical texts from Delehaye are cited in full by Grosdidier de Matons (1977, 161–62).

24. Ὅλος τούτου ὑπῆρχεν ἔμψυχος βίβλος ⟨ὁ βίος⟩ / καὶ πᾶσιν πρὸ τοῦ γνωσθῆναι τῷ κυρίῳ πεφανέρωτο. / Γένος μὲν ἐξ Ἑβραίων, τὸν νοῦν δὲ εἶχεν ἑδραῖον· / οὐ γέγονεν Φαρισαῖος, ἀλλὰ σκεῦος δοκιμώτατον. Text cited from Grosdidier de Matons (1977, 169), who dates the verses to the mid–ninth century on the basis of their attribution to the monk Theophanes of the Lavra monastery.

25. Maas and Trypanis 1963, xix–xx; Grosdidier de Matons 1977, 179–89.

26. From "On Pentecost": τί φυσῶσιν καὶ βομβέουσιν οἱ Ἕλληνες / τί φαντάζονται πρὸς Ἄρατον τὸν τρισκατάρατον; τί πλανῶνται πρὸς Πλάτωνα; / τί Δημοσθένην στέργουσι τὸν ἀσθενῆ; / τί μὴ νοοῦσιν Ὅμηρον ὄνειρον ἀργόν; / τί Πυθαγόραν θρυλλοῦσιν τὸν δικαίως φιμωθέντα. For discussion of this passage and for Romanos' treatment of heresies, see Maas and Trypanis 1963, xxii–xxiii, and Grosdidier de Matons 1977, 184–85. Some six centuries later, Theodore Prodromos invokes a similar "litany of names" (Plato, Aristotle, Pythagoras, Euclid, Antisthenes, Kleanthes), this time in praise of Plato; see Theodoros Prodromos, Λόγος εἰς τὸν πορφυρογέννητον κυρὸν Ἰσαάκιον τὸν Κομνηνόν, ed. Kurtz 1907, 114.91–115.127.

27. 1910, 285–306.

28. Maguire 1981, 55–83.

29. Browning 1978a, 111–12.

30. Grosdidier de Matons 1977, 303–19. On the language of the liturgy and its affinities with that of ancient mystical traditions, see Antoniades 1939, pt. 2: "Vocabulaire, style, rythme."

31. Grosdidier de Matons 1977, 181. His position is refuted in a well-documented article by Petersen (1985) proving Romanos' familiarity with his native Syriac hymn forms and with Ephrem in particular. On "semitisms," see Mitsakis 1967.

32. Pitra 1876, vol. 1; Christ in Christ and Paranikas 1871; Wellesz 1961.

33. Norden 1923, 1898.

34. Nilsson (1945, 63–69) notes the ritual prominence of lamps and torches.

35. Text of "Hymn to Christ" in Cantarella 1948: 1, 36.

36. Ibid., 3–7. Greek use of acrostic is found in "Hymn to Dionysos," *Anthologia Palatina* 9.524. Compare examples in Dieterich 1901, 77; Norden 1923, A.1.

37. Texts in Cantarella 1948:1, 14–15, lines 34–35; Wellesz 1957; Grosdidier de Matons 1965: 2,14–41.

38. Grosdidier de Matons (1977, 4–5) considers it unlikely that any of these early hymns in classicizing meters was intended for liturgical performance.

39. Aubry 1903, pt. 2, "L' ancienne tradition rhythmique"; Antoniades 1939. Werner (1947, 408–70) criticizes one-sided approaches and emphasizes interactions between AG and Near Eastern music in rendition, melodic tradition and structure, and philosophical and theological attitudes, especially in the Hellenistic period. Hoeg (1955–57, 383–412) traces the development of liturgical music up to the seventh century, accepting Syriac and Jewish influence.

40. Norden 1898: 1, 16–23. Some illustrative examples: Herakleitos frags. 20, 21, 66: ἁπτόμενον μέτρα καὶ ἀποσβεννύμενον μέτρα (20). πυρός τροπαὶ πρῶτον θάλασσα, θαλάσσης δὲ τὸ μὲν ἥμισυ γῆ, τὸ δὲ ἥμισυ πρηστήρ (21). τοῦ δὲ βίου οὔνομα βίος, ἔργον δὲ θάνατος (66). Empedokles frag. 63: δοίη δὲ θνητῶν γένεσις, δοίη δ᾽ ἀπόλειψις. On rhythm in prose, see Arist. *Rhet* 3.8, 1408b30: ῥυθμὸν δεῖ ἔχειν τοῦ λόγου, μέτρον δὲ μή· ποίημα γὰρ ἔσται.

41. Norden 1898, 379ff. Melito's *Homily on the Passion* is a particularly interesting composition in that while it displays all the features of "antithetical style," there is no agreement among scholars as to whether a Syriac orginal underlies the extant Greek text. Wellesz (1943, 41–52) argues in favor; against, Grosdidier de Matons (1977, 16) states that there is no evidence. But the very possibility surely suggests continued interaction between the two languages at the time.

42. Herakleitos frag. 66 (cited in note 40, above), and the famous extract from the liturgy for Easter Sunday: Χριστὸς ἀνέστη ἐκ νεκρῶν, θανάτῳ θάνατον πατήσας καὶ τοῖς ἐν τοῖς μνήμασι ζωὴν χαρισάμενος.

43. Cohen 1950, xiii–xiv. Norden (1898), (1898: 2, 813–24 app. 1) distinguishes what he calls the Semitic *Gedankenparallelismus* (thought parallelism) from Greek *Satzparallelismus* (formal parallelism); but the distinction has more to do with genre and context than with linguistic origins.

44. Other Syriac terms relevant to the kontakion are *ma'mitha* "refrain", *bayta* "house; strophe" (Gk. *oikos*), and *qala* "melody" (Gk. *heirmos*). On Syriac literature, Duval (1903) remains a classic. Forms and meters of Syriac religious verse and their interrelatedness to Greek are discussed in Wellesz 1961 and Brock 1986, 61–129.

45. For a general introduction to Ephrem, with fine translations of the best hymns, see Brock 1975. On "Greek Ephrem," or texts attributed to Ephrem but extant in Greek and languages other than Syriac, see Grosdidier de Matons 1977, 19–24. For Syriac memre, attributed to Ephrem and continuing through the eighth century, see Brock 1986 and 1989, 93–113.

46. For parallels in Byzantine art, see Maguire 1981, plates 51–68.

47. For precedents on Joseph's doubts about the virgin birth, referred to in the first hymn on the Nativity, see Proklos' hymn, cited by Grosdidier de Matons 1977, 18–24.

48. For Romanos, *Mary at the Cross* and *On Abraham and Isaak*, see Alexiou 1974, 63–65, 60–61, 142–44, 154–55, 162, 168, 190; 1975, 111–40; 1990, 97–123; 1990 c.

49. A precedent for the lamentations of Adam exists in the early kontakion, θρῆνος Ἀδάμ, probably performed on the Sunday τῆς τυροφάγου during Lent; see Grosdidier de Matons 1977, 30–31.

50. On alleged misogyny in Romanos, see Topping 1983, 7–18.

51. Grosdidier de Matons 1967: 4, 366.

52. Ibid., 409 n. 5, citing Pitra's comparison of verse 17 alongside the liturgy of John Chrysostom.

53. There is some evidence that an actual dance took place after the liturgy; see Clement of Alexandria, *Strom.* 7, although Giet considers it unlikely to have been performed inside the church (1953, 131–33).

54. Migne 88, 1861D, cited in Grosdidiers de Matons 1967, 4:387.

55. Anthony Hirst has kindly provided me with references to Ephrem and his commentators which suggest a conflation of Mary, mother of God, with Mary Magdalene in Syriac tradition; see Leloir 1966. Hirst (1994, 23–7, 29) demonstrates the consistency of Romanos' innovations, based on Syriac, in his treatment of the *myrrhophóroi*. Correcting a common misapprehension, he points out that προέφθασαν in stanza 1 is used intransitively, "they got there first," pp. 8–10.

Chapter 3

1. Turner (1968) 1980, 151–53. See also Gignac 1976, 1981; Palmer 1945, 1980.

2. See Anderson 1984, 108, 115, to whom I owe reference to letters of Ilarion and Serenos.

3. Texts cited (without detailed commentary) in Thomson 1966, 46, no. 18, and Moleas 1989, no. 22–23.

4. On incongruity of participle and subject, a phenomenon dating back to the Hellenistic period and especially common in Romanos, see Mitsakis 1967, 158–59, # 306.

5. Text cited in Thomson 1966, 46, no. 19. The use of scribes is discussed by Turner (1980, 130).

6. Text cited in Thomson 1966, 47, no. 20, and Soyter 80, no. 17. Soyter renders ἂν δὲ ἔλθης εἰς Ἀλεξάνδριαν as "wenn du nach Alexandria gehst," whereas I see the particle δὲ as implying "if you really do go to Alexandria [without me]."

7. For parallels, see Soyter 1959, 80.

8. Text cited in Moleas 1989, 23. My translation stays closer to the Greek mood, voice, and tense to render more clearly the shifts from indirect to direct speech.

9. Turner 1980, 130.

10. Example (verbatim, March 1989): Αγαπιτή μας Μαργαρετ. Σε φιλούμε όλοι. Είναι παραπολής ο κερός που πήραμε το γράμασου, και μόλις τώρα κατόρθωσα να σου απαντείσο. Ζηταω χίλια σιγνομην γιαυτήμου την καθιστέρεση. Απο ιγία ίμαστε καλά ολοι και θέλουμε και για σένα το ίδιο . . . Μαργαρίτα σχετικα με καπιο

χόρο που ήχαμε σιζητήση το καλοκέρι όλο και προσπαθούμε για τον καταλιλο και καπως να το μπορούμε ος προς το ικονομικό και σε χόρο που να ειναι καταληλος. Εκεί κοντα στις Αλυκές-και σιγγεκριμένα κοντα στο Αρχέο Θέατρο, που πολιέτε ενας χόρος ειναι πολήμεγαλο. Είναι 9 ½ Στρέμματα και δεν κόβουν καπιο κοματη Μικρότερο . . . Απο ολους εδω έχεις πολα χερετίσματα τα σου στέλουν την Αγαπη τους και σου εύχοντε καλό χειμόνα. Ιδιέτερα σου στέλνει την Αγαπη ημητέρα. Από τον Παύλο το Θαναση και μεν έχεις τη απεριόριστη Αγαπη και σε φιλούμε. Θαπεριμένουμε όταν μπορής δικα σου νέα.

11. Turner (1980, 149–50) cites Egyptian and Greek antecedents for brother-sister marriage, although he notes that the frequency of the form "sister" might indicate a more general term of endearment. Here the possibility that Alis was also Ilarion's wife seems to be precluded by reference to his "lady," Berous, and possibly their son, Apollonaris. πολλαπολλῶν· Liddell and Scott list the form as an adverb of probability; compare πολλάκις, "perchance" (s.v. πολύς, IIIe). However, usage and context suggest "in the end," "at the end of the day."

12. There are several obscurities in this letter. Unlike Ilarion in the previous example, Serenos addresses Isidora as "sister and lady/mistress"; he dispatched her by ship on some mission that turned out badly and is trying to make amends. In addition to orthographic errors, note the aberrant use of the adverbial participle in the genitive absolute, δυναμένου, for which, in general terms, see Mitsakis 1967, 156–61, esp. 160.

13. I cite this letter in its entirety. The more decipherable parts are included in Thomson 1966, 50, no. 25.

14. Newton 1972, 112–13; Andriotis, 1976, 12–13. For other examples in Byzantine Greek, see pages 77–95 below, Browning (1976, 13–14) notes that in papyri there is "no basis for distinguishing what is significant in language from 'merely occasional, or foreigners' Greek,' hence the search for dialect elements in KG has proved so far fruitless."

15. Ekavi has the name "Ekavis Longou" inscribed on the icon she dedicates to Saint Anastasia on the occasion of her daughter's recuperation, only to discover later that the name "Longos" has mysteriously disappeared. Rather than accept Nina's rational explanation that the engraver forgot, Ekavi interprets it as a sign from the saint of her husband's imminent death (Takhtsis [1962] 1974, 77–80). For close allusion to Cavafy's poem "The God Abandons Antony," first pointed out by Holton (Standing Committee on Modern Greek in Universities Conference, Cambridge University, 1985), see Takhtsis 1974, 190–91, 221, 224–25. Reminiscing on the death of her second husband, Antonis, Nina notes how Ekavi seemed to intrude upon her relationship with Antonis, alienating her from him as a kind of third presence, even after death (249), rather in the manner of Cavafy's erotic poems, e.g., "Myris, Alexandria, 340 A.D.," lines 54–70. "Antonis" and "Longos," together with the obsessive but divisive presence of their respective wives, Nina and Ekavi, is part of one of the complex subtexts of this ostensibly readerly, orally flavored novel. The significance of names is further demonstrated by the gentle parody implicit in Nina's reference to Ekavi's father's choice of prestigious ancient names for his numerous—but short-lived and ill-starred—offspring, as if to realize through them the high hopes of the "Great Idea." Like the god's plans in Cavafy's poem "The God Abandons Antony," Nina says οἱ ἐλπίδες τοῦ πατέρα της διαψεύστηκαν, 63–64.

16. Cavafy's enduring interest in fragmented texts as sources for his poetic inspiration is attested by many other poems, notably "Kaisarion" (1917), "Imenos" (1919), and "Mimes of

Herodas" (1892). Lambropoulos (1983, 658–68, esp. 662–66) has exaggerated the "writerly" nature of "In the Month of Athyr," suggesting the impossibility of its oral delivery or interpretation. This is not so; tone of voice, marked by gaps and hesitation, can convey perfectly the poignant contrast between doubt about the person, Lefkios, and the certainty that he was "greatly loved."

17. Maurice, *Strategikon*, ed. Dennis II. 16–17, III. 8–9 provides rich evidence for semantic change in both technical and general vocabulary (e.g., παῖς = "servant," not "child") and for the high frequency of foreign loan words, especially Latin, but also Persian. Kekaumenos testifies more generally to morphological and syntactic development in a style avowedly free of literary pretensions, despite his fondness for biblical citation.

18. Among the more remarkable is a contract from 1081 for the sale of land negotiated between two monasteries on Mt. Athos. The erratic spelling of the pronouns "we" and "you" (ἡμεῖς and ὑμεῖς) testifies equally to the sound change *ü* to *i* and to the ease with which it was accommodated, even in legal documents. Furthermore, as the document moves from defining ownership rights to actual description of the land and its boundary markers, the register shifts from legalistic clichés with little syntactic connection to a much more fluent discourse, with the occasional use of curse formulas to discourage transgressors (Lemerle, Guillou, and Svoronos 1970, 1:233–35, esp. §§42–47. My thanks to A.W. Dunn for first showing me this text.

19. Reiske 1829, 455–508. For text, translation, and commentary, see Haldon 1990. His readings have not superseded the detailed summary by Hendy 1985, 304–7.

20. For the latest documentation on this motif and its parallel use in Eastern and Western court ceremonial, see Hendy 1999.

21. The word κοπή cannot mean "space," rather "cut," or "chafing"; χρεία is attested for "latrine" in Byzantine Greek, but its sense here is surely the more general "use," or "wear." Hendy's rendering of σάγματα τοῦ κουκουμίλιου as "saddles of the chamber-pot type,"and of σιτλολέκανα and γανωτά as "cast" and "tinned" respectively, has the advantage of close familiarity with the material artifacts of imperial ceremonial.

22. On θάλασσα "tunic" and διβιτίσιον "cloak," see Hendy 1999:159–61.

23. Cited in Mackridge 1985, 315.

24. For collection and detailed analysis of acclamations, see Maas 1912, 28–51; for the hymns of the demes, see Lambros 1905, 385–95. The advantage of such texts is that they can be dated with precision; see Magdalino 1993, 240–41 on Theodore Prodromos's historical poems.

25. Maas 1912, 28–51; Politis 1968: 1,187; Baud-Bovy 1973. See now Lauxtermann 1999.

26. The address to the saint, followed by an injunction in the imperative (especially to seek assistance), is the most common formula; see Megas 1956, 34, 45.

27. Cf. examples cited below, pages 89 (Greek) and 90 (English), line 8 (δάμαλιν) and page 398 (ἀλεκτόριν). On the custom of sacrificing animals on feast-days, see Danforth 1989, 73–74.

28. Politis' correction is symptomatic of the philologist's zeal to standardize divergent forms, frequent in medieval Greek, in accordance with modern preconceptions of homogeneity.

29. Again, the correction is unnecessary, since the original form almost certainly reflects received pronunciation. On Byzantine evidence for an unaccented vowel shift of *o* to *u*, see Andriotis 1976, 11, and, more extensively, 1933, 340–52. On the instability of voiced and unvoiced consonants since KG (Egyptian Greek), see Browning 1976, 14–15.

30. Ed. Morgan 1954, 292–97. Cod. Marc. xi. 19 (M) contains a substantial portion of Cretan drama but inserts this poem on a single, smaller leaf, probably interpolated in a later binding of the original codex in the late sixteenth century; the copyist believed it to be some kind of prophecy. Of the two remaining manuscripts, B, entitled "Of Leo the Wise," is from the Brouloi monastery in Crete, occurring alongside other prophecies, also probably included after the completion of most of the codex in 1621 (Bees 1906); K (published in Laourdas 1951), from Cod. Marc. xi.22, was written in 1590 by the Cretan Georgios Klontzas, who ascribes it to the prophet Daniel. All in all, whatever its original textual form, we are clearly dealing with a well-attested Byzantine legend in song. Kazhdan and Sherry (1997, 538–43) cite Slavic versions, based on a Byzantine original, which were possibly composed in Macedonia during the fourteenth century.

31. For historical details, see Ostrogorsky 1968, 284–94.

32. Bakhtin 1986, 60–102. See below, pages 87–94.

33. The reference of καυχοκτόνο cannot be to Theophano, as Morgan (1954) conjectured, because it was Tzimiskes who ascended the throne.

34. For the two manuscripts designated C and V, see Fabre 1905, D198–C451–53, 173, col. 1, lines 7–13, 21–35. Herzfeld's analysis (1972, 57–73) is the most recent to try to make sense of this text in the light of comparative examples, ancient, Byzantine, and modern. Reference to Herzfeld in ensuing discussion and critical apparatus will be to this hitherto unpublished dissertation. For other partial editions, see Tommasini 1901; Krumbacher 1902, Maas 1912, Politis 1911, 645. Baud-Bovy (1946, 23–38) was the first to make a systematic comparison of ancient, medieval, and modern versions of this song, including its melodic structure. Patala's edition of the complete text, based on three manuscripts (1996), appeared only after my own text had gone to press.

35. Contrast extracts from the liturgy, transcribed with consistency in Fabre 1905, 154.

36. For analysis of this song in relation to AG (Aristophanes), see Petropoulos 1994, 5–17.

37. For Neophytos, see Pentekontakephalos biblos, cod. 522, fols. 47.33–34, 48, National Library, Athens (sixteenth century). Reference is owed to the kindness of Catia Galatariotou. For Byzantine parallels, see *Belth.* 129–33: Ὄρη καὶ κάμποι καὶ βουνά, λαγκάδια καὶ νάπαι, / κάμὲ νῦν συνθρηνήσατε τὸν κακομοιρασμένον, / ὁποὺ διὰ μῖσος ἄπειρον καὶ ψόγον οὐκ ὀλίγον / σήμερον τῆς πατρίδος μου καὶ τῆς πολλῆς μου δόξης / χωρίζομαι ὁ δυστυχής. Κ' ἔδε μυστήριον ξένον . . . For formulaic parallels to the second citation from Neophytos, compare the famous "rebels' song" from the island of Crete, possibly dating back to uprisings against Venetian rule, see Morgan 1960, 25–26. It is not fortuitous that this song also evokes the seasons, "clear skies and February" being symbolically identified with freedom: Πότες θὰ κάμη ξαστεργιὰ πότες θὰ φλεβαρίση, / νὰ πάρω τὸ τουφέκι μου, τὴν ὄμορφη πατρόνα, / καὶ ν' ἀνεβῶ στὸν Ὁμαλό, στὴ στράτα τῶ Μουσούρω. On laments for exile, see Chapters 9 and 10.

38. Cod. Veneticus (Zanetti 398), Lambros 1894, 165–166; for corrections (e.g., κύρκας τῆς for κυρ κάτης), see Kyriakidis, 1923, 341–44. L. Politis (1968, 188) makes too many unnecessary corrections. Lambros adds to his text the interesting gloss that F.206 of the same codex contains the scribe's note that he completed his work in just eight months in the year after the fall of Constantinople, January 1454. The months of the girl's separation therefore coincide with the first months of Ottoman rule. For modern Greek songs on the months,

see below, pages 392–94. One might add the popular song, set to music by Mikis Theodor-akis, 'Απρίλη μου, 'Απρίλη μου ξανθέ.

39. The concept of popular culture as "abgesunkenes Kulturgut" was formulated by Naumann; see Lloyd 1967, 53.

Chapter 4

1. Hendy 1970, 31–52; 1985; 1989, no. III. His results have been confirmed and con-solidated with reference to the rural economy by Harvey 1989, and with reference to the reign of Manuel I by Magdalino 1993.

2. Hunger 1968, 59–96; Polyakova 1979; Kazhdan and Franklin 1984; Kazhdan and Epstein 1985. My thanks to Alexander Kazhdan for alerting me to the importance of Polyakova's fine yet extraordinarily wide-ranging study of a single text, Eustathios Makrem-bolites' prose novel, *Hysmine and Hysminias*. Scholars have bandied back and forth the same references to her comparative chronology of Byzantine and Western medieval romance without mentioning her sensitive appreciation of the differences.

3. Magdalino 1993, 332–42, 426–30.

4. Ibid., 355, who cites Wilson 1983, 192–93.

5. For a recidivist viewpoint, see Mango 1980, 233–55.

6. Hunger 1968; Alexiou 1977, 23–44; 1982/83, 29–45; 1986b, 1–40; MacAlister 1987; Beaton 1989; Agapitos 1991. Agapitos and Smith 1992 provide a richly referenced—if daunting—critique of Beaton 1989, while pointing to the urgent need both for new edi-tions of the texts based on contemporary philological principles and for comparative work on Byzantine and "Oriental" narratives.

7. See Kazhdan and Franklin 1984; Kazhdan and Epstein 1985; Macrides and Mag-dalino 1991, 117–56; and Mullet 1990, 258–75.

8. Mango 1980, 251; Tozer 1892, 233–70.

9. Bakhtin 1984, 18–24. See Macrides and Magdalino 1991, 146, for twelfth-century Byzantine anticipations of the "civic humanism" of the Renaissance (as realized in Venice). Antoniades 1951, 1–11, offers a sketch of the *Ptochoprodomika* and their context, with paral-lels cited from medieval England (Chaucer), Italy (Dante, Boccaccio, Pulci), Switzerland, Germany, and France (Villon), culminating with Rabelais' *Gargantua and Pantagruel* (1532). For a rehabilitation of Byzantine humor, see Baldwin 1982, 19–28; 1984, 5–13. Magdalino (1993, 355–57, 395–97) summarizes the "curiously ambivalent qualities of humour and seri-ousness" in Komnenian literature.

10. These questions are raised both in general terms and in relation to specific histori-cal and literary texts by Macrides and Magdalino (1991, 117–56) and by Magdalino (1993).

11. Mango 1980, 241, 254–55.

12. Magdalino in Macrides and Magdalino 1991, 139–56.

13. Van der Valk 1971. His "verbosity" is not always appreciated by modern classicists; see Kazhdan and Franklin 1984, 158, 194–95, Wilson 1983, 198–99. Yet his parallels have proved invaluable to folklorists as a source of information on contemporary popular belief; see Koukoules, 1924, 5–40; 1948–55).

14. Wilson 1983, 191–96.

15. MacAlister (1987, chaps. 9–10) cites new evidence on Makrembolites' and Prodro-

mos' familiarity with Aristotle's lesser-known treatises on animal behavior and dreams, with precise documentation of when, how, and by whom Aristotle's texts were circulated and discussed. On the influence of medical discourse on literary preoccupations with "bodily functions," see Magdalino 1993, 355–57, 395–97.

16. Magdalino 1993, 322–24.

17. *Nicefore Basilace, Progimnasii e Monodie*, ed. Pignani 1983, 169–80, 191–93, 221–24; see esp. 217–21 and 41 for interaction with and possible indebtedness to Makrembolites.

18. Hunger ed. 1968.

19. Cited from Magdalino 1984, 61.

20. This passage is cited and discussed by Kazhdan and Franklin (1984, 111). It is worth providing a fuller context and summary for this remarkable extract, taken from a letter addressed to Alexios Aristenos, orphanotrophos and nomophylax, on the importance of language. Prodromos opens with the usual self-deprecatory topos: how can I dare to address you on such a topic? (Migne 133: 1258D–1259A). He goes on to claim that of all human faculties, language is the chief and most powerful not simply because nature ordained it so but also because it has established itself as the "servant of reason" (ὑπηρέτης λόγου) and messenger of the mind's "movements" (1260 A–B). He gives a brief review of different languages and of differences within the same language (e.g., Greek): just as Morpheus needed the lyre to ride on the dolphin, so the arts are effective only through their instruments.

21. Romano ed. 1974. The English translation by Baldwin (1984) is clear and accurate, although the colloquialisms are sometimes infelicitous. Number references in parentheses in the discussion below are to the chapter headings of the text.

22. Romano 1974, 25–31; Baldwin 1984, 28–37; Tsolakis 1990, 109–17; Beaton 1996.

23. For details, see Alexiou 1982/83, 30–31, 36; Baldwin 1984, 28–37. Hunger's case for Prodromos, based on stylistic and thematic similarities with the *Battle of Cats and Mice* is perhaps the strongest (1968, 61–63).

24. Greek text, first edited by Treu (1892, 361–65), is cited in full by Romano (1974, 42–45) and in English translation by Baldwin (1984, 24–28).

25. Genette 1980, 65–282; Alexiou 1982/83, 31–33 nn. 5–9. My present reservations concern not the rigor of Genette's methodology but the application of such "technical terms" as "intertextuality," "mimesis," and "diegesis" (and all their multiple compounded forms) to a distant culture which had rules of literary execution and performance different from, but no less exacting than, those of modern literary critics; see Magdalino 1993, 354. Genette uses Greek terms for modern concepts; I have tried to respect Byzantine usage.

26. The dubious identification of "Scythians" as either Peçenegs or Seljuk Turks in the late eleventh and early twelfth centuries is discussed by Baldwin (1984, 32) as pointing to the 1090s and 1120s. It could also be read as an ambivalent comment on the dangerously top-heavy concept of the empire and its culture.

27. Baldwin 1984, 13–14, 82 n. 10. The tensions implied in these competing modes of narrative style suggest some, but not all, of the differences between oral and literary discourse analyzed by Ong (1982, 31–116). *Timarion* is a literary composition which was probably performed orally, and it serves as a useful reminder that medieval narrative lies closer to oral discourse than to modern realism in the use of digressions, retrospections, iterative and descriptive parentheses, and interventions.

28. Tozer 1892, 256.

29. Mango 1980, 241; Baldwin 1984, 28–29.

30. Baldwin 1984, 30–34.

31. Tsolakis 1990, 109, 113, 116–17.

32. Polemis 1968, 74–75, 153 n. 5. The identification of Timarion's *dux* with one Andronikos Doukas of Thessaloniki is made by Cheynet and Vannier 1986, 147–49.

33. Magdalino 1993, 332.

34. For details, see commentaries ad loc. in Romano 1974 and Baldwin 1984. On medical references and their relevance to twelfth-century practices, see Kazhdan 1984, 50–51.

35. For analysis of the historical and socioeconomic importance of this passage, see Vryonis 1981, 196–226; Hendy 1985, 55; 1989, 29; and Magdalino 1993, 140, 149, 355.

36. Alexiou 1982/83, 29; Hunger 1978: 2, 152.

37. For references in the text to spectator/spectacle and to use of modalizing locutions, see Alexiou 1982/83, 38–39 n. 21. The verb θεωρῶ and its cognates deserve separate investigation because they connote both presence at a religious ceremony and contemplation of epiphany; see Rutherford forthcoming.

38. Alexiou 1982/83, 45.

39. Magdalino 1992, 197. Magdalino is convincing in his refutation of Cupane's thesis that the figure of Ἔρως Βασιλεύς in Byzantine romance is "inspired by western example" and in his doubts about Beaton's postdating of Makrembolites' novel to the late twelfth or early thirteenth century, based largely on Cupane's hypothesis. The richly documented sources cited throughout show that the figure that "Eros the King" evolved slowly but surely in Byzantine rhetoric and art from the eleventh century and was reinforced in the early years of Manuel's reign. By no means a sudden, Western importation, the figure of Eros as King attracted Byzantine attentions independently of the West, and depictions in Byzantine art and literature are too multiple and complex to be attributed to a single outside model. I am indebted to Henry Maguire for pointing out the following literary and artistic parallels for the motif of loves and graces dancing or running in attendance at ceremonial occasions: the ekphrasis of the jousts of Manuel I (Lambros 1908, 15, line 1); and the Bamberg silk portraying women crowning the emperor on horseback (Bayerisches Landesamt für Denkmalpflege, Munich).

40. See below, Chapter 8: describing how Thymios, the family servant, strapped him round the middle with a broad red sash for the long night ride from the City to his native Vizye, Georgis comments, in almost the same words as those of Timarion: Τοιουτοτρόρως προσηρτημένος πλέον ἀσφαλῶς εἰς αὐτόν, ὡς ἐὰν ἤμην κανὲν ἄψυχον παράρτημα, ἐξ ὅσων φέρουν οἱ χωρικοὶ συνήθως ἐσφιγμένα περὶ τὴν ζώνην των, ἐξηκολούθησα τὸ φανταστικὸν ἐκεῖνο ταξείδιον, τοῦ ὁποίου τὰς ἐντυπώσεις ποτὲ δὲν ἐλησμόνησα (Moullas ed. 1980: 181). It is possible that Vizyenos was acquainted with the *Timarion*, first edited with Latin translation by M. Hase (1813) and republished by the German scholar A. Ellissen (1860).

41. Lambakis 1982.

42. Romano (1974, 141) and Baldwin (1984, 31, 121) consider this reference to Brutus and Cassius a possible allusion to the foul circumstances surrounding the death of John II in 1143, although both judiciously point out that it was also a literary topos.

43. The names are Tozer's apt rendering (1892, 254).

44. I owe this insight to Laurie Hart. On exhumation rites, see Danforth 1982, 48–69.

45. For a convincing identification of the "lisping professor" with Psellos, see Baldwin 1984, 127–29. The identification of the homunculus with Theodore Prodromos is incom-

patible with Kazhdan's careful review of evidence on the life of Prodromos; see Kazhdan and Franklin 1984, 92–101. On Italos, see Clucas 1981, 129 and n. 511.

46. Alexiou ed. 1975; and, from a newly discovered edition of 1509, Panagiotakis 1991. In my analysis of the poem, I draw attention to its literary antecedents (including the *Timarion*) and parallels in folk songs, while leaving open the question of "influence"; see Alexiou 1991, 251–62. David Ricks (*Times Literary Supplement*, 10 January 1992) has taken me to task for assuming an Orthodox background for Bergadis and for the anonymous author of the *Sacrifice of Abraham*. Nowhere do I speculate on the religious beliefs of either poet, about whom very little is known. Reference to "friars" no more makes Bergadis a Catholic than reference to "imams" in a modern work of fiction would make its author a Muslim.

47. Beck 1986, 146–59. I have relied throughout on the text as edited by Hilberg (1876), the only one to contain a critical apparatus.

48. Polyakova 1979, 89–178.

49. Plepelits 1989.

50. Beaton 1989, 84.

51. Plepelits (1989, 75–77) cites forty-three manuscripts, most from the fifteenth and sixteenth centuries, and editions with translations into Latin and other languages, printed in Italy (1550, 1566); France (1559 [reprinted 1582], 1625, 1828); Germany (1573, 1599, 1610, 1663); the Netherlands (1652); and Russia (1965). The first to list the forty-three manuscripts was Palau 1980, 75–113. This number may be compared with the following approximate tally for ancient novels: Achilles Tatius 23 (excluding papyri); Heliodoros 27; Longos 9 or 10. The exception is Xenophon of Ephesos with a single manuscript. I am grateful to Ole Smith and Albert Henrichs for advice on the manuscripts for the Byzantine and ancient novels, respectively.

52. Huet [1670] 1966, 51–52; Krumbacher 1897, 764; Rohde 1960, 560; Perry 1967, 103. For full citations, see Alexiou 1977, 23–24.

53. Gigante 1960, 168–81; Hunger 1968, 59–76.

54. Hunger 1968, 72–76; Kazhdan 1967, 101–17; Tsolakis 1967; Aleksidze 1965, 17; Mazal 1967; Cupane 1974, 1978. Beaton (1989, 70, 72, 220) attempts to refute reference to contemporary events by citing literary precedents dating back to the second century A.D., but there is no reason why one kind of evidence excludes the other.

55. Alexiou 1977. Hägg (1983, 3–80) devotes seven pages to the Byzantine revival, maintaining that in my reevaluation of *Hysmine*, "perhaps the pendulum has swung too far in the positive direction" (75). Cupane has extended her analysis of Western influence on the Byzantine romance to include discussion of *Eros Basileus* and the *Erotokastron* (1986, 1987). Beaton (1989) gives an overview of the Byzantine romance, which, despite stringent criticism by Agapitos and Smith (1992), contains much useful insight and synthesis. MacAlister (1987) provides a full analysis of dreams in the ancient and Byzantine romances.

56. See MacAlister 1987 on the twelfth century; Agapitos and Smith 1992 on the twelfth to fifteenth centuries; and Smith 1991–92, 75–94, on Eros.

57. Granted that my own interpretation of place-names (Eurykomis, Aulikomis, Daphnipolis, Artykomis) as "unreal, but not vague" (1977, 29–33) may not do full justice to the complexities of Makrembolites' naming system, I reject Plepelits's attempt (1989, 23–29) to equate each city with a postulated historical-geographic counterpart as simplistic: if our author wanted to locate Eurykomis as Alexandria, Aulikomis as Constantinople/Thebes,

Artykomis as Ephesos, and Daphnipolis as Antioch, he would have done so. At the same time, I accept his conclusion that the names are intended to be allegorical, not merely fictitious. Albert Henrichs has added the following comments to my analysis: "The novel begins with a description of Eurykomis, a city which celebrates the Diasia and whose religious commitment exceeds even that of Athens. Yet Makrembolites must have known that the Diasia were celebrated in Athens, and in Athens only; according to Lucian, the festival had been discontinued by his time (Deubner 1932, 155–57, esp. 157 n. 9, on Lucian *Ikarom.* 24). I find it hard to believe that an author who explicitly locates an exclusively Athenian festival in a city other than Athens was expecting his audience to find Eurykomis on a real map and to identify it with an actual city, let alone with Alexandria, as Plepelits argues; Alexandria was never 'die Stadt des Zeus,' as he claims (p. 26), but the city of Serapis. The altar of Zeus Xenios at the end of Book 5 again does not suggest Alexandria or any other real city, but it surely fits the particular situation of the narrative" (personal letter, July 1993).

58. The term is borrowed from Winkler 1990 and more especially from his analysis of Longos' *Daphnis and Chloe*, to which Makrembolites was probably more indebted than is usually acknowledged.

59. Migne 114. Hägg (1983, 54–65) surveys interconnections between the ancient novel and the early acts of the apostles and martyrs and between medieval hagiography and the revival of the novel. On the popularity of Byzantine saints' lives, see Browning 1981, 117–27.

60. Among the best examples of temptation dreams are those that beset Saint Antony; see de Montfaucon 1698, 5. For interactions between hagiography and romance in Western medieval tradition, see Clogan 1975. Galatariotou (1989, 95–137) examines the case of Neophytos the Recluse (1134–1215), the Cypriot whose account of his own anachōrēsis from the secular world contains frequent reference to the dangers of "carnal and satanic Eros" (illustrated with lurid stories of people known to him), as opposed to Eros as "godly and saving". She also cites the interpretation of the *Song of Songs* as referring to the Church, bride of Christ, especially strong in the eleventh-century hymns of Symeon the New Theologian and throughout the twelfth century. Makrembolites' use of the *Song of Songs* in his imagery for lovemaking has been pointed out by Polyakova (1979, 89–124), and Plepelits (1989, 29–72) lists striking parallels between Hysmine and the *Hymns* of Symeon the New Theologian. It may be added that Hysminias' case, as herald to Zeus with a strong sense of religious mission (albeit pagan), was not unlike that of Neophytos, even if his response proved different.

61. Mavrogordato ed. 1956, appendix.

62. Galatariotou 1987b, 29–68.

63. Smith (1992, 75–94) argues that the central motif of the Naples version of this fifteenth-century romance is Achilles' disdain for Eros, shared by his girl (κόρη), with fatal consequences for her. Drawing on MacAlister (1987, chap. 9), he concludes that "the nature of Eros in the romances is of primary importance", adducing parallels in *Hysmine* and *Achilleid* (93).

64. For bibliographic references, see Beck 1971, 40–41 (*Barlaam*), 44–45 (*Stephanites*), and 48 (*Syndipas*). Hägg (1983, 164–65) terms *Barlaam* a "hagiographic novel" which does not fit the standard frame.

65. Hägg (1983, 110–18) discusses these texts as Hellenistic heirs to epic under the separate categories of historiography, biography, and fantastic travel tales.

66. For Greek translations from *1001 Nights*, see Beck 1971, 47–48, and Kehayioglou 1988, 156–66. On the influence of Boccaccio on oral traditions, see Stewart 1988.

67. Plepelits 1989, 2–5, 69–73.

68. Cupane 1974, 245–81; 1978, 229–67; Beaton 1989, 77–79.

69. Polyakova 1979, 89–115 (Basilakes), 144–51 (Fablel); Kazhdan and Epstein 1985, 202.

70. Strzygowski (1888, 22–46) considers three cycles from the eleventh century and cites twelfth-century parallels, including a poem by Theodore Prodromos and *Hysmine*; Keil (1889, 94–142) provides text and critical apparatus for verses by Prodromos, by Manuel Philes, and two anonymous poems, which he then compares with the verse romance *Lybistros and Rhodamne* (5.120ff.); and Polyakova (1971, 114–24) analyzes the complete text of the twelfth-century painter's manual, Voltz ed. 1895, 547–58, and comments on its remarkable similarity to the painting of the months described by Makrembolites. My thanks to Alexander Kazhdan for the reference to Polyakova. For an illustrated manuscript of a calendar poem in the vernacular, see Eideneier 1979a, 382–419.

71. Magdalino 1992, 197–204.

72. MacAlister 1987, 356.

73. Alexiou 1977, 26–29; Dunlop 1814, revised by Wilson 1888:1, 77–82.

74. Beaton (1989, 80 n. 13) oddly cites my summary (1977) in support of his threefold division; Plepelits 1989, 66–69.

75. Polyakova (1979, 95–97) and Plepelits (1989, 23–29) interpret place-names as allegorical; see above, note 57.

76. Contrast Makrembolites' use of the myth of Daphne, which mirrors Hysminias' situation but with reversed sex-roles, with Longos' use of the myth of Syrinx in *Daphnis and Chloe* (2.34), interpreted by Winkler (1990, 116) as "deliberately set at odds with Chloe's reality." Ancient myths of maids transformed into trees were creatively elaborated in Byzantine literature: after lengthy praise of the bay tree's divine beauty and comments on the myth of Daphne, Ioannes Geometres (tenth century) tells the sad tale of the maid who turned into an apple tree when rival lovers killed each other in a drunken brawl for her sake: κόρη τις ἦν πάλαι καλή καὶ παρθενική, τοῦ δὲ κάλλους ἐρασταὶ πολλοὶ καὶ ἐρωτικοί, σωφρονοῦσα δὲ καὶ μὴ προδιδοῦσα τὴν ὥραν ἔτι μᾶλλον δυσέρωτας ἐποίει τοὺς ἐραστάς· οἱ δὲ τέως μὲν ἤρως ὡς ἐρασταὶ καὶ ἡμιλλῶντο πρὸς ἀλλήλους, ἔπειτα οἰνωθέντες ἀλλήλους φονεύουσιν ὡς ἀντερασταί, ἐφίσταται ἡ παρθενικὴ καὶ ἐλεεῖ μὲν ἐκείνους, / αἰδεῖται δὲ τοὺς ζῶντας, δακρύει δὲ ἑαυτήν, καὶ γίνεται δι' εὐχῆς φυτόν, καλὸν ὡς καλή, λευκὸν ὡς λευκή, ὡς αἰδουμένη δὲ πορφυροῦν (Littlewood 1972: IV, 17–18). Littlewood notes (p. 70) that this myth is "not attested elsewhere," and is "doubtless an attempt to explain the fruit's erotic symbolism." However, striking parallels with modern Greek folktales suggest to me that Geometres may have drawn some features of his otherwise obscure symbolism from contemporary myth and legend, not just from ancient literature: praising the apple tree's ability to bloom and bear fruit both in the wild (ἐν ἀγρίοις) and under cultivation (ἐν ἡμέροις), he compares rows of wild trees with "good maidens kept close to their chambers" (ὡσπερεὶ κόραι καλαί, θαλαμευομένων). He adds that while other trees, such as the palm, "often trangress the seasons" (τὰς ὥρας πολλάκις παρανομεῖ), the apple "even here observes the law and is chaste" (αὕτη δὲ κἂν τούτοις τηρεῖ τὸν νόμον καὶ σωφρονεῖ), a detail similar to Hysmine's plea to Hysminias not to pluck her "out of season"; see below, pages 123–24. Littlewood notes (p. 67) that the meta-

phor of the tree as a girl in her chamber cannot be traced in earlier texts, but cites from Niketas Eugenianos' novel the simile of closed rosebuds shielding the tree "like a maid in her chamber" (ἐθαλάμευον ὥσπερ παρθένον) (Longos *D.C.* 1.83–85). Parallels between Byzantine erotic imagery and the modern Greek love songs have often been adduced; see Littlewood 1972, 68; 1974, 33–59). But why compare a tree with an "enchambered maiden"? As we shall see in Chapter 7, in modern Greek *paramythia* (tales), one of the most common motifs is that of a maiden who, pursued by an unwanted lover (as in Geometres' tale) or, more frequent, by her father, takes refuge in a tree (bay, myrtle, rose, apple) until, fully ripened, she is discovered by her future husband. On the antiquity of this motif throughout the Mediterranean and Near East, see Merkelbach 1978, 1–16.

77. See 7.9, 9.2, 11.14. Plepelits (1989, 37, 64) nicely cites, as parallels to Eros' injunctions to "leave kinsfolk and follow me" and his union of the pair (to Hysmine: ἔχεις τὸν ἐραστόν; to Hysminias: Ὑσμινία, ἰδοὺ τὴν Ὑσμίνην ἔχεις), Christ's command to Mary to recognize John as her son and to John to recognize Mary as his mother (Γύναι, ἰδὲ ὁ υἱός σου, John 19, 26).

78. ἀρὰ μητρὸς κατεπεγείρει μοι τὸ κλυδώνιον· χεῖρες μητρὸς εἰς οὐρανὸν αἰρόμεναι πρὸς βυθὸν ὠθοῦσιν ἡμᾶς καὶ ὅλους καταποντίζουσιν. Ὦ γλῶσσα μητρὸς ἡμᾶς κατακλύζουσα, ὦ χεῖρες ἐκείνης ὅλας τὰς θαλάσσας ταύτας ταράττουσαι, ὦ ζέσις ψυχῆς ἐκείνης τὰς ἡμετέρας ταύτας παντελῶς καταψύχουσα. . . . Ἀλλ', ὦ μῆτερ, ἐπίσχες τὴν γλῶσσαν, ἵνα καὶ Ποσειδῶν τὸ κλυδώνιον· σύσχες τὰς χεῖρας, ἵνα τῶν κυμάτων ἀπολυθῶμεν ἡμεῖς· φεῖσαι τῶν ἡμετέρων ψυχῶν,

79. Kratisthenes' disappearance coincides with Hysminias' maturation; see Alexiou 1977, 31, and Plepelits 1989, 18–19.

80. Longos *D.C.* 1.13–14; see Winkler 1990, 115–16.

81. See Maehler 1976, 1–20, for introduction, text, and floor mosaics, the last also reproduced in Hägg 1983, 19, 20.

82. Ὑσμινία . . . , φεῖσαι παρθενίας ἐμῆς· μὴ πρὸ τοῦ θέρους ἐκτίλῃς τοὺς στάχυας· μὴ τὸ ῥόδον τρυγήσῃς πρὸ τοῦ προκύψαι τῆς κάλυκος, μὴ τὴν σταφυλὴν ὀμφακίζουσαν, μή πως ἀντὶ νέκταρος ὄξος ἐκθλίψεις ἐξ ὄμφακος. . . . Ἐγώ σοι φύλαξ ἀκοίμητος, ἀπαρεγχείρητος αἱμασιὰ καὶ φραγμὸς ἀνεπίβατος. Note the similarity with Geometres' imagery, above, n. 76.

83. Plepelits 1989, 29–33. I no longer think this evocation is comic, see Alexiou 1977, 37.

84. For close parallels in twelfth-century secular art, see Hunt 1984, 138–57.

85. Littlewood 1979, 103–5; Plepelits 1989, 39–44.

86. See Phaidros' hymn on the all-conquering powers of Eros (Plato *Symp.* 178E–179B), the subject of the second ekphrasis; Pausanias' hymn on πάνδημος Ἀφροδίτη (πονηρὸς δ' ἐστὶν ἐκεῖνος ὁ πάνδημος, ὁ τοῦ σώματος μᾶλλον ἢ τῆς ψυχῆς ἐρῶν, 183D), Hysminias' current state; and Eryximachos' medical perspective on Eros' power to attract and unite opposing forces among gods, humankind, animals, and all nature alike (ὡς μέγας καὶ θαυμαστὸς καὶ ἐπὶ πᾶν ὁ θεὸς τείνει καὶ κατ' ἀνθρώπινα καὶ κατὰ θεῖα πράγματα, 186A–B), a lesson Hysminias has still to learn (cf. 188A–D on the need to observe the seasons of the year).

87. Parallels are noted by Polyakova 1979, 95–115, and by Plepelits 1989, 56–59.

88. Καὶ ἦν ἔρις παρ' ἡμῖν Σωφροσύνης καὶ Ἔρωτος. . . . · ὁ μὲν γὰρ ὡς ἀπὸ γῆς μοι κρατῆρας ἀνῆπτε πυρός, ἡ δ' ὡς ἐξ οὐρανοῦ τὴν κόρην ἐψέκαζεν. . . . Ἀλλ' ὕδωρ Αἰδοῦς Ἔρωτος πῦρ οὐ κατέκλυσεν, ἀλλ' ἤδη στεφανίτης ἐγώ, καὶ Σωφροσύνης

Ἔρως ἐκράτησεν ἄν, εἰ μή τις περὶ τὴν πύλην γενόμενος ... τὴν Ὑσμίνην ἐζήτει. ...
οὕτω γὰρ δοκεῖ Σωφροσύνη καὶ δαίμοσιν πρὸς τῷ φρέατι γέγονε (4.23).

89. On August in the Orthodox calendar, see Hart 1992, 42. On his representation on the frieze as a baptismal figure, see Plepelits 1989, 50–51.

90. Plepelits (1989, 60–61) points to Christian features; yet, if so, they are integrated with depictions in art of Eros riding naked on a sea horse (information owed to Henry Maguire, with special reference to the Walters Art Gallery, Baltimore, Bal. 71.298).

91. Magdalino 1992, 199.

92. Plato *Symp.* 189C–193D. Aristophanes' praise of Eros is hardly meant to be taken seriously, either by Sokrates or by Plato; yet it resonates well with Eros' designs on our homonymous lovers. When one half of the originally separated pair meets the other, it cannot bear to be apart: ὅταν μὲν οὖν καὶ αὐτῷ ἐκείνῳ ἐντύχῃ τῷ αὑτοῦ ἡμίσει καὶ ὁ παιδεραστῆς καὶ ἄλλος πᾶς, τότε καὶ θαυμαστὰ ἐκπλήττονται φιλίᾳ τε καὶ οἰκειότητι καὶ ἔρωτι, οὐκ ἐθέλοντες ... χωρίζεσθαι ἀλλήλων οὐδὲ σμικρὸν χρόνον. Aristophanes then adds an irresistibly funny touch: if we humans annoy God further, he may divide us yet again, making us look like flatfish, or tomb carvings!

93. On history, see Hendy 1985, 514, 588–90; 1989, 23–24; 1999; Harvey 1989, 167, 169, 171–75. On language, see Koukoules 1915, 309–32; 1948–55, 1955, (Indices) 160–64.

94. On food, see Mango 1980, 83, 251; on humor, see Speck 1984, 302–3.

95. Kazhdan and Epstein 1985, 84; cf. Grosdidier de Matons 1976, 4–6, and Beaton 1987, 1–28.

96. Hendy 1985, 588–90; 1989, 23–24; Alexiou 1986b, 25–31.

97. Beaton 1987; Herzfeld 1985b, 1–22.

98. On Rabelais, see Bakhtin 1984, 59–144.

99. Herzfeld 1985b, 22–23.

100. Information thanks to Michael Hendy. There is no need to assume that the dedication dictates a date of composition in the early years of John's reign; it may have been intended as a discreet reminder that emperors, like clients, can pass in and out of favor.

101. The reference is probably to an earlier vernacular poem, acknowledged to have been addressed by Theodore Prodromos to Manuel (Majuri 1919, 397–407).

102. The rank of *sebastokrator*, directly below the emperor, was introduced by Alexios I to accommodate his elder brother Isaak, and to demote the rank of kaisar, held by his brother-in-law, Nikephoros. The sebastokrator was usually related by kinship to the emperor, and there were no more than three. One of John II's four sons is probably indicated here. Information thanks to Michael Hendy.

103. See Gavrilovic 1986, 195–202.

104. "Verses of the grammatikos, kyros Theodoros Prodromos the second book against abbots" (g); "Of Ptochoprodromos to the emperor lord Manuel Komnenos, the Purple-born" (V); "Other verses of Hilarion the monk, Ptochoprodromos, to the most revered emperor Manuel the Purple-born and Komnenos" (S); "Verses of Hilarion the monk, Ptochopdromos, to the emperor Manuel the Purple-born" (A). All references to manuscripts, poems, and line numberings are as given by Hesseling and Pernot 1910.

105. Manuscripts: G, CSA, g. The dedication is "from the same to the same" (G), 'Ptochoprodromos' (g), "Verses of Theodore Ptochoprodromos to the Emperor, lord Manuel, (CS) the Purple-sprung (A).

106. Kazhdan and Franklin 1984, 93.

107. On Manuel's coinage, see Hendy 1985, 517–19, plate 31. See below, note 120, for parody on the Lord's Prayer.

108. On imperial castoffs as favors, see Hendy 1999, 159 and n. 65. On changing fashions in the eleventh and twelfth centuries, see Kazhdan and Epstein 1985, 74–79.

109. Problems in this passage concern the use of Slavic colloquialisms. On "mandragourai," see Theophrastos 9.9.1 for medicinal uses of the mandrake and Papamichael 1975 for its fertilizing and abortifacient powers.

110. Cf. Theophrastos 9.8.8 on "magic circles" in the collection of the mandrake: περιγράφειν δὲ καὶ τὸν μανδραγόραν εἰς τρεῖς ξίφει, τέμνειν δὲ πρὸ ἑσπέραν βλέποντα, τὸν δ' ἕτερον κύκλῳ περιορχεῖσθαι καὶ λέγειν ὡς πλεῖστα περὶ ἀφροδισίων. On nefarious rites conducted on the seashore, see Theodore Balsamon, Migne 137, 740B–741C, cited from Kazhdan and Epstein 1985, 239–40.

111. For twelfth-century monastic typika, see Gautier 1974, 1–145; 1981, 5–143 (diataxis of Michael Attaliates): the parallels with the Prodromic text (especially in the Pantakrator typikon) are remarkable. For a socioeconomic and cultural overview of monastic typika in the eleventh and twelfth centuries, see Galatariotou 1987a, 77–138; on their potential as a literary genre, see Angold 1993, 46–70.

112. Beaton 1990; Kazhdan and Epstein 1985, 86–90.

113. Browning 1975, 3–23; 1978b, 46–48; Konstantinides 1982, 16, 135–66.

114. See Alexiou 1986b, 30–31 n. 64 (information thanks to Catia Galatariotou); Dyck 1990, 45–52.

115. For Prodromos' historical poems, see Hörandner 1974. On doubts about the "authenticity" of the *Ptochoprodromika*, see Eideneier and Eideneier 1982/83, 119–50.

116. For full references to ancient and Byzantine precedents for Prodromic topoi, see Alexiou 1986b, 6–31.

117. Harvey 1989, 167.

118. Alexiou 1986b, 23–24.

119. *Od.* 13.429–35, 14.48–51, 122–32, 151–57, 435–533, 16.69–94, 17.452–57, 550, 19.96–98, 225, 22.486, 24.226–27.

120. For medieval Latin parallels, see Ziolkowski 1987, 31–34.

121. Hendy 1969, 121 and plates 17 and 18.

122. These are proverbially associated with unclean female parts; see Herzfeld 1985b,145.

123. Hendy 1985, 588–90; 1989, 23–24.

Chapter 5

1. Austin 1975.

2. Herzfeld 1985b, 8–26, 36–45, 76–91, 123–49; 1988; 1991, 41–80.

3. Hirschon 1992, 35–56.

4. Winkler 1990, 71–100.

5. The debate on Austin's speech-act theory has taken place at a theoretical level between Derrida and Searle; see Derrida 1972, 107–60; Searle 1977, 198–208; and Derrida 1977, 162–254. For debate on specifics of the Greek case, see du Boulay 1976, 389–406, and Tannen 1990, 205–7.

6. Nagy 1990b, 31–32.

7. Detienne, 1979, 4–5.

8. See Tambiah 1990. On morphological "building blocks" in the folktale, see Propp 1968.

9. Todorov's distinctions between the categories of the fantastic, the marvelous, and the uncanny are unduly schematic, failing to take account of the ambivalence inherent both in oral genres and in literary genres indebted to oral discourse. He states that the fantastic depends on hesitation "common to character and reader, who must decide whether or not what they perceive derives from "reality" as it exists in the common opinion. At the story's end, the reader makes a decision even if the character does not; he opts for one solution or the other, and thereby emerges from the fantastic. If he decides that the laws of reality remain intact and permit an explanation of the phenomena described, we may say that the work belongs to another genre: the uncanny. If, on the contrary, he decides that new laws of nature must be entertained to account for the phenomena, we enter the genre of the marvelous" (1975, 41). The qualities of Greek and African American fiction, sometimes characterized as magic realism, render the reader unable to decide.

10. Ward 1990, 88; cf. Baumann 1986.

11. In Greek, there is little distinction between discussion and argument: συζήτηση is verbal, μάλωμα (AG ὁμαλώνω = "to level down, strike") may include physical violence, as in the Greek proverb, λόγια κόκκαλα τζακίζουν "words break bones": contrast the English "sticks and stones may break my bones, but words shall never harm me")

12. Politis 1904: 1, nos. 31–32, p. 21, 2, 656–58. For a historical interpretation of such legendary material, see Nicol 1979, 84, 87–88; for an anthropological interpretation, see Herzfeld, 1985b.

13. Politis 1904: nos. 31–32; cf. Nagy 1990b, 269–72, for an ancient parallel to the incident of "frying fish."

14. See Politis 1904: 1, nos. 35–36, p. 23; 2, pp. 678–79. For a reliable guide to the ideology of the "Great Idea," or the recovery of the City and empire, see Llewellyn-Smith 1973, 1–34.

15. Sutton (1988, 187–216) uses historical and oral archives to pin down the community's need to locate its origins in the past. Stewart (1991) does the same for religion, as does Herzfeld (1985b) for everyday cultural activities. Records from Sklithron suggest that major relocations of the village site from coastal areas to surrounding mountainous terrain occurred in the early to mid–nineteenth century.

16. Text in Politis 1904: 1, no. 264, 141–42, II, 842–43.

17. Nagy 1990a, 8–9.

18. Stewart 1991, 8–14.

19. Ibid., 84–91. Cf. Herzfeld 1985b, 37–38, and Sutton 1988, 208.

20. Sources cited in Alexiou 1974, 70–77; 1975, 134–40.

21. Alexiou 1974, 74 (Greek). For the "Cherry Tree Carol," see Child 1965: 2, 54.

22. Lawson 1910, 102.

23. Megas 1970, 136–37, 235. For a comparable story illustrating Cretan poniriá (cunning), see Herzfeld 1985b, 40–41.

24. Politis 1904: 1, nos. 742–44, 748–54, 779; cf. narratives collected by Blum and Blum (1970). On Nereids, see Stewart 1991.

25. Politis 1904, I, nos. 916, 917, 920. On *moira* and *moires*, see Krikos-Davis 1982, 106–34.

26. Text in Megas 1970, 20–21. On metamorphosis, see Fernandez 1986, 3–70.

27. Text in: Alexiou 1955, 81–118.

28. I am indebted to Eleni Ioannidou for this proverb (personal communication, 1962).

29. Sources in Politis 1899–1902. See also Kolitsaras 1964–66; Meraklis 1985; Papadimitriou 1987; Loukatos 1977, 122–29.

30. Eur. *Hek.* 1181 schol, A. *Ag.* 650–51; Politis 1899–1902 (Παροιμίαι), s.v. πῦρ.

31. Alexiou 1974, 116, 228 n. 45.

32. The dialogue between Frosyni and Yiannoulis in Chortatsis' *Panoria* (act 3, scene 3) derives much of its humor from the oblique nature of their exchange by means of double-edged proverbs.

33. Papadimitriou (1987, 157–71) provides examples of lexical and semantic shifts in Greek proverbs from antiquity to the present day. For continuity and change in the *adynaton*, see Tuffin, 1972/73, 79–92.

34. Politis 1909a, 6–10; 1914, 1–140.

35. Kyriakidis [1934]1990a, 169–87.

36. Politis 1914, no. 78A.

37. Saunier 1972, II (A4); cf. Alexiou 1978, 227–29. On Cretan male defiance of death expressed through the consumption of food and strong drink, see Herzfeld 1985b, 126–27.

38. For texts, see Politis 1914, no. 89, and Ioannou 1975, 44–48. Mandel (1983, 173–84) considers the song from the perspective of gender and power. For further discussion and bibliography, see below, pages 184–85, 189–93.

39. On ambiguity as a source of anxiety and power, see Douglas 1966, 94–112. For analysis of Greek ballads, see Alexiou 1983, 73–111, and pages 189–210, below.

40. See, for example, Vizyenos' citations of "The Evil Wife" and other songs in his essay Ἀνὰ τὸν Ἑλικῶνα, Panagiotopoulos ed. 1954, 368–69.

41. Zipes 1979, 23–24; Propp 1984, 70. See below, pages 211–13.

42. The archaeologist and folklorist Adamandios Adamandiou (1900, 290–91) cites one of the best tellers on the island of Tinos as insisting that humorous tales are no less "tasty" than those with magic. See below, page 212 for full citation.

43. Politis, 1904: I, no. 362.

44. For critical appraisals of Perrault and the brothers Grimm, see Bottigheimer 1987 and Tatar 1987, 1992. I have to disagree with Tatar's overliteralist and superficial interpretation of the few Greek tales to which she refers (1992, 68).

45. My friend Elli Nika (d. 1988), who came to Athens from Smyrna as a child in the aftermath of 1922, commented to me circa 1963 on the lines from Seferis' poem Ἄρνηση (μὲ τί πάθος καὶ τί πόθους πήραμε τὴ ζωή μας· λάθος, καὶ ἀλλάξαμε ζωή), familiar to her from Theodorakis' Ἐπιφάνεια: "That's just how we felt. We suffered: τραβή-ξαμε τόσα πολλά, καὶ ποῦ βγήκαμε." Of the poets whose verses have been set to music, mostly in excerpts, only Yiannis Ritsos' 18 *Lianotrágouda* were composed for music (Ritsos and Theodorakis 1973). Seferis was displeased by Theodorakis' renderings of his poems, particularly those from *Mythistórēma* ("Λίγο ἀκόμα"). It is true that the poem may be interpreted as a poignant expression of how nearly we missed achieving our goal (see Elli Nika's comment), whereas Theodorakis' setting transforms the poem into a triumphal affirmation of how nearly we are there. The point is that Theodorakis' setting resonated

well with the popular mood of the mid-sixties, rather than with the mood of past unful-filled that pervades the poetry of Seferis and others of the Generation of the Thirties. Seferis' poem remained open to appropriation and reinterpretation in the context of Greek culture.

46. Veyne 1988. For a broader, anthropological perspective, see Needham 1972.

47. Todorov 1975. His approach has been challenged as "narrowly cognitive" by Gilead 1991, 277–93, esp. 289 n. 1.

48. Stewart 1991, 3–16.

49. For detailed discussion and bibliographic references, see below, pages 235–49, 261.

50. Douglas 1966, 114–39; Hart 1992, 190.

51. Stewart 1991, 164–69.

52. Blum and Blum 1970, 328–34; Herzfeld 1983, 169.

53. On the delights of thieving and lying tales, see Stewart 1991, 110–15.

Chapter 6

1. Child's definition and evaluation of the ballad as genre is summarized by Hart 1906, 804–7: "A distinct species of poetry, preceding art poetry, the product of a homogeneous people, the expression of our common human nature, of the mind and heart of the people, never of the personality of an individual man." Child also regarded the ballad as "founded on what is permanent and universal in man," lamenting that "sources of the British ballads are dried up forever" (Hustvedt 1930, 248) cited from Wells, 1950, 257–60.

2. In this chapter I attempt to bring together diverse threads in Greek song, researched over the past fifteen years. Not included, except by barest reference, is my analysis of the Pontic song "Monoyiannes" and its relation to the myth of Alkestis; see Alexiou 1978, 227–29. On themes of death and marriage, see Alexiou 1983, 73–111. On the interactions between Greek and European folklore, see Alexiou 1984/85, pp. 1–28. My comparison of Greek songs with Scottish ballads, part of an earlier draft of this chapter, has been deferred for a future project; but the following publications may be noted: Purser 1992 and Lyle 1994.

3. Martin Crusius, professor of Greek at the University of Tübingen *circa* 1556, cites the complete text of a Greek song (1554), possibly the first non-Greek to do so since Liut-prand of Cremona in the ninth century. Less than one hundred years later, Georges de la Guilletière (also known as Guillet) promised to publish a collection of Greek songs, claiming that they were worthy of comparison with ancient Greek literature (1676, 14). On European travelers who cite or comment on folk songs, see Politis 1984, 67–83; Spencer 1954, 67–68, 131–32; and 1984, 12, 158.

4. European sources (particularly English and Scottish) are documented, with Scandinavian and other examples, by Wells 1950, 223–74. On interesting differences from the Greek case, see Alexiou 1984/85: contrast, for example, the high prestige of the ballad in Denmark, collected by royal decree since 1591, when Anders Vedel published his *Danske Viser*, recommending them to Queen Sophia in his preface as "historical antiquities" and "documents" which celebrate the feats of early kings. One of the earliest and best manuscripts (Hjertebogen) of Danish folk songs was written by noblewoman Karen Brahe (Ole Smith, personal communication 1993). Cocchiara (1981, 136) cites Hernando de Castillo's

Cancionero general (1511) as one of the earliest Spanish collections of old romances handed down from oral tradition.

5. On early modern Europe, see Burke 1978, 286. On Greek elites and popular culture, see above, Chapter 1.

6. Cocchiara 1981, 44–76.

7. Wilson 1974, 819–35, esp. 822.

8. Cocchiara 1981, 116–50.

9. The Swiss cleric J. C. L. Sismondi began collecting material from the early nineteenth century, while Baron Werner von Haxthausen (1935), whose collection (in collaboration with Wilhelm Müller) was close to publication in Germany as early as 1814, was not published until 1935.

10. Herzfeld 1982, 79–80.

11. Geertz (1975, 240–54) defines postcolonial searches for nationhood along the lines of the "essentialist" model, on the one hand, with its appeal to tradition, culture, national character, even race, and the "epochalist" model, on the other, with its appeal to the general outlines of what is understood as the history and spirit of the contemporary age. Geertz's model fits the Greek case at the turn of the eighteenth and in the nineteenth centuries well enough, especially in his paradigmatic example of language choice (241).

12. Dionysios Solomos, later hailed as "national poet," wrote to Tertsetis in 1833, "I am glad that the folk songs are being taken as a starting point [ξεκίνημα]; but I would wish that those that used the Kleftic language [τὴν κλέφτικη γλῶσσα] to take their essence and not their form"; source cited from Tziovas 1986, 240.

13. Herzfeld 1982, 82; see also pp. 75–96 on the collections of Manoussos (1850) and Zambelios (1852).

14. Wachsmuth 1864; Schmidt 1871; Lawson 1910.

15. Herzfeld (1987) implies that the ethnocentric Greek voices analyzed in his earlier study (1982) were only responding to Eurocentrically mirrored models. On the complexities of European attitudes to Greece in the early nineteenth century, see Jusdanis 1991, 22–41, and, more general, Said 1978, 149–97.

16. Meraklis 1984 retains Politis' taxonomy without question.

17. The case of "national folklore" may be compared with that of the first "national poet" of modern Greece, Dionysios Solomos, whose fragmented variants and remains have been fitted onto the Procrustean bed of nationist literary criticism; see Lambropoulos 1988, 85–99, and Calotychos 1993, 46–100.

18. Alexiou (1983 and 1984/85) situates Greek ballads and folklore in sociocultural contexts, from Greek and European perspectives. Reinsch (1990) emphasizes the contamination of oral tales by literary sources since late antiquity, widely disseminated in the vernacular from the sixteenth century onward. Agapitos (1992) offers an overview of Greek and German philology as they converged with local nationalisms.

19. Tziovas 1986, 228–83.

20. Herzfeld 1983, 167–68, and 1985b, 141–46.

21. Haxthausen 1935 and Meyer 1885, 312, cited by Kyriakides 1990, 288.

22. Kyriakids (1990, 168–207) emphasizes late antiquity, Hellenistic and Greco-Roman, rather than the classical age, as the distant "beginnings" of modern Greek folklore; his study is richly documented with reference to ancient texts and sources. For recent analysis of the

ancient *parakatalogē* (melodramatic recitative) and its relation to the tetrameter, see Nagy 1990b, 27–28, 46.

23. On Vizyenos, see below, Chapter 8. For his essay, see Ἑστία (March, 1893), reproduced in part by Panagiotopoulos 1954, 323–61. Further references are included in Alexiou 1993, 263–86.

24. Bold 1979, 1–10, cites respectively Gerould 1932, 3 and Entwistle 1939.

25. On ballad themes in Scots "waulking songs," see Bourke 1988, 1–17; 1991/92, 2, 28–31; and personal communication (1993); and Kerrigan 1980, 1–17. On the transformation of Scottish ballads in Irish song, see Shields 1991, 40–59 (with Irish and French examples).

26. For printed collections with musical notation, see Baud-Bovy 1935 and Spyridakis and Peristeris 1968. For authenticated long-play disks, now available on CDs, see Karas and Vouras 1977–88 and Dragoumis 1990.

27. For a critique of Beaton's analysis of "Mikrokostandinos," see Danforth 1989, 114 n. 20. For questions on Beaton's definition of the oral-formulaic theory, see Sifakis 1988, 145–46.

28. In Peter Loizos' documentary film on the aftermath of 1974 on Cyprus (1985), Maria sings laments for her lost village (while baking for the family business) with such intensity that her memories of the past assert their constant presence. On women from Crete and Nisyros who practice laments while sharing household labor, see Caraveli 1986, 169–71, and Herzfeld 1991.

29. On breathing pauses in the laments, see Seremetakis 1990, 481–511, and Holst-Warhaft, 1992, 70–71.

30. Spyridakis and Peristeris 1968: λς‑ν, 425–40 (English summary by Mary Vouras).

31. Song text made available to me from his own folklore archives by B. A. Rotas in 1961; cf. Megas 1971. My thanks to Katharine Thomson for the musical transcription.

32. See tapes 1–94 (1955) in the James A. Notopoulos Collection, Harvard University.

33. See Gerould 1932; Wells 1950, 41–76; Buchan 1972, 28–61.

34. For a compilation of variants and a review of studies, see Megas 1971. *Laog.* 18 1959, 521–32, includes a number of unusual Greek examples. For a comparative study of pan-Balkan versions, see Vargyas 1967. On gender dialectics in the Greek versions, see Mandel 1983, 173–83.

35. Compare the "table song" in my archives, sung to a doleful tune (1963, cited in Alexiou 1974, 127–28, with opening line Χαρῆτε υἱοί), with Zambelios 1859, 48–49, and Politis 1914, no. 223.

36. For texts and on differing views of ethnic origins, see Vargyas 1967, 173–233, and Megas 1971, 25–212.

37. On this widely diffused song, see Politis 1885, 193–261; Krikos 1975, 23–30; Saunier 1979; Alexiou 1983; Dronke 1976.

38. Kriaris 1920, p. 221–24B, line 70; Pasayanis 1928, 60, lines 77–81; 163, lines 84–88.

39. On ancient myth, see Detienne 1977, 1979, and Burkert 1979. Links between mythical themes in ancient and postclassical texts, such as the personification of death, sacrifice, and the descent to the Underworld, are analyzed by Alexiou, with reference to other Near Eastern and Western traditions (1978, 1990c, 1991).

40. Politis 1888; cf. the Cappadocian version cited by Saunier, 1972: i, 119–52; ii, 335–70.

41. Alexiou and Dronke 1971, 846–51; Saunier 1968, 97.

42. Sultan 1991; Holst-Warhaft 1992, 21, 38.

43. Dronke 1976, 1–40.

44. Galatariotou (1987b, 29–68) analyzes the structural opposition between οἶκος (house) and τένδα (tent), which she shows to be interwoven with the hero's demise.

45. See Schmidt 1877, no. 10, where the Nereid queen undoes the spell she has cast; for parallels in Gypsy tales, compare Tong 1989, 25–29.

46. Schmidt 1877, 115–17. Child (1965: 1,338 n.) aptly cites Schmidt's comment that the Nereid's silence "even seems to explain Sophocles calling the nuptials of Peleus and Thetis 'speechless' ἀφθόγγους γάμους." We are once more reminded of the Gypsy tale "Vana," in which Niglo loses his beloved Vana at the point when he follows the advice of a human "expert" in supernatural affairs (Tong 1989, 22–25). Roasting a child in the oven is a theme central to the "Homeric Hymn to Demeter", where, in contrast to the Cretan tale, it is the (mortal) Metaneira's intervention to save her son from (immortal) Demeter's nightly roastings that affirms his mortality. Seizing and cooking—and eating—are dangerous practices when the boundaries of mortal and immortal worlds are transgressed; and the immortals always win!

47. On south Slavic ballads, see Lord 1995, 167–86. The Slavic ballads cited have more in common with the Greek examples I have analyzed above than with their Scots English counterparts, especially as regards the treatment of themes such as love and death.

Chapter 7

1. Propp (1968, 23) analyzed tales in terms of the binary oppositions hero/villain, seeker/victim, and good/evil and declared that "all fairy tales are of one type in regard to their structure." In subsequent studies these dichotomies have been accepted with modifications, but without challenge to their universal validity. Zipes (1987, 4–11) provides a summary of feminist critiques of fairy tales, in particular those of Lieberman (1972), Dworkin (1972), Gilbert and Gubar (1979, 37–44), and Moore (1975). Their consensus is that fairy tales spread antihumanist stereotypes: females are poor girls or beautiful princesses to be rewarded for passivity, obedience, and submission; stepmothers are evil; the best woman is the housewife; beauty is the highest value for women; men should be aggressive and shrewd; money and property are the highest goals; magic and miracles are means of solving social ills; tales are "racist." Zipes validates feminist rewritings as attempts to replace "the atavistic forms and ideas found in traditional tales" with the "non-sexist social conditions and the different options presented in the feminist fairy tales which are still seeking to prove their humanitarian value" (1987, 33). Whereas here and elsewhere (1979, 160–82) Zipes highlights the flaws in Freudian and Jungian approaches to tales, he fails to challenge the overliteralist interpretations and premises of feminist critics, who rely heavily on the Western literary canon, rather than on traditional tales, including those of non-Western cultures. Female protagonists in the Greek tales do not conform to the stereotyped straitjackets listed above. Alleged racist elements in the tales need closer analysis; see p. 215 below.

2. On openness in traditional tales and teller-audience interaction and debate, see Benjamin 1968, 86–92, and Ward 1990. These qualities are illustrated by Zora Neale Hurston's presentation of Southern black storytelling traditions in *Mules and Men* (1990a [1935]).

3. Tong 1989, 14. Taxonomy of tales into discrete types may accord with the folklorist's desire to treat tales as texts, but it is at variance with performative functions and contexts.

4. Tong 1989, 35. In AG, the verb παραμυθέομαι means "encourage, reassure, console", cf. παραμύθημα, - μυθία "consolation." For the first recorded instance of παραμύθι as "tale", "lie", see Du Cange; Stephanus, s.v.

5. Boccaccio's *Decameron* (mid–fourteenth century) is among the earlier and fuller literary compilations of oral tales, at least in Europe. Thereafter widely translated and circulated, the tales nevertheless reentered the oral traditions of other peoples; see below, n.14. Perrault's *Contes de ma mère Loye* (1697) was diffused and reworked in aristocratic and other circles throughout the eighteenth century; see Zipes 1979, 23. The brothers Grimm, who compiled and revised their collection of German tales between 1812 and 1832, commence a new phase in the process of canonization: recorded from a variety of sources, and very few from performers in context, their tales reflect continual revisions, which pandered—consciously or unconsciously—to the demands of the European market, with its literary taste for tales "educative for children." For recent critiques of the Grimms' sources and editorial practices, see Bottigheimer 1987 and Tatar 1987, 1992. Zipes (1979, 20–40) emphasizes the difference between "folk tale" (oral) and "fairy tale" (literary) that began in Europe with Perrault and culminated with the Grimm brothers, drawing attention to the commercialized, mass-mediated versions of fairy tales handed down to us from the later nineteenth century. Hans Christian Andersen, whose tales were published between 1836 and 1872, provides yet another example of how tales can be absorbed into literarure. See Andersen 1946 for complete English edition.

6. Thompson 1955–58.

7. Lévi-Strauss in Propp 1984, 167–88. For a more recent critique of Propp's selectivity of tales and partial interpretations, see Bremond and Verrier 1982, 61–78.

8. For Freud's theories on joke, myth, and dream, see [1905] 1960; [1913; 1939] Dickson ed. 1986: esp. 132–58, 308–36; and [1900] 1955. For the application of Freudian theories to tales, see Bettelheim 1976 and Dundes 1978. For critiques, see Zipes 1979, 160–69, and Tatar 1987, 53–57.

9. Jung's theses, as developed in his diverse tracts, are applied by Estés (1993) but criticized as reductive and universalist by Goodison (1991, 19–24).

10. Marks and Courtivron 1981, 90–98, 137–41. See also Cixous 1981, 41–55.

11. Gilligan 1982, 22–23 (Demeter and Persephone); 1989 (Oedipus and Psyche). Gordon (1993, 253–65) provides an excellent model for feminist psychoanalytic interpretation of tales.

12. The Jew, Moor, or baldchin of Greek tales is no more "racist" than other such local stereotypes defining "self" as opposed to "other." Stereotypes become racist only when projected onto a national scale and manipulated by politicians.

13. I have borrowed the terms "zooming" and "distancing" from Christiane Sourvinou-Inwood's analysis of ancient Greek myths (Jackson Lectures, Harvard University, April 1994).

14. The Irish tales, not mentioned by Zipes, deserve separate consideration: there were few cities and hence no oppressed industrial class, while the rural inhabitants of the west spoke mainly Irish. Nevertheless, their tales bear striking similarities to the Greek in their reference to the "other world." See O'Sullivan 1966, nos. 26–38.

15. On the prioritization of narrative and heroic songs, see above, Chapter 6. Zuccarini was the first to include three Greek tales in the periodical *Ausland* (1832), followed by a few

more in Evlambios (1843). The earliest collection to be published was von Hahn's (1864), with 114 Greek and 12 Albanian tales, rendered into German translation only, itself heavily tinged with the German of the Brothers Grimm; see Olsen 1990, 79–93. The Danish linguist and mythologist Jean Pio, who had worked with von Hahn in Greece, published the Greek text of 47 of von Hahn's tales, transcribed from manuscripts where possible with the help of D. Mavrophydes, giving careful linguistic annotations in French (Pio 1879). Schmidt 1877 includes several tales and legends in his collection, many of which came to the notice of F. J. Child. Tales collected by Greek scholars were published in the periodicals Ἑστία, Παρνασσός, Νεοελληνικὰ Ἀνάλεκτα, Κυπριακά, and Δελτίον τῆς Ἱστορικῆς καὶ Ἐθνολογικῆς Ἑταιρείας τῆς Ἑλλάδος.

16. On the inferior quality and mixed nature of Greek tales in comparison with other folklore genres, see Politis' review of Pio (1879) in Ἑστία 9 (1880, 9–12, 22–23, 43–47), reprinted in 1 (1920): 196–210. Politis laments (197): Πόσον πτωχὸν ὅμως καὶ στεῖρον ἐκ τῶν ἐρευνῶν τούτων ἀποδεικνύεται τὸ ἀνθρώπινο πνεῦμα! Ἂν ἐπιτρέπετο ἐκ τῶν παραμυθιῶν νὰ κρίνωμεν, οὐχὶ ἀδίκως θὰ διημφισβητοῦμεν πᾶσαν παραγωγικὴν ἱκανότητα αὐτοῦ.... Ὁ πυρὴν ... εἶναι πάντοτε ὁ αὐτός, καὶ μόνον ἡ ἐξωτερικὴ στίλβωσις ποικίλλει ἑκάστοτε. (1920, 197) He points out that the Greek tales took their present form "relatively late" and that they were heavily influenced from the start by translations from Arabic ("Sinbad," "Halima"); by Indian myths about Alexander the Great; and by Egyptian tales deriving from Aesop. He concludes that although tales owe their "first source" to the "remains" (λείψανα) of ancient myths, they were influenced subsequently by Christian apocrypha and hagiographies (themselves a mixture of Greek and Semitic elements); by European tales brought eastward by the Crusaders; and by translations from Arabic and Persian. Wachsmuth declares that although the Grimm brothers used German tales to illuminate German mythology, the Greek *paramythia* are "the least reliable guides for the delineation of the mythology of a people. . . . Unstable and uncertain, they wander from one people to another, mingling with each other, and the distinction between alien [ὀθνείου] and indigenous [ἰθαγενοῦς] becomes extremely difficult" [1864] 1920, 200–201. While I do not dispute their facts, I take issue with their interpretations – namely, that paramythia are less reliable indicators of Greek tradition than songs or other genres because they are "mixed." The problem arises because in the case of Greek the oral-literary interactions with other peoples since late antiquity can be documented with some precision, whereas in German, "indigenous purity" can simply be assumed. Reinsch (1990, 295–313) provides a critique of Megas' assumption that the paramythia reflect "unbroken oral transmission" since antiquity (n.d. and 1970). All three scholars fail to recognize the importance of oral performance in assimilating to their own traditions themes and images borrowed from literary tales. On the Irish storyteller Peig Sayers and her use of Boccaccio, see Stewart 1988.

17. On the assimilation of literary texts into oral tradition by means of chapbooks, see Dawkins 1950, introduction; Politis 1982 and Veloudis 1974.

18. On survivalism in Greek folklore studies, see Herzfeld 1982, 97–110, and Stewart 1991, 5–8. For evidence of arbitrary treatment of dialect elements and linguistic forms in the tales, see Politis' review of D. Kambouroglou and M. Kambouroglou (1912, 341–43, 750–54).

19. Dawkins 1950, 1953 (English translation, sources, and parallels cited), 1955; Megas n.d.; English translation 1970. More recent anthologies include Ioannou 1987; Kafandaris 1988; and Angelopoulou 1991. Of these, Kafandaris offers the best range of tales, chrono-

logically arranged from 1843 onward. But despite a useful glossary, the scholarly value of his collection is reduced by his tendency to "normalize" the language and above all by the difficulty of tracing his sources. Angelopoulou offers both a well-documented introduction and a detailed commentary on her fifty-two tales.

20. Kliapha 1977. Although her book was not intended as a scholarly text, she includes vital information on tellers' age and place of origin and their comments on how they have varied the traditional tales they inherited. One senses that she has *lived* the tales!

21. Cited in Gillies 1945, xxv, 11.

22. For system of reference to tales, see Key (p. 493). I have not included reference to tale types as given in Stith Thompson's *Motif Index*, because the Greek tales are too fluid and diverse to be classified with certainty.

23. On ritual laughter, see Propp 1984, 124–46.

24. See Stewart 1991, 86–95, 172–83.

25. For focus on the eldest of the three siblings, see Bettelheim's analysis of "The Three Little Pigs" (1976, 44).

26. On "Chinese box" structures in vernacular verse romances, see Agapitos 1991, 124–28, 134–40.

27. This happens in other versions; see Dawkins 1953, 1–6.

28. Gould 1989; cf. Tong 1989, 29–33.

29. Adamandiou 1900, 285–6; on Gourioti, see above, pages 167–71.

30. Telling—or refusing to tell—dreams can have consequences on telling and withholding stories; see Dawkins 1953, 346–54.

31. For other examples, see Politis 1904: 1, no. 264.

32. For the motif of color change associated with warrior status, compare the fate of Rotokritos in Kornaros' *Erotokritos*, books 4–5. The device of "story within story" is, of course, common to tales worldwide. In Greek, its most common functions are to reveal the evildoer, as in this example, and to get the silent partner to speak, as in "The Silent Princess" (Dawkins 1953, 323–31).

33. Riddles and enigmas, proverbs, and nonsense rhymes, apart from being a source of entertainment for teller and audience alike, function on metanarrative levels. Although not always directly related to plot, they communicate an inner or hidden "truth" that gives the tale additional meaning and reverses our expectations. "The Mute Violinist" (Kastellorizo: *Deltion* 1892, 696–707) commences with the following nonsense rhyme: *Tereren peteten / A nanny-goat bore chickens and a hen bore kids, / On the cockerel there grew forty squash plants, / The fig tree grew roses, the rosebush wild figs, / Let's leave off lying and get down to the truth. / Beginning of the story, good evening to you!* The "impossibility" of mixed species is made possible in the course of the tale as the poor fisherman's son and the rich man's daughter prove worthy, through suffering, of each other's love. The boy, who turns mute as a result of her taunts at their wedding, concludes as he speaks out at last to save her from execution: *A fisherman's son was not unworthy to take a noblewoman in marriage: see, how a fisherman's son can save a noblewoman from death!* Psychoanalysts, from Ludwig Laistner to Bruno Bettelheim, have emphasized the sexual aspect of the "riddling process," see Holbek 1987: 259–322; I prefer to see it also as a profound folk reflection on the complexities of human communication and the creation of meaning. Nor is it fortuitous that muteness and musicality are so frequently linked with indirect and nonrational forms of discourse. In common with other verbal autistics, my son Dimitri is fascinated by riddles and proverbs, while autistics with little ex-

pressive speech will invariably respond better if addressed either through a third party or object (as in "The Silent Princess") or in enigmatic rather than direct language. On riddling in general and on the diffusion and antiquity of the "miller lass" theme in particular, see Child 1965: 1,6–20. A Greek Gypsy version is given in Tong 1989, 35–41 ("The Clever Tailor's Daughter").

34. Cf. the protagonist of "Ill-Fated Princess," who climbs up the highest mountain on the edge of the world to argue with the oldest and meanest of the Moires to get her fate changed; she succeeds, but only after bartering bread for silk and using native cunning. See Megas 1970, 144–48 (English), 2,172–77 (Greek).

35. For another version of this popular tale with a happier outcome, see Megas 1970, 148–52 (English), 1, 199–204 (Greek).

36. Drakaina's pissing powers of turning seven windmills are matched by the powers of her brother Drakos' penis to become a bridge for all to cross. As George Syrimis has noted in an unpublished paper for my graduate seminar (1992) "Of Dragons and Dungeons: Concepts of Good and Evil in the Greek Wondertales," these grotesque creatures are at least "environmentally friendly"! As for "Cinderello," the name suggests conflation with the Grimms' "Achtenputsel"; see Olsen 1990.

37. For other examples of drakoi turned human or humans turned drakoi, see Kafandaris 1988: 1, 426–36.

38. I borrow the phrase from Palmenfelt 1993, 165.

39. Lord 1991, 41–42, 69–71, 76–77; 1995, 34, 200–201.

40. Adamandiou 1900, 291–92.

41. Charos as peddlar figures in ballads with the theme of the returning husband; see Dronke 1976, 1–40. The configuration of death/husband occurs in both genres, but whereas in the ballad the wife finds herself in the arms of Charos by morning, Trimmatos' metamorphoses are more frequent and sinister in the tale.

42. For a Romanian Gypsy example of this theme, see Tong 1989, 152–56.

43. Scavdi 1984, 160, cites birth customs from the villages of Kyriaki and Stiri in Boiotia.

44. On metamorphosis in ancient myth, see Forbes Irving 1990. The numerous and striking parallels in the modern paramythia, which can be related to wider mythical and ritual contexts than can be attempted in the case of ancient Greece, lead me to suspect that the ritual and religious dimensions of metamorphosis cannot be so easily dismissed as Forbes Irving supposes.

45. Stewart 1991, 140–47.

46. Ibid., 147–61, 180–91. On Christ's metamorphoses at Gethsemane, see Alexiou 1974, 73–74.

47. For another example of this principle, see "The Young Man and His Three Friends" (Dawkins 1953, 270–87), in which the protagonist must find brides for the Son of the Sun, the Son of the Moon, and the Son of the Sea through his own initiative and wit before he can gain access to the Fair One of the World in the Wood of the Golden Boughs. With his three friends' aid, he is pieced together after savage mutilation by a rival and restored to his princess; thanks to her magic powers, they lived in a tower on the edge of the earth "in joy and love, and it may be they are still alive today (287)." Three details of metamorphosis in "Yiankos" can be linked with other genres, modern and ancient. Lover as insect: in love songs, the girl may explain to her suspicious mother that the creaking of her bed as she lay

with her lover and the love bites on her nipples were caused by fleas (Petropoulos 1959: 2,42.4). Warrior as lion and sea as cleansing after battle: in Homer *Il.* 10, Odysseus and Diomedes set out "like lions" (ὡς τε λέοντε δύω, 297) at night into the Trojan camp; on their return, they wash their bodies in the sea before bathing in fresh water and offering libations to Athena (αὐτοὺς ἱδρῶ ἀπενίζοντο θαλάσσηι / ἐσβάντες, κνήμας τε ἰδὲ λόφον ἀμφί τε μηρούς, 572–73). I do not, of course, suggest a direct link between these texts but would point out that metamorphosis in the tales constitutes a literal "acting out" of themes and images with different functions in other genres.

48. The Gypsy tale "Phara-un, God of the Gypsies" (United States) illustrates the same world-view "that neither the good nor the bad exists in isolation" (Tong 1989, 76).

49. On regenerative and fertilizing powers of bodily functions and the grotesque, see Bakhtin 1984, 304–436.

50. See Propp 1968, 77, for the same formulation in Russian tales.

51. For citations, see Alexiou 1984/85, 20–23.

52. On the motif in the Ptochoprodromic Poems, see Chapter 4; for parallels in Cypriot songs, see Papadopoullos 1975, 255–62. Since the similarities between Koan tale and Cypriot song are as close as those between Ovid and Prodromos, it is probable that we are dealing with a traditional topos.

53. The ekphrastic passage from "The Little Deer" exquisitely captures the Ovidian qualities, as tailor and king's men watch in wonder as the sleeping apprentice transforms the sea with its waves and fishes into a beautiful dress, then packs it into a hazelnut, all without magical aids: *[The tailor] was still sunk in wonder and did not perceive the [king's] men. . . . They look where the [tailor] was staring, and what do they see? A swelling wave of the sea and fish in it. "Marvellous", they all cried out in astonishment, and the tailor was so much startled that he leaped like a goat. . . . But the king's men, when they saw him jump suddenly, let out a laugh, and the apprentice woke up and stirred from the place where he was lying, and the swelling wave of the sea with its fishes stirred also, and the master perceived that it was his prentice covered with the dress which the king had ordered . . . "Look now at what my prentice has done. He could find nothing to cover himself, and so he took the dress which was here all finished and covered himself with it". "Oh, oh, it is in fact a dress, and we were taking it for a real swollen wave of the sea with the fish in it . . . "*, (Dawkins 1950, 189–90). The passage delays the plot; but there can be no doubt as to the narrator's delight!

54. Stewart's analysis of Naxiot material (1991, 116–61) is fully consistent with my field experience from Sklithron that, even in the 1960s (and to a much greater extent before World War II), tales of metamorphosis were told not just for entertainment but also to help shape the moral cosmology of the villagers. Despite iconographic evidence to the contrary, there is a curious reluctance on the part of some scholars to credit the notion that the Greeks—particularly the ancients—"believed" in metamorphosis, let alone worshipped their gods and saints in nonhuman form. Thus, Forbes Irving prefers to explain transformation myths in terms of "purely mythical logic" and to minimize the ritual/cultic dimensions (1990, 6, 38–57, 195–96). In a comparative analysis of transformation themes in song and tale, Meraklis (1966, 94–112) concludes that what he considers the greater rationalism (ὀρθ-ολογισμός) and sentiment (συναίσθημα) of the songs renders them superior in poetic expression. For both scholars, metamorphosis is acceptable only if poetic rather than literal. Yet such untranslatable expressions as δεντρίζει for a child who is growing up (literally, "he is becoming a tree") lead one to doubt whether there is a meaningful distinction between the

symbolic and the literal in popular linguistic usage. As for the overlap between myth and ritual, the custom of planting a tree in the courtyard of a newly married couple or on the grave of the deceased both signifies and symbolizes the presence of the loved one in marriage and the world beyond; see below pages 399–404.

55. On the uses of *parēgoriá* and *paramythiá* as "funeral feast," see Du Cange s.vv. and Alexiou 1974:31, 71. For comparative evidence of tales traditionally told at wake, see Tong 1989, 35 (Greek and Bohemian Gypsy) and O'Sullivan 1966, xxxvii (Irish). In view of the general paucity of contextual evidence on performance, no *argumentum ex silentio* can be applied to the Greek tales.

56. Diagrams, as in du Boulay (1974, 104) and Stewart (1991, 146, 153, 161) are indicators of moral values in traditions and legends but cannot express the more complex cosmology of the tales.

57. I owe this insight to Hart, whose charts of calendrical cycles and ritual substances (1992, 231, 238) are invaluable to an understanding of the tales.

58. Stewart 1991, 255–59, 286–92.

59. See Morgan 1960, 178–83, for analysis of the romance and bibliographical references to tale. Holton (1975, 101) traces its parallel passage into narrative song. Both examples demonstrate the interdependence between literary and oral texts, particularly in areas which came under Frankish influence.

60. Dawkins 1950, "Little Deer," 181–99; "Yavrouda," 369–93; and "Yiannakis," 486–524.

61. For romance tradition, see Morgan 1960, 137–51.

62. Citations in Alexiou 1984/85, 20–22.

63. Morgan 1960, 178.

64. Alexiou 1974, 200–201.

65. Branscombe, 1991, 25–27; Thomson 1977, 155–68. Prokofiev's "Love for Three Oranges" is another obvious example.

66. Nagy 1990b, 65–68.

67. See Simonsen 1993, 121–41, and Palmenfelt 1993, 143–67. Dramatized versions of tales have unexploited potential for autistic people, as was exemplified in a remarkable performance of "The Twins" by members of Oakfield House Autistic Community at an International Conference on Greek modernism, University of Birmingham, 4–5 July 1995. Autistics are supposed to lack imagination and team spirit, yet no fewer than nine autistic adults (ages 20–40) worked collaboratively with one another, with the director, Sara Clithero, and with three members of the staff, showing exceptional imagination and musical talent. See below, pages 325–28 and Chap. 9, n. 31.

68. I have listened to many tales and songs in the course of my fieldwork in Greece. Few can have been so moving as the stories told by my former husband and in-laws in the form of "true stories." But likewise, few were as "funny" as the strange tale told in exile on the island of Yioura during the "bad years" after World War II by my brother-in-law Thanasis to his fellow prisoners of how his fictive protagonists rolled themselves into balls, hid inside barrels, set out to sea, and found their way to freedom. He wants to write this story himself, so I have not pressed him for details. It is too late now; he died of cancer, August 1999.

Chapter 8

1. Greek prose fiction has been less well received than poetry in Western literary circles, perhaps because criteria for evaluating the novel are tacitly grounded on modern assumptions of literacy, rationality, and realism. As critic and novelist, David Lodge (1984) has emphasized the need to develop as rigorous a critical language for prose as for poetry, particularly with respect to forms and imagery. Bakhtin (1981) argued for a more diachronic understanding of the dialogic dimensions of fiction. The Greek case deserves reassessment, especially in the light of the recent success (among many others from marginalized cultures) of African American and Latin American writers. Tziovas (1989b) sees MG literature as an expression of "residual orality and belated textuality"; Beaton, as essentially "European" (1994, 10–13).

2. Goldmann 1971, 1986; Lukács 1962; Watt 1957. Bakhtin takes the Russian novel as a focal point in his discussion of the novel over a wide linguistic and chronological range but never quite addresses the question of how and where it may be distinctive. Russian fiction, reflecting an ambivalent relationship to Europe, its imperial past, and its Byzantine heritage, offers a paradigm.

3. On brigandage, see Koliopoulos 1988 and Herzfeld 1982, 60–70. On Kolettis, see Dimaras' introduction to Paparrigopoulos 1970, 11–12.

4. Clogg 1979, 70; Skopetea 1988, 51–63, 66–75; Hirschon 1989, 1–35.

5. Vitti 1991, 19.

6. Beaton 1994, 49; Kehayioglou 1988, 156–66; 1989, 65–76.

7. The term is Bakhtin's; see Bocharov 1994, 1009–24.

8. Sachinis 1957; cf. Moullas 1980, κζ–κθ.

9. For discussion of modernism in Pamuk's novel and in Rea Galanaki's Ὁ βίος τοῦ Ἰσμαῆλ Φερὶκ Πασᾶ (1989), see Calotychos 1998.

10. Jusdanis 1991, 113–18.

11. Gilbert and Gubar 1987: 1, 4–5, 149–62.

12. Panagiotopoulos 1955, κα'–κβ'; George Syrimis, personal communication, 1989).

13. Brubaker, 1989a, 23–89; 1989b, 19–32.

14. For a summary of early critical reception of the novella (by Palamas, Politis, and Xenopoulos), see Vitti 1991, 50–54. On Vikelas' use of second-person address, see Kacandes 1990, 225–28.

15. Ong 1982, 54–55.

16. Dimiroulis 1985, 266–93.

17. Kakavoulia 1985, 294–311.

18. Greek citations are given according to the edition by Moullas 1980 (Greek), followed by reference to the reliable and readable translation by Wyatt 1988 (English). Unless otherwise stated, I have given my own renderings of passages quoted at length where variation of linguistic register is crucial to my argument. The finest literary study of Vizyenos is Chryssanthopoulos' Ph.D. thesis (1986), as yet unpublished in full. To my many discussions in the course of my supervision of his dissertation (1979–85) and to his sensitive insights, I owe more than can be acknowledged by the most scrupulous reference. Athanasopoulos (1992) provides biographical information and demonstrates links between poetic and prose compositions, but criticism is marred by simplistic transpositions between life and literature. The commemorative issue "Γ. Βιζυηνός," Διαβάζω 278 (January 1992),

contains interesting contributions (notably by Wyatt). Chryssanthopoulos 1994 is a summation, with new insights, of his Ph.D. thesis, to which my own studies (1993, 263–86; 1995, 289–98, 351–55), and therefore those of my graduate students (Barbeito 1995; Syrimis 1995), remain indebted.

19. The prize was awarded to Georgios Drosinis' novella, Χρυσοῦλα: both Roidis and Politis sat on the adjudicating committee. Drosinis' Τὸ βοτάνι τῆς ἀγάπης (1884) may seem worlds away from Vizyenos, but it remains a memorable piece of Greek fiction, harking back to Longos' *Daphnis and Chloe* for idyllic love scenes and to Diodoros Siculus for bucolic Euboia, as well as to ballad themes such as "Bridesmaid turned bride", "Mother murderess", "Evil mother-in-law". If Greek fiction between 1880 and 1920 seems unduly concerned with rural life, the period coincides precisely with village expansion; see Sutton 1988, 187–216, esp. 203–8.

20. Tziovas 1986, 18–20; Jusdanis 1991, 88–108.

21. Moullas 1980, ν´, νς´–νξ´. For a sensitive analysis of Ἡ λυγερή, see Politi 1981.

22. These passages, the first from an interview with his doctor, N. Vasiliades, Δυὸ ὥρες εἰς τὸ Δρομοκαΐτιον (1905), and the second quoted by Sachinis (1973,13), are cited from Chryssanthopoulos 1986, 251, nn. 2, 4. Athanasopoulos (1992, 120–21) cites these and other extracts from Vasiliades' notes as signs of "megalomanic delirium"; yet their validity is undisputed.

23. On dates, see Moullas 1980, πδ´–πε´; on artistic unity, see Chryssanthopoulos 1994, 16–30.

24. Chryssanthopoulos 1994, 20–21.

25. Ibid., 76–85.

26. Ibid., 80–82; for more extended discussion, see Chryssanthopoulos 1986, 107–11.

27. On psychoanalytic dimensions of characterization in this story, see Chryssanthopoulos 1994, 141–55.

28. Chryssanthopouos notes that, whereas stories 1–5 draw on genres already established in Greek fiction, story 6 blends elements of realism with elements of fantasy to create a new genre (ibid., 22–23). Kalogeras (1995, 85–114) discusses the fascinating case of K. T. Kazantzes (1864–1927), a "Tourkomeritis" from Ioannina who emigrated to America: his five stories first published in Greek (Chicago 1910), are uncannily reminiscent of Vizyenos', especially in the name of Eulalia, or Evlalia, female protagonist of Kazantzes' last story Ἡ στραγγαλισμένη and silent/absent cause of catastrophe in Vizyenos' "Consequences."

29. On communication and cognition, see Sperber and Wilson 1986, 1–15, 108–224.

30. Lévi-Strauss 1963, 1966; Derrida 1976; Bakhtin 1981, 1984.

31. Wyatt 1987, 47–63. Wyatt concludes, "Why did Vizyenos not write more stories? One cannot know, but I suspect that in having told his own story he had nothing more to say" (60). For a different view, which formed the starting point of my own, see Chryssanthopoulos 1980, 64–69; 1986; 1988, 11–22.

32. Details of Vizyenos' mining ventures in Samokavi, Thrace, and of his interest in mines from as early as 1881, are given by Chryssanthopoulos. 1986, 31–32; cf. Athanosopoulos 1992, 53–56. Neither draws parallels with Goethe's mining activities.

33. Chryssanthopoulos 1986, 145; Moullas 1980, 160.

34. Chryssanthopoulos (1986, 142–45) is the first critic to have understood the significance of the purely coincidental and circumstantial nature of the evidence for identifying Klara with the girl in the asylum. As he says, the reader may *infer* the identification, but nei-

ther narrator nor narrative permit its confirmation: Klara's flowing blonde hair and harp against a blue-domed sky are common attributes of angels in heaven.

35. It is probably pure chance that Eulalios is the name of one of Byzantium's most famous—and rarely named—painters; see Maguire 1981, 11–12. But not quite: the irony of her name is surely deliberate (Eulalie was a well-known French prostitute in the eighteenth century). As Wyatt (1992, 41–42) has argued, it was inspired by Heinrich Heine's reference in *Harzreise* (1824) to the eponymous heroine of August von Kotzebue's play *Menschenhass und Reue* (1789), who committed adultery but won forgiveness through repentance and atonement.

36. Chryssanthopoulos 1986, 41, 138–39. A very thin line is drawn between Herr H★★★ and Rudolf Hermann Lotze, the German philosopher and physiologist, one of the founders of psychopathology, who died in 1881. N's comment on him as μακαρίτης τώρα (105) is consistent with the story's chronology.

37. Beaton 1982/83, 115–16; Chryssanthopoulos 1986, 132.

38. On Goethe's probable debt to Alkman, never fully acknowledged either by poet or by critics, and on Vizyenos' rendering of the Greek via German texts, see Wyatt 1993, 97–106.

39. For the Greek tale, see Megas [n.d.], 156–63; for earlier poems which engage in dialogue with Greek folklore and German lyric poetry, see Makrakis 1959, 5–18, and Vizyenos 1954, 70–93. Vizyenos chooses, through Greek folklore, to invert the German appropriation of Greek myth by Goethe and Schiller.

40. See Campbell 1964, 280, on male virginity among the transhumant pastoralists of northern Greece, known as Sarakatsani; see Herzfeld 1983, 163–68, 171.

41. Galatariotou 1989, 95–137.

42. One is tempted to compare the "courtship on ice" between Levin and Kitty in Tolstoy's *Anna Karenina* (1875–77), pt. 1, chap. 9.

43. Cf. aria from Giuseppe Verdi's *La forza del destino*, "O tu che in segno àgli angeli, eternamente pura"; reference thanks to M. F. Herzfeld.

44. Whereas the Greek *strígla* ("witch") may assume beautiful shape, the German Hexe is an old hag on a broomstick; *kallikántzaros* (Greek equivalent of German "dwarf") is ugly and comic rather than evil.

45. Compare the song and tale motif where the protagonist must ride in the company of Death (see Chapters 6, 7).

46. Compare the mythical hero Andronikos, who fought with his father over the question of his identity (Herzfeld 1980, 64–67, 78–80).

47. Shaw 1976–77: 1, 113–14, 127, 187; Lewis 1979, 35–37. My thanks to Cemal Kafadar for confirming that fears of implementation among non-Muslim subjects lasted beyond legal institution.

48. Stewart (1997) selects this as one of the best literary examples to illustrate links both with the oral-literary past and with present and future, informed by psychoanalysis and literary criticism; it is traditional in imagery and formulation, yet modern in its refusal to be prophetic: the grandson finds grandfather alive and well, and the grandfather dies peacefully.

49. O'Sullivan 1953, 82–83; Thomson 1988, 43.

50. Thomson 1988, 43.

51. Lessing 1962, 11. Steiner (1982, 42), echoes his sentiments; cf. Mitchell 1986, 99, 104. My thanks to Evterpe Mitsi for alerting me to different attitudes to word and picture and for

allowing me to read her Ph.D. diss. (1991). Her title inspired my own article on Vizyenos (1993, 263–86).

52. Reference to Goethe, but not to "Erlkönig", is made in Moullas 1980, οδ΄, and also (rather vaguely) to songs of *xenitiá*. More specifically, see Saunier 1983, 36–37, for songs containing the motif of the girl's dream of her lover's riderless horse. For the motif of dirtied clothes, see Saunier 1983, 168–70 (2a–2c). On the wide acclaim for Schubert's renderings of Goethe's poems, see Grove's *Dictionary of Music* (1883).

53. Cited in Thomson 1988, 59–60.

54. Ibid., 60.

55. My working vocabulary on Vizyenos (twenty-three pages) necessitated recourse to dictionaries in ancient, medieval, and modern Greek (including dialect) and in Turkish. See also Kaligas 1995 on his debt to Plotinus.

56. See the manifesto Ἐλεύθερο πνεῦμα by George Theotokas (1929) 1973.

57. Beaton 1994, 10–11; Jusdanis 1991, 88–121.

58. Bien 1972 and 1989a examines Kazantzakis' language and politics. His essay (1989b) contains many fine insights, to which I am indebted.

59. On the language of Takhtsis' novel, see Kazazis 1979, 17–27.

60. For a fuller assessment of Myrivilis, see Alexiou 1989, 363–92, and 1990b, 67–88.

61. See Zora Neale Hurston's novel *Their Eyes Were Watching God* ([1937] 1990b). At a Harvard Colloquium on the chorus in ancient Greek tragedy (1992), Helen Bacon drew parallels between Euripides' use of choral voice (on Eros) in the *Hippolytos* and Toni Morrison's use of the same in *Song of Solomon* (1987, 128–29).

62. Beaton (1994, 329–68) contrasts the practice of contemporary writers against the precepts of theoreticians on the "language question" (296–329). I disagree with his undocumented footnote (354 n. 132) that present-day writers derive their knowledge of folklore primarily from published texts.

Chapter 9

*I cite the epigraph 9 to Part III from the French because Bouveresse was one of the few to understand Wittgenstein's interest in anthropology; see his "Remarques sur le Rameau d'Or de Frazer" (1977, 16).

1. Vassilikos in BBC2 Greek Language Series (1984), as cited by Beaton 1994, 358.

2. The lack of an appropriate word for "ritual" has rendered problematic the Greek translation of my *Ritual Lament in Greek Tradition*, given as Ὁ θρῆνος στὴν ἑλληνικὴ παράδοση· τελετουργία καὶ κείμενα but in diverse forms in the course of the book (trans. P. Roilos and D. Yatromanolakis, Athens: in press).

3. Jakobson and Halle 1956, 69–96: see above, pages 6–7, and n. 15. For an anthropological critique of these boundaries, see Fernandez 1986, 3–5, 48–50. I have nevertheless resisted the suggestion that I use Fernandez's term "tropes" instead of "metaphor" for my overarching category, because it is a neologism based on the less familiar and more general AG τροπαὶ λέξεως or τρόποι ("figures of speech; style").

4. Sullivan 1986, 32; Tambiah 1973, 199–29.

5. Sullivan 1986, 2: field material, based on work among South American Indians, is used to question text-centered approaches of modern academic discourse.

6. Tambiah 1979, 140–41, 165–66.

7. Blum and Blum 1970, 11–21.

8. Tambiah 1973, 199.

9. Propp 1984, 33, emphasis added.

10. Sullivan 1986, 6–8; Birdwhistell 1970; Leach 1972, 108–16.

11. Frazer 1923–27; Wittgenstein 1976.

12. Goffman 1959; Berne 1964.

13. Hirschon 1989, 195.

14. Dubisch 1986, 201.

15. The concept is best illustrated by du Boulay 1982, 218–38.

16. See the lament for exile cited by Danforth (1982, 92) and above, page 295. Note the cosmic reciprocity between the refusal of mountains and plains to wear snow and frost and the young man's inability to return to his homeland, where the washing of his dirty clothes signifies the ties of kinship.

17. See Hirschon 1981; Dubisch 1986, 195–214.

18. This information indicates some of the negative impulsions toward ritual, when disputes over property are bitter and fed by long memories; yet Katina's motives were far from materialistic. On links between enbroideries and memories, see Leontis 1995.

19. References corroborating my own field experiences include: on gift giving, Hirschon 1989 and Kenna 1995, 133–46; on calls and meeting places, Cowan 1990, 64–88; on name days, Veletza 1994, 7–12, and Hirschon 1995.

20. For more general information on the importance of "passing gifts on," see Hyde 1979, 3–24.

21. Hirschon 1989, 21.

22. Moore and Myerhoff 1977, 3–24; see also Goody 1977, 25–36.

23. Williams (1992, 189–93) records the meaning of ritual and language in "my [autistic] world," as opposed to "the world," with extraordinary perspicacity, from the perspective of a partially recovered autistic adult; compare Grandin (1989) for further documentation of the autistic subject's need for ritual. Material provided by both—highly gifted—autistic writers coincides with my own observations of autistic behavior not only in my twin sons but in members of my elder son's resident community for adult autistics (Oakfield House, Birmingham, England): ritual is above all a means of organizing the body in relation to the outside.

24. Bettelheim (1967) places emphasis on psychological trauma, whereas Rutter (1978) and Sacks (1983, 1995) point to neurological damage.

25. Holst-Warhaft (1992, 35–37) documents the lament as a genre which maps the memory by defining former presences as current absences.

26. Happé 1995, 37. If we think of autistics' world in terms of pictures, their reactions are not unreasonable: when asked how he felt about moving house from Oakfield to a small satellite home nearby, Richard commented, "Moving house? You can't move a house!" while my son Dimitri, when told he would have to wash in the sink while they fixed up the bathroom, said, "There's only one problem: I'm too big to go in there!" Most telling, Grandin describes as the starting point in her "emergence" the moment when the local preacher cited the words, "Knock, and He will answer. . . . 'I am the door: by me if any man enter in, he shall be saved'" (John 10:7, 9). From that moment on, Grandin explored her own literal and metaphorical doors and windows until she found a way through

(1989:79–80). See also Sacks 1995, 253–55. My term "thinking in pictures" was formulated in 1990, before it received startling confirmation by Grandin 1995.

27. Williams 1992, 189–93.

28. Happé 1995, 48, citing Hurlburt, Happé and Frith 1994 and Hurlburt 1990. Less clinical, but more compelling, evidence is cited from interviews with autistic Grandin by Sacks 1995, 254–55, 264, 268–69: scenes from her infancy and childhood flashed into her mind, as, many years later, she gained insights into "how animals feel" as they are led to the slaughter (267); cf. 242 on retention of infantile memories.

29. With insight and humanity, Claiborne-Park (1967) documents her autistic daughter's counterstrategies in language games. This book, given to us as parents in 1969 by Dr. G. B. Simon, director of Lea Castle Hospital, as a means of reconciling us to life with what we then thought was only one autistic son, should be read by *all* parents.

30. σὺ δ' ἐν στροφαλίγγι κονίης / κεῖσο μέγας μαγαλωστί, λελασμένος ἱππο-συνάων (Homer *Od.* 24.39–40, *Il.* 16.775–76. For tree imagery in the lament, see Alexiou 1974, 198–201.

31. For these reasons, I reject the view of Baron-Cohen (1995) that autistics are "mind-blind"; rather, they are uncannily able to read too many "minds" at once, with a preference for the animal and vegetal over the human! This "aberration," which is also shared by some persons with a mental disorder, may indeed afford neurological insights into the phenomenon of metamorphosis as encountered in the paramythia (Chapter 7). For powerful use of metamorphosis in literature to convey a severe mental disorder, see Antonia White's Clara in *Beyond the Glass* (1979: 2, 430–39).

32. Vouras 1968.

33. See Isbell in Urton 1985, 285–313, for insightful discussion of synesthesia in myth and metaphor. See also Sullivan 1986, 6–8.

34. Danforth 1979, 141–63, esp. 149, 155–56; 1982, 135.

35. Brock 1986. In the second verse homily, Sarah's final lament, uttered when told Abraham's lying news that their son was indeed sacrificed, goes like this: "May the soul of my only child be accepted, for he hearkened to the words of his mother / I was wishing I was an eagle, or had the speed of a turtle-dove / so that I might go and behold that place where my only child, my beloved, was sacrificed / that I might see the place of his ashes, and see the place of his binding, / and bring back a little of his blood to be comforted by its smell. / I had some of his hair to place somewhere inside my clothes, / and when grief overcame me, I placed it over my eyes. / I had some of his clothes so that I might imagine (him), putting them in front of my eyes, / and when suffering sorrow overcame me I gained relief through gazing upon them. / I wished I could see his pyre and the place where his bones were burnt, / and could bring a little of his ashes and gaze upon them and always be comforted", (125 lines 112–21). Brock also cites (90) the same motif in a Jewish narrative poem of the sixteenth century.

36. On Greek rites, see Alexiou 1974, 27, 42, 45; on Gypsy rites, see Tong 1989, 12. Peter Bien informs me that on the death of his Greek father-in-law in Thrace, all household linen was destroyed. My autistic son Pavlos first washes, then rips when fabric is tensile, his own most intimate garments, and those of his nearest and dearest. The act marks anger, loss, love.

37. Rosaldo 1987, 239–44. For parallels between Illongot *linget* and AG *ménos*, see Padel 1992, 25–26.

38. Hirschon 1989, 240–41.

39. See feature and leading articles in London's Sunday newspaper the *Observer* (1988) and subsequent television documentaries.

40. Each of these terms (θυσία, ἄνθρωπος, δένω) is culturally loaded with ambivalent meanings.

41. On differences between "the ethics of animism," as practiced in medieval and early modern rural societies in Europe, and the concept of Protestant "brotherly love" that gradually replaced it, see Schneider 1990, 29–54. On notions of reciprocity and sin encountered in a Cretan mountain village, see Herzfeld 1985b, 205–58.

42. See Hart 1992, 193–223, and Alexiou 1974, 170–71, on abuse of saints when things do not turn out well.

43. Meraklis 1984, 19 n. 18.

44. On reciprocity, see Schneider 1990.

45. Hertz 1960; Danforth 1982, 35–77.

46. Tambiah 1979, 140–41; Sullivan 1986, 32.

47. Alexiou 1974, 37–51; Hirschon 1989, 208–9. In Myrivilis' novel 'Η Παναγιὰ Γοργόνα (*Mermaid Madonna*), when old Permahoula eventually dies at the age of 110 (by her reckoning), she blesses her favorite Vatis "from her twenty nails" for granting her last request for a long, strong brandy as she "travels over" to the other side (1956, 348–50).

48. Alexiou 1974, 25–26, 38; Hirschon 1989, 210–11.

49. I cannot resist re-citing the case of my former husband's maternal grandfather, who "instructed his relatives not to lament until he was properly dressed and laid out. Soon after, when he appeared to be dead, the women began keening, but with great effort he raised himself and told them to stop" (Alexiou 1974, 38).

50. Alexiou 1974, 5, 7–8, 39–42; cf. du Boulay (1982).

51. Hirschon 1989, 212.

52. Reference thanks to Scavdi 1984, 119–20.

53. Seremetakis 1990.

54. du Boulay 1982, 218–38.

55. Scavdi (1984, 41ff.) alerted me to the ritual-dramatic potential of this extraordinary lament sequence. For subsequent comments informed by fieldwork, see Seremetakis 1991, 129–44.

56. Scavdi 1984, 41.

57. Danforth 1982, plates 1–4.

58. Politis [1872] 1931: 232–35.

59. When Aspasia and Dimitris' second daughter, Maria, insisted on marrying Pavlos against their wishes because he was related by sponsorship, Maria resorted to desperate measures pouring paraffin over herself and setting light to it: she was rescued and married Pavlos, but received minimal dowry. My second son is named after her husband, found dead on the riverbed of the Peneus during the Civil War. On prohibitions of marrying within sponsorship groups, see du Boulay 1974, 1982.

60. Politis (1872) 1931: 232–22, see especially 232–33, 302–3.

61. Ibid., 259–60.

62. Alexiou and Dronke 1971, 850; cf. Politis 1931, 281.

63. Hear the sequences from Epiros and Thrace on disk, Karas and Vouras 1977–88. They are supported by my field recordings from Thessaly and Macedonia (1963–64, 1965).

64. On the disadvantaged position of the young wife in virilocal societies, see du Boulay 1983, 243–70.

65. See Scavdi 1984, 160–61, on ancient parallels for the custom.

66. Douglas 1966; Hirschon 1978, 66–88.

67. Krikos-Davis 1982, 125–26.

68. Stewart 1991, 100–101, 195–97.

69. Hirschon 1978, 81.

70. Du Boulay, cited in Alexiou 1983, 86 n. 36.

71. See, especially, the bridal 'aubade' Τώρα τὰ πουλιά, discussed below in Chapter 10.

72. Alexiou 1974, 31–35, 42–51; cf. Danforth 1982, 48.

73. We are not in the realm of logic: the dead are seemingly believed to be spiritually in Paradise but corporeally in Hades. Therefore a widow's husband comes to her in a dream, demanding a belt to keep his pants up in Hades (he had been buried summarily during the Civil War, after his body had stiffened, so the new clothes had to be draped over him, rather than put on; Danforth 1982, 135). Danforth's citations from the Orthodox liturgy do not contradict Seremetakis' fieldwork from the Mani (1991, 178). Both testify to the conviction that acts performed for dead loved ones, whether or not they involve the church, can make a real difference. As an example of poetic nonlogic, let me re-cite a love song from the Peloponnese: "I will go down to Hades and to Paradise, / to find Charos and say a few words to him" (Alexiou 1974, 50; cf. Petropoulos 1958–59, 42.4).

74. Migne 79, 1493: κατὰ πᾶσαν τὴν ἑβδοματικὴν αὐτοῦ ζωὴν ὀφείλει περιφέρειν ἐν ἑαυτῷ τὴν νέκρωσιν.

75. Basil of Seleucia (Migne 85, 492): "The essence and purpose of the succession of children begotten from us is therefore this: the eternal renewal of the image of the sowers and planters [that is, fathers] in their sons, resurrected in such a way that those long since dead seem to appear again among the living people around us." Athenagoras spells out, (Migne 6, 996): "(Man) begets sons in order to live and endure for as long as possible, through the sons born from him and through the succession of their sons and grandsons, taking comfort (paramythoúmenos) for his own end (teleutēn), and thinking in this way to immortalize what is mortal (to thnēton apathanatízein)."

76. Migne 31, 432.

77. My former husband's second sister wanted to name her younger daughter after a paternal aunt, Theano; but the godparents named her Sophia, because the aunt was believed to be crazy. To this day she calls herself Sophia, but is known as "Nitsa," (diminutive of Theano) to her nearest kin.

78. Parker 1983.

79. Maguire 1981.

80. On inauguration ceremonies as a form of initiation, see Hart 1992, 121–22, 128–30; on the rites and symbolism of baptism, see Stewart 1991, 203–7.

81. Danforth 1982, 48–69.

82. Bergadis (Panagiotakis ed.) 1991. On the poem's relationship to earlier literary tradition and to the folk songs, see Alexiou 1991, 251–62.

83. For parallels, see Tambiah (1979, 126), who cites evidence to suggest that slang and low comedy intrude on learned discourse ("the polite style") by unfavorable comparison of low to high styles. In Javanese popular theater, he notes (n. 2), refined etiquette is opposed to vulgar manners in order to honor the high-ranked persona. Prodromos' games in Poem I on pejorative associations of the high style throughout would seem to invert the process.

84. Henderson 1975; Bancroft-Marcus 1979, 242–54. Eideneier 1987, 101–19, links

hunger in the Ptochoprodromic Poems with Karaghiozis in the modern shadow theater: although he does not succeed in establishing a direct link, he demonstrates admirably the metaphorical interconnections.

Chapter 10

1. Anthropology: Caraveli-Chaves 1980, 129–57; 1986, 169–94; Seremetakis 1991; Herzfeld 1981, 44–57; 1991; Danforth 1982; Hart 1992, 130–45; Panourgia 1994, 261–69; 1995. Ancient Greek: Vermeule 1979; Humphreys 1983; Garland 1985. Literature: Sacks 1985; Holst-Warhaft 1992.

2. Ariès 1981; Burkert 1983; Girard 1977.

3. On dance, see Torp 1990 for ethnomusicological and ethnochoreographic analysis of the ring dance in the Balkan area, and Cowan 1990 for study of performative and social contexts in the northern Greek town of Sohos. For a sensitive study of lament imagery and its interactions with wedding songs, see Coulton 1983.

4. Major collections referred to in this chapter include Fauriel (1824–25); Politis 1914; Saunier 1968; Spyridakis and Peristeris 1968; Baud-Bovy 1935 (Dodekanese); Yiankas n.d. (Epiros); Romaios 1956 (Thrace); Kavakopoulos 1981 (Thrace); and Papadopoullos 1975 (Cyprus). The most comprehensive recordings of songs on disk are in the series (arranged by region) produced by Karas and Vouras (1978–88); see also the annotated and illustrated disks from Aigina and Asia Minor, produced from the Melpo Merlier Archives by M. Dragoumis (Athens: FA 115/116, 1980; ACBA, 1990). I have also availed myself of recordings from the James A. Notopoulos Collection, Harvard University).

5. Studies on questions of gender include Campbell 1964 (Sarakatsani); Peristiany 1965 (Cyprus/Mediterranean); Friedl 1967 (Vasilika); du Boulay 1974 (Evia); Herzfeld 1985b (Crete); Dubisch ed. 1986; and Loizos and Papataxiarchis 1991.

6. Caraveli 1986; Seremetakis 1991; Holst-Warhaft 1992. Herzfeld (1983, 161–72) was among the first to note the difference between the ideal and the real in attitudes to chastity.

7. Petropoulos 1994. I have not had the opportunity to consult the D.Phil. thesis on which the book is partly based (Oxon., 1989), although the author had the kindness to show me early drafts. For a fine study of the rise of the European love lyric and its relation to medieval Latin, see Dronke 1968.

8. Many of these images, reminiscent of the *Epitaphios Thrēnos*, have also been used by literary writers, for example, Yiannis Ritsos in Ἐπιτάφιος (1936, setting sun) and Stratis Myrivilis in Ἡ Παναγιὰ Γοργόνα (1956, 483, broken wings).

9. Kafandaris 1988, 2:9.

10. For comparable examples from Kokkinia and Crete, see Hirschon 1989, 214, and Herzfeld 1993, 241–55.

11. For a version sung by children, cf. Karas and Vouras, *Songs of Thrace* 2, SDNM 122, A6.

12. If I am not mistaken, the word *yarenopoúla* is derived from Turkish *yaren* "friend," cf. *yarenlık*, "friendly talk; joking." Their function is comparable to that of the *vlámisses* in songs from Roumeli and Epiros.

13. Such wordplay is also found in a Cypriot alphabetic love song, itself strongly remi-

niscent in structure and meter of the twelfth-century swallow song discussed in Chapter 3: Γάμμα, γένομαι γιοφύριν / νὰ περνᾶς, χρυσὸν ζαφείριν (Papadopoullos 1975, 263–65).

14. Aside from its association with mourning, a true black dye can be obtained only from the wool of a black sheep, hence all-black kilims are virtually unknown (information thanks to kindness of M. F. Hendy). On color and use of natural dyes, see also Balamoti 1984, 27–44. For green in association with the death of a young girl before marriage, see Danforth 1982, 146: "In the green and golden fields, they stole Eleni."

15. This curious phrase would appear to be a stylized hyperbole to indicate the girl's purity, rather than a literal statement: women are not permitted to enter the church sanctuary, and ordinary mortals are never buried there. The formula appropriately varies the traditional request of the dying Klepht [bandit-hero]: Πάρτε με, σύρτε με, παιδιά, ἐκεῖ ψηλὰ στὴ ράχη (Yiankas n.d. 95).

16. The motif is too common to cite all examples; but cf. Romaios 1956, 29–30; Papadopoullos 1975, 15–23, 28–29; Karas and Vouras SDNM 113, A6 (Kasos).

17. Cf. the knee song from Kos, in Baud-Bovy 1935, 2:120: Νάνι του καὶ παρήγγειλα στὴν Πόλη τὰ καλά του.../ στὴ Βενετιὰ τὰ ροῦχα του καὶ τὰ διαμαντικά του.

18. As Winkler notes of the papyrus spells, "The systematic interlacing of violence and charm . . . is simply the necessary shape given to aspirations of success in that agonistic, masked and duplicitous society" (1990, 78).

19. On priests, see Blum and Blum 1970, 189, 286, 289, 312. For a parallel to Tsipi's version of vacillation between the deaths of the girl and her lover, see Politis 1914, 128A. As I interpret it, the last line in Tsipi's song may mean both "my own hands shall make his winding-sheet" and "may my own hands be his winding-sheet;" cf. hands as oars in the song cited on pages 382–83 below. Such ambivalence is attested throughout ancient Greek erotic tradition by Carson 1986, 9, 83–85.

20. Dronke 1968, 1:11: "Oh that I were the washerman of my beloved / even for only a month. / Then [. . .] to wash out the oil / that remains in her dress" (Cairo Museum, cat. gen. 25218).

21. See Winkler 1990, 82–84, on ancient texts. For a modern Cretan parallel, to the need for secrecy and silence, Herzfeld has provided me with the following mantinada: οὔτε περνῶ καὶ δὲ μιλῶ, να χαίρει ἡ καρδιά σου / τὸ κάμω γιὰ τὴ γειτονιά, μὴν ἔβγει τ' ὄνομά σου (personal communication, 1991). On Sappho, see also Carson 1986, 12–17.

22. Cf. Karas and Vouras 1977–88, SDNM 113, A1 (Peloponnese), rendered without the last four crucial lines.

23. Nick Germanacos, personal communication, 1990.

24. On the protective and fertilizing properties of bracelets and rings, especially of the octagonal "hooped" variety, see Vikan 1990, 145–63, esp. plate 26. For cyclical symbolism in modern Greek culture, see du Boulay 1982, 219–38; and Stewart 1991, 164–69.

25. On hair in mythical songs and tales, see, for example, "Bridge of Hair" (chapter 6), and "Lord of the lower earth" (chapter 7). More generally, see Obeyesekere, 1981.

26. Durham 1924, 297–304.

27. *Laog.* 11 (1934): 255, lines 48–50.

28. Among the many studies on the garden as an erotic space, the following are of especial relevance to the love lyric: Dronke 1968: 2,323ff. (medieval Latin and vernacular literature); Littlewood 1974, 33–59; 1993, 83–103 (Byzantine and modern Greek, apple theme).

29. For a similar example from Thrace, see Kavakopoulos 1981, 63, no. 67.

30. See above (Chapter 4) for references to Byzantine ekphrasis; cf. Dronke 1968: 1, 181–92, for medieval Latin and vernacular examples.

31. Beaton 1980, 121. Bouvier, (1976: 78.6) provides an interesting parallel to angels sitting in the branches of a tree "down there in Jerusalem" in a version of the Virgin's lament.

32. For similar associations of cinnamon with the beloved in Chaucer's "Miller's Tale" and the Burana lyrics, see Dronke 1968, 1:118, 314.

33. Hirschon 1978, 66–88; 1989, 235–38; Herzfeld 1986, 215–33.

34. For the mother-in-law's "coin of silence," placed on the bride's lips on entering her new household, I am indebted to du Boulay, personal communication, cited in Alexiou 1983, 86 n. 36.

35. On the metonomy of wine as blood, see Herzfeld 1985b, 81, 126: "Drinking red wine is a symbol of manhood, since it is thought to produce the blood that creates sons."

36. Douglas 1966, 129.

37. Alexiou 1974, 203–4; Danforth 1982, 115–20.

38. On the eroticism of this motif in ancient tragedy, see Loraux 1987, 31–48.

39. See Fernandez 1986, 89–99, on empowering ambivalence in the performative context of folk poetry.

40. Cf. Herzfeld 1979, 285–301.

41. Alexiou 1974, 195–205; Danforth 1982, 104–20.

42. On the ambivalent status of nuns, see Iossifides 1991, 135–55.

43. Alexiou 1974, 197.

44. The reference in the Kythniot song is probably to the imminent departure of the young men for reaping and threshing; see J. Petropoulos 1994, 32–33 (Thrace). For the song on disk, hear Karas and Vouras 1977–88, SDNM 105, B2. "Thermia" is a local name for Kythnos.

45. A possible exception is the Cypriot narrative "Song of Armenoués" (Papadopoullos 53–54, A16): one Friday evening, young Armenis accosts Milia (her name means "apple tree") with his intention of entering her bower and plucking her apples; she demurs, telling him her carpenter husband is traveling abroad. On Saturday Armenis enjoys her; on Sunday her husband returns; on Monday he summons both wife and lover to appear before a Turkish judge (lines 1–10). On the way, Milia walks σὰν μῆλον μαραμένον (line 12), Armenis σὰν μῆλον ἀθθισμένον (line 14). The judge hears the husband's and Armenis' suits, both couched in terms of tree cultivation: trespassers on others' courtyard apple trees should be "gathered like apple pips," claims the former; no, responds the latter, a passer by is obliged to keep fertile a lush garden whose gardener is absent. Milia is awarded to Armenis.

46. Herzfeld 1983, 161–72.

47. Sultan 1991a and 1991b; cf. Galatariotou 1987b, 29–68.

48. Hirschon 1989, 222, 239.

49. See the videofilm *Agrapha* (Vouras and Antony 1985).

50. Compare the motif of Charos (Death) invoked as companion to her dead husband by a mourning widow in a lament cited at the beginning of Chapter 10.

51. Compare Janie's similarly concrete image of "something [falling] off the shelf inside her . . . her image of Jody tumbled down and shattered," used in the context of falling out of love with her second husband, in Zora Neale Hurston's *Their Eyes Were Watching God* (1990b, 110–13). For analysis of this text and its relevance to metaphor, metonymy, and voice, see Johnson 1987, 155–71.

Chapter 11

1. Among the most striking examples are θυσία (sacrifice); σκότος/σκοτώνω (darkness to kill); θάμπος/θαμπώνω (brightness to dazzle, blur, grow, dim); φέγγος/φεγγάρι (shining light; moon); θεωρία (contemplation; beholding; theory). The poet Cavafy's understanding of these multidimensional properties of Greek is recorded in his conversations with Sareyiannis (1964, 41–43).

2. I owe this example from the everyday speech of Stemnitsa, Arkadia, to Panagiotis Roilos.

3. Padel 1992, 9–10, 33–40.

Key to References for Songs and Tales

Songs are cited by name of editor or journal, sometimes followed by place of origin, e.g. Yiankas 750: Epiros; *Laog.* 19.250: Crete. Where reference is to song number, rather than page number, (no.) follows each item cited in Bibliography, e.g., Politis (no.).

Tales are cited by name of editor or journal and tale number, followed by place and date of origin. Details of earlier or parallel versions may also be given in parentheses, e.g.

Kafandaris 1: Athens 1843 (Evlambios)
Kafandaris 2: Epiros 1850 (von Hahn: German), 1879 (Pio: Greek)

All abbreviated references are listed alphabetically in Bibliography.

Bibliography

About, E.
1854   *La Grèce contemporaine*. Paris. 2d ed., 1872.

Acad. Ath.
1962   Ἀκαδημία Ἀθηνῶν. Δημοτσιεύματα τοῦ Λαογραφικοῦ Ἀρχείου, 7. Ἑλληνικὰ δημοτικὰ τραγούδια (ἐκλογή), τόμος Α´, Athens.

Adamandiou, A.
1900   Τηνιακὰ παραμύθια, Δελτίον τῆς Ἐθνολογικῆς Ἑταιρείας τῆς Ἑλλάδος 5:277–330.

Agapitos, P. A.
1991   *Narrative structure in the Byzantine vernacular romances: A textual and literary study of "Kallimachos," "Belthandros," and "Libistros."* Miscellanea Byzantina Monacensia 34, Munich.

1992   Byzantine literature and Greek philologists in the nineteenth century. *Classica et Medievalia* 43:231–60.

Agapitos, P. A., and O. L. Smith
1992   *The study of medieval Greek romance: A reassessment of recent work.* Copenhagen: Museum Tusculanum.

Aleksidze, A. D.
1965   *Vizantijskij roman xii veka.* Tbilisi.

Alexiou, L.
1955   Ἡ Φυλλάδα τοῦ Γαδάρου, ἤτοι Γαδάρου, λύκου καὶ ἀλουποῦς διήγησις ὡραία. Κρητικὰ Χρονικὰ 9:81–118.

Alexiou, M.
1963, 1965, 1966   Field recordings from northern Greece: personal archives.
1974   *The ritual lament in Greek tradition.* Cambridge: Cambridge University Press.

1975   The lament of the Virgin in Byzantine literature and modern
                Greek folksong. *Byzantine and Modern Greek Studies* 1:111–40.
1977   A critical reappraisal of Eustathios Makrembolites' *Hysmine and
                Hysminias. Byzantine and Modern Greek Studies* 3:23–44.
1978   Modern Greek folklore and its relation to the past: The evolution
                of Charos in Greek tradition. In Vryonis 1978, 221–36.
1982   Diglossia in Greece. In Haas 1982, 156–92.
1982/83   Literary subversion and the aristocracy in twelfth-century Byzan-
                tium: A stylistic analysis of the *Timarion. Byzantine and Modern
                Greek Studies* 8:29–45.
1983   Sons, wives, and mothers: Reality and fantasy in some modern
                Greek ballads. *Journal of Modern Greek Studies* 1:73–111.
1984/85   Folklore: An obituary? *Byzantine and Modern Greek Studies*
                9:1–28.
1986a   Modern Greek Studies in the West. *Journal of Modern Greek Studies*
                4, 1:3–16.
1986b   The poverty of écriture and the craft of writing: Towards a reap-
                praisal of the Prodromic Poems. *Byzantine and Modern Greek Stud-
                ies* 10:1–40.
1989   Women in two novels by Stratis Myrivilis: Myth, fantasy, and vio-
                lence. *Modern Greek Studies Yearbook* 5:363–92.
1990a   Greek philology: Diversity and difference. *Comparative Literature
                Studies* 27 1:53–61.
1990b   Οἱ γυναῖκες σε δυὸ μυθιστορήματα τοῦ Στράτη Μυριβήλη·
                μῦθος, φαντασία καὶ βία. Νέα Ἑστία 128:67–88.
1990c   Reappropriating Greek sacrifice: *Homo necans,* or ἄνθρωπος
                θυσιάζων? *Journal of Modern Greek Studies* 8, 1:97–123.
1991   Literature and popular tradition. In Holton 1991, 239–74.
1993   Writing against silence: Antithesis and ekphrasis in the prose fic-
                tion of Georgios Vizyenos. *Dumbarton Oaks Papers* 47:263–86.
1995   Why Vizyenos? and review article. *Journal of Modern Greek Studies*
                13, 2:289–98, 351–55.
Alexiou, M., and P. Dronke
1971   The lament of Jephtha's daughter: Tradition and originality. *Studi
                Medievali* 12, 2:819–63.
Alexiou, M., and D. W. Holton
1976   The origins and development of "politikos stichos": A select crit-
                ical bibliography. *Mandatoforos* 9:22–34.
Alexiou, S.
1965   Τὸ Κάστρο τῆς Κρήτης καὶ ἡ ζωή του στὸν ΙΕ καὶ ΙΖ αἰῶνα.
                Κρητικὰ Χρονικὰ 19:146–78.
——, ed. 1975   Μπεργαδής, Ἀπόκοπος· Βοσκοπούλα. Athens: Ermis.
Allen, S. W.
1968   *Vox Graeca: The pronunciation of classical Greek.* Cambridge: Cam-
                bridge University Press.

Aloni, A.
1981   *Le muse di Archiloco: Ricerche sullo stile archiloco.* Copenhagen: Museum Tusculanum.

Alverson, H.
1991   Metaphor and experience: Looking over the notion of image schema. In Fernandez 1991, 94–117.

Andersen, H. C.
1949   *The complete Andersen.* Trans. J. Hersholt. New York: Limited Editions Club.

Anderson, G.
1984   *Ancient fiction: The novel in the Greco-Roman world.* Beckenham, Kent: Croom Helm.

Andriotis, N. P.
1933   Περὶ τῆς ἀρχῆς τῶν βορείων γλωσσικῶν ἰδιωμάτων τῆς νέας ἑλληνικῆς. Ἐπετηρὶς Ἑταιρείας Βυζαντινῶν Σπουδῶν 10:340–52.
1974   *Lexikon der Archaismen in neugriechischen Dialekten.* Vienna.
1976   La genèse des dialectes. In *XV congrès d'études byzantines*, 1. Athens.

Angelopoulou, A.
1991   Ἑλληνικὰ παραμύθια, Α: Οἱ Παραμυθοκόρες. Athens: Estia.

Angold, M.
——, ed. 1984   *The Byzantine aristocracy, IX–XIII centuries.* Oxford: British Archaeological Reports. International series, 221.
1993   Were Byzantine monastic typika literature? In *The making of Byzantine history: Studies dedicated to D. M. Nicol*, ed., R. M. Beaton and C. Roueché, 46–70. Northampton: Variorum.

Ankori, Z.
1968   *Jews and the Jewish community in the history of medieval Crete.* Πεπραγμένα τοῦ 2ου Κρητολογικοῦ Συνεδρίου. Athens.

Antoniades, S. L.
1939   *La place de la liturgie dans la tradition des lettres grecques.* Leiden.
1951   Πτωχοπροδρομικά. In *Extrait des Mélanges offerts à Octave et Melpo Merlier*, 1–11. Athens.

Archeion Pontou.
Ariès, P.
1981   *The hour of our death.* Trans. H. Weaver (French edition, 1977). Harmondsworth: Penguin.

Athanasopoulos, V.
1992   Οἱ μῦθοι τῆς ζωῆς καὶ τοῦ ἔργου τοῦ Γ. Βιζυηνοῦ. Athens: Kardamitsa.

Aubry, P.
1903   *Le rythme tonique dans la poésie liturgique et dans les chants des églises chrétiennes.* Paris.

Austin, J. L.
1975   *How to do things with words.* Cambridge: Cambridge University Press.

Bachtin, N.
1935   Introduction to the study of modern Greek. Birmingham: Frank Juckes.
1985   English poetry in Greek: Notes on a comparative study of poetic
                    idioms, [The Link, vols. 1 and 2. 1938–39] Reprinted in Poetics
                    Today 6, 3: 333–56.
1963   Lectures and essays. University of Birmingham.
Bakhtin, M. M.
1981   The dialogic imagination: Four essays. Ed. M. Holquist. Trans. C.
                    Emerson and M. Holquist. Austin: University of Texas Press.
1984   Rabelais and his world. Trans. H. Iswolsky. Bloomington: Indiana
                    University Press.
1986   Speech genres and other late essays. Ed. C. Emerson and M. Holquist.
                    Trans. V. W. McGee. Austin: University of Texas Press.
Bakker, W. F., and A. F. van Gemert
1977   A check list of published Cretan documents in vernacular Greek.
                    Mandatoforos 10:12–39.

Balamoti, F.
1984   The survival of weaving traditions in Epiros, Greece, M.A. thesis, Uni-
                    versity of Birmingham.

Baldwin, B.
1982   A talent to amuse: Some aspects of Byzantine satire. Byzantinische
                    Forschungen 8:19–28.
1984   Timarion: translated with introduction and commentary. Detroit:
                    Wayne State University Press.

Bancroft-Marcus, R.
1979   George Chortatsis: a critical study. D.Phil. thesis, U. of Oxford.
1983   Women in the Cretan Renaissance. Journal of Modern Greek Stud-
                    ies, 1.1:19–38.

Barbeito, P. F.
1995   Altered states: Space, gender, and the (un)making of identity in the
                    short stories of Georgios M. Vizyenos. Journal of Modern Greek
                    Studies 13.2:299–326.

Baron-Cohen, S.
1995   Mindblindness: An essay on autism and theory of mind. Cambridge,
                    MIT Press.

Baud-Bovy, S.
1935   Chansons du Dodécanèse. 2 vols. Athens: Libraire J. N. Sidéris.
1936   La chanson populaire grecque du Dodécanèse vol. 1. Les Textes.
                    Paris.
1946   Sur le χελιδόνισμα. Byzantina-Metabyzantina I.1: 23–38.
1950   Sur la strophe de la chanson "cleftique." In Mélanges H. Grégoire,
                    2:53–78. Brussels.
1958   Études sur la chanson cleftique. Athens: Institut français d' Athènes.
1973   Ἡ ἐπικράτηση τοῦ δεκαπεντασυλλάβου στὸ ἑλληνικὸ
                    δημοτικὸ τραγούδι. Ἑλληνικά 26:301–13.

Bauman, R.
1986   *Story, performance, and event: Contextual studies of oral narrative.* Cambridge: Cambridge University Press.

Beaton, R. M.
1980   *Folk poetry of modern Greece.* Cambridge: Cambridge University Press.
1982/83   Realism and folklore in nineteenth-century fiction. *Byzantine and Modern Greek Studies* 8:103–22.
1987   The rhetoric of poverty: The lives and opinions of Theodore Prodromos. *Byzantine and Modern Greek Studies* 11:1–28.

Beaton, R. M., ed.
1988   *The Greek novel, A.D. 1–1985.* London: Croom Helm.
1989   *The medieval Greek romance.* Cambridge: Cambridge University Press.
1990   Πτωχοπροδρομικά Γ· ἡ ἠθοποιεΐα τοῦ ἀτάκτου μοναχοῦ. In Μνήμη Σ. Καρατζᾶ. 101–7. Thessaloniki.
1994   *An introduction to modern Greek literature.* Oxford: Clarendon.
1996   Cappadocians at Court:"Digenes" and "Timarion". In: Mullett, M. and D. Smythe (eds.) Alexios I Komnenos, Belfast: 329-38.

Beck, H. G.
1971   *Geschichte der byzantinischen Volksliteratur.* Munich: C. H. Beck.
1986   *Byzantinisches Erotikon.* Munich: C. H. Beck.

Bees, N. A.
1906   Κατάλογος τῶν χειρογράφων κωδίκων τῆς ἐν 'Αρσανείᾳ μονῆς τῶν ἁγίων Θεοδώρων. 'Επετηρὶς Φιλολογικοῦ Συλλόγου Παρνασσοῦ 9:56–57.

Benjamin, W.
1968   Story-teller. In *Illuminations,* 83–109. New York: Harcourt, Brace, World.

Bernal, M.
1987   *Black Athena: The Afro-Asiatic roots of classical civilisation.* London: Free Association Books; Trenton, N.J.: Rutgers University Press, 1988.

Berne, E.
1964   *Games people play: The psychology of human relationships.* Harmondsworth: Penguin.

Bettelheim, B.
1967   *The empty fortress: Infantile autism and the birth of the self.* New York: Free Press.
1976   *The uses of enchantment: The meaning and importance of fairy tales.* New York: Vintage.

Bien, P.
1972   *Kazantzakis and the linguistic revolution in Greek literature.* Princeton: Princeton University Press.
1989a   *Kazantzakis: Politics of the spirit.* Princeton: Princeton University Press.
1989b   *Nikos Kazantzakis, novelist.* Bristol: Classical Press.

Birdwhistell, R. L.

1970   *Kinesics and context: Essays on body motion and communication.*
             Philadelphia: University of Pennsylvania Press.

Bloch, M.

1983   *Marxism and anthropology.* Oxford: Oxford University Press.

Bloch, M., and J. Parry, eds.

1982   *Death and the regeneration of life.* Cambridge: Cambridge University
             Press.

Blum, R., and E. Blum

1970   *The dangerous hour: The lore of crisis and mystery in rural Greece.* Lon-
             don: Chatto and Windus.

Boccaccio, G.

1972   *The Decameron.* Harmondsworth: Penguin Classics.

Bocharov, S.

1994   Conversations with Bakhtin. *Proceedings of the Modern Language As-
             sociation* 109, 5:1009–24.

Bold, A.

1979   *The ballad.* London: Critical Accents.

Bottigheimer, R.

1987   *Grimms' bad girls and bold boys.* New Haven: Yale University Press.

Bourdieu, P.

1977   *Outline of a theory of practice.* Trans. R. Nice. Cambridge: Cam-
             bridge University Press.

Bourke, A.

1988   Working and weeping: Women's oral poetry in Irish and Scottish
             Gaelic. *Women's Studies Forum, Working Papers* 7:1–17.

1991/92   Performing—Not writing. *Graph* 11 (Winter): 28–31.

Bouveresse, J.

1977   Remarques sur le Rameau d'Or de Frazer. *Actes de la recherche en
             sciences sociales,* 35.

Bouvier, B.

1976   *Le mirologue de la Vierge: Chansons et poèmes grecs sur la Passion du
             Christ.* Rome: Bibliotheca Helvetica Romana XVI.

Branscombe, P.

1991   *W.A. Mozart, "Die Zauberflöte."* Cambridge: Cambridge University
             Press.

Bremond, C., and J. Verrier

1982   Afanassiev et Propp. *Littérature* 45:61–78.

Brock, S. P.

1975   The harp of the spirit: Twelve poems of Saint Ephrem. *Studies
             Supplementary to Sobornost* 4.

1986   Two Syriac verse homilies on the Binding of Isaac. *Le Muséon.
             Revue d' Études Orientales,* 99:61–129.

1989   A Syriac verse homily on Elijah and the widow of Sarepta. *Le
             Muséon. Revue d' Etudes Orientales),* 102:93–113.

Broumas, O.
    1977   *Beginning with O.* New Haven: Yale University Press.
    1989   Poetry and Translation Seminar, Boston University: April (unpub-
                    lished).
Browning, R.
    1975   Enlightenment and repression in Byzantium in the eleventh and
                    twelfth centuries. *Past and Present* 69:3–23.
    1976   Problems concerning the genesis of the dialects of modern
                    Greek. *XV congrès d'études byzantines.* Athens.
    1978a   The language of Byzantine literature. In Vryonis ed. 1978,
                    103–33.
    1978b   Literacy in the Byzantine world. *Byzantine and Modern Greek Stud-
                    ies* 4:39–54.
    1981   The "low-level" saint's life in the early Byzantine world. In Hackel
                    1981, 117–27.
    1983   *Medieval and modern Greek*, 2d ed. Cambridge: Cambridge Univer-
                    sity Press.
Brubaker, L.
    1989a   Byzantine art in the ninth century: Theory, practice, and culture.
                    Byzantine and Modern Greek Studies 13:23–93.
    1989b   Perception and conception: Art, theory, and culture in ninth-
                    century Byzantium. *Word and Image* 5:19–32.
Buchan, D.
    1972   *The ballad and the folk.* London: Routledge and Kegan Paul.
Burke, P.
    1978   *Popular culture in early modern Europe.* London: Harper and Row.
Burkert, W.
    1979   *Structure and history in Greek mythology.* Berkeley: University of
                    California Press.
    1983   *Homo necans: The anthropology of ancient Greek sacrificial ritual and
                    myth.* Trans. P. Bing. Berkeley: University of California Press.
Bynon, T.
    1977   *Historical linguistics.* Cambridge: Cambridge University Press.
Calotychos, V.
    1993   Realizing and resisting "self-colonization": Ideology and form in
                    modern Greek Poetics. Ph.D. diss., Harvard University.
    1997   Thorns in the side of Venice? Galanaki's *Pasha* and Pamuk's *White
                    Castle* in the global market. In Tziovas ed. 1997, 243–60.
Campbell, J. K.
    1964   *Honour, family, and patronage.* Oxford: Oxford University Press.
Cantarella, R.
    1948   *I poeti Bizantini.* 2 vols. Milan: Società Editrice "Vita e Pensiero."
Caraveli-Chaves, A.
    1980   Bridge between worlds: The Greek women's lament as commu-
                    nicative event. *Journal of American Folklore* 93:129–57.

(Caraveli)
1986   The bitter wounding: The lament as social protest in rural Greece.
                         In Dubisch ed. 1986, 169–94.
Carson, A.
1986   *Eros the bittersweet: An essay*. Princeton: Princeton University Press.
Cavafy, C. P.
1963a   Ποιήματα. 2 vols. Ed. G. P. Savvidis. Athens: Ikaros.
1963b   Πεζά. Ed. G. Papoutsakis. Athens: Fexis.
Chantraine, P.
1927   *Histoire du parfait grec*. Paris.
Chesnutt, M., ed.
1993   *Telling reality: Folklore studies in memory of Bengt Holbek*. Copen-
                         hagen Folklore Studies 1. Copenhagen: NIF Publications.
Cheynet, J.-C., and J.-F. Vannier
1986   *Études prosopographiques: Byzantina-Sorbonensia*. Paris.
Child, F. J.
1965   *The English and Scottish popular ballads*. 5 vols. 1882–98. Reprint,
                         New York: Dover Publications.
Christ, W., and M. Paranikas
1871   *Anthologia Graeca Carminum Christianorum*. Leipzig
Chryssanthopoulos, M.
1980   Μεταξὺ φαντασίας καὶ μνήμης. Ὁ Πολίτης 38:64–69.
1986   Memory and imagination in the short stories of Georgios M.
                         Vizyenos. Ph.D. diss., University of Birmingham.
1988   Reality and imagination: The use of history in the short stories of
                         Yeóryios Viziinós. In Beaton (ed.) 1988, 11–22.
1994   Γεώργιος Βιζυηνός· μεταξὺ φαντασίας καὶ μνήμης. Athens:
                         Estia.
Cixous, H.
1981   Castration or decapitation? *Signs: Journal of Women in Culture and
                         Society* 7, no. 1:41–55.
1986   *Inside*. Trans. C. Barko. New York: Schocken.
Claiborne-Park, C.
1967   *The siege*. Harmondsworth: Penguin.
Clanchy, M. T.
1979   *From memory to written record*. Cambridge: Harvard University
                         Press.
Clogan, P. M., ed.
1975   Medieval hagiography and romance, *Medievalia et Humanistica* 6.
                         Cambridge: Cambridge University Press.
Clogg, R.
1979   *A short history of modern Greece*. Cambridge: Cambridge University
                         Press.
Clucas, L.
1981   *The trial of John Italos and the crisis of intellectual values in Byzantium in
                         the eleventh century*. Munich: Miscellanea Byzantina Monacensia 26.

Cocchiara, G.
1981   *The history of folklore in Europe.* Trans. J. N. McDaniel. Philadelphia: Institute for the Study of Human Issues. Originally published as *Storia del folklore in Europa* (Turin, 1952).

Cohen, A., ed.
1950   *Psalms.* London.

Cohen, L. J.
1979   Semantics of metaphor. In Ortony (ed.): 69–80.

Constantine, D.
1984   *Early Greek travellers and the Hellenic ideal.* Cambridge: Cambridge University Press.

Cornford, F. M.
1941   *The Republic of Plato.* Oxford: Oxford University Press.

Coulton, M.
1983   *Imagery of marriage and death in Greek folk songs.* M. Litt. thesis, University of Birmingham.

Cowan, J.
1990   *Dance and the body politic in northern Greece.* Princeton: Princeton University Press.

Crick, F.
1988   *What mad pursuit: A personal view of scientific discovery.* New York: Basic.

Crusius, M.
1584   *Turco-Graeciae libri octo, quibus Graecorum status sub imperio Turcico describitur.* Basel.

Cupane, C.
1974   "'Ἔρως-βασιλεύς": La figura di Eros nel romanzo bizantino d'amore. *Atti del Accademia di Arti di Palermo,* 4th ser. 33, 2:243–97.
1978   Il motivo del castello nella narrativa tardo-bizantina: Evoluzione di un' allegoria. *Jahrbuch der Österreichischen Byzantinistik* 27:229–67.
1986   Topica romanzesca in oriente e in occidente: "Avanture" e "amour." In *Il romanzo tra cultura latina e byzantina,* ed. H. G. Beck et al., 47–72. Testi della 3 settimana di studi medievali (1983). Palermo: Biblioteca dell Encheiridion 5.
1987   Byzantinisches Erotikon: Ansichten und Einsichten. *Jahrbuch der Österreichischen Byzantinistik* 37:213–33.

Danforth, L. M.
1979   The role of dance in the ritual therapy of the Anastenaria. *Byzantine and Modern Greek Studies* 4:141–63.
1982   *Death rituals of rural Greece.* Princeton: Princeton University Press.
1984   The ideological context of the search for continuities in Greek culture. *Journal of Modern Greek Studies* 2:53–85.
1989   *Firewalking and religious healing.* Princeton: Princeton University Press.

Das, V.
1983   The language of sacrifice, *Man* 18:445–62.

Dawkins, R. M.

1916   *Modern Greek in Asia Minor.* Cambridge: Cambridge University Press.

1932   *Leontios Makhairas, Recital concerning the Sweet Land of Cyprus, entitled "Chronicle."* 2 vols. Oxford: Oxford University Press.

1940   The dialects of modern Greek. *Transactions of the Philological Society*: 1–38.

1950   *Forty-five stories from the Dodekanese.* Cambridge: Cambridge University Press.

1953   *Modern Greek folktales.* Oxford: Oxford University Press.

1955   *More Greek folktales.* Oxford: Oxford: University Press.

Delehaye, H.

1902   *Propylaeum ad "Acta Sanctorum."* Brussels: Socii J. Bollandi.

Deltion.   Δελτίον τῆς Ἱστορικῆς καὶ Ἐθνολογικῆς Ἑταιρείας τῆς Ἑλλάδος. Athens.

Dennis, G. T.

1981   *Das Strategikon des Maurikios: Einführung, Edition, und Indices.* Trans. E. Gamillscheg. Corpus fontium historiae Byzantinae. Vienna: Verlag der österreichischen Akademie der Wissenschaften.

Derrida, J.

1972   *Marges de la philosophie.* Paris. (*Speech and phenomena*, trans. A. Bass, Brighton, Sussex: Harvester.)

1976   *Of grammatology.* Trans. G. Spivak. Baltimore: Johns Hopkins University Press. (*De la grammatologie.* Paris, 1967).

1977   Limited Inc. *Glyph* 2:162–254.

Detienne, M.

1977   *The gardens of Adonis.* Trans. J. Lloyd. London: Harvester, *Les jardins d'Adonis: La mythologie des aromates en Grèce* (Paris, 1972).

1979   *Dionysos slain.* Trans. M. Muellner and L. Muellner. Baltimore: Johns Hopkins University Press. (*Dionysos mis à mort.* Paris, 1977).

Deubner, L.

1932   *Attische Feste.* Berlin.

Dieterich, A.

1901   ABC Denkmaeler. *Rheinisches Museum* 56:77–105.

Dimaras, K. T.

1964   Ἱστορία τῆς νεοελληνικῆς λογοτεχνίας. Athens: Ikaros.

1970   Εἰσαγωγή· Κ. Παπαρριγόπουλος, ῾῾Ἱστορία τοῦ Ἑλληνικοῦ ἔθνους''. Athens.

Dimiroulis, D.

1985   Ὁ Ἐμμανουὴλ Ροΐδης καὶ ἡ τέχνη τῆς πολεμικῆς. Χάρτης 15:266–93.

Douglas, M.

1966   *Purity and danger.* London: Ark.

Doumani, M.

1983   *Mothering in Greece.* London: Academic Press.

Dragoumis, M.
1990   Τραγούδια ἀπὸ τὴν Αἴγινα (disk). Athens: Ἀρχεῖο Μ. Μερλιέ.
                    Ἱστορικὸ καὶ λαογραφικὸ μουσεῖο Αἴγινας.

Dronke, P.
1968   Medieval Latin and the rise of European love-lyric. 2 vols. Oxford: Ox-
                    ford University Press.
1976   Learned lyric and popular ballad in the early Middle Ages. Studi
                    Medievali 17:1–40. Reprinted in The medieval poet and his world,
                    167–207. Rome: Edizioni di Storia e Letteratura, 1984.
1994   Verse with prose from Petronius to Dante: The art and scope of the mixed
                    form. Cambridge: Harvard University Press.

Dubisch, J.
1986   Women, food, and social boundaries. In Dubisch ed. 1986, 195–
                    214.
———, ed. 1986   Gender and power in rural Greece. Princeton: Princeton University
                    Press.

du Boulay, J.
1974   Portrait of a Greek mountain village. Oxford: Clarendon.
1976   Lies, mockery, and family integrity. In Peristiany 1976, 389–406.
1982   The Greek vampire: A study of cyclic symbolism in marriage and
                    death. Man 17, 2:218–38.
1983   The meaning of dowry: Changing values in rural Greece. Journal
                    of Modern Greek Studies 1, 1:243–70.

Du Cange.
1688   Glossarium ad scriptores mediae et infimae Graecitatis, C. du Fresne,
                    Lugduni. Reprinted 1943.

Dundes, A.
1978   Essays in folkloristics. New Delhi: Folklore Institute.

Dunlop, J. C.
1888   History of prose fiction, revised by H. Wilson from original edition
                    1814, vol. 1. London.

Durham, M. E.
1924   Some tribal origins, laws, and customs of the Balkans. London.

Duval, R.
1903   La littérature syriaque. Paris.

Dworkin, A.
1972   Woman hating. New York: Dutton.

Dyck, A. R.
1990   Ptochoprodromos, "'Ανάθεμαν τὰ γράμματα" and related
                    texts. Byzantinische Zeitschrift 15:45–52.

Eideneier, H.
1979a   Zum fünfzehn Silber der Ptochoprodromika. In Festschrift L.
                    Politis. Thessaloniki.
1979b   Ein byzantinischen Kalendergedicht in der Volkssprache Ἑλλη-
                    νικά 33:368–419.

1987   Der Ptochoprodromos in schriftlicher und mündlicher Ueber-
                       lieferung. In *Neograeca Medii Aevi I. Text und Ausgabe, Akten zum
                       Symposion Köln*, ed. H. Eideneier, 101–19. Köln.
1991   *Ptochoprodromos*. Einführung, kritische Ausgabe, deutsche Ueber-
                       setzung, Glossar. *Neograeca Medii Aevi*. Köln: Romiosini.
Eideneier, H. and N. Eideneier
1982/83   Leser oder Hörerkreis? Zur byzantinischen Dichtung in der Volk-
                       sprache. Ἑλληνικά 34:119–50.
Ekdawi, S., P. Fann, and E. Philokyprou
1993   Bold men, fair maids, and affronts to their sex: The characterisa-
                       tion and structural roles of men and women in the Escorial *Di-
                       genes Akrites*. *Byzantine and Modern Greek Studies* 17:25–42.
Eliade, M.
1954   *The myth of the eternal return: Or, cosmos and history*. Princeton:
                       Princeton University Press; New York: Bollingen.
1960   *Myths, dreams, and mysteries: The encounter between contemporary faiths
                       and archaic realities*. New York: Harper and Row.
1963   *Myth and reality*. New York: Harper and Row.
Ellissen, A.
1860   "Timarion." *Analekten der mittel-und neugriechischen Literatur*, vol. 4:
                       1–185. Leipzig.
Elytis, O.
1970   Τὸ ἄξιον ἐστί, 6th edition. Athens: Ikaros.
Entwistle, W.
1939   *European balladry*. Oxford: Clarendon.
Estés, C. P.
1993   *The gift of story*. New York: Ballantine.
Evlambios, G.
1843   Ὁ Ἀμάραντος, ἤτοι τὰ ρόδα τῆς ἀναγεννηθείσης Ἑλλά-
                       δος, vol. 1. Petrograd.
Fabre, P.
1905   *Le "Liber Censuum" de l'église romaine*. Paris: Bibliothèque des
                       écoles françaises d' Athène et de Rome, A. Fontemoing, Mai.
Fakinou, E.
1987   Ἡ μεγάλη πράσινη. Athens: Kastaniotis.
Fallmerayer, J. P.
1830–36   *Geschichte der Halbinsel Morea während des Mittelalters*. 2 vols.
                       Stüttgart and Tübingen: Cotta.
1845   *Fragmente aus dem Orient*. 2 vols. Stuttgart and Tübingen: Cotta.
Faubion, J.
1993   *Modern Greek lessons: A primer in historical constructivism*. Princeton:
                       Princeton University Press.
Fauriel, C.
1824–25   *Chants populaires de la Grèce moderne*, 2 vols. Paris.
Fentress, J., and C. Wickham
1992   *Social memory*. Oxford: Blackwell.

Ferguson, C. A.
1959   Diglossia. *Word* 15:325–40. Reprinted in *Language structure and language use: Essays by C. A. Ferguson*, Stanford, Calif.: 1971.

Fernandez, J. W.
1986   *Persuasions and performance: The play of tropes in culture*. Bloomington: Indiana University Press.
——, ed. 1991   *Beyond metaphor: The theory of tropes in anthropology*. Stanford: Stanford University Press.

Finnegan, R.
1977   *Oral poetry. Its nature, significance and social context*. Cambridge: Cambridge University Press.

Forbes Irving, P. M. C.
1990   *Metamorphosis in Greek myths*. Oxford: Clarendon.

Forster, E. M.
1962   *Aspects of the novel* (1927). Harmondsworth: Pelican.

Foucault, M.
1970   *The order of things: An archaeology of the human sciences*. Trans. A. M. Sheridan Smith. London: Tavistock. (*Les mots et les choses*. Paris: Gallimard, 1970.)
1972   *The Archaeology of Knowledge*. Trans. A. M. Sheridan Smith. London Tavistock. (*L' archéologie du savoir*. Paris: Gallimard, 1969.)

Fox-Genovese, E.
1982   Placing women's history in history. *New Left Review* 133:5–29.

Frangoudaki, A.
1973   Καὶ πάλι γιὰ τὸ γλωσσικὸ ζήτημα. Συνέχεια, August.

Frazer, J. G.
1922   *The golden bough* (1890). Abridged edition, London: Macmillan.

Freud, S.
1955   *The interpretation of dreams* (1900). Pelican Freud Library, no. 4. Harmondsworth: Pelican.
1960   *Jokes and their relation to the unconscious* (1905). Pelican Freud Library, no. 6. Harmondsworth: Pelican.
1985   *Totem and taboo* (1913) and *Moses and Monotheism* (1939). In: *Freud: The Origins of Religion*, ed. A. Dickson. Pelican Freud Library, no. 13. Harmondsworth: Pelican.

Friedl, E.
1967   The position of women: appearance and reality. *Anthropological Quarterly* 40, no. 3:97–108. Reprinted in Dubisch ed. 1986, 42–52.
1975   *Women and men: An anthropologist's view*. New York: Holt, Rinehart and Winston.

Galatariotou, C.
1984–185   Holy women and witches: Aspects of Byzantine conceptions of gender. *Byzantine and Modern Greek Studies* 9:55–94.
1987a   Byzantine ktetorika typika: A comparative study. *Revue des Études Byzantines* 45:77–138.

1987b   Structural oppositions in the Grottaferrata Digenes Akrites. *Byzantine and Modern Greek Studies* 11:29–68.

1989   Eros and Thanatos: On a Byzantine hermit's conception of sexuality. *Byzantine and Modern Greek Studies* 13:95–137.

1991   *The making of a saint: The life, times, and sanctification of Neophytos the Recluse.* Cambridge: Cambridge University Press.

Garland, R.

1985   *The Greek way of death.* Ithaca: Cornell University Press.

Garnett, L.

1896   *Greek folk prose.* London.

Gast, J.

1782   *A history of Greece, from the accession of Alexander of Macedon, till its final subjection to the Roman power.* London.

Gautier, P.

1974   Le typikon du Christ Sauveur Pantocrator. *Revue des Études Byzantines* 32:1–145.

1981   La diataxis de Michel Attaliate, *Revue des Études Byzantines* 39: 5–143.

Gavrilovic, Z.

1986   The cosmic symbolism of the Cross and the Emperor in Ptochoprodromos, Poem IV. *Byzantine and Modern Greek Studies* 10:195–202.

Geertz, C.

1975   *The interpretation of cultures.* London: Hutchinson.

Genette, G.

1980   *Narrative discourse: An essay in method.* Trans. J. E. Lewin. Ithaca: Cornell University Press. (*"Discours du récit" Essai, Figures III. Collection Poétique*, Paris 1972).

Gentili, B.

1979   *Theatrical performances in the ancient world.* London Studies in Classical Philology, 2. Amsterdam.

1988   *Poetry and its public in ancient Greece: from Homer to the fifth century.* Trans. A. T. Cole. Baltimore: Johns Hopkins UP (*Poesia e pubblico nella Grecia antica: Da Omero al V secolo* Rome and Bari, 1985).

Gernet, L., and P. Vidal-Naquet

1981   "Value" in Greek myth. In Gordon 1981, 111–46.

Gerould, G. H.

1932   *The ballad of tradition.* Oxford: Oxford University Press.

Giet, S.

1953   À propos des danses liturgiques. *Revue des sciences religieuses* 27: 131–33.

Gigante, M.

1960   Il romanzo di Eustathio Macrembolites. *Akten des xi internationalen Byzantinister-Kongresses Müncher 1958*, 168–81. Munich.

Gignac, G.

1976 and 1981.   *A grammar of the Greek papyri of the Roman and Byzantine periods.* Vol. 1, *Phonology*: Milan, 1976. Vol. 2, *Morphology*: Milan, 1981.

Gilbert, S. M., and S. Gubar

1979   *The madwoman in the attic: The woman writer and the nineteenth-century imagination.* New Haven: Yale University Press.

1987   *No man's land: The place of the woman writer in the twentieth century.* Vol. 1, *The war of words.* New Haven: Yale University Press.

Gilead, S.

1991   Magic abjured: Closure in children's fantasy fiction. *Proceedings of the Modern Language Association* 106, 2:277–93.

Gillies, A.

1945   *Herder.* Oxford: Oxford University Press.

Gilligan, C.

1982   *In a different voice: Psychological theory and women's development.* Cambridge, Ma: Harvard University Press.

1989   Oedipus - Psyche: Two stories about love. Modern Language Association Convention, San Francisco.

Girard, R.

1977   *Violence and the sacred.* Trans. P. Gregory. Baltimore: Johns Hopkins University Press. (*La violence et le sacré.* Paris: B. Grasset, 1972.)

Gobineau, J. A.

1853–55   *Essai sur l'inégalité des races humaines.* Trans. A. Collins *The inequality of human races,* 1915. New York: Putnam.

Godelier, M.

1977   *Perspectives in Marxist anthropology.* Trans. R. Brain. Cambridge: Cambridge University Press. (*Horizons: Trajets marxistes en anthropologie* Paris: F. Maspéro, 1973.)

Goffman, E.

1959   *The presentation of self in everyday life.* New York: Anchor.

1967   *Interaction ritual.* Harmondsworth: Penguin.

Goldmann, L.

1971   *La création culturelle dans la société moderne.* Bibliothèque Meditations 84. Paris: Denoël-Gonthier.

1986   *Pour une sociologie du roman.* Paris: Gallimard.

Goodison, L.

1991   *Moving heaven and earth.* London: Pandora.

Goody, J., ed.

1968   *Literacy in traditional societies.* Cambridge: Cambridge University Press.

1977   Against "ritual": Loosely structured thoughts on a loosely defined topic. In Moore and Myerhoff eds. 1977, 25–36.

1987, ed.   *The interface between the written and the oral: Studies in literacy, family, culture, and the state.* Cambridge: Cambridge University Press.

Gordon, R. L., ed.

1981   *Myth, religion, and society.* Structuralist essays by M. Detienne, L. Gernet, J.-P. Vernant, and P. Vidal-Naquet. Cambridge: Cambridge University Press.

Gordon, S.
1993   The powers of the handless maiden. In *Feminist messages: Coding in women's folk culture*, 253–65. Chicago: University of Illinois Press.

Gould, S. J.
1989   *Wonderful life: The Burgess shale and the nature of history*. New York: Norton.

Grandin, T.
1989   *Emergence: Labeled autistic*. Navato, Calif.: Arena Press, 2d ed.
1995   *Thinking in pictures and other reports of my life with autism*. New York: Doubleday. Reprinted 1996: Vintage.

Grenfell, B. P., and A. S. Hunt
1898   *The Oxyrhynchus Papyri*. London

Grimm, J., and W. Grimm.
1856   *Kinder und Hausmärchen* (1812–13). 2 vols. 3d ed. Berlin.

Grosdidier de Matons, J.
1964–67, ed.   *Romanos le Mélode: Hymnes*. 4 vols. Paris: du Cerf.
1976   Courants archaisants et populaires dans la langue et la littérature. *Actes de xv congrès d'études byzantines*. Athens.
1977   *Romanos le Mélode et les origines de la poésie religieuse à Byzance*. Paris: Beauchesne.

Grove, G., ed.
1880–89   *A Dictionary of Music and Musicians*, 4 vols. London: Macmillan.

Guillet, G. de
1676   *Lacedemone ancienne et nouvelle*, où l'on voit les Moeurs et les Coûtumes des Grecs Modernes, des Mahometans, et des Juifs du Pays. Paris.

Haas, W., ed.
1982   *Standard languages, spoken and written*. Mont Follick Series, 5: Manchester University Press.

Hackel, S., ed.
1981   The Byzantine saint. Studies supplementary to *Sobornost* 5:117–27.

Hägg, T.
1983   *The novel in antiquity*. (Swedish edn. 1980), Oxford: Basil Blackwell.

von Hahn, J. G.
1864   *Griechische und albanäsische Märchen*. Leipzig.

Haldon, J. F.
1990   *Three treatises on imperial military expeditions*. Vienna: Akademie der Wissenschaften.

Happé, F.
1995   *Autism*. Cambridge: Harvard.

Hart, J.
1996   *New voices in the nation: Women and the Greek Resistance, 1941–64*. Ithaca: Cornell University Press.

Hart, L.
1992   *Time, religion, and social experience in rural Greece*. Lanham, Md: Rowman and Littlefield.

Hart, W. M.

1906　　　　Professor Child and the ballad. *Publications of the Modern Language Association* 21:804–7.

Harvey, A. E.

1989　　　　*Economic expansion in the Byzantine Empire, 900–1200.* Cambridge: Cambridge University Press.

Havelock, E. A.

1982　　　　*The literary evolution in Greece and its cultural consequences.* Princeton: Princeton University Press.

1984　　　　Oral composition in the *Oedipus Tyrannus* of Sophokles. *New Literary History* 16, 1:175–97.

Hawking, S. W.

1988　　　　*A brief history of time: From the big bang to black holes.* Toronto: Bantam.

Haxthausen, W. von

1935　　　　*Neugriechische Volkslieder.* Münster: Aschendorffsche Verlagsbuchhandlung.

Headlam, W.

1910　　　　*The "Agamemnon" of Aeschylus.* Cambridge: Cambridge University Press.

1922　　　　*The "Mimes" of Herodas.* Cambridge: Cambridge University Press.

Henderson, J.

1975　　　　*The maculate Muse: Obscene language in Attic comedy.* New Haven: Yale University Press.

Hendy, M. F.

1969　　　　*Coinage and money in the Byzantine Empire, 1081–1261.* Washington, D.C.: Dumbarton Oaks Series XII.

1970　　　　Byzantium, 1081–1204: An economic reappraisal. *Transactions of the Royal Historical Society,* ser. 5, 20:31–52. Reprinted in Hendy 1989: no. II.

1985　　　　*Studies in the Byzantine monetary economy, c. 300–1450.* Cambridge: Cambridge University Press.

1989　　　　'"Byzantium, 1081–1204": The economy revisited, twenty years on'. In: Hendy, *The economy, fiscal administration and coinage in Byzantium.* Northampton: Variorum: no. III.

1999　　　　*Byzantine coins in the Dumbarton Oaks Collection and in the Whittemore Collection, IV.* Alexios I to Michael VIII (1081–1261). Washington, D.C.: Dumbarton Oaks Series.

Hertz, R.

1960　　　　*Death and the right hand.* Trans. R. Needham and C. Needham. Aberdeen: Cohen and West. Contribution à une étude sur la représentation collective de la mort. *L'année sociologique* 10 (1907): 48–137.

Herzfeld, M.

1972　　　　The khelidonisma: A study in textual and ritual variation. M.A. thesis: University of Birmingham.

1979　　　　Exploring a metaphor of exposure. *Journal of American Folklore* 92:285–301.

| 1980 | Social borderers: Themes of ambiguity and conflict in Greek folk song. *Byzantine and Modern Greek Studies* 6:61–80. |

1981   Performative categories and symbols of passage in rural Greece. *Journal of American Folklore* 94:41–57.

1982   *Ours once more: Folklore, ideology, and the making of modern Greece.* Austin: University of Texas Press.

1983   Semantic slippage and moral fall: The rhetoric of chastity in rural Greek society. *Journal of Modern Greek Studies* 1:161–72.

1985a   Lévi-Strauss in the nation state. *Journal of American Folklore* 98: 191–208.

1985b   *The poetics of manhood.* Princeton: Princeton University Press.

1986   Within and without: The category of "female" in the ethnography of modern Greece. In Dubisch ed. 1986, 215–33.

1987   *Anthropology through the looking glass.* Cambridge: Cambridge University Press.

1988   Rhetoric and the constitution of social relations. Working Paper Series. Chicago: Chicago Center for Psycho-social Studies.

1991   *A place in history: Social and monumental time in a Cretan town.* Princeton: Princeton University Press.

1993   In defiance of destiny: The management of time and gender at a Cretan funeral. *American Ethnologist* 20, 2:241–55.

Hesseling, D. C., and H. Pernot, eds.

1910   *Poèmes prodromiques en grec vulgaire.* Amsterdam.

1913   Ἐρωτοπαίγνια *(Chansons d'amour), publiées d'après un manuscrit du xve siècle.* Paris: Bibliothèque grecque vulgaire, vol. 10.

Hilberg, I., ed.

1876   Εὐσταθίου Πρωτονωβελεσίμου τοῦ Μακρεμβολίτου τῶν καθ' Ὑσμίνην καὶ Ὑσμινίαν, λόγοι ια'. Vienna: A. Hölder.

Hirschon, R.

1978   Open body, closed space: The transformation of female sexuality. In *Defining females: The nature of woman in society,* ed. S. Ardener, 66–88. London: Croom Helm.

1981   Essential objects and the sacred: Interior and exterior space in an urban Greek locality. In *Women and space,* ed. S. Ardener, 72–88. London: Croom Helm.

1989   *Heirs of the Greek catastrophe: The social life of Asia Minor refugees in the Piraeus.* Oxford: Oxford University Press.

1992   Greek adults' verbal play; or, How to train for caution. *Journal of Modern Greek Studies* 10, 1:35–56.

1995   Individuals in the true sense: The significance of personal celebrations in contemporary Greece. Modern Greek Studies Association Symposium, held at Harvard University.

Hirst, A.

1994   Coherence and complexity in Romanos' Easter kontakion, Τὸν πρὸ ἡλίου ἥλιον, M.A. thesis, King's College, University of London.

Hodges, Z. C., and A. L. Farstad, eds.
1985   *The Greek New Testament according to the majority text.* 2d ed. New
                  York: Thomas Nelson.
Hoeg, C.
1955–57   Les rapports de la musique chrétienne et de la musique de l'anti-
                  quité classique. *Byzantion* 25–27:383–412.
Holbek, B.
1987   *Interpretation of fairy tales.* Helsinki: Academia scientifica fennica.
Holst-Warhaft, G.
1992   *Dangerous voices: Women's laments and Greek literature.* London:
                  Routledge.
Holton, D. W.
1975   "The leprous queen": A ballad from Lesbos. *Byzantine and Modern
                  Greek Studies* 1:97–110.
1990   Modern Greek today: One grammar or two? In *Greek outside
                  Greece II*, 23–33. Athens: Diaspora Books.
——, ed. 1991   *Literature and society in Renaissance Crete.* Cambridge: Cambridge
                  University Press.
Hörandner, W.
1974   *Theodoros Prodromos: Historische Gedichte.* Vienna: Wiener Byzanti-
                  nische Studien, XI.
1982   Zur Frage der Metrik früher Volksprachlicher-Texts: Kann
                  Theodoros Prodromos der Verfasser volksprachlicher Gedichte
                  sein? *Jahrbuch für Oesterreichischen Byzantinistik* 32, 3:375–81.
Huet, P. D.
1966   *Traité de l'origine des romans.* Reprinted from first edition (Paris,
                  1670), Stuttgart: P. Metzler.
Humphreys, S. C.
1983   *The family, women, and death: Comparative studies.* London: Rout-
                  ledge.
Hunger, H.
1953   Zum Epilog der Theogonie des Johannes Tzetzes. *Byzantinische
                  Zeitschrift* 46:302–7. Reprinted in Hunger 1973, XVIII.
1968   Die byzantinische Literatur der Komnenzeit, Versuch einer
                  Neubewertung. *Anzeiger phil.-hist. Klasse Österreichische Akademie
                  der Wissenschaften* 105:59–96. Reprinted in Hunger 1973, XVI.
——, ed. 1968   *Der byzantinischen Katz-Mäuse Krieg. Theodoros Prodromos' "Kato-
                  myomachia": Einleitung, Text, und Uebersetzung.* Graz.
1969/70   On the imitation (μίμησις) of antiquity in Byzantine literature. *Dum-
                  barton Oaks Papers* 23–24:17–38. Reprinted in Hunger 1973, XV.
1973   *Byzantinische Grundlagenforschung.* London: Variorum.
1978   *Die hochsprachliche profane Literatur der Byzantiner*, 2 vols. Byzanti-
                  nische Handbuch: Munich.
Hunt, L. A.
1984   Comnenian aristocratic palace decorations: Descriptions and Is-
                  lamic connections. In Angold 1984, 138–57.

Huntington, R. and P. Metcalf
1979   *Celebrations of death: The anthropology of mortuary ritual.* Cambridge: Cambridge University Press.
Hurlburt, R. T.
1990   *Sampling normal and schizophrenic inner experience.* New York: Plenum.
1994   *Sampling the inner experience of autism: A preliminary report,* with F. Happé and U. Frith. Psychological Medicine, 24.
Hurston, Z. Neale
1990a   *Mules and men* (1935). New York: Harper and Row.
1990b   *Their eyes were watching God* (1937). New York: Harper and Row.
Hustvedt, S. B.
1930   *Ballad books and ballad men.* Cambridge: Harvard University Press.
Hyde, L.
1979   *The gift: Imagination and the erotic life of property.* New York: Vintage.
Ioannou, G.
1975   Τὸ δημοτικὸ τραγούδι· παραλογές. Athens: Ermis.
1987   Παραμύθια τοῦ λαοῦ μας. Athens: Ermis.
Iossifides, A. M.
1991   Sisters in Christ: Metaphors of kinship among Greek nuns. In Loizos and Papataxiarchis 1991, 135–55.
Irigaray, L.
1987   *Speculum of the other woman.* Trans. G. C. Gill. Ithaca: Cornell University Press.
Isbell, B. J.
1985   The metaphoric process: "From nature to culture and back again." In Urton 1985, 285–313.
Jakobson, R., and M. Halle
1956   Two aspects of language and two types of aphasic disturbances. In *Fundamentals of language,* 69–96. The Hague: Mouton.
Jardine, A.
1985   *Gynesis.* Ithaca: Cornell University Press.
Jeffreys, M. J.
1974   The nature and origins of political verse. *Dumbarton Oaks Papers* 28:141–95.
1975   The literary emergence of vernacular Greek. *Mosaic* 8:171–93.
Jeffreys, M. J., and O. Smith
1991   Political verse for Queen Atossa. *Classica et Mediaevalia* 42:301–4.
Jenkins, R.
1961   *The Dilessi murders.* Cambridge: Cambridge University Press.
1963   Byzantium and Byzantinism. In *Lectures in memory of Louise Taft Semple.* Cincinnati: University of Cincinnati Press.
Johnson, B.
1980   *The critical difference: Essays in the contemporary rhetoric of reading.* Baltimore: Johns Hopkins University Press.
1987   *A world of difference.* Baltimore: Johns Hopkins University Press.

Jones, A. H. M.
1971   The cities of the Eastern Roman provinces. Oxford: Oxford University
                  Press.

Joseph, B.
1981   The synchrony and diachrony of modern Greek na. Byzantine and
                  Modern Greek Studies 7:139–54.
1983   The synchrony and diachrony of the Balkan infinitive: A study in areal, gen-
                  eral, and historical linguistics. Cambridge: Cambridge University Press.
1985   European Hellenism and Greek nationalism: Some effects of eth-
                  nocentrism on Greek linguistic scholarship. Journal of Modern
                  Greek Studies 3, 1:87–96.

Jung, C. G.
1968   [1959] Archetypes and the collective unconscious. Trans. R. F. C. Hull.
                  London: Routledge and Kegan Paul.
1969   [1963] Essays on a science of mythology: The myth of the divine child and
                  the mysteries of Eleusis, with C. Kerényi. Trans. R. F. C. Hull. Rev.
                  ed. Bollingen Series, 22. Princeton: Princeton University Press.

Jusdanis, G.
1991   Belated modernity and aesthetic culture: Inventing national literature.
                  Minneapolis: University of Minnesota Press.

Kacandes, I.
1990   Orality, reader address, and the "anonymous you." Journal of Modern
                  Greek Studies 8, 2:225–28.

Kafandaris, K.
1988   Ἑλληνικὰ λαικὰ παραμύθια. 2 vols. Athens: Odysseas.

Kakavoulia, M.
1985   Πάπισσα Ἰωάννα· Πολύτοπο/παλίμψηστο. Χάρτης 15:294–311.

Kaligas, P.
1995   Γεωργίου Βιζυηνοῦ· Ἡ φιλοσοφία τοῦ καλοῦ παρὰ Πλωτίνῳ.
                  Athens: Mouses, Armos.

Kalligas, P.
1991   Θάνος Βλέκας (1855). Introduction by E. N. Chorafas. Athens:
                  Ouranis.

Kalogeras, G.
1995   Ethographia and nationalistic anxieties: The short stories of Kon-
                  stantinos I. Kazantzis. Journal of the Hellenic Diaspora 21, 2:85–114.

Kambouroglou, M. G.
1883   Ἀθηναϊκὰ παραμύθια. Deltion 1:289–348.

Karas, S., and M. Vouras
1977–88   Τραγούδια τῆς Ἑλλάδος. Songs of Greece. 31 records and cas-
                  sette tapes of folk music recorded in the 1970's. Society for Dis-
                  semination of National Music (SDNM), nos. 101–31. Athens.

Kasdagli, A.
1988   Ἕνας νοτάριος στὰ τέλη τοῦ ΙΖ´ αἰώνα. In Μιὰ μέρα·
                  Δεκαπέντε ἱστορίες καθημερινότητας ἀπο τὰ ἀρχαία χρόνια
                  ὡς τὴν ἐποχή μας, 171–99. Athens: Etaireia Spoudon Neoel-
                  lenikou Politismou.

1997   *Land and marriage settlements in the Aegean: The case of seventeenth-century Naxos*. Venice: Hellenic Institute of Byzantine and Post-Byzantine Studies.

Kassis, K. D.
1979–81   Μοιρολόγια τῆς Μέσα Μάνης, 3 vols. Athens: E. Rigas.

Kavakopoulos, P.
1981   Τραγούδια τῆς βορειοδυτικῆς Θράκης. Thessaloniki: Ἵδρυμα Μελετῶν Χερσονήσου τοῦ Αἴμου 178.

Kazazis, K.
1979   Learnedisms in Costas Taktsis' *Third Wedding*. *Byzantine and Modern Greek Studies* 5, 2:17–27.

1992   Sunday Greek revisited. *Journal of Modern Greek Studies* 10, 1:57–70.

Kazhdan, A. P.
1967   Bemerkungen zu Niketas Eugenianos. *Jahrbuch des Oesterreichischen Byzantinistik* 16:101–17.

1984   The image of the medical doctor in Byzantine literature of the 10th to 12th centuries. *Dumbarton Oaks Papers* 38:43–51.

Kazhdan, A. P., and A. W. Epstein
1985   *Change in Byzantine culture in the eleventh and twelfth centuries*. Berkeley: University of California Press.

Kazhdan, A. P., and S. Franklin
1984   *Studies on Byzantine literature of the eleventh and twelfth centuries*. Cambridge: Cambridge University Press.

Kazhdan, A. P., and L. Sherry.
[1997]   *A History of Byzantine Literature*. 7 vols. Athens.

Kehayioglou, G.
1988   Translations of Eastern "novels" and their influence on late Byzantine and modern Greek fiction (11th–18th centuries). In Beaton 1988, 156–66.

1989   The discontinuity of Greek literary responses to the Arab world. *Journal of Modern Greek Studies* 7, 1:65–76.

Keil, B.
1889   Die Monatscycklen der byzantinischer Kunst in spätgriechische Literatur. *Wiener Studien* 11:94–142.

Keller, R. E.
1982   Diglossia in German-speaking Switzerland. In Haas 1982, 70–93.

Kenna, M.
1995   Saying "No" in Greece: Some preliminary thoughts on hospitality, gender, and the evil eye. In *Brothers and others: Essays in honour of John Peristiany*, ed. S. Peristiany, 133–46. Athens: EKKE.

Kerrigan, C., ed.
1980   *An anthology of Scottish women poets*. Edinburgh: Edinburgh University Press.

Kirk, G. S.
1970   *Myth: Its meaning and functions in ancient and other societies*. Cambridge: Cambridge University Press.

Kliapha, M.
1977   Παραμύθια τῆς Θεσσαλίας. Athens: Kedros.
Koliopoulos, G.
1988   Ληστές. Athens. Translated as *Brigands with a cause*. Oxford:
                Clarendon, 1988.
Kolitsaras, I. G.
1964–66   Παροιμίαι τοῦ ἑλληνικοῦ λαοῦ. 3 vols. Athens: Χριστιανικῆς
                Ἐνώσεως.
Konstantinides, K.
1982   *Higher education in Byzantium in the thirteenth and early fourteenth
                centuries.* Cyprus.
Kontosopoulos, N. G.
1981   Διάλεκτοι καὶ ἰδιώματα τῆς νέας ἑλληνικῆς. Athens.
Korais, A.
1833   Ἄτακτα. Athens.
1964   Ἅπαντα τα πρωτότυπα ἔργα. Ed. G. Valetas, 4 vols (Α 1-2,
                Β 1-2). Athens: Dorikos.
1984   Διήμερο Κοραῆ, 29 καὶ 30 Ἀπριλίου 1983· Προσεγγίσεις στὴ
                γλωσσικὴ θεωρία, τὴ σκέψη καὶ τὸ ἔργο τοῦ Κοραῆ. Ἀθήνα:
                Κέντρο Νεοελληνικῶν Ἐρευνων.
Koukoules, Ph.
1915   Προδρόμεια λαογραφικὰ ζητήματα. Λαογραφία 5:309–32.
1924   Λαογραφικὰ παρὰ τῷ Εὐσταθίῳ. Ἐπετηρὶς τῆς Ἑταιρείας
                Βυζαντινῶν Σπουδῶν 1:5–40.
1948–55   Βυζαντινῶν Βίος καὶ πολιτισμός. 6 vols. Athens.
Kriaris, A.
1920   Πλήρης συλλογὴ κρητικῶν δημωδῶν ἀσμάτων. 2d ed.
                Athens.
Krikos, K.
1975   The "Song of the dead brother": A bibliography. *Mandatoforos*
                6:23–30.
Krikos-Davis, K.
1982   Moira at birth in Greek tradition. *Folia Neohellenica* 4:106–34.
Krumbacher, K.
1897   *Geschichte der byzantinischen Litteratur*. 2d ed. Munich. Reprint,
                New York, 1970.
1902   Review of Tommasini 1901. *Byzantinische Zeitschrift* 11:586–88.
Kurtz, B., ed.
1907   Unedierte Texte aus der Zeit des Kaisers Johannes Komnenos:
                Theodoros Prodromos, Λόγος εἰς τὸν πορφυρογέννητον
                κυρὸν Ἰσαάκιον τὸν Κομνηνόν, *Byzantinische Zeitschrift* 16:
                114.91–115.127.
Kyriakidis, S. P.
1923   Περὶ τῆς λέξεως κυρκατης. *Byzantinisch-neugriechische Jahrbücher*
                4:341–44.
1990   Αἱ ἱστορικαί ἀρχαί τῆς δημώδους νεοελληνικῆς ποιήσεως

(1934) and Γιὰ τὴ νεοελληνικὴ μπαλλάντα' (1960). Reprinted in: Kyriakidis, Τὸ δημοτικὸ τραγοῦδι, ed. A. Kyriakidou-Nestoros, (1990): 168–207, 287–301. Athens: Ermis.

Kyriakidou-Nestoros, A.
1978   Ἡ θεωρία τῆς ἑλληνικῆς λαογραφίας· κριτικὴ ἀνάλυση. Athens.
L.A.   Λαογραφικὸν Ἀρχεῖον τῆς Ἀκαδημίας Ἀθηνῶν, Athens.
Lacan, J.
1977   Écrits: A selection. Trans. A. Sheridan. New York: Norton.
Lambakis, S.
1982   Οἱ καταβάσεις στὸν κάτω κόσμο στὴ βυζαντινὴ καὶ στὴ μεταβυζαντινὴ λογοτεχνία. Athens.
Lambropoulos, V.
1983   Περὶ ἀναγνώσεως. Χάρτης 5/6:658–68.
1988   Literature as national institution: Studies in the politics of modern Greek criticism. Princeton: Princeton University Press.
1989   Empiricists and skepticists: A paradigm shift. Journal of Modern Greek Studies 7,1:1–39.
Lambros, S.
1894   Ein byzantinisches Volkslied, Byzantinische Zeitschrift 3:165.
1905   Ὕμνοι τῶν δήμων εἰς τὸν αὐτοκράτορα Ἰω. Κομνηνόν. Νέος Ἑλληνομνήμων 2:385–95.
1908   Ἔκφρασις τῶν ξυλοκονταριῶν τοῦ κραταιοῦ καὶ ἁγίου ἡμῶν αὐθέντου καὶ βασιλέως, Νέος Ἑλληνομνήμων 5:3–18.
Laografia   (1989–96). Irvine, Calif.
Laog.   Λαογραφία. Athens.
Laourdas, B.
1951   Ὁ Μαρκιανὸς κῶδιξ τοῦ Γεωργίου Κλόντζα καὶ οἱ περὶ Κρήτης χρησμοί. Κρητικὰ Χρονικὰ 5:230–42.
L.S.   Λαογραφικὰ Σύμμεικτα, Athens.
Lauxtermann, M.
1999   The spring of rhythm: An essay on the political verse and other Byzantine metres. Byzantina Vindobonensia 22. Vienna: Verlag der österreichisches Akademie.
Lawson, J. C.
1910   Modern Greek folklore and ancient Greek religion. Cambridge: Cambridge University Press. Reprint, New York: University Books, 1964.
Leach, E.
1972   Two essays concerning the symbolic representation of time. In Reader in comparative religion, ed. W. Lessa and E. Vogt. 3d ed. New York: Harper and Row.
1976   Culture and communication. Cambridge: Cambridge University Press.
Legrand, E., ed.
1878   Grammaire grecque moderne, suivie du panorama de la Grèce d'Alexandre Soutsos. Paris: Maisonneuve.

1974   *Collection de monuments pour servir à l'étude de la langue néohellénique,*
               vol. 6 (1880–1902). Athens: B.N. Gregoriades.

Leloir, L.
1966   *Ephrem de Nisibe: Commentaire de l'Évangile concordant ou Diates-*
               saron, Paris: Sources Chrétiennes 121.

Lemerle, P., A. Guillou, and N. Svoronos, eds.
1970   *Actes de Lavra, I: Des origines à 1204.* Paris: Archives de l'Athos V.

Leontis, A.
1995   *Women's fabric arts in Greek America, 1894–1994.* Columbus, Ohio:
               Hellenic Heritage.

Lessing, G. E.
1962   *Laocoön: An essay on the limits of painting and poetry* (1766). Ed. and
               trans. E. A. McCormick. Baltimore: Johns Hopkins University Press.

Lévi-Strauss, C.
1963   *Structural anthropology* (1958). Trans. C. Jakobson and B. G. Schoeff.
               London: Basic Books/Penguin.
1966   *The savage mind* (1962), Eng. ed., London: Weidenfeld and Nichol-
               son.

Lewis, G.
1979   *Modern Turkey.* New York: Praeger.

Liddell-Scott-Jones
1925–40   *A Greek-English Lexicon.* Compiled by H. G. Liddell and R. Scott.
               Revised and augmented by H. S. Jones. Oxford: Clarendon, 9th.
               edition.

Lidderdale, H. A.
1966   *The Memoirs of General Makriyannis.* Oxford: Oxford University Press.

Lieberman, M.
1972   "Some day my prince will come": Female acculturation through
               the fairy tale. *College English* 34:383–95.

Littlewood, A. R.
1972   *The "Progymnasmata" of Ioannes Geometres* (ed.). Amsterdam:
               Hakkert.
1974   The symbolism of the apple in Byzantine literature. *Jahrbuch der*
               Oesterreichischen Byzantinistik 23:33–59.
1979   Romantic paradises: The role of the garden in the Byzantine ro-
               mance. *Byzantine and Modern Greek Studies* 5:95–114.
1993   The erotic symbolism of the apple in late Byzantine and meta-
               Byzantine demotic literature. *Byzantine and Modern Greek Studies*
               17:83–103.

Llewellyn-Smith, M.
1973   *Ionian vision.* London: Allen Lane.

Lloyd, A. L.
1967   *Folk song in England.* London: Lawrence and Wishart.

Lloyd, G. E. R.
1979   *Magic, reason, and experience: Studies in the origins and development of*
               Greek science. Cambridge: Cambridge University Press.

Lodge, D.
1977   *The modes of modern writing: Metaphor, metonymy, and the typology of modern literature*. London: Arnold.
1984   *Language of fiction*. 2d ed. Reading: Cox and Wyman.
Loizos, P., and E. Papataxiarchis, eds.
1991   *Contested identities: Gender and kinship in modern Greece*. Princeton: Princeton University Press.
Loraux, N.
1987   *Tragic ways of killing a woman*. Cambridge: Harvard University Press.
Lord, A.
1991   *Epic singers and oral tradition*. Ithaca: Cornell University Press.
1995   *The singer resumes the tale*. Ed. M. L. Lord. Ithaca: Cornell University Press.
Loukatos, D. S.
1977   Εἰσαγωγή στήν ἑλληνική λαογραφία. Athens: Ethniki Trapeza.
Lukács, G.
1962   *The historical novel*. Trans. H. Mitchell and S. Mitchell. London: Merlin.
Luria, A. B.
1987   *The mind of a mnemonist*. Cambridge: Harvard University Press.
Lyle, E.
1994   *Scottish ballads*. Edinburgh: Canongate Classics.
Maas, P.
1910   Das Kontakion. *Byzantinische Zeitschrift* 19:285–306.
1912   Metrische Akklamationen der Byzantiner. *Byzantinische Zeitschrift* 21:28–51.
Maas, P., and C. Trypanis.
1963   *Sancti Romani melodi cantica: Cantica genuina*. Oxford: Clarendon.
MacAlister, S.
1987   The dream in Greek romance. Ph.D. thesis: University of Sydney. Now published as: *Dreams and Suicides: the Greek novel from antiquity to the Byzantine Empire*. London: Routledge.
Mackridge, P. A.
1985   *The modern Greek language*. Oxford: Oxford University Press.
Macrides, R. J., and P. Magdalino
1991   The fourth kingdom and the rhetoric of Hellenism. In *The perception of the past in twelfth-century Europe*, ed. P. Magdalino, 117–56. London: Hambledon.
Maehler, H.
1976   Der Metiochos-Parthenope Roman. *Zeitschrift für Papyrologie und Epigraphik* 23:1–20.
Magdalino, P.
1984   Byzantine snobbery. In Angold 1984, 58–78.
1992   Eros the King and the King of *Amours*: Some observations on *Hysmine and Hysminias*. *Dumbarton Oaks Papers* 46:197–204.

1993   *The Empire of Manuel I Komnenos, 1143–1180.* Cambridge: Cambridge University Press.

Maguire, H.
1981   *Art and eloquence in Byzantium.* Princeton: Princeton University Press.
1995, ed.   *Byzantine magic.* Dumbarton Oaks: Washington, D.C., and Harvard University Press.

Majuri, A., ed.
1919   Una nuova poesia di Teodoro Prodromo. *Byzantinische Zeitschrift* 23:397–407.

Makrakis, P. I.
1959   Μιὰ ἄγνωστη συλλογὴ τοῦ Γ. Βιζυηνου. Ἑταιρεία Θρακικῶν Μελετῶν 79:5–18.

Makryiannis
n.d.   Ἀπομνημονεύματα. Athens: Byron.

Maltezou, C.
1991   The historical and social context. In Holton 1991, 17–47.

Mandel, R.
1983   Sacrifice at the Bridge of Arta: Sex roles and the manipulation of power. *Journal of Modern Greek Studies* 1, 1:173–84.

Mandilaras, B. G.
1972   *Studies in the Greek Language: Some aspects of the development of the Greek language up to the present day.* Athens: N. Xenopoulos Press.

Mango, C.
1965   Byzantinism and romantic philhellenism. *Journal of the Warburg and Courtauld Institutes* 28:29–43.
1980   *Byzantium: The Empire of New Rome.* New York: Charles Scribner's Sons.

Manoussos, A.
1850   Τραγούδια ἐθνικά. Vol. 1. Corfu. Reprint, Athens: Ermis, 1969.

Mao Tse-Tung
1961–65   On contradiction. In *Selected works of Mao Tse-tung*, Peking: 1.311–47 (1937).

Marks, E., and I. de Courtivron, eds.
1981   *New French feminisms.* New York: Schocken.

Marx, K.
1973   *Grundrisse* (1857–58). London: Harmondsworth.

Marx, K., and F. Engels.
1980   *Collected works.* Vol. 13. London: Lawrence and Wishart.

Mavrogordato, J., ed.
1956   *Digenes Akrites.* Oxford: Clarendon.

Mazal, O.
1967   *Der Roman des Konstantinos Manasses.* Wiener Byzantinische Studien. Vienna.

Megas, G. A.
1956   Ἑλληνικαὶ ἑορταί. Athens: Spyropoulos.

1961   Άναστενάρια καὶ ἔθιμα Τυρινῆς Δευτέρας εἰς τὸ Κωστῆ καὶ
                τὰ πέριξ αὐτοῦ χωρία τῆς Άνατολικῆς Θράκης, Laog.
                19:472–534.
1970   Folktales of Greece. Trans. H. Colaclides. Chicago: University of
                Chicago Press.
1971   Τὸ τραγούδι τοῦ γεφυριοῦ τῆς Άρτας. Συγκριτικὴ μελέτη.
                Laog. 27:212–25.
Meraklis, M. G.
1966   Τὰ θέματα τῆς μεταμορφόσεως καὶ τῆς ἀναστάσεως. Laog.
                24:94–112.
1984   Έλληνικὴ λαογραφία· Κοινωνικὸ συγκρότημα. Athens:
                Odysseas.
1985   Παροιμίες ἑλληνικές καὶ τῶν ἄλλων βαλκανικῶν λαῶν.
                Athens: Pataki.
Merkelbach, R.
1978   The girl in the rosebush: A Turkish tale and its roots in ancient
                ritual. Harvard Studies in Classical Philology 82:1–16.
Meyer, G.
1885   Essays und Studien zur Sprachgeschichte und Volkskunde.
Migne, J.-P.
1855–   Patrologiae cursus completus, ser. Graeca. Paris.
Mirambel, A.
1937   Les "états de langue" dans la Grèce actuelle. In Conférences de l'In-
                stitut de Linguistique, fasc. 5, 19–53. Paris.
1964   Les aspects psychologiques du purisme dans la Grèce moderne.
                Journal de Psychologie, normale et pathologique 4 (October): 405–36.
Mitchell, T. F.
1982   More than a matter of "writing with the learned, pronouncing
                with the vulgar." In Haas 1982, 123–55.
Mitchell, W. J. T.
1986   Iconology: Image, text, ideology. Chicago: University of Chicago
                Press.
Mitsakis, K.
1967   The language of Romanos the Melodist. Munich: C. H. Beck.
Mitsi, E.
1991   Writing against pictures. Ph.D. diss., New York University.
Moi, T., ed.
1986   The Kristeva reader. Oxford: Basil Blackwell.
Moleas, W.
1989   The development of the Greek language. Bristol: Classical Press: A. D.
                Caratzas.
Montfaucon, B. de, ed.
1698   Vita S. Antonii. Paris.
Moore, R.
1975   From rags to witches: Stereotypes, distortions, and anti-humanism
                in fairy tales. Inter-racial Books for Children 6:1–3.

Moore, S. F., and B. Myerhoff, eds.
1977   Secular ritual. Amsterdam: Van Gorcum.
Morgan, G. A.
1954   A Byzantine satirical song? Byzantinische Zeitschrift 47:292–97.
1960   Cretan poetry: Sources and inspiration. Iraklion. Monograph
                     reprinted from Κρητικὰ Χρονικὰ 14 (1960): 7–68, 203–70,
                     379–434.
Morrison, T.
1987   Song of Solomon (1977). London: Penguin; New York: Plume.
1982   Sula (1973). New York: Plume.
Moullas, P., ed.
1980   Γεώργιος Βιζυηνός· Νεοελληνικὰ διηγήματα. Athens: Ermis.
Mullett, M.
1990   Dancing with deconstructionists in the gardens of the Muses: New
                     literary history Vs.? Byzantine and Modern Greek Studies 14:258–75.
Mullett, M., and D. Smythe, eds.
1996   Alexios I Komnenos. Papers given at the second Belfast Interna-
                     tional Colloquium.
Myrivilis, S.
1956   Ἡ Παναγιὰ Γοργόνα (1949). Athens: Estia.
Nagy, G.
1979   The best of the Achaeans. Baltimore: Johns Hopkins University Press.
1990a   Greek mythology and poetics. Ithaca: Cornell University Press.
1990b   Pindar's Homer. Baltimore: Johns Hopkins University Press.
Needham, R.
1972   Belief, language, and experience. Oxford: Blackwell.
Newton, B. E.
1972   The generative interpretation of dialect: A study of modern Greek phonol-
                     ogy. Cambridge: Cambridge University Press.
Nicol, D. M.
1971   Byzantium and Greece. Inaugural Lecture at Korais Chair, King's
                     College. London: Bowman Press.
1979   The end of the Byzantine Empire. London: E. Arnold.
Nilsson, M. P.
1945   Pagan divine service in late antiquity. Harvard Theological Review
                     38:63–69.
Nitschke, A.
1976/77   Soziale Ordnungen im Spielen der Märchen. 2 vols. Stuttgart.
Norden, E. A.
1898   Die antike Kunstprosa. 2 vols. Leipzig.
1923   Agnostos Theos. Leipzig/Berlin.
Notopoulos, J. A.
1955   Recordings from the James A. Notopoulos Collection, tapes 1–94.
                     Harvard University Archives, Cambridge.
Obeyesekere, G.
1981   Medusa's hair. Chicago: University of Chicago Press.

Olsen, B.

1990   Ἡ γερμανοπρέπεια τῶν ἑλληνικῶν παραμυθιῶν στὴ συλλογὴ τοῦ J. G. von Hahn. Ἑλληνικά 41:79–93.

Ong, W. J.

1977   *Interfaces of the word.* Ithaca: Cornell University Press.

1982   *Orality and literacy:The technologising of the word.* London: Methuen.

1984   Orality, literacy, and medieval textualisation. *New Literary History* 16:1–16.

Ortony, A.

1979 (ed.)   *Metaphor and Thought.* Cambridge: Cambridge University Press.

1979   The role of similarity in similes and metaphors. In Ortony ed., 1979: 342–56.

Ostrogorsky, G.

1968   *History of the Byzantine state.* Trans. J. Hussey. Oxford: Basil Blackwell.

O'Sullivan, M.

1953   *Twenty years a-growing.* Trans. G. Thomson. Oxford: Oxford University Press.

O'Sullivan, S., ed.

1966   *Folktales of Ireland.* Chicago: University of Chicago Press.

Padel, R.

1992   *In and out of the mind: Greek images of the tragic self.* Princeton: Princeton University Press.

Palau, A.-C.

1980   La tradition manuscrite d'Eustathe Makrembolitès. *Revue d'histoire de textes* 12:75–113.

Pallis, A.

1910   Ἡ Νέα Διαθήκη κατὰ τὸ Βατικανὸ χερόγραφο. Μεταφρασμένη ἀπὸ τὸν Α. Πάλλη Liverpool.

Palmenfelt, U.

1993   On the understanding of folk legends. In Chesnutt 1993, 143–67.

Palmer, L. R.

1945   *A grammar of the post-Ptolemaic papyri.* Oxford: Oxford University Press.

1980   *The Greek language.* N.J.: Humanities Press.

Panagiotakis, N.

1991   Τὸ κείμενο τῆς πρώτης ἔκδοσης τοῦ ''Ἀπόκοπου.'' Τυπογραφικὴ καὶ φιλολογικὴ διερεύνηση. Venice.

Panagiotopoulos, I. A.

1954   Γ. Μ. Βιζυηνός. Βασικὴ Βιβλιοθήκη. 16. Athens:

1955   Τὸ ἱστορικὸν μυθιστόρημα. Βασικὴ Βιβλιοθήκη, 17. Athens:

Panourgia, N.

1994   Objects at birth, subjects at death. *Journal of Modern Greek Studies* 12, no. 2:261–69.

1995   *Fragments of death, fables of identity.* Madison: University of Wisconsin Press.

Papadimitriou, I. T.
1987   Αἰσώπεια καὶ Αἰσωπικά. Athens.
Papadopoullos, T.
1975   Δημώδη κυπριακὰ ἄσματα. Leukosia: Κέντρον 'Επιστη-
                μονικῶν 'Ερευνῶν.
Papagianni, V.
1990   Κυράνω. Athens: Nefeli.
Papamichael, A. J.
1975   Birth and plant symbolism: Symbolic and magical uses of plants in con-
                nection with birth in modern Greece. Athens.
Parker, R.
1983   Miasma. Oxford: Oxford University Press.
Parry, M.
1971   The making of Homeric verse: The collected papers of Milman Parry. Ed.
                A. Parry. Oxford: Clarendon.
Pasayanis, K.
1928   Μανιάτικα μοιρολόγια καὶ τραγούδια (no.). Athens.
Patala, Z.
1996   "Les chants grecs du Liber Politicus du chanoine Benoit." Byzantion
                66: 512-30.
Peristiany, J. G., ed.
1965   Honour and shame: The values of Mediterranean society. London: Wei-
                denfeld and Nicholson.
1976, ed.   Mediterranean family structures. Cambridge: Cambridge University
                Press.
Pernot, H.
1931   Chansons populaires grecques des xve et xvie siècles. Paris: Les Belles-
                Lettres.
Perrault, C.
1697   Contes du temps passé. Paris.
Perry, B. E.
1967   The ancient romances. Berkeley: University of California Press.
Petersen, W. L.
1985   The dependence of Romanos the Melodist upon the Syriac
                Ephrem: Its importance for the origin of the kontakion. Vigiliae
                Christianae 39:171-87.
Petropoulos, D.
1958-59   'Ελληνικὰ δημοτικὰ τραγούδια. 2 vols. Βασικὴ Βιβλιοθήκη,
                56-57. Athens.
Petropoulos, J. C. B.
1994   Heat and lust: Hesiod's midsummer festival scene revisited. Lanham,
                Md.: Rowman and Littlefield.
Pignani, A., ed.
1983   Nicefore Basilace, progimnasii e monodie. Naples: Bibliopolis.
Pio, J.
1879   Contes populaires grecs. Copenhagen: Libraires de l'Université.

536   Bibliography

Pitra, J. B.
1876   *Analecta Sacra spicilegio Solesmensi parata.* Vol. 1. Paris.
Plepelits, K.
1989   *Hysmine und Hysminias.* Stuttgart: Hiersemann.
Polemis, D.
1968   *The Doukai: A contribution to Byzantine prosopography.* London: University of London Historical Studies XXII.
Politi, G.
1981   Ἡ μυθιστορηματικὴ κατεργασία τῆς ἰδεολογίας· ἀνάλυση τῆς "Λυγερῆς" τοῦ Ἀνδρέα Καρκαβίτσα. Ἐπιστημονικὴ Ἐπετηρίδα Φιλοσοφικῆς Σχολῆς. Thessaloniki.
Politis, A.
1982   Τὸ βιβλίο μέσο παραγωγῆς τῆς προφορικῆς γνώσης. In: Τὸ βιβλίο στὶς προβιομηχανικὲς κοινωνίες. Athens: Κέντρον Νεοελληνικῶν Ερευνῶν.
1984   Ἡ ἀνακάλυψη τῶν ἑλληνικῶν δημοτικῶν τραγουδιῶν. Athens: Themelio.
Politis, L.
1956   Τὸ θέμα τῶν πουλιῶν στὸ δημοτικὸ τραγοῦδι τοῦ νεκροῦ ἀδερφοῦ. Ἐπιστημονικὴ Ἐπετηρὶς τῆς Φιλοσοφικῆς Σχολῆς Θεσσαλονίκης 7:271–80.
1968   Ποιητικὴ ἀνθολογία. Vol. 1. Athens: Galaxia.
Politis, N. G.
1871   Μελέτη ἐπὶ τοῦ βίου τῶν νεωτέρων Ἑλλήνων· Νεοελληνικὴ μυθολογία. Athens: Wilberg and Nakis.
1872   Τὰ κατὰ τὴν γέννησιν. Νεοελληνικὰ Ἀνάλεκτα 1:374–84. Reprinted in Λαογραφικὰ Σύμμεικτα 3 (1931):206–19.
1880   Δημώδη παραμύθια. Ἑστία 9:9–12, 22–23, 43–47. Reprinted in Λαογραφικὰ Σύμμεικτα 1 (1920):196–210.
1885   Τὸ δημοτικὸν ἄσμα περὶ τοῦ Νεκροῦ Ἀδελφοῦ. Δελτίον τῆς Ἱστορικῆς καὶ Ἐθνολογικῆς Ἑταιρείας τῆς Ἑλλάδος 2:193–261.
1899–1902;
1904   Μελέται περὶ τοῦ βίου καὶ τῆς γλώσσης τοῦ ἑλληνικοῦ λαοῦ. 6 Vols. 1–4, Παροιμίαι, 5–6 Παραδόσεις. Athens.
1909a   Λαογραφία. *Laog.* 1: 3-18
1909b   Ἀκριτικὰ ἄσματα· ὁ θάνατος τοῦ Διγενῆ. *Laog.* 1:169–275.
1911   Δημώδη βυζαντινὰ ἄσματα. Λαογραφία 3:622–52.
1912   Διὰ τὰ Ἀθηναϊκὰ παραμύθια (review of D. Kambouroglous and M. Kambouroglou and their response). *Laog.* 4:341–43, 750–54.
1914   Ἐκλογαὶ ἀπὸ τὰ τραγούδια τοῦ ἑλληνικοῦ λαοῦ (no.). Athens.
Pollis, A.
1992   Greek national identity: Religious minorities, rights, and European norms. *Journal of Modern Greek Studies* 10, 2:171–96.

Polyakova, S. V.
1971   Ekfrasa 12 mesjatsev Evmatija Makremvolita. *Palestinskii sbornik* 23:114–24.
1979   *Opyt interpretatsii "Povesti ob Ismini i Isminii" Evmafia Makremvolita.* Moscow: Nauka.
Proïas
n.d.   Λεξικὸν τῆς νέας ἑλληνικῆς γλώσσης. Athens: ᾿εκδοτικός οἶκος Π. Δημητράκου, ἀ.ε.
Propp, V.
1968   *The morphology of the folktale* (1929). Trans. L. Scott. 2d ed. revised and edited by L. A. Wagner. Austin: University of Texas Press.
1984   *Theory and history of folklore.* Trans. A. Y. Martin and R. P. Martin. Ed. A. Liberman. Manchester: Manchester University Press.
Psycharis, Y.
1971   Τὸ ταξίδι μου. Ἔκδοση μὲ ἐπιμέλεια ᾿Α. ᾿Αγγέλου. (1888). Athens: Ermis.
Purser, J.
1992   *Scotland's music.* Edinburgh / London: Mainstream / BBC Scotland.
Quinn, N.
1991   The cultural basis of metaphor. In Fernandez 1991, 56–93.
Reinsch, D. R.
1990   Griechische Märchen und das Problem ihrer mündlichen Quellen. *Neograeca Medii Aevi* III: 295–313.
Reiske, J., ed.
1829   *Constantine Porphyrogenitus: "De Caeremoniis."* Bonn: Corpus Scriptorum Historiae Byzantine.
Renfrew, C.
1987   *Archaeology and linguistics.* Cambridge: Cambridge University Press.
Ricks, D.
1989   *The shade of Homer.* Cambridge: Cambridge University Press.
Ritsos, Y.
1936   Ἐπιτάφιος. Athens: Kedros.
Ritsos, Y. and M. Theodorakis
1973   *Lianotragouda* (Λιανοτράγουδα). Athens.
Rohde, E.
1960   *Der griechische Roman.* 4th ed. Hildesheim.
Roidis, R.
1978   Ἅπαντα, 5 vols. Ed. A. Angelou. Athens: Ermis.
Romaios, K. A., P. Papachristodoulou, and P. Kavakopoulos
1956   Μουσικὰ κείμενα δημοτικῶν τραγουδιῶν τῆς Θράκης. Athens: Academy.
Romano, R., ed.
1974   *Pseudo-Luciano, "Timarione": Testo critico, introduzione, traduzione, commentario e lessico.* Naples.

Rosaldo, M. Z., and L. Lamphere, eds.
1974   *Women in society and culture.* Stanford: Stanford University Press.
Rosaldo, R.
1987   Anthropological commentary. In *Violent origins,* ed. R. G. Hamerton-Kelly, 239–44. Stanford: Stanford University Press.
Rumelhart, D. E.
1979   Problems with literal meanings. In Ortony 1979:78–90.
Russell, J.
1995   The archaeological context of magic during the early Byzantine period. In Maguire 1995, 35–50.
Rutherford, I.
Forthcoming   *Geography of pilgrimage.*
Rutter, M.
1978   Diagnosis and definition of childhood autism. *Journal of Autism and Childhood Schizophrenia* 8:139–61.
Rutter, M., and E. Schopler, eds.
1977   *Autism: A reappraisal of concepts and treatment.* New York: Plenum.
Sachinis, A.
1957   Τὸ ἱστορικὸ μυθιστόρημα. Athens. Reprint, 1981.
1973   Παλαιότεροι πεζογράφοι, Athens. Reprint, 1982.
Sacks, O.
1983   *The man who mistook his wife for a hat.* London: Picador.
1995   *An anthropologist on Mars.* London: Picador.
Sacks, P.
1985   *The English elegy: Studies in the genre from Spenser to Yeats.* Baltimore: Johns Hopkins University Press.
Said, E.
1978   *Orientalism.* Harmondsworth: Penguin.
1983   *The world, the text, and the critic.* Cambridge: Harvard University Press.
Sareyiannis, I. A.
1964   Σχόλια στὸν Καβάφη. Athens: Ikaros.
Sathas, K. N., ed.
1870   Γεωργίου Βουστρώνιου, Διήγησις Κρόνικας Κύπρου ἀρχεύγοντα ἀπὸ τὴν ἐχρονιὰν αυνστ΄ Χριστοῦ. Athens: A. Koromila.
1872–94   Μεσαιωνικὴ Βιβλιοθήκη. 7 vols. Paris and Venice.
Saunier, G.
1968   "Les chansons de noces à thèmes funèbres. Recherches sur la famille et la societé grecques." Paris (dactylographié).
1972   Le combat avec Charos dans les chansons populaires grecques. Ἑλληνικά 25, 1: 119–52; 2: 335–70.
1979   *"Adikia": Le mal et l'injustice dans les chansons populaires grecques.* Paris: Societé d'Éditions des Belles Lettres.
1983   Τὸ δημοτικὸ τραγούδι· τῆς ξενιτιᾶς. Athens: Ermis.

Scavdi, D.

1984   *The lament in Greek traditional society*. Ph.D. thesis: University of Birmingham.

Schmidt, B.

1871   *Das Volksleben der Neugriechen und das hellenische Altertum*. Leipzig: Teubner.

1877   *Griechische Märchen, Sage und Volkslieder*. Leipzig.

Schneider, J.

1990   Spirits and the spirit of capitalism. In *Religious Orthodoxy and popular faith in European society*, ed. E. Badone, 29–54. Princeton: Princeton University Press.

Seaford, R.

1994   *Reciprocity and ritual: Homer and tragedy in the developing city-state*. Oxford: Clarendon.

Searle, J.

1977   Reiterating the differences: A reply to Derrida. *Glyph* 1:198–208.

Seferis, G.

1967   *Collected Poems, 1924-1955*. Translated, edited and introduced by E. Keeley and P. Sherrard. Princeton: Princeton University Press.

Selfe, L.

1977   *Nadia: A case of extraordinary drawing ability in an autistic child*. London: Academic Press.

Seremetakis, N. C.

1990   The ethics of antiphony: The social construction of pain, gender, and power in the southern Peloponnese. *Ethos* 18:481–511.

1991   *The last word: Women, divination, and death in Inner Mani*. Chicago: University of Chicago Press.

Ševčenko, I.

1970   Poems on the deaths of Leo VI and Constantine VII in the Madrid MS of Scylitzes. *Dumbarton Oaks Papers* 23/24:222–25.

1981   Levels of style in Byzantine prose. *Jahrbuch der Oesterreichischen Byzantinistik* 31:289–312.

Shaw, S. J.

1976–77   *History of the Ottoman Empire*. 2 vols. Cambridge: Cambridge University Press.

Shields, H.

1991   Popular modes of narration and the popular ballad. In: *The ballad and oral literature*, ed. J. Harris, 40–59. Cambridge: Harvard University Press.

Siapkaras-Pitsillides, T.

1952   *Le Pétrarquisme en Chypre: Poèmes d'amour en dialecte chypriote d'après un manuscrit du xvi siècle*. Athens: Collection de l'Institut Français.

Sifakis, G. M.

1988   Γιὰ μιὰ ποιητικὴ τοῦ ἑλληνικοῦ δημοτικοῦ τραγουδιοῦ. Iraklio: Πανεπιστημιακὲς Ἐκδόσεις.

Simonsen, M.

1985   Do fairy tales make sense? *Journal of Folklore Research* 22:29–36.

1993   Some remarks on "reflection theory" as applied to folktales. In Chesnutt 1993, 121–41.

Skopetea, E.
1988   Τὸ πρότυπο βασίλειο καὶ ἡ μεγάλη ἰδέα· ὄψεις τοῦ ἐθνικοῦ προβλήματος στὴν Ἑλλάδα (1830–1880). Athens: Poly.

Smith, O.
1991–92   Some features of structure and narrative in the Byzantine Achilleid. Ἑλληνικά 42:75–94.

Sofianos, N.
1870   Grammaire du grec vulgaire, ed. E. Legrand (1660). In: Collection des monuments pour servir à l'étude de la langue néo-hellénique, vol. 6, Paris. Reprint. Athens 1976: B. N. Georglades.

Soutsos, P.
1853   Νέα σχολὴ τοῦ γραφομένου λόγου, ἡ ἀνάστασις τῆς ἀρχαίας ἑλληνικῆς γλώσσης ἐννοουμένης ὑπὸ πάντων. Athens.

Soyter, G.
1959   Griechische Humor von Homers Zeiten bis heute. Berlin: Akademische Verlag.

Spanakis, S.
1969   Ἡ θρησκευτικὸ-ἐκκλησιαστικὴ κατάσταση στὴν Κρήτη τὸν xvi αἰώνα. Κρητικὰ Χρονικὰ 21:134–52.

Speck, P.
1984   "Interpolations et non-sens indiscutables": Das erste Gedicht der Ptochoprodromika. Ποίκιλα Βυζαντινά 4:302–3.

Spencer, T. J.
1954   Fair Greece, sad relic. London: Weidenfeld and Nicholson.

Sperber, D.
1975   Rethinking symbolism. Cambridge: Cambridge University Press.
1982   Evocation. Birmingham: University of Birmingham.

Sperber, D., and D. Wilson
1986   Relevance: Communication and cognition. London: Harper and Row. Reprint, Cambridge: Harvard University Press, 1988.

Spivak, G.
1987   In other worlds: Essays in cultural politics. London: Methuen.

Spyridakis, G. K., and S. A. Peristeris
1968   Ἑλληνικὰ δημοτικὰ τραγούδια (μουσικὴ ἐκλογή). Athens: Academy. Δημοσιεύματα τοῦ Κέντρου Ἐρεύνης τῆς Ἑλληνικῆς Λαογραφίας, 10.

Stamiris, E.
1986   The women's movement in Greece. New Left Review 158:98–113.

Steiner, W.
1982   The colors of rhetoric. Chicago: University of Chicago Press.

Stephanus, H.
1816–18   Thesaurus Linguae Graecae. London.

Stewart, C.
1991   Demons and the Devil: Moral imagination in modern Greek culture. Princeton: Princeton University Press.

1997   Fields in dreams: Anxiety, experience, and limits of social constructions in modern Greek dream narratives. *American Ethnologist* 24.4:877–94.

Stewart, J.
1988   *Boccaccio in the Blaskets*. Galway: Officina Typographica.

Stock, B.
1980   *Implications of literacy*. Princeton: Princeton University Press.
1984   Medieval literacy, linguistic theory, and social organisation. *New Literary History* 16, 1:14–29.

Strzygowski, J.
1888   Die Monatscyklen der byzantinischen Kunst. *Repertorium für Kunsturischenschaft* 11:22–46.

Suleiman, S. R., ed.
1986   *The female body in Western culture*. Cambridge: Harvard University Press.

Sullivan, L. E.
1986   Sound and senses: Towards a hermeneutics of performance. *History of Religions* 26:1–33.

Sultan, N.
1991a   *The wandering hero in Homeric epic and modern Greek folksong*. Ph.D. diss., Harvard University.
1991b   Women in "Akritic" song: The hero's "other" voice. *Journal of Modern Greek Studies* 9, 2:153–70.

Sutton, S. B.
1988   What is a "village" in a nation of migrants? *Journal of Modern Greek Studies* 6, 2:187–216.

Syrimis, G.
1995   Gender, narrative modes, and the procreative cycle: The pregnant word in Vizyenos. *Journal of Modern Greek Studies* 13, 2:327–49.

Takhtsis, K.
1974   Τὸ τρίτο στεφάνι (1962). Athens: Ermis.

Tambiah, S. J.
1973   Form and meaning of magical acts: A point of view. In *Modes of Thought*, ed. R. Horton and R. Finnegan. London: Faber and Faber: 199–219.
1979   A performative approach to ritual. *Proceedings of the British Academy* 65:113–69.
1990   *Magic, science, religion, and the scope of rationality*. Cambridge: Cambridge University Press.

Tannen, D.
1990   *You just don't understand: Women and men in conversation*. New York: Ballantine.

Tarsouli, G.
1942   Μωραΐτικα Τραγούδια (no.). Athens.

Tatar, M.
1987   *The hard facts of the Grimms' fairy tales*. Princeton: Princeton University Press.

1992	*Off with their heads!* Princeton: Princeton University Press.
Theotokas, G.	
1973	Ἐλεύθερο πνεῦμα (1929), ed. K. Dimaras. Athens: Ermis. Reprint, 1988.
Thompson, S.	
1955–58	*Motif Index of Folk Literature.* 6 vols. Rev. ed. Copenhagen and Indiana.
Thomson, G.	
1929	*Greek Lyric Metre.* Cambridge: Cambridge University Press.
1938	*Aeschylus: The Oresteia.* 2 vols. Cambridge: Cambridge University Press. 2d ed. Prague: Czechoslovak Academy of Sciences, 1966.
1945	*Marxism and poetry.* London: Lawrence and Wishart.
1946	*Aeschylus and Athens: A study in the social origins of drama.* London: Lawrence and Wishart.
1949	*Studies in ancient Greek society.* Vol. 1, *The prehistoric Aegean.* London: Lawrence and Wishart.
1955	*Studies in ancient Greek society.* Vol. 2, *The first philosophers.* London: Lawrence and Wishart. 2d ed., 1961.
1964	Ἡ ἑλληνικὴ γλῶσσα, ἀρχαία καὶ νέα. Athens.
1966	*The Greek language* (1960). 2d ed. Cambridge: W. Heffer.
1969	*Kostis Palamas: The twelve lays of the gipsy.* London: Lawrence and Wishart.
1974	*The Human Essence: The sources of science and art.* London: China Policy Study Group.
1988	*Island Home: The Blasket heritage.* Dingle: Brandon Press.
Thomson, K.	
1977	*The Masonic thread in Mozart.* London: Lawrence and Wishart.
Todorov, T.	
1975	*The fantastic: A structuralist approach to a literary genre.* Trans. R. Howard. Ithaca: Cornell University Press.
Tolstoy, L.	
1949 (1857–77)	*Anna Karenina.* Trans. A. Maude. The World's Classics 210. London: Oxford University Press.
Tommasini, B. V.	
1901	Sulle laudi greche conservate nel *Liber Politicus* del canonica Benedetto. A Ernesto Monaci, Rome.
Tong, D.	
1989	*Gypsy folktales.* New York: Harcourt Brace Jovanovich.
Topping, E.	
1983	Patriarchal prejudice and pride in Greek Christianity—Some notes on origins. *Journal of Modern Greek Studies* 1,1:7–18.
Torp, L.	
1990	*Chain and round dance patterns: A method for structural analysis and its application to European material.* 3 vols. Copenhagen: Museum Tusculanum Press.

Tozer, H. F.
1892   Byzantine satire. *Journal of Hellenic Studies* 2:233–70.
Traube, E.
1979   Incest and mythology: Anthropological and Girardian perspec-
                       tives. *Berkshire Review* 14:37–43.
Treu, M., ed.
1892   Ein Kritiker des Timarion. *Byzantinische Zeitschrift* 1:361–65.
Triandafyllidis, M.
1938   Νεοελληνική γραμματική· Ἱστορική εἰσαγωγή. Athens.
1941   Νεοελληνική γραμματική. Athens. Rev. ed., 1976.
Tsolakis, E. T.
1967   Συμβολή στὴ μελέτη τοῦ ποιητικοῦ ἔργου τοῦ Κωνσταντίνου
                       Μανασσῆ καὶ κριτικὴ ἔκδοση τοῦ μυθιστορήματος τοῦ "Τὰ
                       κατ' Ἀρίστανδρον καὶ Καλλιθέαν". Thessaloniki.
1990   Τιμαρίων, μιὰ νέα ἀνάγνωση. Μνήμη Σ. Καρατζᾶ. Thessaloniki.
Tsourkas, C.
1967   *Les débuts de l'enseignement philosophique et de la libre pensée dans les
                       Balkans: La vie et l'oeuvre de Théophile Corydallée (1570–1646).* Thessa-
                       loniki, Institute for Balkan Studies.
Tuffin, P. G.
1972/73   The whitening crow: Some *adynata* in the Greek tradition.
                       Ἐπετηρὶς τοῦ Κέντρου Ἐπιστημονικῶν Ἐρευνῶν 6:79–92.
Turner, E. G.
1980 (1968)   *Greek papyri: An introduction.* Oxford: Oxford University Press.
Turner, T.
1991   "We are parrots," "twins are birds": Play of tropes as operational
                       structure. In Fernandez 1991, 121–58.
Turner, V. W.
1977 (1969)   *The ritual process: Structure and anti-structure.* Ithaca: Cornell Univer-
                       sity Press.
Tzartzanos, A.
1930   Γραμματικὴ τῆς νεοελληνικῆς γλώσσης. Athens.
Tziatzios, E.
1928   Τραγούδια τῶν Σαρακατσαναίων. Athens.
Tziovas, D.
1986   *The nationism of the demoticists and its impact on their literary theory.*
                       Amsterdam: Hakkert.
1989a   George Thomson and the dialectics of Hellenism. *Byzantine and
                       Modern Greek Studies* 13:296–305.
1989b   Residual orality and belated textuality in Greek literature and cul-
                       ture. *Journal of Modern Greek Studies* 7, 1:321–35.
1997   (ed.) *Greek modernism and beyond.* Essays in honor of Peter Bien.
                       Lanham: Rowman and Littlefield.
Urton, G., ed.
1985   *Animal myths and metaphors in South America.* Salt Lake City: Uni-
                       versity of Utah Press.

Valetas, G.
1947   Ἀνθολογία τῆς δημοτικῆς πεζογραφίας, 3 vols. Athens:
                     P. Ranos.

van der Valk, M.
1971   *Eustathii archiepiscopi Thessalonicensis commentarii ad Homeri Iliadem
                     pertinentes.* Vol. 1. Leiden.

Van Dyck, K.
1994   Reading between worlds: Contemporary Greek women's writing
                     and censorship. *Proceedings of the Modern Language Association* 109,
                     1:45–60.

1998   *Kassandra and the Censors:* Greek poetry since 1967. Ithaca: Cornell
                     University Press.

Van Gennep, A.
1960 (1909)   *Rites of passage.* Trans. M. Vizedom and G. L. Caffee. Chicago:
                     University of Chicago Press.

Vargyas, L.
1967   *Researches into the medieval history of folk ballad.* Budapest.

Vassilikos, V.
1966   Ἐκτὸς τῶν τειχῶν. Athens.

Veletza, V.
1994   Celebrating namedays: Now and then. *Laografia* 11, 5:7–12.

Veloudis, G.
1974   *Das griechische Druck- und Verlagshaus "Glikis" in Venedig
                     (1670–1854).* Wiesbaden.

Vermeule, E.
1979   *Aspects of death in early Greek art and poetry.* Berkeley: University of
                     California Press.

Vernant, J. P.
1974   *Mythe et pensée chez les Grecs.* 4th ed. Paris.

Veyne, P.
1988   *Did the Greeks believe in their myths? An essay on the constitutive
                     imagination.* Trans. P. Wissing. Chicago: University of Chicago
                     Press.

Vikan, G.
1990   Art and marriage in Byzantium. *Dumbarton Oaks Papers* 44:
                     145–63.

Vikelas, D.
1991 (1879)   Λουκῆς Λάρας. Ed. M. Ditsa. Athens: Ermis.

Vitti, M.
1991   Ἰδεολογικὴ λειτουργία τῆς ἑλληνικῆς ἠθογραφίας (1974). 3d
                     ed. Athens: Kedros.

Vizyenos, G. M.
1893   Ἀνὰ τὸν Ἑλικῶνα. Ἑστία (Μάρτιος).
1954   Γ. Βιζυηνός. Ed. I. M. Panagiotopoulos. Βασικὴ Βιβλιοθήκη 16.
                     Athens: Aetos.

1980   Νεοελληνικὰ Διηγήματα. Ed. P. Moullas. Athens: Ermis.

Vlastos, P.
1931   Συνώνυμα καὶ συγγενικά. Athens.
Vološinov, V. N.
1986   Marxism and the philosophy of language. Trans. L. Matejka and I. R.
                    Titunic. Cambridge, Ma.: Harvard University Press.
Voltz, L.
1895   Bemerkungen zu byzantinischen Monatshiten. Byzantinische
                    Zeitschrift 4:547–58.
Vouras, M.
1968   Field recordings from Olymbos, Karpathos: personal archives.
Vouras, M., and A. Anthony
1985   'Greek Celebrations: Agrapha', videofilm re-released 1996. Water-
                    town, Mass.
Vryonis, S.
1971   The decline of medieval Hellenism in Asia Minor and the process of Is-
                    lamisation from the eleventh through fifteenth centuries. Berkeley: Uni-
                    versity of California Press.
1978   (ed.) Βυζαντινὰ καὶ Μεταβυζαντινά. Vol. 1. Malibu, Calif.: Un-
                    dena Press.
1978   Recent scholarship on continuity and discontinuity of culture:
                    Classical Greeks, Byzantines, modern Greeks. In Vryonis ed. 1978,
                    237–56.
1981   The panegyris of the Byzantine saint: A study in the nature of a
                    medieval institution, its origins and fate. In Hackel 1981, 196–226.
Wachsmuth, K.
1864   Das alte Griechenland im neuen. Bonn: Max Cohen. Reprint. in
                    Λαογραφικὰ Σύμμεικτα (1920).
Warburton, I. P.
1970   On the verb in modern Greek. Bloomington: Indiana University
                    Press.
Ward, C.
1990   What they told Buchi Emecheta. Proceedings of the Modern Lan-
                    guage Association 105, 1:83–97.
Watson, J. D.
1968   The double helix: A personal account of the structure of DNA. New
                    York: Norton.
Watt, I.
1957   The rise of the novel. London: Chatto and Windus; Berkeley: Uni-
                    versity of California Press.
Wellesz, E. K.
1943   Melito's Homily on the Passion: An investigation into the sources of
                    Byzantine hymnography. Journal of Theological Studies 44:41–52.
1957   The Akathistos Hymn. Monumenta Musicae Byzantinae Copen-
                    hagen.
1961   A history of Byzantine music and hymnography. 2d ed. Oxford: Ox-
                    ford University Press.

Wells, E. K.
1950   *The ballad tree*. New York: Ronald Press.
Werner, E.
1947   Hellenism and Judaism in Christian music. *Hebrew Union College Annual* 20:408–70.
White, A.
1979   *Beyond the glass* (1954). In *Frost in May*. vol. 2. Glasgow: Fontana and Virago.
Williams, D.
1992   *Nobody nowhere*. London: Doubleday.
1993   *Somebody somewhere*. London: Doubleday.
Wilson, N. G.
1983   *Scholars of Byzantium*. London: Duckworth.
Wilson, W. A.
1974   Herder, folklore, and romantic nationalism. *Journal of Popular Culture* 6.4:819–35.
Winkler, J. J.
1990   *The constraints of desire*. Princeton: Princeton University Press.
Wittgenstein, L.
1976   *Philosophical investigations* (1953). Trans. G. E. M. Anscombe. 3d ed. Oxford: Blackwell.
Wyatt, W. J.
1987   Vizyenos and his characters. *Journal of Modern Greek Studies* 5, 1:47–63.
1988   *My mother's sin and other stories by Georgios Vizyenos*. Hanover: University Press of New England.
1992   "Συνέπειαι". Διαβάζω 278:41–42.
1993   Goethe's Wanderer's Night Song. In: Vizyenos, *Journal of Modern Greek Studies* 11, 1:97–106.
Yiankas, A.
n.d.   Ἠπειρώτικα δημοτικὰ τραγούδια (no.). Athens.
Zambelios, S.
1852   Ἄσματα δημοτικὰ τῆς Ἑλλάδος. Corfu.
1859   Πόθεν ἡ λέξη τραγουδῶ. Athens: P. Soutsos and A. Ktenas.
Zateli, Z.
1993   Καὶ μὲ τὸ φῶς τοῦ λύκου ἐπανέρχονται. Athens: Kastanioti.
Zinkeisen, J. W.
1840/63   *Geschichte des osmanliches Reiches in Europa*. Vol. 2. Hamburg: F. Perthes.
Ziolkowski, J.
1987   The erotic paternoster. *Neuphilologische Mitteilungen* 88:31–34.
Zipes, J.
1979   *Breaking the magic spell*. Austin: University of Texas Press.
1987   *Don't bet on the prince*. New York: Methuen and Gower.
Zuccarini, F.
1832   *Das Ausland* 2.

INDEXES

Notes are indexed only when the name or subject does not appear in the text relating to the referent.

 I. General Index.   Authors, names, places, and subjects. See also pages vii–x for itemization of chapters and subheadings.

II. Index of Themes and Images.   A selective guide to key items in texts and rituals.

Cross-references in one index that refer to the other index are set in **bold**.

My thanks to Bearby, Zebedee, and Dimitri for their technical assistance and kind support.

I. General Index

II. Index of Themes and Images

Myth and Poetics

A SERIES EDITED BY

GREGORY NAGY